DATE DUE			
REF.	REF.	REF.	REF.
	REF.	REF.	
	REF.	REF.	

The Who's Who of Nobel Prize Winners

DISCARDED

Edited by Bernard S. Schlessinger
and June H. Schlessinger

Rashelle S. Karp,
Louise Sherby,
and Parvin Kujoory,
Associate Editors

ORYX PRESS
1986

The rare Arabian Oryx is believed to have inspired the myth of the unicorn. This desert antelope became virtually extinct in the early 1960s. At that time several groups of international conservationists arranged to have 9 animals sent to the Phoenix Zoo to be the nucleus of a captive breeding herd. Today the Oryx population is over 400, and herds have been returned to reserves in Israel, Jordan, and Oman.

Library of Congress Cataloging-in-Publication Data

The Who's who of Nobel Prize winners.

Includes indexes.

1. Nobel prizes. 2. Biography—20th century—Dictionaries. I. Schlessinger, Bernard S., 1930-
II. Schlessinger, June H.
AS911.N9W53   1986   001.4′4′0922 [B]   86-42784
ISBN 0-89774-193-5

Contents

Preface

The Who's Who of Nobel Prize Winners originated from the difficulty students in our classes were experiencing in finding biographical material on Nobel Prize winners. We felt that Nobel Prize-winning luminaries deserved coverage in a reference source devoted exclusively to providing biographical information and listings of their accomplishments. Oryx Press agreed, and the project was begun.

Two years later, the project was completed with the help of 177 contributors from 67 institutions in 23 states. We are grateful to all of them for their time and energy. All prize winners, from 1901 (when the first awards were given) through 1985, are included.

Research and writing of the 541 entries required tremendous amounts of painstaking work. In addition to careful searching through standard biographical sources, there were visits to countless large libraries, musty archives, and, finally, dust-covered personal biographies where many silent hurrahs were given as a last bit of an individual biographical puzzle was uncovered and put in place. For living laureates, close to 100 letters were sent to check on missing information.

We cannot pay special tribute by name in this Preface to all of our helpers (their names will be found in the "List of Contributors" in this book), but we owe a special debt of gratitude to our capable, hard-working associate editors—Rashelle S. Karp, Louise Sherby, and Parvin Kujoory—and to our invaluable typists—Barbara McNutt and Carol Somers—who labored long and hard to produce the computer disks that were used to generate the final copy. And our Oryx editors, Jan Krygier and Anne Thompson, kept us working toward the deadline and were as much a part of the project as we were.

Despite conscientious verifying, cross-checking, and all of our best efforts, some readers may find errors in our entries. While every effort has been made to ensure that all information is both accurate and current within the confines of format and scope, the editors cannot assume any responsibility for errors or omissions in *The Who's Who of Nobel Prize Winners,* whether such errors or omissions result from accident, negligence, or any other cause. In the event of publication error or omission, the sole responsibility of the editors will be the entry of corrected information in succeeding editions. Please direct all such information to: Bernard S. Schlessinger and June H. Schlessinger, in care of The Oryx Press, 2214 North Central at Encanto, Phoenix, Arizona 85004-1483.

We hope that *The Who's Who of Nobel Prize Winners* will prove to be a useful and valued resource.

Bernard S. Schlessinger, Professor and Associate Dean, Texas Woman's University
June H. Schlessinger, Assistant Professor, North Texas State University

Using this Book

Each entry in this book is composed of 15 fields of information. The format of each field, and some further information about the nature of each field, are explained here.

NAME

The most complete name found for the individual has been used. If a pseudonym was found, it is included in parentheses. If a person's name changed, the former name is included in parentheses. The last name is always given first. Also included as part of the name are titles of nobility, when applicable. Examples of entries are:

Angell, Norman, Sir (Lane, Ralph Norman Angell)

Agnon, Shmuel Yosef (Czaczkes, Shmuel Yosef)

Sienkiewicz, Henryk Adam Aleksandr Pius (Litwos)

All such name variations are included in the Name Index of this book, with "see references" given to direct the user to the main name entry.

PRIZE

The prize awarded is listed, followed by the year in which the prize was won. Thus, this field appears as follows:

Peace, 1931

In those cases where a prize was awarded posthumously or the laureate refused the prize, a notation to that effect is included in the entry. Multiple winners are listed under each applicable category, with "see references" given to direct the user to the first full listing for the winner.

BIRTH AND DEATH DATES

The birth date and death date (when applicable) of each Nobel Prize winner are listed, along with birthplace and location of death (when applicable). States in the United States are abbreviated with standard two-letter codes. Otherwise, the fullest information is presented, as can be seen here:

January 27, 1903; Melbourne, Australia
September 26, 1888; St. Louis, MO

For individuals who were born in the Austro-Hungarian empire prior to 1918, place of birth is given as region of the empire (i.e., Poland or Czechoslovakia) rather than Austria-Hungary.

PARENTS

The names of the winner's father and mother in the fullest form found are included. Mothers' names especially were often difficult to find. The absence of a first or maiden name indicates that only an incomplete name could be found. If no record was found, the term "No record found" is used. Thus, an entry such as the one shown below can be considered to be complete.

Father, Ezra Flory; Mother, Martha Brumgraph Flory

However, entries will also be found in less complete form, such as these:

Father, Muhammed El-Sadat; Mother, no record found

Father, Panayiotis Alepoudelis; Mother, Maria Alepoudelis

NATIONALITY OR CITIZENSHIP

In cases where the laureate was born and remained in the country of birth throughout his or her career, a single notation is given, as in the following example:

German

If the laureate was born in one country, then later moved to and became a citizen of another country, the country of birth is given first, followed by a notation for the country to which the laureate moved and became a citizen. An example is:

German; later American citizen

In cases where laureates spent significant parts of their lives in several countries and obtained multiple citizenships, each of those is identified in the entry. Here is an example:

German; later Swiss and American citizen

In cases where it is known that a laureate resided in a certain country, but citizenship for that country cannot be determined, the entry is arranged as follows:

Dutch; later French resident and American citizen

RELIGION

Of all the fields researched for this book, this was by far the most difficult for which to locate definitive information. Whether the Nobel Prize winner was in Literature, Peace, Economics, Medicine and Physiology, Chemistry, or Physics, there were scant data on religious preference and ofttimes contradictory data. The Literature and Peace winners were more likely to have religion identified, but even in these cases, it was more often a passing (and sometimes puzzling) reference, rather than a clear statement (for example, "Jewish/Evangelical" or "Freethinker; from Lutheran background"). Unless a specific narrow religious preference was stated in the literature consulted, generic terms (such as "Christian") were used. In instances where we were fairly certain of religion, but not positive, we used the term "Most probably." When not even a good guess could be made, we used the notation "No record found." Where a person's religious preference changed, we used statements such as "Agnostic; from Christian background." Also, in some cases, the laureate's parents were of different religious persuasions; that fact has been noted, when known, in the field. Here is an example:

Areligious; from Anglican/Methodist background.

Even when the literature consulted was definite about religious preference, there is still some question as to religious affiliation in some instances because of the highly personal and variable nature of a person's preference in this area. The user should read all entries with that thought in mind; any new information made available will be included in later editions.

EDUCATION

In citing the university name and the the degree name, the format found in the sources consulted was followed. For universities in the United States, the abbreviation of the state in which the university is located is used. For universities outside the United States, the country of location is given. Some country identifications may look odd, as may some spellings, but it must be remembered that both geographic locations and spelling customs changed markedly between 1901 and 1985. Our rule was that we used the data presented in the sources consulted unless an obvious error would thus result. Where the laureate did not receive any degree, the entry reads "No college degrees."

SPOUSE

The full name of the spouse is presented, followed by as full a date of marriage as was available. If the person married more than once, the death or divorce of the previous spouse is noted, with a date, if available. Where it was not possible to determine whether the previous spouse had died or been divorced, that information was omitted. In some cases, the term "dissolved" (used in some sources) is carried into this book as well. If the person did not marry, the notation "None" is used. If it was impossible to determine whether a marriage had occurred, the notation "No record found" is used.

CHILDREN

Where names of children were found, the name plus the term "son" or "daughter" are included. If numbers of children were found, but no names, the numbers are given, sometimes as totals and sometimes broken down by daughters and sons, as available. Interestingly, where names were not found, it was most often the names of daughters; in some cases, sons' names were given, but daughters' names were omitted! Where applicable, and where such information is available, adopted children, stepchildren, and stillborn children are listed as well.

CAREER

In its most complete form, career information is presented this way:

Organization name, geographic location, title, years of employment.

The career entry generally begins with the first "professional" position held by the winner. Thus, for most science-oriented laureates, the first position listed will be after the year of the terminal degree. For academics, the title "Professor" is used, no matter what the rank or the distribution between teaching, research, and service. In the case of the Literature winners, where the person's sole involvement was in writing, the title "Writer" is used. In the case of the Peace winners, where the person's career was spent in a variety of activist and political roles, appropriate general titles such as "Political Activist" or "political posts" are used. For military career years, no specific titles are given.

Many laureates have periods in their careers where they occupied concurrent positions. In these cases, the principal position, as interpreted by the editors, is listed, except in a few extraordinary entries. Occasionally, there will be a gap in coverage, often due to a return to educational pursuit.

OTHER AWARDS

The listings for this field are those taken directly from the sources consulted. Where dates were available, they are included. The awards are listed in chronological order. Knighthood is noted where appropriate, but peerages are not.

SELECTED PUBLICATIONS

For all entries, the publications listed are not exhaustive or comprehensive, but representative of the winners' works. Generally, the recommendations of the contributors to this book were followed. In some few cases, either the winners did not write any works or no titles attributed to them could be found.

Literature and Peace winners' bibliographic listings are more complete than those for the laureates in Economics, Medicine and Physiology, Chemistry, and Physics. For the laureates in Literature and Peace, the total significant output was limited in numbers of titles, unlike the other four areas, in which it was not uncommon to find one laureate with a production of several hundred titles. For the latter four areas, contributors were asked to limit themselves to four to six important contributions representative of the work for which the Prize was awarded or representative of the career work of the laureate.

The titles of works included are given in the most complete form available. For books, both the English title and the original language title, if applicable, are given as presented in standard cataloging sources. For periodical material, the most complete article information and periodical name available in the standard indexing sources consulted are included. If a "Collected Works" was found, it was listed as one of the bibliographic entries. Bibliographic items in this field are in chronological order, and the laureate's name as author is not included.

BIOGRAPHICAL SOURCES

Where a book-length biography or autobiography on the winner was available, it has been listed in this field. For these laureates, usually in Literature or Peace, for whom several biographies were found, the contributors' recommendations were followed.

For many of the science laureates, especially those of more recent vintage, no book-length biographical treatment was found. In those cases, the listings are of either journal articles about the person, the publicity attending the receipt of the prize, or a specialty encyclopedia's treatment of the individual.

Bibliographic items in this field are arranged in alphabetical order. If the title is autobiographical, the author is not listed. For those sources (for example, a *New York Times* article), where the title would be a headline such as "Nobel Prize Announced," the title has been omitted.

COMMENTARY

The commentary provides a brief explanation of why the laureate received his or her prize as well as summarizes other important contributions made by the individual. In this field, the laureate is referred to by his or her familiar name rather than the full name used to head the entry. Where the language of the Academy's citation was available (either in the Nobel Academy's publications or in such standard sources as the *New York Times* or *The Times*), it has been included. Each commentary concludes with a parenthetical abbreviation of the entry editor's name. The complete listing of abbreviations and full editor names can be found in the "List of Contributors" in this volume.

LIST OF CONTRIBUTORS

A.C. - Dr. Ana Cleveland, Professor, Texas Woman's U., Denton, TX

A.D. - Dr. Anne Day, Professor, Clarion U. of PA, Clarion, PA

A.D.J. - Dr. Ada D. Jared, Librarian, Louisiana State U., Alexandria, LA

A.J. - Alice Johnson, Librarian, Texas Woman's U., Denton, TX

A.N. - Dr. Al Nicosia, Professor, Texas Woman's U., Denton, TX

A.S. - Alison Staton, Librarian, McKinney Public Library, McKinney, TX

B.E. - Barbara Edmanson, Texas Woman's U., Denton, TX

B.E.M. - Barbara E. Mooschekian, Librarian, Infomart, Dallas, TX

B.F. - Brenda Flowers, Librarian, Flower Mound Public Library, Flower Mound, TX

B.I.M. - Barbara I. McNutt, Librarian, Monmouth County Library, Freehold, NJ

B.L. - Dr. Bullit Lowry, Professor, North Texas State U., Denton, TX

B.L.W. - Bryan L. Wagner, Student, Clarion U. of PA, Clarion, PA

B.M. - Barbara McCracken, Librarian, Tarrant County Community College, Fort Worth, TX

B.N.L. - Barbara N. List, Librarian, Columbia U., New York, NY

B.R.W. - Beverly R. Wester, Librarian, Health Sciences Library, U. of Maryland, Baltimore, MD

B.S. - Barbara Spencer, Texas Woman's U., Denton, TX

B.S.S. - Dr. Bernard S. Schlessinger, Professor, Texas Woman's U., Denton, TX

B.W. - Brenda Westbrook, Library Consultant, Fort Worth, TX

C.B. - Dr. Charles Bruce, Professor, Texas Woman's U., Denton, TX

C.B.B. - Charlotte B. Brown, Librarian, Franklin and Marshall College, Lancaster, PA

C.C. - Cheryl Chan, Librarian, Texas Woman's U., Denton, TX

C.D. - Connie Dowell, Librarian, U. of California, Santa Barbara, CA

C.E. - Carlyle Edwards, Librarian, Cumberland County Public Library, Fayetteville, NC

C.G. - Carol Godt, Librarian, U. of Michigan, Ann Arbor, MI

C.H.W. - Carol H. Wing, Librarian, Rhode Island College, Providence, RI

C.M. - Carolyn Meanley, Librarian, Jacobs Engineering, Houston, TX

C.N.B. - Cheryl N. Broome, Librarian, Texas Woman's U., Denton, TX

C.R.L. - Charles Logan, Librarian, Naval Underwater Systems Center, New London, CT

C.S. - Carol Somers, Student, Clarion U. of PA, Clarion, PA

C.T. - Clarabel Tanner, Library Consultant, Fort Worth, TX

D.B. - Dr. Daniel Bergen, Professor, U. of Rhode Island, Kingston, RI

D.C. - Dr. Donald Cleveland, Professor, North Texas State U., Denton, TX

D.C.S. - Dr. Darrel C. Sheraw, Professor, Clarion U. of PA, Clarion, PA

D.E.S. - Doreen E. Stevens, Librarian, Cleburne Public Library, Cleburne, TX

D.G. - Diane Grund, Librarian, Moraine Valley Community College, Palos Hills, IL

D.H. - Diane Hudson, Librarian, Texas Woman's U., Denton, TX

D.K. - Deborah Kane, Librarian, Dallas Transportation System, Dallas, TX

D.N.S. - Dr. David N. Shavit, Professor, Northern Illinois U., DeKalb, IL

D.N.W. - David N. Weatherby, Professor, Clarion U. of PA, Clarion, PA

D.O.F. - Dr. Darlene O. Ford, Adjunct Professor, North Texas State U., Denton, TX

D.P. - Dolores Payette, Librarian, Bartlett Public Library, Bartlett, IL

D.P.K. - David P. Karp, Student, Clarion U. of PA, Clarion, PA

D.P.N. - Darlene P. Nichols, Librarian, U. of Michigan, Ann Arbor, MI

D.R. - Dorothy Riemenschneider, Librarian, Columbia U., New York, NY

D.S. - Delbye Sessions, Librarian, Norwich U., Norwich, VT

D.T. - Diane Tilson, Student, Texas Woman's U., Denton, TX

D.V. - Dr. Don Vann and Dolores Vann, Professors, North Texas State U., Denton, TX

D.W. - Diane Whitt, Librarian, De Soto, Inc., Des Plaines, IL

E.B. - Dr. Edra Bogle, Professor, North Texas State U., Denton, TX

E.E.G. - Dr. Elizabeth E. Gunter, Professor, North Texas State U., Denton, TX

E.G. - Elizabeth Gwyn, Librarian, Bridgeport Public Library, Bridgeport, CT

E.L. - Elaine Lowenthal, Librarian, Flossmoor Public Library, Flossmoor, IL

F.K. - Frank Kellerman, Librarian, Brown U., Providence, RI

F.L.T. - Dr. Frank L. Turner, Professor, Texas Woman's U., Denton, TX

F.R.P. - Dr. Francisco R. Perez, Professor, Southwestern Texas State U., San Marcos, TX

G.E.M. - Glenn E. Mensching, Librarian, U. of Michigan, Ann Arbor, MI

G.K. - Dr. Gerald Kirk, Professor, North Texas State U., Denton, TX

G.S. - Dr. Gene Sessions, Professor, Norwich U., Norwich, VT

G.W. - Dr. George Wollaston, Professor, Clarion U. of PA, Clarion, PA

H.J.W. - Henry J. Watkin, Librarian, Columbia U., New York, NY

H.L.F. - Dr. Howard L. Ford, Professor, North Texas State U., Denton, TX

I.H.G. - I. Helen Gross, Librarian, Texas Woman's U., Denton, TX

I.S.Z. - Irwin S. Zeidman, Librarian, Columbia U., New York, NY

J.A. - John Adcox, Student, North Texas State U., Denton, TX

J.A.S. - Joanne A. Saale, Student, Texas Woman's U., Denton, TX

J.B. - Dr. Joni Bodart, Professor, Emporia State U., Emporia, KS

J.B.T. - Dr. Julie B. Todaro, Professor, U. of Michigan, Ann Arbor, MI

J.C. - Joyce Chesher, Student, Texas Woman's U., Denton, TX

J.C.H. - John C. Hepner, Librarian, Texas Woman's U., Denton, TX

J.E.H. - Dr. James E. Hardcastle, Professor, Texas Woman's U., Denton, TX

J.F. - John Ferguson, Professor, Richland Community College, Dallas, TX

J.F.K. - Dr. Jake F. Kobler, Professor, North Texas State U., Denton, TX

J.G. - Dr. James Galloway, Librarian, Texas Woman's U., Denton, TX

J.H. - Joyce Hughes, Librarian, Lewisville Public Schools, Lewisville, TX

J.H.S. - Dr. June H. Schlessinger, Professor, North Texas State U., Denton, TX

J.J.S. - Joel J. Schlessinger, M.D., U. of Alabama, Birmingham, AL

J.L. - Dr. James Lee, Professor, North Texas State U., Denton, TX

J.L.K. - J. Lawrence Kelland, Librarian, U. of Rhode Island, Kingston, RI

J.M.S. - Jeanne M. Stevens, Librarian, Hamline U. School of Law, St. Paul, MN

J.N.B. - Jill N. Bergahn, Student, Texas Woman's U., Denton, TX

J.N.F. - Janice N. Franklin, Student, Texas Woman's U., Denton, TX

J.N.L. - Jeanne N. Leader, Librarian, Bozeman Public Library, Bozeman, MT

J.N.S. - Janice N. Sieburth, Librarian, U. of Rhode Island, Kingston, RI

J.P. - Jeanette Prasifka, Librarian, Anderson Accounting, Dallas, TX

J.S. - Dr. John Smith, Professor, North Texas State U., Denton, TX

J.V. - June Vanderryst, Librarian, Richardson Public Library, Richardson, TX

J.V.S. - Junko V. Stuveras, Librarian, Columbia U., New York, NY

J.W. - Jack Weigel, Librarian, Columbia U., New York, NY

K.C. - Dr. Katherine Cveljo, Professor, North Texas State U., Denton, TX

K.F. - Kay Frey, Librarian, Northern Michigan U., Marquette, MI

K.G. - Kathleen Gunning, Librarian, U. of Houston, Houston, TX

K.H. - Kay Harvey, Librarian, East Texas State U., Commerce, TX

K.J.H. - Kathleen J. Haynes, Librarian, Texas Woman's U., Denton, TX

K.M. - Keith McCreary, North Texas State U., Denton, TX

K.N.M. - Kathleen N. Murray, Librarian, Mount Prospect Public Library, Mount Prospect, IL

L.A. - Linda Arny, Librarian, U. of Massachusetts, Amherst, MA

L.B. - Louise Blalock, Librarian, Darien Public Library, Darien, CT

L.B.W. - Dr. L.B. Woods, Library Director, Henderson State U., Arkadelphia, AR

L.C. - Linda Clary, Student, Texas Woman's U., Denton, TX

L.C.B. - Linda C. Bradley, Student, Texas Woman's U., Denton, TX

L.D. - Lisa Dalton, Librarian, U. of North Carolina, Chapel Hill, NC

L.I.S. - Louise I. Saul, Librarian, Texas Woman's U., Denton, TX

L.I.W. - Lisa I. White, Librarian, Duncanville Public Library, Duncanville, TX

L.K. - Lisa Kammerlocher, Librarian, North Texas State U., Denton, TX

L.M. - Lynda Maceachron, Student, Texas Woman's U., Denton, TX

L.M.W. - Dr. Lucille M. Wert, Librarian, U. of Illinois, Champaign, IL

L.N.W. - Laura N. Windsor, Librarian, U. of Michigan, Ann Arbor, MI

L.P. - Dr. Lloyd Parks, Professor, North Texas State U., Denton, TX

L.R.S. - Dr. L. Robert Stevens, Professor, North Texas State U., Denton, TX

L.S. - Leslie Sandlin, Librarian, Mount Pleasant Public Library, Mount Pleasant, TX

L.S.S. - Louise S. Sherby, Librarian, Columbia U., New York, NY

L.T. - Linda Tashbook, Librarian, Texas Woman's U., Denton, TX

L.W. - Loralyn Whitney, Librarian, Villa Maria College Library, Erie, PA

M.A.V.C. - Mary Ann Van Cura, Librarian, Hamline U. School of Law, St. Paul, MN

M.B. - Martha Babula, Student, Northern Illinois U., DeKalb, IL

M.C. - Mary Coleson, Student, Texas Woman's U., Denton, TX

M.D.C. - Marcy Ducca Carrick, Teacher, Cortez High School, Phoenix, AZ

M.E.T. - Mary E. Teasdale, Student, Texas Woman's U., Denton, TX

M.F. - Maurice Fortin, Librarian, North Texas State U., Denton, TX

M.F.L. - Maureen F. Logan, Teacher, Westerly High School, Westerly, RI

M.G.R. - Dr. Martha G. Randiro, Professor, Texas Woman's U., Denton, TX

M.H. - Marguerite Horn, Librarian, Brown U., Providence, RI

M.J.B. - Marsha J. Blair, Librarian, East Texas State U., Commerce, TX

M.J.H. - Mary Jane Hilburger, Librarian, Northeastern Illinois U., Chicago, IL

M.K. - Mona Kerby, Librarian, Arlington District, Arlington, TX

M.L. - Marlene Latuch, Librarian, Somerset District, Somerset, PA

M.L.L. - Marlene L. Lopes, Librarian, Rhode Island College, Providence, RI

M.N. - Metta Nicewarmer, Librarian, Texas Woman's U., Denton, TX

M.N.C. - Mary N. Cargill, Librarian, Columbia U., New York, NY

M.N.K. - Mary N. Kay, Librarian, Columbia U., New York, NY

M.P. - Mary Porrett, Librarian, Texas Woman's U., Denton, TX

N.H. - Nancy Humphreys, Librarian, U. of Wisconsin, Whitewater, WI

N.L. - Nolan Lushington, Librarian, Greenwich Public Library, Greenwich, CT

N.R.H. - Nancy R. Hessler, Librarian, Moraine Valley Community College, Palos Hills, IL

P.A.C. - Patricia A. Cannon, Librarian, Amarillo Public Library, Amarillo, TX

P.A.G. - Dr. Pete A. Gunter, Professor, North Texas State U., Denton, TX

P.E.J. - Dr. Patricia E. Jensen, Professor, U. of Rhode Island, Kingston, RI

P.H. - Phillip Hight, Librarian, Northeastern Illinois U., Chicago, IL

P.K. - Dr. Parvin Kujoory, Professor, Prairie View A & M U., Prairie View, TX

P.M. - Patricia Montrose, Student, Texas Woman's U., Denton, TX

P.P. - Patricia Peak, Librarian, Texas Woman's U., Denton, TX

P.P.F. - Pamela P. Feather, Librarian, Oswego Public Library, Oswego, IL

P.P.H. - Dr. Pamela P. Hufnagel, Professor, Pennsylvania State U., Dubois, PA

P.S. - Patricia Squires, Librarian, Northern Telecom, Dallas, TX

R.A. - Dr. Reynaldo Ayala, Professor, U. of San Diego, Calexico, CA

R.G. - Dr. Ray Granade, Professor, Ouachita Baptist U., Arkadelphia, AR

R.J. - Ralph Johnson, Librarian, North Texas State U., Denton, TX

R.K. - Dr. Rashelle Karp, Professor, Clarion U. of PA, Clarion, PA

R.P. - Robert Peden, Librarian, Infomart, Dallas, TX

R.R. - Richard Russell, Librarian, Glenville State College, Glenville, WV

R.S.L. - Dr. Robert S. La Forte, Professor, North Texas State U., Denton, TX

R.W.S. - Robert W. Sears, Librarian, Dallas Public Library, Dallas, TX

S.B. - Shelly Blakeley, Librarian, Texas Woman's U., Denton, TX

S.C. - Sharon Charette, Librarian, Wheaton College, Norton, MA

S.D. - Sara Davis, Librarian, Jacobs Engineering, Houston, TX

S.D.S. - Sarah D. Smith, Librarian, Indian Trails Public Library, Wheeling, IL

S.G. - Sandy Gallup, Librarian, Brown U., Providence, RI

S.H.S. - Sarah H. Spurgin, Librarian, Columbia U., New York, NY

S.K. - Stephen Kochoff, Librarian, Columbia U., New York, NY

S.K.A. - Sheila K. Arestad, Librarian, Franklin and Marshall College, Lancaster, PA

S.M. - Dr. Samuel Marino, Professor, Texas Woman's U., Denton, TX

S.O. - Dr. Solveig Olsen, Professor, North Texas State U., Denton, TX

S.R. - Susan Roosth, Librarian, Southern Methodist U., Dallas, TX

S.W. - Dr. Steve Wood, Professor, U. of Rhode Island, Kingston, RI

S.W.C. - Sarah W. Cogan, Librarian, U. of Michigan, Ann Arbor, MI

T.B. - Teresa Bungard, Librarian, U. of Michigan, Ann Arbor, MI

T.K. - Taissa Kuzma, Librarian, American Mathematical Society, Providence, RI

T.M. - Thomas McGinty, Librarian, LTV Corporation, Dallas, TX

T.N.B. - Thomas N. Booker, Student, Texas Woman's U., Denton, TX

T.S. - Tony Stankus, Librarian, Holy Cross College, Worcester, MA

T.S.K. - Dr. Turner S. Kobler, Professor, Texas Woman's U., Denton, TX

V.A.H. - Virginia A. Hooton, Librarian, U. of Texas at Dallas, Dallas, TX

V.B. - Veronica Beasley, Student, Texas Woman's U., Denton, TX

V.C. - Victoria Clayton, Librarian, Queens College, Flushing, NY

V.V.M. - Dr. Vandelia Van Meter, Professor, University of Southern Mississippi, Hattiesburg, MS

W.E.W. - Wynne E. Weiss, Librarian, Des Plaines Public Library, Des Plaines, IL

W.G. - Wendy Graham, Librarian, Montana State Library, Helena, MT

W.K. - Dr. William Kamman, Professor, North Texas State U., Denton, TX

W.L.N. - Dr. W. Lee Nahrgang, Professor, North Texas State U., Denton, TX

MAIN ENTRY SECTION

Chemistry

1901

Van't Hoff, Jacobus Henricus   **1**
PRIZE: Chemistry, 1901. BORN: August 30, 1852; Rotterdam, Netherlands. DIED: March 1, 1911; Berlin, Germany. PARENTS: Father, Jacobus Henricus Van't Hoff; Mother, Alida Jacoba Kalff Van't Hoff. NATIONALITY: Dutch. RELIGION: No organized religion; most probably Christian/Protestant background. EDUCATION: Polytechnic School, Netherlands, technology diploma, 1871; Univ. of Utrecht, Netherlands, doctorate, 1874. SPOUSE: Johanna Francina Mees, married 1878. CHILDREN: Johanna Francina, daughter; Aleida Jacoba, daughter; Jacobu Henricus, son; Govert Jacob, son. CAREER: Veterinary College, Utrecht, Netherlands, Professor, 1876-77; Univ. of Amsterdam, Netherlands, Professor, 1877-78; Univ. of Leipzig, Germany, Professor, 1878-96; Univ. of Berlin, Germany, Professor, 1896-1911. OTHER AWARDS: Davy Medal, 1893; Chevalier de la Legion d'Honneur, 1894; Helmholtz Medal, Prussian Academy of Sciences, 1911.

Selected Publications: *La Chimie dans l'Espace.* Rotterdam: P.M. Bazendijk, 1875. *Ansichten Uber die Organische Chemie.* 2 volumes. Braunschweis, Germany: F. Viewes, 1878-81. *Etudes de Dynamique Chimique.* Amsterdam: F. Muller & Co., 1884. *Lois de l'Equilibre Chimique dans l'Etate Dilue, Gazeux on Dissous.* Stockholm: P.A. Norstedt, 1886. *Vorlesunsen uber Theoretischen und Physikalischen Chemie.* 3 volumes. Braunschweig, Germany: F. Vieweg und Sohn, 1898-1900.

For More Information See: Cohen, E. *Jacobus Henricus Van't Hoff. Sein Leben und Werken.* Leipzig, Germany: Akademische Verlags-gesellschaft, 1912. *Dictionary of Scientific Biography.* New York: Scribner's, 1976 (Volume 13), 575-81.

Commentary: Jacobus Van't Hoff was awarded the Nobel Prize "in recognition of the extraordinary services he has rendered by the discovery of the laws of chemical dynamics and osmotic pressure in solutions." In addition to this work, he was also noted for his research on structural formulas in space (stereochemistry) and on chemical equilibrium. (W.G.)

1902

Fischer, Emil Herman   **2**
PRIZE: Chemistry, 1902. BORN: October 9, 1852; Euskirchen, Germany. DIED: July 15, 1919; Berlin, Germany. PARENTS: Father, Laurenz Fischer; Mother, Julie Poensgen Fischer. NATIONALITY: German. RELIGION: Protestant. EDUCATION: Univ. of Bonn, Germany, B.S., 1871; Univ. of Strasbourg, France, Ph.D., 1874. SPOUSE: Agnes Gerlach, married 1888. CHILDREN: Hermann Otto Laurenz, son; 2 other sons. CAREER: Univ. of Munich, Germany, Professor, 1875-82; Univ. of Erlangen, Germany, Professor, 1882-85; Univ. of Wurzberg, Germany, Professor, 1885-92; Univ. of Berlin, Germany, Professor, 1892-1919. OTHER AWARDS: Davy Medal, 1890; Hofman Medal, German Chemical Society, 1906; Elliot Cresson Gold Medal, Franklin Institute, Philadelphia, PA, 1913.

Selected Publications: *Anleitung zur Darstellung Organischer Präparate.* Würzburg, Germany: Verlag der Stahel'schen kgl. Hof-und Universitäts-Buch und Kunstbandlung, 1893. *Untersuchungen über Aminosäuren, Polypeptide, und Proteine, 1899-1906.* Berlin: Springer, 1906. *Untersuchungen in der Puringrupp, 1882-1906.* Berlin: Springer, 1907. *Untersuchungen über Triphenylmethanfarbstoffe, Hydrazine, und Indole.* Berlin: Springer, 1924.

For More Information See: *Aus Meinem Leben.* Berlin: Verlang Julius Springer, 1921. *Dictionary of Scientific Biography.* New York: Scribner's, 1972 (Volume 5), 1-5. Forster, Martin Onslow. "Emil Fischer Memorial Lecture." *Journal of the Chemical Society* 117 (1920): 1157-1201. Hoesch, Kurt. *Emil Fischer, Sein Leben und Sein Werk.* Berlin: Verlag Chemie, 1921.

Commentary: Emil Fischer was awarded the Nobel Prize for his work with the carbohydrate and purine chemical groups. In addition, he was recognized for his work in the areas of enzyme chemistry and aniline dyestuffs, his syntheses of previously unknown amino acids, and the fatty acid esterification of glycerol to produce margarine. Fischer greatly expanded the science of biochemistry by elucidating basic chemical structures, clarifying structural relationships within chemical groups, and synthesizing new variations and configurations of organic substances. A practical aspect of his research was the development of laboratory principles which were applicable in the technological production of synthetic chemicals and foodstuffs. (D.O.F.)

1903

Arrhenius, Svante August   **3**
PRIZE: Chemistry, 1903. BORN: February 19, 1859; Wijk, Sweden. DIED: October 2, 1927; Stockholm, Sweden. PARENTS: Father, Svante Gustav Arrhenius; Mother, Carolina Christina Thunberg Arrhenius. NATIONALITY: Swedish. RELIGION: Lutheran. EDUCATION: Univ. of Uppsala, Sweden, Ph.D., 1884. SPOUSE: Sofia Rudbeck, married 1894; Maria Johansson, married 1905. CHILDREN: Olof, son; Sven, son; Ester, daughter; Anna-Lisa, daughter. CAREER: Univ. of Uppsala, Sweden, Professor, 1884-91; Univ. of Stockholm, Sweden, Professor and Administrator, 1891-1905; Nobel Institute

for Physical Chemistry, Sweden, Director, 1905-27. OTHER AWARDS: Davy Medal, Royal Society, 1902; Willard Gibbs Medal, United States, 1911; Faraday Medal, 1914.

Selected Publications: *Lehrbuch der Elektrochemie.* Leipzig, Germany: Quandt & Handell, 1901 (*Textbook on Electrochemistry.* Tr. by John McCrae. New York: Longmans Green & Co., 1902). *Theorien der Chemie.* Leipzig, Germany: Akademische Verlagsegesellschaft, 1906 (*Theories of Chemistry.* Tr. by T. Slater Price. New York: Longmans Green & Co., 1907). *The World in the Making: Evolution of the Universe.* New York: Harper & Brothers, 1908. *The Silliman Lectures and Theories of Solutions.* New Haven, CT: Yale U. Press, 1912. *The Quantitative Laws in Biological Chemistry.* London: G. Bell & Sons, 1915.

For More Information See: *Dictionary of Scientific Biography.* New York: Scribner's, 1973 (Volume 1), 296-302. "Svante August Arrhenius." *Zeitschrift fur Physikalische Chemie* 69 (1909): 5-20. *Svenst Biografiskt Lexikon.* Stockholm: Albert Bonniers Forlag, 1920 (Volume 2), 287-301.

Commentary: Svante Arrhenius received the Nobel "in recognition of the extraordinary services he has rendered to the advancement of chemistry by his electrolytic theory of dissociation." He was also notable for his work in electrical conductivity, in serology and immunochemistry, and in physical processes in the universe. Arrhenius participated actively in nonscientific affairs and was instrumental in negotiating the release of German-Austrian scientists who were prisoners of war in World War I. (B.S.S.)

1904

Ramsay, William, Sir   4

PRIZE: Chemistry, 1904. BORN: October 2, 1852; High Wycombe, Buckinghamshire, Glasgow, Scotland. DIED: July 23, 1916; High Wycombe, Buckinghamshire, Glasgow, Scotland. PARENTS: Father, Robertson W. Ramsay; Mother, Catherine Robertson Ramsay. NATIONALITY: Scottish. RELIGION: Calvinist. EDUCATION: Univ. of Tübingen, Germany, Ph.D., 1872. SPOUSE: Margaret Stevenson Buchanan, married August 1881. CHILDREN: 1 son; 1 daughter. CAREER: Anderson College, Glasgow, Scotland, Professor, 1872-74; Univ. of Glasgow, Scotland, Professor, 1874-80; Bristol Univ., England, Professor, 1880-87; Univ. of London, England, Professor, 1887-1913. OTHER AWARDS: Davy Medal, Royal Society, 1895; Hodgkins Prize, Smithsonian Institution, 1895; French Academy of Scientists Prize, 1895; Knighthood, 1902; A.W. Hoffman Medal, German Chemical Society, 1903; Prussian Order of Merit; Commander of the Crown of Italy.

Selected Publications: *The Gases of the Atmosphere: The History of Their Discovery.* New York: Macmillan, 1896. *Modern Chemistry: Theoretical.* London: J. Dent, 1900. *Modern Chemistry: Systematic.* London: J. Dent, 1900. *Introduction to the Study of Physical Chemistry.* London: Joseph Black, 1904. *Essays Biographical and Chemical.* London: A. Constable & Co., 1908. *Elements and Electrons.* New York: Harper, 1912.

For More Information See: *Dictionary of Scientific Biography.* New York: Scribner's, 1973 (Volume 11), 277-84. Travers, Morris W. *A Life of William Ramsay.* London: Edward Arnold, 1956.

Commentary: William Ramsay's Nobel was "in recognition of his services in the discovery of the inert gaseous elements in air, and his determination of their place in the periodic system." His interests, however, were far-ranging and included significant work on the pyridine bases, on evaporation and dissociation, on molecular surface energy, and on radioactivity. (B.S.S.)

1905

Von Baeyer, Adolf Johann Friedrich Wilhelm   5

PRIZE: Chemistry, 1905. BORN: October 31, 1835; Berlin, Germany. DIED: August 20, 1917; Starnberg, Bavaria, Germany. PARENTS: Father, Johann Jakob von Baeyer; Mother, Eugenie Hitzig von Baeyer. NATIONALITY: German. RELIGION: Jewish/Evangelical. EDUCATION: Univ. of Berlin, Germany, Ph.D., 1858. SPOUSE: Adelheid Bendemann, married 1868. CHILDREN: Eugenie, daughter; Hans, son; Otto, son. CAREER: Kekule Laboratory, Heidelberg, Germany, Researcher, 1858-60; Trade Academy, Berlin, Germany, Professor, 1860-66; Univ. of Berlin, Germany, Professor, 1866-69; War Academy, Germany, Professor, 1869-71; Univ. of Strassburg, Germany, Professor, 1871-73; Univ. of Munich, Germany, Professor, 1873-1917. OTHER AWARDS: Davy Medal, Royal Society, 1881.

Selected Publications: *Adolph von Baeyer's Gesammelte Werke* (*Collected Works*). 2 volumes. Brunswick, Germany: F. Viewig und Sohn, 1905.

For More Information See: *Dictionary of Scientific Biography.* New York: Scribner's, 1970 (Volume 2), 389-91. Rupe, H. *Adolf von Baeyer als Lehrer und Forscher.* Stuttgart, Germany: F. Enke, 1932.

Commentary: Adolf von Baeyer was granted the Nobel "in recognition of his services in the advancement of organic chemistry and the chemical industry, through his work on organic dyes and hydroaromatic compounds." One of the fathers of organic chemistry, Baeyer's work encompassed the study of uric acid, barbituric acid, indigo, indole, indigotin, zinc-dust distillation, condensation reactions, the phthaleins, acetylene, polyacetylene, organic peroxides, oxonium compounds, benzene and cyclic terpene. (B.S.S.)

1906

Moissan, Ferdinand Frederick Henri   6

PRIZE: Chemistry, 1906. BORN: September 28, 1852; Paris, France. DIED: February 20, 1907; Paris, France. PARENTS: Father, no record found; Mother, Mitelle Moissan. NATIONALITY: French. RELIGION: Jewish. EDUCATION: Univ. of Paris, France, baccalaureate, 1874; Univ. of Paris, France, licence, 1877; Univ. of Paris, France, docteur es sciences physiques, 1880. SPOUSE: Leonie Lugan, married 1882. CHILDREN: Louis, son. CAREER: École Superieure de Pharmacie, France, Professor, 1879-83, 1886-1900; Univ. of Sorbonne, France, Professor, 1900-07. OTHER AWARDS: Lacaze Prize, Academy of Sciences, 1887; Davy Medal, Royal Society, 1896; Hoffman Medal, German Chemical Society, 1903.

Selected Publications: *Le Four Electrique.* Paris: G. Steinheil, 1897. *Le Fluor et ses Composes.* Paris: G. Steinheil, 1900. *Le Chimie Minerale, ses Relations avec les Autres Sciences.* Paris: G. Steinheil, 1904. *Traite de Chimie Minerale.* Paris: Masson, 1904-06.

For More Information See: *Dictionary of Scientific Biography.* New York: Scribner's, 1970 (Volume 9), 450-52. Lebeau, Paul. "Henri Moissan." *Bulletin de la Societe Chimique de France* (4th series) 3 (1908): 1-38.

Commentary: Henri Moissan was awarded the Nobel Prize "in recognition of the great services rendered by him in his investigation and isolation of the element fluorine, and for the adoption in the service of science of the electric furnace called after him." Moissan used the high temperatures attainable in the electric furnace he developed to prepare numerous new compounds and to vaporize substances previously regarded as infusible. In addition, he discovered silicon carbide (carborundum), produced artificial diamonds, and devised a commercially profitable method of producing acetylene. The development of high-temperature chemistry was greatly inspired by his electric furnace. (D.R.)

1907

Buchner, Eduard   7
PRIZE: Chemistry, 1907. BORN: May 20, 1860; Munich, Germany. DIED: August 13, 1917; Focsani, Rumania. PARENTS: Father, Ernst Buchner; Mother, Friederike Martin Buchner. NATIONALITY: German. RELIGION: Most probably Christian/Protestant. EDUCATION: Univ. of Munich, Germany, Ph.D., 1888. SPOUSE: Lotte Stahl, married 1900. CHILDREN: 2 sons; 1 daughter. CAREER: Univ. of Munich, Germany, Professor, 1889-93; Univ. of Kiel, Germany, Professor, 1893-96; Univ. of Tubingen, Germany, Professor, 1896-98; Agricultural College, Berlin, Germany, Professor, 1898-1908; Univ. of Breslau, Germany, Professor, 1908-11; Univ. of Wurzburg, Germany, Professor, 1911-17.

Selected Publications: *Die Zymassegarung* (*Zymosis*). Munich: R. Oldenbourg, 1903 (with H. Buchner and M. Hahn).

For More Information See: *Biographical Dictionary of Scientists.* London: A. and C. Black, 1969, 87-88. *Dictionary of Scientific Biography.* New York: Scribner's, 1970 (Volume 2), 560-63.

Commentary: Eduard Buchner was awarded the Nobel Prize in chemistry in 1907 "for his biochemical researches and his discovery of cell-free fermentation," the turning point for the study of enzymes and the beginning of modern enzyme chemistry. By grinding yeast cells with sand at a controlled temperature, he was able to prepare a cell-free extract that would ferment sucrose to ethanol. He called the active, fermentation-producing agent of the expressed fluid "zymase." The work showed that living yeast cells were not essential for fermentation as others had supposed. Buchner's revolutionary discoveries in biochemistry overshadowed his work in preparative organic chemistry, one result of which was the syntheses of cycloheptatriene and cycloheptane-carboxylic acid. (D.R.)

1908

Rutherford, Ernest, Sir   8
PRIZE: Chemistry, 1908. BORN: August 30, 1871; Spring Grove, New Zealand. DIED: October 19, 1937; Cambridge, England. PARENTS: Father, James Rutherford; Mother, Martha Thompson Rutherford. NATIONALITY: British. RELIGION: Protestant. EDUCATION: Canterbury College, New Zealand, B.A., 1892; Canterbury College, New Zealand, M.A., 1893; Canterbury College, New Zealand, B.Sc., 1894. SPOUSE: Mary Georgina Newton, married 1900. CHILDREN: Eileen, daughter. CAREER: McGill Univ., Canada, Professor, 1898-1907; Victoria Univ., Manchester, England, Professor, 1907-19; Cambridge Univ., England, Professor, 1919-37. OTHER AWARDS: Rumford Medal, Royal Society, 1904; Bressa Prize, 1910; Knighthood, 1914; Copley Medal, Royal Society, 1922; Order of Merit, 1925; Albert Medal, Royal Society of Arts, 1928; Faraday Medal, 1930.

Selected Publications: *Radioactivity.* Cambridge: Cambridge U. Press, 1904. *Radioactive Transformations.* London: A. Constable, 1906. *Radioactive Substances and Their Radiations.* Cambridge: Cambridge U. Press, 1913. *Radiations from Radioactive Substances.* Cambridge: Cambridge U. Press, 1930 (with J. Chadwick and C.D. Ellis). *The Newer Alchemy.* New York: Macmillan, 1937. *Collected Papers of Lord Rutherford of Nelson.* 3 volumes. New York: Interscience Publishers, 1962-65.

For More Information See: *Dictionary of Scientific Biography.* New York: Scribner's, 1975 (Volume 12), 25-36. Feather, Norman. *Lord Rutherford.* London: Blackie and Son, Ltd., 1940. *Obituary Notices of the Royal Society of London.* Cambridge: Royal Society, 1938 (Volume 2), 395-423.

Commentary: Ernest Rutherford was honored by the Academy "for his investigations into the disintegration of the elements, and the chemistry of radioactive substances." While still in New Zealand, Rutherford studied the magnetic properties of iron in high-frequency discharges and designed a time-measuring device. In England, he invented an electromagnetic wave detector and studied x-ray bombardment and uranium radiations. During his time in Canada, he continued his studies of radioactivity and radon. Back in England, his further studies on radioactivity led to his concept of nuclear structure and eventually to the bombardment studies that elaborated this, and produced transmutations. In addition to his own work, he developed a multitude of great researchers. (L.K.)

1909

Ostwald, Friedrich Wilhelm   9
PRIZE: Chemistry, 1909. BORN: September 2, 1853; Riga, Latvia. DIED: April 4, 1932; Grossbothen, Germany. PARENTS: Father, Gottfried Ostwald; Mother, Elizabeth Leuckel Ostwald. NATIONALITY: Latvian; later German citizen. RELIGION: Christian. EDUCATION: Univ. of Dorpat, Latvia, graduate, 1875; Univ. of Dorpat, Latvia, M.A., 1876; Univ. of Dorpat, Latvia, Ph.D., 1878. SPOUSE: Helene von Reyher, married April 24, 1880. CHILDREN: Carl Wilhelm Wolfgang, son; Grete, daughter; 3 other children. CAREER: Riga Polytechnic Institute, Latvia, Professor, 1881-87; Univ. of Leipzig, Germany, Professor, 1887-1906. OTHER AWARDS: Faraday Medal, Royal Society, 1904.

Selected Publications: *Lehrbuch der Allgemeinen Chemie.* Leipzig, Germany: Engleman, 1891-1902. *Hand-und Hilfsbuch zur Ausfuhrung Physikochemischer Messungen.* Leipzig, Germany: W. Englemann, 1893. "Uber Physikochemische Messmethoden." *Zeitschrift fur Physikalische Chemie* 17 (1895): 427-45. *Grundlinien der Anorganischen Chemie.* Leipzig, Germany:

W. Englemann, 1900. "Uber Katalyse." *Verhandlungen der Gesellschaft Deutsch Naturforscher und Arzte* 73 (1901): 184-201.

For More Information See: *Dictionary of Scientific Biography.* New York: Scribner's, 1978 (Volume 15), 455-69. *Lebenslinien.* 3 volumes. Berlin: Klasing and Co., 1926-27. Ostwald, Grete. *Wilhelm Ostwald, Mein Vater.* Stuttgart, Germany: Berliner Union, 1953.

Commentary: The Nobel Prize was presented to Wilhelm Ostwald "for his work on catalysis and on the conditions of chemical equilibrium and velocities of chemical reactions." Ostwald's early research on chemical dynamics and his efforts to develop new methods of measurement prompted his emergence as one of the central figures in the development of the new field of physical chemistry. His studies of catalysis, seminal in this field, led to his patenting of the Ostwald process of oxidizing ammonia to nitric acid. Ostwald's writings were basic to the developing fields of inorganic, analytical, and physical chemistry. His later philosophical and "universal" scientific writings were equally important. (L.K.)

1910

Wallach, Otto   10

PRIZE: Chemistry, 1910. BORN: March 27, 1847; Koenigsberg, Germany. DIED: February 26, 1931; Goettingen, Germany. PARENTS: Father, Gerhard Wallach; Mother, Otillia Thoma Wallach. NATIONALITY: German. RELIGION: Jewish. EDUCATION: Univ. of Gottingen, Germany, Ph.D., 1869. SPOUSE: None. CHILDREN: None. CAREER: Aktiengesellschaft fuer Anilinfabrikation, Germany, Researcher, 1871-73; Univ. of Bonn, Germany, Professor, 1873-89; Univ. of Gottingen, Germany, Professor, 1889-1915. OTHER AWARDS: Davy Medal, 1912.

Selected Publications: "Zur Kentniss de Terpene und Atherischen Oele IV." *Justus Liebigs Annalen der Chemie* 238 (1887): 78-89. "Zur Constitutionsbestimmung des Terpineols." *Berichte der Deutschen Chemischen Gesellschaft* 28 (1895): 1773-77. *Die Terpene und Campher.* Leipzig, Germany: Veit, 1909.

For More Information See: *Dictionary of Scientific Biography.* New York: Scribner's (Volume 14), 141-42. Partridge, William S., and Schierz, Ernest R. "Otto Wallach: The First Organizer of the Terpenes." *Journal of Chemical Education* 24 (1947): 106-08.

Commentary: The Nobel Award to Otto Wallach was "in recognition of his services to organic chemistry and the chemical industry by his pioneer work in the field of alicyclic compounds." Although he was also responsible for some of the key research on organic structure determination and on organic syntheses and transformations, his research in the area of oils and perfumes is usually cited because of its impetus in the development of a major industry. (J.H.)

1911

Curie, Marie (Sklodowska, Maria)   11

PRIZE: Physics, 1903; Chemistry, 1911. BORN: November 7, 1867; Warsaw, Poland. DIED: July 4, 1934; Sancellemoz, France. PARENTS: Father, Wladyslaw Sklodowska; Mother, Bronislawa Boguska Sklodowska. NATIONALITY: Polish; later French citizen. RELIGION:

Anticlerical; from Catholic background. EDUCATION: Univ. of Paris-Sorbonne, France, licence es sciences physiques, 1893; Univ. of Paris-Sorbonne, France, licence es sciences mathematiques, 1894; Univ. of Paris-Sorbonne, France, Ph.D., 1904. SPOUSE: Pierre Curie, married July 25, 1895. CHILDREN: Irene, daughter; Eve, daughter. CAREER: Governess, 1885-91; École Normale Supérieur, Sevres, France, Professor, 1900; Univ. of Sorbonne, France, Professor, 1904-34. OTHER AWARDS: Berthelot Medal, Academie des Sciences, 1902; Gegner Prize, 1902; Davy Medal, Royal Society, 1903; Elliott Cresson Medal, 1909.

Selected Publications: *Recherches sur les Substances Radioactives.* Paris: Gauthier-Villars, 1904. *Traité de Radioactivité.* 2 volumes. Paris: Gauthier-Villars, 1910. "Les Mesures en Radioactivité et l'Etalon du Radium." *Journal de Physique* 2 (1912): 715. *Oeuvres de Marie Sklodowska-Curie.* Warsaw: Panstwowie Widawnictwo Naukowe, 1954.

For More Information See: Cotton, Eugene. *Les Curies.* Paris: Seghers, 1963. Curie, Eve. *Madame Curie.* Paris: Gallimard, 1939. *Dictionary of Scientific Biography.* New York: Scribner's, 1971 (Volume 3), 497-503.

Commentary: Marie Curie was the first woman to win a Nobel Prize and the first person to receive two Nobel Prizes. She shared the first Nobel, in Physics, with her husband, Pierre, and A.H. Becquerel "in recognition of the special services rendered by them in the work they jointly carried out in investigating the phenomena of radiation discovered by Professor Becquerel." Her second unshared Nobel Prize, in Chemistry, came "in recognition of the services rendered by her to the development of chemistry: by her discovery of the elements radium and polonium, by her determination of the nature of radium and isolation of it in a metallic state, and by her investigations into the compounds of this remarkable element." (V.C.)

1912

Grignard, Francois Auguste Victor   12

PRIZE: Chemistry, 1912. BORN: May 6, 1891; Cherbourg, France. DIED: December 13, 1935; Lyons, France. PARENTS: Father, Theophile Henri Grignard; Mother, Marie Hebert Grignard. NATIONALITY: French. RELIGION: Most probably Christian/Protestant. EDUCATION: Univ. of Lyons, France, Licencie es Sciences Mathematiques, 1893; Univ. of Lyons, France, Licencie es Sciences Physiques, 1898; Univ. of Lyons, France, Docteur es Sciences, 1901. SPOUSE: Augustine Marie Boulant, married 1910. CHILDREN: Roger, son; 1 daughter. CAREER: Univ. of Lyons, France, Professor, 1894-1905; Univ. of Besancon, France, Professor, 1905-06; Univ. of Lyons, France, Professor, 1906-09; Univ. of Nancy, France, Professor, 1909-32. OTHER AWARDS: Cahours Prize (Institute de France), 1901 and 1902; Bertholet Medal, 1902; Prix Jecker, 1905; Lavoisier Medal, 1912.

Selected Publications: "Sur Quelques Nouvelles Combinaisons Organometalliques du Magnesium et Leur Application a des Syntheses d'Alcohols et d'Hydrocarbures." *Comptes Rendus de l'Academie des Sciences* 126 (1898): 1322. "Sur les Combinaisons Organomagnesiennes Mixtes et Leur Application a des

Syntheses d'Acides, d'Alcohols, et d'Hydrocarbures."
Annales de l'Universite de Lyon 6 (1901): 1-116. *Traite de Chimie Organique*. Paris: Masson, 1935-59.

For More Information See: *Dictionary of Scientific Biography*. New York: Scribner's, 1972 (Volume 5), 540-41. "Victor Grignard." *Journal of the American Chemical Society* 59 (1937): 17-19.

Commentary: The award to Victor Grignard was "for the discovery of the so-called Grignard reagent, which in recent years has greatly advanced the progress of organic chemistry." He first studied ethyl beta-isopropylacetobutyrate, the diisopropylbutenedicarboxylic acids and branched unsaturated hydrocarbons, moving on then to the organomagnesium compounds. After preparation of the magnesium alkyl halides, he used them to prepare alcohols, ketones, keto-esters, nitriles, terpene compounds, and fulvenes. Grignard also studied hydrocarbon cracking and catalytic hydrogenation and dehydrogenation. (M.E.T.)

Sabatier, Paul 13

PRIZE: Chemistry, 1912. BORN: November 5, 1854; Carcassone, France. DIED: August 14, 1941; Toulouse, France. PARENTS: No record found. NATIONALITY: French. RELIGION: Catholic. EDUCATION: École Normale Supérieure, France, Agrege in Physical Sciences, 1877; College de France, Doctor of Science, 1880. SPOUSE: (No first name found) Herail, married (no date found). CHILDREN: 4 daughters. CAREER: Lycée of Nimes, France, Professor, 1877-78; College de France, Professor, 1878-80; Univ. of Bordeaux, France, Professor, 1880-82; Univ. of Toulouse, France, Professor, 1882-1929. OTHER AWARDS: Prix La Caze, Academy of Sciences, 1897; Prix Jecker, Academy of Sciences, 1905; Davy Medal, Royal Society, 1915; Special Award, American Chemical Society, 1926; Franklin Medal, Franklin Institute of Philadelphia, 1933; Commander, Legion d'Honneur.

Selected Publications: *Leçons Elementaires de Chimie Agricole* (*Elementary Lessons in Agricultural Chemistry*). Paris: G. Masson, 1890. *La Catalyse en Chimie Organique* (*Catalysis in Organic Chemistry*). Paris: Beranger, 1913. "How I Have Been Led to the Direct Hydrogenation Method by Metallic Catalysts." *Industrial and Engineering Chemistry* 18 (October 1926): 1005-08.

For More Information See: *Biographical Memoirs of the Fellows of the Royal Society*. London: Royal Society, 1942-44 (Volume 4), 63-66. *Dictionary of Scientific Biography*. New York: Scribner's, 1975 (Volume 12), 46-47. "Paul Sabatier, 1854-1941." *Nature* 174 (November 6, 1954): 859-60.

Commentary: Recognized early for his work in physical chemistry, Paul Sabatier expanded his studies to include organic processes and molecular structure, culminating in the Nobel Prize awarded "for his method of hydrogenating organic compounds in the presence of finely divided metals whereby the progress of organic chemistry has been greatly advanced in recent years." In 1897, in collaboration with the Abbé Jean-Baptiste Senderens, he initiated over 30 years of research and refinement of the chemical theory involved. He elaborated on his hypothesis in *La Catalyse en Chimie Organique*, considered a fundamental title in organic catalysis. Sabatier sparked broader provincial

participation in French scientific institutions and, through his advocacy of new techniques, expanded scientific accomplishment. (P.A.C.)

1913

Werner, Alfred 14

PRIZE: Chemistry, 1913. BORN: December 12, 1866; Mulhausen, France. DIED: November 15, 1919; Zurich, Switzerland. PARENTS: Father, Jean-Adam Werner; Mother, Salome Jeannette Tesche Werner. NATIONALITY: French; later Swiss citizen. RELIGION: Catholic. EDUCATION: Zurich Polytechnikum, Switzerland, baccalaureate, 1889; Univ. of Zurich, Switzerland, doctorate, 1890. SPOUSE: Emma Wilhelmine Giesker, married 1894. CHILDREN: Alfred, son; Charlotte, daughter. CAREER: Zurich Polytechnikum, Switzerland, Professor, 1889-91; College de France, 1891-92; Zurich Polytechnikum, Switzerland, Professor, 1892-93, Univ. of Zurich, Switzerland, Professor, 1893-1919. OTHER AWARDS: Leblanc Medal, Societe Chimique; Officier de l'Instruction Publique, Societe Chimique.

Selected Publications: "Bieträge Zur Theorie der Affinität Und Valenz." *Vierteljahrsschrift der Naturforschenden Gesellschaft in Zurich* 36 (1891): 129-69. *Lehrbuch der Stereochemie* (*Textbook of Stereochemistry*). Jena, Germany: G. Fischer, 1904. *Neuere Anschauungen auf dem Gebiete der Anorganischen Chemie*. Brunswick, Germany: Viewig and Son, 1905.

For More Information See: *Dictionary of Scientific Biography*. New York: Scribner's, 1976 (Volume 14), 264-72. Kaufmann, G.B. *Alfred Werner, Founder of Coordination Chemistry*. New York: Springer-Verlag, 1966.

Commentary: Alfred Werner was awarded the Nobel Prize "in recognition of his work on the linkage of atoms in molecules, by which he has thrown fresh light on old problems and opened up new fields of research, particularly in inorganic chemistry." Having established an early reputation in organic chemistry by extending LeBel and Van't Hoff's ideas and questioning Kekulé's concept of valences, Werner developed a comprehensive coordination theory. When, after nearly 20 years of application, he discovered optically active inorganic compounds predicted by the theory, its wide applicability was recognized. (P.A.C.)

1914

Richards, Theodore William 15

PRIZE: Chemistry, 1914. BORN: January 31, 1868; Germantown, PA. DIED: April 2, 1928; Cambridge, MA. PARENTS: Father, William T. Richards; Mother, Anna Matlack Richards. NATIONALITY: American. RELIGION: Protestant. EDUCATION: Haverford College, PA, S.B., 1885; Harvard Univ., MA, A.B., 1886; Harvard Univ., MA, A.M., Ph.D., 1888. SPOUSE: Miriam Stuart Thayer, married May 28, 1896. CHILDREN: Grace Thayer, daughter; William Theodore, son; Greenough Thayer, daughter. CAREER: Harvard Univ., MA, Professor, 1894-1928. OTHER AWARDS: Davy Medal, Royal Society, 1910; Faraday Medal, Chemical Society, 1911; Willard Gibbs Medal, American Chemical Society, 1912; Franklin Medal, Franklin Institute of Philadelphia, 1916; Lavoisier Medal, Paris, 1922; Le Blanc Medal, Paris, 1922.

Selected Publications: "The Relative Values of the Atomic Weights of Hydrogen and Oxygen." *Proceedings of the American Academy of Arts and Sciences* 23 (1887): 149 (with J. Cooke, Jr.). "A Revision of the Atomic Weights of Sodium and Chlorine." *Journal of the American Chemical Society* 27 (1905): 459 (with R.C. Wells). "The Atomic Weight of Lead of Radioactive Origin." *Journal of the American Chemical Society* 36 (1914): 1329.

For More Information See: *Dictionary of Scientific Biography.* New York: Scribner's, 1975 (Volume 11), 416-18. "Theodore William Richards Memorial Lecture." *Journal of the American Chemical Society* (1930): 1930-68.

Commentary: The Academy cited Theodore Richards "in recognition of his accurate determinations of the atomic weight of a large number of chemical elements." Richards developed the techniques and determined 30 atomic weights, including such fundamental atomic weights as those of oxygen, silver, chlorine, bromine, iodine, potassium, sodium, nitrogen, and sulfur. He was also a notable researcher in the areas of crystal growth, gas expansion, electrical resistance, and spectra. (B.S.S.)

1915

Willstäter, Richard Martin 16

PRIZE: Chemistry, 1915. BORN: August 13, 1872; Karlsruhe, Germany. DIED: August 3, 1942; Locarno, Switzerland. PARENTS: Father, Max Willstäter; Mother, Sophie Ulmann Willstäter. NATIONALITY: German. RELIGION: Jewish. EDUCATION: Univ. of Munich, Germany, Ph.D., 1894. SPOUSE: Sophie Lester, married 1903. CHILDREN: Ludwig, son; Ida Margarete, daughter. CAREER: Univ. of Munich, Germany, Professor, 1905-12; Univ. of Berlin, Germany, Professor and Administrator, 1912-16; Univ. of Munich, Germany, Professor, 1916-25. OTHER AWARDS: Davy Medal, 1932; Gibbs Medal, 1933.

Selected Publications: *Untersuchungen über Chlorophyll.* Berlin: J. Springer, 1913 (with Arthur Stoll). *Untersuchungen über die Assimilation der Kohlensaure.* Berlin: J. Springer, 1918 (with Arthur Stoll). *Untersuchungen über Enzyme.* 2 volumes. Berlin: J. Springer, 1928.

For More Information See: *Aus Meinem Leyben.* Weinheim, Germany: Verlag Chemie, 1948. *Dictionary of Scientific Biography.* New York: Scribner's, 1976 (Volume 14), 411-12.

Commentary: The Nobel Award to Richard Willstäter was "for his research on plant pigments, especially chlorophyll" and recognized his contribution in elaborating the structure and function of chlorophyll. He was equally noted for his work on plant pigments, especially the study of the blue and red pigments of flowers, and for the studies of carbonic acid assimilation by plants, of enzymes, and of synthesis and structure of atropine and cocaine. His development of the techniques of partition chromatography changed the nature of research in organic chemistry. (J.H.)

1918

Haber, Fritz 17

PRIZE: Chemistry, 1918. BORN: December 9, 1868; Breslau, Germany. DIED: January 29, 1934; Basel, Switzerland. PARENTS: Father, Siegfried Haber; Mother, Paula Haber. NATIONALITY: German. RELIGION: Jewish. EDUCATION: Technische Hochschule, Germany, Ph.D., 1891. SPOUSE: Clara Immewhar, married 1901, died 1914; Charlotta Nathan, married 1917, divorced 1927. CHILDREN: Herman, son; Ludwig, son; Eva, daughter. CAREER: Univ. of Jena, Germany, Researcher, 1892-94; Technische Hochschule, Karlsruhe, Germany, Professor, 1894-1911; Kaiser Wilhelm Institute, Dahlem, Germany, Director, 1911-33. OTHER AWARDS: Rumford Medal, Royal Society, 1932.

Selected Publications: *Experimentelle Untersuchungen uber Zertsetzung und Verbrennung von Kohlenwasserstoffen.* Munich: R. Oldenbourg, 1896. *Grundriss der Technischen Elektrochemie auf Theoretischer Grundlage.* Munich: R. Oldenbourg, 1898. *Thermodynamik Technisher Gasreaktionen Vorlesungen.* Munich: R. Oldenbourg, 1905. "Processes for the Preparation of Ammonia." U.S. Patent 971501, 1910 (with R. Le Rossignol). "Production of Synthetic Ammonia." U.S. Patent 1, 149, 510, 1915 (with K. Bosch and A. Mittasch).

For More Information See: *Dictionary of Scientific Biography.* New York: Scribner's, 1972 (Volume 5), 620-23. Goran, Morris. *The Story of Fritz Haber.* Norman, OK: U. of Oklahoma Press, 1967.

Commentary: Fritz Haber received the Nobel Prize for his development of the Haber process, which combined nitrogen and hydrogen under pressure with an iron catalyst, producing ammonia, which could be used in production of fertilizer or explosives. His productive career also included a number of other pioneering contributions: the development of the glass pH electrode, the study of chemical reactions in a flame, the applications of chemicals in gas warfare, and his research into catalysis. (C.N.B.)

1920

Nernst, Walther Hermann 18

PRIZE: Chemistry, 1920. BORN: June 25, 1864; Briesen, Germany. DIED: November 18, 1941; Muskau, Germany. PARENTS: Father, Gustav Nernst; Mother, Ottilie Nerger Nernst. NATIONALITY: German. RELIGION: Christian. EDUCATION: Univ. of Würzburg, Germany, Ph.D., 1887. SPOUSE: Emma Lohmeyer, married 1892. CHILDREN: 2 sons; 3 daughters. CAREER: Univ. of Leipzig, Germany, Researcher, 1887-90; Univ. of Gottingen, Germany, Professor, 1890-1904; Univ. of Berlin, Germany, 1904-33.

Selected Publications: *Theoretische Chemie vom Standpunkte der Avogadroschen Regel und der Thermodynamik.* Goettingen, Germany: F. Enke, 1893 (*Theoretical Chemistry from the Standpoint of Avogadro's Rule and Thermodynamics.* Tr. by Prof. Charles Skeele Palmer. New York: Macmillan and Co., 1895). *Einfuhrung in die Mathematische Behandlung der Naturwissenschaften-Kurzgefasstes Lehrbuch der Differential-und Integralrechnung mit Besonderer Berucksichtigung der Chemie.* Munich: Dr. E. Wolff, 1895. *Experimental and Theoretical Applications of Thermodynamics to Chemistry.* New York: C. Scribner's Sons, 1907. *Die Theoretischen und Experimentellen Grundlagen des Neuen Warmesatzes.* Halle-Salle, Germany: W. Knapp, 1918. *Das Weltgebaude im Lichte der Neueren Forschung.* Berlin: Julius Springer, 1921.

For More Information See: Bodenstein, Max. "Walther Nernst." *Berichte der Deutschen Chemischen Gesellschaft* 75 (1942): 79-104. *Dictionary of Scientific Biography.* New York: Scribner's, 1978 (Volume 15), 432-53. Mendelsohn, Kurt. *The World of Walther Nernst. The Rise and Fall of German Science, 1864-1941.* New York: Macmillan, 1973.

Commentary: Walther Nernst received the Nobel Prize "in recognition of his work in thermochemistry." Nernst's early research was in electrochemistry. During this period, he formulated the theory of galvanic cells. This was followed by his famous heat theorem, also known as the Third Law of Thermodynamics, which became the basis for the solution of many industrial problems. He participated in the development of quantum theory, especially with his determination of specific heats at low temperature and vapor densities at high temperature. Nernst's studies of photochemistry led him to the atom chain reaction theory. His later research was in astrophysical theories. (L.K.)

1921

Soddy, Frederick　　　　　　　　　**19**
PRIZE: Chemistry, 1921. BORN: September 2, 1877; Eastbourne, Sussex, England. DIED: September 22, 1956; Brighton, England. PARENTS: Father, Benjamin Soddy; Mother, Hannah Green Soddy. NATIONALITY: British. RELIGION: Calvinist. EDUCATION: Oxford Univ., England, B.A., 1898; Oxford Univ., England, M.A., 1910. SPOUSE: Winifred Moller Beilby, married March 3, 1908. CHILDREN: None. CAREER: McGill Univ., Montreal, Canada, Researcher, 1900-02; Univ. of London, England, Researcher, 1903-04; Univ. of Glasgow, Scotland, Professor, 1904-14; Aberdeen Univ., Scotland, Professor, 1914-19; Oxford Univ., England, Professor, 1919-36. OTHER AWARDS: Cannizzaro Prize, Academia dei Lincei, Rome, 1913.

Selected Publications: *Radio-Activity: An Elementary Treatise from the Standpoint of the Disintegration Theory.* London: The Electrician Printing and Publishing, 1904. *The Interpretation of Radium.* London: J. Murray, 1908. *The Chemistry of the Radio-Elements.* London: Longmans, Green, 1911-14. *Science and Life.* London: J. Murray, 1920.

For More Information See: *Biographical Memoirs of Fellows of the Royal Society.* London: Royal Society, 1957 (Volume 3), 203-16. *Dictionary of Scientific Biography.* New York: Scribner's, 1981 (Volume 12), 504-09. Howorth, Muriel. *Pioneer Research on the Atom, Rutherford and Soddy in a Glorious Chapter of Science, the Life of Frederick Soddy.* London: New World Publications, 1958.

Commentary: The award to Frederick Soddy was "for his contributions to our knowledge of the chemistry of radioactive substances, and his investigations into the origin and nature of isotopes." Soddy worked with Lord Rutherford on the theory of radioactive decay. His work on helium and other elements helped clarify the relations of elements in the periodic table. Throughout his career, but especially after his retire-

ment in 1936, Soddy was also outspoken regarding social issues. He blamed scientists for their disregard for the social consequences of their work, including radioactivity. (F.K.)

1923

Pregl, Fritz　　　　　　　　　　　**20**
PRIZE: Chemistry, 1923. BORN: September 3, 1859; Laibach, Austria. DIED: December 13, 1930; Graz, Austria. PARENTS: Father, Raimund Pregl; Mother, Friderike Schlacker Pregl. NATIONALITY: Austrian. RELIGION: Catholic. EDUCATION: Univ. of Graz, Austria, M.D., 1894. SPOUSE: None. CHILDREN: None. CAREER: Univ. of Graz, Austria, Professor, 1893-1907; Medico-Chemical Institute, Graz, Austria, Forensic Chemist, 1907-10; Univ. of Innsbruck, Austria, Professor, 1910-13; Univ. of Graz, Austria, Professor, 1913-30. OTHER AWARDS: Lieben Prize, Imperial Academy of Science, Vienna, Austria, 1914.

Selected Publications: *Die Quantitative Organische Mikroanalyse (Quantitative Organic Microanalysis).* Berlin: J. Springer, 1917.

For More Information See: *Dictionary of Scientific Biography.* New York: Scribner's, 1975 (Volume 11), 128-29. "Fritz Pregl." *Berichte der Deutschen Chemischen Gesellschaft* 64A (1931): 113.

Commentary: Fritz Pregl's Nobel Prize was "for his invention of the method of micro-analysis of organic substances," a result of his dissatisfaction with the lengthy, complicated, and inexact analytical methods for organic chemistry of his time. The use of very small quantities for analysis made possible the progress in many areas of biochemistry. (P.H.)

1925

Zsigmondy, Richard Adolf　　　　　**21**
PRIZE: Chemistry, 1925. BORN: April 1, 1865; Vienna, Austria. DIED: September 24, 1929; Gottingen, Germany. PARENTS: Father, Adolf Zsigmondy; Mother, Irma von Szakmary Zsigmondy. NATIONALITY: Austrian; later German resident. RELIGION: Most probably Christian/Protestant. EDUCATION: Univ. of Munich, Germany, Ph.D., 1890. SPOUSE: Laura Louise Muller, married 1903. CHILDREN: Annemarie, daughter; Kathe, daughter. CAREER: Univ. of Berlin, Germany, Researcher, 1891-92; Technische Hochschule, Graz, Austria, Professor, 1893-97; Schott und Genossen, Jena, Germany, Researcher, 1897-1900; Personal Researcher, 1900-07; Univ. of Gottingen, Germany, Professor and Administrator, 1907-29.

Selected Publications: *Zur Erkenntnis der Kolloide (Colloids and the Ultramicroscope).* Jena, Germany: G. Fischer, 1905. *Kolloidchemie: ein Lehrbuch (The Chemistry of Colloids).* Leipzig, Germany: Otto Spamer, 1912. *Das Kolloid Gold (Colloidal Gold).* Leipzig, Germany: Akademische Verlagsgesellschaft, 1925 (with P. A. Thiessen).

For More Information See: *Asimov's Biographical Encyclopedia of Science and Technology.* Garden City, NY: Doubleday, 1982, 603-04. *Dictionary of Scientific Biography.* New York: Scribner's, 1976 (Volume 14), 632-34.

Commentary: Richard Zsigmondy won the Nobel Prize for his "elucidation of the heterogeneous nature of colloidal solutions." He started on this path early in his career, when he became interested in the colors produced by organic solutions of gold. Later, he worked in a related area, studying properties of colored glass. He formulated a variety of white glass, called milk glass, which became famous. These investigations led to work on colloids. With H.F.W. Siedentopf, Zsigmondy invented the ultramicroscope, a tool which enabled him to study the movement of colloidal particles, to determine their quantity in a particular solution, and to learn something of their shape, all of which was impossible before his discoveries. (P.H.)

1926

Svedberg, Theodor H.E.   22
PRIZE: Chemistry, 1926. BORN: August 30, 1884; Flerang, Valbo, Sweden. DIED: February 25, 1971; Orebro, Sweden. PARENTS: Father, Elias Svedberg; Mother, Augusta Alstermark Svedberg. NATIONALITY: Swedish. RELIGION: Lutheran. EDUCATION: Univ. of Uppsala, Sweden, B.S., 1905; Univ. of Uppsala, Sweden, Ph.D., 1907. SPOUSE: Andrea Andreen, married 1909; Jane Frodi, married 1916; Ingrid Bloomquist, married 1938; Margit Hallen, married 1948. CHILDREN: 12 children. CAREER: Univ. of Uppsala, Sweden, Professor, 1912-49; Gustaf Werner Institute of Nuclear Chemistry, Sweden, Director, 1949-67. OTHER AWARDS: Scheele Award, Royal Swedish Academy of Sciences, 1907, 1916; Oscar II Reward, U. of Uppsala, Sweden, 1908; Edlund Award, Royal Swedish Academy of Sciences, 1909; Bergstedt Reward, Royal Society of Sciences, Sweden, 1910; Wallmark Award, Royal Swedish Academy of Sciences, 1910; Bjorken Prize, 1913, 1923, 1926; Berzelius Medal, 1941; Medal, City of Uppsala, Sweden, 1948; Franklin Medal, Franklin Institute, PA, 1949; Gustaf Adolf Medal, 1964.

Selected Publications: *Die Methoden zur Herstellung Kolloider Losungen Anorganischer Stoffe.* Dresden, Germany: T. Steinkopff, 1909. *Die Existenz der Molekule.* Leipzig, Germany: Academische Verlagsgesselschaft, 1912. *Colloid Chemistry.* New York: Chemical Catalog Company, 1924. *The Ultracentrifuge.* Oxford: Clarendon Press, 1940 (with K.O. Pedersen). "The Osmotic Balance." *Nature* 153 (1944): 523 (with I. Jullander). "The Cellulose Molecule. Physical-Chemical Studies." *Journal of Physical and Colloid Chemistry* 51 (1947): 1-18.

For More Information See: *Biographical Memoirs of Fellows of the Royal Society.* Cambridge: Royal Society, 1972 (Volume 18), 595-627. *Dictionary of Scientific Biography.* New York: Scribner's, 1976 (Volume 13), 158-64.

Commentary: Theodor Svedberg was given the Nobel Prize for his lifelong involvement with colloidal chemistry in its various forms. His early research dealt with the preparation and study of colloidal suspensions of metals. Svedberg developed the ultracentrifuge so that he could use centrifugal force to separate colloidal particles from solution and used it to characterize and study protein molecules. It was later adapted to the study of polymers. With Tiselius, he also later developed the techniques of electrophoresis. (C.N.B.)

1927

Wieland, Heinrich Otto   23
PRIZE: Chemistry, 1927. BORN: June 4, 1877; Pforzheim, Germany. DIED: August 5, 1957; Starnberg, Germany. PARENTS: Father, Theodor W. Wieland; Mother, Elise Blum Wieland. NATIONALITY: German. RELIGION: Christian. EDUCATION: Univ. of Munich, Germany, Ph.D., 1901. SPOUSE: Josephine Bartmann, married 1908. CHILDREN: Wolfgang, son; Theodor, son; Otto, son; Eva, daughter. CAREER: Univ. of Munich, Germany, Professor, 1901-17; Technische Hochschule, Munich, Germany, Professor, 1917-21; Univ. of Freiburg, Germany, Professor, 1921-25; Univ. of Munich, Germany, Professor, 1925-50. OTHER AWARDS: Lavoisier Medal, France, 1938; Order Pour le Merite, 1952; Otto Hahn Prize, 1955.

Selected Publications: *Die Hydrazine.* Stuttgart, Germany: F. Enke, 1913. "Die Chemie der Gallensauren." *Zeitschrift fur Angewandte Chemie und Zentralblate fur Technische Chemie* 42 (1929): 421-24. "Recent Researches on Biological Oxidation." *Journal of the Chemical Society* (1931): 1055-64. *On the Mechanism of Oxidation.* New Haven, CT: Yale U. Press, 1932.

For More Information See: "Autobiography." *Nachrichten aus Chemie und Technik* (1955): 222-23. *Dictionary of Scientific Biography.* New York: Scribner's, 1976 (Volume 14), 334-35. Lunde, Gulbrand. "The 1927 and 1928 Nobel Chemistry Prize Winners, Wieland and Windaus." *Journal of Chemical Education* 7 (1930): 763-71.

Commentary: Heinrich Wieland's Nobel Prize was awarded "for his investigations of the constitution of the bile acids and related substances." Wieland's earlier work dealt with organic nitrogen-containing compounds, moving from studies of nitrogen oxide reactions with olefins and aromatic compounds through studies of polymerization and synthesis to production and characterization of short-lived radicals. His later research was on the chemistry of natural substances such as morphine, strychnine, the alkaloids, crystalline cyclopeptides, and pterin compounds. Wieland's major contributions were the study of bile acids which led to the recognition of the carbon framework of the steroids and the study of oxidation processes in living cells. (R.J.)

1928

Windaus, Adolf Otto Reinhold   24
PRIZE: Chemistry, 1928. BORN: December 25, 1876; Berlin, Germany. DIED: June 9, 1959; Goettingen, Germany. PARENTS: Father, Adolf Windaus; Mother, Margarete Elster Windaus. NATIONALITY: German. RELIGION: Most probably Christian. EDUCATION: Univ. of Berlin, Germany, medical license, 1897; Univ. of Freiburg, Germany, Dr. phil., 1900. SPOUSE: Elizabeth Resau, married 1915. CHILDREN: Gunter, son; Gustav, son; Margarete, daughter. CAREER: Univ. of Berlin, Germany, Researcher, 1900-01; Univ. of Freiburg, Germany, Professor, 1901-06; Innsbruck Univ., Austria, Professor, 1906-15; Univ. of Gottingen, Germany, Professor, 1915-44. OTHER AWARDS: Pasteur Medal, 1938; Goethe Medal, 1941; Grand Order of Merit, 1951; Order Pour le Merite, 1952; Grand Order of Merit with Star, 1956.

Selected Publications: "Die Konstitution des Cholesterins." *Nachrichten Gesellschaft d. Wissenschaften.* Goettingen, Germany: 1919. "Anwendungen der Spannungstheorie." *Nachrichten Gesellschaft d. Wissenschaften.* Goettingen, Germany: 1921. "Ultraviolet Bestrahlung von Ergasterin." *Nachrichten Gesellschaft d. Wissenschaften, Goettingen* (1929): 45-59 (with others). "Chemistry of Irradiated Ergosterol." *Proceedings of the Royal Society* B 108 (1931): 568-75.

For More Information See: Butenandt, Adolf. *Proceedings of the Chemical Society* (1961): 131-38. *Dictionary of Scientific Biography.* New York: Scribner's, 1976 (Volume 14), 443-46.

Commentary: Adolf Windaus was cited by the Academy "for the services rendered through his research into the constitution of the sterols and their connection with the vitamins." Windaus, in accordance with his view that sterols were parents to other groups of natural substances, converted cholesterol to cholanic acid, proving the relationship of sterols to bile acids. He also showed that histidine, a protein component, was an imidazole alanine, and discovered histamine. His later researches centered around the antirachitic and antineuritic vitamins, whose structural components he investigated; the stereochemistry of hydrogenated rings; and chemotherapy. (B.S.S.)

1929

Euler-Chelpin, Hans Karl August Simon von   25

PRIZE: Chemistry, 1929. BORN: February 15, 1873; Augsburg, Germany. DIED: November 6, 1964; Stockholm, Sweden. PARENTS: Father, Rigas von Euler-Chelpin; Mother, Gabrielle Furtner von Euler-Chelpin. NATIONALITY: German; later Swedish citizen. RELIGION: Most probably Christian/Protestant. EDUCATION: Univ. of Berlin, Germany, doctorate, 1895. SPOUSE: Astrid Cleve, married 1902, divorced 1912; Elizabeth Baroness Ugglas, married 1913. CHILDREN: 9 children. CAREER: Univ. of Stockholm, Sweden, Professor, 1906-41. OTHER AWARDS: Lindblom Prize, Germany, 1898; Grand Cross for Federal Services with Star, Germany, 1959.

Selected Publications: *Chemie der Hefe und der Alkoholischen Gärung.* Leipzig, Germany: Akademische Verlagsgesellschaft, 1915 (with Paul Lindner). *Chemie der Enzyme.* Munich: J. F. Bergman, 1920-27. *Biokatalysatoren.* Stuttgart, Germany: F. Enke, 1930. *Biochemie der Tumoren.* Stuttgart, Germany: Enke, 1942 (with Bol Skarzynski).

For More Information See: *Dictionary of Scientific Biography.* New York: Scribner's, 1971 (Volume 4), 485-86. "Hans von Euler-Chelpin." *Bayerische Akademie der Wissenschaften, Jahrbuch* (1965): 206-12.

Commentary: Hans von Euler-Chelpin won the Nobel (along with Arthur Harden) for his "investigation on the fermentation of sugar and fermentative enzymes." Euler-Chelpin's initial interest was in catalysis. He moved on to study the chemistry of plants, the chemistry of fungi, and the chemistry of enzymes. In addition, he played an important part in explaining the chemistry of vitamins and the biochemistry of tumors. His German patriotism was reflected in his voluntary service in both world wars. (L.C.B.)

Harden, Arthur, Sir   26

PRIZE: Chemistry, 1929. BORN: October 12, 1865; Manchester, England. DIED: June 17, 1940; Bourne End, England. PARENTS: Father, Albert Tyas Harden; Mother, Eliza MacAlister Harden. NATIONALITY: British. RELIGION: Christian. EDUCATION: Univ. of Manchester, England, B.S., 1885; Univ. of Erlangen, Germany, Ph.D., 1888. SPOUSE: Georgina Sydney Bridge, married 1900. CHILDREN: None. CAREER: Univ. of Manchester, England, Researcher, 1888-97; British Institute of Preventive Medicine, Professor, 1897-1930. OTHER AWARDS: Davy Medal, Royal Society, 1935; Knighthood, 1936.

Selected Publications: *An Elementary Course of Practical Organic Chemistry.* London: Longmans, Green, 1897 (with F.C. Garrett). *Inorganic Chemistry for Advanced Students.* London: Macmillan and Co., 1899 (with H.E. Roscoe). "The Alcoholic Ferment of Yeast Juice." *Proceedings of the Royal Society* 77B (1907): 405-20 (with W.J. Young). *Alcoholic Fermentations.* London: Longmans, Green, and Company, 1911.

For More Information See: *Dictionary of Scientific Biography.* New York: Scribner's, 1972 (Volume 6), 110-12. *Obituary Notices of Fellows of the Royal Society.* Cambridge: Royal Society, 1942-44 (Volume 4), 3-14. Smedley-Maclean, Ida. "Arthur Harden (1865-1940)." *Biochemical Journal* 35 (1941): 1071-81.

Commentary: Arthur Harden and Hans von Euler-Chelpin shared the Nobel Prize "for their investigations on the fermentation of sugar and fermentative enzymes." Harden's early research was on the effect of light on chlorine mixtures with carbon dioxide and on biological reactions such as bacterial action and alcoholic fermentation. His classic work was on sugar fermentation by yeast juice—work which added much to later studies of metabolic processes in life. He also studied vitamins. (L.K.)

1930

Fischer, Hans   27

PRIZE: Chemistry, 1930. BORN: July 27, 1881; Hochstam-Main, Germany. DIED: March 31, 1945; Munich, Germany. PARENTS: Father, Eugen Fischer; Mother, Anna Herdegen Fischer. NATIONALITY: German. RELIGION: Most probably Christian/Protestant. EDUCATION: Univ. of Marburg, Germany, doctorate, 1904; Univ. of Munich, Germany, M.D., 1908. SPOUSE: Wiltrud Haufe, married 1935. CHILDREN: None. CAREER: Univ. of Berlin, Germany, Researcher, 1908-10; Univ. of Munich, Germany, Professor, 1910-16; Univ. of Innsbruck, Austria, Professor, 1916-18; Univ. of Vienna, Austria, Professor, 1918-21; Technische Hochschule, Germany, Professor, 1921-45. OTHER AWARDS: Liebig Memorial Medal, 1929; Davy Medal, Royal Society, 1937.

Selected Publications: *Die Chemie des Pyrrols.* 3 volumes. Leipzig, Germany: Akademische Verlagsgesellschaft, 1934-40 (with H. Orth). *Vorlesungen uber Organische Chemie.* 2 volumes. Munich: P. Beleg, 1950.

For More Information See: *Biographical Dictionary of Scientists.* New York: John Wiley, 1982, 181. *Dictionary of Scientific Biography.* New York: Scribner's, 1978 (Volume 15), 157-58.

Commentary: Hans Fischer won the Nobel Prize "for his works on the structural composition of the coloring matter of blood, and of leaves, and for his synthesis of hemin." Later he worked out the structural formulas for both biliverdin and bilirubin, and in 1942 he synthesized biliverdin, with the synthesis of bilirubin following in 1944. He also worked out the complete structure of chlorophylls, demonstrating that chlorophylls were substituted porphins with an atom of magnesium at the center, thus paving the way for their synthesis by his pupils following his untimely death. (K.H.)

1931

Bergius, Friedrich Karl Rudolph   28
PRIZE: Chemistry, 1931. BORN: October 11, 1884; Goldschmieden, Germany. DIED: March 30, 1949; Buenos Aires, Argentina. PARENTS: Father, Heinrich Bergius; Mother, Marie Haase Bergius. NATIONALITY: German. RELIGION: Protestant. EDUCATION: Univ. of Leipzig, Germany, Ph.D, 1907. SPOUSE: Ottilie Krazert, married (no date found). CHILDREN: 2 sons; 1 daughter. CAREER: Technical Univ., Hanover, Germany, Professor, 1909-14; Goldschmidt Company, Essen, Germany, Research Director, 1914-45; Argentine Ministry of Industries, Researcher, 1946-49. OTHER AWARDS: Liebig Medal, Germany.

Selected Publications: *Die Anwendung Hoher Drucke bei Chemischen Vorgangen und Eine Nachbildung des Entstehungsprozesses der Steinkohle.* Halle, Germany: W. Knapp, 1913. "Die Verflussigung der Kohle." *Zeitschrift des vereins Deutscher Ingenieure* 69 (1926). "Gewinnung von Alkohol und Glucose aus Holz." *Chemical Age (London)* 29 (1933): 481-83.

For More Information See: *Biographical Dictionary of Scientists.* New York: John Wiley & Sons, 1982, 48. *Dictionary of Scientific Biography.* New York: Scribner's, 1970 (Volume 2), 3-4.

Commentary: Friedrich Bergius was awarded the Nobel for his "services regarding the invention and development of chemical high-pressure methods." Beginning with his work on the dissociation of calcium peroxide, he developed methods for laboratory work at high pressures and applied them to the liquefaction of coal. After successfully commercializing this process, he solved the problem of obtaining sugar from the cellulose in wood. (M.P.)

Bosch, Carl   29
PRIZE: Chemistry, 1931. BORN: August 27, 1874; Cologne, Germany. DIED: April 26, 1940; Heidelberg, Germany. PARENTS: Father, Carl Bosch; Mother, Paula Liebst Bosch. NATIONALITY: German. RELIGION: Most probably Christian/Protestant. EDUCATION: Univ. of Leipzig, Germany, Ph.D., 1898. SPOUSE: Married 1902. CHILDREN: 1 daughter; 1 son. CAREER: Badische Anilin- und Sodafabrik, Germany, Researcher and Administrator, 1899-1925; I.G. Farben Industrie, Researcher and Administrator, 1925-40. OTHER AWARDS: Liebig Medal, Germany; Bunsen Medal, Germany; Siemens Ring, Germany; Exner Medal, Austria; Carl Lueg Medal, Germany.

Selected Publications: "Verfahren Zur Herstellung von Ammoniak aus Seinen Elementen mit Hilfe von Katalysatoren." *Chemisches Zentralblatt* (1913): 195. "Stickstoff in Wihtschaft und Technik." *Naturwissen-*

schaften 8 (1920): 867-68. "Probleme Grosstechnischer Hydrierung-Verfahren." *Chemische Fabrik* 7 (1934): 1-10.

For More Information See: "Carl Bosch, 1874-1940." *Chemische Berichte* 90 (1957): 19-39. *Dictionary of Scientific Biography.* New York: Scribner's, 1970 (Volume 2), 323-24.

Commentary: Carl Bosch received the Nobel Prize for his "discovery and development of chemical high-pressure methods," most particularly for the work he did in fixing of nitrogen. Beginning with the production of barium cyanide, he succeeded in commercializing the high-pressure synthesis of ammonia. He then developed the methods for practical production of nitrogen fertilizers. (M.P.)

1932

Langmuir, Irving   30
PRIZE: Chemistry, 1932. BORN: January 31, 1881; Brooklyn, NY. DIED: August 16, 1957; Falmouth, MA. PARENTS: Father, Charles Langmuir; Mother, Sadie Comings Langmuir. NATIONALITY: American. RELIGION: Protestant. EDUCATION: Columbia Univ., NY, B.S., 1903; Univ. of Gottingen, Germany, Ph.D., 1906. SPOUSE: Marion Mersereau, married April 27, 1912. CHILDREN: Kenneth, son; Barbara, daughter. CAREER: Stevens Institute of Technology, Hoboken, NJ, Professor, 1906-09; General Electric Research Laboratory, Schenectady, NY, Researcher and Administrator, 1909-50. OTHER AWARDS: Hughes Medal, Royal Society, 1918; Rumford Medal, 1920; Nichols Medal, American Chemical Society, 1920; Gibbs Medal, 1930; Franklin Medal, 1934; Faraday Medal, Chemical Society, 1938; Faraday Medal, Institute of Electrical Engineers, 1943; Medal for Merit, U. S. Army and Navy, 1948; John Carty Medal, National Academy of Sciences, 1950.

Selected Publications: *The Collected Works of Irving Langmuir.* New York: Pergamon Press, 1962.

For More Information See: *Current Biography Yearbook.* New York: H. W. Wilson, 1950, 320-22. *Dictionary of American Biography.* New York: Scribner's, 1980 (Supplement 6), 363-65. Rosenfeld, Albert. *The Quintessence of Irving Langmuir.* Volume 12 of *Collected Works.* New York: Pergamon Press, 1962.

Commentary: Irving Langmuir was cited by the Academy "for his discoveries and researches in the field of surface chemistry." Langmuir, in the course of pursuing theoretical studies in chemistry, physics, and engineering, managed to provide some of the major practical advances of the twentieth century. His achievements included the development of the gas-filled light bulb, the high-vacuum radio tube, the atomic hydrogen welding torch, and many other electronic devices. The general theory of absorbed films was another of his contributions, as was the initial work on production of artificial rainfall. (L.C.B.)

1934

Urey, Harold Clayton   31
PRIZE: Chemistry, 1934. BORN: April 29, 1893; Walkerton, IN. DIED: January 5, 1981; La Jolla, CA. PARENTS: Father, Samuel Clayton Urey; Mother, Cora Rebecca Reinoehl Urey. NATIONALITY: American. RELIGION:

Christian. EDUCATION: Univ. of Montana, B.S., 1917; Univ. of California, Ph.D., 1923. SPOUSE: Frieda Daum, married June 12, 1926. CHILDREN: Gertrude Elizabeth, daughter; Frieda Rebecca, daughter; Mary Alice, daughter; John Clayton, son. CAREER: Univ. of Copenhagen, Denmark, Researcher, 1923-24; Johns Hopkins Univ., MD, Professor, 1924-29; Columbia Univ., NY, Professor and Administrator, 1929-42; Manhattan Project, United States, Director of War Research, 1940-45; Univ. of Chicago, IL, Professor, 1945-58; Univ. of California, La Jolla, Professor, 1958-70. OTHER AWARDS: Gibbs Medal, American Chemical Society, 1934; Davy Medal, Royal Society, 1940; Franklin Medal, Franklin Institute, PA, 1943; Medal for Merit, 1946; Distinguished Service Award, Phi Beta Kappa, 1950; Cordoza Award, 1954; Priestley Award, Dickenson College, PA, 1955; Hamilton Award, Columbia U., NY, 1961; Remsen Award, 1963; Medal, U. of Paris, 1964; National Medal of Science for Astronomy, 1964; Achievement Award, American Academy, 1966; Gold Medal, Royal Astronomical Society, 1966; Leonard Medal, Meteoritical Society, 1969; Day Award, Geological Society of America, 1969; Chemical Pioneer Award, American Institute of Chemists, 1969; Linus Pauling Award, Oregon State U., 1970; Johann Kepler Medal, American Society for the Advancement of Science, 1971; Gold Medal, American Institute of Chemists, 1972; Priestley Medal, American Chemical Society, 1973; Exceptional Scientific Achievement Award, NASA, 1973; Knight of Malta, 1973; Headliner Award, San Diego Press Club, 1974; Goldschmidt Medal, Geochemical Society, 1975.

Selected Publications: *Atoms, Molecules and Quanta*. New York: McGraw-Hill, 1930 (with A.E. Ruark). *The Planets: Their Origin and Development*. New Haven, CT: Yale U. Press, 1952. *Production of Heavy Water*. New York: McGraw-Hill, 1955 (with others). *Some Cosmochemical Problems*. University Park, PA: Pennsylvania State U. Press, 1963.

For More Information See: *Current Biography Yearbook*. New York: H.W. Wilson, 1960, 441-42. *New York Times* (January 7, 1981): 1+.

Commentary: Harold Clayton Urey was awarded the Nobel Prize for Chemistry in 1934 "for his discovery of heavy hydrogen" known as deuterium, a key factor in the development of the atomic bomb. He was also known for his research on thermodynamic properties of gases, atomic structure, absorption spectra and structure of molecules, properties and separation of isotopes, exchange reactions, measurement of paleotemperature, and chemical problems relative to the origin of the earth, meteorites, the moon, and the solar system. (D.R.)

1935

Joliot-Curie, Frédéric 32

PRIZE: Chemistry, 1935. BORN: March 19, 1900; Paris, France. DIED: August 14, 1958; Paris, France. PARENTS: Father, Henri Joliot; Mother, Émilie Roederer Joliot. NATIONALITY: French. RELIGION: Atheist; from Protestant background. EDUCATION: École de Physique et de Chimie Industrielle, France, engineering degree, 1923; École de Physique et de Chimie Industrielle, France, licencié-és science, 1927; Univ. of Paris, France, docteur-és-sciences, 1930. SPOUSE: Irène Curie, married October 9, 1926. CHILDREN: Héléne, daughter; Pierre, son. CAREER: Radium Institute, Paris, France, Researcher, 1925-31; Caisse Nationale des Sciences, Researcher, 1931-37; Collège de France, Professor, 1937-44; Centre National de la Recherche Scientifiques, Director, 1944-46; Atomic Energy Commission, France, Commissioner, 1946-50; Univ. of Paris, France, Professor and Researcher, 1956-58. OTHER AWARDS: Henri Wilde Prize, France, 1933; Marquet Prize, France, 1934; Barnard Gold Medal, Columbia U., 1940.

Selected Publications: *Oeuvres Scientifiques Completes*. Paris: Presses Universitaires de France, 1961.

For More Information See: *Current Biography Yearbook*. New York: H.W. Wilson, 1946, 294-96. *Dictionary of Scientific Biography*. New York: Scribner's, 1973 (Volume VII), 151-57. Goldsmith, Maurice. *Frédéric Joliot-Curie, A Biography*. London: Laurence and Wishart, 1976.

Commentary: This joint award to Frédéric and Irène Joliot-Curie (the fifth Nobel for the Curie extended family) was made "for their jointly performed synthesis of the new radioactive elements," referring to experiments in which alpha-particle bombardment produced radioactive phosphorus from aluminum, radioactive nitrogen from boron, and radioactive silicon from magnesium. The team had previously produced neutrons by bombardment of beryllium. Frédéric's earlier work was on the electrochemical properties of radioactive elements. He was later involved with producing high-energy particles, with the theory of nuclear fission, and with the development of France's Atomic Energy Commission, on which he served as high commissioner. In his nonscientific endeavors, he became a hero of the underground resistance during the Second World War, an active member of the French Communist Party, and a prime mover in the World Peace Movement. (L.B.W.)

Joliot-Curie, Irène 33

PRIZE: Chemistry, 1935. BORN: September 12, 1897; Paris, France. DIED: March 17, 1956; Paris, France. PARENTS: Father, Pierre Curie; Mother, Marie Sklodowska Curie. NATIONALITY: French. RELIGION: Atheist; from Catholic (mother)/Protestant (father) background. EDUCATION: Collège Sévigné, France, baccalauréat, 1914; Univ. of Paris, France, licentiate, 1920; Univ. of Paris, France, Sc.D., 1925. SPOUSE: Frédéric Joliot, married October 9, 1926. CHILDREN: Héléne, daughter; Pierre, son. CAREER: Curie Laboratory, Paris, France, Researcher, 1921-35; Caisse Nationale de la Recherche, Researcher, 1935-36; Univ. of Paris and Radium Institute, France, Researcher, 1937-56. OTHER AWARDS: Henri Wilde Prize, France, 1933; Marquet Prize, France, 1934; Barnard Gold Medal, Columbia U., NY, 1940.

Selected Publications: *Oeuvres Scientifiques Complètes*. Paris: Presses Universitaires de France, 1961.

For More Information See: *Current Biography Yearbook*. New York: H.W. Wilson, 1940, 435-36. McKown, Robin. *She Lived for Science: Irene Joliot-Curie*. New York: Messner, 1961. Curie, Eve. "Madame La Secrétaire." *The Living Age* 351 (September 1936): 40-42.

Commentary: The joint award of the Nobel Prize to Irène and Frédéric Joliot-Curie was made "for their jointly performed synthesis of the new radioactive elements," referring to the experiments in which alpha-particle bombardment produced radioactive phosphorus from aluminum, radioactive nitrogen from boron, and radioactive silicon from magnesium. The team had previously produced neutrons by bombardment of beryllium. Irene later demonstrated the splitting of uranium. Together, the Joliot-Curies were also instrumental in developing atomic energy in France, and were active in the underground of the Second World War, in Communist activities, and in the World Peace Movement. (L.B.W.)

1936

Debye, Peter Josephus Wilhelmus   34
PRIZE: Chemistry, 1936. BORN: March 24, 1884; Maastricht, Netherlands. DIED: November 2, 1966; Ithaca, NY. PARENTS: Father, Wilhelmus Debye; Mother, Maria Reumkens Debye. NATIONALITY: Dutch; later American citizen. RELIGION: Catholic. EDUCATION: Aachen Institute of Technology, Germany, electrical technology degree, 1905; Univ. of Munich, Germany, Ph.D., 1908. SPOUSE: Mathilde Alberer, married April 10, 1913. CHILDREN: Peter Paul Rupprecht, son; Mathilde Maria, daughter. CAREER: Aachen Technological Institute, Germany, Researcher, 1905-06; Univ. of Munich, Germany, Researcher, 1906-10; Univ. of Zurich, Switzerland, Professor, 1910-12; Univ. of Utrecht, Netherlands, Professor, 1912-14; Univ. of Gottingen, Germany, Professor, 1914-20; Univ. of Zurich, Switzerland, Professor, 1920-27; Univ. of Leipzig, Germany, Professor, 1927-34; Univ. of Berlin, Germany, Professor, 1934-39; Cornell Univ., NY, Professor, 1939-52. OTHER AWARDS: Rumford Medal, Royal Society; Franklin Medal, Philadelphia, PA; Faraday Medal; Lorentz Medal, Royal Netherlands Academy; Willard Gibbs Medal, 1949; Max Planck Medal, West German Physical Society, 1950; Kendall Award, 1957; Nichols Medal, 1961; Priestley Medal, American Chemical Society, 1963; American Physics Society High-Polymer Physics Prize, Ford Motor Co., 1965; Madison Marshall Award, American Chemical Society, 1965; National Medal of Science, 1965.

Selected Publications: *The Dipole Moment and Chemical Structure.* London: Blakiston, 1932. "Energy Absorption in Dielectrics with Polar Molecules." *Faraday Society* 30 (1934): 679-84. *Collected Papers.* New York: Interscience, 1954.

For More Information See: Davies, Mansel. *Journal of Chemical Education* 45 (1968): 467-73. *Dictionary of Scientific Biography.* New York: Scribner's, 1971 (Volume 3), 617-21.

Commentary: The Academy honored Peter Debye "for his contributions to our knowledge of molecular structure through his investigations on dipole moments and on the diffraction of x-rays and electrons in gases." By utilizing techniques of measuring dipole moments and of electron and x-ray diffraction, Debye established invaluable tools for structure determination. Debye also made significant contributions in the areas of specific heats of bodies at various temperatures, magnetic cooling, crystal structure determination, the theory of solutions, and polymer size determinations. (B.S.S.)

1937

Haworth, Walter Norman, Sir   35
PRIZE: Chemistry, 1937. BORN: March 19, 1883; Chorley, Lancashire, England. DIED: March 19, 1950; Birmingham, England. PARENTS: Father, Thomas Haworth; Mother, Hannah Haworth. NATIONALITY: British. RELIGION: Christian. EDUCATION: Univ. of Manchester, England, baccalaureate, 1906; Univ. of Gottingen, Germany, Ph.D., 1910; Univ. of Manchester, England, D.Sc., 1911. SPOUSE: Violet Chilton Dobbie, married 1922. CHILDREN: James, son; David, son. CAREER: Univ. of London, England, Professor, 1911-12; Univ. of St. Andrews, Scotland, Professor, 1912-20; Univ. of Durham, England, Professor, 1920-25; Univ. of Birmingham, England, Professor and Administrator, 1925-48. OTHER AWARDS: Longstaff Medal, 1933; Davy Medal, 1934; Royal Medal, 1942; Knighthood, 1947.

Selected Publications: *The Constitution of Sugars.* London: E. Arnold & Company, 1929. "The Constitution of Some Carbohydrates." *Chemische Berichte* (1932): 43-65. "Synthesis of Ascorbic Acid." *Chemistry and Industry* (1933): 2790-806 (with E.L. Hirst). "Starch." *Journal of the Chemical Society* (1946): 543-549. "The Structure, Function and Synthesis of Polysaccharides." *Proceedings of the Royal Society* (1946): 1-9.

For More Information See: *Dictionary of Scientific Biography.* New York: Scribner's, 1972 (Volume 6), 184-85. "Walter Norman Haworth." *Journal of the Chemical Society* (1951): 2790-806.

Commentary: Walter Haworth received the Nobel Prize "for his researches into the constitution of carbohydrates and vitamin C." His elaborations of the structure of the simple sugars, his studies in cellulose chemistry, and his investigations of vitamin C were all pioneer landmark efforts. In addition, he took part in the chemical work of the atomic energy project in World War II. (B.E.)

Karrer, Paul   36
PRIZE: Chemistry, 1937. BORN: April 21, 1889; Moscow, Russia. DIED: June 18, 1971; Zurich, Switzerland. PARENTS: Father, Paul Karrer; Mother, Julie Lerch Karrer. NATIONALITY: Russian; later Swiss citizen. RELIGION: Protestant. EDUCATION: Univ. of Zurich, Switzerland, doctorate, 1911. SPOUSE: Helene Frolich, married April 14, 1914. CHILDREN: Jurg, son; Heinz, son. CAREER: Univ. of Zurich, Switzerland, Researcher, 1911-12; Georg Speyer Haus, Frankfurt-am-Main, Germany, Researcher and Administrator, 1912-18; Univ. of Zurich, Switzerland, Professor and Administrator, 1918-59. OTHER AWARDS: Marcel Benoist Prize, Switzerland, 1923; Cannizzaro Prize, Italy, 1935; Officier de la Legion d'Honneur, 1954.

Selected Publications: *Einführung in die Chemie der Polymeren Kohlehydrate, ein Grundiss der Chemie der Starke, des Glykogen, der Zellulose und Anderer Polysaccharide.* Leipzig, Germany: Akademische Verlagsgesellschaft, 1925. *Lehrbuch der Organischen Chemie.* Leipzig, Germany: Thieme, 1928. *Die Carotenoids.* Basel, Switzerland: Birkhäuser, 1948 (with E. Jucker).

For More Information See: *Biographical Memoirs of Fellows of the Royal Society.* London: Royal Society, 1978 (Volume 24), 244-321. *Dictionary of Scientific Biography.* New York: Scribner's, 1978 (Volume 15), 257-58.

Commentary: Paul Karrer was awarded the Nobel prize "for his researches into the constitution of carotenoids, flavins and vitamins A and B2." He synthesized vitamin E; isolated vitamin K1, determined its structure, and synthesized it; contributed greatly to an understanding of the structure and function of nicotin-amide-adenine dinucleotide (NAD); worked on many of the carotenoids; carried out the total synthesis of carotene hydrocarbons; synthesized and determined the structure of toxiferine and related alkaloids; and synthesized canthaxanthin from B-carotene. In addition, he also founded two important foundations for the advancement of science: the Fritz Hoffman-La Roche Foundation for the advancement of interdisciplinary study groups in Switzerland and the Foundation for Scholarships in Chemistry. (K.H.)

1938

Kuhn, Richard   37

PRIZE: Chemistry, 1938. BORN: December 3, 1900; Vienna, Austria. DIED: August 1, 1967; Heidelberg, Germany. PARENTS: Father, Hofrat Richard Clemens Kuhn; Mother, Angelika Rodler Kuhn. NATIONALITY: Austrian; later German citizen. RELIGION: Most probably Christian/Protestant. EDUCATION: Univ. of Munich, Germany, Ph.D., 1922. SPOUSE: Daisy Hartman, married 1928. CHILDREN: 2 sons; 4 daughters. CAREER: Univ. of Munich, Germany, Professor, 1925-26; Eidgenossische Technische Hochschule, Zurich, Switzerland, Professor, 1926-28; Univ. of Heidelberg, Germany, Professor, 1928-67. OTHER AWARDS: Pour le Merite fur Wissenschaften und Kunste, 1958.

Selected Publications: "Materials of Living Nature." *Naturwissenschaften* 25 (1937): 225-31. "Fertilizing (Gamones) and Sex-Determining Substances (Termones) in Plants and Animals." *Angewandte Chemie* 53 (1940): 1-6. "Carotene Dyes." German Patent 719845 (March 26, 1942) (with H. Bielig). "Vitamins and Medicines." *Die Chemie* 55 (1942): 1-6.

For More Information See: *Biographical Encyclopedia of Scientists.* New York: Facts on File, 1981, 455. *Dictionary of Scientific Biography.* New York: Scribner's, 1973 (Volume 7), 517-18.

Commentary: Richard Kuhn was awarded the Nobel "for his work on carotenoids and vitamins." He began his career working on enzyme specificity in carbohydrate metabolism and moved on to study optical stereochemistry. Among the many areas in which he worked were additions to ethylene bonds, the diphenyls, the diphenylpolyenes, colored hydrocarbons, crocetin, bixin, carotene, water-soluble vitamins, and factors effective against infection. (M.F.)

1939

Butenandt, Adolf Friedrick Johann   38

PRIZE: Chemistry, 1939. BORN: March 24, 1903; Bremerhaven-Lehe, Germany. PARENTS: Father, Otto Louis Max Butenandt; Mother, Wilhelmina Thomfohrde Butenandt. NATIONALITY: German. RELIGION: Most probably Christian/Protestant. EDUCATION: Univ. of Gottingen, Germany, Ph.D., 1927. SPOUSE: Erika von Ziegner, married February 28, 1931. CHILDREN: Ina, daughter; Otfrid, son; Heide, daughter; Eckart, son; Anke, daughter; Imme, daughter; Maike, daughter. CAREER: Univ. of Gottingen, Germany, Professor, 1931-33; Technische Hochschule, Danzig, Germany, Professor, 1933-36; Kaiser-Wilhelm Institute for Biochemistry, Berlin, Germany, Director, 1936-45; Max-Planck Institute for Biochemistry, Germany, Professor and Administrator, 1945-85.

Selected Publications: *Untersuchungen uber das Weibliche Sexualhormon (Follikel-oder Brunsthormon).* Berlin: Weidmannsche Buchhandlung, 1931. *Die Biologische Chemie im Dienste der Volkagesundheit.* Berlin: W. de Gruyter, 1941. *Uber die Biochemische Analyse einer Gen-Wirkkette der Pigmentbildung bei Insekten.* Debrecen, Hungary: Tisza Istvan-Tudomanyegyetemi Nyomda, 1943. *Zur Feinstruktur des Tabakmosaik-Virus.* Berlin: Akademie der Wissenschaften, W. de Gruyter, 1944.

For More Information See: "Adolf Butenandt." *Journal of Chemical Education* 26 (February 1949): 91. *Asimov's Biographical Encyclopedia of Science and Technology.* Garden City, NY: Doubleday, 1982, 792.

Commentary: The award to Adolf Butenandt was "for his work on sex hormones." He was forced by the German government to refuse the prize but was able to accept the honor later in 1949. In 1929, Butenandt isolated estrone, one of the hormones responsible for female sexual development and functioning; in 1931, androsterone, a male sex hormone; and in 1934, the hormone progesterone, which plays an important part in the female reproductive cycle. He also studied the interrelationships of sex hormones and their possible carcinogenic properties. (C.D.)

Ruzicka, Leopold Stephen   39

PRIZE: Chemistry, 1939. BORN: September 13, 1887; Vukovar, Yugoslavia. DIED: September 26, 1976; Zurich, Switzerland. PARENTS: Father, Stjepan Ruzicka; Mother, Ljubica Sever Ruzicka. NATIONALITY: Yugoslavian; later Swiss citizen. RELIGION: Christian. EDUCATION: Technische Hochschule, Germany, Dr. Ing., 1910. SPOUSE: Anna Hausman, married 1912, divorced (no date found); Gertrud Frei Acklin, married July 1951. CHILDREN: None. CAREER: Federal Institute of Technology, Zurich, Switzerland, Professor, 1923-26; Univ. of Utrecht, Netherlands, Professor, 1926-29; Federal Institute of Technology, Zurich, Switzerland, Professor, 1929-57.

Selected Publications: *Uber den Bau der Organischen Materie; Antrittarede Gehalten am 10.* Utrecht, Netherlands: Aula der Reichsuniversitat, 1926. *Uber Konstitution und Zusammenhange in der Sesquiterpenreihe.* Berlin: Gebruder Borntraeger, 1928. *Conferenze di Chimica Organica, Tenute Nell'Instituto Chimico dell'Universita di Roma.* Rome: Academia Nazionale dei Lincei, 1951. "The Isoprene Rule and the Biogenesis of Terpenic Compounds." *Experimentia* 9 (1953): 357-65.

For More Information See: *Asimov's Biographical Encyclopedia of Science and Technology.* Garden City, NY: Doubleday, 1982, 712. *Biographical Memoirs of the Fellows of the Royal Society.* London: Royal Society, 1980 (Volume 26), 411-501. "Dr. Leopold Ruzicka Dies in Switzerland at Age 89; Won Nobel in Chemistry." *The New York Times* (September 27, 1976): 34.

Commentary: The award to Leopold Ruzicka was "for his work on polymethylenes and higher terpenes." In 1916, he began researching natural odoriferous compounds, which culminated in the discovery that the molecules of muskone and civetone, important to the perfume industry, contain rings of 15 and 17 carbon atoms respectively. Prior to his work, rings with more than eight atoms were thought to be unstable, if they did exist. By 1933/34, Ruzicka was able to offer the first complete proof of the constitution of a sex hormone and accomplish the first artificial production of a sex hormone. His patent for the preparation of testosterone from cholesterol earned him a fortune as well as international acclaim. (C.D.)

1943

Hevesy, George Charles von (Hevesy, George Charles De) 40

PRIZE: Chemistry, 1943. BORN: August 1, 1885; Budapest, Hungary. DIED: July 5, 1966; Freiburg, Germany. PARENTS: Father, Louis de Hevesy; Mother, Eugenie Schosberger de Hevesy. NATIONALITY: Hungarian; later German resident, Danish resident, and Swedish citizen. RELIGION: Jewish. EDUCATION: Univ. of Freiburg, Germany, Ph.D., 1908. SPOUSE: Pia Riis, married September 26, 1924. CHILDREN: George Louis, son; Jenny, daughter; Ingrid, daughter; Pia, daughter. CAREER: Technical High School, Zurich, Switzerland, Teacher, 1908-10; Austrian-Hungarian Government Worker, 1910-12; Univ. of Budapest, Hungary, Professor, 1912-20; Institute of Theoretical Physics, Copenhagen, Denmark, Researcher, 1920-26; Univ. of Freiburg, Germany, Professor, 1926-34; Institute of Theoretical Physics, Copenhagen, Denmark, Researcher, 1934-43; Univ. of Stockholm, Sweden, Professor, 1943-55. OTHER AWARDS: Canizzaro Prize, Academy of Sciences, Rome, 1929; Copley Medal, 1949; Faraday Medal, 1950; Bailey Medal, 1951; Sylvanus Thompson Medal, 1955; Atoms for Peace Award, United Nations, 1959; Niels Bohr Medal, 1961; Rosenberger Medal, U. of Chicago, 1961.

Selected Publications: *Adventures in Radioisotope Research: The Collected Papers of George Hevesy.* New York: Pergamon Press, 1962.

For More Information See: *Current Biography Yearbook.* New York: H. W. Wilson, 1959, 186-88. *Dictionary of Scientific Biography.* New York: Scribner's, 1972 (Volume 6), 365-67.

Commentary: George von Hevesy received the Nobel Prize "for his work on the use of isotopes as tracer elements in researches on chemical processes." Early in his career he attempted unsuccessfully to separate radium-D from lead and instead used the radioactivity of the radium-D to follow the reactions of lead, introducing the concept of radioactive labeling and tracing. Hevesy was instrumental later in achieving physical separations and applying tracer techniques in biology. He also was the codiscoverer of the element hafnium. (M.F.)

1944

Hahn, Otto 41

PRIZE: Chemistry, 1944. BORN: March 8, 1879; Frankfurt am Main, Germany. DIED: July 28, 1968; Gottingen, Germany. PARENTS: Father, Heinrich Hahn; Mother, Charlotte Stutzmann Giese Hahn. NATIONALITY: German. RELIGION: Protestant. EDUCATION: Univ. of Marburg, Germany, Ph.D., 1901. SPOUSE: Edith Junghans, married March 22, 1901. CHILDREN: Hanno, son. CAREER: Univ. of Berlin, Germany, Professor, 1907-33; Kaiser Wilhelm Institute of Chemistry, Germany, Professor, 1928-45; Max Planck Society for the Advancement of Science, Germany, President, 1946-60. OTHER AWARDS: Grand Cross of the Order of Merit, Germany, 1959; Fermi Award, United States Atomic Energy Commission, 1966.

Selected Publications: *Applied Radiochemistry.* Ithaca, NY: Cornell U. Press, 1936. *New Atoms, Progress and Some Memories: A Collection of Papers.* New York: Elsevier, 1950.

For More Information See: *Dictionary of Scientific Biography.* New York: Scribner's, 1972 (Volume 6), 14-17. *Otto Hahn: A Scientific Autobiography.* New York: Scribner's, 1966.

Commentary: Otto Hahn received the Nobel "for his discovery of the fission of heavy nuclei." Hahn's early discoveries included the identification of radiothorium and protactinium, research which laid the foundation for the new field of radiochemistry. His interest in the effects of thermal neutrons on uranium and thorium led to the recognition of the theory of fission. Hahn was exceedingly concerned over the application of his discoveries in atomic energy and was responsible for the "Mainau Declaration" in 1955, which warned of the dangers in misusing atomic energy. In 1957, he was one of 18 eminent German scientists who publicly protested any German acquisition of nuclear weapons. (J.L.)

1945

Virtanen, Artturi Ilmari 42

PRIZE: Chemistry, 1945. BORN: January 15, 1895; Helsinki, Finland. DIED: November 11, 1973; Helsinki, Finland. PARENTS: Father, Kaarlo Virtanen; Mother, Serafüna Isotalo Virtanen. NATIONALITY: Finnish. RELIGION: Most probably Christian. EDUCATION: Univ. of Helsinki, Finland, M.Sc., 1916; Univ. of Helsinki, Finland, Ph.D., 1919. SPOUSE: Lilja Moisio, married 1920. CHILDREN: 2 sons. CAREER: Central Laboratory of Industry, Finland, Researcher, 1916-17; Government Butter and Cheese Control Station, Finland, Researcher, 1919; Finnish Cooperative Dairies Association, Researcher, 1919-24; Univ. of Helsinki, Finland, Professor, 1924-48; Academy of Finland, President, 1948-63. OTHER AWARDS: Friesland Prize, Netherlands, 1967; Atwater Prize, 1968; Siegfried Thannhauser Medal, 1969; Gold Medal, Germany, 1971; Gold Medal and Prize, Spain, 1972; Uovo d'oro, Italy, 1973.

Selected Publications: *Cattle, Fodder and Human Nitrogen: With Special Reference to Biological Nitrogen Fixation.* Cambridge: Cambridge U. Press, 1938. *Kirjakauppojen Liiketalous ja Kannattavuus, 1952.* Helsinki: Liiketalous tieteellinen Tutkimuslaitos, 1954. *On Nitrogen Metabolism in Milking Cows.* Helsinki:

Suomalainen Tiedeakatemia, 1968. *Fundamental Studies of Organic Compounds in Plants, Especially Vegetables and Fodder Plants, and Their Enzymic and Chemical Splitting Products Which Often Have Physiological Effects, in Order to Improve the Utilization Potential for Their Products, Final Report.* Helsinki: Biochemical Research Institute, 1969.

For More Information See: *Biographical Encyclopedia of Scientists.* New York: Facts on File, 1981, 812. *Dictionary of Scientific Biography.* New York: Scribner's, 1976 (Volume 14), 454-56.

Commentary: Artturi Virtanen received the Nobel Prize for "his researches and inventions in agricultural and nutritive chemistry, especially for his method of fodder preservation." He studied the process of fermentation that occurs in stored green fodder and determined that acidifying the fodder to a pH level slightly under 4 would halt the deterioration of the forage. Tests showed that the acidified fodder not only kept well but also continued to be satisfactory in taste and nutrition. This discovery was particularly important for countries with long winters, as it ensured a constant supply of feed regardless of the time of harvest. Virtanen did additional research on leguminous, nitrogen-fixing plants; the chemical composition of higher plants; and on the methods by which plants synthesize vitamins. (L.D.)

1946

Northrop, John Howard 43

PRIZE: Chemistry, 1946. BORN: July 5, 1891; Yonkers, NY. PARENTS: Father, John I. Northrop; Mother, Alice Belle Rich Northrop. NATIONALITY: American. RELIGION: Protestant. EDUCATION: Columbia Univ., NY, B.S., 1912; Columbia Univ., NY, M.A., 1913; Harvard Univ., MA, Ph.D., 1915. SPOUSE: Louise Walker, married 1917. CHILDREN: Alice, daughter; John, son. CAREER: Rockefeller Institute, NY, Professor, 1916-49; Univ. of California, Los Angeles, Professor, 1949-59. OTHER AWARDS: Stevens Prize, Columbia U., 1931; Daniel Giraud Elliot Medal, National Academy of Sciences, 1939; Certificate of Merit, United States, 1948; Alexander Hamilton Award, Columbia U., 1961.

Selected Publications: "Crystalline Pepsin." *Science* 69 (1929): 580. "Crystalline Pepsin.I. Isolation and Tests of Purity." *Journal of General Physiology* 13 (1930): 739-66. "The Isolation of Crystalline Pepsin and Trypsin." *Scientific Monthly* 35 (1932): 333-40. "Concentration and Partial Purification of Bacteriophage." *Science* 84 (1936): 90-91. *Crystalline Enzymes.* New York: Columbia U. Press, 1939 (with others).

For More Information See: *Biographical Encyclopedia of Scientists.* New York: Facts on File, 1981, 599-600. *Current Biography Yearbook.* New York: H.W. Wilson, 1947, 472-74.

Commentary: John Northrop shared the Nobel Prize for his contributions to the "preparation of enzymes and virus proteins in a pure form." His major efforts dealt with the crystallization of a number of enzymes and the proof of their protein nature. The techniques he developed were used in his laboratory to isolate pepsin, trypsin, chymotripsin, ribonuclease, and deoxyribonuclease. He worked later with isolation and characterization of a bacterial virus and also studied temperature effects on life span. (J.B.)

Stanley, Wendell Meredith 44

PRIZE: Chemistry, 1946. BORN: August 16, 1904; Ridgeville, IN. DIED: April 15, 1971; Salamanca, Spain. PARENTS: Father, James G. Stanley; Mother, Claire Plessinger Stanley. NATIONALITY: American. RELIGION: Most probably Christian. EDUCATION: Earlham College, IN, B.S., 1926; Univ. of Illinois, M.A., 1927; Univ. of Illinois, Ph.D., 1929. SPOUSE: Marian Staples Jay, married June 15, 1929. CHILDREN: Wendell Meredith, Jr., son; Marjorie Jean, daughter; Dorothy Claire, daughter; Janet Elizabeth, daughter. CAREER: Univ. of Illinois, Professor, 1929-30; Univ. of Munich, Germany, Researcher, 1930-31; Rockefeller Institute, NY, Professor, 1931-48; Univ. of California, Professor and Administrator, 1948-71. OTHER AWARDS: American Association for the Advancement of Science Prize, 1937; Isaac Adler Award, Harvard U., MA, 1938; Rosenburger Medal, U. of Chicago, IL, 1938; Scott Award, Philadelphia, PA, 1938; Gold Medal, American Institute of New York, 1941; Copernican Citation, 1943; Nichols Medal, American Chemical Society, 1946; Gibbs Medal, American Chemical Society, 1947; Franklin Medal, Franklin Institute, Philadelphia, PA, 1948; Certificate of Merit, United States, 1948; Modern Medicine Award, 1958; Distinguished Service Medal, American Cancer Society, 1963; Scientific Achievement Award, American Medical Association, 1966.

Selected Publications: "Chemical Studies on the Virus of Tobacco Mosaic. VI. The Isolation from Diseased Turkish Tobacco Plants of a Crystalline Protein Possessing the Properties of Tobacco-Mosaic Virus." *Phytopathology* 26 (1936): 305-20. "The Isolation of a Crystalline Protein Possessing the Properties of Ancuba-Mosaic Virus." *Journal of Bacteriology* 31 (1936): 52-53. "The Isolation of Crystalline Tobacco Mosaic Virus Protein from Diseased Tomato Plants." *Science* 83 (1936): 85 (with H.S. Loring).

For More Information See: *Asimov's Biographical Encyclopedia of Science and Technology.* Garden City, NY: Doubleday, 1982, 801-02. *Current Biography Yearbook.* New York: H.W. Wilson, 1947, 604-07. *National Cyclopedia of American Biography.* Clifton, NJ: James T. White, 1977 (Volume 57), 161-63.

Commentary: Wendell Stanley won his Nobel Prize for his contributions to the "preparation of enzymes and virus proteins in a pure form." Stanley used John Northrop's techniques to crystallize tobacco mosaic virus, which retained its infective properties. Later, he isolated the influenza virus and prepared a vaccine against it. (J.B.)

Sumner, James Batcheller 45

PRIZE: Chemistry, 1946. BORN: November 19, 1887; Canton, MA. DIED: August 12, 1955; Buffalo, NY. PARENTS: Father, Charles Sumner; Mother, Elizabeth Rand Kelly Sumner. NATIONALITY: American. RELIGION: Unitarian. EDUCATION: Harvard Univ., MA, B.A., 1910; Harvard Univ., MA, M.A., 1913; Harvard Univ., MA, Ph.D., 1914. SPOUSE: Bertha Louise Ricketts, married 1915, divorced 1930; Agnes Paulina Lundquist, married 1931, divorced 1942; Mary Morrison Beyer, married 1943. CHILDREN: Roberta Rand, daughter; Prudence Avery, daughter; Nathanial, son;

James Cosby Ricketts, son; Frederick Overton Burnley, son; John Increase, son; Samuel Beyer, son. CAREER: Cornell Univ., NY, Professor, 1914-55. OTHER AWARDS: Scheele Medal, Sweden, 1937.

Selected Publications: "The Isolation and Crystallization of the Enzyme Urease." *Journal of Biological Chemistry* 69 (1926): 435-41. *Textbook of Biological Chemistry.* New York: Macmillan Company, 1927. "Crystalline Catalase." *Journal of Biological Chemistry* 121 (1937): 417-24. *Chemistry and Methods of Enzymes.* New York: Academic Press, 1943. *The Enzymes, Chemistry and Mechanism of Action.* 2 volumes. New York: Academic Press, 1950-52 (with K. Myrback).

For More Information See: *Biographical Memoirs of the National Academy of Sciences.* Washington, DC: National Academy of Sciences, 1958 (Volume 31), 376-96. *Current Biography Yearbook.* New York: H.W. Wilson, 1947, 620-22. *Dictionary of Scientific Biography.* New York: Scribner's, 1976 (Volume 13), 152-53.

Commentary: James Sumner shared the Nobel Prize "for his discovery that enzymes can be crystallized," stemming from his work with urease. His work also included the crystallization of catalase and contributions to the chemistry of the peroxidases and lipoxidase. (J.B.)

1947

Robinson, Robert, Sir   46

PRIZE: Chemistry, 1947. BORN: September 13, 1886; Chesterfield, Derbyshire, England. DIED: February 8, 1975; Great Missenden, Bucks, England. PARENTS: Father, W.B. Robinson; Mother, Jane Davenport Robinson. NATIONALITY: British. RELIGION: Freethinker; from Congregationalist background. EDUCATION: Univ. of Manchester, England, baccalaureate, 1906; Univ. of Manchester, England, D.Sc., 1910. SPOUSE: Gertrude Maud Walsh, married 1922, died 1954; Stearn Sylvia Hershey Hillstrom, married 1957. CHILDREN: Marion, daughter; Michael, son. CAREER: Univ. of Sydney, Australia, Professor, 1912-15; Univ. of Liverpool, England, Professor, 1915-20; British Dyestuffs Corporation, Director of Research, 1920; Univ. of St. Andrews, Scotland, Professor, 1921; Univ. of Manchester, England, Professor, 1922-28; Univ. of London, England, Professor, 1928-30; Oxford Univ., England, Professor, 1930-55. OTHER AWARDS: Davy Medal, 1930; Royal Medal, 1932; Knighthood, 1939; Copley Medal, 1942; Franklin Medal, PA, 1947.

Selected Publications: "A Synthesis of Tropinone." *Journal of the Chemical Society* 111 (1917): 762-68. "A Theory of the Mechanism of the Phytochemical Synthesis of Certain Alkaloids." *Journal of the Chemical Society* 111 (1917): 876-99. "An Electrochemical Theory of the Mechanism of Organic Reactions." *Inst. Internat. Chim. Solvay Conseil Chim* 4e Conseil, Brussels (1932): 423-50.

For More Information See: *Biographical Memoirs of the Fellows of the the Royal Society.* London: Royal Society, 1976, 415-527. *Memoirs of a Minor Prophet.* New York: Elsevier, 1976.

Commentary: The Nobel Prize was granted to Robert Robinson "for research on certain vegetable products of great biological importance, particularly alka-

loids." His contributions included important research on sterols, pyrimidine analogs, the artificial sex hormones, and penicillin. (B.E.)

1948

Tiselius, Arne Wilhelm Kaurin   47

PRIZE: Chemistry, 1948. BORN: August 10, 1902; Stockholm, Sweden. DIED: October 29, 1971; Stockholm, Sweden. PARENTS: Father, Hans Abraham J:son Tiselius; Mother, Rosa Kaurin Tiselius. NATIONALITY: Swedish. RELIGION: Lutheran. EDUCATION: Univ. of Uppsala, Sweden, M.A., 1924; Univ. of Uppsala, Sweden, Ph.D., 1930. SPOUSE: Ingrid Margareta Dalén, married November 26, 1930. CHILDREN: Per, son; Eva, daughter. CAREER: Univ. of Uppsala, Sweden, Researcher and Professor, 1925-68. OTHER AWARDS: Bergstedt Prize, Royal Swedish Scientific Society, 1926; Paterno Medal, 1954; Hoffman Medal, 1955; Franklin Medal, 1956; Mookerjee Medal, 1959; Karrer Medal, 1961; Messel Medal, 1962.

Selected Publications: "A New Method for Determination of the Mobility of Proteins." *Journal of the American Chemical Society* 48 (September 1926): 2272-78 (with T. Svedberg). "The Moving Boundary Method of Studying the Electrophoresis of Proteins." *Nova Acta Regiae Societatis Scientiarium Upsaliensis* 4th series, 7 (1930): 1-107. "Adsorption and Diffusion in Zeolite Crystals." *Journal of Physical Chemistry* 40 (February 1936): 223-32. "A New Apparatus for Electrophoretic Analysis of Colloidal Mixtures." *Transactions of the Faraday Society* 33 (1937): 524-31. "Electrophoresis of Serum Globulin II. Electrophoretic Analysis of Normal and Immune Sera." *Biochemical Journal* 31 (July 1937): 1464-77. "Separation and Fractionation of Macromolecules and Particles." *Science* 141 (July 1963): 13-20 (with J. Parath and P.A. Albertsson).

For More Information See: *Biographical Memoirs of the Fellows of the Royal Society.* London: Royal Society, 1974 (Volume 20), 401-28. *Current Biography Yearbook.* New York: H.W. Wilson, 1949, 603-04. *Dictionary of Scientific Biography.* New York: Scribner's, 1976 (Volume 13), 418-22.

Commentary: Arne Tiselius received the Nobel Prize for his work with two methods of biochemical study of proteins and other large molecules: electrophoresis and adsorption analysis. The awards committee specifically cited his use of electrophoretic methods to separate the proteins of blood serum; Tiselius had developed apparatus which separated albumin from globulin and led to the discovery of alpha, beta, and gamma globulins and the immunoglobulins (antibodies). He later worked with adsorption methods for separating substances and through this work made major contributions to the field of protein chromatography. (D.O.F. and H.L.F.)

1949

Giauque, William Francis   48

PRIZE: Chemistry, 1949. BORN: May 12, 1895; Niagara Falls, Ontario, Canada. DIED: March 29, 1982; Berkeley, CA. PARENTS: Father, William Tecumseh Sherman Giauque; Mother, Isabella Jane Duncan Giauque. NATIONALITY: American. RELIGION: Most probably Christian. EDUCATION: Univ. of California, B.S., 1920; Univ. of California, Ph.D., 1922. SPOUSE: Murill Francis Ashley, married July 19, 1932. CHILDREN: William Francis Ashley, son; Robert David Ashley, son. CAREER: Univ. of California, Berkeley, Professor, 1922-62. OTHER AWARDS: Pacific Division Prize, American Association for the Advancement of Science, 1929; Medal, Chandler Foundation, Columbia U., NY, 1936; Elliot Cresson Medal, Franklin Institute, 1937; Gibbs Medal, American Chemical Society, 1951; Lewis Medal, 1956.

Selected Publications: "Thermodynamic Treatment of Certain Magnetic Effects: A Proposed Method of Producing Temperatures Considerably Below 1° Absolute." *Journal of the American Chemical Society* 49 (1927): 1864-70. "Temperatures Below 1° Absolute." *Industrial and Engineering Chemistry* 28 (1936): 743-45.

For More Information See: *The Annual Obituary, 1982.* New York: St. Martin's Press, 1983, 143-45. *Current Biography Yearbook.* New York: H. W. Wilson, 1950, 170-72.

Commentary: William Francis Giauque won the Nobel Prize "for his contributions in the field of chemical thermodynamics, particularly concerning the behaviour of substances at extremely low temperatures." Beginning with his interest during his Ph.D. research, he embarked on research that would cool elements to zero degrees absolute and then tested their molecular order. In 1933, he first approached his goal, having invented most of the equipment needed to measure and test at such low temperatures. In the course of his experiments, he discovered two new isotopes of oxygen (17 and 18). Giauque also was a key worker in the area of statistical mechanics and the measurement of entropies at low temperatures. (L.T.)

1950

Alder, Kurt   49
PRIZE: Chemistry, 1950. BORN: July 10, 1902; Koenigshuette, Germany. DIED: June 20, 1958; Cologne, Germany. PARENTS: Father, Joseph Alder; Mother, Maria Alder. NATIONALITY: German. RELIGION: Most probably Christian. EDUCATION: Univ. of Kiel, Germany, Ph.D., 1926. SPOUSE: No record found. CHILDREN: No record found. CAREER: Univ. of Kiel, Germany, Professor, 1930-36; I.G. Farben Industrie, Administrator, 1936-40; Univ. of Cologne, Germany, Professor and Administrator, 1940-58. OTHER AWARDS: Emil Fischer Memorial Medal, Association of German Chemists, 1938.

Selected Publications: "Synthesen in der Hydroaromatischen Reihe. I. Mitteilung, Anlagerungen von 'Di-en'-kohlenwasserstoffen." *Annalen die Chemie* 460 (1928): 98-122 (with O. Diels). "Die Methode der Dien-Synthese." *Handbuch der Biologischen Arbeitsmethoden.* Berlin: Urban and Schwartzenburg, 1933 (Volume 2), 3171. *Neuere Methoden der Praeparativen Organischen Chemie.* Berlin: Verlag Chemie, 1943. "Über den Sterischen Verlauf von Dien-Synthesen mit Acyclischen Dienen. Die Allgemeine Sterische Formel." *Annalen die Chemie* 571 (1951): 157-66.

For More Information See: *Dictionary of Scientific Biography.* New York: Scribner's, 1970 (Volume 1), 105-06. Guenzl-Schumacher, M. "Kurt Alder." *Chemikerzeitung* 82 (1958): 489-90.

Commentary: Kurt Alder was awarded the Nobel Prize for his contributions to the "discovery and development of the diene synthesis," which involves addition of unsaturated compounds with alternating double bonds to compounds with a double bond activated by a carbonyl or carboxyl group in near proximity to form a new compound. Alder continued to study the conditions and applications of the Diels-Alder reaction throughout his career. He also had an industrial interest in production of synthetic rubbers, and he showed his interest in the external world by joining in the Nobel laureate renunciation of war in 1955. (T.K.)

Diels, Otto Paul Herman   50
PRIZE: Chemistry, 1950. BORN: January 23, 1876; Hamburg, Germany. DIED: March 7, 1954; Kiel, Germany. PARENTS: Father, Hermann Diels; Mother, Bertha Duebell Diels. NATIONALITY: German. RELIGION: Most probably Christian. EDUCATION: Univ. of Berlin, Germany, Ph.D., 1899. SPOUSE: Paula Geyer, married 1909. CHILDREN: 3 sons; 2 daughters. CAREER: Univ. of Berlin, Germany, Professor, 1899-1916; Univ. of Kiel, Germany, Professor and Administrator, 1916-48. OTHER AWARDS: Gold Medal, St. Louis Exposition, MO, 1906; Adolf von Baeyer Memorial Medal, Society of German Chemists, 1931.

Selected Publications: "Ueber das Kohlensuboxyd I." *Berichte der Deutschen Chemischen Gesellschaft* 39 (1906): 689 (with B. Wolf). *Einfuhrung in die Organische Chemie.* Leipzig, Germany: Weinheim, 1907. "Synthesen in der Hydroaromatischen Reihe. I. Mitteilung, Anlagerungen von 'si-en-'kohlenwasserstoffen." *Annalen die Chemie* 460 (1927): 98-122 (with K. Alder).

For More Information See: *Dictionary of Scientific Biography.* New York: Scribner's, 1971 (Volume 4), 90-92. Olsen, S. "Otto Diels." *Chemische Berichte* 95 (1962): 5-46.

Commentary: Otto Diels shared the Nobel Prize for his work in the "discovery and development of the diene synthesis," in which an organic compound with a set of double-bonded carbons around a single-bonded set combines with an organic compound that contains a double bond activated by a nearby carbonyl or carboxyl group to form a new compound. Diels continued to study Diels-Alder reactions and their applications throughout his career. He also isolated, earlier in his career, carbon suboxide, and developed a method for removing hydrogen from steroids, using selenium. (T.K.)

1951

McMillan, Edwin Mattison   51
PRIZE: Chemistry, 1951. BORN: September 12, 1907; Redondo Beach, CA. PARENTS: Father, Edwin Hargauh McMillan; Mother, Anna Marie Mattison McMillan. NATIONALITY: American. RELIGION: Christian. EDUCATION: California Institute of Technology, B.S., 1928; California Institute of Technology, M.S., 1929; Princeton Univ., NJ, Ph.D., 1932. SPOUSE: Elsie Walford Blumer, married 1941. CHILDREN: Ann, daughter; David, son; Stephen, son. CAREER: Univ. of California, Berkeley, Professor, 1932-73. OTHER AWARDS: Research Corporation Scientific Award, 1951; Atoms for Peace

Award, 1963; Alumni Distinguished Service Award, California Institute of Technology, 1966; Centennial Citation, U. of California, Berkeley, 1968.

Selected Publications: "The Synchrotron—A Proposed High-Energy Particle Accelerator." *Physical Review* 68 (September 1945): 143-44. *Lecture Series in Nuclear Physics*. Washington, DC: United States Government Printing Office, 1947. "Production of Mesons by X-rays." *Science* 110 (1949): 579-83 (with J. Peterson and R. White).

For More Information See: *Current Biography Yearbook*. New York: H.W. Wilson, 1952, 382-84. *National Cyclopedia of American Biography*. New York: J.T. White, 1952 (Volume H), 236-37.

Commentary: Edwin McMillan won the 1951 Nobel Prize for chemistry for "his discovery of element 93, neptunium, the first element beyond uranium." He shared the prize with Glenn Seaborg, who had been instrumental in discovering elements 94-102. McMillan was involved also in the wartime work on radar, sonar, and the atomic bomb, and devised the theory of phase stability used in the construction of high-energy atom-smashing equipment. (B.F.)

Seaborg, Glenn Theodore   52

PRIZE: Chemistry, 1951. BORN: April 19, 1912; Ishpeming, MI. PARENTS: Father, Herman Theodore Seaborg; Mother, Selma Erickson Seaborg. NATIONALITY: American. RELIGION: Protestant. EDUCATION: Univ. of California, Los Angeles, A.B., 1934; Univ. of California, Ph.D., 1937. SPOUSE: Helen Lucille Griggs, married 1942. CHILDREN: Peter, son; David, son; Stephen, son; John Eric, son; Lynne, daughter; Diane, daughter. CAREER: Univ. of California, Berkeley, Professor and Administrator, 1937-. OTHER AWARDS: Award in Pure Chemistry, 1947; Perkin Medal, 1957; Enrico Fermi Award, United States Atomic Energy Commission, 1959; Priestley Memorial Award, 1960; Franklin Medal, 1963; Charles Lathrop Parsons Award, 1964; Chemistry Pioneer Award, 1968; Gold Medal Award, 1973; Arches of Science Award, 1968; John R. Kuebler Award, Alpha Chi Sigma, 1978; Priestley Medal, American Chemical Society, 1979; Henry DeWolf Smyth Award, American Nuclear Society, 1982; Actinide Award, 1984.

Selected Publications: *The Chemistry of the Actinide Elements*. New York: Wiley, 1958 (with Joseph J. Katz). *The Transuranium Elements*. New Haven, CT: Yale U. Press, 1958. *Education and the Atom*. New York: McGraw-Hill, 1964 (with Daniel M. Wilkes). *Man and Atom*. New York: E.P. Dutton, 1971 (with William R. Corliss). *Nuclear Milestones*. San Francisco, CA: W.H. Freeman, 1972. *Transuranium Elements: Products of Modern Alchemy*. New York: Academic Press, 1978 (with others).

For More Information See: *Asimov's Biographical Encyclopedia of Science and Technology*. Garden City, NY: Doubleday, 1982, 842-43. *Biographical Encyclopedia of Scientists*. New York: Facts on File, 1981, 721-22. *Current Biography Yearbook*. New York: H.W. Wilson, 1961, 413-15.

Commentary: Glenn Seaborg's Nobel Prize (shared with Edwin McMillan) came "for discoveries in the chemistry of the transuranium elements." Of the 13 such elements known in the 70s, he was involved in the identification of nine (atomic numbers 94 through 102). He also studied the chemistry and physics of the

actinide series, especially of neptunium and plutonium. In addition, Seaborg was an active scientist outside of the laboratory and served a term as chair of the Atomic Energy Commission. (B.F.)

1952

Martin, Archer John Porter   53

PRIZE: Chemistry, 1952. BORN: March 1, 1910; London, England. PARENTS: Father, William A.P. Martin; Mother, Lillian Kate Brown Martin. NATIONALITY: British. RELIGION: Most probably Christian/Protestant. EDUCATION: Cambridge Univ., England, B.A., 1932; Cambridge Univ., England, M.A., 1935; Cambridge Univ., England, Ph.D., 1936. SPOUSE: Judith Bagenal, married 1943. CHILDREN: 2 sons; 3 daughters. CAREER: Cambridge Univ., England, Researcher, 1933-38; Wool Industries Research Association, Leeds, England, Researcher, 1938-46; Boots Pure Drug Company, Nottingham, England, Researcher, 1946-48; Medical Research Council, England, Researcher, 1948-52; National Institute for Medical Research, London, England, Researcher, 1952-56; Consultant, England, 1956-59; Abbotsbury Laboratories, England, Director, 1959-70; Wellcome Foundation, England, Consultant, 1970-73; Univ. of Houston, TX, Professor, 1974-79. OTHER AWARDS: Berzelius Gold Medal, Swedish Medical Society, 1951; John Scott Award, 1958; John Price Wetherill Medal, 1959; Franklin Institute Medal, 1959; Leverhulme Medal, 1963; Kolthoff Medal, 1969; Callendar Medal, 1971; Achievement Award, The Worshipful Company of Scientific Instrument Makers, 1972; Randolf Major Medal, 1979.

Selected Publications: "A New Form of Chromatography Employing Two Liquid Phases." *Biochemical Journal* 35 (1941): 1358-68 (with R. Synge). "Identification of Lower Peptides in Complex Mixtures." *Biochemical Journal* (February 1947): 595-96 (with R. Consden and A. Gordon). "Separation of the C12-C13 Fatty Acids by Reversed-Phase Partition Chromatography." *Biochemical Journal* (May 1950): 532-38 (with G. Howard).

For More Information See: *Asimov's Biographical Encyclopedia of Science and Technology*. Garden City, NY: Doubleday, 1964, 599. *Current Biography Yearbook*. New York: H.W. Wilson, 1953, 417-19.

Commentary: A.J.P. Martin was awarded the Nobel Prize for his invention of partition chromatography, which combines the principles of countercurrent solvent extraction and chromatography. Small quantities of closely related chemical substances can be separated from one another by partition chromatography. Martin also was instrumental in the development of paper chromatography and gas chromatography. (J.H.)

Synge, Richard Laurence Millington   54

PRIZE: Chemistry, 1952. BORN: October 28, 1914; Liverpool, England. PARENTS: Father, Laurence Millington Synge; Mother, Katharine Charlotte Swan Synge. NATIONALITY: British. RELIGION: Most probably Christian/Protestant. EDUCATION: Cambridge Univ., England, baccalaureate, 1936; Cambridge Univ., England, Ph.D., 1941. SPOUSE: Ann Stephen, married 1943. CHILDREN: Jane, daughter; Elizabeth, daughter; Thomas Millington, son; Matthew Millington, son; Patrick Millington, son. CAREER: Wool Industries Research Association, Leeds, England, Researcher, 1941-

43; Lister Institute of Preventive Medicine, London, England, Researcher, 1943-48; Rowett Research Institute, Aberdeen, Scotland, Researcher and Administrator, 1948-67; Food Research Institute, Researcher, Norwich, England, 1967-76; Univ. of East Anglia, England, Professor, 1967-84. OTHER AWARDS: John Price Wetherill Medal, Franklin Institute, Philadelphia, PA, 1959.

Selected Publications: "A New Form of Chromatography Employing Two Liquid Phases." *Biochemical Journal* 35 (1941): 1358-68 (with A. Martin). *Science in Society*. London: Edward Arnold, 1969.

For More Information See: *A Biographical Encyclopedia of Scientists*. New York: Facts on File, 1981, 769. *Current Biography Yearbook*. New York: H.W. Wilson, 1953, 611-12.

Commentary: The Nobel Prize was awarded to R.L.M. Synge for the research that led to the development of partition chromatography. Synge immediately used this technique to separate the 20 closely related amino acids of which proteins are composed. Also, Synge used chromatographic techniques in his "elegant investigation" of the chemical structure of the antibiotic gramicidin. (L.D. and J.H.)

1953

Staudinger, Hermann   55

PRIZE: Chemistry, 1953. BORN: March 23, 1881; Worms, Germany. DIED: September 8, 1965; Freiburg-im-Breisgau, Germany. PARENTS: Father, Franz Staudinger; Mother, no record found. NATIONALITY: German. RELIGION: Most probably Christian. EDUCATION: Univ. of Halle, Germany, Ph.D., 1907. SPOUSE: Magda Woit, married 1927. CHILDREN: No record found. CAREER: Technische Hochschule, Karlsruhe, Germany, Professor, 1907-12; Federal Technical Institute, Zurich, Switzerland, Professor, 1912-26; Univ. of Freiburg, Germany, Professor and Administrator, 1926-56. OTHER AWARDS: Cannizzaro Prize, Reale Academia Nazionale dei Lincei, Rome, Italy, 1933.

Selected Publications: *Die Ketene* (*Ketenes*). Stuttgart, Germany: Enke, 1912. *Anleitung zur Organischen Qualitativen Analyse* (*Introduction to Organic Qualitative Analysis*). Berlin: Springer, 1923. *Die Hochmolekularen Organischen Verbindungen, Kautschuk und Cellulose* (*The High-Molecular Organic Compounds, Rubber and Cellulose*). Berlin: Springer, 1932. *Organische Kolloid Chemie* (*Organic Colloid Chemistry*). Braunschweig, Germany: Vieweg, 1940. *Makromolekulare Chemie und Biologie* (*Macromolecular Chemistry and Biology*). Basel, Switzerland: Wepf and Co., 1947.

For More Information See: *Arbeitserrinnerungen* (*Working Memoirs*). Heidelberg, Germany: A. Huthig, 1961. *Dictionary of Scientific Biography*. New York: Scribner's, 1976 (Volume 13), 1-4.

Commentary: Hermann Staudinger was cited by the Academy "for his discoveries in the field of macromolecular chemistry." His work, which was the foundation of much of macromolecular chemistry, was concentrated mostly on cellulose, rubber, and isoprene, but there were significant contributions as well to the chemistry of ketenes, oxalyl chloride, outoxidation, aliphatic diazo-compounds, explosions, and insecticides. (T.K.)

1954

Pauling, Linus Carl   56

PRIZE: Chemistry, 1954; Peace, 1962. BORN: February 28, 1901; Portland, OR. PARENTS: Father, Herman William Pauling; Mother, Lucy Isabelle Darling Pauling. NATIONALITY: American. RELIGION: No record found. EDUCATION: Oregon State College, B.Sc., 1922; California Institute of Technology, Ph.D., 1925. SPOUSE: Ava Helen Miller, married 1923. CHILDREN: Linus Carl, Jr., son; Peter Jeffress, son; Linda Helen, daughter; Edward Crellin, son. CAREER: Oregon State College, Corvallis, Professor, 1919-20; California Institute of Technology, Professor, 1925-64; Center for Study of Democratic Institutions, Professor, 1964-67; Univ. of California, San Diego, Professor, 1967-69; Stanford Univ., CA, Professor, 1969-74. OTHER AWARDS: Langmuir Prize, American Chemical Society, 1931; Nichols Medal, 1941; Davy Medal, Royal Society, 1947; Medal for Merit, 1948; Pasteur Medal, Biochemical Society of France, 1952; Addis Medal, National Nephrosis Federation, 1955; Phillips Memorial Award, American College of Physicians, 1956; Avogadro Medal, Italian Academy of Science, 1956; Fermat Medal, 1957; Sabatier Medal, 1957; International Grotius Medal, 1957; Order of Merit, Republic of Italy, 1965; Medal, Academy of Rumanian People's Republic, 1965; Linus Pauling Medal, 1966; Silver Medal, Institute of France, 1966; Supreme Peace Sponsor, World Fellowship of Religion, 1966.

Selected Publications: *Introduction to Quantum Mechanics*. New York: McGraw-Hill, 1935 (with E.B. Wilson, Jr.). *The Nature of the Chemical Bond*. Ithaca, NY: Cornell U. Press, 1939. *No More War!* New York: Dodd, Mead, 1958. *The Architecture of Molecules*. San Francisco, CA: W.H. Freeman, 1964 (with R. Hayward). *Vitamin C and the Common Cold*. San Francisco, CA: W.H. Freeman, 1970.

For More Information See: *Asimov's Biographical Encyclopedia of Science and Technology*. Garden City, NY: Doubleday, 1964, 477. *Current Biography Yearbook*. New York: H.W. Wilson, 1964, 339-42.

Commentary: Linus Pauling was the first person to receive two unshared Nobel Prizes in two different fields. His prize in chemistry was granted for his work on chemical bonds and molecular structure, while his peace prize cited his writings and lectures warning against the dangers of radioactive fallout in weapons testing and war. Pauling's applications of quantum mechanics to chemistry began his career, but it ventured far afield, investigating such varying areas as crystal structure, bonding, the resonance theory, protein structure, antibodies, hereditary diseases, anesthesia, and Vitamin C therapy. Since World War II, Pauling also devoted large amounts of time to the cause of peace and disarmament, in debates, lectures, articles, petitions, and books. (M.E.T. and B.S.S.)

1955

Du Vigneaud, Vincent   57

PRIZE: Chemistry, 1955. BORN: May 18, 1901; Chicago, IL. DIED: December 11, 1978; White Plains, NY. PARENTS: Father, Alfred Joseph Du Vigneaud; Mother, Mary Theresa O'Leary Du Vigneaud. NATIONALITY: American. RELIGION: Most probably Christian. EDUCA-

TION: Univ. of Illinois, B.Sc., 1923; Univ. of Illinois, M.Sc., 1924; Univ. of Rochester, NY, Ph.D., 1927. SPOUSE: Zella Zon Ford, married June 12, 1924. CHILDREN: Vincent, son; Marilyn Renee, daughter. CAREER: DuPont Laboratory, DE, Researcher, 1924; Philadelphia General Hospital, PA, Researcher, 1924-25; Univ. of Rochester, NY, Researcher, 1925-27; Johns Hopkins Univ., MD, Researcher, 1927-28; Univ. of Illinois, Professor, 1929-32; George Washington Univ., Washington, DC, Professor, 1932-38; Cornell Univ., NY, Professor, 1938-75. OTHER AWARDS: Hildebrand Award, Washington Chemical Society, 1936; Mead-Johnson Vitamin B Complex Award, American Institute of Nutrition, 1942; Nichols Medal, New York Section, American Chemical Society, 1945; Borden Award, American Association of American Medical Colleges; Lasker Award, American Public Health Association, 1948; Award of Merit for War Research, 1948; Osborne and Mendel Award, 1953; John Scott Medal and Award, American Pharmaceutical Manufacturers' Association, 1954; Passano Foundation Award, 1955; Willard Gibbs Medal, American Chemical Society, 1956.

Selected Publications: *A Trail of Research in Sulphur Chemistry and the Metabolism and Related Fields.* Ithaca, NY: Cornell U. Press, 1952. "Tritiation of Oxytocin by the Wilzbach Method and the Synthesis of Oxytocin from Tritium-Labeled Leucine." *Journal of the American Chemical Society* 84 (1962): 409-13 (with others). "The Hormones of the Posterior Pituitary Gland with Special Reference to Their Milk-Ejecting Ability." *Bulletin of the New York Academy of Medicine* 41 (1965): 802-03.

For More Information See: *Biographical Encyclopedia of Scientists.* New York: Facts on File, 1981, 222. *Current Biography Yearbook.* New York: H.W. Wilson, 1956, 160-62.

Commentary: Vincent Du Vigneaud was cited by the Academy "for his work on biochemically important sulphur compounds, especially for the first synthesis of a polypeptide hormone." Du Vigneaud began his research on the sulphur of insulin, studied other sulphur-containing compounds and the role of the methyl group in biology, and contributed to the knowledge about biotin, coenzyme R, and penicillin. His later research centered on oxytocin and vasopressin, two pituitary hormones. (L.T.)

1956

Hinshelwood, Cyril Norman, Sir   58
PRIZE: Chemistry, 1956. BORN: June 19, 1897; London, England. DIED: October 9, 1967; London, England. PARENTS: Father, Norman Macmillan Hinshelwood; Mother, Ethel Frances Smith. NATIONALITY: British. RELIGION: Most probably Christian/Protestant. EDUCATION: Oxford Univ., England, B.A., 1920; Oxford Univ., England, M.A., 1924. SPOUSE: None. CHILDREN: None. CAREER: Oxford Univ., England, Professor, 1921-64. OTHER AWARDS: Lavoisier Medal, Société Chimique de France, 1935; Davy Medal, Royal Society, 1943; Royal Medal, Royal Society, 1947; Longstaff Medal, Chemical Society, 1948; Knighthood, 1948; Guldberg Medal, U. of Oslo, 1952; Faraday Medal, Chemical Society, 1953; Order of the Republic, Italy, 1956.

Selected Publications: *Kinetics of Chemical Change in Gaseous Systems.* Oxford: Clarendon Press, 1926. *Thermodynamics for Students of Chemistry.* London: Methuen, 1926. *The Reaction Between Hydrogen and Oxygen.* Oxford: Clarendon Press, 1934 (with A.T. Williamson). *The Chemical Kinetics of the Bacterial Cell.* London: Clarendon Press, 1947. *The Structure of Physical Chemistry.* Oxford: Clarendon Press, 1951. *Growth, Function and Regulation in Bacterial Cells.* Oxford: Clarendon Press, 1966 (with A.C.R. Dean).

For More Information See: *Current Biography Yearbook.* New York: H.W. Wilson, 1957, 259-60. *Dictionary of Scientific Biography.* New York: Scribner's, 1972 (Volume 6), 404-05.

Commentary: The Nobel Prize was awarded to Sir Cyril Hinshelwood (and Nikolai Semenov) for "their researches into the mechanism of chemical reactions." Working independently, each discovered that a series of molecules could react in one sequence without the addition of new outside energy but could also be forced to so react. By speeding up changes in the structure of molecules, the resulting chain reactions could produce sudden or controlled violent explosions. These discoveries paved the way for more efficient automobile engines and for the modern plastics industry. Later work by Hinshelwood centered on investigation of chemical reactions in living organisms. (B.M.)

Semenov, Nikolai Nikolaevich   59
PRIZE: Chemistry, 1956. BORN: April 16, 1896; Saratov, Russia. PARENTS: Father, Nikolai Alex Semenov; Mother, Elena Dmitrieva Semenov. NATIONALITY: Russian. RELIGION: Most probably Eastern Orthodox. EDUCATION: Leningrad State Univ., USSR, graduate, 1917. SPOUSE: Natalia Nikolaevna Burtseva, married September 15, 1924. CHILDREN: Yurii Nikolaevich, son; Ludmilla Nikolaevna, daughter. CAREER: Leningrad Poly-Technical Institute, USSR, Professor, 1920-31; Institute of Chemical Physics of the Academy of Sciences, USSR, Director, 1932-. OTHER AWARDS: Stalin Prize; Order of the Red Banner of Labor; Order of Lenin (7 times); Lomonosov Gold Medal, USSR.

Selected Publications: *Chain Reactions.* Tr. by Prof. Frenkel and Judviga Smidt-Chernysheff. Oxford: Clarendon Press, 1935. *Chemical Kinetics and Chain Reactions.* Tr. by Prof. Frenkel and Judviga Smidt-Chernysheff. Oxford: Clarendon Press, 1935. *Some Problems of Chemical Kinetics and Reactivity.* Tr. by Michel Boudart. Princeton, NJ: Princeton U. Press, 1958-59.

For More Information See: *Current Biography Yearbook.* New York: H.W. Wilson, 1957, 498-500. *New York Times* (November 2, 1956): 1.

Commentary: Nikolai Semenov was the first Soviet citizen living in his homeland to win the Nobel Prize. His research on chemical processes led him to believe physics might be the key to many of the problems of chemistry. In pursuing this idea, he developed the science of chemical kinetics. In 1956, Semenov, with Sir Cyril Hinshelwood, was awarded the Nobel Prize in Chemistry for "researches into the mechanism of chemical reactions." Some contend that their work led to the capability of controlled atomic chain reactions; it is more generally agreed that their work paved the way for the development of more efficient automobile engines and the foundation of the plastics industry.

Semenov's early work dealt with molecular physics and the splitting off of electrons by electrical force. As early as 1927, he developed a theory of the thermal explosion of gaseous mixtures. (B.M.)

1957

Todd, Alexander Robertus, Sir 60

PRIZE: Chemistry, 1957. BORN: October 2, 1907; Glasgow, Scotland. PARENTS: Father, Alexander Todd; Mother, Jane Lowrei Todd. NATIONALITY: British. RELIGION: Christian. EDUCATION: Glasgow Univ., Scotland, baccalaureate, 1928; Univ. of Frankfurt, Germany, Ph.D., 1931; Oxford Univ., England, Ph.D., 1933. SPOUSE: Alison Sarah Dale, married January 10, 1937. CHILDREN: Alexander Henry, son; Helen Jean, daughter; Hilary Alison, daughter. CAREER: Edinburgh Univ., Scotland, Researcher, 1934-36; Lister Institute for Preventive Medicine, England, Researcher, 1936-38; Manchester Univ., England, Professor, 1938-44; Cambridge Univ., England, Professor, 1944-78. OTHER AWARDS: Lavoisier Medal, French Chemical Society, 1948; Davy Medal, Royal Society, 1949; Knighthood, 1954; Royal Medal, 1955; Cannizzaro Medal, Italian Chemical Society, 1958; Longstaff Medal, Chemical Society of London, 1963; Copley Medal, Royal Society, 1970; Ordre Pour Le Merite, Federal Republic of Germany; Second Class Order of Rising Sun, Japan; Lomonosov Gold Medal, USSR.

Selected Publications: "Chemical Structure and Properties of Tocopherol (Vitamin E). I. Chemistry." *Soc. Chem. Ind., Food Group* (April 1939): 3-8. "Vitamins of the B Group." *Journal of the Chemical Society* (1941): 427-32. "Synthesis in the Study of Nucleotides." *Journal of the Chemical Society* (1946): 647-53. "Synthesis of Nucleotides." *Bull. Soc. Chem. France* (1948): 933-38. "A Hundred Years of Organic Chemistry." *Advancement of Science* 8 (1952): 393-96. *Perspectives in Organic Chemistry*. New York: Interscience, 1956.

For More Information See: *Biographical Encyclopedia of Scientists*. New York: Facts on File, 1981, 789. *Current Biography Yearbook*. New York: H.W. Wilson, 1958, 437-39.

Commentary: Alexander Todd was awarded the Nobel Prize for his contributions to biochemistry and to the understanding of the gene. At the beginning of his impresssive career, Todd synthesized and determined the structure of vitamin B-1 and also studied vitamins E and B-12, as well as isolating the active entity from Cannabis. He later synthesized and determined the structures of the purine and pyrimidine bases in nucleic acids, synthesized coenzymes related to the nucleic acid systems, and synthesized the energy-transfer compounds (adenosine diphosphate and adenosine triphosphate). (C.T.)

1958

Sanger, Frederick 61

PRIZE: Chemistry, 1958; Chemistry, 1980. BORN: August 13, 1918; Rendcomb, Gloucestershire, England. PARENTS: Father, Frederick Sanger; Mother, Cicely Crewdson Sanger. NATIONALITY: British. RELIGION: Agnostic; from Quaker/Anglican background. EDUCATION: Cambridge Univ., England, B.A., 1940; Cambridge Univ., England, Ph.D., 1943. SPOUSE: Margaret Joan Howe, married 1940. CHILDREN: Robin, son; Peter Frederick, son; Sally Joan, daughter. CAREER: Cambridge Univ., England, Professor, 1944-. OTHER AWARDS: Corday-Morgan Medal and Prize, Chemical Society, 1951; Gairdner Foundation Annual Award, 1971, 1979; William Bate Hardy Prize, Cambridge Philosophical Society, 1976; Copley Medal, Royal Society, 1977.

Selected Publications: "The Free Amino Groups of Insulin." *Biochemical Journal* 39 (1945): 507-15. "The Amino-Acid Sequence in the Glycyl Chain of Insulin. The Identification of Lower Peptides from Partial Hydrolysates." *Biochemical Journal* 53 (1953): 353-66 (with E.O.P. Thompson). "DNA Sequencing with Chain-Terminating Inhibitors." *Proceedings of the National Academy of Sciences, USA* 74 (1977): 5463-67 (with A.R. Coulson and S. Nicklen). "Nucleotide Sequence of Bacteriophage Phi X174 DNA." *Nature (London)* 265 (1977): 687-95 (with others).

For More Information See: *Asimov's Biographical Encyclopedia of Science and Technology*. Garden City, NY: Doubleday, 1982, 1426. *Biographical Encyclopedia of Scientists*. New York: Facts on File, 1981, 708. *Current Biography Yearbook*. New York: H.W. Wilson, 1981, 354-56.

Commentary: Frederick Sanger, the recipient of two Nobel Prizes in Chemistry, received the first "for his work on the structure of proteins, especially that of insulin" and the second for his work in determining the base sequences of nucleic acids. The methods which Sanger developed in painstaking years of effort were successfully used by others in determining the structures of complicated compounds. In his work on DNA, Sanger also found two cases of genes located within genes, previously thought to be impossible. (M.B.)

1959

Heyrovsky, Jaroslav 62

PRIZE: Chemistry, 1959. BORN: December 20, 1890; Prague, Czechoslovakia. DIED: March 27, 1967; Prague, Czechoslovakia. PARENTS: Father, Leopold Heyrovsky; Mother, Clara Hanl Heyrovsky. NATIONALITY: Czechoslovakian. RELIGION: Christian. EDUCATION: Univ. of London, England, B.Sc., 1913; Charles Univ., Czechoslovakia, Ph.D., 1918; Charles Univ., Czechoslovakia, D.Sc., 1921. SPOUSE: Marie Koran, married February 22, 1926. CHILDREN: Michael, son; Judith Cěrny, daughter. CAREER: Univ. of London, England, Professor, 1913-14; Charles Univ., Prague, Czechoslovakia, Professor and Administrator, 1919-54; Institute of Physical Chemistry, Prague, Czechoslovakia, Director, 1926-54; Central Polarographic Institute, Prague, Czechoslovakia, Director, 1950-63. OTHER AWARDS: First State Prize, Czechoslovakia, 1951; Order of the Czechoslovak Republic, 1955.

Selected Publications: "Electrolysis with a Dropping Mercury Cathode, Part I. Deposition of Alkali and Alkaline Earth Metals." *Philosophical Magazine* 45 (1923): 303-14. "Researches with the Dropping Mercury Cathode, Part II. The Polarograph." *Recueil des Travaux Chimiques des Pays-Bas* 44 (1925): 496-98 (with M. Shikata). *A Polarographic Study of the Electrokinetic Phenomena of Adsorption, Electroreduction and Overpotential Displayed at the Dropping Mercury*

Cathode. Paris: Hermann, 1934. *Polarographie: Theoretische Grundlagen, Praktische Ausfuhrung und Anwendungen der Elektrolyse mit der Tropfenden Quecksilberelektrode.* Vienna: Springer, 1941. *Bibliography of Publications Dealing with the Polarographic Method.* 5 volumes. Prague: Nakladatelství Československé akademie véd, 1960-1964.

For More Information See: *Current Biography Yearbook.* New York: H.W. Wilson, 1961, 202-04. *Dictionary of Scientific Biography.* New York: Scribner's, 1975 (Volume 6), 370-76.

Commentary: Jaroslav Heyrovsky was cited by the Academy as "the originator of one of the most important methods of contemporary chemical analysis." At the presentation it was said "your polarograph...can be used for the most diverse purposes. Steadily your method has won the confidence of analytical chemists." Heyrovsky's career was unusual in that he spent it entirely on the study of the polarograph, the device that he invented, and on its application in polarography, the electrochemical means of determining the chemical composition of oxidizable substances. (D.W.)

1960

Libby, Willard Frank   63
PRIZE: Chemistry, 1960. BORN: December 17, 1908; Grand Valley, CO. DIED: September 8, 1980; Los Angeles, CA. PARENTS: Father, Ora Edward Libby; Mother, Eva May Rivers Libby. NATIONALITY: American. RELIGION: Most probably Christian/Protestant. EDUCATION: Univ. of California, B.S., 1931; Univ. of California, Ph.D., 1933. SPOUSE: Leonor Hickey, married 1940, divorced 1966; Leona Woods Marshall, married 1966. CHILDREN: Janet Eva, daughter; Charlotte, daughter. CAREER: Univ. of California, Berkeley, Professor, 1933-45; Univ. of Chicago, IL, Professor, 1945-54; United States Atomic Energy Commission, 1954-59; Univ. of California, Los Angeles, Professor and Administrator, 1959-80. OTHER AWARDS: Research Corporation Award, 1951; Chandler Medal, Columbia U., 1954; Remsen Memorial Lecture Award, 1955; Bicentennial Lecture Award, City College of New York, 1956; Nuclear Applications in Chemistry Award, 1956; Cresson Medal, Franklin Institute, 1957; Willard Gibbs Medal, 1958; Priestley Memorial Award, Dickinson College, 1959; Albert Einstein Medal Award, 1959; Day Medal, Geological Society of America, 1961; Gold Medal, American Institute of Chemists, 1970; Lehman Award, New York Academy of Science, 1971.

Selected Publications: "Stability of Uranium and Thorium for Natural Fission." *Physical Review* 55 (1939): 1269. *Radiocarbon Dating.* Chicago: U. of Chicago Press, 1952. "Chemistry and the Peaceful Uses of the Atom." *Chemical and Engineering News* 35 (1957): 14-17.

For More Information See: *Biographical Encyclopedia of Scientists.* New York: Facts on File, 1981, 490-91. *Current Biography Yearbook.* New York: H.W. Wilson, 1954, 406-07.

Commentary: The award to Willard Libby was made "for his method to use carbon-14 for age determination in archaeology, geology, geophysics, and other branches of science." He developed sensitive techniques to detect the amount of carbon-14 activity in a sample, and by relating the amount found to the constant amount when the substance was a living plant or animal, he determined the age of the sample. Libby also participated in the Manhattan Project during World War II as part of the group that developed the gaseous-diffusion method of separating uranium isotopes, and he was an important member of the Atomic Energy Commission in its deliberations in the 50s. (G.W.)

1961

Calvin, Melvin   64
PRIZE: Chemistry, 1961. BORN: April 8, 1911; St. Paul, MN. PARENTS: Father, Elias Calvin; Mother, Rose Hervitz Calvin. NATIONALITY: American. RELIGION: Jewish. EDUCATION: Michigan College of Mining and Technology, B.S., 1931; Univ. of Minnesota, Ph.D., 1935. SPOUSE: Genevieve Jemtegaard, married 1942. CHILDREN: Noel, son; Elin, daughter; Karole, daughter. CAREER: Univ. of Manchester, England, Researcher, 1935-37; Univ. of California, Berkeley, Professor, 1937-80. OTHER AWARDS: Davy Medal, Royal Society, 1964; Priestley Medal, American Chemical Society, 1978; Gold Medal, American Institute of Chemists, 1979.

Selected Publications: "The Path of Carbon in Photosynthesis." *Science* 107 (1948): 476. *The Path of Carbon in Photosynthesis.* Englewood Cliffs, NJ: Prentice-Hall, 1957 (with J.A. Bassham). "Quantum Conversion in Photosynthesis." *Journal of Theoretical Biology* 1 (1961): 258. *Photosynthesis of Carbon Compounds.* New York: W.A. Benjamin, 1962.

For More Information See: *Asimov's Biographical Encyclopedia of Science and Technology.* Garden City, NY: Doubleday, 1982, 837. *Current Biography Yearbook.* New York: H.W. Wilson, 1962, 68-70.

Commentary: Melvin Calvin's Nobel Prize was earned "for his research on the carbon dioxide assimilation in plants," the process of photosynthesis. He pioneered the use of radioactive isotopes, particularly carbon-14, in the tracing of the metabolism of chemical substances in biochemical pathways. His research on the metal chelate compounds and in the area of biology was also significant. (J.E.H.)

1962

Kendrew, John Cowdery, Sir   65
PRIZE: Chemistry, 1962. BORN: March 24, 1917; Oxford, England. PARENTS: Father, W.G. Kendrew; Mother, Evelyn May Graham Sandberg Kendrew. NATIONALITY: British. RELIGION: Agnostic. EDUCATION: Cambridge Univ., England, B.A., 1939; Cambridge Univ., England, M.A., 1943; Cambridge Univ., England, Ph.D., 1949; Cambridge Univ., England, D.Sc., 1962. SPOUSE: None. CHILDREN: None. CAREER: British Military Service, 1939-46; Cambridge Univ., England, Researcher and Professor, 1947-74; European Molecular Biology Laboratory, Heidelberg, Germany, Director, 1975-82. OTHER AWARDS: Royal Medal, Royal Society, 1965; Knighthood, 1974; Order of the Madara Horsemen, Bulgaria, 1980.

Selected Publications: "The Crystal Structure of Horse Myoglobin." *Haemoglobin (Symposium on Conference at Cambridge in Memory of Joseph Barcroft)*

(June 1948): 131-49. "The Crystal Structure of Horse Metmyoglobin I. General Features: The Arrangement of the Polypeptide Chains." *Proceedings of the Royal Society (London)* A201 (1950): 62-89. "A Three-Dimensional Model of the Myoglobin Molecule Obtained by X-ray Analysis." *Nature* 181 (1958): 666 (with others). "The Molecular Structures of Myoglobin and Hemoglobin." *New Perspectives in Biology, Proceedings of the Symposium, Rehovoth, Israel* (1963): 18-27.

For More Information See: *Asimov's Biographical Encyclopedia of Science and Technology*. Garden City, NY: Doubleday, 1982, 863-64. *Biographical Encyclopedia of Scientists*. New York: Facts on File, 1981, 434. *Current Biography Yearbook*. New York: H.W. Wilson, 1963, 215-17.

Commentary: John Kendrew shared the Nobel Prize for his contributions to the "studies of the structures of globular proteins," using x-ray crystallography. Kendrew determined the structure of myoglobin, a protein containing approximately 2,600 atoms. Another major interest was the highly respected *Journal of Molecular Biology*, which he founded in 1959, and for which he served as editor throughout the remainder of his career. (J.E.H.)

Perutz, Max Ferdinand 66

PRIZE: Chemistry, 1962. BORN: May 19, 1914; Vienna, Austria. PARENTS: Father, Hugo Perutz; Mother, Adele Goldschmidt Perutz. NATIONALITY: Austrian; later British citizen. RELIGION: Jewish. EDUCATION: Cambridge Univ., England, Ph.D., 1940. SPOUSE: Gisela Clara Peiser, married March 28, 1942. CHILDREN: Robin, son; Vivien, daughter. CAREER: Cambridge Univ., England, Researcher and Professor, 1939-. OTHER AWARDS: Royal Medal, Royal Society, 1971; Copley Medal, Royal Society, 1979.

Selected Publications: *Proteins and Nucleic Acids: Structure and Function*. New York: Elsevier Publishing Company, 1962. *Haemoglobin and Myoglobin* (Atlas of Molecular Structures in Biology Series: No. 2). New York: Oxford U. Press, 1981 (with G. Fermi).

For More Information See: *Biographical Encyclopedia of Scientists*. New York: Facts on File, 1981. *Current Biography Yearbook*. New York: H.W. Wilson, 1963, 324-26.

Commentary: Max Perutz shared the Nobel Prize for his contribution to the "studies of the structures of globular proteins." In particular, Perutz determined the structure of hemoglobin, using X-ray diffraction analysis of hemoglobin crystals. His research interests centered on molecular biology, and his discoveries led to a greater understanding of the relationship between the structure and function of macromolecules in living systems. (J.E.H.)

1963

Natta, Giulio 67

PRIZE: Chemistry, 1963. BORN: February 26, 1903; Imperia, Italy. DIED: May 2, 1979; Bergamo, Italy. PARENTS: Father, Francesco Natta; Mother, Elena Crespi Natta. NATIONALITY: Italian. RELIGION: Catholic. EDUCATION: Polytechnic Institute, Italy, Ph.D., 1924. SPOUSE: Rosita Beati, married April 25, 1935. CHILDREN: Franca, daughter; Giussepe, son. CAREER: Polytechnic Institute, Milan, Italy, Professor, 1924-33;

Univ. of Pavia, Italy, Professor and Administrator, 1933-35; Univ. of Rome, Italy, Professor and Administrator, 1935-37; Polytechnic Institute, Turin, Italy, Professor and Administrator, 1937-74. OTHER AWARDS: Gold Medal, Milan, Italy, 1960; Gold Medal, President of Italy, 1961; Gold Medal, Synthetic Rubber Industry, 1961; Stas Medal, Belgian Chemical Society, 1962; Gold Medal, Society of Plastic Engineers, NY, 1963; Perrin Medal, French Chemical Physical Society, 1963; Lavoisier Medal, French Chemical Society, 1963; Perkin Gold Medal, English Society of Dyers and Colourists, 1963; John Scott Award, Philadelphia, PA, 1964; Lomonosov Gold Medal, Academy of Sciences, USSR, 1969.

Selected Publications: "The Kinetics of the Stereospecific Polymerization of A-Olefins." *Advances in Catalysis* 11 (1959): 1-66 (with I. Pasquon). "Organometallic Complexes As Catalysts in Ionic Polymerization." *Tetrahedron* 8 (1960): 86-100 (with G. Mazzanti). "Precisely Constructed Polymers." *Scientific American* 205 (August 1961): 33-41. "Alternating Copolymer of Dimethylketene with Acetone." *Macromolecular Syntheses* 4 (1972): 73-75 (with G.F. Pregaglia and M. Binaghi). *Polymerization Reactions*. New York: Springer, 1975 (with others). *Structure and Behavior of 3-Dimensional Molecules. An Introduction to Stereochemistry*. Weinheim, Germany: Verlag Chemie, 1976 (with Mario Farino).

For More Information See: *Asimov's Biographical Dictionary of Science and Technology*. Garden City, NY: Doubleday, 1982, 792. *Current Biography Yearbook*. New York: H.W. Wilson, 1964, 312-14.

Commentary: Giulio Natta's life as a teacher, administrator, and researcher spanned over 50 years of work in industrial and chemical engineering, which resulted in the discovery of basic chemical techniques and their practical applications for business and industry. Natta's major research focus in macromolecular chemistry was the study of petrochemicals, specifically olefins. Working independently but cooperatively with Karl Ziegler, and using his background in polymers, Natta discovered the process of stereospecific polymerization. For these studies, for discoveries in polymerization, for "bridging the gap between natural and synthetic macromolecules, and for developing practical methods for linking simple atoms into complex molecular networks," Natta and Ziegler won the Nobel Prize. (J.B.T.)

Ziegler, Karl 68

PRIZE: Chemistry, 1963. BORN: November 26, 1898; Helsa, Oberhausen, Germany. DIED: August 12, 1973; Mulheim, Germany. PARENTS: Father, Karl Ziegler; Mother, Luise Rall Ziegler. NATIONALITY: German. RELIGION: Lutheran. EDUCATION: Univ. of Marburg, Germany, Ph.D., 1920. SPOUSE: Maria Kurtz, married 1923. CHILDREN: 1 son, 1 daughter. CAREER: Marburg Univ., Germany, Professor, 1923-27; Heidelberg Univ., Germany, Professor, 1927-36; Univ. of Halle, Germany, Professor and Administrator, 1936-43; Kaiser Wilhelm Institute, Germany, Director, 1943-69. OTHER AWARDS: Leibig Medal, 1935; Swinburne Medal, 1964.

Selected Publications: "Catalysis of the Polymerization of Unsaturated Hydrocarbons by Alkali Organic Compounds." *Annalen* 511 (1934): 45-63 (with L. Jakob). "The Importance of Alkali Metallo-organic Compounds for Synthesis." *Angewandte Chemie* 49

(1936): 455-60. "The Polymerization of Butadiene and the Production of Artificial Rubber." *Rubber Chem. Tech* 11 (1938): 501-07. "Organoalkali Compounds. XV. Controlled 1,2- and 1,4-Polymerization of Butadiene." *Annalen* 542 (1940): 90-122 (with H. Grimm and R. Willer). *Praparative Organische Chemie.* Wiesbaden, Germany: Dieterichsche Verlags, 1948. "The Polymerization of Ethylene." *Bull. Soc. Chim. France* (1956): 1-6.

For More Information See: *Biographical Encyclopedia of Scientists.* New York: Facts on File, 1981, 871. *Chemical and Engineering News* 41 (November 11, 1963): 22.

Commentary: Karl Ziegler shared the Nobel Prize for his work on catalysis of polymerization. His early research centered on the Grignard reactions, which prompted his interest in metallo-organic compounds. In the 1950s, Ziegler discovered that he could use aluminum- or titanium-imbedded resins as catalysts in the production of polyethylene, producing a stronger, unbranched polymer. He and his colaureate, Giulio Natta, continued to develop this fertile field of chemistry over the course of their careers. (R.P.)

1964

Hodgkin, Dorothy Crowfoot   69
PRIZE: Chemistry, 1964. BORN: May 12, 1910; Cairo, Egypt. PARENTS: Father, John Winter Crowfoot; Mother, Grace Mary Hood Hodgkin. NATIONALITY: British. RELIGION: Most probably Christian/Protestant. EDUCATION: Oxford Univ., England, baccalaureate, 1932; Cambridge Univ., England, Ph.D., 1937. SPOUSE: Thomas L. Hodgkin, married December 16, 1937. CHILDREN: Luke, son; Tobias, son; Elizabeth, daughter. CAREER: Oxford Univ., England, Professor, 1934-77. OTHER AWARDS: Royal Medal, Royal Society, 1957; Copley Medal, Royal Society, 1976; Mikhail Lomonosov Gold Medal, 1982.

Selected Publications: "X-ray Analysis and Protein Structure." *Cold Spring Harbor Symposia on Quantitative Biology* 14 (1949): 79-84. "X-ray Analysis of the Structure of Penicillin." *Advancement Sci* 6 (1949): 85-89. "X-ray Crystallographic Study of the Structure of Vitamin B-12." *Bull. Soc. Franc. Mineral et Cryst* 78 (1955): 106-15. *Wandering Scientists.* New Delhi: Indian Council for Cultural Relations, 1974. *Structural Studies on Molecules of Biological Interest.* New York: Oxford U. Press, 1981.

For More Information See: *Asimov's Biographical Encyclopedia of Science and Technology.* Garden City, NY: Doubleday, 1982, 834. *Biographical Encyclopedia of Scientists.* New York: Facts on File, 1981, 386-87.

Commentary: Dorothy Hodgkin spent her career working on the determination of the structure of complex organic molecules and was awarded the Nobel Prize for her structural determination on vitamin B-12. She was the first to use the computer successfully in such work to determine the structure of penicillin (1949) and later also studied the structure of insulin. Hodgkin was also an inveterate traveler, an avocation inherited from her archaeologist father. (J.L.)

1965

Woodward, Robert Burns   70
PRIZE: Chemistry, 1965. BORN: April 10, 1917; Boston, MA. DIED: July 8, 1979; Cambridge, MA. PARENTS: Father, Arthur Chester Woodward; Mother, Margaret W. Burns Woodward. NATIONALITY: American. RELIGION: Protestant. EDUCATION: Massachusetts Institute of Technology, B.S., 1936; Massachusetts Institute of Technology, Ph.D., 1937; Wesleyan Univ., CT, D.Sc., 1945. SPOUSE: Irji Pullman, married July 30, 1938; Eudoxia M.M. Muller, married September 14, 1946. CHILDREN: Siiri Anne, daughter; Jean Kristen, daughter; Crystal Elisabeth, daughter; Eric Richard Arthur, son. CAREER: Harvard Univ., MA, Professor, 1937-79. OTHER AWARDS: Ledlie Prize, Harvard U., MA, 1955; Davy Medal, Royal Society, 1959; Pius XI Gold Medal, Pontifical Academy of Sciences, 1961; Priestley Medallion, Dickinson College, NJ, 1962; National Medal of Science, USA, 1964; Lavoisier Medal, Societe Chimique de France, 1968; Decorated Order of the Rising Sun, Japan, 1970; Science Achievement Award, American Medical Association, 1971; Arthur C. Cope Award, American Chemical Society, 1973; Copley Medal, Royal Society, 1978.

Selected Publications: "Total Synthesis of Quinine." *Journal of the American Chemical Society* 66 (1944): 849 (with W.E. Doering). "Total Synthesis of a Steroid." *Journal of the American Chemical Society* 73 (1951): 2403-04 (with others). "The Total Synthesis of Cholesterol." *Journal of the American Chemical Society* 73 (1951): 3548 (with F. Sondheimer and D. Taub). "The Total Synthesis of Cortisone." *Journal of the American Chemical Society* 73 (1951): 4057 (with F. Sondheimer and D. Taub). "The Total Synthesis of Reserpine." *Journal of the American Chemical Society* 78 (1956): 2023-25 (with others). "Total Synthesis of Vitamin B12." *Pure and Applied Chemistry* 33 (1973): 145-77.

For More Information See: *Asimov's Biographical Encyclopedia of Science and Technology.* Garden City, NY: Doubleday, 1982, 1416-17. *Current Biography Yearbook.* New York: H.W. Wilson, 1952, 647-49.

Commentary: Robert Woodward's Nobel recognized "his meritorious contributions to the art of chemical synthesis." A brilliant laboratory worker, Woodward developed techniques for total synthesis and achieved total synthesis of quinine (1944), penicillin (1945), strychnine (1947), cholesterol and cortisone (1951), lysergic acid (1954), reserpine (1956), tetracycline (1962), chlorophyll (1966), and vitamin B12 (1971). (E.G.)

1966

Mulliken, Robert Sanderson   71
PRIZE: Chemistry, 1966. BORN: June 7, 1896; Newburyport, MA. PARENTS: Father, Samuel Parsons Mulliken; Mother, Katherine Mulliken. NATIONALITY: American. RELIGION: Most probably Christian. EDUCATION: Massachusetts Institute of Technology, B.S., 1917; Univ. of Chicago, IL, Ph.D., 1921. SPOUSE: Mary Helen Noe, married December 24, 1929. CHILDREN: Lucia Maria, daughter; Valerie Noe, daughter. CAREER: Bureau of Mines, United States, Engineer, 1917; United States Army, 1918-19; Univ. of Chicago, IL, Professor, 1919-61; Florida State Univ., Professor, 1965-72.

OTHER AWARDS: Lewis Gold Medal, American Chemical Society; Richards Gold Medal, 1960; Debye Award, 1963; Kirkwood Medal, 1964; Willard Gibbs Gold Medal, 1965.

Selected Publications: "The Assignment of Quantum Numbers for Electrons in Molecules." *Physics Review* 32 (1928): 186-222. "The Assignment of Quantum Numbers for Electrons in Molecules. II. Correlation of Molecular and Atomic Electron States." *Physics Review* 32 (1928): 761-72. "Electronic States of Diatomic Carbon, and the C-C Bond." *Physics Review* 56 (1939): 778-81. "Quantum-Mechanical Methods and the Electronic Spectra and Structure of Molecules." *Chemical Reviews* 41 (1947): 201-06.

For More Information See: *Asimov's Biographical Encyclopedia of Science and Technology.* Garden City, NY: Doubleday, 1982, 579. *Biographical Encyclopedia of Scientists.* New York: Facts on File, 1981, 752-53.

Commentary: Robert Mulliken's Nobel was presented "for his fundamental work concerning chemical bonds and the electronic structure of molecules by the molecular-orbital method." Mulliken, over a long and fruitful career, developed the theory and interpretation of molecular spectra and applied quantum theory to the electronic states of molecules, eventually providing the molecular orbital theory of electrons moving in a field produced by all the nuclei present. He also worked in the areas of isotope separation by evaporative centrifuging and in electronegativity. (P.P.)

1967

Eigen, Manfred 72

PRIZE: Chemistry, 1967. BORN: May 9, 1927; Bochum, Germany. PARENTS: Father, Ernst Eigen; Mother, Hedwig Feld Eigen. NATIONALITY: German. RELIGION: Lutheran. EDUCATION: Univ. of Gottingen, Germany, Doctor Rerum Naturalium, 1951. SPOUSE: Elfriede Müller, married 1952. CHILDREN: Gerald, son; Angela, daughter. CAREER: Univ. of Gottingen, Germany, Researcher, 1951-53; Max Planck Institut, Germany, Professor and Administrator, 1953-. OTHER AWARDS: Otto Hahn Prize, German Chemical Society, 1962.

Selected Publications: "Methods for Investigation of Ionic Reactions in Aqueous Solutions with Half Times as Short as 10^{-9} Sec.: Application to Neutralization and Hydrolysis Reactions." *Discussions of the Faraday Society* 17 (1954): 194-205. "Kinetics of Neutralization." *Zeitschrift für Elektrochemie* 59 (1955): 986-93 (with Leo De Maeyer). "Potential-Impulse Method for the Investigation of Very Rapid Ionic Reactions in Aqueous Solution." *Zeitschrift für Elektrochemie* 59 (1955): 483-94 (with J. Schoen). "A Temperature-Jump Method for the Examination of Chemical Relaxation." *Zeitschrift für Elektrochemie* 63 (1959): 652-61 (with G. Czerlinski). "Eine Kinetische Methode zur Untersuchung Schneller Prototroper Tautomerisierungsreaktionen." *Chemische Berichte* 98 (May 1965): 1623-38 (with G. Ilgenfritz and W. Kruse).

For More Information See: *Contemporary Authors.* Detroit, MI: Gale Research Company, 1983 (Volume 108), 140. *Science* 158 (November 10, 1967): 748-68.

Commentary: Manfred Eigen was awarded the Nobel Prize for developing techniques to measure rapid chemical reactions. Ronald G.W. Norrish and George Porter jointly shared the other half of the prize. The relaxation methods developed by Eigen, beginning in the mid-1950s, revolutionized chemical research by making possible the study of chemical reactions with half times from one second to fractions of a millimicrosecond. By disturbing the equilibrium of a solution and electronically measuring the time necessary for the solution to return to equilibrium, Eigen provided a way to study the reaction rates of previously unmeasurable chemical processes. (J.C.H.)

Norrish, Ronald George Wreyford 73

PRIZE: Chemistry, 1967. BORN: November 9, 1897; Cambridge, England. DIED: June 7, 1978; Cambridge, England. PARENTS: Father, Herbert Norrish; Mother, Amy Norrish. NATIONALITY: British. RELIGION: Most probably Christian/Protestant. EDUCATION: Cambridge Univ., England, baccalaureate, 1921; Cambridge Univ., England, Ph.D., 1924. SPOUSE: Anne Smith, married 1926. CHILDREN: 2 daughters. CAREER: British Army, 1916-19; Cambridge Univ., England, Professor, 1925-65. OTHER AWARDS: Liversidge Medal, Chemical Society, 1958; Davy Medal, Royal Society, 1958; Bernard Lewis Gold Medal, Combustion Institute, 1964; Faraday Medal, Chemical Society, 1965; Longstaff Medal, Chemical Society, 1969.

Selected Publications: "Chemical Reactions Produced by Very High Light Intensities." *Nature* 164 (1949): 658 (with G. Porter). "The Application of Flash Techniques to the Study of Fast Reactions." *Discussions of the Faraday Society* 17 (1954): 40-46 (with G. Porter). "The Gas Phase Oxidation of n-Butenes." *Proceedings of the Royal Society (London)* Series A272 (1963): 164-91 (with K. Porter). "The Kinetics and Analysis of Very Fast Reactions." *Chemistry in Britain* 1 (1965): 289-311.

For More Information See: *Biographical Memoirs of Fellows of the Royal Society.* London: Royal Society, 1981 (Volume 27), 379-424. "Obituary R.G.W. Norrish, 1897-1978." *Nature* 275 (September 7, 1978): 78-79.

Commentary: Ronald Norrish was awarded the prize for his "studies of extremely fast chemical reactions, effected by disturbing the equilibrium by means of very short pulses of energy." The chemical reactions studied lasted only for one-billionth of a second, but the techniques developed allowed for the observation of short-lived intermediate species, such as free radicals, and for complete elaborations of reaction kinetics. The techniques of flash photolysis have been used in liquids, gases, and for the study of biological materials. Norrish also further developed the theory of photochemical reactions. (M.F.)

Porter, George, Sir 74

PRIZE: Chemistry, 1967. BORN: December 6, 1920; Stainforth, England. PARENTS: Father, John Smith Porter; Mother, Alice Ann Roebuck Porter. NATIONALITY: British. RELIGION: Agnostic; from Methodist background. EDUCATION: Univ. of Leeds, England, B.Sc., 1941; Cambridge Univ., England, M.A., 1947; Cambridge Univ., England, Ph.D., 1949. SPOUSE: Stella Jean Brooke, married 1949. CHILDREN: John Brooke, son; Christopher, son. CAREER: British Navy, 1941-45; Cambridge Univ., England, Professor, 1949-55; Univ. of Sheffield, England, Professor, 1955-63; Royal Institution, England, Professor and Administrator, 1963-. OTHER AWARDS: Corday-Morgan Medal, Chemical Society, 1955; Silvanus Thompson Medal, 1969; Davy Medal, Royal Society, 1971; Knighthood, 1972; Kalinga Prize, 1977; Robertson Prize, National Academy of Sciences, 1978; Rumford Medal, Royal Society, 1978; Communications Award, European Physical Society, 1978; Faraday Medal, Chemical Society, 1979; Longstaff Medal, 1981.

Selected Publications: "Chemical Reactions Produced by Very High Light Intensities." *Nature* 164 (1949): 658 (with R. Norrish). "The Application of Flash Techniques to the Study of Fast Reactions." *Discussions of the Faraday Society* 17 (1954): 40-46 (with R. Norrish). *Chemistry for the Modern World.* New York: Barnes and Noble, 1962. *Progress in Reaction Kinetics.* New York: Pergamon Press, 1965.

For More Information See: *Biographical Encyclopedia of Scientists.* New York: Facts on File, 1981, 647-48. *Science* 158 (November 10, 1967): 746-48.

Commentary: George Porter shared the Nobel for his "studies of extremely fast chemical reactions, effected by disturbing the equilibrium by means of very short pulses of energy." The chemical reactions studied lasted only for one-billionth of a second, but the techniques that were developed became standard for observing short-lived intermediates that permitted elucidating chemical reaction kinetics. Flash photolysis was used in important studies of gases, liquids, and biochemical systems. (M.F.)

1968

Onsager, Lars   75

PRIZE: Chemistry, 1968. BORN: November 20, 1903; Oslo, Norway. DIED: October 5, 1976; Coral Gables, FL. PARENTS: Father, Erling Onsager; Mother, Ingrid Kirkeby Onsager. NATIONALITY: Norwegian; later American citizen. RELIGION: Protestant. EDUCATION: Norges Tekniske Hogskale, Norway, Chem. E., 1925; Yale Univ., CT, Ph.D., 1935. SPOUSE: Margarete Arledter, married September 7, 1933. CHILDREN: Inger Marie, daughter; Erling Frederick, son; Hans Tanberg, son; Christian Carl, son. CAREER: Brown Univ., Providence, RI, Professor, 1928-33; Yale Univ., New Haven, CT, Professor, 1933-72. OTHER AWARDS: Rumford Medal, American Academy of Sciences, 1953; Lorenz Medal, 1958; G.N. Lewis Medal, 1962; J.J. Kirkwood Medal, 1962; Willard Gibbs Medal, 1962; T.W. Richards Medal, 1964; Debye Award, 1965; Belfer Award, 1966.

Selected Publications: "Reciprocal Relations in Irreversible Processes." *Physical Review* 37 (1931): 405-26. "Reciprocal Relations in Irreversible Processes." *Physical Review* 38 (1931): 2265-79. "Initial Recombination of Ions." *Physical Review* 54 (1938): 554-57. "de Haas-van Alphen Effect in Zinc." *Physical Review* 74 (1948): 1235 (with J.E. Robinson). "Fluctuations and Irreversible Processes." *Physical Review* 91 (1953): 1505-12 (with S. Machlup).

For More Information See: *Biographical Memoirs of Fellows of the Royal Society.* London: Royal Society, 1978 (Volume 24), 445. *Current Biography Yearbook.* New York: H.W. Wilson, 1958, 321-23.

Commentary: Lars Onsager was awarded the Nobel Prize "for the discovery of the reciprocal relations bearing his name which are fundamental for the thermodynamics of irreversible processes." His theoretical treatments provided the foundation for the study of

nonequilibrium thermodynamics. Earlier in his career, he also modified the Debye-Huckel equations for ion motion in solution to include the effect of Brownian motion. (W.G.)

1969

Barton, Derek Harold Richard, Sir   76

PRIZE: Chemistry, 1969. BORN: September 8, 1918; Gravesend, Kent, England. PARENTS: Father, William Thomas Barton; Mother, Maude Henrietta Barton. NATIONALITY: British. RELIGION: Most probably Christian. EDUCATION: Imperial College, England, B.Sc., 1940; Imperial College, England, Ph.D., 1942; Univ. of London, England, D.Sc., 1949. SPOUSE: Jeanne Wilkins, married December 20, 1944; Christiane Cognet, married November 5, 1969. CHILDREN: William Godfrey Lukes, son. CAREER: British Government Service, Researcher, 1942-45; Imperial College, England, Professor, 1945-49; Harvard Univ., MA, Professor, 1949-50; Univ. of London, England, Professor, 1950-55; Univ. of Glasgow, Scotland, Professor, 1955-57; Imperial College, England, Professor, 1957-78; Institute of Chemistry and Natural Substances, France, Director, 1978-. OTHER AWARDS: Hoffman Prize, Imperial College, England, 1940; Harrison Memorial Prize, Chemical Society, 1948; Corday-Morgan Medal, Chemical Society, 1951; Fritzsche Award, American Chemical Society, 1959; Roger Adams Award, American Chemical Society, 1959; Davy Medal, Royal Society, 1961; Knighthood, 1972.

Selected Publications: "The Conformation of the Steroid Nucleus." *Experienta* 6 (1950): 316-20. "The Stereochemistry of Cyclohexane Derivatives." *Journal of the Chemical Society* (1953): 1027-40. "The Inaugural Simonsen Lecture. Some Aspects of Sesquiterpenoid Chemistry." *Proceedings of the Chemical Society* (1958): 61-66. "Recent Progress in Conformational Analysis." *Theoret Org. Chem., Papers Kekule Symposium, London* (1958): 127-43. "Recent Progress in Conformational Analysis." *Suomen Kemistilehte* 32A (1959): 27-33.

For More Information See: *Chemical and Engineering News* 47 (November 10, 1969): 11. *Science* 166 (November 7, 1969): 715-22.

Commentary: Derek Barton shared the Nobel Prize with Odd Hassel for contributions "to the development of the concept of conformation and its application in chemistry." Barton's landmark paper proposed that functional group orientations in space affect the reaction rates in isomers. He applied his views to six-membered organic rings and explained the stability of cyclohexane, building on Hassel's work. Barton's later work dealt with steroids, terpenes, and oxyradicals. (J.R.F.)

Hassel, Odd   77

PRIZE: Chemistry, 1969. BORN: May 17, 1897; Oslo, Norway. DIED: May 15, 1981; Oslo, Norway. PARENTS: Father, Ernst Hassel; Mother, Mathilde Klaveness Hassel. NATIONALITY: Norwegian. RELIGION: Lutheran. EDUCATION: Univ. of Oslo, Norway, Candidate Real degree, 1920; Univ. of Berlin, Germany, D. Phil., 1924. SPOUSE: None. CHILDREN: None. CAREER: Univ. of Oslo, Norway, Professor, 1925-64. OTHER AWARDS: Knight Order of St. Olav; Guineras Medal, 1964; Guldberg Waage Medal, 1964.

Selected Publications: *Crystal Chemistry*. London: Heinemann, 1935. *U.S. Dept. Com., Office Tech. Serv.* AD267293 (1961): 1-37. "Weak Intermolecular Bonds in Solids." *Dansk. Tidsskr. Farm* 36 (1962): 41-54. "Investigation of Molecular Structures." *Selected Topics in Structure Chemistry*. Oslo: Universitetsforlaget, 1967.

For More Information See: *Chemical and Engineering News* 47 (November 10, 1969): 11. *Science* 166 (November 7, 1969): 715-22.

Commentary: Odd Hassel and Derek Barton shared the Nobel Prize for their contributions "to the development of the concept of conformation and its application in chemistry." Hassel's early career centered on the investigation of silver halide photosensitization by organic dyes, in the course of which he discovered adsorption indicators. However, it was his landmark papers on conformational analysis of cyclohexane (which showed the chair form of the compound to be more stable than the boat form) that brought him to prominence. His later studies of charge-transfer bonding were also important. (J.R.F.)

1970

Leloir, Luis Federico   78

PRIZE: Chemistry, 1970. BORN: September 6, 1906; Paris, France. PARENTS: Father, Federico R. Leloir; Mother, Hirtensia Aguirre Leloir. NATIONALITY: Argentinian. RELIGION: Catholic. EDUCATION: Univ. of Buenos Aires, Argentina, M.D., 1932. SPOUSE: Amelie Zuherbuhler, married November 26, 1943. CHILDREN: Amelia, daughter. CAREER: Univ. of Buenos Aires, Argentina, Researcher, 1932-35; Cambridge Univ., England, Researcher, 1935-37; Institute of Physiology, Argentina, Researcher, 1937-44; United States, Exile, 1944-47; Biochemical Research Institute, Argentina, Researcher, 1947-.

Selected Publications: "The Enzymic Transformation of Uridine Diphosphate into a Galactose Derivative." *Arch. Biochem. Biophys* 33 (1951): 186-90. "Carbohydrate Metabolism." *Ann. Rev. Biochem* 22 (1953): 179-210 (with C.E. Cardini). "Uridine Coenzymes." *Proc. 3rd Intern. Congr. Biochem., Brussels* (1955): 154-62. "Nucleotide and Saccharide Synthesis." *Conf. on Polysaccharides in Biol., Trans* (1958): 155-234.

For More Information See: *Chemical and Engineering News* 48 (November 2, 1970): 13. *Science* 170 (November 6, 1970): 604-09.

Commentary: Luis Leloir was awarded the Nobel Prize for "his discovery of sugar nucleotides and their role in the biosynthesis of carbohydrates." Leloir, working in simple circumstances, isolated uridine diphosphate glucose and showed that it was incorporated into glycogen in the presence of a liver enzyme. He also worked out the mechanism of synthesis of starch. Leloir's discoveries—that the sugar nucleotides are principal actors in interconversion of sugars and polysaccharide formation—led to additional research in carbohydrate metabolism and on the medical implications of the discoveries. (C.N.B.)

1971

Herzberg, Gerhard   79

PRIZE: Chemistry, 1971. BORN: December 25, 1904; Hamburg, Germany. PARENTS: Father, Albin Herzberg; Mother, Ella Biber Herzberg. NATIONALITY: German; later Canadian citizen. RELIGION: Jewish. EDUCATION: Darmstadt Institute of Technology, Germany, Doctor of Engineering, 1928. SPOUSE: Luise H. Oettinger, married December 29, 1929. CHILDREN: Paul Albin, son; Agnes Margaret, daughter. CAREER: Darmstadt Institute of Technology, Germany, Professor, 1930-35; Univ. of Saskatchewan, Canada, Professor, 1935-45; Univ. of Chicago, IL, Professor, 1945-48; National Research Council, Canada, Researcher and Administrator, 1949-69. OTHER AWARDS: U. of Liege Medal, 1950; Henry Marshall Tory Medal, Canadian Royal Society, 1953; Jay Kissen Mookerjee Gold Medal, Indian Association for the Cultivation of Science, 1957; Frederic Ive Medal, Optical Society of America, 1964; Willard Gibbs Medal, American Chemical Society, 1969; Faraday Medal, Chemical Society of London, 1970; Royal Medal, Royal Society, 1971; Linus Pauling Medal, American Chemical Society, 1971.

Selected Publications: *Atomic Spectra and Atomic Structure*. New York: Prentice-Hall, 1937. *Molekulspektren und Molekulstructur. Zweiatomige Molekule*. Dresden, Germany: T. Steinkopff, 1939. *Infrared and Roman Spectra of Polyatomic Molecules*. New York: D. Van Nostrand, 1945. "The Electronic Structure of the Nitrogen Molecule." *Physical Review* 69 (1946): 362-65. "Lamb Shift of the 1(2)S Ground State of Deuterium." *Proceedings of the Royal Society of London* 234A (1956): 516-28.

For More Information See: *Chemical and Engineering News* 49 (November 1, 1971): 5. *Current Biography Yearbook*. New York: H.W. Wilson, 1973, 185-87.

Commentary: The Nobel Prize was given to Gerhard Herzberg for his "contributions to the knowledge of electronic structure and geometry of molecules, particularly free radicals." Herzberg was responsible for development of techniques and measurement and interpretation of the spectra of molecules, including hydrogen, oxygen, nitrogen, and CO. He also measured the Lamb shifts in D, He, and Li (+) and the spectra of interstellar gas. His work was used in the explanation of the properties of radicals and ions present as intermediates in chemical reactions. (L.I.S.)

1972

Anfinsen, Christian Boehmer   80

PRIZE: Chemistry, 1972. BORN: March 26, 1916; Monessen, PA. PARENTS: Father, Christian Boehmer Anfinsen; Mother, Sophie Rasmussen Anfinsen. NATIONALITY: American. RELIGION: Most probably Christian. EDUCATION: Swarthmore College, PA, B.A., 1937; Univ. of Pennsylvania, M.S., 1939; Harvard Univ., MA, Ph.D., 1943. SPOUSE: Florence Bernice Kenenger, married November 29, 1941, divorced 1978; Libby Esther Shulman Ely, married 1979. CHILDREN: Carol, daughter; Margot, daughter; Christian, son. CAREER: Univ. of Pennsylvania, Professor, 1938-39; Carlsberg Univ., Denmark, Researcher, 1939-40; Harvard Univ., MA, Professor, 1941-50; National Heart Institute, Researcher, 1950-62; Harvard Univ., MA, Professor,

1962-63; National Institute of Arthritis, Metabolism, and Digestive Diseases, Researcher, 1963-81; Johns Hopkins Univ., MD, Professor, 1982-. OTHER AWARDS: Public Service Award, Rockefeller Foundation, 1954; Myrtle Wreath, Hadassah, 1977.

Selected Publications: "Method for the Specific Proteolytic Cleavage of Protein Chains." *Archives of Biochemistry and Biophysics* 65 (1956): 156-63 (with Michael Sela and Harold Tritsch). "Reductive Cleavage of Disulfide Bridges in Ribonuclease." *Science* 125 (1957): 691-92 (with Michael Sela and Frederick H. White). *The Molecular Basis of Evolution.* New York: Wiley, 1959. "The Ribonucleases-Occurrence, Structure and Properties." In *Enzymes.* New York: Academic Press, 1961 (Volume 5), 95-122.

For More Information See: "The 1972 Nobel Prize for Chemistry." *Science* (November 3, 1972): 492-93. "Nobel Winners in Physics, Chemistry." *New York Times* (October 21, 1972) 1: L14.

Commentary: The Nobel citation commends Christian Anfinsen's "work on ribonuclease, especially concerning the connection between the amino acid sequence and the biologically active conformation." His pioneering work on enzymes relating protein organization and function and on the genetic basis of protein organization have been landmark studies in the field. (A.S.)

Moore, Stanford   81

PRIZE: Chemistry, 1972. BORN: September 4, 1913; Chicago, IL. DIED: August 23, 1982; Manhattan, NY. PARENTS: Father, John Howard Moore; Mother, Ruth Fowler Moore. NATIONALITY: American. RELIGION: Catholic. EDUCATION: Vanderbilt Univ., TN, A.B., 1935; Univ. of Wisconsin, Ph.D., 1938. SPOUSE: None. CHILDREN: None. CAREER: Rockefeller Institute for Medical Research, NY, Professor, 1939-42; Office of Scientific Research and Development, Washington, DC, Researcher, 1942-45; Rockefeller Institute for Medical Research, NY, Professor, 1945-82. OTHER AWARDS: Founder's Medal, Vanderbilt U., TN, 1935; Chromatography Award, American Chemical Society, 1963; Richard's Medal, American Chemical Society, 1972; Linderstrom-Lang Medal, Copenhagen, Denmark, 1972.

Selected Publications: "Structure and Activity of Pancreatic Ribonuclease." *Soc. Chim. Biol., Celebration Cinquantenaire, Conf. Rappt., Paris* (1964): 189-94. "Amino Acid Analysis: Aqueous Dimethyl Sulfoxide as Solvent for the Ninhydrin Reaction." *Journal of Biological Chemistry* 243 (1968): 6281-83. "Chemical Structures of Pancreatic Ribonuclease and Deoxyribonuclease." *Science* 180 (1973): 458-64 (with William H. Stein). "The Precision and Sensitivity of Amino Acid Analysis." *Kagaku No Ryoiki Zokan* 106 (1976): 136-75.

For More Information See: *Science* 178 (November 3, 1972): 492-93. *Science News* 102 (October 28, 1972): 276.

Commentary: Stanford Moore, with his colaureate William Stein, received the Nobel Prize for painstaking, lengthy research which established the amino-acid sequence of the enzyme ribonuclease. In the process, they developed an invaluable tool for later research—the automatic amino acid analyzer—as well as iden-

tifying critical solvents and techniques for use in such work. Moore and Stein also identified the most likely active site on the ribonuclease molecule. (M.N.)

Stein, William Howard   82

PRIZE: Chemistry, 1972. BORN: June 25, 1911; New York, NY. DIED: February 2, 1980; New York, NY. PARENTS: Father, Fred M. Stein; Mother, Beatrice Borg Stein. NATIONALITY: American. RELIGION: Jewish. EDUCATION: Harvard Univ., MA, B.S., 1933; Columbia Univ., NY, Ph.D., 1938. SPOUSE: Phoebe L. Hockstader, married June 22, 1936. CHILDREN: William Howard, Jr., son; David F., son; Robert J., son. CAREER: Rockefeller Institute, NY, Researcher, 1938-80. OTHER AWARDS: Award in Chromatography and Electrophoresis, 1964.

Selected Publications: "Amino-Acid Composition of Human Hemoglobin." *Biochimica et Biophysica Acta* 24 (1957): 640-42 (with others). "Chemical Modifications of Ribonuclease." *Brookhaven Symposia in Biology* 13 (1960): 104-14. "Relations Between Structure and Activity of Ribonuclease." *Proc. Intern. Congr. Biochem., 5th, Moscow* 4 (1961): 33-38 (with Stanford Moore). "Structure-Activity Relations in Ribonuclease." *Federation Proceedings* 23 (1964): 599-608. "Structure and the Activity of Ribonuclease." *Israel Journal of Medical Science* 1 (1965): 1229-43.

For More Information See: *Chemical and Engineering News* 50 (October 30, 1972): 2-3. *Science* 178 (November 3, 1972): 492-93.

Commentary: William Stein was awarded the Nobel Prize for his careful elucidation, with Stanford Moore, of the amino-acid sequence of the enzyme ribonuclease. Stein devised an automatic amino acid analyzer and chromatographic methods for determining the hydrolysis products of proteins and used the technology he had developed to solve the puzzle of the amino-acid sequence. (J.A.S.)

1973

Fischer, Ernst Otto   83

PRIZE: Chemistry, 1973. BORN: November 10, 1918; Muchen-Solln, Germany. PARENTS: Father, Karl Tobias Fischer; Mother, Valentine Danzer Fischer. NATIONALITY: German. RELIGION: Lutheran. EDUCATION: Univ. of Munich, Germany, Dipl. Chem., 1949; Univ. of Munich, Germany, Doctor Rerum Naturalium, 1952. SPOUSE: None. CHILDREN: None. CAREER: Univ. of Munich, Germany, Professor, 1954-. OTHER AWARDS: Gottingen Academy Prize, 1957; Alfred Stock-Gedachtnis Prize, 1959.

Selected Publications: "The Nomenclature of Metal Compounds Containing Two Cyclopentadienyl Rings." *Z. Naturforsch* 9b (1954): 619-20. "New Results on Aromatic Metal Carbonyls." *Journal of Inorganic and Nuclear Chemistry* 8 (1958): 268-72. *Metal (pi)-Complexes.* New York: Elsevier, 1966 (with H. Werner). "Transition Metal Carbonyl Carbene Complexes." *Pure and Applied Chemistry* 30 (1972): 353-72.

For More Information See: *Biographical Encyclopedia of Scientists.* New York: Facts on File, 1981, 264-65. *Science* 182 (November 16, 1973): 699-700.

Commentary: The award to Ernst Otto Fischer was "for his pioneering research in organometallic chemistry...in particular, his independent and imaginative efforts in the development of the chemistry of sandwich complexes of the transition metals." His work on the structure of ferrocene gave impetus to the study of sandwich complexes. His later work on transition metal complexes with organic compounds was prolific and notable. (L.I.W.)

Wilkinson, Geoffrey 84

PRIZE: Chemistry, 1973. BORN: July 14, 1921; Todmorden, England. PARENTS: Father, Henry Wilkinson; Mother, Ruth Crowther Wilkinson. NATIONALITY: British. RELIGION: Agnostic; from Anglican and Methodist background. EDUCATION: Univ. of London, England, B.Sc., 1941; Univ. of London, England, Ph.D., 1946. SPOUSE: Lise Sölver, married July 17, 1951. CHILDREN: Anne, daughter; Pernille, daughter. CAREER: National Research Council of Canada, Scientific Officer, 1943-46; Univ. of California, Researcher, 1946-50; Massachusetts Institute of Technology, Professor, 1950-51; Harvard Univ., MA, Professor, 1951-55; Univ. of London, England, Professor, 1956-. OTHER AWARDS: Inorganic Chemistry Award, American Chemical Society, 1966; Lavoisier Medal, French Chemical Society, 1968; Transition Metal Chemistry Award, Royal Society, 1972; Hiroshima U. Medal, Japan, 1978; Royal Medal, Royal Society, 1981; Galileo Medal, U. of Pisa, Italy, 1983.

Selected Publications: "The Structure of Iron Biscyclopentadienyl." *Journal of the American Chemical Society* 74 (1952): 2125-26 (with M. Rosenblum, M.C. Whiting, and R.B. Woodward). *Advanced Inorganic Chemistry.* New York: Interscience, 1962 (with F.A. Cotton). "Catalytically Active Rhodium (I) Complexes." German Patent 2, 136, 470 (February 10, 1972). "Hexamethyltungsten." U.S. Patent 3, 816, 491 (June 11, 1974). *Basic Inorganic Chemistry.* New York: Wiley, 1976 (with F.A. Cotton).

For More Information See: "The 1973 Nobel Prize for Chemistry." *Science* (November 16, 1973): 699-701. "Three Win Nobel Physics Prize and Two the Chemistry Award." *New York Times* (October 24, 1973) 1: L1, L26.

Commentary: Geoffrey Wilkinson was cited by the Academy for his "pioneering work, performed independently, on the chemistry of the organometallic so-called sandwich compounds." His earlier work on the preparation and elaboration of structure of iron biscyclopentadienyl was followed by other important work on the preparation and structure of transition metal compounds with organic entities, such as hexamethyltungsten. His later work on the catalytic activity of rhodium (II) complexes is another step in developing manufactured compounds that may have far-reaching consequences in the use of metal-based industrial materials. (A.S.)

1974

Flory, Paul John 85

PRIZE: Chemistry, 1974. BORN: June 19, 1910; Sterling, IL. DIED: September 9, 1985; Big Sur, CA. PARENTS: Father, Ezra Flory; Mother, Martha Brumgraph Flory. NATIONALITY: American. RELIGION: Protestant. EDUCATION: Manchester College, IN, B.Sc., 1931; Ohio State U., M.S., 1931; Ohio State U., Ph.D., 1934. SPOUSE: Emily Catharine Tabor, married March 7, 1936. CHILDREN: Susan, daughter; Malinda, daughter; Paul, Jr.,

son. CAREER: DuPont Experimental Station, DE, Researcher, 1936-38; Univ. of Cincinnati, OH, Professor, 1938-40; Standard Oil Development, OH, Researcher, 1940-43; Goodyear Tire and Rubber, OH, Administrator, 1943-48; Cornell Univ., NY, Professor, 1948-56; Mellon Institute, Pittsburgh, PA, Administrator, 1956-61; Stanford Univ., CA, Professor, 1961-75. OTHER AWARDS: Sullivant Medal, 1945; Baekeland Award, 1947; Cowyn Medal, 1954; Nichols Medal, 1962; High-Polymer Physics Prize, 1962; International Award in Plastics, 1967; Goodyear Medal, 1968; Debye Award, 1969; Chandler Medal, 1970; First Award for Excellence, 1971; Cresson Medal, 1971; Kirkwood Medal, 1971; National Medal of Science, 1975.

Selected Publications: *Principles of Polymer Chemistry.* Ithaca, NY: Cornell U. Press, 1953. *Statistical Mechanics of Chain Molecules.* New York: Interscience Publishers, 1969. *Selected Works of Paul J. Flory.* Stanford, CA: Stanford U. Press, 1985.

For More Information See: *Biographical Encyclopedia of Scientists.* New York: Facts on File, 1981, 271-72. *Current Biography Yearbook.* New York: H.W. Wilson, 1975, 127-30.

Commentary: The award to John Flory was for his "fundamental achievements, both theoretical and experimental, in the field of macromolecules." Flory used statistical mechanics early in his career to develop expressions for the chain-length distribution in polymer molecules. He later presented a theory of nonlinear polymer structure and introduced the idea of a Flory temperature, at which polymer properties can be measured. His work on the elasticity of polymer materials was also noteworthy. Flory spent his later years as a leading spokesperson for activist groups working to protect Soviet scientists. (J.A.S.)

1975

Cornforth, John Warcup, Sir 86

PRIZE: Chemistry, 1975. BORN: September 7, 1917; Sidney, Australia. PARENTS: Father, J.W. Cornforth; Mother, Hilda Eippern Cornforth. NATIONALITY: British. RELIGION: Most probably Christian. EDUCATION: Univ. of Sidney, Australia, B.S., 1937; Oxford Univ., England, M.Sc., 1938; Oxford Univ., England, D.Phil., 1941. SPOUSE: Rita H. Harradence, married 1941. CHILDREN: John, son; Brenda, daughter; Philippa, daughter. CAREER: Medical Research Council, London, England, Researcher, 1946-62; Shell Research Laboratory, Kent, England, Director, 1962-75; Univ. of Sussex, Brighton, England, Professor, 1975-82. OTHER AWARDS: Corday-Morgan Medal, Chemistry Society, 1953; Flintoff Medal, Chemistry Society, 1966; CIBA Medal, 1966; Stouffer Prize, 1967; Davy Medal, Royal Society, 1968; Ernest Gunther Award, American Chemical Society, 1969; Prix Roussel, 1972; Royal Medal, Royal Society, 1976; Knighthood, 1977; Copley Medal, Royal Society, 1982.

Selected Publications: *The Chemistry of Penicillin.* Princeton, NJ: Princeton U. Press, 1949 (with others). "Absolute Configuration of Cholesterol." *Nature* 173 (1954): 536 (with I. Youhotsky and G. Popjack). "Total Synthesis of Steroids." *Progress in Organic Chemistry* 3 (1955): 1-43. "Stereoselective Synthesis of Squalene." *Journal of the Chemical Society* (1959):

2539-47 (with R.H. Cornforth and K.K. Mathew). "Absolute Stereochemistry of Some Enzymic Processes." *Biochemical Journal* 86 (1963): 7.

For More Information See: *Biographical Encyclopedia of Scientists*. New York: Facts on File, 1981, 163. *Science* 190 (November 21, 1975): 772-73.

Commentary: The award to John Cornforth was "for his researches on the stereochemistry of enzyme-catalyzed reactions." Cornforth began his research with work on the structure of penicillin but was most noted for his elucidation of the steps in the biosynthesis of cholesterol from acetic acid. His synthesis of alkenes, oxazoles, and abscisic acid was also notable. (L.I.W.)

Prelog, Vladimir   87

PRIZE: Chemistry, 1975. BORN: July 23, 1906; Sarajevo, Yugoslavia. PARENTS: Father, Milan Prelog; Mother, Mara Cettolo Prelog. NATIONALITY: Yugoslavian; later Swiss citizen. RELIGION: Agnostic; from Catholic background. EDUCATION: Institute of Technology and School of Chemistry, Czechoslovakia, doctorate, 1929. SPOUSE: Kamila Vitek, married October 31, 1933. CHILDREN: Jan, son. CAREER: G.Z. Driza Laboratories, Prague, Czechoslovakia, Researcher, 1929-35; Univ. of Zagreb, Yugoslavia, Professor, 1935-42; Eidgenossische Technische Hochschule, Switzerland, Professor, 1942-76. OTHER AWARDS: Warner Medal, 1945; Stas Medal, 1962; Medal of Honor, Rice U., 1962; Marcel Benoist Award, 1965; Roger Adams Award; A.W. Hofman Medal; Davy Medal, Royal Society.

Selected Publications: "Conformation and Reactivity of Medium-sized Ring Compounds." *Pure Applied Chemistry* 6 (1963): 545-60. "Constitution of Rifamycins." *Pure Applied Chemistry* 7 (1963): 551-64. "Role of Certain Microbial Metabolites as Specific Complexing Agents." *Pure Applied Chemistry* 25 (1971): 197-210. "Chiral Ionophores." *Pure Applied Chemistry* 50 (1978): 893-904. "Structure and Properties of Boromycin and Products of Its Degradation." *Front. Bioorg. Chem. Mol. Biol* (1979): 87-96.

For More Information See: *Biographical Encyclopedia of Scientists*. New York: Facts on File, 1981, 651-52. *Chemical and Engineering News* 53 (October 27, 1975): 4-5.

Commentary: Vladimir Prelog received the Nobel Prize for his contributions in the area of the "stereochemistry of organic molecules and reactions," specifically for the techniques and rules which can determine whether a partially asymmetric compound is dextra or levo. His early research included notable advances in the areas of the structure of the alkaloids, microorganism metabolites, the discovery of boromycin, the stereospecificity of microorganisms, and the relationship between conformation and chemical activity of medium-sized ring structures. (J.P.)

1976

Lipscomb, William Nunn   88

PRIZE: Chemistry, 1976. BORN: December 9, 1919; Cleveland, OH. PARENTS: Father, William Nunn Lipscomb; Mother, Edna Patterson Porter Lipscomb. NATIONALITY: American. RELIGION: Most probably Christian. EDUCATION: Univ. of Kentucky, B.S., 1941; California Institute of Technology, Ph.D., 1946. SPOUSE: Mary Adele Sergeant, married May 20, 1944,

divorced August 14, 1983; Jean Craig Evans, married August 1983. CHILDREN: Dorothy Jean, daughter; James Sargent, son. CAREER: United States Office of Scientific Research and Development, Chemist, 1942-46; Univ. of Minnesota, Professor, 1946-59; Harvard Univ., MA, Professor, 1959-. OTHER AWARDS: Harrison Howe Award, American Chemical Society, 1958; Distinguished Service Award, American Chemical Society, 1968; George Ledlie Prize, Harvard U., MA, 1971; Peter Debye Award, American Chemical Society, 1973; Evans Award, Ohio State U.; Remsen Award, American Chemical Society, Maryland Section, 1976; Alexander von Humboldt-Stiftung, 1979.

Selected Publications: "Valence in the Boron Hydrides." *Journal of Physical Chemistry* 61 (1957): 23-27. "Boron Hydrides." *Advances in Inorganic Chemistry and Radiochemistry* 1 (1959): 117-56. *Boron Hydrides*. New York: W.A. Benjamin, 1963. "Geometrical Theory of Boron Hydrides." *Inorganic Chemistry* 3 (1964): 1683-85. *Nuclear Magnetic Resonance Studies of Boron Hydrides and Related Compounds*. New York: W.A. Benjamin, 1969.

For More Information See: *Chemistry* 49 (December 1976): 2. *Science* 194 (November 1976): 709-10.

Commentary: William Lipscomb received his Nobel for his research which explained the molecular structure and chemical bonding in the boranes, using the concept of two electrons binding together three atoms. He went on to study chemical effects in nuclear magnetic resonance studies of complex molecules and the quantum mechanics of large molecules. Lipscomb used low-temperature x-ray diffraction to research the structure of other crystals and compounds, including biochemical substances. (L.C.)

1977

Prigogine, Ilya   89

PRIZE: Chemistry, 1977. BORN: January 25, 1917; Moscow, Russia. PARENTS: Father, Roman Prigogine; Mother, Julie Wichmann Prigogine. NATIONALITY: Russian; later Belgian citizen and American resident. RELIGION: Most probably Christian. EDUCATION: Universite Libre de Bruxelles, Belgium, baccalaureate, 1939; Universite Libre de Bruxelles, Belgium, doctorate, 1942. SPOUSE: Marina Prokopowicz, married February 25, 1961. CHILDREN: Yves, son; Pascal, son. CAREER: Universite Libre de Bruxelles, Belgium, Professor and Administrator, 1947-; Univ. of Texas, Austin, Professor and Administrator, 1967-. OTHER AWARDS: Prix Francqui, 1955; Prix Solvay, 1965; Bourke Medal, Chemical Society, England, 1972; Rumford Medal, Royal Society, 1976; Karcher Medal, American Crystallographic Association, 1978; Descartes Medal, U. of Paris, France, 1979; Honda Prize, 1983.

Selected Publications: *Thermodynamique Chimique Conformement aux Methodes de Gibbs et De Donder*. Liege, Belgium: Desoer, 1944-51 (*Treatise on Thermodynamics Based on the Methods of Gibbs and De Donder*. London: Longmans, Green, 1954) (with R. Defay). *Introduction to Thermodynamics of Irreversible Processes*. New York: Interscience, 1962 (with A. Bellemans and V. Mathot). *Order Out of Chaos*. New York: Bantam Books, 1984.

For More Information See: *Chemical and Engineering News* 55 (October 17, 1977): 4. *Physics Today* 30 (December 1977): 79-80.

Commentary: Ilya Prigogine was awarded the Nobel Prize for "his successful development of a satisfactory theory of nonlinear thermodynamics in states which are far removed from equilibrium." The "generalized, nonlinear and irreversible thermodynamics," especially the method used by Prigogine to study the stability of the dissipative structures which "live in their symbiosis with their environment," has possible applications in a very wide range of problems; his researches have created "theories to bridge the gaps between chemical, biological and social scientific fields of inquiry." He has been called "the poet of thermodynamics" for his elegant and lucid presentation of innovative theories. (J.V.S.)

1978

Mitchell, Peter Denis   90
PRIZE: Chemistry, 1978. BORN: September 20, 1920; Mitcham, Surrey, England. PARENTS: Father, Christopher Gibbs Mitchell; Mother, Kate Beatrice Dorothy Taplin Mitchell. NATIONALITY: British. RELIGION: Atheist; from Atheist/Agnostic Christian background. EDUCATION: Cambridge Univ., England, B.A., 1943; Cambridge Univ., England, Ph.D., 1950. SPOUSE: Patricia Helen Mary ffrench, married November 1, 1958. CHILDREN: Jeremy, son; Daniel, son; Jason, son; Gideon, son; Julia, daughter; Vanessa, daughter. CAREER: Cambridge Univ., England, Professor, 1943-55; Univ. of Edinburgh, Scotland, Professor, 1955-63; Glynn Research Institute, England, Director, 1964-. OTHER AWARDS: CIBA Medal and Prize, Biochemical Society, England, 1973; Warren Triennial Prize, Massachusetts General Hospital, 1974; Louis and Bert Freedman Foundation Award, New York Academy of Sciences, 1974; Wilhelm Feldberg Foundation Prize, Anglo/American Science Exchange, 1976; Lewis S. Rosenstiel Award, Brandeis U., 1977; Medal, Federal European Biochemistry Society, 1978; Copley Medal, Royal Society, 1981.

Selected Publications: *Chemiosmotic Coupling in Oxidative and Photosynthetic Phosphorylation.* Bodmin, Cornwall, England: Glynn Research, 1966. *Chemiosmotic Coupling and Energy Transduction.* Bodmin, Cornwall, England: Glynn Research, 1968. *Chemiosmotic Proton Circuits in Biological Membranes.* Reading, MA: Addison-Wesley, 1981 (with P.C. Hinkle and V.P. Skulachev).

For More Information See: *Biographical Encyclopedia of Scientists.* New York: Facts on File, 1981, 564. *Science* 202 (December 8, 1978): 1174-76.

Commentary: Peter Mitchell was awarded the Nobel Prize in Chemistry for his once-controversial chemiosmotic theory regarding energy coupling oxidation and photosynthetic phosphorylation. He proposed that hydrogen ions are transported across the membranes of a cell's mitochondria during the production of adenosine triphosphate (ATP) through the creation of an electrochemical gradient. Previously, it was thought that energy was transported down the respiratory chain by an elusive high-energy intermediate compound generated during oxidation. Mitchell was also unconventional in his creation of his own laboratory, in its architecture, and in his interest in local affairs, building restoration, and history. (L.C.)

1979

Brown, Herbert Charles (Brovarnik, Herbert Charles)   91
PRIZE: Chemistry, 1979. BORN: May 22, 1912; London, England. PARENTS: Father, Charles Brovarnik; Mother, Pearl Gorinstein Brovarnik. NATIONALITY: British; later American citizen. RELIGION: Jewish. EDUCATION: Wright Junior College, IL, A.S., 1935; Univ. of Chicago, IL, B.S., 1936; Univ. of Chicago, IL, Ph.D., 1938. SPOUSE: Sarah Baylen, married February 6, 1937. CHILDREN: Charles Allan, son. CAREER: Univ. of Chicago, IL, Professor, 1936-43; Wayne State Univ., MI, Professor, 1943-47; Purdue Univ., IN, Professor, 1947-78. OTHER AWARDS: Purdue Sigma Xi Research Award, 1951; Nichols Medal, American Chemical Society, 1959; American Chemical Society Award for Creative Research in Synthetic Organic Chemistry, 1960; H.N. McCoy Award, 1965; Linus Pauling Medal, 1968; National Medal of Science, 1969; Roger Adams Medal, 1971; Charles Frederick Chandler Medal, 1973; Madison Marshall Award, 1975; Chemical Pioneer Award, 1975; CCNY Scientific Achievement Award Medal, 1976; Elliot Cresson Medal, 1978; C.K. Ingold Medal, 1978; Priestley Medal, 1981; Perkin Medal, 1982.

Selected Publications: *Hydroboration.* New York: W.A. Benjamin, 1962. *Boranes in Organic Chemistry.* Ithaca, NY: Cornell U. Press, 1972. *Organic Syntheses via Boranes.* New York: Wiley-Interscience, 1975 (with others). *The Nonclassical Ion Problem.* New York: Plenum Press, 1977.

For More Information See: *Asimov's Biographical Encyclopedia of Science and Technology.* Garden City, NY: Doubleday, 1982, 843. *Biographical Encyclopedia of Scientists.* New York: Facts on File, 1981, 114.

Commentary: Herbert C. Brown received the Nobel Prize for his "discovery and exploration of borohydrides and organoboranes." Beginning with the development of a practical method for diborane synthesis, Brown later produced sodium borohydride, used extensively in organic chemistry. He was responsible for the introduction of a new class of compounds, the organoboranes, which also became valuable in organic chemistry. His work on steric effects was also noteworthy. (I.S.Z.)

Wittig, Georg Friedrich Karl   92
PRIZE: Chemistry, 1979. BORN: June 16, 1897; Berlin, Germany. PARENTS: Father, Gustav Wittig; Mother, Martha Dombrowski Wittig. NATIONALITY: German. RELIGION: Most probably Christian. EDUCATION: Univ. of Marburg, Germany, Ph.D., 1923. SPOUSE: Waltraut Ernst, married 1930. CHILDREN: 2 daughters. CAREER: Univ. of Marburg, Germany, Professor, 1926-32; Technische Hochschule, Braunschweig Institute of Technology, Germany, Professor, 1932-37; Univ. of Freiburg, Germany, Professor, 1937-44; Univ. of Tubingen, Germany, Professor, 1944-56; Univ. of Heidelberg, Germany, Professor, 1956-. OTHER AWARDS: Adolf von Baeyer Medal, Society of German Chemists, 1953; Silver Medal, U. of Helsinki, 1957; Dannie Heineman Award, Göttinger Academy of Sciences, 1965; Otto Hahn Prize, Germany, 1967; Silver Medal, City of Paris, 1969; Paul Karrer Medal, U. of Zurich, 1972; Medal of the Bruylants Chair, U. of Leuwen, 1972;

Roger Adams Award, American Chemical Society, 1973; Karl Ziegler Prize, Society of German Chemists, 1975; Ordens Grosses Verdienstkreuz, 1980.

Selected Publications: "Course of Reactions of Pentaphenylphosphorus and Certain Derivatives." *Annalender Chemie, Justus Liebigs* 580 (1953): 44-57. "Triphenylphosphinemethylene as an Olefin-forming Reagent." *Chemisches Berichte* 87 (1954): 1318-30. "Triphenylphosphinemethylenes as Olefin-forming Reagents." *Chemisches Berichte* 88 (1955): 654-66. "Metallizability of Quaternary Ammonium and Phosphonium Salts." *Annalender Chemie, Justus Liebigs* 562 (1956): 177-78.

For More Information See: *Biographical Dictionary of Scientists, Chemists.* New York: Peter Bedrick Books, 1983, 148-49. *Modern Scientists and Engineers.* 3 volumes. New York: McGraw-Hill, 1980 (Volume 3), 341-42.

Commentary: Georg Wittig won the Nobel Prize for "the discovery of the rearrangement reaction that bears his name," which caused phosphorus ylides to react with ketones and aldehydes to form alkenes. The reactions, commonly known as the Wittig reaction, introduced double bonds between carbons in specified locations and led to the synthesis of pharmaceuticals and other complex organic substances, including Vitamin A, Vitamin D derivatives, prostaglandin, and insect pheromones. (M.B.)

1980

Berg, Paul   93

PRIZE: Chemistry, 1980. BORN: June 30, 1926; New York, NY. PARENTS: Father, Harry Berg; Mother, Sarah Brodsky Berg. NATIONALITY: American. RELIGION: Jewish. EDUCATION: Pennsylvania State U., B.S., 1948; Western Reserve Univ., OH, Ph.D., 1952. SPOUSE: Mildred Levy, married September 13, 1947. CHILDREN: John, son. CAREER: Washington Univ., St. Louis, MO, Professor, 1955-59; Stanford Univ., CA, Professor, 1959-. OTHER AWARDS: Eli Lilly Award, 1959; California Scientist of the Year, 1964; V.D. Mattia Prize, Roche Institute for Molecular Biochemistry, 1972; Albert Lasker Medical Research Award, 1980; Gairdner Foundation Award, 1980

Selected Publications: "Contributions of Nucleic Acids to the Specificity of Protein Synthesis." *Probl. Neoplastic Disease; Symp., New York* (1962): 15-34. "Viral Genome in Transformed Cells." *Proceedings of the Royal Society, Series B* (1971): 65-76. "Potential Biohazards of Recombinant DNA Molecules." *Proceedings of the National Academy of Sciences U.S.A.* (1974): 2593-94 (with others).

For More Information See: *New York Times Biographical Service* (October 1980): 1359. *Science* 210 (November 21, 1980): 887-89.

Commentary: Paul Berg was cited for "his fundamental studies of the biochemistry of nucleic acids, with particular regard to recombinant DNA," and for his development of the new technology of genetic engineering. He had been one of the leaders in studying the molecular biology of nucleic acids throughout his career. His work on bacterial protein synthesis was followed by his studies of gene expression in higher

organisms. He was also notable for leading molecular biologists in calling for a cessation of recombinant DNA research until the risks could be assessed. (P.P.)

Gilbert, Walter   94

PRIZE: Chemistry, 1980. BORN: March 21, 1932; Boston, MA. PARENTS: Father, Richard V. Gilbert; Mother, Emma Cohen Gilbert. NATIONALITY: American. RELIGION: Jewish. EDUCATION: Harvard Univ., MA, B.A., 1953; Harvard Univ., MA, A.M., 1954; Cambridge Univ., England, D. Phil., 1957. SPOUSE: Celia Stone, married December 29, 1953. CHILDREN: John Richard, son; Kate, daughter. CAREER: Harvard Univ., MA, Professor, 1957-. OTHER AWARDS: U.S. Steel Foundation Award, National Academy of Sciences, 1968; Ledlie Prize, Harvard U., MA, 1969; Warren Triennial Prize, Massachusetts General Hospital, 1977; Louis and Bert Freedman Foundation Award, New York Academy of Sciences, 1977; Prix Charles-Leopold Mayer, Academie des Sciences, France, 1977; Louisa Gross Horowitz Prize, Columbia U., NY, 1979; Gairdner Prize, 1979; Albert Lasker Basic Science Award, 1979.

Selected Publications: "Protein Synthesis in Escherichia Coli." *Cold Spring Harbor Symposium on Quantitative Biology* 28 (1963): 287-97. "Isolation of the Lac Repressor." *Proceedings of the National Academy of Sciences U.S.* 56 (1966): 1891-98 (with Benno Mueller-Hill). "DNA Replication. The Rolling Circle Model." *Cold Spring Harbor Symposium on Quantitative Biology* 33 (1968): 473-84 (with David Dressler). "The Lac Operator in DNA." *Proceedings of the National Academy of Sciences U.S.* 58 (1968): 2415-21 (with Benno Mueller-Hill). "Repressors and Genetic Control." *Neurosci: Second Study Program* (1970): 946-54.

For More Information See: *Physics Today* 34 (January 1981): 17-18. *Science* 210 (November 21, 1980): 887-89.

Commentary: Walter Gilbert shared the Nobel Prize for his work on determination of the sequence of bases in DNA by a method applicable to single- and double-stranded DNA. He was equally well-known for his use of equilibrium dialysis to isolate the lac repressor, the element in the Monod-Jacob model that determined whether or not the gene in Escherichia coli would cause production of the enzyme beta-galactosidase, which is dependent on the presence or absence of lactose. (B.S.S.)

Sanger, Frederick *see* entry 61

1981

Fukui, Kenichi   95

PRIZE: Chemistry, 1981. BORN: October 4, 1918; Nara, Japan. PARENTS: Father, Ryokichi Fukui; Mother, Chie Fukui. NATIONALITY: Japanese. RELIGION: No record found. EDUCATION: Kyoto Imperial Univ., Japan, Bachelor's in Engineering, 1941; Kyoto Imperial Univ., Japan, Ph.D., 1948. SPOUSE: Tomoe Horie, married 1947. CHILDREN: Tetsuya, son; Miyako, daughter. CAREER: Japanese Army Fuel Laboratory, Researcher, 1941-44; Kyoto Imperial Univ., Japan, Professor, 1944-82; Kyoto Univ. of Industrial Arts, Japan, President, 1982-. OTHER AWARDS: Japan Academy Medal, 1962; Order of Culture, Japan, 1981; Person of Cultural Merit, Japan, 1981.

Selected Publications: "Developments in Quantum-Mechanical Interpretation of the Reactivity of Unsaturated Hydrocarbons." *Journal of Japanese Chemistry* 6 (1952): 379-85. "Further Studies on the Frontier Electrons." *Journal of Japanese Chemistry* 8 (1954): 73-74. "Molecular Orbital Theory of Orientation in Aromatic, Heteroaromatic, and Other Conjugated Molecules." *Journal of Chemical Physics* 22 (1954): 1433-42 (with others). "Theoretical Reactivity Index of Addition in the Frontier Electron Theory." *Bulletin of the Chemical Society of Japan* 34 (1961): 230-32 (with others).

For More Information See: *Chemical and Engineering News* 59 (October 26, 1981): 6-7. *Science* 214 (November 6, 1981): 627-29.

Commentary: Kenichi Fukui was cited by the Academy "for his frontier orbital theory of chemical reactivity," which stated that the progress of a reaction depends on the geometries and relative energies of the highest occupied molecular orbital of one reactant and the lowest unoccupied molecular orbital of the other. His theory was extended by his colaureate Roald Hoffman, while Fukui continued to work on calculations and applications to many specific reactions during his career. (D.P.N.)

Hoffman, Roald (Hoffman, Ronald) 96

PRIZE: Chemistry, 1981. BORN: July 18, 1937; Zloczow, Poland. PARENTS: Father, Hillel Satran; Stepfather, Paul Hoffman; Mother, Clara Rosen Satran Hoffman. NATIONALITY: Polish; later American citizen. RELIGION: Jewish. EDUCATION: Columbia Univ., NY, B.S., 1958; Harvard Univ., MA, M.A., 1960; Harvard Univ., MA, Ph.D., 1962. SPOUSE: Eva Borjesson, married 1960. CHILDREN: Hillel Jan, son; Ingrid Helena, daughter. CAREER: Harvard Univ., MA, Researcher, 1962-65; Cornell Univ., NY, Professor, 1965-. OTHER AWARDS: American Chemical Society Award, 1969; Fresenius Award, 1969; Harrison Howe Award, 1969; Annual Award of International Academy of Quantum Molecular Sciences, 1970; Arthur C. Cope Award, American Chemical Society, 1973; Linus Pauling Award, 1974; Nichols Medal, 1980; Inorganic Chemistry Award, American Chemical Society, 1982.

Selected Publications: "Orbital Symmetries and Endo-exo Relationships in Concerted Cycloaddition Reactions." *Journal of the American Chemical Society* 87 (1965): 4388-89 (with R.B. Woodward). "Orbital Symmetries and Orientational Effects in a Sigmatropic Reaction." *Journal of the American Chemical Society* 87 (1965): 4389-90 (with R.B. Woodward). "Selection Rules for Concerted Cycloaddition Reactions." *Journal of the American Chemical Society* 87 (1965): 2046-48 (with R.B. Woodward). "Stereochemistry of Electrocyclic Reactions." *Journal of the American Chemical Society* 87 (1965): 395-97 (with R.B. Woodward). *Conservation of Orbital Symmetry.* Weinheim, Germany: Verlag Chemie, 1970 (with R.B. Woodward). "Theoretical Aspects of the Coordination of Molecules to Transition Metal Centers." *Pure Applied Chemistry* 50 (1978): 1-9 (with T.A. Albright and D.L. Thorn).

For More Information See: *Biographical Encyclopedia of Scientists.* New York: Facts on File, 1981, 387-88. *Science* 214 (November 6, 1981): 627-29.

Commentary: Roald Hoffman's Nobel was granted for his applications of molecular orbital theory to chemical reactions. He and Robert Woodward formulated the Woodward-Hoffman rules of orbital sym-

metry, which permitted predictions of reaction results. Hoffman continued in the study of chemical reactions, as affected by the interactions between the molecular orbitals of reactants and products. (J.P.)

1982

Klug, Aaron 97

PRIZE: Chemistry, 1982. BORN: August 11, 1926; Dunbar, South Africa. PARENTS: Father, Lazar Klug; Mother, Bella Silin Klug. NATIONALITY: South African; later British resident. RELIGION: Jewish. EDUCATION: Univ. of Witwatersrand, South Africa, B.Sc., 1946; Univ. of Cape Town, South Africa, M.Sc., 1947; Cambridge Univ., England, Ph.D., 1949. SPOUSE: Liebe Bobrow, married 1948. CHILDREN: Adam, son; David, son. CAREER: Cambridge Univ., England, Professor, 1949-53; Birkbeck College, London, England, Professor and Administrator, 1954-61; Cambridge Univ., England, Professor and Administrator, 1962-. OTHER AWARDS: Heineken Prize, Royal Netherlands Academy of Science, 1979; Louisa Gross Horowitz Prize, Columbia U., 1981.

Selected Publications: "Reaggregation of the A-protein of Tobacco Mosaic Virus." *Biochim. et Biophys. Acta* 23 (1957): 199-201 (with R.E. Franklin). "Joint Probability Distributions of Structure Factors and the Phase Problem." *Acta Cryst* 11 (1958): 515-43. "Architecture of Plant Viruses." *Biochemical Journal* 88 (1963): 24. "An Optical Method for the Analysis of Periodicities in Electron Micrographs, and Some Observations on the Mechanism of Negative Staining." *Journal of Molecular Biology* 10 (1964): 565-69 (with J. Berger).

For More Information See: *Chemical and Engineering News* 60 (October 25, 1982): 4-5. *Science* 218 (November 12, 1982): 653-55.

Commentary: Aaron Klug was cited by the Academy "for his development of crystallographic electron microscopic techniques and for elucidation of biologically important nucleic acid-protein complexes." Klug's work refined electron microscopy so that it could be used quantitatively to permit three-dimensional images. His structural research included time spent successfully with transfer-RNA, tobacco mosaic virus, chromatin, and the structures within the purple membrane of a selected bacterium. (S.B.)

1983

Taube, Henry 98

PRIZE: Chemistry, 1983. BORN: November 30, 1915; Neudorf, Saskatchewan, Canada. PARENTS: Father, Samuel Taube; Mother, Albertina Tiledetzki Taube. NATIONALITY: Canadian; later American resident. RELIGION: Lutheran. EDUCATION: Univ. of Saskatchewan, Canada, B.S., 1935; Univ. of California, M.S., 1937; Univ. of California, Ph.D., 1940. SPOUSE: Mary Alice Wesche, married November 27, 1952. CHILDREN: Linda, daughter; Marianna, daughter; Heinrich, son; Karl, son. CAREER: Univ. of California, Professor, 1940-41; Cornell Univ., NY, Professor, 1941-46; Univ. of Chicago, IL, Professor, 1946-62; Stanford Univ., CA, Professor, 1961-. OTHER AWARDS: Harrison Howe Award, 1961; Chandler Medal, Columbia U., NY, 1964; Kirkwood Award, Yale U. and American Chemical Society,

1966; Distinguished Service in Advancement of Inorganic Chemistry Award, 1967; National Medal of Science, 1977; Monsanto Co. Award, 1981; Welch Award, 1983; Priestley Medal, 1984.

Selected Publications: "Rates and Mechanisms of Substitution in Inorganic Complexes in Solution." *Chemical Reviews* 50 (1952): 69-126. "Evidence for a Bridged Activated Complex for Electron Transfer Reactions." *Journal of the American Chemical Society* 76 (1954): 2103-11 (with Howard Myers). "Electron-Transfer Reactions of Ruthenium Ammines." *Inorganic Chemistry* 7 (1968): 2369-79 (with T.J. Meyer). "A Direct Approach to Measuring the Franck-Codon Barrier to Electron Transfer Between Metal Ions." *Journal of the American Chemical Society* 91 (1969): 3988-89 (with C. Creutz). *Electron Transfer Reactions of Complex Ions in Solution.* New York: Academic Press, 1970. "Redetermination of the Hexaaminecobalt (III/II) Electron-Self-Exchange Rate." *Inorganic Chemistry* 23 (1984): 979-82 (with Anders Hammershoi and Daniel Geselowitz).

For More Information See: "Electron-Transfer Work Earns Taube a Nobel." *Chemical Week* (October 26, 1983): 15-16. "The 1983 Nobel Prize in Chemistry." *Science* (December 1983): 986-87. "Nobel Prize Winner Henry Taube Discusses His Research." *Science* (January 9, 1984): 43-44.

Commentary: Henry Taube received the Nobel Prize for "his work in the mechanism of electron transfer reactions, especially in metal complexes." His career research answered the question of how an electron moves from one place to another, via a "chemical bridge." Taube also studied the transfers of electrons in metals through chemical reactions as exemplified in the formation of rust and other oxidations. His research had great applicability in industry. (B.W.)

1984

Merrifield, Robert Bruce   99
PRIZE: Chemistry, 1984. BORN: July 15, 1921; Fort Worth, TX. PARENTS: Father, George E. Bruce; Mother, Lorene Lucas Bruce. NATIONALITY: American. RELIGION: Methodist. EDUCATION: Univ. of California, Los Angeles, B.A., 1943; Univ. of California, Los Angeles, Ph.D., 1949. SPOUSE: Elizabeth Furlong, married June 20, 1949. CHILDREN: Nancy, daughter; James, son; Betsy, daughter; Cathy, daughter; Laurie, daughter; Sally, daughter. CAREER: Philip R. Park Research Foundation, Researcher, 1943-44; Univ. of California, Los Angeles, Medical School, Researcher, 1948-49; Rockefeller Institute for Medical Research, NY, Researcher, 1949-57; Rockefeller Univ., NY, Professor, 1957-. OTHER AWARDS: Lasker Award, 1969; Gairdner Award, 1970; Intra-Sci Award, 1970; Award for Creative Work in Synthetic Organic Chemistry, American Chemical Society, 1972; Nichols Medal, 1973; Alan E. Pierce Award, American Peptide Symposium, 1979.

Selected Publications: "Solid-Phase Peptide Synthesis: The Synthesis of a Tetrapeptide." *Journal of the American Chemical Society* 85 (1963): 2149-54. "Solid-Phase Synthesis of the Cyclododecadepsipeptide Valinomycin." *Journal of the American Chemical Society* 91 (1969): 2691-95 (with B.F. Gisin and D.C. Tosteson). "An Assessment of Solid Phase Peptide Synthesis." *Peptides: Structural Function, Proceedings of the American Peptide Symposium, 8th*(1983): 33-44.

"SN2 Deprotection of Synthetic Peptides with a Low Concentration of Hydrogen Fluoride in Dimethyl Sulfide: Evidence and Application in Peptide Synthesis." *Journal of the American Chemical Society* 105 (1983): 6442-55 (with James P. Tam and William F. Heath). "Solid-Phase Synthesis of Cecropin A and Related Peptides." *Proceedings of the National Academy of Sciences USA* 80 (1983): 6475-79 (with D. Andreu and H.G. Boman).

For More Information See: *Current Biography Yearbook.* New York: H.W. Wilson, March 1985, 20-22. "R. Bruce Merrifield: Designer of Protein-Making Machine." *Chemical and Engineering News* (August 2, 1971): 22-26.

Commentary: Robert Bruce Merrifield was awarded the Nobel Prize for his development of a "simple and ingenious automated laboratory technique for rapidly synthesizing peptide chains in large quantities on a routine basis, called 'solid-phase peptide synthesis.'" The technique has aided in the treatment and prevention of a number of diseases and genetic disorders and has greatly stimulated progress in genetic engineering. (B.W.)

1985

Hauptman, Herbert Aaron   100
PRIZE: Chemistry, 1985. BORN: February 14, 1917; Bronx, NY. PARENTS: No record found. NATIONALITY: American. RELIGION: Jewish. EDUCATION: City College of New York, B.S., 1937; Columbia Univ., NY, M.A., 1939; Univ. of Maryland, Ph.D., 1955. SPOUSE: Edith Citrynell, married 1940. CHILDREN: Barbara, daughter; Carol, daughter. CAREER: United States Census Bureau, Statistician, 1940-42; United States Air Force, 1942-43, 1946-47; United States Naval Research Laboratory, Researcher, 1947-70; Medical Foundation of Buffalo, NY, Administrator, 1970-. OTHER AWARDS: Belden Prize, 1934; Pure Science Award, Sigma Xi, 1959; A.L. Paterson Award, American Crystallographic Association, 1984.

Selected Publications: "The Phases and Magnitudes of the Structure Factors." *Acta Cryst* 3 (1950): 181-87 (with J. Karle). "Solution of Structure-Factor Equations." *Acta Cryst* 4 (1951): 188-89 (with J. Karle). *Solution of the Phase Problem. I. The Centrosymmetric Crystal.* Ann Arbor, MI: American Crystallographic Association, 1953 (with J. Karle). "A Theory of Phase Determination for the Four Types of Non-centrosymmetric Space Groups." *Acta Cryst* 9 (1956): 635-51 (with J. Karle). *Table of All Primitive Roots for Primes Less than 5000.* Washington, DC: Naval Research Laboratory, 1970. *Crystal Structure Determination: The Role of the Cosine Seminvariants.* New York: Plenum Press, 1972.

For More Information See: *New York Times* (October 27, 1985): 1. *Science* 231 (January 24, 1986): 362-64.

Commentary: Now considered one of the "founders of a new era in research on molecular structure," Herbert Hauptman was cited by the Academy for the "development of direct methods for the determination of crystal structures." The original work was considered "unaccepted and controversial" for more than 15 years after its publication. By analyzing the intensity of the structure of a molecule directly, it is now possible to quickly analyze the three-dimensional structure of the molecule. Adapting these techniques for use by computers, scientists are now able to determine the structure of complex molecules in just a few days. (L.S.S.)

Karle, Jerome   101

PRIZE: Chemistry, 1985. BORN: June 18, 1918; Brooklyn, NY. PARENTS: Father, Louis Karle; Mother, Sadie Karfunkle Karle. NATIONALITY: American. RELIGION: Most probably Jewish. EDUCATION: City College of New York, B.S., 1937; Harvard Univ., MA, A.M., 1938; Univ. of Michigan, Ph.D., 1943. SPOUSE: Isabella Helen Lugoski, married June 4, 1942. CHILDREN: Louise Isabella, daughter; Jean Marianne, daughter; Madeline Diane, daughter. CAREER: Manhattan Project, Chicago, IL, Researcher, 1943-44; United States Navy Project, MI, Researcher, 1944-46; Naval Research Laboratory, MD, Researcher and Administrator, 1946-. OTHER AWARDS: Pure Science Award, Sigma Xi, 1959; Navy Distinguished Civilian Service Award, 1968; Hillebrand Award, American Chemical Society, 1969; Robert Dexter Conrad Award, 1976; A.L. Paterson Award, American Crystallographic Association, 1984.

Selected Publications: "The Phases and Magnitudes of the Structure Factors." *Acta Cryst* 3 (1950): 181-87 (with H. Hauptman). "Solution of Structure-Factor Equations." *Acta Cryst* 4 (1951): 188-89 (with H. Hauptman). *Solution of the Phase Problem. I. The Centrosymmetric Crystal.* Ann Arbor, MI: American Crystallographic Association, 1953 (with H. Hauptman). "A Theory of Phase Determination for the Four Types of Non-centrosymmetric Space Groups." *Acta Cryst* 9 (1956): 635-51 (with H. Hauptman).

For More Information See: *New York Times* (October 27, 1985): 1. *Science* 231 (January 24, 1986): 362-64.

Commentary: Jerome Karle, whose work was not accepted until the mid-1960s, was cited by the Academy for "the development of direct methods for the determination of crystal structures." The mathematical techniques allowed the use of x-ray crystallography for directly determining the structure of three-dimensional molecules, particularly hormones, vitamins, and antibiotics. (L.S.S.)

Economics

1969

Frisch, Ragnar Kittil, Anton 102

PRIZE: Economics, 1969. BORN: March 3, 1895; Oslo, Norway. DIED: January 31, 1973; Oslo, Norway. PARENTS: Father, Anton Frisch; Mother, Ragna Fredrikke Kittilsen Frisch. NATIONALITY: Norwegian. RELIGION: Most probably Christian/Protestant. EDUCATION: Univ. of Oslo, Norway, M.A., 1919; Univ. of Oslo, Norway, Ph.D., 1926. SPOUSE: Marie Smedal, married April 28, 1920, died; Astrid Johannessen, married 1953. CHILDREN: Ragna, daughter. CAREER: Univ. of Oslo, Norway, Professor, 1931-71. OTHER AWARDS: Schumpeter Prize, Harvard U., MA, 1955; Antonio Feltrinelli Prize, Academia Nacionale dei Lincei, Rome, Italy, 1961.

Selected Publications: *Maxima and Minima. Theory and Economic Applications.* Tr. by Express Translation Service. Chicago: Rand McNally, 1966. *Economic Planning Studies.* Dordrecht, Netherlands: D. Reidel, 1976. *New Methods of Measuring Marginal Utility.* Philadelphia, PA: Porcupine Press, 1978.

For More Information See: "Ragnar Frisch and Business Cycle Research during the Interwar Years." *History of Political Economy* 13 (1981): 695-725. *Science* 166 (1969): 715-17. *Thinkers of the Twentieth Century.* Detroit, MI: Gale, 1983, 184-85.

Commentary: Ragnar Frisch was awarded the Nobel Prize for his contributions in establishing the subjects of econometrics and mathematical economics. Frisch's research was important to establishing theories for: models of whole economics, production, consumer behavior, index numbers, and planning. His work was not restricted to economics, since his statistical and mathematical methodologies could be applied elsewhere as well. (J.F.)

Tinbergen, Jan 103

PRIZE: Economics, 1969. BORN: April 12, 1903; The Hague, Netherlands. PARENTS: Father, Dirk Cornelis Tinbergen; Mother, Jeanette Van Eek Tinbergen. NATIONALITY: Dutch. RELIGION: Agnostic; from Protestant background. EDUCATION: Leiden Univ., Netherlands, Ph.D., 1929. SPOUSE: Tine Johanna DeWit, married July 19, 1929. CHILDREN: Adriaan M., daughter; Elsje, daughter; Hanneke, daughter; Marianne, daughter. CAREER: Central Bureau of Statistics, Netherlands, Statistician, 1929-36; League of Nations Secretariat, Statistician, 1936-38; Central Bureau of Statistics, Netherlands, Statistician, 1938-45; Central Planning Bureau, Netherlands, Director, 1945-55; Netherlands School of Economics, Professor, 1933-73; Leiden Univ., Netherlands, Professor, 1973-75. OTHER AWARDS: Erasmus Prize, 1967; Order of the Lion; Order of Orange Nassau.

Selected Publications: *An Economic Approach to Business Cycle Problems.* Paris: Hermann, 1937. *Statistical Testing of Business Cycle Theories.* Geneva: League of Nations, 1939. *Business Cycles in the United Kingdom, 1870-1914.* Amsterdam: North-Holland, 1951. *On the Theory of Economic Policy.* Amsterdam: North-Holland, 1952. *Economic Policy: Principles and Design.* Amsterdam: North-Holland, 1956.

For More Information See: *Science* 166 (1969): 715-17. *Thinkers of the Twentieth Century.* Detroit, MI: Gale, 1983, 567-68.

Commentary: Jan Tinbergen was awarded the Nobel Prize for his work in econometrics, the mathematical representation of economic theory. During his impressive career, he worked with statistical models of economies, the mathematical analysis of economic cycles, and several theories: of income distribution, of economic growth, of economic planning, and of economic development. (J.F.)

1970

Samuelson, Paul Anthony 104

PRIZE: Economics, 1970. BORN: May 15, 1915; Gary, IN. PARENTS: Father, Frank Samuelson; Mother, Ella Lipton Samuelson. NATIONALITY: American. RELIGION: Jewish. EDUCATION: Univ. of Chicago, IL, B.S., 1935; Harvard Univ., MA, M.A., 1936; Harvard Univ., MA, Ph.D., 1941. SPOUSE: Marion Crawford, married July 2, 1938, died 1978; Risha Eckaus, married 1981. CHILDREN: Jane Kendall, daughter; Margaret Wray, daughter; William Frank, son; Robert James, son; John Crawford, son; Paul Reid, son. CAREER: Massachusetts Institute of Technology, Professor, 1940-. OTHER AWARDS: John Bates Clark Medal, American Economic Association, 1947; Guggenheim Fellow, 1948; Ford Foundation Fellow, 1958; Medal of Honor, U. of Evansville, IL, 1970; Albert Einstein Commemorative Award, 1971; Distinguished Service Award, National Association of Investment Clubs, 1974; Alumni Medal, U. of Chicago, IL, 1983.

Selected Publications: *Foundations of Economic Analysis.* Cambridge, MA: Harvard U. Press, 1947. *Economics: An Introductory Analysis.* New York: McGraw-Hill, 1948. *Linear Programming and Economic Analysis.* New York: McGraw-Hill, 1958 (with Robert Dorfman and Robert Solow). *The Collected Scientific Papers of Paul A. Samuelson.* 3 volumes. Cambridge, MA: Harvard U. Press, 1966-72.

For More Information See: *Current Biography Yearbook.* New York: H.W. Wilson, 1965, 356-59. *Science* 170 (November 13, 1970): 720-21. Silk, Leonard. *The Economists.* New York: Basic Books, 1976, 3-43.

Commentary: The Nobel Committee cited Paul Samuelson for doing "more than any other contemporary economist to raise the level of scientific analysis in economic theory." Most contemporaries would probably agree that this is because of Samuelson's ability to express in mathematical terms and lucid prose the economic theories of the day. However, his greatest impact has been through his classic textbook, *Economics*, and his popular writings which have educated the general public to the world of economics. (B.S.S.)

1971

Kuznets, Simon Smith   105

PRIZE: Economics, 1971. BORN: April 30, 1901; Kharkov, Russia. PARENTS: Father, Abraham Kuznets; Mother, Pauline Friedman Kuznets. NATIONALITY: Russian; later American citizen. RELIGION: Jewish. EDUCATION: Columbia Univ., NY, B.A., 1923; Columbia Univ., NY, M.A., 1924; Columbia Univ., NY, Ph.D., 1926. SPOUSE: Edith Handler, married June 29, 1929. CHILDREN: Paul Kuznets, son; Mrs. Norman Stein, daughter. CAREER: National Bureau of Economic Research, Researcher, 1927-30; Univ. of Pennsylvania, Professor, 1930-54; Johns Hopkins Univ., MD, Professor, 1954-60; Harvard Univ., MA, Professor, 1960-71. OTHER AWARDS: Robert Troup Paine Prize, 1970.

Selected Publications: *Commodity Flow and Capital Formation.* New York: National Bureau of Economic Research, 1938. *National Product Since 1869.* New York: National Bureau of Economic Research, 1946. *Economic Change.* New York: Norton, 1953. *Capital In the American Economy.* Princeton, NJ: Princeton U. Press, 1961. *Economic Growth of Nations: Total Output and Production Structure.* Cambridge, MA: Harvard U. Press, 1971. *National Income and Its Composition, 1919-1935.* New York: National Bureau of Economic Research, 1971.

For More Information See: *Current Biography Yearbook.* New York: H.W. Wilson, 1972, 266-68. *Science* 174 (October 27, 1971): 481-83.

Commentary: Simon Kuznets was recognized for his "empirically founded interpretation of economic growth" and "for illuminating with facts—and explaining through analysis—the economic growth from the middle of the last century." His contribution consisted of developing a system for national income accounting and applying statistical methods to measure the sources and uses of the annual production of a country. Later in his career, Kuznets studied the changing roles of capital, labor, and productivity in the United States economy and became a leader in socioeconomic theory. (B.S.S.)

1972

Arrow, Kenneth Joseph   106

PRIZE: Economics, 1972. BORN: August 23, 1921; New York, NY. PARENTS: Father, Harry I. Arrow; Mother, Lillian Greenberg Arrow. NATIONALITY: American. RELIGION: Jewish. EDUCATION: City College of New York, B.S., 1940; Columbia Univ., NY, M.A., 1941; Columbia Univ., NY, Ph.D., 1951. SPOUSE: Selma Schweitzer, married August 31, 1947. CHILDREN: David Michael, son; Andrew, son. CAREER: Cowles Commission for Research in Economics, Univ. of Chicago, IL, Researcher, 1947-49; Stanford Univ., CA, Professor, 1949-68; Harvard Univ., MA, Professor, 1968-. OTHER AWARDS: John Bates Clark Medal, American Economic Association, 1957.

Selected Publications: *Social Choice and Individual Values.* New York: Wiley, 1951. *Studies in Linear and Nonlinear Programming.* Stanford, CA: Stanford U. Press, 1958 (with others). *Studies in the Mathematical Theory of Inventory and Production.* Stanford, CA: Stanford U. Press, 1958. *Essays in the Theories of Risk-Bearing.* Chicago: Markham Publishing Co., 1971. *Studies in Resource Allocation.* New York: Cambridge U. Press, 1977. *Social Choice and Justice: Collected Papers of Kenneth J. Arrow.* Oxford: Blackwell, 1984.

For More Information See: *New York Times Biographical Edition* (October 1972): 1737-38. *Science* 178 (November 3, 1972): 487-89.

Commentary: The Nobel Prize was awarded to Kenneth Arrow for his "pioneering work on the theory of general economic equilibrium." Arrow's doctoral research was on social choice and individual values (the title of his dissertation), and he continued over the course of his career to apply economic theory to all types of social problems—medical care, education, water resources, etc. His later research concerned the role of information in the behavior of businesspeople and consumers. Arrow was also heavily involved with students at all levels and with university affairs wherever he taught. (B.S.S.)

Hicks, John Richard, Sir   107

PRIZE: Economics, 1972. BORN: April 8, 1904; Leamington Spa, England. PARENTS: Father, Edward Hicks; Mother, no record found. NATIONALITY: British. RELIGION: Most probably Christian. EDUCATION: Oxford Univ., England, B.A., 1927; Oxford Univ., England, M.A., 1931. SPOUSE: Ursula Kathleen Webb, married 1935. CHILDREN: None. CAREER: London School of Economics, England, Professor, 1926-35; Cambridge Univ., England, Professor, 1935-38; Univ. of Manchester, England, Professor, 1938-46; Oxford Univ., England, Professor, 1946-65. OTHER AWARDS: Knighthood, 1964.

Selected Publications: *The Theory of Wages.* London: Macmillan, 1932. *Value and Capital: An Inquiry into Some Fundamental Principles of Economic Theory.* Oxford: Clarendon Press, 1939. *The Social Framework: An Introduction to Economics.* Oxford: Clarendon Press, 1942. *A Contribution to the Theory of the Trade Cycle.* Oxford: Clarendon Press, 1950. *Capital and Growth.* Oxford: Clarendon Press, 1965. *The Crisis in Keynesian Economics.* Oxford: Basil Blackwell, 1974.

For More Information See: Baumol, William J. "John R. Hicks' Contribution to Economics." *The Swedish Journal of Economics* 74 (December 1972): 503-27. Morgan, Brian. "Sir John Hicks's Contributions to Economic Theory." In *Twelve Contemporary Economists.* New York: John Wiley, 1981, 108-40. Reid, G.C., and Wolfe, J.N. "Hicks, John R." *International Encyclopedia of the Social Sciences.* New York: Free Press, 1979 (Volume 18), 300-02.

Commentary: Although honored for his "pioneering contributions to general economic equilibrium theory and welfare theory," the work of John Hicks also influenced such areas as monetary theory and stability analysis, as his writings became the foundation for much of the economic thought of the time. Hicks was perhaps best known for *Value and Capital* (1939), in which he set forth his general economic equilibrium theory. Considered an economic classic, few works had such a profound effect on the basic structure of economic theory. (R.W.S.)

1973

Leontief, Wassily W.   108

PRIZE: Economics, 1973. BORN: August 5, 1906; St. Petersburg, Russia. PARENTS: Father, Wassily Leontief; Mother, Eugenia Bekker Leontief. NATIONALITY: Russian; later American citizen. RELIGION: Eastern Orthodox. EDUCATION: Leningrad Univ., USSR, Learned Economist, 1925; Univ. of Berlin, Germany, Ph.D., 1928. SPOUSE: Estella Helena Marks, married 1932. CHILDREN: Svetlana Eugenia Alpers, daughter. CAREER: Univ. of Kiel, Germany, Research Economist, 1927-30; National Bureau of Economic Research, NY, Research Associate, 1931; Harvard Univ., MA, Professor, 1931-75; New York Univ., Professor, 1975-. OTHER AWARDS: Guggenheim Fellowship, 1940, 1950; Bernhard-Harms Prize, Germany, 1970.

Selected Publications: "Quantitative Input and Output Relations in the Economic System of the United States." *Review of Economic Statistics* 18 (August 1936): 105-25. *The Structure of the American Economy, 1919-1929: An Empirical Application of Equilibrium Analysis.* Cambridge, MA: Harvard U. Press, 1941. "Exports, Imports, Domestic Output and Employment." *Quarterly Journal of Economics* 60 (February 1946): 171-93. "Factor Proportions and the Structure of American Trade: Further Theoretical and Empirical Analysis." *Review of Economics and Statistics* 38 (November 1956): 386-407. "The Economic Impact—Industrial and Regional—of an Arms Cut." *Review of Economics and Statistics* 47 (August 1965): 217-41. "The Distribution of Work and Income." *Input-Output Economics.* New York: Oxford U. Press, 1966. *Scientific American* (September 1982): 188-190.

For More Information See: Dorfman, Robert. "Wassily Leontief's Contribution to Economics." *Swedish Journal of Economics* 75 (December 1973): 442-49. Samuelson, Paul A. "Nobel Laureate Leontief." *Newsweek* (November 5, 1973): 94. Seligman, Ben B. *Main Currents in Modern Economics: Economic Thought Since 1870.* New York: Free Press of Glencoe, 1962, 434-41. Silk, Leonard. *The Economists.* New York: Basic Books, 1976, 151-90.

Commentary: Wassily Leontief won his award for the "development of the input-output method of economic analysis, used in various forms in more than 50 industrialized countries for planning and forecasting." He has used his methods to study the effects of various factors on the U.S. economy—the end of World War II, military spending, environment, and world development. (N.H.)

1974

Hayek, Friedrich August Von   109

PRIZE: Economics, 1974. BORN: May 8, 1899; Vienna, Austria. PARENTS: Father, August Von Hayek; Mother,

Felizitas Juraschek Von Hayek. NATIONALITY: Austrian; later British, American, and German resident. RELIGION: Catholic. EDUCATION: Univ. of Vienna, Austria, Dr. Jur., 1921; Univ. of Vienna, Austria, Ph.D., 1923. SPOUSE: Helene von Fritsch, married 1926, divorced 1950; Helene Bitterlich, married 1950. CHILDREN: Christine, daughter; Lawrence, son. CAREER: Austrian Institute of Economic Research, Director, 1927-31; Univ. of London, England, Professor, 1931-50; Univ. of Chicago, IL, Professor, 1950-62; Univ. of Freiburg, Germany, 1962-70. OTHER AWARDS: Ordre pour le merite.

Selected Publications: *Geldtheorie und Konjunkturtheorie.* Vienna: Hoelder-Pichler-Tempsky, 1929 (*Monetary Theory and the Trade Cycle.* London: Harcourt, 1933). *Prices and Production.* London: G. Routledge, 1933. *The Pure Theory of Capital.* London: G. Routledge, 1941. *The Road to Serfdom.* Chicago: U. of Chicago Press, 1944. *Individualism and Economic Order.* Chicago: U. of Chicago Press, 1949. *The Counter-Revolution of Science.* Chicago: U. of Chicago Press, 1952. *The Constitution of Liberty.* Chicago: U. of Chicago Press, 1960. *Denationalization of Money.* London: Institute of Economic Affairs, 1976.

For More Information See: *Contemporary Authors.* Detroit, MI: Gale, 1980 (Volumes 93-96), 218-19. *Current Biography Yearbook.* New York: H. W. Wilson, 1945, 271-73.

Commentary: Friedrich Hayek shared the Nobel Prize for "pioneering work in the theory of money and economic fluctuations" and for "penetrating analysis of the interdependence of economic, social, and institutional phenomena." Beginning with work on theoretical economic thought, Hayek later combined these writings with analyses of the viability of different economic systems that made him a world figure. (S.K.)

Myrdal, Karl Gunnar   110

PRIZE: Economics, 1974. BORN: December 6, 1898; Gustafs Parish, Sweden. PARENTS: Father, Karl Adolf Myrdal; Mother, Anna Sophia Carlson Myrdal. NATIONALITY: Swedish. RELIGION: Lutheran. EDUCATION: Univ. of Stockholm, Sweden, law degree, 1923; Univ. of Stockholm, Sweden, doctorate, 1927. SPOUSE: Alva Riemer, married 1924. CHILDREN: Jan, son; Kaj, daughter; Sissela, daughter. CAREER: Stockholm, Sweden, Attorney, 1923-27; Univ. of Stockholm, Sweden, Professor, 1927-38; Carnegie Corp., NY, Researcher, 1938-42; then Writer and Political Activities. OTHER AWARDS: Peace Prize, West Germany, 1970; Seidman Award, Memphis, TN, 1973; Felix Newburgh Award, Sothonburg, Sweden, 1977.

Selected Publications: *Population: A Problem for Democracy.* Cambridge, MA: Harvard U. Press, 1940. *An American Dilemma: The Negro Problem and Modern Democracy.* New York: Harper & Brothers, 1944. *Challenge to Affluence.* New York: Pantheon, 1963. *Asian Drama: An Inquiry Into the Poverty of Nations.* New York: Pantheon, 1968.

For More Information See: *Contemporary Authors.* New Revision Series. Detroit, MI: Gale, 1981 (Volume 4), 447-48. *Current Biography Yearbook.* New York: H.W. Wilson, 1975, 295-98.

Commentary: Gunnar Myrdal received the Nobel Prize for his "pioneering work in the theory of money and economic fluctuations" and for his "penetrating analysis of the interdependence of economic, social and institutional phenomena." Myrdal's studies of and influence on economic and social affairs began in Sweden and extended to the United States. His treatments of economic policy in both countries and his study of the population question in Sweden and the race issue in America were classics. He was also an active United Nations worker, especially in Asia, and a campaigner for peace. (S.K.)

1975

Kantorovich, Leonid Vital'evich 111
PRIZE: Economics, 1975. BORN: January 19, 1912; St. Petersburg, Russia. PARENTS: Father, Vitalij M. Kantorovich; Mother, Pauline G. Saks Kantorovich. NATIONALITY: Russian. RELIGION: Jewish. EDUCATION: Leningrad State Univ., USSR, B.A., 1930; Leningrad State Univ., USSR, Ph.D., 1935. SPOUSE: Natalja Vladimirovna, married 1938. CHILDREN: Ien, son; Vselovod, daughter. CAREER: Leningrad State Univ., USSR, Professor, 1934-60; Academy of Sciences, USSR, Administrator, 1960-71; Institute of National Economy Control, Moscow, USSR, Administrator, 1971-76; Academy of Sciences, USSR, Administrator, 1976-. OTHER AWARDS: State Prize, USSR, 1949; Lenin Prize, USSR, 1965; Order of Lenin, USSR, 1967, 1982.

Selected Publications: *Mathematicheskie Metody Organizatsii i Planirovaniia Proizvodstva.* Leningrad: Leningradskogo Gov. Univ, 1939 "Mathematical Methods of Organizing and Planning Production." *Management Science* 6 (July 1960): 366-422. *Ekonomicheskii Raschet Nailuschshego Ispol'zogvaniia Resursov.* Moscow: Izdvo Akademii Nauk SSSR, 1959 (*The Best Use of Economic Resources.* Tr. by P.F. Knightsfield. Cambridge, MA: Harvard U. Press, 1965). *Optimal'nye Resheniia v Ekonomike* (*Optimal Solution in Economics*). Moscow: Nauka, 1972 (with A.V. Gorstko). *Funktsionalyi Analiz* (*Functional Analysis*). Moscow: Nauka, 1977 (with G.P. Akilov).

For More Information See: Johansen, Leif. "L.V. Kantorovich's Contribution to Economics." *The Scandinavian Journal of Economics* 78 (1976): 61-80. Stuart, Robert C. "Leonid Vitalevich Kantorovich." In *Soviet Leaders.* New York: Thomas Y. Crowell, 1967, 187-93.

Commentary: Leonid Kantorovich won the Nobel Prize for his "contributions to the theory of optimum allocation of resources." His 1939 treatise, *Mathematical Methods of Organizing and Planning Production,* introduced linear programming as a solution to the problems of resource allocation. Received unfavorably by the Soviet government, his theories were not recognized until the publication in the 1950s of works such as *The Best Use of Economic Resources.* (R.W.S.)

Koopmans, Tjalling Charles 112
PRIZE: Economics, 1975. BORN: August 28, 1910; Graveland, Netherlands. DIED: February 26, 1985; New Haven, CT. PARENTS: Father, Sjoerd Koopmans; Mother, Wijkje van der Zee Koopmans. NATIONALITY: Dutch; later American citizen. RELIGION: Most probably Christian/Protestant. EDUCATION: Univ. of Utrecht, Netherlands, M.A., 1933; Univ. of Leiden, Netherlands, Ph.D., 1936. SPOUSE: Truus Wanningen, married 1936. CHILDREN: Ann W., daughter; Helen J.,

daughter; Henry S., son. CAREER: Netherlands School of Economics, Professor, 1936-38; League of Nations, Specialist Financial Secretary, 1938-40; Princeton Univ., NJ, Researcher, 1940-41; Penn Mutual Life Insurance Company, Economist, 1941-42; Combined Shipping Adjustment Board, Statistician, 1942-44; Univ. of Chicago, IL, Professor, 1944-55; Yale Univ., CT, Professor, 1955-85.

Selected Publications: *Three Essays on the State of Economic Science.* New York: McGraw-Hill, 1957. *Scientific Papers of Tjalling C. Koopmans.* New York: Springer-Verlag, 1970, V-VII, 595-600.

For More Information See: *New York Times Biographical Service* (1975): 1285-86. *Science* 190 (November 14, 1975): 649, 710-12.

Commentary: Tjalling Koopmans received the Nobel Prize for his contributions to the theory of optimum allocation of resources. Beginning with his work on efficient use of shipping facilities, Koopmans applied brilliant mathematical techniques to develop the complicated equations of this field. His work in econometrics and mathematical programming developed entire new areas of economic studies. (M.C.)

1976

Friedman, Milton 113
PRIZE: Economics, 1976. BORN: July 31, 1912; Brooklyn, NY. PARENTS: Father, Jeno Saul Friedman; Mother, Sarah Ethel Landau Friedman. NATIONALITY: American. RELIGION: Jewish. EDUCATION: Rutgers Univ., NJ, A.B., 1932; Univ. of Chicago, IL, A.M., 1933; Columbia Univ., NY, Ph.D.; 1946. SPOUSE: Rose Director, married June 25, 1938. CHILDREN: Janet, daughter; David, son. CAREER: National Resources Committee, Washington, DC, Assistant Economist, 1935-37; National Bureau of Economic Research, NY, Researcher, 1937-45; Univ. of Minnesota, Professor, 1945-46; Univ. of Chicago, IL, Professor, 1946-. OTHER AWARDS: Clark Medal, American Economic Association, 1951; Chicagoan of the Year, Chicago Press Club, 1972; Private Enterprise Exemplar Medal, Freedoms Foundation, 1978.

Selected Publications: Friedman, Milton. *Capitalism and Freedom.* Chicago: U. of Chicago Press, 1962. Friedman, Milton, and Schwartz, Anna Jacobson. *A Monetary History of the United States, 1867-1960.* Princeton, NJ: Princeton U. Press, 1963. Friedman, Milton. *The Counter-Revolution in Monetary Theory.* London: Institute of Economic Affairs, 1970. Friedman, Milton, and Director, Rose. *Free to Choose.* New York: Harcourt, Brace, Jovanovich, 1980.

For More Information See: *Current Biography Yearbook.* New York: H.W. Wilson Co., 1969, 151-54. Shackleton, J.R. "Milton Friedman, Superstar?" *Political Quarterly* 51 (July/September 1980): 349-54. Tobin, James, and Johnson, Harry. "Nobel Milton." *The Economist* 261 (October 23, 1976): 94-95. Viorst, Milton. *Hustlers and Heroes.* New York: Simon and Schuster, 1971.

Commentary: The Nobel citation notes Milton Friedman's work, *Capitalism and Freedom,* but also states that it is "very rare for an economist to wield such influence, directly or indirectly, not only on the direction of scientific research but also on the actual practise." His clear statements in conservative economics and in the areas of monetary and quantity theory have influenced economists and policy makers in the United States and throughout the world. (M.J.B.)

1977

Meade, James Edward   114

PRIZE: Economics, 1977. BORN: June 23, 1907; Swanage, Dorset, England. PARENTS: Father, Charles Hippisley Meade; Mother, Kathleen Cotton-Stapleton Meade. NATIONALITY: British. RELIGION: Most probably Christian/Protestant. EDUCATION: Oxford Univ., England, B.A., 1930. SPOUSE: Elizabeth Margaret Wilson, married March 14, 1933. CHILDREN: Thomas Wilson, son; Charlotte Elizabeth, daughter; Bridget Ariane, daughter; Carol Margaret, daughter. CAREER: Oxford Univ., England, Professor, 1930-37; League of Nations, Economist, 1938-47; London School of Economics, Professor, 1947-57; Cambridge Univ., England, Professor, 1957-68. OTHER AWARDS: Companion of the Order of Bath, 1947.

Selected Publications: *The Theory of International Economic Policy.* 2 volumes. London: Oxford U. Press, 1951-55. *A Geometry of International Trade.* London: Allen & Unwin, 1952. *A Neo-Classical Theory of Economic Growth.* London: Allen & Unwin, 1962. *The Principles of Political Economy.* 4 volumes. Albany, NY: State U. of New York Press, 1965-76. *The Intelligent Radical's Guide to Economic Policy.* London: Allen & Unwin, 1975.

For More Information See: *Science* 198 (1977): 813-14+. *Twentieth Century Culture: A Biographical Companion.* New York: Harper and Row, 1983.

Commentary: James Meade won the Nobel Prize for his work as a pioneer in the area of macroeconomics, the economic behavior of large systems. A prolific writer, Meade's influence was felt primarily through his books and his work on important British committees studying the economy. His books that dealt with foreign trade in an "open" world economy and with the dangers, as well as benefits, of employers' associations and trade unions, are representative of his influence. (J.F.)

Ohlin, Bertil Gotthard   115

PRIZE: Economics, 1977. BORN: April 23, 1899; Klippan, Sweden. DIED: August 3, 1979; Northern Sweden. PARENTS: Father, Elis Vilhelm Ohlin; Mother, Ingeborg Sandberg Ohlin. NATIONALITY: Swedish. RELIGION: Lutheran. EDUCATION: Lund Univ., Sweden, B.A., 1917; Harvard Univ., MA, M.A., 1923; Univ. of Stockholm, Sweden, Ph.D., 1924. SPOUSE: Evy Kruse, married May 2, 1931. CHILDREN: Helen, daughter; Thomas, son; Anne Marie, daughter. CAREER: Univ. of Copenhagen, Denmark, Professor, 1925-30; Stockholm School of Economics, Sweden, Professor, 1930-65; Sweden, Member of Parliament, 1938-70. OTHER AWARDS: Commander with the Great Cross, Royal North Star, Sweden, 1961; Commander, First Order of the Dannebrogen, Denmark.

Selected Publications: *Handelns Teori* (*The Theory of Trade*). Stockholm: Centraltryckeriet, 1924. *The Course and Phases of the World Economic Depression; Report Presented to the Assembly of the League of Nations.* Geneva: The Secretariat of the League of Nations, 1931. *Interregional and International Trade.* Cambridge, MA: Harvard U. Press, 1933. *The Problem*

of Economic Stabilization. New York: Columbia U. Press, 1949. *Bertil Ohlin's Memoarer* (*Bertil Ohlin's Memoirs*). Stockholm: Bonnier, 1972.

For More Information See: *International Encyclopedia of the Social Sciences Biographical Supplement.* New York: The Free Press, 1979, 603-07. Lundberg, Erik. "Portrait: Bertil Ohlin." *Challenge* 23 (September-October 1980): 54-57. Samuelson, Paul A. "Bertil Ohlin: 1899-1979." *Journal of International Economics Supplement* (January 1982): 31-49.

Commentary: Bertil Ohlin received the Nobel award for his "pathbreaking contribution to the theory of international trade and international capital movements." Although a prominent economist and a member of the Swedish Academy of Science, Ohlin was probably better known in his native Sweden as a politician and a journalist. For more than two decades he was the leader of the Swedish Liberal Party and served as the Minister of Trade at the close of World War II. Ohlin produced the majority of the economic work for which the prize was awarded prior to the start of his political career, but beginning in the 1920s and continuing until his death, he regularly contributed material on economic policy to the Swedish daily newspapers. (D.G.)

1978

Simon, Herbert Alexander   116

PRIZE: Economics, 1978. BORN: June 15, 1916; Milwaukee, WI. PARENTS: Father, Arthur Simon; Mother, Edna Merkel Simon. NATIONALITY: American. RELIGION: Unitarian; from Jewish background. EDUCATION: Univ. of Chicago, IL, A.B., 1936; Univ. of Chicago, IL, Ph.D., 1943. SPOUSE: Dorothea Pye, married December 25, 1937. CHILDREN: Katherine, daughter; Barbara, daughter; Peter Arthur, son. CAREER: Univ. of Chicago, IL, Researcher, 1936-38; International City Managers Association, Chicago, IL, Editor, 1938-39; Univ. of California, Berkeley, Administrator, 1939-42; Illinois Institute of Technology, Professor, 1942-49; Carnegie-Mellon Univ., PA, Professor and Administrator, 1949-. OTHER AWARDS: Administrator's Award, American College of Hospital Administrators, 1957; Distinguished Scientific Contributions Award, American Psychological Association, 1969; Frederick Mosher Award, American Society for Public Administration, 1974; Turing Award, Association for Computing Machinery, 1975; Dow-Jones Award, 1983; Scholarly Contributions Award, Academy of Management, 1983; National Medal of Science, United States, 1986.

Selected Publications: *Administrative Behavior: A Study of Decision-Making Processes in Administrative Organization.* New York: Macmillan Co., 1947. *Models of Man: Social and Rational; Mathematical Essays on Rational Human Behavior in a Social Setting.* New York: Wiley, 1957. *Organizations.* New York: Wiley, 1958 (with J. G. March and H. Guetzkow). *New Science of Management Decision.* New York: Harper, 1960. *Human Problem Solving.* Englewood Cliffs, NJ: Prentice-Hall, 1972 (with Allen Newell). *Reason in Human Affairs.* Stanford, CA: Stanford U. Press, 1983.

For More Information See: *Contemporary Authors.* New Revision Series. Detroit, MI: Gale, 1983 (Volume 9), 456-57. *Current Biography Yearbook.* New York: H. W. Wilson Co., 1971, 358-61.

Commentary: Thirty years after he published his research results in the now classic text *Administrative Behavior*, Herbert Simon received the Nobel Prize in recognition of his "pioneering research into the decision making process in economic organization." His concept of "bounded rationality" acknowledged the human element in problem solving and showed that decision makers choose not the optimum solution but rather the first alternative "good enough" to meet predefined needs. Later, Simon, working with Allen Newell, used computer simulation to study problem solving and thereby became a pioneer in the field of artificial intelligence. Described as a true Renaissance man because of the variety and scope of his knowledge and talents, Simon has written on subjects ranging from economics and political science to psychology and computers. (M.L.L.)

1979

Lewis, William Arthur, Sir   117
PRIZE: Economics, 1979. BORN: January 23, 1915; Castries, St. Lucia. PARENTS: Father, George F. Lewis; Mother, Ida Barton Lewis. NATIONALITY: St. Lucian; later British and American resident. RELIGION: Anglican. EDUCATION: St. Mary's College, British West Indies, Bachelor of Commerce, 1929; London School of Economics, England, Ph.D., 1937. SPOUSE: Gladys Isabel Jacobs, married May 5, 1947. CHILDREN: Elizabeth Anne, daughter; Barbara Jean, daughter. CAREER: London School of Economics, England, Lecturer, 1938-47; Univ. of Manchester, England, Professor, 1948-58; Univ. of West Indies, Professor and Administrator, 1959-63; Princeton Univ., NJ, Professor, 1963-. OTHER AWARDS: Knighthood, 1963.

Selected Publications: *Economic Survey, 1919-39.* Philadelphia, PA: Blakiston Co., 1950. *Development Planning.* New York: Harper and Row, 1966. *Aspects of Tropical Trade, 1883-1965.* Stockholm: Almqvist and Wiksell, 1969. *The Evolution of the International Economic Order.* Princeton, NJ: Princeton U. Press, 1978. *Selected Economic Writings of W. Arthur Lewis.* New York: New York U. Press, 1983.

For More Information See: Crittenden, Ann. "1979 Nobel Economics Award Shared by Two Experts on Poorer Nations." *New York Times* (October 17, 1979): 1: 1+. "Nobel Laureate Sir William Arthur Lewis 1980." *Black Enterprise* 10 (July 1980): 34. Ranis, Gustan. "The 1979 Nobel Prize in Economics." *Science* 206 (December 1979): 1389-91.

Commentary: Sir William Arthur Lewis is most noted for his models for developing the economics of Third World nations, based on work with the developing nations in Africa and the English-speaking Caribbean. The Nobel Prize award was a recognition of his "lifelong concerns with poverty and growth, agricultural and human development in developing countries," in contrast to other years, when the award was given strictly for theoretical breakthroughs. Lewis was the first Black to receive a Nobel Prize in a category other than Peace. (E.L.)

Schultz, Theodore William   118
PRIZE: Economics, 1979. BORN: April 30, 1902; Arlington, SD. PARENTS: Father, Henry Edward Schultz; Mother, Anna Elizabeth Weiss Schultz. NATIONALITY: American. RELIGION: Most probably Christian/Protestant. EDUCATION: South Dakota State College, B.S., 1927; Univ. of Wisconsin, M.S., 1928; Univ. of Wisconsin, Ph.D., 1930. SPOUSE: Esther Florence Werth, married (no date found). CHILDREN: Elaine, daughter; Margaret, daughter; T. Paul, son. CAREER: Iowa State College, Professor, 1930-43; Univ. of Chicago, IL, Professor, 1943-72. OTHER AWARDS: Francis A. Walker Medal, American Economic Association, 1972; Leonard Elmhirst Medal, International Agriculture Economic Association, 1976.

Selected Publications: *The Economic Value of Education.* New York: Columbia U. Press, 1963. *Transforming Traditional Agriculture.* New Haven, CT: Yale U. Press, 1964. *Economic Growth and Agriculture.* New York: McGraw-Hill, 1968. *Investments in Human Capital: The Role of Education and of Research.* New York: Macmillan Co., 1971.

For More Information See: *New York Times Biographical Service* (October 1979): 1414. *Science* 206 (December 21, 1979): 1389-91.

Commentary: Theodore Schultz was awarded the Nobel Prize in recognition of his work which stressed the importance of human resources in agriculture. The citation noted his importance in pointing out that there "has been a considerably higher yield on human capital than on physical capital in the American economy." His thinking was a prime factor in the development of human resources in the United States and developing countries. (M.C.)

1980

Klein, Lawrence Robert   119
PRIZE: Economics, 1980. BORN: September 14, 1920; Omaha, NE. PARENTS: Father, Leo Byron Klein; Mother, Blanche Monheit Klein. NATIONALITY: American. RELIGION: Most probably Jewish. EDUCATION: Univ. of California, B.A., 1942; Massachusetts Institute of Technology, Ph.D., 1944; Oxford Univ., England, M.A., 1957. SPOUSE: Sonia Adelson, married February 15, 1947. CHILDREN: Hannah, daughter; Rebecca, daughter; Rachel, daughter; Jonathan, son. CAREER: Univ. of Chicago, IL, Professor, 1944-47; National Bureau of Economic Research, Researcher, 1948-50; Univ. of Michigan, Professor, 1949-54; Oxford Univ., England, Researcher, 1954-58; Univ. of Pennsylvania, Professor, 1958-. OTHER AWARDS: John Bates Clark Medal, American Economic Association, 1959; William F. Butler Award, New York Association of Business Economists, 1975; Golden Slipper Club Award, 1977; President's Medal, U. of Pennsylvania, 1980.

Selected Publications: *The Keynesian Revolution.* New York: Macmillan, 1947. *Economic Fluctuations in the United States, 1921-1941.* New York: Wiley, 1950. *A Textbook of Econometrics.* Evanston, IL: Row, Peterson, 1953. *An Econometric Model of the United States, 1929-1952.* Amsterdam: North-Holland Publishing Company, 1955 (with A. S. Goldberger). *An Introduction to Econometrics.* Englewood Cliffs, NJ: Prentice-Hall, 1962. *Economic Theory and Econometrics.* Philadelphia, PA: U. of Pennsylvania Press, 1985.

For More Information See: Ball, R. J. "On Lawrence R. Klein's Contributions to Economics." *Scandinavian Journal of Economics* 83 (1981): 81-95. Maugh, Thomas H., II. "The 1980 Nobel Memorial Prize in Economics." *Science* 210 (November 14, 1980): 758-59.

Commentary: Citing Lawrence Klein as the leading researcher in the field of econometrics, the Academy acknowledged three decades of achievement by awarding him the Nobel Prize for "the creation of econometric models and their application to the analysis of economic fluctuations and economic policies." Not the first to study the relationship of individual variables within a total economy, Klein revived Jan Tinbergen's 1930s model, added a system of equations based upon the economic theory of John Maynard Keynes, applied modern statistical analysis and computer technology, and therewith pioneered a practical instrument that could both forecast business fluctuations and portray economic interrelationships. Klein's writings clarified theory; his projects became training grounds for economists and government officials throughout the world. (M.L.L.)

1981

Tobin, James   120
PRIZE: Economics, 1981. BORN: March 5, 1918; Champaign, IL. PARENTS: Father, Louis Michael Tobin; Mother, Margaret Anketell Edgerton Tobin. NATIONALITY: American. RELIGION: Most probably Christian. EDUCATION: Harvard Univ., MA, A.B., 1939; Harvard Univ., MA, M.A., 1940; Harvard Univ., MA, Ph.D., 1947. SPOUSE: Elizabeth Fay Ringo, married September 14, 1946. CHILDREN: Margaret Ringo, daughter; Louis Michael, son; Hugh Ringo, son; Roger Gill, son. CAREER: Office of Price Administration, Economist, 1941-42; U.S. Navy, Lieutenant, 1942-46; Harvard Univ., MA, Professor, 1946-50; Yale Univ., CT, Professor, 1950-. OTHER AWARDS: Clark Medal, American Economics Association, 1955.

Selected Publications: *National Economic Policy.* New Haven, CT: Yale U. Press, 1966. *Essays in Economics.* Volume 1, Macroeconomics. Chicago: Markham, 1972. *The New Economics: One Decade Older.* Princeton, NJ: Princeton U. Press, 1974. *Essays in Economics.* Volume 2, Consumption and Economics. New York: Elsevier, 1975. *Asset Accumulation and Economic Activity.* Chicago: U. of Chicago Press, 1980. *Essays in Economics.* Volume 3, Theory and Policy. Cambridge, MA: MIT Press, 1982.

For More Information See: *Current Biography Yearbook.* New York: H.W. Wilson Co., 1984, 393-96. *The National Cyclopedia of American Biography.* New York: James T. White and Co., 1964 (Volume J), 280-81. Samuelson, Paul A. "1981 Nobel Prize in Economics." *Science* (October 30, 1981): 520-22.

Commentary: James Tobin's award citation noted that he had provided "a basis for understanding how subjects actually behave when they acquire different assets and incur debts" by his statement of the "portfolio selection theory" of investment. His work was in the areas of economic theory, econometrics, monetary theory, and policy and consumer behavior, but his major concern was to modify, in terms of the later U.S. economy, the original Keynesian theory that the federal government should pursue an aggressive fiscal and monetary policy to attain rapid growth and full employment. (B.E.M.)

1982

Stigler, George Joseph   121
PRIZE: Economics, 1982. BORN: January 17, 1911; Renton, WA. PARENTS: Father, Joseph Stigler; Mother, Elizabeth Hungler Stigler. NATIONALITY: American. RELIGION: Most probably Christian. EDUCATION: Univ. of Washington, BBA, 1931; Northwestern Univ., IL, MBA, 1932; Univ. of Chicago, IL, Ph.D., 1938. SPOUSE: Margaret Mack, married December 26, 1936. CHILDREN: Stephen, son; David, son; Joseph, son. CAREER: Iowa State Univ., Professor, 1936-38; Univ. of Minnesota, Professor, 1938-46; Brown Univ., RI, Professor, 1946-47; Columbia Univ., NY, Professor, 1947-57; Center for Advanced Studies in Behavioral Sciences, Fellow, 1957-58; Univ. of Chicago, IL, Professor, 1958-.

Selected Publications: *Production and Distribution Theories.* New York: Macmillan, 1941. *The Theory of Price.* New York: Macmillan, 1942. *Five Lectures on Economic Problems.* New York: Longmans Green, 1949. *The Citizen and the State: Essays on Regulation.* Chicago: U. of Chicago Press, 1975. *The Economist as Preacher.* Chicago: U. of Chicago Press, 1982. *The Organization of Industry.* Chicago: U. of Chicago Press, 1983. *The Intellectual and the Marketplace.* Cambridge, MA: Harvard U. Press, 1984.

For More Information See: *Current Biography Yearbook.* New York: H.W. Wilson, 1983, 372-375. *Science* 218 (November 12, 1982): 655-57.

Commentary: George Stigler was awarded the Nobel Prize for his "seminal studies of industrial structures, functioning of markets and the causes and effects of public regulations. His studies of the forces which give rise to regulatory legislation have opened up a completely new area of economic research," the Academy's citation said. The Academy also praised his work in explaining price variations and his explanations of the effect in the marketplace of households and companies making similar economic decisions with different amounts of information. (V.B.)

1983

Debreu, Gerard   122
PRIZE: Economics, 1983. BORN: July 4, 1921; Calais, France. PARENTS: Father, Camille Debreu; Mother, Fernande Decharne Debreu. NATIONALITY: French; later American citizen. RELIGION: Most probably Christian. EDUCATION: École Normale Supérieure, France, Agrégé de l'Université, 1946; Univ. of Paris, France, D.Sc., 1956. SPOUSE: Françoise Bled, married June 14, 1945. CHILDREN: Chantal, daughter; Florence, daughter. CAREER: French Army, 1944-45; Center National de la Rocherche Scientifique, Paris, France, Researcher, 1946-48; Rockefeller Fellow, U.S., Sweden, and Norway, 1948-50; Univ. of Chicago, IL, Researcher, 1950-55; Yale Univ., CT, Professor, 1955-61; Univ. of California, Berkeley, Professor, 1962-. OTHER AWARDS: Chevalier de Légion d'Honneur, 1976; Commander de l'Ordre Nationale du Mèrite, 1984.

Selected Publications: *Theory of Value: An Axiomatic Analysis of Economic Equilibrium.* New Haven, CT: Yale U. Press, 1959. *Professor Debreu's "Market Equilibrium" Theorem: An Expository Note.* West

Lafayette, IN: Purdue U. Press, 1973. *Mathematical Economics: Twenty Papers of Gerard Debreu.* Cambridge, MA: Cambridge U. Press, 1983.

For More Information See: Samuelson, Paul. "The 1983 Nobel Prize in Economics." *Science* 222 (December 2, 1983): 987-89. *Time* 122 (October 31, 1983): 93.

Commentary: Gerard Debreu was awarded the Nobel Prize for three decades of work on one of the most basic of economic problems: the equilibrium between prices in a free-market economy and what producers supplied and consumers demanded. Debreu's work, though little known outside of the economic community, is the basis on which many other economists concerned with micro-economics have built their own work. The Academy said Debreu's book, *The Theory of Value*, is "a classic both for its universality and for its elegant analytical approach." They further stated that Debreu's theoretical contributions lent themselves to "far-reaching interpretations and applications." (V.B.)

1984

Stone, John Richard Nicholas, Sir 123

PRIZE: Economics, 1984. BORN: August 30, 1913; London, England. PARENTS: Father, Gilbert Stone; Mother, no record found. NATIONALITY: British. RELIGION: Most probably Christian/Protestant. EDUCATION: Cambridge Univ., England, baccalaureate, 1935; Cambridge Univ., England, M.A., 1938; Cambridge Univ., England, D.Sc., 1957. SPOUSE: Feodora Leontinoff, married 1941, died 1956; Giovanna Saffi Croft-Murray, married 1960. CHILDREN: 1 daughter. CAREER: C.E. Heath and Co., London, England, Economist, 1936-39; British Government Offices, Economist, 1939-45; Cambridge Univ., England, Professor, 1945-80. OTHER AWARDS: Knighthood, 1978.

Selected Publications: *Quantity and Price Indexes in National Accounts.* Paris: Organization for Economic Cooperation and Development, 1956. *Mathematics in the Social Sciences and Other Essays.* London: Chapman & Hall, 1966. *Demographic Accounting and Model Building.* Paris: Organization for Economic Cooperation and Development, 1971. *National Income and Expenditure.* London: Bowes & Bowes, 1977.

For More Information See: *New York Times Biographical Service* 15 (1984): 1397-98. *Science* 227 (1985): 20-22.

Commentary: Richard Stone's achievements which earned him the Nobel Prize lay in developing complex economic models, particularly those which led to accounting systems that could be used to chart the economic activity of nations. His work was responsible for standardization of national income reports throughout the world and by the United Nations. Early in his career, Stone also developed statistical techniques for economics and studied consumer reaction to changes in income and prices. (J.F.)

1985

Modigliani, Franco 124

PRIZE: Economics, 1985. BORN: June 18, 1918; Rome, Italy. PARENTS: Father, Enrico Modigliani; Mother, Olga Flaschel Modigliani. NATIONALITY: Italian; later American citizen. RELIGION: Jewish. EDUCATION: Univ. of Rome, Italy, law degree, 1939; New School for Social Research, NY, Ph.D., 1944. SPOUSE: Serena Calabi, married 1939. CHILDREN: Andre, son; Sergio, son. CAREER: New Jersey College for Women, Professor, 1942; Bard College, NY, Professor, 1942-44; New School for Social Research, NY, Professor, 1945-48; Univ. of Illinois, Professor, 1949-52; Carnegie-Mellon Univ., PA, Professor, 1952-60; Northwestern Univ., IL, Professor, 1960-62; Massachusetts Institute of Technology, Professor, 1962-.

Selected Publications: *The Collected Papers of Franco Modigliani.* 3 volumes. Cambridge, MA: MIT Press, 1980.

For More Information See: *Business Week* (October 28, 1985): 32. *New York Times Biographical Service* (October 16, 1985): 1259-60.

Commentary: Franco Modigliani was given the Nobel Prize for two major theories. The first, on personal finance, stated that persons save when their income is highest to allow for financial security throughout life. The second, on corporate finance, noted that a company's market value was not altered by the distribution of shares or bonds in its balance sheet. The two theories are well accepted in economic circles and provide the basis for much work in the field. (D.P.K.)

Literature

1901

Prudhomme, René-François-Armend (Sully Prudhomme, René-François-Armend) 125

PRIZE: Literature, 1901. BORN: March 16, 1839; Paris, France. DIED: September 6, 1907; Châtenay, France. PARENTS: Father, M. Sully Prudhomme; Mother, Clotilde Caillat Sully Prudhomme. NATIONALITY: French. RELIGION: Catholic. EDUCATION: Lycée Bonaparte, France, Bachelier ès Sciences, 1856. SPOUSE: None. CHILDREN: None. CAREER: Paris, France, Clerk, 1859-60; Writer.

Selected Publications: *Les Solitudes: Poèsies.* Paris: A. Lemerre, 1869. *Poèsie, 1865-88.* Paris: A. Lemerre, 1883-88. *Le Prisme, Poèsies Diverses.* Paris: A. Lemerre, 1886. *Psychologie du Arbitre de Definitions Fondamentales: Vocabulaire Logiquement Ordonné des Idées les Plus Generals et des Idées les Plus Abstraites.* Paris: A. Lemerre, 1896. *Oeuvres de Sully Prudhomme.* Paris: A. Lemerre, 1900-01. *Epaves.* Paris: A. Lemerre, 1908. *Patrie et Humanité (Essai de Solution Collective).* Paris: Edition de "La Revue," 1913. *Journal Intime: Lettres-Pensée.* Paris: A. Lemerre, 1922.

For More Information See: *Columbia Dictionary of Modern European Literature.* New York: Columbia U. Press, 1947, 791. Esteve, Edmond. *Sully Prudhomme.* Paris: Boivin, 1925.

Commentary: René Sully-Prudhomme, French poet, was the recipient of the first Nobel Prize for literature. His work is generally considered to fall into two stylistic groups. The earlier is lyrical, typified by his most famous poem, "Vase Brisé," which was published in his first book of poems, *Stances et poèmes* (1865). Later in his life, Sully-Prudhomme's poetry grew increasingly abstract and concerned with philosophic and didactic issues. Sully-Prudhomme was given the Nobel Prize "in special recognition of his poetic composition, which gives evidence of lofty idealism, artistic perfection, and a rare combination of the qualities of both heart and intellect." (S.W.C.)

1902

Björnson, Björnstjerne Martinius 126

PRIZE: Literature, 1902. BORN: December 8, 1832; Kvikne, Norway. DIED: April 26, 1910; Paris, France. PARENTS: Father, Peder Björnson; Mother, Inger Elise Nordraak Björnson. NATIONALITY: Norwegian. RELIGION: Freethinker; from Lutheran background. EDUCATION: No college degrees. SPOUSE: Karoline Reimers, married 1857. CHILDREN: Björn, son; Bergljot, daughter. CAREER: *Morgenbladet*, Theater Critic, 1854-56; *Illustreret Folkeblad*, Editor, 1856; *Bergensposten*, Editor, 1858; *Aftenbladet*, Editor, 1859-60; *Norsk Folkeblad*, Editor, 1866-71. OTHER AWARDS: Norwegian Government's Author's Salary, first recipient, 1863.

Selected Publications: *Synnöve Solbakken.* Kristiania: Dahl, 1857 (*Synnöve Solbakken.* Tr. by Julie Sutter. New York: Macmillan, 1912). *Sigurd Slembe.* Copenhagen: Gyldendal, 1862 (*Sigurd Slembe.* Tr. by William Morton Payne. Boston: Houghton, Mifflin & Co., 1888). *En Gead Gutt.* Copenhagen: Gyldendal, 1868. *Arnl jot Gelline.* Copenhagen: Gyldendal, 1870. *Digte og Sange.* Copenhagen: Gyldendal, 1870 (*Poems and Songs.* Tr. by Arthur Hubbel Palmer. New York: American-Scandinavian Foundation, 1915). *Sigurd Jorsalfar (Sigurd the Crusader).* Copenhagen: Gyldendal, 1872. *Over Aevne* (Volume I, 1883) and *Over Aevne* (Volume II, 1895). Copenhagen: Gyldendal, 1883-95 (*Beyond Our Power* (Volume I)). *Modern Continental Plays.* Tr. by Edwin Bjorkman. Ed. by S.M. Tucker. New York, 1929 and *Beyond Human Might* (Volume II). Tr. by Edwin Bjorkman. *Nobel Prize Library* (volume on Beckett, Björnson, Buck, Bunin). New York: Gregory, 1971, 85-136. *Nār den ny Vin Blomstrer.* Gyldendal, 1909 (*When the New Wine Blooms.* Tr. by Lee M. Hollander. Boston: R.G. Badger, 1911).

For More Information See: Anker, Öyvind. *Björnstjerne Björnson: The Man and His Work* (with Björnson's *Modern Norwegian Literature*). Follebu: Aulestad, 1955. Beyer, Harald. *A History of Norwegian Literature.* Tr. by Einar Haugen. New York: New York U. Press, 1970. Brandes, Georg Morris Cohen. *Henrik Ibsen: A Critical Study with a 42-Page Essay on Björnstjerne Björnson.* London: Macmillan, 1899; New York: Arno Press, 1977. *Cyclopedia of World Authors.* Englewood Cliffs, NJ: Salem Press, 1974, 180-82. *European Authors, 1000-1900.* New York: H.W. Wilson, 1967, 98-100. Payne, William Morton. *Björnstjerne Björnson, 1832-1910.* Chicago: McClurg, 1910.

Commentary: Björnstjerne Björnson was 71 years old when he received the Nobel Prize as "a tribute to his noble, magnificent, and versatile work as a poet, which has always been distinguished by both the freshness of its inspiration and the rare purity of its spirit." Besides poetry, he wrote numerous novels and plays, ranging from early peasant stories and historical dramas to contemporary works. His most famous poem is the Norwegian national anthem. An untiring writer, orator, and champion of the oppressed, Björnson was always involved in public debate and surrounded by controversy. Even today his status as author is rivaled by the memory of his fearless and flamboyant personality. (S.O.)

Mommsen, Christian Matthias Theodor **127**
PRIZE: Literature, 1902. BORN: November 30, 1817;
Garding, Schleswig, Germany. DIED: November 1,
1903; Berlin-Charlottenburg, Germany. PARENTS: Father, Jens Mommsen; Mother, Sophie Elisabeth Krum-
bhaur Mommsen. NATIONALITY: German. RELIGION:
Atheist; from Protestant background. EDUCATION: Un-
iversität zu Kiel, Germany, Doctor of Law, 1843.
SPOUSE: Marie Auguste Reimer, married 1854. CHIL-
DREN: Marie, daughter; Lisbet, daughter; Käthe, daughter; Hildegard, daughter; Adelheid, daughter; Luise,
daughter; Anna, daughter; Wolfgang, son; Karl, son;
Kurt, son; Ernst, son; Oswald, son; Konrad, son; Hans,
son; Max, son; Otto, son. CAREER: Danish Government
Traveling Fellowship, 1844-46; *Schleswig-Holsteinische
Zeitung*, Editor, 1848; Univ. of Leipzig, Germany,
Professor, 1848-51; Univ. of Zurich, Switzerland, Professor, 1852-54; Univ. of Breslau, Germany, Professor,
1854-58; Königlich Preussischen Akademie der Wissenschaften, Professor, 1858-61; Univ. of Berlin, Germany, Professor, 1861-1903.

Selected Publications: *Inscriptiones regni Neapolitani
Latinae.* Leipzig, Germany: G. Wigand, 1852.
Romische Geschichte. Berlin: Weidmann, 1854-85
(*History of Rome.* Volumes I-III. Tr. by W.P. Dickson.
New York: Scribner's, 1862-75; *The Provinces of the
Roman Empire.* Volume V. Tr. by W.P. Dickson. Lon-
don: Bentley, 1886). *Geschichte der Römische Munz-
wesen.* Berlin: Weidmann, 1860. *Römisches Staats-
recht.* Leipzig, Germany: S. Hirzel, 1871-88. *Romisches
Strafrecht.* Leipzig, Germany: Duncker und Humblot,
1899. *Gesammelte Schriften* (*Collected Writings*). Berlin: Weidmann, 1905-13.

For More Information See: Fowler, W. Warde,
"Theodor Mommsen: His Life and Work." In *Roman
Essays and Interpretations.* Oxford: Clarendon Press,
1920, 250-68. Hartmann, Ludo Moritz. *Theodor Mom-
msen: Eine Biographische Skizze.* Gotha, Germany: F.
A. Perthes, 1908. Wikert, Lothar. *Theodor Mommsen:
Eine Biographie.* Frankfurt: V. Klosterman, 1958-80.

Commentary: The Nobel Committee cited Theodor
Mommsen as "the greatest living master of historical
writing, with special reference to his monumental
work, *History of Rome.*" In this work, he demonstrated unparalleled ability to combine minute detail
with a sweeping breadth of view, and passionate feeling with sober critical judgment. Particularly memorable are his battle scenes and character portraits
which, though thoroughly historical, are painted with
consummate artistic skill. His other scholarly achievements include his work as an editor of the *Corpus
Inscriptionum Latinarum*, a collection of all known
Latin inscriptions. Mommsen was not only chiefly responsible for organizing this publication, which extended the range of research on Roman civilization
immeasurably, but was also its most important contributor. A researcher of Herculean productivity who was
also intimately involved in the political life and
thought of his time, Mommsen ranks as one of the
greatest minds of the nineteenth century. (H.J.W.)

1904

Echegaray Y Eizaguirre, José **128**
PRIZE: Literature, 1904. BORN: April 19, 1832; Madrid,
Spain. DIED: September 14, 1916; Madrid, Spain. PAR-
ENTS: Father, José Echegary y Lacosta; Mother, Man-
uela Eizaguirre Chaler. NATIONALITY: Spanish. RELI-
GION: Christian. EDUCATION: Escuela de Caminos,
Madrid, Spain, engineering degree, 1853. SPOUSE: Ana
Perfecta Estrada, married 1857. CHILDREN: 1 daughter.
CAREER: Escuela de Caminos, Madrid, Spain, Profes-
sor, 1854-68; Political posts and Writer, 1868-1916.
OTHER AWARDS: Cortina Award, Real Academia Es-
panola de La Lengua, Spain, 1892; Grand Cross of
Alfonso XII, 1904; Premio Echegaray, Royal Academy
of the Exact, Physical and Natural Sciences, 1907;
Knight of the Golden Fleece; Grand Cordon of the
Legion of Honor; Grand Cross of San Mauricio and
San Lazaro, Italy.

Selected Publications: *O Locura o Santidad, Drama
en Tres Actos y en Drosa.* Madrid: J.M. Duncazcal,
1877 (*Madman or Saint.* Tr. by H. Lynch. Boston: L.
Wolfe, 1895). *El Gran Galeoto, Drama en Tres Actos y
en Verso, Precedido de un Dialogo en Prosa.* Madrid: J.
Rodrignes, 1881 (*The Great Galeoto, a Drama in Four
Acts: a Prologue.* Tr. by Jacob F. Fassett. Boston: R.
G. Badger, 1914). *El Loco Dios; Drama en Cuatro
Actos, en Prosa.* Madrid: Velasco, 1900 (*The Madman
Divine, a Prose Drama in Four Acts.* Tr. by Elizabeth
Howard West. Boston: Poet Lore, 1908).

For More Information See: Matias, Julio.
Echegaray-Su Vida y Obra. Madrid: E.P.S.A., 1970.
Oxford Companion to Spanish Literature. Oxford:
Clarendon Press, 1978, 176.

Commentary: The Nobel Prize was given to José
Echegaray "in recognition of the numerous and brilliant compositions which in an individual and original
manner have revived the great traditions of the Spanish drama." Echegaray excelled as a professor of mathematics, as a high political figure in the Spanish government and as a leader in Spanish drama. Remembered as a dramatist, his output included a dozen
competent works in science. It wasn't until early middle age that he turned to writing plays; in the 30
following years, he produced more than 60 works in
the melodramatic vein; his greatest strength lay in his
power to create and maintain suspense and to stimulate the imagination with stage effects. (D.C.)

Mistral, Frederic **129**
PRIZE: Literature, 1904. BORN: September 8, 1830;
Maillane, Bouches-du-Rhone, France. DIED: March 25,
1914; Maillane, France. PARENTS: Father, Francois
Mistral; Mother, Adelaide Poulinet Mistral. NATIONAL-
ITY: French. RELIGION: Catholic. EDUCATION: Univ. of
Aix-en-Provence, France, licence en droit, 1851.
SPOUSE: Marie Riviére, married 1876. CHILDREN:
None. CAREER: Writer. OTHER AWARDS: French Acad-
emy Prize, 1861; Reynaud Prize, Institute of France.

Selected Publications: *Mireio, Poémes Provençau de
Frederic Mistral.* Avignon, France: J. Roumanille,
1859 (*Mireille, A Pastoral Epic of Provence from the
Provencal of F. Mistral.* Tr. by H. Crichton. London:
Macmillan, 1868). *Calendau.* Avignon, France: J.
Roumanille, 1867. *La Reine Jeanne: Tragedie Proven-
çale en Cinq Actes.* Paris: A. Lemerre, 1879. *Lou Tres-
or d'ou Felibridge ou Dictionaire Provençal-Français.*
Aix-en-Provence, France: Veue Remondet-Aubin,
1879-1887. *Nerte, Nouvelle Provencale.* Paris: Hachette,
1884. *Le poème du Rhône, xii Chantes: Texte, Pro-

vençal et Traduction Française. Paris: A. Lemerre, 1897 (*The Poem of the Rhone*. Tr. by M.B. Jones. Claremont, CA: Claremont College Press, 1914).

For More Information See: Downer, Charles. *Frederic Mistral*. New York: Columbia U. Press, 1901. *European Authors, 1000-1900*. New York: H.W. Wilson, 1967, 641-42. *Memoirs of Mistral*. Tr. by Constance Maud. London: E. Arnold, 1907.

Commentary: The Nobel Award was conferred on Frederic Mistral "in recognition of the fresh originality and true artistic genius of his poetry, which faithfully mirrors the native spirit of his people, and of his important work as a Provençal philologist." Mistral's love of Provence translated itself into an outpouring of poetry about its people and its natural beauties, as well as the founding of the Association of Provençal Poets, whose members standardized the language and presented it in dictionary form. (P.K.)

1905

Sienkiewicz, Henryk Adam Aleksander Pius (Litwos) 130

PRIZE: Literature, 1905. BORN: May 5, 1846; Wola Okrzejska, Lithuania. DIED: November 15, 1916; Vevey, Switzerland. PARENTS: Father, Jozef Sienkiewicz; Mother, Stefania Cieciszowska Sienkiewicz. NATIONALITY: Polish. RELIGION: Catholic. EDUCATION: No college degrees. SPOUSE: Maria Szetkiewicz, married 1881, died October 19, 1885; Maria Romanowska, married 1893, separated shortly thereafter, marriage later annulled; Maria Babska, married May 5, 1904. CHILDREN: Henryk Jozef, son; Jadwiga, daughter. CAREER: Writer, Journalist, and Editor. OTHER AWARDS: Oblegorek Estate, received as national gift, 1900.

Selected Publications: *Dziela*. 60-volume collective edition. Ed. by Julian Krzyzanowski. Warsaw: Pantsworog Instytut Wydawniczy, 1947-55. Contains Polish versions of all below. *Janko Muzykant*. 1879 (*Yanko, the Musician and Other Stories*. Tr. by Jeremiah Curtin. Boston: Little, Brown & Co., 1893). *Ogniem i Mieczem*. 1884 (*With Fire and Sword: An Historical Novel of Poland and Russia*. Tr. by Jeremiah Curtin. Boston: Little, Brown & Co., 1890). *Potop*. 1886 (*The Deluge: An Historical Novel of Poland, Sweden, and Russia*. Tr. by Jeremiah Curtin. Boston: Little, Brown & Co., 1891). *Pan Wolodyjowski*. 1888 (*Pan Michael: An Historical Novel of Poland, the Ukraine, and Turkey*. Tr. by Jeremiah Curtin. Boston: Little, Brown and & Co., 1893). *Bez Dogmatu*. 1891 (*Without Dogma*. Tr. by Iza Young. Boston: Little, Brown & Co., 1893). *Rodzina Polanieckich*. 1894 (*Children of the Soil*. Tr. by Jeremiah Curtin. Boston: Little, Brown & Co., 1895). *Quo Vadis*. 1895 (*Quo Vadis*. Tr. by Jeremiah Curtin. Boston: Little, Brown & Co., 1896). *Na Polu Chwaly*. 1906 (*The Field of Glory: An Historical Novel*. Tr. by Henry Britoff. New York: J.S. Ogilvie Publishing Co., 1906). *Wiry*. 1910 (*Whirlpools*. Tr. by Max A. Drezmal. Boston: Little, Brown & Co., 1910). *W Pustyni i w Puszczy*. 1912 (*In Desert and Wilderness*. Tr. by Max A. Drezmal. Boston: Little, Brown & Co., 1912).

For More Information See: Giergielewicz, Mieczyslaw. *Henryk Sienkiewicz*. New York: Twayne Publishers, 1968. *Modern Slavic Literatures: A Library of Literary Criticism*. New York: Frederick Ungar Publishing Co., 1976 (Volume 2), 394-99.

Commentary: Henryk Sienkiewicz's award was "because of his outstanding merits as an epic writer," with a style distinguished by naive and striking metaphors. In his historical novels, Sienkiewicz maintained the objectivity of an historian while demonstrating uncompromising loyalty to his country and fellow Poles. Writing about Poland's past, Sienkiewicz inspired faith in the country's future. With remarkable insight and rich imagination he created characters that belong in the gallery of immortal characters of world literature. (S.R.)

1906

Carducci, Giosuè Alessandro Guiseppe 131

PRIZE: Literature, 1906. BORN: June 27, 1835; Valdicastello, Italy. DIED: February 16, 1907; Bologna, Italy. PARENTS: Father, Michele Carducci; Mother, Idegonde Celli Carducci. NATIONALITY: Italian. RELIGION: Anti-church; from Catholic background. EDUCATION: Univ. of Pisa, Italy, Ph.D., 1855. SPOUSE: Elvira Manicucci, married 1859. CHILDREN: Beatrice, daughter; Laura, daughter; Dante, son; Liberta, daughter. CAREER: Univ. of Bologna, Italy, Professor, 1860-1904.

Selected Publications: *Levia Gravia* (*Light and Heavy*). Pistoia Tip, Italy: Niccolai e Quarteroi, 1868. *Odi Barbare* (*The Barbarian Odes*). Bologna: Presso Nicola Zanichelli, 1877 (*The Barbarian Odes of Giosue Carducci*. Tr. by W.F. Smith et al. Menasha, WI: George Bante Co., 1939). *Giambi ed Epodi* (*Iambics and Epodes di Giosue Carducci 1867-1872*). Bologna: N. Zanichelli, 1882 (*Political and satiric verse of Giosue Carducci*. Tr. by W.F. Smith. Colorado Springs, CO: Private Printing, 1942). *Rime Nuove* (*New Rhymes*). Bologna: N. Zanichelli, 1887 (*The New Lyrics of Giosue Carducci*. Tr. by W.F. Smith. Colorado Springs, CO: private printing, 1942). *Bozzetti e Scherme*. Bologna: Carducci, 1889. *Primi Saggi*. Bologna: Carducci, 1889. *Confessioni e Battaglie* (*Confessions and Battles*. Bologna: Carducci, 1890). *Giambi ed Epodi e Rime*. Bologna: N. Zanichelli, 1894. *Studi Saggi e Discorsi*. Bologna: Carducci, 1898. *Su Ludovico Aristo e Taquarto Tasso: Studi*. Bologna: Carducci, 1905. *Archelogia Poetica*. Bologna: N. Zanichelli, 1908. *Edizione Nazionale Delle Opere di Giosuè Carducci*. Bologna: N. Zanichelli, 1935-40.

For More Information See: Bailey, John. *Carducci*. Oxford: Clarendon, 1926. *Columbia Dictionary of Modern European Literature*. New York: Columbia U. Press, 1947, 143-44.

Commentary: Giosuè Carducci, Italian poet, politician, and literary historian, was awarded the Nobel Prize "not only in consideration of his deep learning and critical research, but above all as a tribute to the creative energy, freshness of style, and lyrical force which characterize his poetic masterpieces." An ardent patriot known for his radical opinions, Carducci strove in his poetry to fuse the modern with the ancient. He was viewed as the greatest figure in Italian literature of his time. (S.W.C.)

1907

Kipling, Joseph Rudyard 132

PRIZE: Literature, 1907. BORN: December 30, 1865; Bombay, India. DIED: January 18, 1936; London, England. PARENTS: Father, John Lockwood Kipling; Mother, Alice MacDonald Kipling. NATIONALITY: British. RELIGION: Methodist. EDUCATION: No college degrees. SPOUSE: Caroline Starr Bolestier, married 1892. CHILDREN: Josephine, daughter; Elsie, daughter; John, son. CAREER: *Civil and Military Gazette*, India, Editor, 1882-87; *Pioneer*, India, Editor, 1887-89; Writer. OTHER AWARDS: Order of Merit, 1916, 1921, 1924 (refused); Gold Medal, 1926.

Selected Publications: *Barrack Room Ballads and Other Verses*. Leipzig, Germany: Heinemann and Balestier, 1892. *The Jungle Book. The Second Jungle Book*. Garden City, NY: Doubleday, Page, 1895. *From Sea to Sea: Letters of Travel*. New York: Scribner's, 1900. *Kim*. Leipzig, Germany: B. Tauchnitz, 1901. *Just So Stories for Little Children*. Leipzig, Germany: B. Tauchnitz, 1902. *The Five Nations*. Leipzig, Germany: B. Tauchnitz, 1903. *Puck of Pook's Hill*. Leipzig, Germany: B. Tauchnitz, 1906. *Soldier Stories*. Garden City, NY: Doubleday, Page, 1920.

For More Information See: Amis, Kingsley. *Rudyard Kipling and His World*. New York: Scribner's, 1975. Clemens, William Montgomery. *A Ken of Kipling Being a Biographical Sketch of Rudyard Kipling*. Toronto: G. N. Norang, 1899. *Dictionary of National Biography, 1931-1940*. London: Oxford U. Press, 1949, 512-16. Dobree, Bonamie. *Rudyard Kipling: Realist and Fabulist*. New York: Oxford U. Press, 1967. *Something of Myself. An Autobiography*. London: Macmillan, 1937.

Commentary: Rudyard Kipling received the Nobel Prize "in consideration of the power of observation, originality of imagination, and also the manly strength in the art of perception and delineation that characterize the writings of this world-renowned author." Kipling, only 42 years of age, was the first English person to receive the award. The author's early fame and critical acclaim were products of his stories and poems of colonial India. His patriotism and support of British colonialism, however, brought him disapproval and critical dismissal, although his stories remained favorites with the British and with international readers. Kipling's poetry ranged from music hall ballads to serious poems for public occasions (*Recessional*, 1897). His beloved works for children include such titles as *Kim* (1901), *Just So Stories for Little Children* (1902), and *Puck of Pook's Hill* (1906). Kipling is remembered as one of England's greatest short story writers, a genuinely popular poet, and a classic author for children. (A.D.J.)

1908

Eucken, Rudolph Christoph 133

PRIZE: Literature, 1908. BORN: January 5, 1846; Aurich, Ostfriesland, Germany. DIED: September 15, 1926; Jena, Germany. PARENTS: Father, Ammo Becker Eucken; Mother, Ida Maria Gitterman Eucken. NATIONALITY: German. RELIGION: Freethinker; from Lutheran background. EDUCATION: Univ. of Gottingen, Germany, Dr. Philos., 1866. SPOUSE: Irene Passow, married 1882. CHILDREN: Arnold Thomas, son; Walter, son; 1 daughter. CAREER: Germany, Schoolteacher, 1867-71; Univ. of Basel, Switzerland, Professor, 1871-74; Univ. of Jena, Germany, Professor, 1874-1920.

Selected Publications: *Geschichte und Kritik der Grundbegriffe der Gegenwart*. Leipzig, Germany: Veit & Comp., 1878 (*The Fundamental Concepts of Modern Philosophic Thought*. Tr. by M. Stuart Phelps. New York: Appleton & Co., 1880). *Grundlinien Einer Neuen Lebensanschauung*. Leipzig, Germany: Veit, 1907 (*Life's Basis and Life's Ideal*. Tr. by Alan G. Widgery. London: Black, 1911). *Der Sinn und Wert des Lebens*. Leipzig, Germany: Quelle & Meyer, 1908 (*The Meaning and Value of Life*. Tr. by Lucy Judge Gibson and W.R. Boyce Gibson. London: Black, 1916). *Können Wir Noch Christen Sein?* Leipzig, Germany: Veit, 1911 (*Can We Still Be Christians?* Tr. by Lucy Judge Gibson. New York: Macmillan, 1914). *Ethics and Modern Thought: A Theory of Their Relations*. New York: Putnam, 1913.

For More Information See: Hermann, Emily. *Eucken and Bergson: Their Significance for Christian Thought*. Boston: Pilgrim Press, 1912. Raeber, Thomas. "Rudolph Christoph Eucken." In *Neue Deutsche Biographie* (Volume 4), 670-72. Berlin: Duncker & Humblot, 1959.

Commentary: Rudolph Eucken did not receive the Nobel Prize for poetry or fiction but "in recognition of his earnest search for truth, his penetrating power of thought, the warmth and strength of presentation with which in his numerous works he has vindicated and developed an idealistic philosophy of life." He diagnosed the malaise of his age as a spiritual confusion and provided a constructive response in his writings. One of his most influential works is *The Meaning and Value of Life*. His philosophy stresses "activism" and spirituality as a creative and renovating force. (S.O.)

1909

Lagerlöf, Selma Ottilian Lovisa 134

PRIZE: Literature, 1909. BORN: November 20, 1858; Ostra Emtervik, Marbacka Farm, Varmland, Sweden. DIED: March 16, 1940; Marbacka, Sweden. PARENTS: Father, Erik Gustaf Lagerlöf; Mother, Louisa Elizabeth Wallrock Lagerlöf. NATIONALITY: Swedish. RELIGION: Freethinker; from Christian, most probably Lutheran, background. EDUCATION: Royal Woman's Superior Training College, Sweden, graduate, 1885. SPOUSE: None. CHILDREN: None. CAREER: Girls' High School, Landskrona, Sweden, Teacher, 1885-95. OTHER AWARDS: Gold Medal, Swedish Academy, 1904.

Selected Publications: *Gösta Berling's Saga*. Stockholm: Bonnier, 1891 (*The Story of Gösta Berling*. Tr. by Pauline Flach. Garden City, NY: Doubleday, Page, 1917). *Antikrists Mirakler*. Stockholm: Bonnier, 1897 (*The Miracles of Antichrist*. Tr. by Pauline Flach. Boston: Little, Brown, 1910). *Jerusalem*. Stockholm: Bonnier, 1901-02 (Tr. by Velma Swanston Howard. Garden City, NY: Doubleday, 1915). *Nils Holgerssons underbara Resa Gennom Sverige*. Stockholm: Bonnier, 1906 (*The Wonderful Adventures of Nils*. Tr. by Velma Swanston Howard. Garden City, NY: Doubleday, 1907). *Nils Holgersson 2*. Stockholm: Bonnier, 1907 (*The Further Adventures of Nils*. Tr. by Velma Swanston Howard. New York: Grosset and Dunlap, 1911). *Tosen Frän Stormyrtorpet och Andra Sagor*. Göteborg,

Sweden: Ahlen and Akerlund, 1908 (*The Girl from the Marsh Croft*. Tr. by Velma Swanston Howard. Boston: Little, Brown and Co., 1912).

For More Information See: *The Diary of Selma Lagerlöf*. Tr. by Velma Swanston Howard. Garden City, NY: Doubleday, Doran, 1936. Larsen, Hanna. *Selma Lagerlöf*. New York: Doubleday, Doran, 1936. *Memories of My Childhood*. Tr. by Velma Swanston Howard. Garden City, NY: Doubleday, Doran, 1934. *Something About the Author*. Detroit, MI: Gale, 1979 (Volume 15), 160-74.

Commentary: Selma Lagerlöf won the Nobel Prize "in appreciation of the lofty idealism, vivid imagination, and spiritual perception that characterize her writings." The first woman to win the prize for literature, her works were in contrast to the prevailing Swedish writers' realism of her day. The Swedish educator, novelist, short story writer, poet, biographer, autobiographer, and dramatist was the leading figure in the romantic revival in Swedish literature. (L.B.)

1910

Heyse, Paul Johann Ludwig von　135

PRIZE: Literature, 1910. BORN: March 15, 1830; Berlin, Germany. DIED: April 2, 1914; Munich, Germany. PARENTS: Father, Karl Ludwig Heyse; Mother, Julie Saaling Heyse. NATIONALITY: German. RELIGION: Protestant and Jewish. EDUCATION: Univ. of Bonn, Germany, doctorate, 1852. SPOUSE: Margaretha Kugler, married May 15, 1854, died 1862; Anna Schubart, married 1867. CHILDREN: 3 sons; 3 daughters. CAREER: King Maximilian II of Bavaria, Germany, Court Poet, 1854-1914. OTHER AWARDS: Schiller Prize, Germany, 1884.

Selected Publications: *L'Arrabbiata*. Berlin: Hertz, 1853 (*L'Arrabbiata and Other Tales*. Tr. by Mary Wilson. New York: Leypold and Holt, 1867). *Kinder der Welt*. 2 volumes. Berlin: Hertz, 1872 (*Children of the World*. New York: Munro, 1883). *Im Paradiese*. 3 volumes. Berlin: Hertz, 1875 (*In Paradise*. New York: Appleton, 1878). *Der Weinhüter*. In *Novellen*. 7 volumes. Berlin: Hertz, 1882. *Selected Stories*. Chicago: Schick, 1886. *Merlin*. Berlin: Hertz, 1892.

For More Information See: Bianquis, Genevieve. "The Life and Works of Payl Heyse." In *Nobel Prize Library*. New York: Gregory, 1971, 347-53. Brandes, Georg. *Creative Spirits of the Nineteenth Century*. Tr. by Rasmas B. Anderson. New York: Crowell, 1923. *European Authors 1000-1900*. New York: H.W. Wilson, 1967, 413-15. *Jugenderinnerungen und Bekenntnisse* (*Memories of My Youth and Confessions*). Berlin: Hertz, 1900.

Commentary: Paul Heyse's Nobel award was "as a tribute to the consummate artistry, permeated with idealism, which he has demonstrated during his long and productive career as a lyric poet, dramatist, novelist, and writer of world-renowned short stories." He was a prolific writer of novellas, plays, poems, novels, and translated works, as attested to by the 38-volume edition of works completed between 1871 and 1914. Although liberal and progressive, his creative work was in traditional forms considered old-fashioned by the naturalists. He excelled particularly in his tightly constructed novellas and developed this genre to a mastery rarely matched. (S.O.)

1911

Maeterlinck, Mauritius Polydorus Maria Bernardus (Maeterlinck, Maurice)　136

PRIZE: Literature, 1911. BORN: August 29, 1862; Ghent, Belgium. DIED: May 6, 1949; Nice, France. PARENTS: Father, Polydore Maeterlinck; Mother, Mathilde Colette Françoise Van den Bossche Maeterlinck. NATIONALITY: Belgian. RELIGION: Agnostic; from Catholic background. EDUCATION: Jesuit Collége de Sainte-Barbe, Belgium, baccalaureate, 1881; Univ. of Ghent, Belgium, law degree, 1885. SPOUSE: Companion Georgette Le Blanc, 1895-1918; Renée Dahon, married 1919. CHILDREN: 1 stillborn child. CAREER: Belgium, Attorney, 1886-89; Writer thereafter. OTHER AWARDS: Triennial Prize for Dramatic Literature, Belgium, 1891 (refused), 1903; Grand Officer of the Ordre de Léopold, Belgium, 1920; made Count, 1932; Medal of the Order of St. James of the Sword, Portugal, 1939.

Selected Publications: *La Princesse Maleine*. Paris: Lacomblez, 1891 (*The Princess Maleine*. Tr. by Gerard Harry. London: W. Heinemann, 1892). *Pelleas et Melisande*. Brussels: P. Lacomblez, 1892 (*Pelleas and Melisanda*. Tr. by Laurence Alma Tadem. London: G. Allen & Unwin, 1915). *Aglavaine et Selysette*. Paris: Societé du Mercure de France, 1896 (*Aglavaine and Selysette: A Drama in Five Acts*. Tr. by Alfred Sutro. London: G. Richards, 1897). *Les Aveugles*. Brussels: Lacomblez, 1897 (*Buried Temple*. Tr. by Alfred Sutro. New York: Dodd, Mead, and Company, 1902). *La Sagesse et la Destinée*. Paris: Bibliothéque-Charpentier, E. Fasquelle, 1898 (*Wisdom and Destiny*. Tr. by Alfred Sutro. Dodd, Mead, and Company, 1898). *Mona Vanna*. Paris: Fasquelle, 1902 (Tr. by Alfred Sutro. London: G. Allen, 1904). *L'oiseau Bleu: Féerie en Cinq Actes et Dix Tableau*. Paris: Charpentier et Fasquelle, 1909 (*The Blue Bird: A Fairy Play in Five Acts*. Tr. by Alexander Teixeira de Mattos. London: Methuen, 1909). *La Vie des Abeilles*. Paris: Charpentier, 1912 (*The Life of the Ant*. Tr. by Bernard Miall. New York: John Day, 1930).

For More Information See: Andrieu, Jean-Marie. *Maeterlinck*. Paris: Éditions Universitaires, 1962. *Encyclopedia of World Literature in the 20th Century*. New York: Ungar Publishing, 1969 (Volume 2), 367-68. Halls, W.D. *Maurice Maeterlinck: A Study of His Life and Thought*. Oxford: Clarendon Press, 1960. Knapp, Bettina. *Maurice Maeterlinck*. Boston: Twayne, 1975.

Commentary: Maurice Maeterlinck received the prize in honor of "his diverse literary activity and especially his dramatic works, which are outstanding for their richness of imagination and for poetic realism, which sometimes in the dim form of the play of legend display a deep intimacy of feeling, and also in a mysterious way appeal to the reader's sentiment and sense of foreboding." Maeterlinck first achieved fame for his symbolist dramas, in which Death seemed triumphant. Late in the 1890s, his works showed a more optimistic attitude, and after 1900, he rejected symbolism, turning to a more realistic style as he wrote of moral and philosophical problems. The Committee's reference to Maeterlinck's diversity also took note of his poems and such famous essays as *Wisdom and Destiny* (1898) and *The Life of the Bees* (1901). (H.L.F.)

1912

Hauptmann, Gerhart Johann 137

PRIZE: Literature, 1912. BORN: November 15, 1862; Bad Salzbrunn, Silesia, Germany. DIED: June 8, 1946; Agnetendorf, Silesia, Germany. PARENTS: Father, Robert Hauptmann; Mother, Marie Straehler Hauptmann. NATIONALITY: German. RELIGION: Rejected organized Christianity; from Protestant background. EDUCATION: No college degrees. SPOUSE: Marie Thienemann, married 1885, divorced 1895; Margarete Marschalk, married 1904. CHILDREN: Ivo, son; Eckart, son; Klaus, son; Bonvenuto, son. CAREER: Germany, Sculptor and Writer. OTHER AWARDS: Gullparzer Prize, Austria, 1896, 1898, 1900; Pour Le Mérite, Peace, 1924; Goethe Prize, 1932.

Selected Publications: *Vor Sonnenaufgang.* Berlin: Fischer, 1889 (*Before Sunrise.* Tr. by James Joyce. San Marino, CA: Huntington Library, 1978). *Die Weber.* Berlin: Fischer, 1892 (*The Weavers.* Tr. by Mary Morison. New York: Huebsch, 1911). *Der Biberpelz, eine Diebskomödie.* Berlin: Fischer, 1893 (*The Beaver Coat: A Thieves' Comedy.* Tr. by Ludwig Lewisohn. In *Contemporary Drama: European Plays.* Ed. by E.B. Watson. New York, 1931). *Der Narr in Christo Emanuel Quint.* Berlin: Fischer, 1910 (*The Fool in Christ: Emanuel Quint.* Tr. by T. Seltzer. New York: Viking, 1926). *Die Ratten: Berliner Tragikomödie.* Berlin: Fischer, 1911 (*The Rats.* Tr. by Ludwig Lewisohn. In *Modern Continental Plays.* Ed. by S.M. Tucker. New York: Harper & Bros., 1929, 415-68). *The Dramatic Works.* 7 volumes. New York: Huebsch, 1912-17. *Der Ketzer von Soana.* Berlin: Fischer, 1918 (*The Heretic of Soana.* Tr. by Bayard Quincy Morgan. 2d ed. London: Calder, 1960). *Die Atriden-Tetralogie.* Berlin: Suhrkamp, 1949. *Three Plays: The Weavers, Hannele, the Beavercoat.* Tr. by Horst Frenz and Miles Waggoner. New York: Ungar, 1977.

For More Information See: Behl, Carl Fr. Wm. *Gerhart Hauptmann: His Life and Works.* Tr. by Helen Taubert. Würzburg: Holzner, 1956. *Encyclopedia of World Biography.* New York: McGraw-Hill, 1973, 135-37. Garten, Hugh F. *Gerhart Hauptmann.* New Haven, CT: Yale U. Press, 1954. Maurer, Warren R. *Gerhart Hauptmann.* Boston: Hall, 1982. *Twentieth Century Authors.* New York: H.W. Wilson, 1942, 625-27.

Commentary: Gerhart Hauptmann was awarded the Nobel Prize "primarily in recognition of his fruitful, varied, and outstanding production in the realm of dramatic art." At that time he was famous internationally for his naturalist plays, which voice a strong social compassion. Later works reflect his lifelong preoccupation with religious studies, philosophy, and ancient Greece. (S.O.)

1913

Tagore, Rabindranath, Sir (Thakura, Ravindranatha) 138

PRIZE: Literature, 1913. BORN: May 7, 1861; Calcutta, India. DIED: August 7, 1941; Calcutta, India. PARENTS: Father, Debendranath Marashi; Mother, Sarada Devi. NATIONALITY: Indian. RELIGION: "Pirali" Brahmin. EDUCATION: No college degrees. SPOUSE: Bhavatarini Benimadhav Raichaudhuri, married 1936. CHILDREN: Madhurilata, daughter; Rathindranath, son; 1 other son. CAREER: India, Writer, Poet, Landowner, and Activist. OTHER AWARDS: Knighthood, 1915.

Selected Publications: *Gitanjali (Song Offerings).* London: The India Society, 1912. *The Gardener.* London: Macmillan, 1913. *Glimpses of Bengal Life.* Tr. by Rajani Ranjan. Madras, India: G.A. Natesan, 1913. *Sadhana (Essays and Lectures).* London: Macmillan, 1913. *The King of the Dark Chamber.* Tr. by K.C. Sen. London: Macmillan, 1914. *The Fugitive.* Sankiniketan, India: Sankiniketan Press, 1919. *Gora.* Tr. by W.W. Pearson. London: Macmillan, 1924. *The Child.* London: Allen & Unwin, 1931. *The Religion of Man.* London: Allen & Unwin, 1931. *Collected Poems and Plays of Rabindranath Tagore.* London: Macmillan, 1936. *Farewell, My Friend.* Tr. by Krishna Kripalani. London: The New India Publishing Co., 1946. *A Flight of Swans.* Tr. by Aurobindo Bose. London: John Murray, 1955. *Letters from Russia.* Tr. by Sasadhar Sinha. Calcutta: Visva-Bharati, 1960.

For More Information See: Kripalani, Krishna. *Rabindranath Tagore: A Biography.* New York: Grove Press, 1962. *My Boyhood Days*(autobiography). Tr. by Marjorie Sykes. Sankiniketan, India: Visva-Bharati, 1940. Sykes, Marjorie. *Rabindranath Tagore.* London: Longmans, 1947. Thomson, Edward John. *Rabindranath Tagore: His Life and Works.* New York: Haskell House, 1974. *Twentieth Century Authors.* New York: H.W. Wilson, 1942, 1381-82.

Commentary: Rabindranath Tagore received the Nobel "because of his profoundly sensitive, fresh and beautiful verse, by which, with consummate skill, he has made his poetic thought, expressed in his own English words, a part of the literature of the West." Although noted for his poetry, because of its "rhythmically balanced style" and "taste in the choice of words," Tagore was also an accomplished playwright, novelist, short-story writer, essayist, musician, and artist. In all his output, he displayed the wisdom and religious mysticism of his Indian background. Tagore was also well known as an educator and a politician. (J.H.S.)

1915

Rolland, Romain (Saint Just) 139

PRIZE: Literature, 1915. BORN: January 29, 1866; Clamecy, Nievre, France. DIED: December 30, 1944; Vezelay, France. PARENTS: Father, Romain Edmé Paul Émile Rolland; Mother, Antoinette Marie Courot Rolland. NATIONALITY: French. RELIGION: Catholic. EDUCATION: École Normale, France, Agrégation d'histoire, 1889; École Française d'Archéologie, Italy, Docteur-ès-Lettres, 1895. SPOUSE: Clotilde Bréal, married October 31, 1892, divorced May 1901; Veuve Marie Koudachev, married 1934. CHILDREN: None. CAREER: École Normale Superieure, Paris, France, Professor, 1895-1900; Sorbonne, Paris, France, Professor, 1900-12. OTHER AWARDS: Grand Prix, French Academy, 1913; Goethe Medal, Germany, 1933 (refused).

Selected Publications: *Les Loups.* Paris: Albin Michel, 1898 (*The Wolves.* Tr. by Barrett H. Clark. New York: Random House, 1937). *Le Quatorze Juillet.* Paris: Cahier de la Quinzaine, 1902 (*The Fourteenth of July.* Tr. by Barrett H. Clark. New York: H. Holt and Company, 1918). *Beethoven.* Paris: Fischbacher, 1903

(*Beethoven*. Tr. by B. Constance Hull. New York: H. Holt and Company, 1917). *Le Théatre du Peuple*. Paris: Suresnes, 1903 (*The People's Theatre*. Tr. by Barrett H. Clark. New York: H. Holt and Company, 1918). *Jean-Christopher*. 10 volumes. Paris: Ollendorff, 1904-12 (Tr. by Gilbert Cannan. New York: H. Holt and Company, 1910-13). *Michel-Ange*. Paris: Librairie Plon, 1906. *Danton*. Paris: Librairie Ollendorff, 1909 (*Danton*. Tr. by Katherine Miller. New York: H. Holt and Company, 1919). *Colas Breugnon*. Paris: Albin Michel, 1918 (*Colas Breugnon*. Tr. by Katherine Miller. New York: H. Holt and Company, 1919).

For More Information See: *McGraw-Hill Encyclopedia of World Biography*. New York: McGraw-Hill, 1973 (Volume 9), 255-56. Zweig, Stefan. *Romain Rolland*. New York: Haskell, 1970. Zweig, Stefan. *Romain Rolland: The Man and His Works*. Salem, NH: Ayer Co., 1973.

Commentary: The citation to Romain Rolland noted "a tribute to the lofty idealism of his literary production and to the sympathy and love of truth with which he has described different types of human beings." His backgrounds in history, literature, and music produced writing of noteworthy character in all three fields, especially the biographical material on such greats as Handel, Beethoven, Michelangelo, Gandhi, and Tolstoi. The same background helped to produce his most memorable work, *Jean Christophe*. In addition, Rolland was involved in theater and in a lifelong quest for peace among nations. (P.K.)

1916

Von Heidenstam, Carl Gustaf Verner   140
PRIZE: Literature, 1916. BORN: July 6, 1859; Olshammer, Sweden. DIED: May 20, 1940; Övralid, Sweden. PARENTS: Father, Nils Gustaf von Heidenstam; Mother, Magdalena Rytterskjöld von Heidenstam. NATIONALITY: Swedish. RELIGION: Atheist; from Christian background. EDUCATION: No college degrees. SPOUSE: Emilia Uggla, married 1880, died 1883; Oldj Wiberg, married 1886, divorced 1888; Greta Sjoberg, married 1889. CHILDREN: No record found. CAREER: Writer. OTHER AWARDS: Henrik Steffens Prize, 1938.

Selected Publications: *Valfart Och Vandringsår* (*Pilgrimage: The Wander Years*). Stockholm: A. Bonnier, 1888. *Endymion*. Stockholm: F. Hegel & Son, 1889. *Renassans*. Stockholm: A. Bonnier, 1889. *Hans Alienus*. Stockholm: A. Bonnier, 1892. *Dikter* (*Poems*). Stockholm: A. Bonnier, 1895. *Karolinerna Berattelser*. Stockholm: A. Bonnier, 1897-98 (*The Charles Men*. Tr. by Charles W. Stork. New York: American Scandinavian Foundation, 1920). *Sankt Goran Och Drahen* (*Saint George and the Dragon*). Stockholm: A. Bonnier, 1900. *Heliga Birgittas Pilgrimsfard* (*Saint Bridget's Pilgrimage*). Stockholm: A. Bonnier, 1901. *Ett Folk* (*One People*). Stockholm: A. Bonnier, 1902. *Folkungatradet*. *Folke Filbyter Berattelse*. Stockholm: A. Bonnier, 1905 (*The Tree of the Folkungs*. Tr. by Arthur G. Chater. London: Glydendal, 1925). *Folkungatradet Bjalboarfvet* (*TheBjalbo Inheritance*). Stockholm: A. Bonnier, 1907. *Svenskarna Och Deras Havdingar*. Stockholm: A. Bonnier, 1908-10 (*The Swedes and Their Chieftains*. Tr. by Charles W. Stork. New York: American Scandinavian Foundation, 1925). *Nya Dikter* (*New Poems*). Stockholm: A. Bonnier, 1915.

For More Information See: *Cyclopedia of World Authors*. New York: Harper and Row, 1958, 495-96. Gustafson, Alrik. *History of Swedish Literature*. Minneapolis, MN: U. of Minneapolis Press, 1961. *Twentieth Century Authors*. New York: H.W. Wilson, 1942, 663-64.

Commentary: Verner von Heidenstam was the recipient of the Nobel Prize "in recognition of his significance as the leading representative of a new era in our literature." Von Heidenstam broke with the Swedish realistic school of gloomy poetry and prose and, using his studies of painting and interest in travel as the source, produced a literature of explosive beauty, filled with an enjoyment of life and of the Swedish countryside and history. As noted in the Nobel presentation, he is "a manly poet and a master of the lyric genre." (J.H.S.)

1917

Gjellerup, Karl Adolph (Epigonos)   141
PRIZE: Literature, 1917. BORN: June 2, 1857; Praestö, Roholte, Denmark. DIED: October 13, 1919; Klotzsche, Germany. PARENTS: Father, Ryde Carl Adolph Gjellerup; Mother, Anna Johanne Fibiger Gjellerup. NATIONALITY: Danish. RELIGION: Atheist; from Lutheran background. EDUCATION: Univ. of Copenhagen, Denmark, B.D., 1878. SPOUSE: Eugenia Anna Caroline Heusinger, married 1887. CHILDREN: None. CAREER: Writer. OTHER AWARDS: Poet's Pension, Denmark, 1889.

Selected Publications: *En Idealist* (*An Idealist*). Copenhagen: R.A. Reitzel, 1878. *Germanerness Loerling* (*The Teuton's Apprentice*). Copenhagen: A. Schau, 1882. *Brynhild*. Copenhagen: A. Schau, 1884. *Minna*. Copenhagen: P.G. Philipsens, 1889 (Tr. by C.L. Nielsen. London: W. Heinemann, 1913). *Mollen* (*The Mill*). Copenhagen: Gyldendal, 1896. *Pilgrimmen Kamanita*. Copenhagen: Gyldendal, 1906 (*The Pilgrim Kamanita*. Tr. by John Logie. London: W. Heinemann, 1911). *Den Fuldentes Husfru* (*The Wife of the Perfect One*). Copenhagen: Glydendalske Boghandel, 1907. *Verdens Vandrerne* (*World Wanderers*). Copenhagen: Gyldendal, 1910.

For More Information See: *European Authors, 1000-1900*. New York: H.W. Wilson, 1967, 330-31. *Karl Gjellerup, Der Dichter und Denker; sein Leben in Selbstzeugnissen und Briefen*. Leipzig, Germany: Quelle and Meyer, 1923.

Commentary: Karl Gjellerup became a Nobel laureate "for his many-sided, rich and inspired writing with high ideals." He is typical of late-nineteenth-century writers trying to discover meaning in a life without Christianity, turning first to an artistic defense of atheism and naturalism, and later developing a more humanistic and idealistic vision. Gjellerup moved from Lutheran to atheist/naturalist to Buddhism and mystical Christianity. Few of his works were translated and he has been considered by some undeservedly forgotten, by others "the dullest writer of the century." (M.F.L.)

Pontoppidan, Henrik   142
PRIZE: Literature, 1917. BORN: July 24, 1857; Frederica, Jutland, Denmark. DIED: August 21, 1943; Charlottenlund, Denmark. PARENTS: Father, Dines Pontop-

pidan; Mother, M. Marie Kirstina Oxenboll Pontoppidan. NATIONALITY: Danish. RELIGION: Freethinker; from Lutheran background. EDUCATION: No college degrees. SPOUSE: Mette Marie Hansen, married December 1881, divorced 1892; Antoinette Cecilia Kofoed, married April 9, 1892. CHILDREN: None. CAREER: Folk High School, Denmark, Teacher, 1879-82.

Selected Publications: *Stalkkede Vinger* (*Clipped Wings*). Copenhagen: Andr. Schous Forlag, 1881. *Spogelser* (*Ghosts*). Copenhagen: Gyldendalske Boghandel Forlag, 1888. *Skyer* (*Clouds*). Copenhagen: Gyldendalske Boghandel Forlag, 1890. *Det Forjaettede Land*. Copenhagen: Philipsen, 1892 (*The Promised Land*. Tr. by Ms. Edgar Lucas. London: J.M. Dent, 1896). *Emmanuel*. Tr. by Mrs. Edgar Lucas. London: J.M. Dent, 1896. *Lykke-Per* (*Lucky Peter*). Copenhagen: Det Nordiske Forlag, 1898-1904. *Kjobenhavn Kristiania*. Copenhagen: Gyldendalske Bohgandel Forlag, 1907. *De Dodes Rige* (*The Kingdom of the Dead*). Copenhagen: Gyldendalske Boghandel, 1917. *Mand's Himmerig* (*Man's Heaven*). Copenhagen: Hyldendal, Norkiske Forlag, 1927.

For More Information See: *Masterplots Cyclopedia of World Authors*. New York: Salem Press, 1958, 852-53. *Twentieth Century Authors*. New York: H.W. Wilson, 1942, 115-16.

Commentary: Henrik Pontoppidan received the Nobel Prize "for his profuse descriptions of Danish life of today" and is recognized as the classic Danish novelist, especially for his trilogy of *The Promised Land*, which dealt with Danish life in the countryside; *Lucky Peter*, which treated Danish life in Copenhagen; and *The Kingdom of the Dead*, a pessimistic social novel of Danish life in the early twentieth century. Beginning as a naturalist, he ends as a philosophical and psychological novelist searching for enduring values. (C.R.L.)

1918

Karlfeldt, Erik Axel 143
PRIZE: Literature, 1918; Literature, 1931 (posthumous). BORN: July 20, 1864; Folkarna, Sweden. DIED: April 8, 1931; Stockholm, Sweden. PARENTS: Father, Erik Errson Janson; Mother, Anna Stina Jansdotter. NATIONALITY: Swedish. RELIGION: Lutheran. EDUCATION: Univ. of Uppsala, Sweden, licentiate, 1898. SPOUSE: Married. CHILDREN: 2 daughters. CAREER: Djursholm Grammar School, Teacher, 1893-96; Stockholm, Sweden, Newspaper Reporter, 1896-98; Royal Library, Stockholm, Sweden, Librarian, 1898-03; Agricultural Academy, Sweden, Librarian, 1903-05.

Selected Publications: *Vidmarks-och Karlekvisor*. Stockholm: J. Seligman, 1906. *Flora och Pomona*. Stockholm: Wahlstrom & Widstrand, 1906. *Fridolins Visor och Andra Dikter*. Stockholm: Wahlstrom & Widstrand, 1914. *Flora och Bellona; Dikter*. Stockholm: Wahlstrom & Widstrand, 1918. *Hosthorn; Dikter*. Stockholm: Wahlstrom & Widstrand, 1927.

For More Information See: *Columbia Dictionary of Modern European Literature*. New York: Columbia U. Press, 1947, 436-37. *Twentieth Century Authors*. New York: H.W. Wilson, 1942, 746.

Commentary: Erik Karlfeldt won the prize in 1918, but refused it, instead devoting himself to the affairs of the Academy as member and secretary from 1904 until his death. He was awarded a second prize posthumously in 1931 for his body of poetry. The presentation talked about representing "...our character with a style and a genuineness that we should like to be ours..." and about singing "...with singular power and exquisite charm of the tradition of our people...." (P.K.)

1919

Spitteler, Carl Friedrich Georg (Felix Tan'-dem) 144
PRIZE: Literature, 1919. BORN: April 24, 1845; Liesthal, Switzerland. DIED: December 28, 1924; Lucerne, Switzerland. PARENTS: Father, Carl Spitteler; Mother, Anna Dorothea Brodbeck. NATIONALITY: Swiss. RELIGION: Rejected doctrine; from Protestant background. EDUCATION: Univ. of Basel, Switzerland, theology degree, 1870. SPOUSE: Marie Opden Hoff, married 1883. CHILDREN: 2 daughters. CAREER: Saint Petersburg, Russia, Private Tutor, 1871-79; Neuveville Schools, Berne, Switzerland, Teacher, 1881-85; *Grenzpost*, Basel, Switzerland, Reporter, 1885-86; *Neue Zurcher Zeitung*, Reporter, 1890-92.

Selected Publications: *Lachende Wahrheiten*. Leipzig, Germany: E. Diederichs, 1898 (*Laughing Truths*. Tr. by James F. Muirhead. New York: G.P. Putnam's Sons, 1927). *Der Olympischer Fruhling* (*Olympian Spring*). Leipzig, Germany: E. Diederichs, 1900-05. *Glockenlieder* (*Bell Songs*). Jena, Germany: E. Diederichs, 1906. *Imago*. Jena, Germany: E. Diederichs, 1906. *Prometheus and Epimetheus*. Jena, Germany: E. Diederichs, 1906 (*Prometheus and Epimetheus*. Tr. by James F. Muirhead. New York: Scribner's, 1931). *Die Madchenfeinde*. Jena, Germany: E. Diederichs, 1907 (*Two Little Misogynists*. Tr. by Mme. la Vicomtesse Le Roquette-Buisson. New York: H. Hold, 1922). *Meine Fruhesten Erlebnisse* (*My Earliest Experiences*). Jena, Germany: E. Diederichs, 1914. *Prometheus der Dulder*. Jena, Germany: E. Diederichs, 1924.

For More Information See: Boesche, A. *The Life and Works of Carl Spitteler*. Albany, NY: J.B. Lyon, 1913-14. "Carl Spitteler." *The London Mercury* 16 (1927): 53-61. *Columbia Dictionary of Modern European Literature*. New York: Columbia U. Press, 1947, 775-76.

Commentary: Carl Spitteler was awarded the Nobel Prize "in special appreciation of his epic, *Olympischer Frühling*." It was compared to the writings of Homer and to *Faust* by the presenter. Spitteler's work is notable for its blend of idealistic hope in the individual and pessimistic view of the world as a whole. (C.C. and J.H.S.)

1920

Hamsun, Knut (Hamsund, Knud Pedersen) 145
PRIZE: Literature, 1920. BORN: August 4, 1859; Lom, Norway. DIED: February 19, 1952; Nörholmen, Norway. PARENTS: Father, Peder Pedersen Hamsund; Mother, Tora Olsdatter Garmostraeet Hamsund. NATIONALITY: Norwegian. RELIGION: Rejected organized Christianity; from Lutheran background. EDUCATION: No college degrees. SPOUSE: Bergljot Beck, married 1898, divorced 1906; Marie Andersen, married 1908.

CHILDREN: Victoria, daughter; Arild, son; Tore, son; Ellinor, daughter; Cecilia, daughter. CAREER: Norway, World Traveler early in life; Farmer and Writer in adult life. OTHER AWARDS: Goethe Prize, 1934 (accepted medal, refused money).

Selected Publications: *Sult.* Copenhagen: Jörgensen, 1890 (*Hunger.* Tr. by George Egerton. London: Smithers, 1899). *Pan.* Copenhagen: Philipsen, 1894 (*Pan.* Tr. by W.W. Worster. London: Gyldendal, 1920). *Victoria, en Kaerligheds Historie.* Kristiania: Cammermeyer, 1898 (*Victoria: A Love Story.* Tr. by Oliver Stallybrass. New York: Farrar, Straus, Giroux, 1969). *Markens gröde.* Kristiania: Gyldendal, 1920 (*Growth of the Soil.* Tr. by W.W. Worster. New York: Knopf, 1923). *Landstrykere.* Oslo: Gyldendal, 1927 (*Wayfarers.* Tr. by James McFarlane. New York: Farrar, Straus, Giroux, 1980). *August.* Oslo: Gyldendal, 1930 (*August.* Tr. by Eugene Gay-Tifft. New York: Coward-McCann, 1931). *Men livet lever.* Oslo: Gyldendal, 1933 (*The Road Leads On.* Tr. by Eugene Gay-Tifft. New York: Coward-McCann, 1934).

For More Information See: Buttry, Dolores. "Knut Hamsun: A Scandinavian Rousseau." Ph.D. diss. U. of Illinois at Urbana-Champaign, 1978. *Cyclopedia of World Authors.* Englewood Cliffs, NJ: Salem Press, 1974, 788-90. Ostby, Arvid. *Knut Hamsun: En bibliografi.* Oslo: Gyldendal, 1972. Naess, Harald. *Knut Hamsun.* Boston: Twayne, 1984. *Paa gjengrodde stier.* Oslo: Gyldendal, 1949 (Memoirs) (*On Overgrown Paths.* Tr. by Carl L. Anderson. New York: Paul Ericksson, 1967). *Twentieth Century Authors.* New York: H.W. Wilson, 1942, 609-11.

Commentary: Knut Hamsun received the Nobel Award "for his monumental work, *Growth of the Soil*," which depicted an archetypal pioneer farmer, the love of nature, and the simple life. His output of poetry, short stories, and novels reflects his development from a restless vagabond to farmer and family man. Because of his reverence for everything German, his countrymen's admiration for him cooled after the Nazi occupation of Norway. He remains more respected abroad than in his home country. (S.O.)

1921

France, Anatole (Thibault, Jacques Anatole-François) 146

PRIZE: Literature, 1921. BORN: April 16, 1844; Paris, France. DIED: October 12, 1924; La Bechéllerie, France. PARENTS: Father, François-Noël Thibault; Mother, Antoinette Gallas Thibault. NATIONALITY: French. RELIGION: "Neo-pagan"; from Catholic background. EDUCATION: College Stanislas, France, baccalaureate, 1864. SPOUSE: Marie-Valérie Guérin de Sauville, married April 28, 1877, divorced August 3, 1893; Marie-Héloïse Laprévotte, married 1920. CHILDREN: Suzanne, daughter. CAREER: Bibliothéque du Sénat, Librarian, 1876-90; France, Free-lance Journalist, 1862-77; *Le Temps*, Editor, 1888.

Selected Publications: *Le Crime de Sylvestre Bonnard, membre de l'Institute.* Paris: Calmann-Lévy, 1881 (*Crime of Sylvester Bonnard.* Tr. by Lafcadio Hearn. New York: Dodd-Mead, 1918). *Thaïs.* Paris: Calmann-Lévy, 1890 (*Thaïs.* Tr. by Robert Douglas. New York: Macmillan, 1929). *L'Étui de Nacre.* Paris: Calmann-Lévy, 1892 (*The Mother of Pearl.* Tr. by

Frederic Chapman. London: John Lane, 1908). *La Rotisserie de la Reine Pedauque.* Paris: Calmann-Lévy, 1893 (*At the Sign of the Reine Pedauque.* Tr. by Wilfred Jackson, London: John Lane, 1912). *Le Lys Rouge.* Paris: Calmann-Lévy, 1899 (*The Red Lily.* Tr. by Wilfred Stephens. London: John Lane Company, 1912). *Sur la Pièrre Blanche.* Paris: Calmann-Lévy, c 1900 (*The White Stone.* Tr. by Charles E. Roche. London: John Lane, 1909-23). *L'île des Pinqouins.* Paris: Calmann-Lévy, 1908 (*Penquin Island.* Tr. by A.W. Evans. New York: Grosset & Dunlap, 1909). *Les Dieux ont Soif.* New York: Macmillan; Paris: Calmann-Lévy, 1912 (*The Gods are Athirst.* Tr. by Alfred Allison. London: John Lane, 1913). *La Revolte des Anges.* Paris: Calmann-Lévy, 1914 (*The Revolt of the Angels.* Tr. by Mrs. Wilfred Jackson. New York: John Lane, 1914). *Histoire Contémporaine.* Paris: Calmann-Lévy, 1920-21. *La Vie en Fleur.* Paris: Calmann-Lévy, 1922 (*The Bloom of Life.* Tr. by James Lewis May. New York: Dodd, Mead & Co., n.d.). *Works of Anatole France in English Translation.* Ed. by Frederic Chapman. 39 volumes. New York: John Lane Co., 1928.

For More Information See: Axelrad, Jacob. *Anatole France: A Life Without Illusions, 1844-1924.* New York: Harper, 1944. *Cyclopedia of World Authors.* New York: Harper, 1958, 376-78. Dargan, Edwin Preston. *Anatole France (1844-1896).* New York: Oxford U. Press, 1937. *The Oxford Companion to French Literature.* Harvey, Sir Paul, and Heseltine, J.E., eds. Oxford: The Clarendon Press, 1969, 286-87. Jefferson, Carter. *Anatole France: The Politics of Skepticism.* New Brunswick, NJ: Rutgers U. Press, 1965. Sareil, Jean. *Anatole France et Voltaire.* Geneva: Droz, 1961. Tylden-Wright, David. *Anatole France.* New York: Walker & Co., 1967. Virtanen, Reino. *Anatole France.* New York: Twayne, 1968.

Commentary: The award to Anatole France was given "in recognition of his splendid activity as an author—an activity marked by noble style, large hearted humanity, charm and French spirit." This activity covered a span of more than five decades, from publication of his first book, *Alfred de Vigny,* in 1868, to *La Vie en Fleur,* in 1922. During this period France labored as novelist, critic, reviewer, essayist, and editor. In this diverse work he displayed a rich erudition, a subtle irony, and a constant strain of skepticism. By the end of the 1890s, he was the leading French literary figure. Within a few years after his death, however, there was a reaction against his work—partly literary, partly political—from which his reputation has never recovered. As one scholar puts it: He "offers an interesting case of great fame followed by abrupt decline." (G.K.)

1922

Benavente y Martinez, Jacinto 147

PRIZE: Literature, 1922. BORN: August 12, 1866; Madrid, Spain. DIED: July 14, 1954; Madrid, Spain. PARENTS: Father, Mariano Benavente y Gonzáles; Mother, Venancia Martinez. NATIONALITY: Spanish. RELIGION: Catholic. EDUCATION: No college degrees. SPOUSE: None. CHILDREN: None. CAREER: Writer, Editor, Theatrical Worker, Spain. OTHER AWARDS: Gran Cruz de Alphonso XIII, Spain, 1923.

Selected Publications: *El Nido Ajeno* (*The Intruder*). (Premiered October 6, 1894). *La Noche del Sabado*. Barcelona: Editorial Cisne, 1903 (*Saturday Night*. Tr. by John Garrett Underhill. Boston: R.G. Badger, 1918). *Los Intereses Creados* (*Bonds of Interest*). (Premiered December 9, 1907). In *Los Intereses Creados*. Madrid: Anaya, 1965, 5-28. *Senora Ama* (*The Lady of the House*). (Premiered February 22, 1908). *La Fuerza Brutta*. Barcelona: Teatralia, 1909 (*Brute Force*. Tr. by John Garrett Underhill. New York: S. French, 1935). *El Principe Que Todo Lo Aprendio en Los Libros*. San Juan: Editorial Teresa Martinez, 1909 (*The Prince Who Learned Everything Out of Books*. Tr. by John Garrett Underhill. Boston: R.G. Badger, 1919). *La Malquerida* (*The Ill-Beloved*). (Premiered December 12, 1913). *Pepa Doncel* (*Don Juan's Servant*). Madrid: Hernando, 1928. *La Honradez de la Cerradura* (*The Secret of the Keyhole*). Buenos Aires: Espasa-Calpe Argentina, 1943. *Su Amante Esposa* (*An Enchanted Hour*). Madrid: Aguilar, 1951.

For More Information See: *Encyclopedia of World Literature*. Englewood Cliffs, NJ: Salem Press, 1958 (Volume 1), 117-18. Penuelas, Marcelino. *Jacinto Benavente*. Tr. by Kay Engler. New York: Twayne, 1968. Starkie, Walter. *Jacinto Benavente*. New York: H. Milford, 1982.

Commentary: The Nobel Prize was awarded to Jacinto Benavente y Martinez for "the talent that he has shown, as a continuator of the illustrious traditions of Spanish drama." Essayist and literary critic, Benavente is best remembered for his theatre, throughout which the theme of love is most important. In his vast and productive literary life, his preoccupation was to show that love was the definitive and certain way to reach sincere kindness, truth, and justice. His best and most popular plays, *The Bonds of Interest* (1907), *The Lady of the House* (1908), and *The Passion Flower* (1913), attest to this goal. (F.R.P.)

1923

Yeats, William Butler   148

PRIZE: Literature, 1923. BORN: June 13, 1865; Dublin, Ireland. DIED: January 28, 1939; Cap Martin, France. PARENTS: Father, John Butler Yeats; Mother, Susan Pollexfen Yeats. NATIONALITY: Irish. RELIGION: Antireligious; from Protestant (Church of Ireland) background. EDUCATION: No college degrees. SPOUSE: Georgie Hyde-Lees, married October 21, 1917. CHILDREN: Ann Butler, daughter; Michael, son. CAREER: *Beltaine*, Editor, 1899-1900; *Samhain*, Editor, 1901-08; *The Arrow*, Editor, 1908-09; Abbey Theatre, Dublin, Ireland, Director, 1904-39. OTHER AWARDS: Royal Academy Prize, 1899; Knighthood, 1915 (refused).

Selected Publications: *The Celtic Twilight. Men and Women, Dhouls and Faeries*. London: Lawrence and Bullen, 1893. *The Wind among the Reeds*. London: John Lane, 1899. *The Collected Works*. 8 volumes. London: Chapman & Hall, 1908. *Responsibilities, and Other Poems*. London: Macmillan and Co., 1916. *Essays*. London: Macmillan and Co., 1924. *The Tower*. London: Macmillan and Co., 1928. *The Winding Stair*. New York: The Foundation Press, 1929. *The Collected Poems*. London: Macmillan and Co., 1933. *The Collected Plays*. London: Macmillan and Co., 1934. *Last Poems and Plays*. London: Macmillan and Co., 1940.

For More Information See: Cowell, Raymond. *W.B. Yeats*. New York: Arco, 1970. Ellman, Richard. *Yeats: The Man and the Masks*. New York: Norton, 1948. *Encyclopedia of World Biography*. New York: McGraw-Hill, 1973, 480-83. Jeffares, Alexander. *W.B. Yeats: Man and Poet*. New York: Barnes and Noble, 1966. *Twentieth Century Authors*. New York: H.W. Wilson, 1942, 1560-62.

Commentary: William Butler Yeats received the Nobel Prize "for his consistently emotional poetry, which in the strictest artistic form expresses a people's spirit." He went on to become what many critics consider the most important poet of the twentieth century, integrating into his poetry and plays lifelong concerns with theosophy, symbolism, Irish folklore, the Irish cause, and occultism. His contributions extended to development of the arts and to personal involvement in the politics of the Irish cause. (L.P.)

1924

Reymont, Wladyslaw Stanislaw (Rejment, Wladyslaw Stanislaw)   149

PRIZE: Literature, 1924. BORN: May 7, 1867; Kobiele Weilkie, Poland. DIED: December 5, 1925; Warsaw, Poland. PARENTS: Father, Jozef Rejment; Mother, Antonia Kupcynska Rejment. NATIONALITY: Polish. RELIGION: Catholic. EDUCATION: No colleges degrees. SPOUSE: None. CHILDREN: None. CAREER: Writer.

Selected Publications: *The Commedienne*. Tr. by Edmund Obecny. New York: G. P. Putman's Sons, 1920. *The Peasants*. Tr. by Michael H. Dziewicki. 4 volumes. New York: Knopf, 1924-25. *The Promised Land*. Tr. by Michael H. Dziewicki. 2 volumes. New York: Knopf, 1927.

For More Information See: *Columbia Dictionary of Modern European Literature*. New York: Columbia Press, 1947, 671-72. Krzyzanowski, Jerzy K. *Wladyslaw Stanislaw Reymont*. New York: Twayne, 1972.

Commentary: Wladyslaw Reymont received the Nobel Prize "for his great national epic, *The Peasants*," which described in imaginative form the rural life and landscape of Poland. His early work was naturalistic and gradually developed into the blend of realism and symbolism that characterized *The Peasants* and later work. (J.H.S.)

1925

Shaw, George Bernard   150

PRIZE: Literature, 1925. BORN: July 26, 1856; Dublin, Ireland. DIED: November 2, 1950; Hertfordshire, England. PARENTS: Father, George Carr Shaw; Mother, Elizabeth Gurly Shaw. NATIONALITY: Irish. RELIGION: Antifundamentalist; from Christian background. EDUCATION: No college degrees. SPOUSE: Charlotte Payne-Townshend, married 1898. CHILDREN: None. CAREER: Edison Telephone Company, London, England, Clerk, 1879-80; *Star*, Critic, 1888-90; *The World*, Critic, 1890-94; *Saturday Review*, Critic, 1895-98; Writer. OTHER AWARDS: Order of Merit (refused).

Selected Publications: *Widowers' Houses: A Comedy*. London: Henry, 1893. *The Devil's Disciple: A Melodrama in Three Acts*. London: Grant Richards, 1901.

Mrs. Warren's Profession: A Play in Four Acts. London: Grant Richards, 1902. *Man and Superman.* Cambridge, MA.: The University Press, 1903. *Arms and the Man: A Pleasant Play.* New York: Brentano's, 1905. *Caesar and Cleopatra: A History.* London: Constable, 1905. *Candida: A Mystery.* London: Constable, 1905. *The Philanderer: An Unpleasant Play.* New York: Brentano's, 1905. *Captain Brassbound's Conversion: An Adventure.* London: Constable, 1906. *Major Barbara.* New York: Brentano's, 1907. *The Doctor's Dilemma.* New York: Brentano's, 1911. *Pygmalion: A Play in Five Acts.* London: Constable, 1912. *Heartbreak House.* Leipzig, Germany: Tauchnitz, 1921. *Back to Methuselah: A Metabiological Pentateuch.* London: Constable, 1921. *The Apple Cart: A Political Extravaganza.* London: Constable, 1930. *The Political Madhouse in America and Nearer Home: A Lecture.* London: Constable, 1933.

For More Information See: Chappelow, Allan. *Shaw the Villager and Human Being: A Biographical Symposium.* New York: Macmillan, 1962. Harris, Frank. *Bernard Shaw.* Garden City, NY: Garden City Publishing Company, Inc., 1931. Henderson, Archibald. *George Bernard Shaw: Man of the Century.* New York: Appleton-Century Crofts, 1956.

Commentary: George Bernard Shaw was the Nobel recipient "for his work which is marked by both idealism and humanity, its stimulating satire often being infused with a singular poetic beauty." Shaw's writings owed much to his lifelong espousal of socialism and his impressive knowledge of music, drama, philosophy, and biology. He was not only a great playwright, but a brilliant music and drama critic, a noted essayist, and a novelist of some repute. (J.L. and J.H.S.)

1926

Deledda, Grazia (Madesani, Grazia)   151
PRIZE: Literature, 1926. BORN: September 27, 1871; Nuoro, Sardinia, Italy. DIED: August 16, 1936; Cervia, Italy. PARENTS: Father, Giovantonio Deledda; Mother, Chrisceda Cambosu Deledda. NATIONALITY: Italian. RELIGION: Catholic. EDUCATION: No college degrees. SPOUSE: Palmiro Madesani; married January 11, 1900. CHILDREN: Sardus, son; Franz, son. CAREER: Writer.

Selected Publications: *Il Vecchio della Montagna* (*The Old Man of the Mountain*). Milan: Fratelli Treves, 1900. *Elias Portolu: Romanzo.* Milan: Fratelli Treves, 1903. *Cenere: Romanzo.* Rome: Nuova Antologia, 1904 (*Ashes: A Sardinian Story.* Tr. by Helen Hester Colvell. London: J. Lane, 1908). *L'Edera: Romanzo* (*The Ivy*). Rome: Nuova Antologia, 1908. *Chiaroscuro: Novella* (*Light and Dark*). Milan: Fratelli Treves, 1912. *Il Fanciulla Nascosto* (*The Hidden Boy*). Milan: Fratelli Treves, 1915. *La Madre: Romanzo.* Milan: Fratelli Treves, 1920 (*The Mother.* Tr. by Mary G. Steegmann. New York: Macmillan, 1928).

For More Information See: Mundula, Mercede. *Grazia Deledda.* Rome: A. F. Forniggini, 1929. *Twentieth Century Authors.* New York: H. W. Wilson, 1942, 368-69.

Commentary: The Academy recognized Grazia Deledda "for her idealistically inspired writings which with plastic clarity picture the life on her native island and with depth and sympathy deal with human problems in general." Deledda's earlier material revolved around the life and the customs of Sardinia, with theme a less important part of the writing. Gradually, and more powerfully in her later works, her only message—"everything is hatred, blood and pain; but, perhaps, everything will be conquered one day by means of love and good will"—emerges in her writings. (J.H.S.)

1927

Bergson, Henri Louis   152
PRIZE: Literature, 1927. BORN: October 18, 1859; Paris, France. DIED: January 4, 1941; Paris, France. PARENTS: Father, Varsovie Michael Bergson; Mother, Katharine Levinson Bergson. NATIONALITY: French. RELIGION: Jewish. EDUCATION: École Normale Supérieure, France;, Licencié és Lettres, 1881; Univ. of Paris, France, Docteur-és-Lettres, 1889. SPOUSE: Louise Neuburger, married 1891. CHILDREN: Jeanne Bergson, daughter. CAREER: Lycée of Angers, France, Professor, 1881-83; Lycée of Clermont-Ferrand, France, Professor, 1883-88; College Rollin and Lycée Henry IV, France, Professor, 1888-98; École Normale Supérieure, France, Professor, 1898-1900; Collège de France, Professor, 1900-18. OTHER AWARDS: Nicholas Murray Butler Gold Medal, 1940.

Selected Publications: *Essai Sur les Données Immédiates de la Conscience.* Paris: Félix Alcan, 1889 (*Time and Free Will: An Essay on the Immediate Data of Consciousness.* Tr. by F.L. Pogson. New York: Macmillan, 1910). *Matiére et Mémoire: Essai Sur la Relation du Corps Avec L'Spirit.* Paris: Félix Alcan, 1896 (*Matter and Memory.* Tr. by Nancy Paul and W. Scott Palmer. New York: Macmillan, 1911). *Le Rire: Essai Sur la Signification du Comique.* Paris: Félix Alcan, 1900 (*Laughter: An Essay on the Meaning of the Comic.* Tr. by Cloudesly Brereton and Fred Rothwell. New York: Macmillan, 1911). "Introduction à la Métaphysique." *Revue de Métaphysique et de Morale* (29 Janvier 1903): 1-36. *L'Evolution Creatrice.* Paris: Félix Alcan, 1907 (*Creative Evolution.* Tr. by Arthur Mitchell. New York: Holt and Co., 1911). *L'Energie Spirituelle.* Paris: Félix Alcan, 1919 (*Mind Energy, Lectures and Essays.* Tr. by H. Wildon Carr. London: Macmillan and Co., 1920). *Durée et Simultaneite.* Paris: Félix Alcan, 1922 (*Duration and Simultaneity, with Reference to Einstein's Theory.* Tr. by Leon Jacobson. New York: Bobbs-Merrill, 1966). *Les Deux Sources de la Morale et de la Religion.* Paris: Félix Alcan, 1932 (*The Two Sources of Morality and Religion.* Tr. by Ashley Andra, Cloudesly Brereton, and W. Horsfal Carter. London: Macmillan and Co., 1935).

For More Information See: Alexander, Ian W. *Bergson, Philosopher of Reflection.* New York: Hillary House, 1957. *Encyclopedia of World Biography.* New York: McGraw-Hill, 1973, 517-19. Gunter, Pete A.Y. *Bergson and the Evolution of Physics.* Knoxville, TN: U. of Tennessee Press, 1969. LeRoy, Edouard. *The New Philosophy of Henri Bergson.* New York: Holt, 1913.

Commentary: Although Henri Bergson's Nobel Prize has been linked in the public mind with his masterwork *Creative Evolution*, the prize was awarded him for the full scope of his writings, which provided a forum for new ideas in aesthetics, psychology, biology, and philosophy. The citation read "in recognition of his rich and vitalizing ideas and the brilliant skill with which they are presented." In the first three decades of the twentieth century, Bergson's books, translated into more than 20 languages, extended his influence throughout the world. (P.A.G.)

1928

Undset, Sigrid   **153**
PRIZE: Literature, 1928. BORN: May 20, 1882; Kalundborg, Denmark. DIED: June 10, 1949; Lillehammer, Norway. PARENTS: Father, Ingvald Martin Undset; Mother, Anna Charlotte Gyth Undset. NATIONALITY: Danish; later Norwegian citizen. RELIGION: Catholic; from Lutheran background. EDUCATION: No college degrees. SPOUSE: Anders Castus Svarstad, married 1912, divorced 1925. CHILDREN: Anders, son; Maren Charlotte, daughter; Hans, son. CAREER: Secretary, 1898-1909; Writer. OTHER AWARDS: Grand Cross of the Order of St. Olaf, Norway, 1947.

Selected Publications: *Viga Ljot og Vigdis: Roman.* Olten, Denmark: Walter, 1909 (*Gunnar's Daughter.* Tr. by Arthur G. Chater. London: Cassell, 1931). *Vaaren* (*Spring*). Oslo: H. Aschehoug, 1914. *Kristin Lavansdatter.* 3 volumes. Oslo: H. Aschehoug, 1920-22. *Fru Marta Oulie.* Oslo: H. Aschehoug, 1921. *Olav Audunsson: Hestviken.* 2 volumes. Oslo: H. Aschehoug, 1925. *Olav Audunsson og Hans Börn.* Oslo: H. Aschehoug, 1927. *Gymnadenia.* Oslo: H. Aschehoug, 1929 (*The Wild Orchid.* Tr. by Arthur G. Chater. New York: Alfred A. Knopf, 1931). *Den Braendende Busk.* Oslo: H. Aschehoug, 1930 (*The Burning Bush.* Tr. by Arthur G. Chater. London: Cassell, 1932). *Elleve år.* Oslo: H. Aschehoug, 1934 (*The Longest Years.* Tr. by Arthur G. Chater. New York: A.A. Knopf, 1935). *Madam Dorthe.* Frankfurt am Main: Buchergilde, 1939 (*Madam Dorothea.* Tr. by Arthur G. Chater. 2 volumes. New York: A.A. Knopf, 1940).

For More Information See: Bayerschmidt, Carl. *Sigrid Undset.* New York: Twayne Publishers, 1970. *Encyclopedia of World Biography.* New York: McGraw-Hill, 1973 (Volume 11), 56-57. *Encyclopedia of World Literature in the 20th Century.* New York: Ungar Publishing, 1971 (Volume 3), 451-52.

Commentary: Sigrid Undset's prize was awarded "mainly in her view of her splendid descriptions of Scandinavian life in the Middle Ages." Her early novels dealt with the problems of young women in a man's world looking for meaning in life. Her psychological insights and religious convictions were then turned to the writing of the historical sagas cited by the Committee. Throughout her writing career, Undset continued to explore woman's role and the erotic life. (J.H.S.)

1929

Mann, Paul Thomas   **154**
PRIZE: Literature, 1929. BORN: June 6, 1875; Lübeck, Germany. DIED: August 12, 1955; Zurich, Switzerland. PARENTS: Father, Johann Heinrich Mann; Mother, Julia da Silva-Bruhns Mann. NATIONALITY: German; later Czechoslovakian and American citizen. RELIGION: Protestant. EDUCATION: No college degrees. SPOUSE: Katja Pringsheim, married 1905. CHILDREN: Erika Julia Hedwig, daughter; Monika, daughter; Elisabeth

Veronika, daughter; Klaus Heinrich, son; Angelus Gottfried, son; Michael Thomas, son. CAREER: Germany and United States, Writer. OTHER AWARDS: Prussian Academy of Arts, 1926; Medal of Service, American Academy of Arts and Letters, 1949; Goethe Prize, Frankfurt, Germany, 1949; Goethe Prize, Weimar, Germany, 1949; Pegasus Medallion, American Academy of Art and Literature, 1950; Antonio Feltrinelli Prize, Academia Nazionale dei Lincei, 1952; Cross of the Legion of Honor, France, 1952.

Selected Publications: *Buddenbrooks.* Berlin: S. Fischer, 1901. *Der Tod in Venedig.* Munich: Hyperion Verlag Hans von Weber, 1912 (*Death in Venice.* London: Martin Secker, 1928). *Der Zauberberg.* Berlin: S. Fischer, 1924 (*The Magic Mountain.* New York: Knopf, 1927). *Joseph und Seine Brüder.* Berlin: S. Fischer, 1933 (*Joseph and His Brothers.* Tr. by H. T. Lowe-Porter. New York: A.A. Knopf, 1934). *Doktor Faustus.* Frankfurt: S. Fischer, 1947 (*Doctor Faustus.* Tr. by H.T. Lowe-Porter, New York: Modern Library, 1948). *Confessions of Felix Krull, Confidence Man.* Tr. by Denver Lindley. New York: New American Library, 1957.

For More Information See: Bürgin, Hans, and Mayer, Hans-Otto. *Thomas Mann: A Chronicle of His Life.* Tr. by Eugene Dobson. University, AL: Alabama U. Press, 1969. *Current Biography Yearbook.* New York: H.W. Wilson, 1942, 561-64. Feuerlicht, Ignace. *Thomas Mann.* New York: Twayne, 1968.

Commentary: When Thomas Mann's award cited "his great novel, *Buddenbrooks*, which in the course of the years has found greater and greater recognition as a classic work of the present day," nearly half of his writing career remained before him and many of his greatest works had not yet been written. A study of the decline of four generations of a German family, the novel expressed Nietzchean themes of the rift between health and will on one hand, and the artist and sensitivity on the other. This theme was further developed in other works such as *Death in Venice. The Magic Mountain* paralleled a young man's musings on death with World War I Germany, as later *Doctor Faustus* found parallels between a possessed composer and Germany under the Nazis. Political essays opposing the Nazis forced him to leave Germany in the '30s. He also wrote many essays on literary figures. In his Nobel acceptance speech, Mann said he put the prize "at the feet of my country and people...dedicated to the German soul," and throughout his exile Mann expressed that soul at its best, with his love for family, intellectualism, satiric bent, and humanity. (E.B.)

1930

Lewis, Harry Sinclair   **155**
PRIZE: Literature, 1930. BORN: February 7, 1885; Sauk Centre, MN. DIED: January 10, 1951; Rome, Italy. PARENTS: Father, Emmet J. Lewis; Mother, Emma Kermott Lewis. NATIONALITY: American. RELIGION: Areligious; from Congregationalist background. EDUCATION: Yale Univ., CT, A.B., 1908. SPOUSE: Grace Hegger, married 1914, divorced 1925; Dorothy Thompson, married 1928, divorced 1942. CHILDREN: Wells, son; Michael, son. CAREER: *New Haven (CT) Journal and Courier, San Francisco (CA) Evening Bulletin*, Reporter, 1908-10; George H. Doran Co., Editor, 1910-14. OTHER AWARDS: Pulitzer Prize, 1926 (refused).

Selected Publications: *Main Street.* New York: Harcourt, Brace, 1920. *Babbitt.* New York: P.F. Collier, 1922. *Arrowsmith.* New York: Harcourt, Brace, 1925. *Elmer Gantry.* New York: Harcourt, Brace, 1927. *Dodsworth.* New York: Harcourt, Brace, 1929. *It Can't Happen Here.* New York: P.F. Collier, 1935. *Cass Timberlane.* New York: P.F. Collier, 1945. *Kingsblood Royal.* New York: Random House, 1947.

For More Information See: *Dictionary of American Biography, Supplement Five, 1951-55.* New York: Charles Scribner's Sons, 1977, 421-24. Gribstein, Sheldon. *Sinclair Lewis.* New York: Twayne Publishers, 1962. Schorer, Mark. *Sinclair Lewis: An American Life.* New York: McGraw-Hill, 1961. *Twentieth Century Authors.* New York: H.W. Wilson, 1942, 821-23. Van Doren, Carl. *Sinclair Lewis: A Biographical Sketch.* Garden City, NY: Doubleday, Doran, 1933.

Commentary: Sinclair Lewis's citation reads "for his great and living art of painting life, with a talent for creating types, with wit and humor," but as the first American recipient, his award also represented the international recognition of modern American writing. Lewis's five novels published in the 20s created from his background a mythical world that has density and vitality and provided a framework for his attacks on those values he both understood and scorned. Although Lewis wrote before and after, he was scarcely noticed by critics and readers except for the work he produced in the 20s. (J.S.)

1931

Karlfeldt, Erik Axel *see* entry 143

1932

Galsworthy, John   156
PRIZE: Literature, 1932. BORN: August 14, 1867; Kingston Hill, Surrey, England. DIED: January 31, 1933; Grove Lodge, Hampstead, London, England. PARENTS: Father, John Galsworthy; Mother, Blanche Bailey Bartleet. NATIONALITY: British. RELIGION: No organized religion; from Anglican background. EDUCATION: Oxford Univ., England, Bachelor in Law, 1890. SPOUSE: Ada Cooper, married September 23, 1905. CHILDREN: None. CAREER: Independently wealthy, Writer. OTHER AWARDS: Knighthood, 1918 (refused); Les Palmes D'Or, Belgium, 1919; Order of Merit, 1929.

Selected Publications: *From the Four Winds.* London: T. Fisher Unwin, 1897. *Jocelyn.* London: Duckworth and Co., 1898. *The Island Farisees.* London: W. Heinemann, 1904. *The Man of Property.* London: W. Heinemann, 1906. *Fraternity.* Leipzig, Germany: B. Tauchnitz, 1909. *Plays: The Silver Box: Joy: Strife.* London: Duckworth and Co., 1909. *The Silver Box.* New York; London: G.P. Putnam's Sons, 1909. *Justice: A Tragedy in Four Acts.* London: Duckworth and Co., 1910. *Strife: A Drama in Three Acts.* London: Duckworth and Co., 1910. *The Pigeon: A Fantasy in Three Acts.* London: Duckworth and Co., 1912. *The Dark Flower.* London: W. Heinemann, 1913. *The Fugitive: A Play in Four Acts.* London: Duckworth and Co., 1913. *The Freelands.* London: W. Heinemann, 1915. *Beyond.* London: W. Heinemann, 1917. *Saint's Progress.* London: W. Heinemann, 1919. *Villa Rubein,*

and Other Stories. London: W. Heinemann, 1923. *A Modern Comedy.* New York: C. Scribner's Sons, 1924-28. *Flowering Wilderness.* London: W. Heinemann, 1932.

For More Information See: Barker, Dudley. *The Man of Principle: A View of John Galsworthy.* Toronto: W. Heinemann, 1963. *Dictionary of Literary Biography.* Detroit, MI: Gale Research, 1985 (Volume 34), 153-74. Dupré, Catherine. *John Galsworthy: A Biography.* London: Collins, 1976. Marrot, H.V. *The Life and Letters of John Galsworthy.* London: W. Heinemann, 1935.

Commentary: John Galsworthy's award was for "his distinguished art of narration," with *The Forsyte Saga* (1922) being singled out for attention. The first work in this trilogy was *The Man of Property* (1906), which satirized the Forsyte family for their obsession with property; to this he added two other novels, *In Chancery* (1920) and *To Let* (1921). Galsworthy was also a successful playwright, frequently defending the underprivileged and condemning the British system of justice for its harshness; the play *Justice*(1910) so impressed Home Secretary Winston Churchill that he immediately initiated reforms in the prison system. (H.L.F.)

1933

Bunin, Ivan Alexeievich   157
PRIZE: Literature, 1933. BORN: October 22, 1870; Voronezh, Russia. DIED: November 8, 1953; Paris, France. PARENTS: Father, Aleksej Nikolaevic Bunin; Mother, Ljudmila Aleksandrovna Cubarova Bunin. NATIONALITY: Russian; later French resident. RELIGION: Eastern Orthodox. EDUCATION: No college degrees. SPOUSE: Anna Nikolaevna Cakni, married September 23, 1898, divorced 1902; Vera Nikolaevna Muromceva, married 1922. CHILDREN: Nicholas, son; Alexei, son; Ludmilla Chubarova, daughter. CAREER: Writer. OTHER AWARDS: Pushkin Prize, Russia, 1903.

Selected Publications: *The Dreams of Chang.* Tr. by Bernard Gilbert Guerney. New York: A.A. Knopf, 1923. *The Village.* Tr. by Isabel F. Hapgood. London: M. Secker, 1923. *Mitya's Love.* Tr. by Madelaine Boyd. New York: Holt, 1926. *The Gentleman from San Francisco.* Tr. by Bernard Gilbert Guerney. New York: A.A. Knopf, 1927. *Well of Days.* Tr. by Gleb Struve and Hamish Miles. London: Hogarth Press, 1933. *Elaghin Affair.* Tr. by Bernard Gilbert Guerney. New York: Funk and Wagnalls, 1935. *Dark Avenues.* Tr. by Richard Hare. London: J. Lehmann, 1949. *Memories and Portraits.* Tr. by Vera Traill and Robin Chancellor. London: J. Lehmann, 1951.

For More Information See: Connolly, Julian W. *Ivan Bunin.* Boston: Twayne, 1982. *Twentieth-Century Russian Literature.* London: Feffer and Simons, 1974, 31-32.

Commentary: Ivan Bunin won the Nobel Prize "for the strict artistry with which he has carried on the classical Russian traditions in prose writing." An accomplished translator and writer of both prose and poetry, his work was laden with symbolism and the recurrent themes of the uselessness of vanity and the nobility of human spirit. His most quoted work remains *The Gentleman from San Francisco.* (C.C. and J.H.S.)

1934

Pirandello, Luigi   158

PRIZE: Literature, 1934. BORN: June 28, 1867; Girgenti, Sicily. DIED: December 10, 1936; Rome, Italy. PARENTS: Father, Stefano Pirandello; Mother, Caterina Ricci-Gramitto Pirandello. NATIONALITY: Italian. RELIGION: Catholic. EDUCATION: Univ. of Bonn, Germany, Dr. Phil., 1891. SPOUSE: Marie Antonietta Portulano, married January 27, 1894. CHILDREN: Stefano, son; Fausto, son; Lietta, daughter. CAREER: Writer, 1891-98; R. Instituto Superiore di Majistero Femminile, Rome, Italy, Professor, 1898-1921; Teatro d'Arte di Roma, Italy, Director, 1925-28.

Selected Publications: *Erma Bifronte* (*Two-Faced Erma*). Milan, Italy: Fratelli Treves, 1906. *L'Escula* (*The Outcasts*). Milan, Italy: Treves, 1908. *Co si e (Se vi pare).* Rome: Nuova Antologia, 1918 (*Right You Are, If You Think You Are.* Tr. by Arthur Livingston. New York: Rialto Service Bureau, 1927). *Maschere Nude.* Milan, Italy: Fratelli Treves, 1918-20. *Ciascuno a Suo Modo.* Florence, Italy: R. Bemporad, 1920 (*Each in His Own Way.* Tr. by J. M. Dent. New York: E. P. Dutton & Co., 1923). *Sie Personnaggi in Cerca d'Autore.* Florence, Italy: R. Bemporad, 1921 (*Six Characters in Search of an Author.* Tr. by Frederick May. London: Heinemann, 1954). *Enrico IV.* Florence, Italy: R. Bemporad, 1922 (*Henry IV.* Tr. by J. M. Dent, New York: Dutton, 1923).

For More Information See: Guidice, Gaspare. *Pirandello: A Biography.* New York: Oxford U. Press, 1975. Ragusa, Olga. *Luigi Pirandello.* New York: Columbia U. Press, 1968. *Twentieth-Century Authors, First Supplement.* New York: H.W. Wilson, 1955, 778-79.

Commentary: "For his bold and ingenious revival of Italian dramatic and scenic art," Luigi Pirandello received the Nobel Prize. Pirandello's influence as a modern dramatist was not confined to the Italian theater. He was recognized as a major international figure in the theater of the twentieth century for his innovative techniques of philosophical and psychological drama, and he produced notable works as dramatist, novelist, short story writer, poet, and critic. (A.D.J.)

1936

O'Neill, Eugene Gladstone   159

PRIZE: Literature, 1936. BORN: October 16, 1888; New York, NY. DIED: November 27, 1953; Boston, MA. PARENTS: Father, James O'Neill; Mother, Ella Quinlan O'Neill. NATIONALITY: American. RELIGION: Catholic. EDUCATION: No college degrees. SPOUSE: Kathleen Jenkins, married October 4, 1909, divorced 1912; Agnes Boulton, married April 12, 1918, divorced July 1929; Carlotta Monterey, married July 1929. CHILDREN: Eugene Gladstone, son; Shane Rudreighe, son; Oona, daughter. CAREER: New England, Clerical and Manual Laborer, 1907-12; *New London (CT) Telegraph*, Reporter, 1912. OTHER AWARDS: Pulitzer Prize, 1920; Pulitzer Prize, 1922; Gold Medal, National Institute of Arts and Letters, 1923; Pulitzer Prize, 1928; Pulitzer Prize, 1957 (posthumous).

Selected Publications: *Beyond the Horizon.* 1920. *The Emperor Jones.* 1920. *Anna Christie.* 1921. *The Hairy Ape.* 1922. *Desire Under the Elms.* 1924. *The Great God Brown.* 1925. *Strange Interlude.* 1928.

Mourning Becomes Electra. 1931. *Ah, Wilderness!*. 1933. *The Iceman Cometh.* 1938. *A Moon for the Misbegotten.* 1943. *A Long Day's Journey into Night.* 1955.

For More Information See: *American Writers: A Collection of Literary Biographies.* New York: Charles Scribner's Sons, 1974 (Volume III), 385-408. Berlin, N. *Eugene O'Neill.* New York: Grove Press, 1982. *The National Cyclopedia of American Biography.* New York: James T. White and Co., 1924 (Current Volume A), 443-44. Skinner, Richard Dana. *Eugene O'Neill: A Poet's Quest.* New York: Longman's, Green, 1935. Winther, S.K. *Eugene O'Neill: A Critical Study.* New York: Russell, 1961.

Commentary: The Nobel Prize was awarded to Eugene O'Neill "for dramatic works of vital energy, sincerity and intensity of feeling, stamped with an original conception of tragedy." Although there has been disagreement with that evaluation, the corpus of O'Neill's work now seems to justify that selection of an important and memorable American dramatist whose influential dramas have been read, translated, and acted out around the world. (C.B.)

1937

Martin du Gard, Roger   160

PRIZE: Literature, 1937. BORN: March 22, 1881; Neuilly-sur-Seine, France. DIED: August 22, 1958; Belleme, France. PARENTS: Father, Paul Martin du Gard; Mother, Madeleine Winy Martin du Gard. NATIONALITY: French. RELIGION: No organized religion; from Catholic background. EDUCATION: Ecole des Chartes, France, baccalaureate, 1906. SPOUSE: Helene Foucault, married February 1906. CHILDREN: Christiane, daughter. CAREER: Writer.

Selected Publications: *Devener.* Paris: Societe d'Editions Litteraire et Artistique, 1908. *Jean Barois.* Paris: Edition de la Nouvelle Revue Française, 1913 (*Jean Barois.* Tr. by Stuart Gilbert. New York: Viking, 1949). *Les Thibaults.* 8 volumes. Paris: Gallimard, 1922-40. *Vieille France.* Paris: Gallimard, 1933 (*The Postman.* Tr. by John Russell. New York: Viking, 1955). *Note sur André Gide, 1913-1951.* Paris: Gallimard, 1951 (*Recollections of Andre Gide.* Tr. by John Russell. New York: Viking, 1953).

For More Information See: *The Oxford Companion to French Literature.* Oxford: Clarendon Press, 1959, 458-59. Savage, Catherine. *Roger Martin du Gard.* New York: Twayne Publishers, 1968.

Commentary: Roger Martin du Gard, novelist and playwright, received his Nobel Prize "for the artistic vigor and truthfulness with which he has pictured human contrasts as well as some fundamental aspects of contemporary life in the series of novels entitled *Les Thibault.*" The eight-part novel cited is one of a genre called the "roman-fleuve," a popular novelistic style of French writers in the twentieth century characterized by basing a collection of novels around a central character or theme. Martin du Gard's works illustrate his ability to observe and describe human nature with precision and detail, making his novels realistic psychological studies. His works are marked by central themes of turmoil caused by illness, suffering and death, evil, and loss of faith, all reflecting his own early religious upbringing and subsequent abandonment of his religion. (S.C.)

1938

Buck, Pearl Comfort Sydenstricker   161
PRIZE: Literature, 1938. BORN: June 26, 1892; Hillsboro, WV. DIED: March 6, 1973; Danby, VT. PARENTS: Father, Absalom Andrew Sydenstricker; Mother, Caroline Stulting Sydenstricker. NATIONALITY: American. RELIGION: Presbyterian. EDUCATION: Randolph-Macon College, VA, A.B., 1914; Cornell Univ., NY, M.A., 1926. SPOUSE: John Lossing Buck, married 1917, divorced 1935; Richard John Walsh, married 1935. CHILDREN: Carol, daughter; legally adopted children include Janice, daughter; Richard, son; John, son; Edgar, son; Jean, daughter; Henrietta, daughter; Theresa, daughter; Chieko, daughter; Johanna, daughter. CAREER: Univ. of Nanking, China, Intermittent Instructor, 1921-31. OTHER AWARDS: Laura Messenger Prize, Cornell U., 1926; Pulitzer Prize, 1931; Howells Medal, American Academy of Arts and Letters, 1935.

Selected Publications: *East Wind, West Wind.* New York: John Day, 1930. *The Good Earth.* New York: John Day, 1931. *Sons.* New York: John Day, 1932. *The Mother.* New York: John Day, 1934. *A House Divided.* New York: John Day, 1935. *The Exile.* New York: John Day, 1936. *Fighting Angel.* New York: John Day, 1936. *The Patriot.* New York: John Day, 1939. *Dragon Seed.* New York: John Day, 1941. *A Bridge for Passing.* New York: John Day, 1962.

For More Information See: *Current Biography Yearbook.* New York: H.W. Wilson, 1956, 82-84. Doyl, Paul A. *Pearl S. Buck.* New York: Twayne, 1965. Harris, Theodore. *Pearl S. Buck: A Biography.* 2 volumes. New York: John Day, 1969-71.

Commentary: Pearl Buck won the Nobel Prize "for her rich and genuine epic pictures of Chinese life, and for her masterly biographies." She saw herself as an interpreter of the nature of China and its people, among whom she lived, and brought into focus in her novels the conflict between the old and the new and the problems faced by Chinese women in both the old and new world. (V.V.M.)

1939

Sillanpää, Frans Eemil (Taata)   162
PRIZE: Literature, 1939. BORN: September 16, 1888; Hämeen Kyro, Finland. DIED: June 3, 1964; Helsinki, Finland. PARENTS: Father, Frans Henrik Sillanpää; Mother, Louisa Vilhelmüna Iisaksdottor Sillanpää. NATIONALITY: Finnish. RELIGION: Most probably Christian/Protestant. EDUCATION: No college degrees. SPOUSE: Sigrid Maria Salomäki, married September 11, 1916, died April 1939; Anna Armia von Hertzen, married November 1939. CHILDREN: 8 children. CAREER: Writer. OTHER AWARDS: Finnish State Pension, 1919; Aleksis Kivi Prize, 1937; Kordelin Foundation Prize, 1938; Frenckell Foundation Prize, 1938.

Selected Publications: *Hiltu ja Ragner* (*Hiltu and Ranger*). Porvoo, Finland: Soderström, 1923. *Hurskhas Kurjuus.* Helsinki: Otava, 1930 (*Meek Heritage.* Tr. by Alex Matson. London: Putnam, 1938). *Nuorena Nukkunut.* Helsinki: Otava, 1931 (*The Maid Silja: The*

History of the Last Offshoot of an Old Family Tree. Tr. by Alexander Matson. New York: The Macmillan Co., 1933). *Ihmiset Suviyossa, eepillinen sarja.* Helsinki: Otava, 1934 (*People in a Summer Night: An Epic Suite.* Tr. by Alexander Matson. Madison, WI: U. of Wisconsin Press, 1966). *Manniskor i Sommarnatten* (*A Man's Way*). Stockholm: Holger Schildt, 1935. *Miehentie Ahrolan Talon Oloista Paavon Isännyyden Vakiintuessa.* Helsinki: Otava, 1948.

For More Information See: *Encyclopedia of World Literature in the Twentieth Century.* New York: Frederick Publishing, 1975 (Volume 3), 273-74. *Twentieth Century Authors.* New York: H.W. Wilson, 1942, 1286-88.

Commentary: Frans Sillanpää received the Nobel "for his deep comprehension and exquisite art in painting the nature of his country and the life of its peasants in their mutual relations." The Finnish novelist and short-story writer wrote around elemental themes about the life and struggles of his people, and was a favorite both in Finland and Sweden before receiving world-wide acclaim. (J.H.S.)

1944

Jensen, Johannes Vilhelm (Lykke, Ivar)   163
PRIZE: Literature, 1944. BORN: January 20, 1873; Farso, Denmark. DIED: November 25, 1950; Copenhagen, Denmark. PARENTS: Father, Hans Jensen; Mother, Marie Kirstine Jensen. NATIONALITY: Danish. RELIGION: Freethinker; from Lutheran background. EDUCATION: Univ. of Copenhagen, Denmark, M.D., 1896. SPOUSE: Else Marie Ulrik, married 1904. CHILDREN: 3 sons. CAREER: Writer.

Selected Publications: *Himmerlandshistorier* (*Himmerland Stories*). Copenhagen: Gyldendal, 1898-1910. *Madame d'Ora.* Copenhagen: Gyldendal, 1904. *Hjulet* (*The Wheel*). Copenhagen: Gyldendal, 1905. *Den Lange Rejse.* Copenhagen: Gyldendal, 1908-22 (*The Long Journey.* Tr. by Arthur Chater. London: Gyldendal, 1922).

For More Information See: *Columbia Dictionary of Modern European Literature.* New York: Columbia U. Press, 1947, 544-45. Rossel, Sven H. *Johannes V. Jensen.* Boston: Twayne, 1984. *Twentieth Century Authors.* New York: H.W. Wilson, 1942, 723-24.

Commentary: Johannes Jensen received the Nobel Prize "for the rare strength and fertility of his poetic imagination, with which is combined an intellectual curiosity of wide scope and a bold, freshly creative style." Jensen was notable for his epic historical and imaginative prose, particularly the multivolume *Himmerlandshistorier* and *Den Lange Rejse.* He was also recognized as an accomplished poet, translator, essayist, and a lucid advocate of Darwin's theories. (P.K.)

1945

Mistral, Gabriela (Godoy y Alcayaga, Lucila)   164
PRIZE: Literature, 1945. BORN: April 7, 1889; Vicuna, Chile. DIED: January 10, 1957; New York, NY. PARENTS: Father, Jeronimo Godoy Villanueva; Mother, Petronila Alcayaga de Molina. NATIONALITY: Chilean. RELIGION: Catholic. EDUCATION: Pedagogical College, Chile, teacher's training, 1909. SPOUSE: None. CHIL-

DREN: Juan Miguel Godoy, son (adopted). CAREER: Liceo de Antofagasta, Chile, Teacher and Administrator, 1911-12; Liceo de los Andes, Chile, Teacher and Administrator, 1912-18; Liceo de Punte Arenas, Chile, Teacher and Administrator, 1918-20; Liceo de Temuco, Chile, Teacher and Administrator, 1920-21; Ministry of Education, Mexico, Adviser, 1922-24; Writer, Lecturer, and Diplomat thereafter. OTHER AWARDS: Laurel Wreath and Gold Crown, Writer's Society, Santiago, Chile, 1914.

Selected Publications: *Desolaçion* (*Despair*). New York: Spanish Institute, 1922. *Ternura* (*Tenderness*). Madrid: Satunio Calleja, 1924. *Tala* (*Ravage*). Buenos Aires: SUR, 1938. *Lagar* (*The Wine Press*). Santiago: Editorial del Pacifico, 1954.

For More Information See: *Current Biography Yearbook.* New York: H.W. Wilson, 1946, 397-400. De Vazquez, Margot Arce. *Gabriela Mistral: The Past and Her Work.* Tr. by Helene Masslo Anderson. New York: New York U. Press, 1964. Gazarian-Gautier, Marie-Lise. *Gabriela Mistral: The Teacher from the Valley of Elqui.* Chicago: Franciscan Herald Press, 1975.

Commentary: The Nobel Academy cited Gabriela Mistral "for her lyric poetry which, inspired by powerful emotions, has made her name a symbol of the idealistic aspirations of the entire Latin American world." Her despair on the loss of her lover through suicide led to her first powerful poetry, *Desolaçion*, her love for children to *Ternura* and *Tala*. In addition, Mistral was a guiding force in education in Chile and Mexico and a gifted Chilean diplomat in several countries and in international activities. (D.K.)

1946

Hesse, Herman (Lauscher, Hermann; Sinclair, Emil)   **165**
PRIZE: Literature, 1946. BORN: July 2, 1877; Calw, Germany. DIED: August 9, 1962; Montagnola, Switzerland. PARENTS: Father, Johannes Hesse; Mother, Marie Gundert Hesse. NATIONALITY: German; later Swiss citizen. RELIGION: Lutheran. EDUCATION: No college degrees. SPOUSE: Marie Bernoulli, married 1904, divorced 1923; Ruth Wenger, married January 1924, divorced 1927; Ninon Auslaender Dobrin, married November 1931. CHILDREN: Bruno, son; Heiner, son; Martin, son. CAREER: Clock Factory, Calw, Germany, Apprentice, 1894; Tubingen, Germany, Bookseller, 1895-99. OTHER AWARDS: Bauernfeld Prize, Vienna, 1904; Fontane Prize, 1920 (refused); Keller Prize, Zurich, 1936; Goethe Prize, Frankfurt, 1946; Raabe Prize, Brunswick, Germany, 1950; German Book Trade Peace Prize, 1955; Knight of the Order Pour le Merite, Germany, 1955.

Selected Publications: *Peter Camenzind.* Berlin: S. Fischer, 1904 (Tr. by Michael Roloff. New York: Farrar, Straus, 1968). *Unterm Rad.* Berlin: S. Fischer, 1906 (*Beneath the Wheel.* Tr. by Michael Roloff. New York: Farrar, Straus, 1968). *Gertrude.* Munich: A. Langen, 1910 (Tr. by Ralph Manheim. New York: Farrar, Straus, 1970). *Rosshalde.* Berlin: S. Fischer, 1914 (Tr. by Ralph Manheim. New York: Farrar, Straus, 1970). *Knulp: Drei Geschichten aus dem Leben Knulps.* Berlin: S. Fischer, 1915 (*Three Tales from the Life of Knulp.* Tr. by Ralph Manheim. New York: Farrar, Straus, 1971). *Maerchen.* Berlin: S. Fischer, 1918 (*Strange*

News from Another Star and Other Tales. Tr. by Denver Lindley. New York: Farrar, Straus, 1971). *Demian.* Berlin: S. Fischer, 1919 (Tr. by Michael Roloff and Michael Lebeck. New York: Harper, 1965). *Klingsors Letzter Sommer.* Berlin: S. Fischer, 1920 (*Klingsor's Last Summer.* Tr. by Richard Winston and Clara Winston. New York: Farrar, Straus, 1970). *Wanderung, Aufzeichnungen.* Berlin: S. Fischer, 1920 (*Wandering: Notes and Sketches.* Tr. by James Wright. New York: Farrar, Straus, 1972). *Siddhartha.* Berlin: S. Fischer, 1922 (Tr. by Hilda Rosner. New York: New Directions, 1951). *Der Steppenwolf.* Berlin: S. Fischer, 1927 (*Steppenwolf.* Tr. by Basil Creighton. New York: Holt, 1970). *Narziss und Goldmund.* Berlin: S. Fischer, 1930 (*Narcissus and Goldmund.* Tr. by Ursula Molinaro. New York: Farrar, Straus, 1968). *Die Morgenlandfahrt: Eine Erzaehlung.* Berlin: S. Fischer, 1932 (*The Journey to the East.* Tr. by Hilda Rosner. New York: Farrar, Straus, 1968). *Das Glasperlenspiel: Versuch einer Lebensbeschreibung des Magister Ludi Josef Knecht samt Knechts hintelassenen Schriften.* Zurich: Fretz & Wasmuth, 1943 (*Magister Ludi: The Glass Bead Game.* Tr. by Richard Winston and Clara Winston. New York: Holt, 1969). *Krieg und Frieden: Betrachtungen zu Krieg und Politik seit dem Jahre 1914.* Zurich: Fretz & Wasmuth, 1949 (*If the War Goes on: Reflections on War and Politics.* Tr. by Ralph Manheim. New York: Farrar, Straus, 1971). *My Belief: Essays on Life and Art.* Ed. by Theodore Ziolkowski, Tr. by Denver Lindley and Ralph Manheim. New York: Farrar, Straus, 1974. *Hours in the Garden and Other Poems*(Tr. by Rika Lesser. New York: Farrar, Straus, 1979).

For More Information See: *Contemporary Authors Permanent Series.* Detroit, MI: Gale Research, 1978 (Volume 2), 252-60. *Cyclopedia of World Authors.* New York: Harper, 1958, 849-50. Freedman, Ralph. *Hermann Hesse, Pilgrim of Crisis.* New York: Pantheon, 1978. Mileck, Joseph. *Hermann Hesse, Life and Art.* Berkeley, CA: U. of California Press, 1978. *Twentieth Century Authors.* New York: H.W. Wilson, 1942, 645-46.

Commentary: Herman Hesse's award was "for his inspired writings which, while growing in boldness and penetration, exemplify the classical humanitarian ideals and high qualities of style." His work, which examined the theme of man's search for his essential, true self as it conflicts with the world, and mirrored the stages of his own life, was nominated for the award by Thomas Mann. (M.K.)

1947

Gide, André Paul Guillaume   **166**
PRIZE: Literature, 1947. BORN: November 22, 1869; Paris, France. DIED: February 19, 1951; Paris, France. PARENTS: Father, Paul Gide; Mother, Juliette Rondeaux. NATIONALITY: French. RELIGION: Protestant; from Huguenot background. EDUCATION: École Alsaçienne, France, baccalaureate, 1889. SPOUSE: Madeleine Rondeaux, married 1895. CHILDREN: None. CAREER: *La Nouvelle Revue Française*, Founder and Editor, 1908-41.

Selected Publications: *L'Immoraliste.* Paris: Merceure de France, 1902 (*The Immoralist.* Tr. by Dorothy Bussy. New York: A.A. Knopf, 1930). *La Porte*

Étroite. Paris: Merceure de France, 1909 (*Strait Is the Gate*. Tr. by Dorothy Bussy. New York: A.A. Knopf, 1924). *Les Caves du Vatican*. Paris: Librarie Stock, 1914 (*The Vatican Swindle*. Tr. by Dorothy Bussy. New York: A.A. Knopf, 1925). *La Symphonie Pastorale*. Paris: Éditions de La Nouvelle Revue Française, 1919 (*The Pastoral Symphony*. Tr. by Dorothy Bussy. New York: A.A. Knopf, 1925). *Les Faux-Monnayeurs*. Paris: Éditions de La Nouvelle Revue Française, 1925 (*The Counterfeiters*. Tr. by Dorothy Bussy. New York: A.A. Knopf, 1927). *Journals 1889-1939*. Paris: Gallimard, 1939 (Tr. by Justin O'Brien. New York: A.A. Knopf, 1947).

For More Information See: "André Gide." *Saturday Review* (November 29, 1947): 20. Brèe, Germaine. *Gide*. New Brunswick, NJ: Rutgers U. Press, 1963. Guérard, Albert J. *André Gide*. 2d ed. Cambridge, MA: Harvard U. Press, 1969. O'Brien, Justin. "The Barely Posthumous Gide." *Saturday Review* (March 22, 1952): 21, 41-42. O'Brien, Justin. *Portrait of André Gide: A Critical Biography*. New York: A.A. Knopf, 1953. *The Reader's Encyclopedia*, 2d edition. New York: Crowell, 1965, 394-95.

Commentary: André Gide wrote over 50 volumes of novels, plays, poems, translations, criticism, journals, and travel books. Not surprisingly, the Nobel award was given not for any one work but "for his comprehensive and artistically significant writings, in which human problems and conditions have been presented with a fearless love of truth and keen psychological insight." Although Gide has had a broad and diverse influence on the twentieth-century French novel, he remains better known as an "emancipator of the mind" who, discontented with himself and the world, fought against social and moral conventions while insisting on rigorous personal honesty and authentic affirmation of the individual. (E.E.G.)

1948

Eliot, Thomas Stearns   167
PRIZE: Literature, 1948. BORN: September 26, 1888; St. Louis, MO. DIED: January 4, 1965; London, England. PARENTS: Father, Henry Ware Eliot; Mother, Charlotte Champe Stearns Eliot. NATIONALITY: American; later British citizen. RELIGION: Anglican; from Unitarian background. EDUCATION: Harvard Univ., MA, B.A., 1909; Harvard Univ., MA, M.A., 1910. SPOUSE: Vivienne Haigh-Wood, married June 26, 1915, separated 1932, died 1947; Valerie Fletcher, married January 10, 1957. CHILDREN: None. CAREER: High Wycombe and Highgate, Teacher, 1915-16; *Egaist*, Editor, 1917-19; Lloyds Bank, Clerk, 1917-23; *Criterion*, Editor, 1922-39; Faber and Gwyer, Editor and Director, 1925-65. OTHER AWARDS: Order of Merit, 1948; French Legion of Honor, 1948; Hanseatic Goethe Prize, 1954; Dante Medal, 1959; German Order of Merit, 1959; United States Medal of Freedom, 1964.

Selected Publications: *The Waste Land*. New York: Boni and Liveright, 1922. *Ash-Wednesday*. London: Faber & Faber Ltd., 1930. *Murder in the Cathedral*. London: Faber & Faber Ltd., 1935. *Four Quartets*. New York: Harcourt, Brace and Co., 1943. *The Cocktail Party*. London: Faber & Faber Ltd., 1950.

For More Information See: *Current Biography Yearbook*. New York: H.W. Wilson, 1962, 121-24. Headings, Philip. *T. S. Eliot*. New York: Twayne, 1964. Margolis, John D. *T. S. Eliot's Intellectual Development, 1922-1939*. Chicago: U. of Chicago Press, 1972. Mattheissen, Francis O. *The Achievement of T. S. Eliot: An Essay on the Nature of Poetry*. 3d edition. New York: Oxford U. Press, 1958.

Commentary: T.S. Eliot's Nobel was "for his outstanding pioneer contribution to present-day poetry." An individualist throughout his lifetime, Eliot pioneered many techniques in his poetry that developed as a result of his life experience and the influence of such writers as Laforgue, the Elizabethans, Gautier, and others. His early pessimistic writings were later tempered by his increasing understanding and elaboration of the relationships among religion, politics, and culture. (G.K.)

1949

Faulkner, William Cuthbert   168
PRIZE: Literature, 1949. BORN: September 25, 1897; New Albany, MS. DIED: July 6, 1962; Oxford, MS. PARENTS: Father, Murry Cuthbert Faulkner; Mother, Maud Butler Faulkner. NATIONALITY: American. RELIGION: Episcopalian. EDUCATION: No college degrees. SPOUSE: Estelle Oldham Franklin, married June 20, 1929. CHILDREN: Alabama, daughter; Jill, daughter. CAREER: First National Bank, Oxford, MS, Clerk, 1915; Winchester Repeating Arms, New Haven, CT, Clerk, 1918; Royal Air Force, Canada, Cadet, 1918; Bookstore, NY, Clerk, 1921; Oxford, MS, Postmaster, 1921-24; Power Company, Oxford, MS, Night Superintendent, 1929. OTHER AWARDS: Howells Medal for Fiction, American Academy of Arts and Letters, 1950; National Book Award for Fiction, 1951; Member of the French Legion of Honor, 1951; National Book Award for Fiction, 1955; Pulitzer Prize, 1955, 1963; Silver Medal of the Greek Academy, 1957; Gold Medal for Fiction, National Institute of Arts and Letters, 1962.

Selected Publications: *Sartoris*. New York: Grosset & Dunlap, 1929. *The Sound and the Fury*. New York: J. Cape and H. Smith, 1929. *As I Lay Dying*. New York: J. Cape and H. Smith, 1930. *Sanctuary*. New York: J. Cape and H. Smith, 1930. *Light in August*. New York: H. Smith and R. Hass, 1932. *Absalom, Absalom!* London: Chatto and Windus, 1934. *The Hamlet*. London: Chatto and Windus, 1940. *Intruder in the Dust*. New York: The Modern Library, 1948.

For More Information See: Blotner, Joseph. *Faulkner: A Biography*. 2 volumes. New York: Random House, 1974. *Contemporary Authors*. Detroit, MI: Gale Research, 1979 (Volumes 81-84), 157-65. *Current Biography Yearbook*. New York: H.W. Wilson, 1951, 191-93.

Commentary: The award to William Faulkner was "for his powerful and artistically unique contribution to the modern American novel." In the presentation, Gustaf Hellstroem called Faulkner "the unrivalled master of all living British and American novelists as a deep psychologist" and "the greatest experimentalist among twentieth-century novelists." He used the setting and characters of fictional Yoknapatawpha County in Mississippi to expound his philosophy of the suffering and overall dignity of man. (J.F.K.)

1950

Russell, Bertrand Arthur William 169

PRIZE: Literature, 1950. BORN: May 18, 1872; Monmouthshire, Wales. DIED: February 3, 1970; Merionethshire, Wales. PARENTS: Father, John Russell; Mother, Katharine Stanley Russell. NATIONALITY: British. RELIGION: Agnostic; from Anglican background. EDUCATION: Cambridge Univ., England, M.A., 1894. SPOUSE: Alys Pearsall Smith, married 1894, divorced 1921; Dora Winifred Black, married 1921, divorced 1935; Patricia Helen Spence, married 1936, divorced 1952; Edith Finch, married 1952. CHILDREN: John Conrad, son; Katharine Jane, daughter; Conrad Sabastian Robert, son. CAREER: Cambridge Univ., England, Professor, 1894-16; National Univ. of Peking, China, Professor, 1920-21; Beacon Hill School, England, Founder and Director, 1927-32; Univ. of California, Los Angeles, Professor, 1939-40; Barnes Foundation, Merion, PA, Lecturer, 1941-42. OTHER AWARDS: Nicholas Murray Butler Medal, 1915; Sylvester Medal, London, 1934; Order of Merit, England, 1949; Pears Cyclopedia Prize, London, 1955; Kalinga Prize, UNESCO, 1957; Sonning Prize, Denmark, 1960.

Selected Publications: *The Principles of Mathematics.* Cambridge: Cambridge U. Press, 1903. *Principia Mathematica.* 3 volumes. Cambridge: Cambridge U. Press, 1910-13. *The Problems of Philosophy.* New York: Holt, 1912. *Our Knowledge of the External World as a Field for Scientific Method in Philosophy.* Chicago: Open Court, 1914. *The Analysis of Mind.* New York: Macmillan, 1921. *The Analysis of Matter.* New York: Harcourt, 1927. *Marriage and Morals.* New York: Liveright, 1929. *Education and the Modern World.* New York: Norton, 1932. *Religion and Science.* New York: Holt, 1935. *An Inquiry into Meaning and Truth.* New York: Norton, 1940. *A History of Western Philosophy and Its Connection with Political and Social Circumstances from the Earliest Times to the Present Day.* New York: Simon and Schuster, 1945. *Authority and the Individual.* New York: Simon and Schuster, 1948. *Human Knowledge: Its Scope and Limits.* New York: Simon and Schuster, 1948. *My Philosophical Development.* New York: Simon and Schuster, 1959.

For More Information See: Clark, Ronald. *Bertrand Russell.* New York: Thames and Hudson, 1981. *Contemporary Authors Permanent Series.* Detroit, MI: Gale Research, 1975 (Volume 1), 552-55. *Contemporary Authors Permanent Series.* Detroit, MI: Gale Research, 1975 (Volume 11), 552-55. *Encyclopedia of World Biography.* New York: McGraw-Hill, 1973, 327-30. Gottschalk, Herbert. *Bertrand Russell.* New York: Roy Publishing, 1965. Russell, Bertrand. *The Autobiography of Bertrand Russell.* 2 volumes. Boston: Little, Brown, 1967-68. Russell, Bertrand. *The Autobiography of Bertrand Russell, 1944-1969.* New York: Simon and Schuster, 1969.

Commentary: Bertrand Russell was granted the Nobel Prize "in recognition of his varied and significant writings, in which he champions humanitarian ideals and freedom of thought." He could have claimed worldwide impact for his work in mathematics, history, philosophy, education, or politics, but his greatest impact was in the model he set for the world of an individual who felt a responsibility for the welfare of the whole and spoke out, unafraid, in defense of his three passions: "the longing for love, the search for knowledge, and unbearable pity for the suffering of mankind." (M.K.)

1951

Lagerkvist, Par Fabian 170

PRIZE: Literature, 1951. BORN: May 23, 1891; Vaxjo, Sweden. DIED: July 11, 1974; Stockholm, Sweden. PARENTS: Father, Anders Johan Lagerkvist; Mother, Johanna Blad Lagerkvist. NATIONALITY: Swedish. RELIGION: Atheist; from Protestant background. EDUCATION: No college degrees. SPOUSE: Karen Dagmar Johanne Sorensen, married 1918, divorced 1925; Elaine Luella Hallberg, married 1925. CHILDREN: None. CAREER: Writer. OTHER AWARDS: Samfundet Prize, Sweden, 1928; Sante-Beuve Prize, 1946; Prix du Meilleur Livre Etranger, 1951; Ameties Francaises Award, France, 1956.

Selected Publications: *Det Eviga Leendet.* Stockholm: Bonniers, 1920 (*The Eternal Smile.* Tr. by Denys Harding and Eric Masterton. Cambridge: Fraser, 1934). *Bödeln.* Stockholm: Bonniers, 1933 (*The Hangman.* Tr. by Denys Harding and Eric Masterton. Cambridge: Fraser, 1934). *Mannen Utan Själ.* Stockholm: Bonniers, 1936 (*The Man Without a Soul.* Tr. by Helge Kokeritz in *Scandinavian Plays of the Twentieth Century,* First Series. Princeton, NJ: Princeton U. Press, 1944). *Barabbas.* Stockholm: Bonniers, 1950 (*Barabbas.* Tr. by Ann Blair. New York: Random House, 1951). *Sibyllan.* Stockholm: Bonniers, 1956 (*The Sibyl.* Tr. by Naomi Walford. New York: Random House, 1958). *Pilgrim Pa Havet.* Stockholm: Bonniers, 1962 (*Pilgrim at Sea.* Tr. by Naomi Walford. New York: Random House, 1964). *Mariamne.* Stockholm: Bonniers, 1967 (*Herod and Mariamne.* Tr. by Naomi Walford. New York: A. A. Knopf, 1968).

For More Information See: *Current Biography Yearbook.* New York: H. W. Wilson, 1952, 321-24. Spector, Robert Donald. *Par Lagerkvist.* New York: Twayne, 1973. Syoberg, Leig. *Par Lagerkvist.* New York: Columbia U. Press, 1976.

Commentary: Par Lagerkvist, equally heralded as a dramatist and novelist, won the Nobel Prize "for the artistic vigor and true independence of mind with which he endeavors in his poetry to find answers to the eternal questions confronting mankind." Early in his writings, perhaps in rebellion against his conservative and religious upbringing, Lagerkvist focused pessimistically on themes such as the cruelty of humankind, humanity's cosmic loneliness, and the futility of hope/love. Later, although his works continued to contain corrupt characters, he tempered pessimism with hope and visions of morality. (J.H.S.)

1952

Mauriac, Francois 171

PRIZE: Literature, 1952. BORN: October 11, 1885; Bordeaux, France. DIED: September 1, 1970; Paris, France. PARENTS: Father, Jean-Paul Mauriac; Mother, Marguerite Coiffard Mauriac. NATIONALITY: French. RELIGION: Catholic. EDUCATION: Univ. of Bordeaux, France,

Licence es Lettres, 1904. SPOUSE: Jeanne Lafont, married June 3, 1913. CHILDREN: Claude, son; Claire, daughter; Luce, daughter; Jean, son. CAREER: Writer. OTHER AWARDS: Grand Prix du Roman, L'Academie Francaise, 1926.

Selected Publications: *L'Enfant Chargé de Chaines.* Paris: Grasset, 1913 (*Young Man in Chains.* Tr. by Gerard Hopkins. London: Eyre and Spottiswoode, 1961). *La Robe Prétexte.* Paris: Grasset, 1914 (*The Stuff of Youth.* Tr. by Gerard Hopkins. London: Eyre and Spottiswoode, 1960). *La Chair et le Sang.* Paris: Emile-Paul, 1920 (*Flesh and Blood.* Tr. by Gerard Hopkins. London: Eyre and Spottiswoode, 1954). *Le Baiser au Lépreux.* Paris: Grasset, 1922 (*A Kiss for the Leper.* Tr. by Gerard Hopkins. London: Eyre and Spottiswoode, 1950). *Le Désert de L'Amour.* Paris: Grasset, 1925 (*The Desert of Love.* Tr. by Gerard Hopkins. London: Eyre and Spottiswoode, 1949). *Ce Qui Était Perdu.* Paris: Grasset, 1930 (*That Which Was Lost.* Tr. by J.H. McEwen. London: Eyre and Spottiswoode, 1950). *Le Mystère Frontenac.* Paris: Grasset, 1933 (*Frontenac Mystery.* Tr. by Gerard Hopkins. London: Eyre and Spottiswoode, 1961). *Les Anges Noirs.* Paris: Grasset, 1936 (*The Dark Angels.* Tr. by Gerard Hopkins. London: Eyre and Spottiswoode, 1950). *Asmodée.* Paris: Grasset, 1938 (*Asmodée or the Intruder.* Tr. by Basil Bartlett. London: Secker and Warburg, 1939). *La Pharisienne.* Paris: Grasset, 1941 (*A Woman of the Pharisees.* Tr. by Gerard Hopkins. New York: Farrar, Straus, 1946). *L'Agneau.* Paris: Flammarion, 1954 (*The Lamb.* Tr. by Gerard Hopkins. London: Eyre and Spottiswoode, 1955).

For More Information See: Alyn, Marc. *Francois Mauriac.* Paris: P. Seghers, 1960. Jenkins, Cecil. *Mauriac.* London: Oliver and Boyd, 1965. Smith, Maxwell Austin. *Francois Mauriac.* New York: Twayne Publishers, 1970.

Commentary: Francois Mauriac received his Nobel "for the deep spiritual insight and the artistic intensity with which he has in his novels penetrated the drama of human life." Though known primarily as a novelist, Mauriac also was a successful playwright, biographer, poet, and journalist. His novels deal with psychological struggles of good versus evil and weaknesses of the flesh versus the spirit. The religious overtones of Mauriac's semi-autobiographical novels are the result of a pious upbringing, which would later cause him to be identified as a Catholic novelist. In addition to his full-length fictional works, he also published two volumes of short stories, four plays, four books of poetry, a number of volumes of literary criticism, and several biographies (most notably *De Gaulle*—1964, *La Vie de Jesus*—1936, and *La Vie de Racine*—1928). (S.C.)

1953

Churchill, Winston Leonard Spencer, Sir   172
PRIZE: Literature, 1953. BORN: November 30, 1874; Blenheim Palace, England. DIED: January 24, 1965; London, England. PARENTS: Father, Randolph Spencer Churchill; Mother, Jennie Jerome Churchill. NATIONALITY: British. RELIGION: Anglican. EDUCATION: Royal Military College, England, baccalaureate, 1895. SPOUSE: Clementine Ogilvy Hozier, married September 12, 1908. CHILDREN: Diana, daughter; Randolph Frederick Edward Spencer, son; Sarah, daughter; Mary, daughter;

Marigold Frances, daughter. CAREER: Great Britain, various military and governmental posts up through Prime Minister, 1898-1955. OTHER AWARDS: Literary Award, *Sunday Times*, 1938, 1949; Man of the Year, *Time*, 1949; Charlemagne Prize, 1955; Freedom House Award, United States, 1955; Williamsburg Award, 1955; Humanitarian Award, 1954, 1956; Sonning Foundation Award, Denmark, 1959; Companion of Literature Prize, United Kingdom Royal Society, 1961; Theodore Herzl Award, Zionist Organization of America, 1964.

Selected Publications: *The River War: An Historical Account of the Reconquest of the Sudan.* London: Eyre & Spottiswood, 1899. *Lord Randolph Churchill.* London: Macmillan, 1906. *The World Crisis.* 4 volumes. London: T. Butterworth, 1923-29. *Marlborough, His Life and Times.* 4 volumes. London: G.G. Harrap, 1933-38. *The Second World War.* 6 volumes. Boston: Houghton-Mifflin, 1948-53. *A History of the English-Speaking Peoples.* 4 volumes. New York: Dodd, Mead, 1956-58.

For More Information See: Broad, Lewis. *Winston Churchill: A Biography.* 2 volumes. New York: Hawthorn Books, 1958-63. Churchill, Randolph Spencer. *Winston S. Churchill.* Boston: Houghton-Mifflin, 1966. *Current Biography Yearbook.* New York: H.W. Wilson, 1953, 116-20. Pelling, Henry. *Winston Churchill.* New York: Dutton, 1974.

Commentary: Winston Churchill's Nobel Award was "for his mastery of historical and biographical description as well as for brilliant oratory in defending exalted human values." It was a fitting tribute to an heroic soldier, an ingenious politician, a tirelessly intelligent organizer and manager, and an international political figure, who managed to leave, despite all of his other activities, an impressive output of writings of magnificent quality for future generations. (N.L.)

1954

Hemingway, Ernest Miller   173
PRIZE: Literature, 1954. BORN: July 21, 1899; Oak Park, IL. DIED: July 2, 1961; Ketchum, ID. PARENTS: Father, Clarence Edmonds Hemingway; Mother, Grace Hall Hemingway. NATIONALITY: American. RELIGION: Catholic. EDUCATION: No college degrees. SPOUSE: Hadley Richardson, married September 3, 1921, divorced January 27, 1927; Pauline Pfeiffer, married May 10, 1927, divorced November 4, 1940; Martha Gellhorn, married November 21, 1940, divorced December 21, 1945; Mary Welsh, married March 14, 1946. CHILDREN: John Hadley Nicanor, son; Patrick, son; Gregory Hancock, son. CAREER: *Kansas City Star*, Reporter, 1917-18; American Red Cross, Ambulance Driver in Italy, 1918; *Toronto Star Weekly*, Canada, Writer, 1920; *Cooperative Commonwealth*, Writer, 1921; *Toronto Star*, Canada, Correspondent, 1922-24; North American Newspaper Alliance, Correspondent in Spain, 1937-38; *PM*, Correspondent, 1941; *Colliers*, Correspondent, 1944. OTHER AWARDS: Pulitzer Prize, 1952.

Selected Publications: *The Sun Also Rises.* New York: Grosset & Dunlap, 1926. *A Farewell to Arms.* New York: Scribner's, 1927. *Death in the Afternoon.* New York: Scribner's, 1932. *For Whom the Bell Tolls.* Garden City, NJ: Sun Dial Press, 1940. *The Old Man* *and the Sea*. London: Jonathan Cape, 1952. *A Moveable Feast*. New York: Scribner's, 1964.

For More Information See: Baker, Carlos. *Ernest Hemingway: A Life Story*. New York: Charles Scribner's Sons, 1969. *Dictionary of American Biography: Supplement 7*. New York: Scribner's, 1981, 333-39. *Encyclopedia of World Biography*. New York: McGraw-Hill, 1973 (Volume 5), 182-85.

Commentary: The Nobel Prize citation commended Ernest Hemingway for his "powerful, stylemaking mastery of the art of modern narration, most recently displayed in *The Old Man and the Sea*, and for his influence on contemporary style." His early work was described as "brutal, cynical, and callous," but the citation also spoke of his "heroic pathos" that formed "the basic element of his awareness of life," and of his "manly love of danger and adventure." Hemingway was praised for his "natural admiration for every individual who fights the good fight in a world of reality overshadowed by violence and death." (J.K.)

1955

Laxness, Halldor Kiljan (Gudjonsson, Halldor) 174

PRIZE: Literature, 1955. BORN: April 23, 1902; Reykjavik, Iceland. PARENTS: Father, Gudjon Helgi Helgason; Mother, Sigridur Halldordottir. NATIONALITY: Icelandic. RELIGION: Christian by birth; Catholic in young manhood; devoted to the class struggle later; with no religious affiliation. EDUCATION: No college degrees. SPOUSE: Ingibjorg Einarsdottir, married 1930, divorced 1940; Audur Sveinsdottir, married 1945. CHILDREN: None. CAREER: Writer. OTHER AWARDS: Stalin Prize, 1943; Sonning Prize, 1969.

Selected Publications: *Vafarinn Mikli fra Kasmir* (*The Great Weaver from Kashmir*). Reykjavik: Acta, 1927. *Altydubokin* (*The Book of the People*). Reykjavik: Alpyouflokkurin, 1929. *Pu Vinvidur Hreini* (*O Thou Pure Vine*). Reykjavik: Bokadeild, Menningarsjoos, 1931. *Fuglinn i Fjorunni* (*The Bird on the Beach*). Reykjavik: Bokadeild, Menningarsjoos, 1932. *Salka Valka*. Copenhagen: Steen Hasselbach, 1934 (Tr. by F. H. Lyon. London: Allen and Unwin, 1963). *Sjalfstaett Folk*. 2 volumes. Reykjavik: E.P. Briem, 1934-35 (*Independent People*. Tr. by J.A. Thompson. London: Allen and Unwin, 1945). *Ljos Heimsins* (*The Light of the World*). Reykjavik: Heimskringla, 1937. *Atomstodin*. Reykjavik: Helgafell, 1948 (*The Atom Station*. Tr. by M. Magnusson. London: Methuen and Company, 1961). *Gerpla*. Reykjavik: Helgafell, 1952 (*The Happy Warriors*. Tr. by K. John. London: Methuen and Company, 1958). *Paradisarheimt*. Reykjavik: Helgafell, 1960 (*Paradise Reclaimed*. Tr. by M. Magnusson. London: Methuen and Company, 1962).

For More Information See: Hallberg, Peter. *Halldor Laxness*. New York: Twayne Publishers, 1971. *Twentieth Century Authors. First Supplement*. New York: H.W. Wilson, 1955, 561-62.

Commentary: The Academy cited Halldor Laxness "for his vivid epic power, which has renewed the great narrative art of Iceland." All of Laxness's important books have Icelandic themes and explore social and sometimes political issues, which relates to his own strong positive feelings about his country and its language, as well as to his lifelong struggles with personal religious and political beliefs. (J.H.S.)

1956

Jiménez, Juan Ramón 175

PRIZE: Literature, 1956. BORN: December 24, 1881; Moguer, Spain. DIED: May 29, 1958; San Juan, Puerto Rico. PARENTS: Father, Víctor Jiménez y Jiménez; Mother, Purificación Mantecón y López Parejo. NATIONALITY: Spanish. RELIGION: Catholic. EDUCATION: Colegio de los Jesuitas del Puerto de Santa María de Cádiz, Spain, bachillerato, 1896. SPOUSE: Zenobia Camprubí Aymar, married 1916. CHILDREN: None. CAREER: Writer.

Selected Publications: *Almas de Violeta* (*Violet Souls*). Madrid: Tipografia Moderna, 1900. *Ninflas* (*Water Lilies*). Madrid: Tipografia Moderna, 1900. *Arias Tristes* (*Sad Airs*). Madrid: Fernando Fe, 1903. *Rimas* (*Rhymes*). Madrid: Fernando Fe, 1903. *Jardines Lejanos* (*Distant Gardens*). Madrid: Fernando Fe, 1904. *Elejías Puras*. (*Pure Elegies*). Madrid: Revista de Archivas, 1908. *Pastorales* (*Pastorals*). Madrid: Biblioteca Renacimiento, 1911. *La Soledad Sonora* (*The Sonorous Solitude*). Madrid: Revista de Archives, 1911. *Platero y Yo*. Madrid: La Lectura, 1914 (*Platero and I*. Tr. by William and Mary Roberts. Oxford: Dolphin, 1956). *Estio* (*Summer*). Madrid: Calleja, 1916. *Sonetos Esperituales* (*Spiritual Sonnets*). Madrid: Colleja, 1917. *Diario de Un Poeta Recién Casado* (*Diary of a Newly-Wed Poet*). Madrid: Calleja, 1917. *Espanoles de Tres Mundos* (*Spaniards of Three Worlds*). Buenos Aires: Losada, 1942. *Animal de Fondo* (*Animal of Depth*). Buenos Aires: Pleamar, 1949. *Selected Writings*. Tr. by H.R. Hays. New York: Farrar, Straus and Cudahy, 1957. *Three Hundred Poems*. Tr. by Eloise Roach. Austin, TX: U. of Texas Press, 1962.

For More Information See: *Current Biography Yearbook*. New York: H.W. Wilson, 1957, 280-82. Fogelquist, Donald F. *Juan Ramón Jiménez*. Boston: Twayne Publishers, 1976. Grafias, Francisco. *Juan Ramón Jiménez*. Madrid: Taurus Ediciones, 1958.

Commentary: The Nobel Prize was granted to Juan Ramón Jiménez "for his lyrical poetry which constitutes an inspiring example in the Spanish language of spirituality and artistic poetry." Influenced by Bécquer, Darío, and other modernists, as well as by French symbolists, Jiménez created his own unique style—metaphysical, abstract, pure, lyrical, and spiritual. His work, in turn, greatly influenced many Hispanic poets—Alberti, Guillén, Salinas, Lorca, Mistral. (M.G.R.)

1957

Camus, Albert 176

PRIZE: Literature, 1957. BORN: November 7, 1913; Mondovi, Algeria. DIED: January 4, 1960; Petit-Villeblevin, France. PARENTS: Father, Lucien Camus; Mother, Catherine Sintes Camus. NATIONALITY: French. RELIGION: "Atheistic Humanist;" from Christian background. EDUCATION: Univ. of Algiers, Algeria, Diplôme d'études superieurs, 1936. SPOUSE: Simone Hie, married June 16, 1936, divorced 1940; Francine Faure, married December 3, 1940. CHILDREN: Jean, son; Catherine, daughter. CAREER: Theatre du Travail, France, Actor, Writer, Producer, 1935-38; *Alger-Républicain*, Algiers, Journalist, 1938-40; *Paris-Soir*,

France, Journalist, 1940; Oran, Algeria Public School, Teacher, 1941-42; Paris, France, Free-lance Journalist, 1942-45; *Combat*, Paris, France, Editor, 1944-47; Editions Gallimard, Reader, 1943-60. OTHER AWARDS: Medal of the Liberation, French Government, 1946; Prix des Critiques, 1947; Legion of Honor (refused).

Selected Publications: *L'Étranger*. Paris: Gallimard, 1942 (*The Stranger*. Tr. by Stuart Gilbert. New York: A. Knopf, 1946). *Le Mythe de Sisyphe*. Paris: Gallimard, 1942 (*The Myth of Sisyphus*. Tr. by Justin O'Brien. London: H. Hamilton, 1955). *La Peste*. Paris: Gallimard, 1947 (*The Plague*. Tr. by Stuart Gilbert. New York: A. Knopf, 1948). *L'Homme Révolté*. Paris: Gallimard, 1951 (*The Rebel*. Tr. by Anthony Bower. New York: A. Knopf, 1954). *La Chute*. Paris: Gallimard, 1956 (*The Fall*. Tr. by Justin O'Brien. New York: A. Knopf, 1957). *L'Exil et Le Royaume*. Paris: Gallimard, 1957 (*Exile and the Kingdom*. Tr. by Justin O'Brien. New York: A. Knopf, 1958).

For More Information See: Brée, Germaine. *Camus*. New Brunswick, NJ: Rutgers U. Press, 1972. Camus, Albert. *Notebooks 1935-1942*. New York: Alfred A. Knopf, 1963. *Contemporary Authors*. Detroit, MI: Gale, 1980 (Volume 89-92), 83-88. Lottman, Herbert. *Albert Camus, a Biography*. Garden City, NY: Doubleday, 1979. Thody, Philip. *Albert Camus*. New York: Macmillan, 1957.

Commentary: Albert Camus was awarded the Nobel Prize "for his important literary production, which with clear sighted earnestness illuminates the problems of the human conscience in our times." His work expressed the concerns of his generation and the moral climate of the mid-twentieth century. Confronted with war's atrocities, Camus expressed despair but looked beyond nihilism to find a reason for human existence and the possibility of happiness. (K.G.)

1958

Pasternak, Boris Leonidovich   177

PRIZE: Literature, 1958 (refused). BORN: February 10, 1890; Moscow, Russia. DIED: May 30, 1960; Peredelkino, USSR. PARENTS: Father, Leonid Ossipovich Pasternak; Mother, Rosa Isodornovna Kaufman Pasternak. NATIONALITY: Russian. RELIGION: Jewish. EDUCATION: Moscow Univ., USSR, baccalaureate, 1913. SPOUSE: Evgeniia Vladimirovna Lourie, married 1922, divorced 1931; Zinaida Nikolaevna Neuhaus Ereemeev, married 1934. CHILDREN: Evgenii Borisovich, son; Leonid Borisovich, son. CAREER: Moscow, Russia, Tutor, 1914-16; Moscow, Russia, Clerk, 1916-17; Soviet Commissariat for Education, USSR, Librarian, 1918; Writers Bookshop, Moscow, USSR, Salesclerk, 1921; Commissariat of Foreign Affairs, Librarian, 1924; Translator, 1932-43. OTHER AWARDS: Bancarella Prize, 1958.

Selected Publications: *The Collected Prose Works*. Arranged by Stefan Schimanski. London: L. Drummond, 1945. *Doctor Zhivago*. Tr. by Max Hayward and Manya Harari. New York: Pantheon, 1958. *The Last Summer*. Tr. by George Reavy. New York: Avon Book Division, Hearst Corp., 1959. *The Poetry of Boris Pasternak, 1914-1960*. Tr. by George Reavy. New York: Putnam, 1960. *The Blind Beauty*. Tr. by Max Hayward and Manya Harari. New York: Harcourt, Brace & World, 1969.

For More Information See: *An Essay in Autobiography*. Tr. by Manya Harari. London: Collins & Harvill Press, 1959. Conquest, Robert. *Pasternak: A Biography*. New York: Octagon Books, 1979. *Current Biography Yearbook*. New York: H.W. Wilson, 1959, 346-47. de Mallac, Guy. *Boris Pasternak: His Life and Art*. Norman, OK: U. of Oklahoma Press, 1981. Hingley, Robert. *Pasternak: A Biography*. New York: Knopf, 1983. *I Remember: Sketch for an Autobiography*. Tr. by David Magarshack. New York: Pantheon, 1959.

Commentary: The Committee cited Boris Pasternak "for his important achievement both in contemporary lyrical poetry and in the field of the great Russian epic tradition." Some felt that the award was based solely on *Doctor Zhivago*, but the importance of Pasternak's poetry is underscored by the fact that he was also nominated in 1953. Anders Oesterling, permanent secretary of the Academy, compared Pasternak's novel to Tolstoy's *War and Peace* and spoke of the book's "pure and powerful genius." He also said that the award was in honor of Pasternak's courage in producing a work of such independence: "It is indeed a great achievement to have been able to complete under difficult circumstances a work of such dignity, high above all political party frontiers and rather anti-political in its entirely humane outlook." (D.V.)

1959

Quasimodo, Salvatore   178

PRIZE: Literature, 1959. BORN: August 20, 1901; Modica, Sicily, Italy. DIED: June 14, 1968; Naples, Italy. PARENTS: Father, Gaetano Quasimodo; Mother, Clotilde Ragusa Quasimodo. NATIONALITY: Italian. RELIGION: Catholic. EDUCATION: No college degrees. SPOUSE: Maria Cumani, married 1948. CHILDREN: Orietta, daughter; Alessandro, son. CAREER: Italian Ministry of Public Works, Engineer, 1926-38; *Il Tempo*, Editor, 1938-40; Giuseppe Verdi Conservatory of Music, Milan, Italy, Professor, 1941-64. OTHER AWARDS: Etna-Taormina International Poetry Prize, 1953; Viareggio Prize, 1958.

Selected Publications: *Edè Subito Sera*. Milan: Mondadori, 1942. *Giorno Dopo Giorno*. Milan: Mondadori, 1947. *La Vita Non è Sogno*. Milan: Mondadori, 1949. *Il Falso e Vero Verde*. Milan: Schwarz, 1954. *La Terra Impareggiabile*. Milan: Mondadori, 1958. *Selected Writings of Salvatore Quasimodo*. Tr. by Allen Mandelbaum. New York: Farrar, Straus & Cudahy, 1960.

For More Information See: *Contemporary Authors, Permanent Series*. Detroit, MI: Gale, 1975 (Volume 1), 524-25. *Current Biography Yearbook*. New York: H.W. Wilson, 1960, 325-27.

Commentary: Salvatore Quasimodo, Italian poet and translator, was awarded the Nobel Prize "for his lyrical poetry, which with classical fire expresses the tragic experience of life in our times." In the 1930s, he was considered to be a leader of the Italian hermetic poetry movement. After World War II, his poetry, while retaining classical imagery and themes, became an instrument for social and political reform. It is this later poetry that the Nobel Committee expressly cited in awarding the prize. (S.W.C.)

1960

Saint-John Perse (Léger, Marie-Rene Auguste Alexis Saint-Léger)   179

PRIZE: Literature, 1960. BORN: May 31, 1887; Saint-Léger-les-Feuilles, French West Indies. DIED: September 20, 1975; Giens, France. PARENTS: Father, Amedée Léger; Mother, Françoise-Renée Dormoy Léger. NATIONALITY: French. RELIGION: Spiritualist; from Protestant background. EDUCATION: Univ. of Bordeaux, France, Licencie in Law, 1908. SPOUSE: Dorothy Milburn Russell, married 1958. CHILDREN: None. CAREER: French Government Positions, 1914-40; United States Library of Congress, Consultant, 1941-45. OTHER AWARDS: Grand Officer of Legion of Honor; Knight of the Grand Cross of the British Empire; Award of Merit, American Academy of Arts and Letters, 1950; Grand Prix National des Letters, 1959; Grand Prix International de Poesie, Belgium, 1959.

Selected Publications: *Eloges*. Paris: Gallimard, 1911 (*Eloges and Other Poems*. Tr. by Louise Varese. New York: Norton, 1944). *Anabase*. Paris: Gallimard, 1924 (*Anabasis*. Tr. by T.S. Eliot. London: Faber, 1930). *Exil, Suivi de Poemes a L'Étrangere, Pluies, Neiges*. Paris: Gallimard, 1945 (*Exile, and Other Poems*. Tr. by Denis Devlin. New York: Pantheon, 1949). *Vents*. Paris: Gallimard, 1946 (*Winds*. Tr. by Hugh Chisholm. New York: Pantheon, 1952). *Amers*. Paris: NRF, 1953 (*Seamarks*. Tr. by Wallace Fowlie. New York: Pantheon, 1958).

For More Information See: *Current Biography Yearbook*. New York: H.W. Wilson, 1961, 262-64. Galand, Rene. *Saint-John Perse*. New York: Twayne, 1972. Knodel, Arthur. *Saint-John Perse: A Study of His Poetry*. Edinburgh: Edinburgh U. Press, 1966.

Commentary: Saint-John Perse's Nobel was "for the soaring flight and the evocative imagery of his poetry, which in a visionary fashion reflects the conditions of our times." His impressive diplomatic career and the destruction of his manuscripts by the Nazis left a rather small total body of work. Never closely allied with any school of poetry though a friend of many poets, Saint-John Perse began by evoking his childhood by the tropical sea. *Anabasis* continues the exotic background, in his own words "a poem of personal and public solitude in the midst of action." *Exile* deals with more personal subjects in a nevertheless epic fashion; *Winds*, too, is epic, and like *Anabasis* can be read on another level as about literature's ability to make passing time eternal. *Seamarks* pictures human life centered about the sea and features a discussion between Man and Woman concerning human life, love, and eternity. Little-known in or out of France, Saint-John Perse is an author whose work is not easy but is extremely rewarding for those who will live with it and absorb its grand scope, its clarity of image, and its levels of meaning. (E.B.)

1961

Andrič, Ivo   180

PRIZE: Literature, 1961. BORN: October 10, 1892; Dolac, Yugoslavia. DIED: March 13, 1975; Belgrade, Yugoslavia. PARENTS: No record found. NATIONALITY: Yugoslavian. RELIGION: Eastern Orthodox. EDUCATION: Univ. of Graz, Austria, Ph.D., 1923. SPOUSE: Milica Babic, married 1959. CHILDREN: None. CAREER: Yugoslavian Diplomatic Service, 1923-41; Yugoslavian Politics, 1946-52. OTHER AWARDS: Prize for Life Work, Yugoslavia.

Selected Publications: *Gospodica* (*The Woman from Sarajevo*). Sarajevo, Yugoslavia: Sjetlost, 1945. *Travnick Hronika* (*Bosnian Chronicle*). Belgrade: Drez. Izdavacki Zavad Jugoslavije, 1945. *Na Drini Cuprija*. Sarajevo, Yugoslavia: Sjetlost, 1947 (*The Bridge on the Drina*. Tr. by Lovett F. Edwards. London: George Allen & Unwin, Ltd., 1959). *Prokleta Avlija*. Belgrade: Prosveta, 1954 (*Devil's Yard*. Tr. by Kenneth Johnstone. New York: Grove Press, 1962).

For More Information See: *Contemporary Literary Criticism*. Detroit, MI: Gale, 1978 (Volume 8), 19-22. *Current Biography Yearbook*. New York: H.W. Wilson, 1962, 13-15.

Commentary: The Nobel Prize was presented to Ivo Andrič "for the epic force with which he has traced themes and depicted human destinies from his country's history." Especially in his Bosnian trilogy, Andrič presented the panorama of Serbian history and life, from the sixteenth-century action around the bridge in *The Bridge on the Drina* to the rivalry between the Austrian and French consuls in Travnick of the Napoleonic Wars in *Bosnian Story* and finally to the psychological study of the merchant's daughter in the present-day *The Woman from Sarajevo*. (K.C.)

1962

Steinbeck, John Ernst   181

PRIZE: Literature, 1962. BORN: February 27, 1902; Salinas, Calfornia. DIED: December 28, 1968; New York, NY. PARENTS: Father, John Ernst Steinbeck; Mother, Olive Hamilton Steinbeck. NATIONALITY: American. RELIGION: Protestant. EDUCATION: No college degrees. SPOUSE: Carol Henning, married 1930, divorced 1943; Gwyn Conger, married 1943, divorced 1949; Elaine Scott, married 1950. CHILDREN: Tom, son; John, son. CAREER: Writer and Free-lance Journalist. OTHER AWARDS: Gold Medal, Commonwealth Club of California, 1936, 1937, 1940; Circle Silver Plaque, New York Drama Critics, 1938; Pulitzer Prize, 1940.

Selected Publications: *To a God Unknown*. New York: Covici-Freide, 1933. *Tortilla Flat*. New York: Covici-Freide, 1935. *In Dubious Battle*. New York: Covici-Freide, 1936. *Of Mice and Men*. New York: Covici-Freide, 1937. *The Red Pony*. New York: Viking Press, 1937. *The Grapes of Wrath*. New York: Viking Press, 1939. *The Forgotten Village*. New York: Viking Press, 1941. *The Moon Is Down*. New York: Viking Press, 1942. *The Pearl*. New York: Viking Press, 1947. *East of Eden*. New York: Viking Press, 1952. *Sweet Thursday*. New York: Viking Press, 1954. *Once There Was a War*. New York: Viking Press, 1958. *The Winter of Our Discontent*. New York: Viking Press, 1961. *The Short Novels of John Steinbeck*. New York: Viking Press, 1963.

For More Information See: *Current Biography Yearbook*. New York: H. W. Wilson, 1963, 397-99. Fontenrose, Joseph. *John Steinbeck*. New York: Barnes & Noble, 1963. French, Warren. *John Steinbeck*. Boston: Twayne Publishers, 1961.

Commentary: John Steinbeck was cited by the Academy "for his one and at the same time realistic and imaginative writings distinguished as they are by a sympathetic humour and a social perception." An author whose critical acclaim seemed to rise or fall almost with each literary contribution, Steinbeck appeared to be most in his element when writing about "the simple joy of life." The Nobel jurors cited his "great feeling for nature—the tilled soil, the wasteland, the mountains and the ocean coasts" in his writing. The American proletariat was the model for Steinbeck's most memorable characters and formed the nucleus around which some of his most recognized themes revolved—such topics as the Depression, realities of nature, responsibility and human suffering, moral neutrality, and eccentric loneliness. (J.H.S.)

1963

Seferis, Giorgos (Seferiádis, Yorgos)   182

PRIZE: Literature, 1963. BORN: February 29, 1900; Smyrna, Turkey. DIED: September 20, 1971; Athens, Greece. PARENTS: Father, Stelios Seferiádis; Mother, Dhespo Tinekidhis Seferiádis. NATIONALITY: Greek. RELIGION: Eastern Orthodox. EDUCATION: Univ. of Paris-Sorbonne, France, law degree, 1924. SPOUSE: Maria Zannou, married 1941. CHILDREN: None. CAREER: Greek Diplomat, 1931-62.

Selected Publications: *Six Poems from the Greek of Sikelianos and Seferis.* Tr. by L. Durell. Athens: Rhodes, 1946. *The King of Asine and Other Poems.* Tr. by B. Spencer, N. Valaoritis, and L. Durell. London: Lehmann, 1948. *Poems.* Tr. by Rex Warner. London: Bodley Head, 1960. *Collected Poems, 1924-1955.* Tr. by Edmund Keeley and Philip Sherrard. Princeton, NJ: Princeton U. Press, 1967. *Three Secret Poems.* Tr. by Walter Kaiser. Cambridge, MA: Harvard U. Press, 1969.

For More Information See: *Current Biography Yearbook.* New York: H.W. Wilson, 1964, 402-04. *Days of 1945-1951: A Poet's Journal.* Tr. by Athan Anagnostopoulos. Cambridge, MA: Harvard U. Press, 1974.

Commentary: Giorgos Seferis was cited by the Academy for "the unique thought and style and beauty of his language, which has become a lasting symbol of all that is indestructible in the Hellenic acceptance of life." In his poetry, Seferis immortalized the glory and the pain of the Greek experience, investigating in depth the themes of modern tensions, war, exile, and nostalgia. In his life's work, meanwhile, the poet carried forward the history of Greece in a series of important diplomatic posts held over a period of 31 years. (J.H.S.)

1964

Sartre, Jean-Paul Charles Aymard   183

PRIZE: Literature, 1964 (refused). BORN: June 21, 1905; Paris, France. DIED: April 15, 1980; Paris, France. PARENTS: Father, Jean Baptiste Sartre; Mother, Anne Marie Schweitzer. NATIONALITY: French. RELIGION: Atheist in adult years; from Lutheran/Catholic background. EDUCATION: École Normale Supérieure, France, "Agrege de philosophie," 1929. SPOUSE: Unmarried, but lived with life-long companion Simone De Beauvoir for almost 50 years. CHILDREN: None; but

legally adopted his editorial assistant, Miss Arlette Kaim. CAREER: French Army, Sergeant, 1929-31; Lycée du Havre, France, Professor, 1931-33; Institute Français, Berlin, Germany, Teaching Fellow, 1933-34; Lycée de Laon, France, Professor, 1936-37; Lycée Pasteur de Neuilly-sur-Seine, France, Professor, 1937-39; French Army, 1939-41; Lycée Condorcet, France, Professor, 1941-44; *Les Temps Moderne*, Paris, France, Editor, 1944-80. OTHER AWARDS: French Popular Novel Prize, 1940; Legion d'honneur (refused), 1945; New York Drama Critics Award, 1947; French Grand Novel Prize, 1950; Omega Prize, Italy, 1950.

Selected Publications: *La Nausée.* Paris: Gallimard, 1938 (*Nausea.* Tr. by R. Baldick. Harmondsworth, England: Penguin, 1965). *L'imagination.* Paris: F. Alcan, 1939 (*Imagination.* Tr. by F. Williams. Ann Arbor, MI: U. of Michigan Press, 1962). *Le Mur.* Paris: Gallimard, 1939 (*The Wall.* Tr. by L. Alexander. Norfolk, CT: Penguin 1948). *L'imaginaire: Psychologie Phenomenologie.* Paris: Gallimard, 1940 (*The Psychology of Imaginatio.n.* Tr. by B. Frechtman. New York: Philosophical Library, 1948). *L'être et le Néant: Essais d'Ontologie Phenomenologique.* Paris: Gallimard, 1943 (*Being and Nothingness: An Essay on Phenomenological Ontology.* New York: Philosophical Library, 1956). *Huis clos.* Paris: Gallimard, 1943 (*In Camera.* Tr. by S. Gilbert. New York: Alfred A. Knopf, 1946. Also Tr. as *No Exit* by P. Bowles. New York, 1958). *Les Chemins de la Liberté.* Paris: Gallimard, 1945-49, comprising: 1. *L'âge de Raison, Roman,* 1945 (*The Age of Reason.* Tr. by E. Sutton. New York: Alfred A. Knopf, 1947); 2. *Le Sursis,* 1945 (*The Reprieve.* Tr. by E. Sutton. London: Hamish Hamilton, 1947); 3. *La Mort dans l'Âme,* 1949 (*Iron in the Soul.* Tr. by G. Hopkins. London: Hamish Hamilton, 1950). *Mort sans Sépulture.* Lausanne: Marguerat, 1946 (*Men without Shadows.* Tr. by Kitty Black. London: H. Hamilton, 1949). *Les mouches.* Paris: Gallimard, 1946 (*The Flies.* Tr. by S. Gilbert. New York: Alfred A. Knopf, 1946). *La Putain Respectueuse.* Paris: Nagel, 1946 (*The Respectful Prostitute.* Tr. by K. Black. London: Hamish Hamilton, 1949). *Réflexion sur la Question Juive.* Paris: Morihien, 1946 (*Portrait of the Anti-Semite.* Tr. by Mary Guggenheim. New York: Partisan Review, 1946). *Situations,* 9 volumes (collected articles and criticism). Paris: Gallimard, 1947-72 (*What is Literature?* Tr. by B. Frechtman. New York: Philosophical Library, 1949—from *Situation III*). *Literary and Philosophical Essays.* (Tr by A. Michelson. London: Rider, 1955—selections). *Situations.* (Tr. by B. Eisler. London: Fawcitt, 1965—*Situations IV*). *Les Jeux sont Faits.* French and European Publications, 1947 (*The Chips are Down.* Tr. by L. Vares. New York: Lear, 1948). *L'engrenage.* Paris: Nagel, 1948 (*In the Mesh.* Tr. by M. Savill. London: A. Dakers). *Les Mains Sales.* Paris: Gallimard, 1948 (*Dirty Hands.* Tr. by L. Abel. New York: Vintage Books, 1949). *Le Diable et le bon Dieu.* Paris: Gallimard, 1951 (*Lucifer and the Lord.* Tr. by Kitty Black. London: H. Hamilton, 1953). *Les Séquestrés d'Altona.* Paris: Gallimard, 1955 (*The Condemned of Altona.* Tr. by G. and S. Leeson. New York: Vintage Books, 1961). *Les Mots.* Paris: Gallimard, 1964 (*Words.* Tr. by I. Clephane. London: H. Hamilton, 1964).

For More Information See: *Current Biography Yearbook.* New York: H.W. Wilson Co., 1971, 366-69. *The New York Times Biographical Service.* New York:

Arno Press, 1980. Podell, Janet, ed. *The Annual Obituary, 1980.* New York: St. Martin's Press, 1981, 231-37. *The Reader's Encyclopedia,* 2d ed. New York: Thomas Y. Crowell Co., 1965, 898-99. Suhl, Benjamin. *Jean-Paul Sartre: The Philosopher as Literary Critic.* New York: Columbia University Press, 1970. Thody, Philip Malcolm. *Sartre: A Biographical Introduction.* New York: Scribner's, 1972.

Commentary: The award to Jean-Paul Sartre was "for his work which, rich in ideas and filled with the spirit of freedom and the quest for truth, has exerted a far-reaching influence on our age." Although Sartre is primarily known for his contributions in the areas of drama and psychological biography, he is equally well known for his notable contributions in literary criticism and political journalism. Probably most know him for his development of the philosophy of existentialism and for the play *No Exit* (1947), still frequently read in college literature courses. (P.K.)

1965

Sholokov, Mikhail Aleksandrovich 184
PRIZE: Literature, 1965. BORN: May 24, 1905; Veshenskaya, Rostov, Russia. DIED: February 21, 1984; Veshenskaya, Rostov, USSR. PARENTS: Father, Aleksander Mikhailovich Sholokov; Mother, Anastasiya Danilovna Chernikova Sholokov. NATIONALITY: Russian. RELIGION: Atheist; from Eastern Orthodox background. EDUCATION: No college degrees. SPOUSE: Maria Petrovna Gromoslakskaya, married 1923. CHILDREN: 4 children. CAREER: Soviet Army, 1918-22; Moscow, USSR, Manual Laborer, 1922-26; Writer and Politician thereafter. OTHER AWARDS: Stalin Prize, 1941; Order of the Fatherland; Lenin Prize, 1960; Hero of Socialist Labor, 1967; Order of Lenin, 8 times.

Selected Publications: *Nakhalenof.* Moscow: n.p., 1925. *Lazorevaya Steppe.* Moscow: n.p., 1925. *Donskie Rasskazy.* Originally published in 1925. Available through Moscow: Gosud. Izd-vo, Khudozh Lit-ry, 1958 (*Tales of the Don.* Tr. by H. C. Stevens. New York: Knopf, 1962). *Tikhii Don.* Originally published, 1926-40. Available through Moscow: Gosud. Izd-vo, Khudozh Lit-ry, 1945 (Translation of volumes 1 and 2 by Stephen Garry published as *And Quiet Flows the Don.* New York: Putman, 1934; translation of volumes 3 and 4 by Stephen Garry published as *The Don Flows Home to the Sea.* New York: Putman, 1940). *Seeds of Tomorrow.* Tr. by Stephen Garry. New York: Knopf, 1935. *Nauka Nenavisti.* Originally published in 1942. Available through Moscow: Sovremennik, 1975 (*Hate.* Moscow: Foreign Language Publishing House, 1942). *Oni Srazhalis' Za Rodinu.* Volume 1. Moscow: Pravda, 1943. *Shornik Statei.* Leningrad: Izdvo Leningradskogo Universiteta, 1956. *Sobraine Sochinenii.* 8 volumes. Moscow: Goslitzdat, 1956-60. *Sud'ba Cheloveka.* Moscow: Gos. Izd-vo Khudozh, Lit-ry, 1957 (*The Fate of Man.* Tr. by Robert Daglish. Moscow: Foreign Languages Press, 1957). *Harvest on the Don.* Tr. by H. C. Stevens. New York: Putnam, 1960. *Rannie Rasskazy.* Moscow: Sovetskaiia Rossia, 1961. *Pleswns, Romans.* Moscow: Riga, 1961. *Put'dorozhen'ka.* Moscow: Molodaia Gvardiia, 1962. *Slovo o Rodine.* Moscow: n.p., 1965. *Izbrannoe.* Moscow: Molodaia Gvardiia, 1968. *Po Veleniiu Dushi.* Moscow: Molodaia Gvardiia, 1970 (*At the Bidding of the Heart.* Tr. by Olga Shartse.

Progress Publishers, 1973). *Rosii v Serdtse.* Moscow: Sovremennik, 1975. *Slovo k Molodym.* Moscow: n.p., 1975. *Stories.* Moscow: Progress Publishers, 1975.

For More Information See: Slonim, Marc. *Soviet Russian Literature, 1917-77.* New York: Oxford U. Press, 1977, 188-97. *Twentieth-Century Authors: A Biographical Dictionary of Modern Literature.* New York: H. W. Wilson, 1942, 1280-82.

Commentary: Mikhail Sholokhov's award was for "artistic strength and honesty when depicting a historical epoch in the life of the Russian people." His major work, *The Quiet Don* (a 1934 work which took him 14 years to write and which is published in the U.S. as *Quiet Flows the Don*), is an epic novel steeped heavily in nineteenth century realism. The work, an outstanding representative of the so-called "proletarian" current in Russian literature, has been compared by some to *War and Peace*, and it was instrumental in his becoming, at age 50, the most renowned writer in the Soviet Union. The struggle between the old and the new, the difficulty in choosing between white and red Russia, dominates his work. Sholokhov was often a controversial figure in the Kremlin because his position was so high that he could afford to be very outspoken. (D.S. and R.P.)

1966

Agnon, Shmuel Yosef (Czaczkes, Shmuel Yosef) 185
PRIZE: Literature, 1966. BORN: July 17, 1888; Buczacz, Galicia (Austria). DIED: February 17, 1970; Rehovat, Israel. PARENTS: Father, Shalom Czaczkes; Mother, Esther Farb Czaczkes. NATIONALITY: Austrian; later Israeli citizen. RELIGION: Jewish. EDUCATION: No college degrees. SPOUSE: Esther Marx, married 1920. CHILDREN: Emuna, daughter; Hemdat, son. CAREER: Israel, Governmental Agency Secretary, 1907-13. OTHER AWARDS: Ussishkin Prize, 1950; Bialik Prize, Israel, 1954, 1958.

Selected Publications: *Hakhnasat Kalah.* Berlin: Schocken, 1931 (*The Bridal Canopy.* Tr. by I.M. Lask. New York: Doubleday, 1937). "Sefer Hamaasim" (*The Book of Deeds). Davar (Musaf)* VII (April 20, 1932). "Pat Shlema." *Moznayim* IV (January 5, 1933): 50-53. In *A Whole Loaf.* Tr. by I.M. Lask. Jerusalem: Schocken, 1958, 316-331. *Oreach Nata Lalun.* In *Kol Sippurav*(Volume VII). Berlin: Schocken, 1939 (*Wayfarer Stopped for a Night.* Tr. by R. Alter. *Mosaic*II (Winter 1961): 37-41). *Shevuat Emunim.* Jerusalem: Schocken, 1943 ("Betrothed." In *Two Tales.* Tr. by W. Lever. New York: Schocken, 1966). *Temol Shilshom*(*Only Yesterday*). In *Kol Sipurav* (Volume IX). Berlin: Schocken, 1945. *Kol Sipurav*(*Collected Works*). 11 volumes. Berlin: Schocken, 1931-53.

For More Information See: Band, Arnold J. *Nostalgia and Nightmare.* Berkeley, CA: U. of California Press, 1968. *Contemporary Authors. Permanent Series.* Detroit, MI: Gale, 1978 (Volume 2), 16-18. *Current Biography Yearbook.* New York: H.W. Wilson, 1967, 1-3.

Commentary: "For his profoundly distinctive narrative art with motifs from the life of the Jewish people," S.Y. Agnon was given the Nobel Prize. Over six decades, Agnon produced poems, stories, and novels that first lovingly and simply told of the life of the

Jewish communities in Eastern Europe and later introduced overtones of fantasy and nightmare in the Kafka tradition. His *The Bridal Canopy* has been referred to as a Hebrew *Don Quixote*. Agnon also produced critically acclaimed books on the Days of Awe, the giving of the Torah, and Hassidic lore. (J.H.S.)

Sachs, Leonie Nelly   186

PRIZE: Literature, 1966. BORN: December 10, 1891; Berlin, Germany. DIED: May 12, 1970; Stockholm, Sweden. PARENTS: Father, William Sachs; Mother, Margaretha Karger. NATIONALITY: German; later Swedish citizen. RELIGION: Jewish. EDUCATION: No college degrees. SPOUSE: None. CHILDREN: None. CAREER: Berlin, Germany and Stockholm, Sweden, Translator. OTHER AWARDS: Kulturpreis der Deutschen Industrie, 1959; Jahrestring Literary Prize, 1959; Annette von Droste-Hülshoff Prize, 1960; Peace Prize, German Bookseller's Association, 1966.

Selected Publications: *Eli: Ein Mysterienspiel vom Leiden Israels.* Stockholm: Walter A. Berendsohn, 1943 (*Eli: A Mystery Play of the Sufferings of Israel.* Tr. by Christopher Holme. New York: Kurt Bernheim, 1970). *In den Wohnungen des Todes* (*In the Habitations of Death*). Berlin: Aufbau-Verlag, 1947. *Sternverdunkelung* (*Eclipse of the Stars*). Amsterdam: Berman-Fischer, 1949. *Und Neimand Weiss Weiter* (*And Noone Knows Where to Go*). Hamburg: Heinrich Ellerman, 1957. *Flucht und Verwandlung* (*Flight and Metamorphosis*). Stuttgart, Germany: Deutsche Verlags-Anstalt, 1959. *Fahrt ins Staublose* (*Journey to the Beyond*). Frankfurt: Suhrkamp Verlag, 1961. *Zerchen im Sand* (*Signs in the Sand*). Frankfurt: Suhrkamp Verlag, 1962. *O the Chimneys. Selected Poems, Including the Verse Play, "Eli."* Tr. by Michael Hamburger, Christopher Holme, Ruth and Matthew Mead, and Michael Raloff. New York: Farrar, Straus and Giroux, 1967.

For More Information See: *Current Biography Yearbook.* New York: H.W. Wilson, 1967, 365-67. Hermann, Armin. *German Nobel Prizewinners.* Munich: Heinz Moos Verlagsgesellschaft, 1968, 32, 39, 40. Opfell, Olga S. *The Lady Laureates.* Metuchen, NJ: Scarecrow Press, 1978, 135-46.

Commentary: The Holocaust, from which she escaped, transformed Nelly Sachs from a minor German poet writing rhymed forms about nature and mythological figures to a powerful voice that reached into the hearts of the world with echoes of Jewish mysticism in works that were her "mute outcry" against her people's sufferings. Her later work identified Jewish suffering with the suffering of all humanity and led to a final message of forgiveness, peace, and hope resting in new generations. The Committee cited her "for her outstanding lyrical and dramatic writings, which interpret Israel's destiny with touching strength." (J.H.S.)

1967

Asturias, Miguel Angel   187

PRIZE: Literature, 1967. BORN: October 19, 1899; Guatemala City, Guatemala. DIED: June 9, 1974; Madrid, Spain. PARENTS: Father, Ernesto Asturias; Mother, Maria Rosales de Asturias. NATIONALITY: Guatemalan. RELIGION: Most probably Christian/Catholic. EDUCATION: San Carlos Univ., Guatemala, law degree, 1923.

SPOUSE: Clemencia Amado, married (no date found); Blanca Mora y Araujo, married (no date found). CHILDREN: Rodrigo, son; Miguel Angel, son. CAREER: Guatemala, Newspaper Correspondent, 1923-33; Writer/Diplomat. OTHER AWARDS: Chavez Prize, 1923; Prix Sylla Monsegur, Paris, 1931; Lenin Peace Prize, 1966.

Selected Publications: *Leyendas de Guatemala.* Madrid: Ediciones Oriente, 1930. *El Senor Presidente.* Mexico City: Editorial Costa-Amic, 1946 (*The President.* Tr. by Frances Partridge. London: V. Gollancz, 1963). *Viento Fuerte.* Buenos Aires: Losada, 1950 (*The Cyclone.* Tr. by Dawin Flahall and Claribel Alegaria. London: Owen, 1967). *Bolivar.* Guatemala City: Editorial Landiver, 1961. *Emulo Lipolidan Fantomina por Miguel Angel Asturias.* Guatemala City: Editorial Landiver, 1961. *Mulata de Tal.* Buenos Aires: Editorial Losada, 1963 (*Mulata.* Tr. by Gregory Ratassa. New York: Delacorte Press, 1967).

For More Information See: Callan, Richard. *Miguel Angel Asturias.* New York: Twayne, 1970. *Current Biography Yearbook.* New York: H.W. Wilson, 1975, 35-38.

Commentary: Miguel Asturias received the Nobel "for his highly colored writings, rooted in a national individuality and Indian traditions." In his many novels, stories, poems, and plays, Asturias displayed his concern for the South American Indian traditions, mythology, and folklore; the national identity for which he fought; and the compassion for the underdog in which he believed. His writing was a true reflection of his beliefs, which led to many years in exile because of his opposition to dictatorships in power in his native Guatemala. (J.H.S.)

1968

Kawabata, Yasunari   188

PRIZE: Literature, 1968. BORN: June 11, 1899; Osaka, Japan. DIED: April 16, 1972; Zushi, Japan. PARENTS: No record found. NATIONALITY: Japanese. RELIGION: Influenced by Buddhist literature. EDUCATION: Tokyo Imperial Univ., Japan, baccalaureate, 1924. SPOUSE: Hideko Kawabata, married (no date found). CHILDREN: 1 daughter. CAREER: Japan, Writer and Editor. OTHER AWARDS: Bungei Konwa Kai Prize, 1937; Geijutsuinsho Literary Prize, 1952; Noma Literary Prize, 1954; Goethe Medal, Germany, 1959; Ordre des Arts et Lettres, France, 1960; French Prix du Meilleur Livre Etranger, 1961; Cultural Medal, Japan, 1961; Akutagawa Prize.

Selected Publications: *Yukiguni* (*Snow Country*). Tr. by Edward G. Seidensticker. New York: Knopf, 1956. *Sembazuru* (*Thousand Cranes*). Tr. by Edward G. Seidensticker. New York: Knopf, 1959. *Nemureru bijo* (*The House of the Sleeping Beauties and Other Stories*). Tr. by Edward G. Seidensticker. Tokyo: Kodansha International, 1969. *Yama No Oto* (*The Sound of the Mountain*). Tr. by Edward G. Seidensticker. New York: Knopf, 1970. *Meijin* (*The Master of Go*). Tr. by Edward G. Seidensticker. New York: Knopf, 1972. *Utsukshisa To Kanashimi To* (*Beauty and Sadness*). Tr. by Howard Hibbett. New York: Knopf, 1975.

For More Information See: *Contemporary Authors.* Detroit, MI: Gale Research, 1980 (Volume 93-96), 265-68. *Current Biography Yearbook.* New York: H.W. Wilson, 1969, 231-33.

Commentary: The award to Yasunari Kawabata was "for his narrative mastership, which with sensibility expresses the essence of the Japanese mind." The first Japanese writer to win the Nobel Prize in literature, Kawabata rejected earlier experiments with the "automatic writing" of Gertrude Stein as well as the "stream of consciousness" method of James Joyce in favor of a more traditional Japanese style of writing that is lyrical and deceptively simple. Kawabata's works are characteristically melancholic and deal with such major themes as alienation, guilt, love, old age, and the acceptance of death. Prior to winning the Nobel Prize, Kawabata was virtually unknown outside of Japan. His winning of the award surprised many Western critics, who were often puzzled by the episodic structure found in his impressionistic novels. (K.M.)

1969

Beckett, Samuel Barclay   189
PRIZE: Literature, 1969. BORN: April 13, 1906; Dublin, Ireland. PARENTS: Father, William Frank Beckett; Mother, Mary Roe Beckett. NATIONALITY: Irish; later French resident. RELIGION: Protestant. EDUCATION: Trinity College, Ireland, B.A., 1927; Trinity College, Ireland, M.A., 1931. SPOUSE: Suzanne Dechevaux-Dumesnil, married 1948. CHILDREN: None. CAREER: Campbell College, Belfast, Ireland, Professor, 1927-28; Ecole Normale Superieure, Paris, France, Professor, 1928-31; Trinity College, Dublin, Ireland, Professor, 1931-32; Writer. OTHER AWARDS: Evening Standard Award, 1955; Obie Award, 1958, 1960, 1962; Italia Prize, 1959; International Publishers Prize, 1961; Prix Filmcritice, 1965; Tours Film Prize, 1966.

Selected Publications: *En Attendant Godot.* Paris: Edition de Minuit, 1952 (*Waiting for Godot.* London: Faber, 1956). *Malloy.* Paris: Olympia Press, 1955. *Malone Dies.* New York: Grove Press, 1956. *All That Falls.* New York: Grove Press, 1957. *Murphy.* New York: Grove Press, 1957. *Proust.* New York: Grove Press, 1957. *The Unnamable.* New York: Grove Press, 1958. *Watt.* Paris: Olympic Press, 1958. *Endgame.* London: Faber, 1959. *Krapp's Last Tape, and Embers.* London: Faber, 1959. *Happy Days.* New York: Grove Press, 1961. *More Pricks than Kicks.* London: Calder & Boyars, 1966. *No's Knife: Collected Shorter Prose, 1945-1966.* London: Calder & Boyars, 1967. *Collected Works.* New York: Grove Press, 1970. *First Love and Other Shorts.* New York: Grove Press, 1974.

For More Information See: Bair, Dierdre. *Samuel Beckett: A Biography.* New York: Harcourt, 1978. *Current Biography Yearbook.* New York: H. W. Wilson, 1970, 30-33. Lyons, Charles. *Samuel Beckett.* New York: Grove Press, 1983. Tindall, William York. *Samuel Beckett.* New York: Columbia U. Press, 1964.

Commentary: Samuel Beckett's Nobel citation recognized him "for introducing new forms to the novel and the drama." Known for his contributions to the theater of the absurd, Beckett himself said "The major sin is the sin of being born." His works portrayed life as "buzzing confusion all around us" centered on Beckett's view of human beings' futile existence. His characters buzz away their existence in pointless, absurd, confusing activity. They exist in settings and engage in discussions from which the only hope for relief is a return to a prefetal nothingness. Using parables to define human beings' completely rudderless spiritual desolation, Beckett conveys the absurdity of life by showing reality as nothingness and theater—a representation of life—as absurd. (J.H.S.)

1970

Solzhenitsyn, Alexander   190
PRIZE: Literature, 1970. BORN: December 11, 1918; Kislorodsk, USSR. PARENTS: Father, Isai Solzhenitsyn; Mother, Taisya Zakharovna Shcherbak Solzhenitsyn. NATIONALITY: Russian; later American resident. RELIGION: Eastern Orthodox. EDUCATION: Rostov Univ., USSR, baccalaureate, 1941. SPOUSE: Natalya Reshetovskaya, married April 27, 1940, divorced 1949, remarried 1956, redivorced 1972; Natalya Svetlova, married 1973. CHILDREN: Yermoli, son; Ignat, son; Stepan, son. CAREER: Secondary School, USSR, Teacher, 1941; Soviet Army, 1941-45; Prisoner, Exile, Writer, 1945-. OTHER AWARDS: Lenin Prize, 1964; Prix du Meilleur Livre Etranger, France, 1969; Templeton Prize, 1983.

Selected Publications: *Odin den' Ivana Denisovicha Matrenin Dvor.* Paris: YMCA Press, 1973 (first published in 1963) (*One Day in the Life of Ivan Denisovich.* Tr. by Ralph Parker. New York: Dutton, 1963). *V Kruge Pervom.* Paris: YMCA Press, 1968 (*First Circle.* Tr. by Thomas P. Whitney. New York: Harper and Row, 1968). *Rakovyī Korpus.* Paris: YMCA Press, 1969 (*Cancer Ward. Sobranie Sochinenii.* (Collected Works). 5 volumes. Frankfurt: Possev Verlag, 1969-70. Tr. by Nicholas Bethel and David Burg. New York: Farrar, Straus and Giroux, 1969). *August Chetyrnadtsatogo.* Paris: YMCA Press, 1971 (*August 1914.* Tr. by Michael Glenny. New York: Farrar, Straus and Giroux, 1972). *Arkhipelag Gulag.* Paris: YMCA Press, 1973 (*Gulag Archipelago.* Tr. by Thomas Whitney. New York: Harper and Row, 1974-78).

For More Information See: *Contemporary Authors.* Detroit, MI: Gale Research, 1978 (Volume 69-72), 543-50. *Current Biography Yearbook.* New York: H.W. Wilson, 1969, 410-13. Scammel, Michael. *Solzhenitsyn.* New York: W.W. Norton, 1984.

Commentary: Alexander Solzhenitsyn's Nobel Award was "for the ethical force with which he has pursued the indispensable traditions of Russian literature." Both his written work and his personal life—rooted in his own country, his own people, his own religion—embody the heritage of the great Russian novelists—like Dostoevsky in his prison experiences and in his spiritual conversion, like Tolstoy in his moral approach to literature and life, and like both in the immense range of his work. (T.S.K.)

1971

Neruda, Pablo (Eliecer Neftali Reyes y Basoalto, Ricardo)   191
PRIZE: Literature, 1971. BORN: July 12, 1904; Parral, Chile. DIED: September 23, 1973; Santiago, Chile. PARENTS: Father, José del Carmen Reyes; Mother, Rosa de Basoalto. NATIONALITY: Chilean. RELIGION: Christian background. EDUCATION: No college degrees. SPOUSE: Marie Antonieta Maruca Hagenaar Vogelzanz, married 1930, separated 1936; Delia del Caroul, married 1934;

Matilde Urrutia, married 1955. CHILDREN: Malva Marina, daughter. CAREER: Diplomat/Writer. OTHER AWARDS: Premio Municipal de Literatura, Chile, 1944.

Selected Publications: *Veinte Poemas de Amor y Una Cancion Desesperada.* Santiago: Nascimento, 1924 (*Twenty Poems: A Disdaining Song.* Tr. by W.S. Merwin. New York: Grossman, 1970). *Residencia en la Tierra.* Madrid: Ediciones del arbol, 1935 (*Residence on Earth.* Tr. by Angel Flores. New York: New Directions, 1947). *Espana en el Corazo* (*Spain in the Heart*). Santiago: Ediciones Ercilla, 1937. *Canto General.* Santiago: n.p., 1950 (*General Song.* Tr. by Nathaniel Tarn. New York: Farrar, Straus, 1967). *Odas Elementales.* Buenos Aires: Editorial Losada, 1954 (*The Elementary Odes of Pablo Neruda.* Tr. by Carlos Lozano. New York: Las Americas, 1961). *Bestiario; Bestiary; a Poem.* Tr. by Elsa Neuberger. New York: Harcourt, 1965.

For More Information See: *Current Biography Yearbook.* New York: H.W. Wilson, 1970, 312-15. *Memoirs.* Tr. by Hardie St. Martin. New York: Farrar, Straus, and Giroux, 1977.

Commentary: Pablo Neruda won the Nobel Prize for "a poetry that, with the action of an elementary force, brings alive a continent's destiny and dreams." His work, utilizing surrealist techniques and exploring his inner self against the broad background of South America, was critically acclaimed throughout his career. He also was a force in the political arena as a Chilean diplomat and through his deep commitment to Communism. (J.H.S.)

1972

Böll, Heinrich   192

PRIZE: Literature, 1972. BORN: December 21, 1917; Cologne, Germany. DIED: July 16, 1985; Bornheim-Merten, Germany. PARENTS: Father, Viktor Böll; Mother, Maria Hermanns Böll. NATIONALITY: German. RELIGION: Catholic. EDUCATION: No college degrees. SPOUSE: Annemarie Cech, married 1942. CHILDREN: Christoph, son; Raimund, son; René, son; Vincent, son. CAREER: Bonn, Germany, Bookshop Apprentice, 1937-38; Germany, Civilian Labor Service, 1938-39; Germany, Army, 1939-45. OTHER AWARDS: Prize of "Group 47," Bad Dürkheim, 1951; René-Schickele Prize, 1952; German Critics Prize, 1953; Prize of the *Tribune de Paris*, 1955; Eduard-von-der-Heydt Prize, Wuppertal, 1958; Prize of the State of Nordrhein-Westfalen, 1959; Charles-Veillon Prize, 1960; Literary Prize of the City of Cologne, 1961; Literary Prize Isola d'Elba, Italy, 1965; Georg-Büchner Prize, 1967; Carl-von-Ossietzky Medal, International League for Human Rights, 1974.

Selected Publications: *Und Sagte Kein Einziges Wort.* Cologne: Kiepenheuer and Witsch, 1953 (*And Never Said a Word.* Tr. by Leila Vennewitz. New York: McGraw-Hill, 1978). *Haus ohne Hüter.* Cologne: Kiepenheuer and Witsch, 1954 (*The Unguarded House.* Tr. by Mervyn Savill. London: Arco, 1957). *Billard um Halbzehn.* Cologne: Kiepenheuer and Witsch, 1959 (*Billiards at Half-Past Nine.* New York: McGraw-Hill, 1973). *Ansichten eines Clowns.* Cologne: Kiepenheuer and Witsch, 1963 (*The Clown.* Tr. by Leila Vennewitz. New York: McGraw-Hill, 1965). *Gruppenbild mit Dame.* Cologne: Kiepenheuer and Witsch, 1971 (*Group Portrait with Lady.* Tr. by Leila Vennewitz. New York:

McGraw-Hill, 1973). *Fürsorgliche Belagerung.* Cologne: Kiepenheuer and Witsch, 1979 (*The Safety Net.* Tr. by Leila Vennewitz. New York: Penguin, 1983).

For More Information See: Conard, Robert C. *Heinrich Böll.* Boston: Twayne Publishers, 1981. *Current Biography Yearbook.* New York: H.W. Wilson Co., 1972, 44-47. Friedrichsmeyer, Erhard. *The Major Works of Heinrich Böll: A Critical Commentary.* New York: Monarch Press, 1974. Macpherson, Enid. *A Student's Guide to Böll.* London: Heinemann, 1972. Reid, James H. *Heinrich Böll: Withdrawal and Re-emergence.* London: Oswald Wolff, 1973. Yuill, W.E., "Heinrich Böll." In *Essays on Contemporary German Literature,* edited by Brian Keith-Smith, London: Oswald Wolff, 1966, 141-58.

Commentary: Heinrich Böll received the award for his "literary works, which represent a renewal of the German literary tradition and which combine a clear vision of contemporary history with an art of representation characterized by sensitivity as well as emotional penetration." Set in modern Germany, but symbolic of conditions throughout the world, Böll's works exhibit a steadfast humanitarianism, which is marked by unwavering compassion for the victims of society as well as by resolute condemnation of the various individuals, groups and economic, historical, political, or social forces which in his opinion precipitated the widespread human suffering of this century. (W.L.N.)

1973

White, Patrick Victor Martindale   193

PRIZE: Literature, 1973. BORN: May 28, 1912; London, England. PARENTS: Father, Victor Martindale White; Mother, Ruth Withycombe White. NATIONALITY: Australian. RELIGION: No organized religion; from Anglican background. EDUCATION: Cambridge Univ., England, B.A., 1935. SPOUSE: None. CHILDREN: None. CAREER: Royal Air Force, Writer, 1940-45. OTHER AWARDS: Gold Medal, Australian Literary Society, 1956; Miles Franklin Award, 1958, 1962; W.H. Smith and Son Literary Award, 1959; Brotherhood Award, National Conference of Christians and Jews, 1962.

Selected Publications: *Happy Valley.* London: Harrap, 1939. *The Living and the Dead.* New York: Viking, 1941. *The Aunt's Story.* New York: Viking, 1948. *The Tree of Man.* New York: Viking, 1955. *The Burnt Ones.* London: Eyre & Spottiswoode, 1957. *Voss.* London: Eyre & Spottiswoode, 1957. *Riders in the Chariot.* New York: Viking, 1961. *The Solis Mandala.* New York: Viking, 1966. *The Vivisector.* New York: Viking, 1970. *The Eye of the Storm.* New York: J. Cape, 1973. *The Cockatoos: Shorter Novels and Stories.* New York: J. Cape, 1974. *A Fringe of Leaves.* New York: J. Cape, 1976.

For More Information See: Colmer, John. *Patrick White.* New York: Methuen Inc., 1984. *Current Biography Yearbook.* New York: H.W. Wilson, 1974, 434-36. Lawson, Alan. *Patrick White.* New York: Oxford U. Press, 1974.

Commentary: The Nobel presentation noted that Patrick White's work "for the first time has given the continent of Australia an authentic voice that carries across the world" by creating "Epic and Psychological narrative art which has introduced a new continent in Literature." The Royal Academy concluded by saying his works "show White's unbroken creative power, an ever deeper restlessness and seeking urge, an onslaught against vital problems that have never ceased to engage him and a wrestling with the language in order to extract all its power and nuances, to the verge of the unobtainable." (D.E.S.)

1974

Johnson, Eyvind Olof Verner   194

PRIZE: Literature, 1974. BORN: July 29, 1900; Overlulea, Sweden. DIED: August 25, 1976; Stockholm, Sweden. PARENTS: Father, Olof Johnson; Mother, Cevia Gustafsdotter Johnson. NATIONALITY: Swedish. RELIGION: Most probably Christian/Protestant. EDUCATION: No college degrees. SPOUSE: Aase Christofferson, married 1927, died 1938; Cilla Frankenhaeuser, married 1940. CHILDREN: 3 children. CAREER: Writer. OTHER AWARDS: Samfundet De Nio's Award, 1936; Swedish Academy Award, 1944; Nordic Council Prize for Literature, Helsinki, 1962.

Selected Publications: *An En Gang, Kapten* (*Once More, Captain*). Stockholm: A. Bonnier, 1934. *Nu Var Det, 1914.* Stockholm: A. Bonnier, 1934 (*1914*. Tr. by Mary Sandbach. New York: Adama Books, 1970). *Grupp Krilon* (*Krilon's Group*). Stockholm: A. Bonnier, 1941. *Krilons Resa* (*Krilon's Journey*). Stockholm: A. Bonnier, 1942. *Krilon Sjalv* (*Krilon Himself*). Stockholm: A. Bonnier, 1943. *Strandernas Svall.* Stockholm: A. Bonnier, 1946 (*Return to Ithaca*. Tr. by M. A. Michael. New York: Thames & Hudson, 1952). *Romantisk Berattelse* (*Romantic Tale*). Stockholm: A. Bonnier, 1955. *Tidens Gang* (*The Course of Time*). Stockholm: A. Bonnier, 1955. *Hans Naades Tid.* Stockholm: A. Bonnier, 1960 (*The Days of His Grace*. Tr. by Elspeth Harley Schubert. New York: Vanguard, 1968). *Livsdagen Lang* (*Life's Long Day*). Stockholm: A. Bonnier, 1964. *Favel Ansam* (*Favel Alone*). Stockholm: A. Bonnier, 1968.

For More Information See: *Contemporary Authors.* Detroit, MI: Gale Research, 1978 (Volume 73-76), 317-18. Orton, G. *Eyvind Johnson.* New York: Twayne, 1972.

Commentary: Eyvind Johnson received the Nobel Prize for "a narrative art, far-seeing in lands and ages." Many objected at the time because his reputation was national rather than international. Johnson's writings fell into several periods. His novels and short stories first explored socialism and world reform, moved to representations of Swedish life with psychological and intellectually questioning overtones, and, with the growth of Naziism, became pleas for freedom and against dictatorship. Johnson devoted considerable time after 1945 to representing Sweden in UNESCO activities. (J.H.S.)

Martinson, Harry Edmund   195

PRIZE: Literature, 1974. BORN: May 6, 1904; Jamshog, Sweden. DIED: February 11, 1978; Stockholm, Sweden. PARENTS: Father, Martin Olofsson; Mother, Betty Olofsson. NATIONALITY: Swedish. RELIGION: Lutheran background; with Taoist orientation. EDUCATION: No college degrees. SPOUSE: Moa Swartz, married 1929, divorced 1940; Ingrid Lindcrantz, married 1942. CHILDREN: None. CAREER: Seaman, 1918-27; Writer. OTHER AWARDS: Henrik Steffins Prize, 1972.

Selected Publications: *Kap Faerval.* Stockholm: A. Bonnier, 1933 (*Cape Farewell*. Tr. by Naomi Walford. New York: Putnam, 1934). *Naesslorna Blomma.* Stockholm: A. Bonnier, 1935 (*Flowering Nettle*. Tr. by Naomi Walford. New York: Cresset, 1935). *Verlighet Till Dods* (*Realism Unto Death*). Stockholm: P. A. Norstedt and Soner, 1940. *Passad* (*Trade Wind*). Stockholm: A. Bonnier, 1945. *Vagen Till Klockrile.* Stockholm: A. Bonnier, 1948 (*The Road*. Tr. by M. A. Michael. New York: J. Cape, 1955). *Cikada* (*Cecada*). Stockholm: A. Bonnier, 1953. *Aniara.* Stockholm: A. Bonnier, 1956 (*Aniara*. Tr. by Hugh McDiarmid and Elspeth Harley Shubert. New York: Knopf, 1963).

For More Information See: *Encyclopedia of World Literature in the Twentieth Century.* New York: Frederick Ungar Publishing Co., 1964 (Volume 2), 387-88. Holm, I. *Harry Martinson: Myster Malningar Motiv.* Stockholm: A. Bonnier, 1960. Kristensen, Tom. *Harry Martinson, den Fribaarne Fyrboder.* Copenhagen: Glydendal, 1941.

Commentary: Harry Martinson—poet, novelist, dramatist, and essayist—shared the Nobel Prize for "writings that catch the dewdrops and reflect the cosmos." His award was looked upon as Swedish nationalism at the time, since his international reputation was slight. Martinson's early work dealt with his hardships as a child and his extensive travels, and exhibited his lack of education and acquaintance with standard writing forms, while capturing the imagination with its unorthodox qualities. The primitivism of his early work matured into the philosophical, cosmic nature of his later efforts, which dealt with the disorientation of modern humanity and have been called "a unique contribution to poetic science fiction." (J.H.S.)

1975

Montale, Eugenio   196

PRIZE: Literature, 1975. BORN: October 12, 1896; Genoa, Italy. DIED: September 12, 1981; Milan, Italy. PARENTS: Father, Domenico Montale; Mother, Guiseppina Ricci Montale. NATIONALITY: Italian. RELIGION: Catholic. EDUCATION: No college degrees. SPOUSE: Drusilla Tanzi, married 1950. CHILDREN: None. CAREER: Italy, Writer, Editor, Critic, Translator. OTHER AWARDS: Antico Fattore Poetry Prize, Italy, 1932; Premio Manzotto, Italy, 1956; Dante Medal, Italy, 1959; Feltrinelli Prize, Italy, 1962; Calouste Gulbenkian Prize, Paris, 1971.

Selected Publications: *Ossi Di Seppia.* Turin, Italy: Gobetti, 1925 (*Cuttlefish Bones*. Tr. by Edith Farnsworth. Chicago: Regnery, 1970). *La Occasioni.* Turin, Italy: Einaudi, 1939. *Finistere.* Lugano, Italy: Quaredeni di Lugano, 1943. *La Bufera e Alto.* Venice: Edizione Nero Pozza, 1956 (*The Storm and Other Things*. Tr. by Edith Farnsworth. Chicago: Regnery, 1970). *La Farfalla di Dinard.* Venice: Nero Puzzo, 1956 (*The Butterfly of Dinard*. Tr. by G. Singh. Lexington, KY: Kentucky U. Press, 1971). *Xenia* (bilingual). Tr. by G. Singh. Los Angeles: Black Sparrow Press, 1970. *Satura.* Milan: Mondadori, 1971 (*Satura and Diario del '71-'72* (selections). Tr. by G. Singh. New York: New Directions Publishing Corp., 1976). *Nel Nostro Tempo.* Rome: Rizzoli Editore, 1972 (*Poets in our Time*. Tr. by Alastair Hamilton. New York: Urizen Books, 1976).

For More Information See: *Current Biography Yearbook.* New York: H.W. Wilson, 1976, 265-68. Singh, Ghan Shyam. *Eugenio Montale: A Critical Study of His Poetry, Prose, and Criticism.* New Haven, CT: Yale U. Press, 1973. West, Rebecca. *Eugenio Montale: Poet on the Edge.* Cambridge, MA.: Harvard U. Press, 1981.

Commentary: Eugenio Montale, Italian poet, translator, and journalist, was cited by the Academy, which noted that his "poetry with great artistic sensitivity, has interpreted human values under the sign of an outlook on life with no illusions." His poetic output of five volumes of poetry at the time of the prize, although small, has ranked him as one of the world's great poets. His public involvement as a journalist in serving as a conscience for his generation is also worthy of note. (A.N.)

1976

Bellow, Saul   197

PRIZE: Literature, 1976. BORN: June 10, 1915; Lachine, Quebec, Canada. PARENTS: Father, Abraham Bellow; Mother, Liza Gordon Bellow. NATIONALITY: Canadian; later American citizen. RELIGION: Jewish. EDUCATION: Northwestern Univ., IL, B.S., 1937. SPOUSE: Anita Goshkin, married December 31, 1937, divorced 1955; Alexandra Tschacbasov, married February 1, 1956, divorced 1956; Susan Glassman, married 1961, divorced 1968; Alexandra Ionescu Tulcea, married October 1974. CHILDREN: Gregory, son; Adam, son; Daniel, son. CAREER: Pestalozzi-Froebel Teachers College, Chicago, IL, Professor, 1938-42; *Encyclopedia Britannica,* Editor, 1943-46; Univ. of Minnesota, Professor, 1946-49; New York Univ., Professor, 1950-52; Princeton Univ., NJ, Fellow, 1952-53; Bard College, NJ, Professor, 1953-54; Univ. of Minnesota, Professor, 1954-59. OTHER AWARDS: Guggenheim Fellowship, 1948, 1955; National Institute of Arts and Letters Award, 1952; American Academy Grant, 1952; National Book Award, 1953; Ford Grant, 1959; Friends of Literature Fiction Award, 1960; National Book Award, 1964; James D. Dow Award, 1964; Prix International de Literature, 1965; Jewish Heritage Award, 1968; Pulitzer Prize, 1976; Neil Gunn International Fellowship, 1977; American Academy Gold Medal, 1977; Brandeis U. Creative Arts Award, 1978.

Selected Publications: *Dangling Man.* New York: Vanguard, 1944. *The Victim.* New York: Vanguard, 1947. *Adventures of Augie March.* New York: Viking Press, 1953. *Seize the Day, and Three Short Stories.* New York: Viking Press, 1956. *Henderson, the Rain King.* New York: Viking Press, 1959. *Herzog.* New York: Viking Press, 1964. *The Last Analysis.* New York: Viking Press, 1965. *Mosby's Memories and Other Stories.* New York: Viking Press, 1968. *Mr. Sammler's Planet.* New York: Viking Press, 1970. *Humboldt's Gift.* New York: Viking Press, 1975. *The Dean's December.* New York: Harper, 1981.

For More Information See: Clayton, John J. *Saul Bellow: In Defense of Man.* Bloomington, IN: Indiana U. Press, 1979. Cohen, Sara B. *Saul Bellow's Enigmatic Laughter.* Urbana, IL: U. of Illinois Press, 1974. *Contemporary Authors.* Detroit, MI: Gale Research, 1969 (Volume 5-8 First Revision), 94-96. *Current Bi-*

ography *Yearbook.* New York: H.W. Wilson, 1965, 23-25. Tanner, Tony. *Saul Bellow.* Edinburgh: Oliver and Boyd, 1965.

Commentary: Saul Bellow received the Nobel Prize in literature "for the human understanding and subtle analysis of contemporary culture that are combined in his works." At the time of the award Bellow had written seven major novels, one novella, and a number of short stories as well as essays and plays. This serious novelist of the post-World War II generation was speaking for the humanistic purposes of the novel. The prize recognized Bellow's "exuberant ideas, flashing irony...and burning compassion" in his depiction of modern man as one "who keeps trying to find a foothold during his wanderings in our tottering world, one who can never relinquish his faith that the value of life depends on its dignity not its success." (C.B.)

1977

Aleixandre y Merlo, Vicente Pio Marcelino Cirilo
198

PRIZE: Literature, 1977. BORN: April 26, 1898; Seville, Spain. PARENTS: Father, Cirilo Aleixandre Ballester; Mother, Elvira Merlo Garcia de Pruneda. NATIONALITY: Spanish. RELIGION: Catholic. EDUCATION: Univ. of Madrid, Spain, law degree, 1919; Univ. of Madrid, Spain, Diploma in Business Administration, 1919. SPOUSE: None. CHILDREN: None. CAREER: Central School of Commerce, Madrid, Spain, Professor, 1919-21; Residentia de Estudiantes, Madrid, Spain, Professor, 1921-22; Writer, 1922-. OTHER AWARDS: National Prize for Literature, Spain, 1933; Spanish Critics Prize, 1969; Ceraud Cross of Order of Carlos III, 1977.

Selected Publications: *Ambito, 1924-1927.* Malaga, Spain: Impresa Sur, 1928. *Espadas Como Labios, 1930-31.* Madrid: Espasa-Calpe, 1932. *Pasion de la Tierra.* Mexico City: Fabula, 1935. *Sombra del Paradiso.* Madrid: Adan, 1944. *Mundo a Solas.* Madrid: Clan, 1950. *Nacimiento Ultimo.* Madrid: Insula, 1953. *Es Un Vasto Dominio.* Madrid: Revista del Occidente, 1962. *Poemas de la Consumacion.* Barcelona: Plaza y Janes, 1968. *Dialogos del Conocimiento.* Barcelona: Plaza y Janes, 1974. *Poemas Paradisiacos.* Madrid: Editiones Catedra, 1981.

For More Information See: *Current Biography Yearbook.* New York: H.W. Wilson, 1978, 4-8. Luis, Leopoldo. *Vida y Obra de Vicente Aleixandre.* Madrid: Espasa-Calpe, 1978. Schwartz, Kessel. *Vicente Aleixandre.* New York: Twayne Publishers, 1970.

Commentary: The Nobel Prize was granted to Vicente Aleixandre "for a creative poetic writing which illuminates men's condition in the cosmos and present-day society, at the same time representing the great renewal of the traditions of Spanish poetry between the wars." Aleixandre was highly admired in Spain and in Latin America as a lifelong poet of the people, beginning with his membership in the so-called Poetic Group of 1927, with roots in both the Spanish lyric tradition and in modernism. His poems are free verse and deal with love, death, and eternity. Most of his early poems were sad love poems, but later, his writings rose above the early pessimistic emptiness. (D.C.)

1978

Singer, Isaac Bashevis   199

PRIZE: Literature, 1978. BORN: July 14, 1904; Leoncin, Poland. PARENTS: Father, Pinchas Mendel Singer; Mother, Bathsheba Zylberman Singer. NATIONALITY: Polish; later American citizen. RELIGION: Jewish. EDUCATION: No college degrees. SPOUSE: Rachel, married 1927 (?), divorced 1935; Alma Haiman, married February 14, 1940. CHILDREN: Israel, son. CAREER: Writer. OTHER AWARDS: Louis Lamed Prize, 1950, 1956; American Academy Award, 1959; Harry and Ethel Daroff Memorial Fiction Award, 1963; National Endowment for the Arts Grant, 1966, 1967; *Playboy* Magazine Award, 1967; Newbery Honor Book Award, 1967, 1968; Bancarella Prize, 1968; Brandeis U. Creative Arts Medal, 1970; National Book Award, 1970, 1974; Agnon Gold Medal, 1975.

Selected Publications: *The Family Moskat.* New York: Knopf, 1950. *Satan in Goray.* New York: Noonday, 1955. *The Magician of Lublin.* New York: Noonday, 1960. *The Slave.* New York: Farrar, Straus, 1962. *Zlateh the Goat and Other Stories.* New York: Harper, 1966. *The Fearsome Inn.* New York: Scribner, 1967. *The Manor.* New York: Farrar, Straus, 1967. *Mazel and Schlimazel.* New York: Farrar, Straus, 1967. *When Schlemiel Went to Warsaw and Other Stories.* New York: Farrar, Straus, 1968. *The Estate.* New York: Farrar, Straus, 1969. *Joseph and Koza.* New York: Farrar, Straus, 1970. *Alone in the Wild Forest.* New York: Farrar, Straus, 1971. *Topsy Turvy Emperor of China.* New York: Harper, 1971. *Enemies: A Love Story.* New York: Farrar, Straus, 1972. *The Fools of Chelm and Their History.* New York: Farrar, Straus, 1973. *Naftali the Storyteller and His Horse, Sus, and Other Stories.* New York: Farrar, Straus, 1976. *Tale of Three Wishes.* New York: Farrar, Straus, 1976. *Shosha.* New York, Farrar, Straus, 1978. *Stories for Children.* New York: Farrar, Straus, 1985.

For More Information See: Alexander, Edward. *Isaac Bashevis Singer.* Boston: Twayne Publishers, 1980. *Current Biography Yearbook.* New York: H.W. Wilson, 1969, 402-04. Kresh, Paul. *Isaac Bashevis Singer: The Magician of West 86th St.* New York: Dial Press, 1970.

Commentary: Isaac Bashevis Singer received the Nobel Prize "for his impassioned narrative art which, with roots in a Polish-Jewish cultural tradition, brings universal human conditions to life." Singer's writings bring to life the shtetl world of East European Jewry in his time of growth and maturing. Based on his own childhood, adolescence, and youthful and mature experiences, his writings vividly portray "the clash between tradition and renewal, between otherworldliness and pious mysticism on the one hand, free thought, doubt, and nihilism on the other." His adult works have been supplemented by a much-loved and admired set of children's books and stories, which have endeared him to children and adults alike. (J.V.)

1979

Elytis, Odysseus (Alepoudelis)   200

PRIZE: Literature, 1979. BORN: November 2, 1911; Crete, Greece. PARENTS: Father, Panayiotis Alepoudelis; Mother, Maria Alepoudelis. NATIONALITY: Greek. RELIGION: Eastern Orthodox. EDUCATION: No college degrees. SPOUSE: None. CHILDREN: None. CAREER: *Kathimerini*, Athens, Greece, Art Critic, 1946-48; Writer. OTHER AWARDS: National Poetry Prize, 1960; National Book Award, 1960; Order of the Phoenix, 1965; Benson Silver Medal, Royal Society of Literature, 1981.

Selected Publications: *To Axion Esti.* Athens: Ikaros, 1959 (*The Axion Esti of Odysseus Elytis.* Tr. by Edmund Keeley and George Savadis. Pittsburgh, PA: U. of Pittsburgh Press, 1974). *O Ilios Oiliatorus.* Athens: Ikaros, 1971 (*The Sovereign Sun: Selected Poems.* Tr. by Kimon Friar. Philadelphia, PA: Temple U. Press, 1974). *To Fotodhendro Ke i Dhekati Tetarti Omorfia* (*The Light Tree and the Fourteenth Beauty*). Athens: Ikaros, 1971. *O Fillomandis* (*The Leaf Diviner*). Athens: Asterias, 1973. *Anihta Hartia* (*Open Book*). Athens: Asterias, 1974. *Maria Nefeli: Shiniko Pūma.* Athens: Ikaros, 1978 (*Maria Nefephele.* New York: Houghton-Mifflin, 1981).

For More Information See: *Contemporary Authors.* Detroit, MI: Gale, 1981 (Volume 102), 171-73. *Current Biography Yearbook.* New York: H.W. Wilson, 1980, 94-96.

Commentary: The Academy praised Odysseus Elytis's "poetry, which against the background of Greek tradition, depicts with sensuous strength and intellectual clearsightedness modern man's struggle for freedom and creativity." It was further noted that by "its combination of fresh sensuous flexibility and strictly disciplined implacability in the face of all compulsion, Elytis's poetry gives shape to its distinctiveness, which is not only very personal but also represents the traditions of the Greek People." (D.E.S.)

1980

Milosz, Czeslaw   201

PRIZE: Literature, 1980. BORN: June 30, 1911; Seteiniai, Lithuania. PARENTS: Father, Aleksander Milosz; Mother, Weronika Kunat Milosz. NATIONALITY: Polish; later American citizen. RELIGION: Catholic. EDUCATION: Univ. of Wilno, Poland, Master Juris, 1934. SPOUSE: Janina (Janka) Dluska, married January 1, 1944. CHILDREN: Anthony, son; John Peter, son. CAREER: Polish National Radio, Programmer, 1935-39; Polish Foreign Affairs Ministry, Diplomat, 1945-50; Univ. of California, Berkeley, Professor, 1960-. OTHER AWARDS: Polish Writers Union Award, 1934; Prix Litteraire Europeen, Les Guildes du Livre, Geneva, 1953; Marian Kister Literary Award, 1967; Jurzykowski Foundation Award for Creative Work, 1968; Polish PEN Club Award for Poetry Translations, 1974; Neustadt International Prize for Literature, U. of Oklahoma, 1978.

Selected Publications: *Trzy Zimy* (*Three Winters*). Warsaw: Wilno, 1936. *Ocalenie* (*Rescue*). Cracow: Spoldzielnia Wydawnicza "Cytelnik," 1945. *Zdobycie Wladzy.* Paris: Instytut Literacki, 1953 (*The Seizure of Power.* Tr. by Celina Viennaiewska. New York: Criterion Books, 1955). *Zniewolony Umysl.* Paris: Institut

Litteraire, 1953 (*The Captive Mind*. Tr. by Jane Zielonko. New York: Knopf, 1953). *Dolina Issy*. Paris: Institut Litteraire, 1955 (*The Issa Valley*. Tr. by Louis Iribarne. New York: Farrar, Straus, Giroux, 1981). *Swiatlo Dzienne* (*Daylight*). Paris: Institut Litteraire, 1955. *Traktat Poetycki* (*Poetic Treatise*). Paris: Institut Litteraire, 1957. *Rodzinna Europa*. Paris: Institut Litteraire, 1958 (*Native Realm: A Search for Self-Definition*. Tr. by Catherine S. Leach. Garden City, NY: Doubleday, 1968). *Widzenia Nad Zatoka*. Paris: Institut Litteraire, 1969 (*Visions from San Francisco Bay*. Tr. by Riczard Lourie. New York: Farrar, Straus, Giroux, 1982). *Prywatne Obowiazki* (*Private Obligations*). Paris: Institut Litteraire, 1972. *Emperor of the Earth: Modes of Eccentric Vision*. Berkeley, CA: U. of California Press, 1977. *Ziemia Ulro* (*The Land of Ulro*). Paris: Institut Litteraire, 1977. *Bells in Winter*. New York: Ecco Press, 1978.

For More Information See: *Current Biography Yearbook*. New York: H.W. Wilson, 1981, 305-08. *Modern Slavic Literatures: A Library of Literary Criticism*. New York: Frederick Ungar Publishing Co., 1976 (Volume 2), 340-46. *Native Realm: A Search for Self-Definition*. Tr. by Catherine S. Leach. Berkeley, CA: U. of California Press, 1981.

Commentary: Czeslaw Milosz's award was for voicing "with uncompromising clearsightedness...man's exposed condition in a world of severe conflicts." Milosz is an exiled writer, "a stranger for whom physical exile is really a reflection of a...spiritual exile applying to humanity in general." His works as a poet, novelist, essayist, translator, critic, and literary scholar are of great historical, sociological, political, and spiritual value. Having experienced the devastation of Hitler's Naziism and the repression of Russian communism, he depicts in his writing the meanness and cruelty of the world; but his writing, of itself, is an expression of hope. (S.R.)

1981

Canetti, Elias   202
PRIZE: Literature, 1981. BORN: July 25, 1905; Ruschuk, Bulgaria. PARENTS: Father, Jacques Canetti; Mother, Mathilde Arditti. NATIONALITY: Bulgarian; later Austrian and British resident. RELIGION: Jewish. EDUCATION: Univ. of Vienna, Austria, D.Sc., 1929. SPOUSE: Benetia Taubner-Calerón, married 1934, died 1963; Hera (no last name found), married 1967. CHILDREN: Johanna, daughter. CAREER: France, Writer and Freelance Journalist. OTHER AWARDS: Prix International, Paris, 1949; Author's Prize, Vienna, 1966; Austrian Prize for Literature, 1968; Georg Buchner Prize, Munich, 1972; Franz Nabe Prize, Graz, 1975; Nelly Sachs Prize, Dartmund, 1976; Kafka Prize, Austria, 1981.

Selected Publications: *Die Komödie der Eitelkeit*. München: W. Weismann, 1934 (*Comedy of Vanity and Life-Terms*. Tr. by Getta Honegger. New York: Performing Arts, 1983). *Die Blendung*. Vienna: H. Reichner, 1935 (*Auto-da-Fé*. Tr. by C.V. Wedgwood. London: J. Cape, 1946). *Masse und Macht*. Dusseldorf, West Germany: Claasen, 1962 (*Crowds and Power*. Tr. by Carol Stewart. New York: Viking, 1962). *Die Andere Prozess: Kafka's Briefe an Felice*. Munich: Hanser, 1969 (*Kafka's Other Trial: The Letters of Felice*. Tr. by Christopher Middleton. New York: Schocken Books,

1974). *Die Ohrenzeuge: 50 Charaktere*. Munich: Hanser, 1974 (*Earwitness: Fifty Characters*. Tr. by Joachim Neugroschel. New York: Seabury, 1979). *Das Gewissen der Worte*. Munich: Hanser, 1975 (*The Conscience of Words*. Tr. by Joachim Neugroschel. New York: Continuum, 1979). *The Plays of Elias Canetti*. Tr. by Getta Honegger. New York: Farrar, Straus and Giroux, 1984.

For More Information See: *Current Biography Yearbook*. New York: H.W. Wilson, 1983, 48-51. Sontag, Susan. *Under the Sign of Saturn*. New York: Farrar, 1980, 181-204. *Die Gerettete Zunge. Geschichte einer Jugend*. Munich: Hanser, 1977 (*The Tongue Set Free*. Tr. by Joachim Neugroschel. New York: Seabury, 1979). *Die Fackel im Ohr*. Munich: Hanser, 1980 (*The Torch in My Ear*. Tr. by Joachim Neugroschel. London: Farrar, 1982). *World Authors*. New York: H.W. Wilson, 1975, 270-72.

Commentary: The Nobel Prize was awarded to Elias Canetti for "writings marked by a broad outlook, a wealth of ideas and artistic power." The modest and humble Canetti paradoxically spent a lifetime studying and writing about power. The Bulgarian-born writer's first languages were Spanish and Ladino; his education was in the sciences (a doctorate in Chemistry) in Britain, Germany, Switzerland, and Austria; and he identified himself as a "Viennese" writer, following the traditions of Goethe and the circle of writers he knew and admired (Brecht, Broch, Kafka, and Kraus). This author was relatively unknown to the English-speaking world until the Nobel Prize was granted in 1981. His most cited works are the nightmarish *Auto-da-Fé*, written in the Kafka tradition of horror and comedy imbedded in a story simply told, and his "life work," *Crowds and Power*, with its paranoic ruler, which has been referred to as "the nearest thing to a book of wisdom we are likely to get in the twentieth century." (J.H.S.)

1982

Garcia Márquez, Gabriel José   203
PRIZE: Literature, 1982. BORN: March 6, 1928; Aracataca, Colombia. PARENTS: Father, Gabriel Eligio Garcia; Mother, Luisa Santiaga Márquez Iquaràn. NATIONALITY: Colombian. RELIGION: No organized religion; from Catholic background. EDUCATION: No college degrees. SPOUSE: Mercedes Barcha, married 1958. CHILDREN: Rodrigo, son; Gonzalo, son. CAREER: *El Heraldo*, Barranquilla, Colombia, Journalist, 1950-54; *El Espectador*, Bogota, Colombia, Rome, Italy, and Paris, France, Journalist, 1954-55; Europe, Free-lance Journalist, 1956-57; *Momento*, Caracas, Venezuela, Journalist, 1957-59; *Presna Latina*, Bogota, Colombia and Havana, Cuba, Journalist, 1959-61; Mexico City, Free-lance Editor, Screenwriter, Copywriter, 1961-65; Mexico City and Barcelona, Spain, Writer, 1965-. OTHER AWARDS: Colombian Association of Writers and Artists Award, 1954; Premio Literario Esso, Colombia, 1961; Premio Chianciano, Italy, 1969; Prix du Meilleur Livre Etranger, France, 1969; Romulo Gallegos Prize, Venezuela, 1972; Books Abro ad, Neustadt International Prize for Literature, 1972

Selected Publications: *La Hojarasca*. Bogota: Ediciones S.L.B., 1955 (*Leaf Storm, and Other Stories*. Tr. by Gregory Rabassa. New York: Harper & Row, 1978). *El Coronel No Tiene Quien Le Escriba*. Medellin: Aqirre, 1961 (*No One Writes to the Colonel, and Other Stories*. Tr. by J.S. Bernstein. New York: Harper & Row, 1979). *La Mala Hora*. Madrid: 1962. (*The Evil Hour*. Tr. by Gregory Rabassa. New York: Harper & Row, 1979). *Cien Anos de Soledad*. Buenos Aires: Editorial Sudamericana, 1967 (*One Hundred Years of Solitude*. Tr. by Gregory Rabassa. New York: Harper & Row, 1970).

For More Information See: *Current Biography Yearbook*. New York: H.W. Wilson, 1973, 146-48. Kennedy, William. "The Yellow Trolley Car in Barcelona: A Profile of Gabriel Garcia Márquez." *The Atlantic* 231 (January 1973): 50-59. McMurray, Robert R. *Gabriel Garcia Márquez*. New York: Ungar, 1984. Williams, Raymond L. *Gabriel Garcia Márquez*. Boston: G.K. Hall, 1984.

Commentary: Gabriel Garcia Márquez was awarded the Nobel Prize "for his novels and short stories, in which the fantastic and the realistic are combined in a richly composed world of imagination, reflecting a continent's life and conflicts." The fictional world created by Garcia Márquez centers around the jungle town of Macondo, which reappears in many novels and stories, including his outstanding achievement *One Hundred Years of Solitude*. The central themes of solitude, time, and death are portrayed through comedy, surrealism, and mythical allegory. Garcia Márquez is committed politically to the side of the poor and, in addition to his literary works, has been very active as a journalist writing on politics and the arts. (K.G.)

1983

Golding, William Gerald 204

PRIZE: Literature, 1983. BORN: September 19, 1911; St. Columb, Cornwall, England. PARENTS: Father, Alec A. Golding; Mother, Mildred A. Golding. NATIONALITY: British. RELIGION: Belongs to no organized church; from Christian background. EDUCATION: Oxford Univ., England, B.A., 1935; Oxford Univ., England, M.A., 1960. SPOUSE: Ann Brookfield, married 1939. CHILDREN: David, son; Judith, daughter. CAREER: Bishop Wordsworth's School, England, Teacher, 1939-40; British Navy, 1940-45; Bishop Wordsworth's School, England, Teacher, 1945-61; Hollins College, VA, Writer-In-Residence, 1961-62. OTHER AWARDS: Commander, Order of the British Empire, 1965; Booker Prize, 1979; Black Memorial Award, 1980; Booker McConnell Prize, 1981.

Selected Publications: *Lord of the Flies*. London: Faber and Faber, 1954. *The Inheritors*. London: Faber and Faber, 1955. *Pincher Martin*. London: Faber and Faber, 1956. *Free Fall*. London: Faber and Faber, 1959. *The Spire*. London: Faber and Faber, 1964. *Darkness Visible*. London: Faber and Faber, 1979. *Rites of Passage*. London: Faber and Faber, 1980.

For More Information See: *Contemporary Authors New Revision Series*. Detroit, MI: Gale Research, 1984 (Volume 13), 219-26. *Current Biography Yearbook*. New York: H.W. Wilson, 1964, 152-154. Hynes, Samuel. *William Golding*. New York: Columbia U. Press, 1964. Kinkead-Weekes, Mark, and Gregor, Dan. *William Golding: A Critical Study*. London: Faber and Faber, 1983.

Commentary: The body of William Golding's works, which "illustrate the human condition in the world today" and demonstrate that "evil springs from the depth of man himself," won him the Nobel Prize. *Lord of the Flies*, the novel that brought literary recognition, shows a group of English schoolboys on a deserted island reverting to primal savagery; in his other novels, Golding, who has been called an allegorist and fabulist, develops the theme of humans' tendency toward evil. (J.A.)

1984

Seifert, Jaroslav 205

PRIZE: Literature, 1984. BORN: September 23, 1901; Prague, Czechoslovakia. DIED: January 10, 1986; Prague, Czechoslovakia. PARENTS: No record found. NATIONALITY: Czechoslovakian. RELIGION: Catholic. EDUCATION: No college degrees. SPOUSE: Marie Ulrichova, married 1928. CHILDREN: Jana, daughter; Jaroslav, son. CAREER: Prague, Czechoslovakia, Writer/Journalist, 1921; *Srĕatec*, Editor, 1922-25; *KSČ Reflektor*, Editor, 1927-29; *Nová scéna*, Editor, 1929-31; *Pestré kvĕty*, Editor, 1931-33; *Ranni noviny*, Editor, 1933-39; *Národní práce*, Editor, 1939-45; *Práce*, Editor, 1945-49. OTHER AWARDS: Czechoslovak State Prize, 1936, 1955, 1968; Union of Czechoslovak Writers Publishing House Prize, 1966; Czechoslovak National Artist, 1967.

Selected Publications: *Jablko z Klína* (*An Apple from the Lap*). Prague: Melantrich, 1933. *Ruce Venušing* (*The Hands of Venus*). Toronto: Sixty-Eight Publishers, 1934. (Also Prague: Melantrich, 1936). *Zhasnĕti Svĕtla* (*Put Out the Lights*). Prague: Fr. Borovy, 1940. *Svĕtlem Odĕná* (*Dressed in Light*). Prague: Nákl. Fr. Borovéha, 1940. *Ruka a Plamen* (*The Hand and the Flame*). Praze: F. Borovy, 1943. *Kammený Most* (*The Stone Bridge*). Prague: Fr. Borovy, 1944. *Prilba Hlíny* (*The Helmut of Clay*). Praze: Práce, 1945. *Mozart v Praze*. Praze, Jarsoslav Pica, 1948. (*Mozart in Prague* (no record found), 1970). *Pisĕn o Viktorce*. Praze: Ceskoslovensky spisovatel, 1950. *Maminka* (*Mother*). Prague: Ceskoslovensky Spisovatel, 1955. *Odlévání Zvonú*. Praze: Ceskoslovensky spis, 1967 (*The Casting of the Bells*. Tr. by Tom O'Grady and Paul Jagasich. Iowa City, IA: The Spirit That Moves Us Press, 1983). *Koncert no Ostrovĕ* (*Concert on the Island*). Prague: Ceskoslovensky spisovatel, 1967. *Moró Sloup*. Cologne: Index, 1977 (*The Plague Monument*. Tr. by Lyn Coffin. New York: Czechoslovak Society of Arts and Sciences, 1980). *Destník z Picadilly*. Prague: Cs. spis, 1979 (*Umbrella from Picadilly*. Tr. by Ewald Osers. San Francisco, CA: Parsons Books, 1984).

For More Information See: "Czech Poet Wins Nobel Prize for Literature." *Publisher's Weekly* (October 26, 1984): 26-27. French, Alfred. *The Poets of Prague*. London: Oxford U. Press, 1969, 20-35. Skvorecky, Josef. "Czech Mate." *The New Republic* (February 18, 1985): 27-32.

Commentary: The Nobel announcement cited Jaroslav Seifert's work, which "endowed with freshness, sensuality and rich inventiveness, provides a liberating image of the indomitable spirit and versatility of man." Seifert's defense of and call for greater freedom is also noted in that "he conjures up another world than that of tyranny and desolation—a world that exists both here and now, although it may be hidden from our view and bound in chains, and one that exists in our dreams and our will and our art and our indomitable spirit. His poetry is a kind of maieutics—an act of deliverance." (D.W.)

1985

Simon, Claude Eugene Henri 206

PRIZE: Literature, 1985. BORN: October 10, 1913; Tananarive, Madagascar. PARENTS: Father, Louis d'Antoine Simon; Mother, Suzanne Denamiel Simon. NATIONALITY: French. RELIGION: No record found. EDUCATION: No college degrees. SPOUSE: Yvonne Ducing, married 1951, divorced (no date found); Rhea Axelos Karavas, married May 29, 1978. CHILDREN: No record found. CAREER: Writer. OTHER AWARDS: Prix de l'Express, 1960; Prix Medicis, 1967.

Selected Publications: *Le Tricheur* (*The Cheat*). Paris: Editions de Minuit, 1945. *La Corde Raide* (*The Tightrope*). Paris: Editions de Minuit, 1947. *Gulliver*. Paris: Calmann-Lévy, 1952. *Le Sacre du Printemps* (*The Annointment of Spring*). Paris: Calmann-Lévy, 1952. *Le Vent, Tentative de Restitution d'un Retable Baroque* (*The Wind*). Paris: Editions de Minuit, 1957. *L'Herbe* (*The Grass*). Paris: Editions de Minuit, 1958. *La Route des Flandres* (*The Flanders Road*). Paris: Editions de Minuit, 1960. *Le Palace* (*The Palace*). Paris: Editions de Minuit, 1962. *Histoire*. Paris: Editions de Minuit, 1967. *La Bataille de Pharsale* (*The Battle of Pharsalus*). Paris: Editions de Minuit, 1969. *Orion Aveugle* (*Blind Orion*). Geneva: Editions Albert Skira, 1970. *Les Corps Conducteurs* (*Conducting Bodies*). Paris: Editions de Minuit, 1971. *Triptyque*. Paris: Editions de Minuit, 1973 *Leçon de Choses* (*Lesson in Things*). Paris: Editions de Minuit, 1975.

For More Information See: Fletcher, John. *Claude Simon*. London: Calder and Boyars, 1975. Jimenez-Fajardo, Salvador. *Claude Simon*. Boston: Twayne, 1975.

Commentary: Claude Simon was cited by the Academy because he "in his novels combines the poet's and the painter's creativeness with a deepened awareness of time in the depiction of the human condition." Simon combined his lifelong interest in painting with linguistic and literary experimentation to become a leader among French experimentalist novelists, basing his work on remembered images, especially of war. Although Simon's initial works contained long, involved sentences, many parentheses, and present participles, his later works were composed of short sentences that require careful reading for emotional and literal comprehension. (J.H.S.)

Medicine and Physiology

1901

von Behring, Emil Adolph   207

PRIZE: Medicine and Physiology, 1901. BORN: March 15, 1854; Hansdorf, Germany. DIED: March 31, 1917; Marburg, Germany. PARENTS: Father, August Georg Behring; Mother, Augustine Zech Behring. NATIONALITY: German. RELIGION: Agnostic; most probably from Protestant background. EDUCATION: Friedrich-Wilhelms Univ., Germany, M.D., 1878; Friedrich-Wilhelms Univ., Germany, Ph.D., 1880. SPOUSE: Elsie Spinola, married 1896. CHILDREN: 6 sons. CAREER: Charité Hospital, Berlin, Germany, Intern, 1880-81; Prussian Army, Surgeon, 1881-87; Academy for Military Medicine, Berlin, Germany, Professor, 1888-89; Institute of Hygiene, Berlin, Germany, Researcher, 1889-93; Univ. of Halle, Germany, Professor, 1894-95; Univ. of Marburg, Germany, Professor and Administrator, 1895-1917. OTHER AWARDS: Officer, Legion of Honor, 1895; Prize, Paris Academie d' Medicine, 1895; Prize, Institute of France, 1895; Nobility, Prussia, 1901; Iron Cross, Germany, World War I.

Selected Publications: "Uber das Zustandekommen der Diptherie-Immunität und der Tetanus-Immunität bei Thieren." *Deutsche Medizinische Wochenschrift* 16 (1890): 113-14 (with S. Kitasato). *Gesammelte Abhandlungen zur Atiologischen Therapie von Ansteckenden Krankheiten.* Leipzig, Germany: Thieme, 1893. *Gesammelte Abhandlungen. Nene Folge.* Bonn: A. Marcus and E. Webers, 1915.

For More Information See: *Dictionary of Scientific Biography.* New York: Scribner's, 1970 (Volume 1), 574-78. Macnalty, A.S. "Emil von Behring." *British Medical Journal* 1 (1954): 668-70. Unger, Hellmuth. *Emil von Behring, Sein Lebenswerk Als Vovergangliches Erbe.* Hamburg: Hoffmann und Campe, 1948. Zeiss, Heinz, and Bieling, R., *Behring, Gestalt und Werk.* Berlin: Grunewald, B. Schultz, 1940.

Commentary: The Nobel citation for Emil von Behring reads "for his work on serum therapy, especially its application against diptheria, by which he has opened a new road in the domain of medical science and thereby placed in the hands of the physician a victorious weapon against illness and death." Von Behring is considered one of the founders of immunology, introduced the term "antitoxin," and successfully used antitoxins against diphtheria, tetanus, and bovine tuberculosis. (L.W.)

1902

Ross, Ronald, Sir   208

PRIZE: Medicine and Physiology, 1902. BORN: May 13, 1857; Almora, India. DIED: September 16, 1932; London, England. PARENTS: Father, Campbell Claye Grant Ross; Mother, Matilda Charlotte Elderton Ross. NATIONALITY: British. RELIGION: Anglican. EDUCATION: St. Bartholomew's Medical School Hospital, England, MRCS diploma (medical degree), 1879. SPOUSE: Rosa Bessie Bloxam, married April 25, 1889. CHILDREN: Charles Claye, son; Dorothy, daughter; Sylvia, daughter; Ronald, son. CAREER: Indian Medical Service, Doctor, 1881-89; School of Tropical Medicine, Liverpool, England, Professor, 1899-1917; London, England, Physician, 1917-23; Hospital for Tropical Diseases, Ross Institute, London, England, Director, 1923-32. OTHER AWARDS: Parke Gold Medal, 1895; Cameron Prize, 1901; Royal Medal, Royal Society, 1909; Knighthood, 1911.

Selected Publications: "On Some Peculiar Pigmented Cells Found in Two Mosquitoes Fed on Malarial Blood." *British Medical Journal* 2 (1897): 1786-88. *The Prevention of Malaria.* London: J. Murray, 1910. *Studies on Malaria.* London: J. Murray, 1928.

For More Information See: *Dictionary of Scientific Biography.* New York: Scribner's, 1975 (Volume 11), 555-57. Megroz, R.L. *Ronald Ross, Discoverer and Creator.* London: Allen and Unwin, 1931. Ross, Sir Ronald. *Memoirs, with a Full Account of the Great Malaria Problem and Its Solution.* London: J. Murray, 1923.

Commentary: Ronald Ross's Nobel Prize came for his work on malaria. His research proved that the Anopheles mosquito was the intermediate host in malaria's transmission, and he later developed the methods for destroying the mosquito. Ross was also an accomplished doctor, mathematician, author, editor, musician, and composer. (R.K.)

1903

Finsen, Niels Ryberg   209

PRIZE: Medicine and Physiology, 1903. BORN: December 15, 1860; Thorshavn, Denmark. DIED: September 24, 1904; Copenhagen, Denmark. PARENTS: Father, Hannes Steingrin Finsen; Mother, Johanne Froman Finsen. NATIONALITY: Danish. RELIGION: Lutheran. EDUCATION: Univ. of Copenhagen, Denmark, M.D., 1890. SPOUSE: Ingeborg Balslev, married 1892. CHILDREN: Halldor, son; Gudrun, daughter; Valgerda, daughter. CAREER: Univ. of Copenhagen, Denmark, Professor, 1890-93; Finsen Ray Institute, Copenhagen, Denmark, Founder and Director, 1896-1904. OTHER AWARDS: Knight of the Order of Dannebrog, 1899; Danish Gold Medal for Merit; Cameron Prize, U. of Edinburgh, Scotland, 1904.

Selected Publications: "Red Light Treatment of Smallpox." *British Medical Journal* 2 (1895): 1412-14. *Om Anvendelse i Medicinen af Koncentrede Kemiske Lysstraaler* (On the use in medicine of concentrated chemical rays). Copenhagen: F. Hegel and Son, 1896. *Phototherapy*. London: E. Arnold, 1901. *Om Bekaempelse af Lupus Vulgaris Med Rede Görelse for de i Danmark Opnaaede Resultater*. Copenhagen: Gyldendalske Boghandels Forlag, 1902. *Die Bekampfung des Lupus Vulgaris*. Jena, Germany: G. Fischer, 1903.

For More Information See: De Kruif, Paul. *Men Against Death*. New York: Harcourt, Brace, 1934, 283-99. *Dictionary of Scientific Biography*. New York: Scribner's, 1970 (Volume 4), 620-21.

Commentary: The Nobel Prize was awarded to Niels Finsen "in recognition of his treatment of disease, especially lupus vulgaris, with concentrated light rays, whereby he opened up new channels for the art of medicine." His frail health and short years prevented further successes, but Finsen's discovery that the bactericidal effect of sunlight was due to the blue, violet, and ultraviolet portions of the spectrum; his development of the instrumentation and the mechanism for screening out heat; and his applications to treatment of disease states left a valuable legacy. (B.I.M.)

1904

Pavlov, Ivan Petrovich   210

PRIZE: Medicine and Physiology, 1904. BORN: September 14, 1849; Ryazan, Russia. DIED: February 27, 1936; Leningrad, USSR. PARENTS: Father, Pyotr Dmitrievich Pavlov; Mother, Varvara Ivanova Pavlov. NATIONALITY: Russian. RELIGION: Agnostic; from Eastern Orthodox background. EDUCATION: Military Medical Academy, Russia, graduate, 1879; Military Medical Academy, Russia, M.D., 1883. SPOUSE: Serafina Vasilievna Karchevskaya, married May 1, 1881. CHILDREN: Mirchik, son; Vladmir, son; Vera, daughter; Victor, son; Vsevolod, son. CAREER: Military Medical Academy, St. Petersburg, Russia, Professor, 1888-1924; Institute of Experimental Medicine, St. Petersburg, Russia, Director, 1891-1936. OTHER AWARDS: Gold Medal, U. of St. Petersburg, Russia, 1875; Copley Medal, Royal Society, 1915.

Selected Publications: *The Work of the Digestive Glands*. Philadelphia, PA: J.B. Lippincott, 1910. *Conditioned Reflexes*. London: Oxford U. Press, 1927. *Polnoe Sobranie Sochineny*(complete collected works) Moscow: Academy of Sciences, USSR, 1954.

For More Information See: Babkin, Boris P. *Pavlov: A Biography*. Chicago: U. of Chicago Press, 1949. *Dictionary of Scientific Biography*. New York: Scribner's, 1974 (Volume 10), 431-36. Parry, Albert. *The Russian Scientist*. New York: Macmillan, 1973, 78-89.

Commentary: The Nobel Award citation to Ivan Pavlov read "in recognition of his work on the physiology of digestion, by which, in essential respects, he has transformed and enlarged our knowledge of the subject." During his long career, Pavlov contributed impressively to the understanding of the heart, of blood circulation, and of digestion, but his name today is remembered principally for the concept of "conditioned reflexes," discovered while studying the digestive process. (L.W.)

1905

Koch, Heinrich Hermann Robert   211

PRIZE: Medicine and Physiology, 1905. BORN: December 11, 1843; Clausthal, Germany. DIED: May 27, 1910; Baden-Baden, Germany. PARENTS: Father, Hermann Koch; Mother, Mathilde Julie Henriette Biewend Koch. NATIONALITY: German. RELIGION: Lutheran. EDUCATION: Univ. of Gottingen, Germany, M.D., 1866. SPOUSE: Emmy Adolfine Josefine Frantz, married July 1867, divorced 1893; Hedwig Freiberg, married 1893. CHILDREN: Gertrud, daughter. CAREER: Hamburg, Germany, Doctor, 1866; Lagenhagen Lunatic Asylum, Germany, Doctor, 1866-68; Poznan, Germany, Doctor, 1868; Rakwitz, Germany, Doctor, 1869; German Army, Doctor, 1870-71; Wollstein, Germany, Doctor, 1872-80; Health Department, Berlin, Germany, Doctor, 1880-85; Berlin Univ., Germany, Professor and Administrator, 1885-90; Institute for Infectious Diseases, Berlin, Germany, Director, 1891-1904. OTHER AWARDS: Harben Medal, 1901; Prussian Order Pour le Merite, 1906; Robert Koch Medal, 1908.

Selected Publications: *Investigations into the Etiology of Traumatic Infective Diseases*. London: The New Sydenham Society, 1880. "Etiology of Terberculosis." *American Review of Tuberculosis* 25 (1932): 285-323. "Etiology of Anthrax, Bases on the Ontogeny of the Anthrax Bacillus." *Medical Classics* 2 (1937-38): 787-820. "Methods for Studying, Preserving and Photographing Bacteria." In *Microbiology Contributions from 1776-1908*. New Brunswick, NJ: Rutgers U. Press, 1960, 67-73.

For More Information See: Barlowe, C. *Robert Koch*. Portland, OR: Heron Books, 1971. *Dictionary of Scientific Biography*. New York: Scribner's 1973 (Volume 7), 420-35.

Commentary: For his work on tuberculosis, Robert Koch was awarded the Nobel Prize. Koch is regarded as the founder of modern medical bacteriology, in recognition of his discoveries as well as development of rigorous research methods. His most important work included proving that anthrax, tuberculosis, and cholera were caused by bacteria. (L.W.)

1906

Golgi, Camillo   212

PRIZE: Medicine and Physiology, 1906. BORN: July 7, 1843; Corteno, Italy. DIED: January 21, 1926; Pavia, Italy. PARENTS: Father, Alessandro Golgi; Mother, Carolina Papini Golgi. NATIONALITY: Italian. RELIGION: Christian. EDUCATION: Univ. of Padua, Italy, M.D., 1865. SPOUSE: Lina Bizzozero, married (no date found). CHILDREN: Perroncito, son (adopted). CAREER: Pavia, Italy, Doctor and Researcher, 1865-72; Univ. of Pavia, Italy, Professor, 1875-78; Univ. of Siena, Italy, Professor, 1879-80; Univ. of Pavia, Italy, Professor, 1880-1918.

Selected Publications: *Opera Omnia*(collected works) 4 volumes. Milan: U. Hoepli, 1903-29.

For More Information See: Chorobski, J. "Camillo Golgi, 1843-1926." *Archives of Neurology* (Chicago) 33 (1935): 163-70. *Dictionary of Scientific Biography*. New York: Scribner's, 1973 (Volume 5), 459-61.

Commentary: Camillo Golgi shared the Nobel Prize for "work on the structure of the nervous system." A prominent neurohistologist, pathologist, and malariologist, his major contributions are usually listed as the development of a staining technique using silver (the Golgi method) for nerve substances, the portrayal of the cytoplasmic reticular substance of nerve and other cells, and the investigation of the fever curve as related to the parasite development in malaria. (R.K.)

Ramón y Cajal, Santiago 213

PRIZE: Medicine and Physiology, 1906. BORN: May 1, 1852; Petilla de Aragón, Spain. DIED: October 18, 1934; Madrid, Spain. PARENTS: Father, Justo Ramón y Casasûls Cajal; Mother, Antonia Cajal. NATIONALITY: Spanish. RELIGION: Catholic. EDUCATION: Univ. of Zaragoza, Spain, licentiate in medicine, 1873; Univ. of Zaragoza, Spain, doctorate in medicine, 1877. SPOUSE: Silveria Fananás García, married 1880. CHILDREN: Paula, daughter; Fe, daughter; Pilar, daughter; Santiago, son; Jorge, son; Luis, son. CAREER: Army Medical Service, 1874-76; Univ. of Zaragoza, Spain, Professor, 1876-83; Univ. of Valencia, Spain, Professor, 1883-87; Univ. of Barcelona, Spain, Professor, 1887-92; Univ. of Madrid, Spain, Professor, 1892-1922; Institute Cajal, Madrid, Researcher, 1922-34. OTHER AWARDS: Fauvelle Prize, 1896; Rubio Prize, 1897; Moscow Prize, 1900; Martinez y Molina Prize, 1902; Helmholtz Gold Medal, 1905; Echegaray Medal, 1922.

Selected Publications: *Manual de Anatomia Pathologica General*. Madrid: Moya, 1896. *Textura del Systema Nervioso del Hombre y de los Vertebrados*. Madrid: Moya, 1899-1904. *Degeneration and Regeneration of the Nervous System*. Tr. by Raoul M. Day. London: Oxford U. Press, 1928.

For More Information See: Cannon, Dorothy F. *Explorer of the Human Brain: The Life of Santiago Ramón y Cajal. 1852-1934*. New York: Schuman, 1949. *Dictionary of Scientific Biography*. New York: Scribner's, 1975 (Volume 11), 273-76. Ramón y Cajal, Santiago. *Recollections of My Life*. Cambridge, MA: Massachusetts Institute of Technology, 1966.

Commentary: Santiago Ramón y Cajal was awarded the Nobel Prize for his work on the structure of the nervous system. His major contributions were in adapting Golgi's silver nitrate staining techniques to thick sections of embryonic material, in formulating theories of nervous system structure and nerve impulse transmission, and in explaining the areas of traumatic degeneration and regeneration of nervous structures. He was also a notable author and Spanish statesman, always concerned about the status of Spain and the Spanish language. (A.C.)

1907

Laveran, Charles Louis Alphonse 214

PRIZE: Medicine and Physiology, 1907. BORN: June 18, 1845; Paris, France. DIED: May 18, 1922; Paris, France. PARENTS: No record found. NATIONALITY: French. RELIGION: Christian. EDUCATION: Univ. of Strasbourg, France, M.D., 1867. SPOUSE: No record found. CHILDREN: No record found. CAREER: French Army, Surgeon, 1870-96; Pasteur Institute, Paris, France, Researcher, 1897-1922. OTHER AWARDS: Breant Prize, 1884; Commander of Legion of Honor, 1912.

Selected Publications: *Traite des Fieures Palustres avec la Description des Microbes du Paludisme*. Paris: O. Doin, 1884. *Du Paludisme et de Son Hematozoaire*. Paris: G. Masson, 1891 *Les Hematozoaires de L'Homme et des Animaux*. Paris: Rueff, 1895. *Trypanosome et Trypanosomiases*. Paris: Masson, 1912.

For More Information See: *Dictionary of Scientific Biography*. New York: Scribner's, 1973 (Volume 8), 65-66. "Le Professeur Laveran." *Bulletin de la Societe de Pathologie Exotique* 15 (1922): 373-78.

Commentary: Charles Laveran was cited "for his work on the part played by protozoa in the generation of disease." His early observation, that protozoa caused malaria, was followed by careful study of the trypanosome diseases of cattle and human sleeping sickness. (D.W.)

1908

Ehrlich, Paul 215

PRIZE: Medicine and Physiology, 1908. BORN: March 14, 1854; Strehlen, Germany. DIED: August 20, 1915; Hamburg, Germany. PARENTS: Father, Ismar Ehrlich; Mother, Rosa Weigert Ehrlich. NATIONALITY: German. RELIGION: Jewish. EDUCATION: Univ. of Leipzig, Germany, M.D., 1878. SPOUSE: Hedwig Pinkus, married 1883. CHILDREN: Steffa, daughter; Marianne, daughter. CAREER: Charité Hospital and Univ. of Berlin, Germany, Doctor and Researcher, 1878-87; Robert Koch Institute, Berlin, Germany, Researcher and Administrator, 1890-95; State Institute for the Investigation and Control of Serum, Stieglitz, Germany, Director, 1896-99; Royal Institute for Experimental Therapy, Frankfurt, Germany, Director, 1899-1915. OTHER AWARDS: Geheimer Obermedizinalrat, 1907; Privy Councilor, 1911; Liebig Medal, Society of German Chemists, 1911; Cameron Prize, Edinburgh, 1914.

Selected Publications: *The Collected Papers of Paul Ehrlich*. Ed. by F. Himmelwert. New York: Pergamon Press, 1956-58.

For More Information See: *Dictionary of Scientific Biography*. New York: Scribner's, 1971 (Volume 4), 295-305. Marquandt, Martha. *Paul Ehrlich*. New York: Henry Schuman, 1951.

Commentary: Paul Ehrlich was awarded the Nobel Prize "in recognition of his work on immunity," specifically the work which led to a diphtheria antitoxin serum dosage which could be safely used in clinical practice. In the process, he developed a method for measuring the effectiveness of sera that was widely adopted, and a theory of immunity. His work in histology produced tissue-staining techniques that were also acclaimed. But the work for which he is remembered is in the field of chemotherapy, particularly his treatment of syphilis with the arsenic compound, Number 606. (L.W.)

Metchnikoff, Elie (Mechnikov, Ilya Ilyich) 216

PRIZE: Medicine and Physiology, 1908. BORN: May 15, 1845; Kharkov, Russia. DIED: July 15, 1916; Paris, France. PARENTS: Father, Ilya Ivanovich Mechnikov; Mother, Emilia Nevakhovich Mechnikov. NATIONALITY: Russian; later French resident. RELIGION: Jewish; with record of unsuccessful conversion to Lutheranism as a child; mother was Jewish; father was not. EDUCATION: Univ. of Kharkov, Russia, graduate, 1864; Univ. of St. Petersburg, Russia, M.S., 1867; Univ. of St.

Petersburg, Russia, doctorate, 1868. SPOUSE: Lyudmilla Fedorovich, married 1868, died 1873; Olga Belokopytova, married 1875. CHILDREN: None. CAREER: Univ. of Odessa, Russia, Professor, 1867-69; Univ. of St. Petersburg, Russia, Professor, 1870; Univ. of Novorossiia, Russia, Professor, 1870-72; Messina, Sicily, Researcher, 1882-86; Bacteriological Institute, Odessa, Russia, Director, 1886-87; Pasteur Institute, Paris, France, Administrator to Director, 1888-1916.

Selected Publications: *Lectures on the Comparative Pathology of Inflammation, Delivered at the Pasteur Institute in 1891.* London: K. Pau, Trench, Trubner and Co., 1893. *Immunity in Infectious Diseases.* Cambridge: Cambridge U. Press, 1907. *The Prolongation of Life: Optimistic Studies.* New York: G.P. Putnam's Sons, 1912. *The Nature of Man: Studies in Optimistic Philosophy.* London: Watts and Company, 1938.

For More Information See: *Dictionary of Scientific Biography.* New York: Scribner's, 1973 (Volume 9), 331-35. Mechnikov, Olga. *The Life of Elie Metchnikoff, 1845-1916.* New York: Houghton-Mifflin, 1921.

Commentary: Elie Metchnikoff was cited by the Academy for his "work on immunity," especially for the formulation of the "cellular" theory of immunity, which states that certain cells of the body (phagocytes) are able to capture and destroy bacteria which have invaded the body. His early career produced important discoveries in comparative anatomy, establishing an evolutionary link between invertebrates and vertebrates. His later career led to an increasing interest by scientists in the process of aging, especially in the role diet and body bacterial processes played. (L.W.)

1909

Kocher, Emil Theodor   217

PRIZE: Medicine and Physiology, 1909. BORN: August 25, 1841; Berne, Switzerland. DIED: July 27, 1917; Berne, Switzerland. PARENTS: Father, Jacob Alexander Kocher; Mother, Maria Wermuth Kocher. NATIONALITY: Swiss. RELIGION: Protestant. EDUCATION: Univ. of Berne, Switzerland, M.D., 1869. SPOUSE: Marie Witschi-Courant, married 1869. CHILDREN: 3 sons. CAREER: Univ. of Berne, Switzerland, Professor, 1872-1911.

Selected Publications: *Chirurgische Operationslehre.* Jena, Germany: G. Fischer, 1892. *Operative Surgery.* New York: W. Wood and Co., 1894. *Vorlesungen über Chirurgische Infektionskrankheiten.* 2 volumes. Basel, Switzerland: C. Sallman, 1895-1909 (with E. Tavel).

For More Information See: *A Biographical Dictionary of Scientists.* New York, Wiley, 1969, 295-96. Bonjour, Edgar. *Theodor Kocher.* Berne: P. Haupt, 1981.

Commentary: Emil Kocher won the Nobel Prize "for his work on the physiology, pathology and surgery of the thyroid gland." Kocher also pioneered in aseptic methods and in surgery of many types. (C.E. and D.W.)

1910

Kossel, Karl Martin Leonhard Albrecht   218

PRIZE: Medicine and Physiology, 1910. BORN: September 16, 1853; Rostock, Germany. DIED: July 5, 1927; Heidelberg, Germany. PARENTS: Father, Albrecht Kos-

sel; Mother, Clara Jeppe Kossel. NATIONALITY: German. RELIGION: Christian. EDUCATION: Univ. of Strasbourg, France, M.D., 1878. SPOUSE: Luise Holtzmann, married 1886. CHILDREN: Walther, son; 1 daughter. CAREER: Univ. of Strasbourg, Germany, Professor, 1877-83; Berlin Physiological Institute, Germany, Director, 1883-87; Univ. of Berlin, Germany, Professor, 1887-95; Univ. of Marburg, Germany, Professor, 1895-1901; Univ. of Heidelberg, Germany, Professor and Administrator, 1901-27.

Selected Publications: *Leitfaden für Medicinisch-Chemische Kurse.* Berlin: Fischer Medecin, 1888. *Die Gewebe des Menschlichen Körpers und Ihre Mikroskopische Untersuchung.* Brunswick, Germany; Herald Braha, 1889 (with W. Behrens and P. Schiefferdecker). *The Protamines and Histones.* New York: Longmans, Green and Co., 1928.

For More Information See: "Albrecht Kossel zum Gedächtnis." *Hoppe-Seyler's Zeitschrift für Physiologische Chemie* 177 (1928): 1-14. *Dictionary of Scientific Biography.* New York: Scribner's, 1973 (Volume 7), 466-68.

Commentary: Albrecht Kossel was the Nobel Award recipient "in recognition of the contributions to the chemistry of the cell made through his work on proteins, including the nucleic substances." Kossel separated nucleoproteins into two parts—a protein and a nucleic acid composed of sugar, phosphoric acid, and nitrogen-containing compounds. He later found that the sugar was a hexose. His writings foresaw the modern investigations of nucleic acids as the storers and transmitters of genetic information. (L.W.)

1911

Gullstrand, Allvar   219

PRIZE: Medicine and Physiology, 1911. BORN: June 5, 1862; Landskrona, Sweden. DIED: July 28, 1930; Uppsala, Sweden. PARENTS: Father, Fehr Alfred Gullstand; Mother, Sophia Matilda Korsell Gullstrand. NATIONALITY: Swedish. RELIGION: Most probably Christian/Protestant. EDUCATION: Royal Caroline Institute, Sweden, M.D., 1888; Royal Caroline Institute, Sweden, Ph.D., 1890. SPOUSE: Signe Christina Breitholz, married 1885. CHILDREN: 1 daughter. CAREER: Royal Caroline Institute, Stockholm, Sweden, Lecturer, 1892-94; Univ. of Uppsala, Sweden, Professor, 1894-1930. OTHER AWARDS: Grafe Medal, Deutsche Opthalmologische Gesellschaft, 1927.

Selected Publications: *Allgemeine Theorie der Monochromatischen Aberrationen und Ihre Nachsten Ergebnisse für die Opththalmologie.* Uppsala, Sweden: Berling, 1900. *Die Optische Abbildung in Heterogenen Medien und die Dioptrik der Kristallinge des Menschen.* Uppsala, Switzerland: Almquist & Wiksells, 1908. *Einführung in die Methoden der Dioptrik des Auges des Menschen.* Leipzig, Germany: S. Hirzil, 1911.

For More Information See: "Allvar Gullstrand." *Zeitschift fur Opthalmologische Optik* 18 (1930): 129-34. *Dictionary of Scientific Biography.* New York: Scribner's, 1972 (Volume 5), 590-91.

Commentary: The Nobel Prize was awarded to Allvar Gullstrand "for his work on the dioptrics of the eye." With a sound medical and scientific background, he explained mathematically and physiologically the basis of the operation of the eye, with special attention to accommodation and astigmatism. He also was an active writer in the area of geometrical optics and an inventor of note of several optical instruments. (R.R.)

1912

Carrel, Alexis 220
PRIZE: Medicine and Physiology, 1912. BORN: June 28, 1873; Sainte Foy-les-Lyon, France. DIED: November 5, 1944; Paris, France. PARENTS: Father, Alexis Carrel-Billiard; Mother, Anne Marie Ricard Carrel. NATIONALITY: French; later American resident. RELIGION: Catholic. EDUCATION: Univ. of Lyons, France, Bachelor of Letters, 1889; Univ. of Lyons, France, Bachelor of Science, 1890; Univ. of Lyons, France, M.D., 1900. SPOUSE: Anne-Marie Laure Gourley de la Motte de Meyrie, married 1913. CHILDREN: None. CAREER: Lyons Hospital, France, Intern, 1896-1900; Univ. of Lyons, France, Professor, 1900-02; Univ. of Chicago, IL, Researcher, 1905-06; Rockefeller Institute, NY, Researcher, 1906-44. OTHER AWARDS: Legion d'Honneur, France; Nordhoff-Jung Prize for Cancer Research, 1930; Newman Foundation Award, U. of Illinois, 1937; Rotary Club of New York Service Award, 1939.

Selected Publications: *Treatment of Infected Wounds.* New York: Hoeber, 1917 (with George Dehelly). *The Culture of Organs.* New York: Hoeber, 1938 (with Charles A. Lindbergh). *Man, the Unknown.* New York: Harper and Brothers, 1939.

For More Information See: *Dictionary of Scientific Biography.* New York, Scribner's, 1971 (Volume 3), 90-91. Soupalt, Robert. *Alexis Carrel, 1873-1944.* Paris: Plon, 1952.

Commentary: The Academy cited Alexis Carrel "for his work on vascular suturing, and on the grafting of blood vessels and organs." In addition to his notable medical work, Carrel was a philosopher and philosophical writer. In later life, he headed the Vichy government's Carrel Foundation for the Study of Human Problems. (B.I.M.)

1913

Richet, Charles Robert 221
PRIZE: Medicine and Physiology, 1913. BORN: August 26, 1850; Paris, France. DIED: December 4, 1935; Paris, France. PARENTS: Father, Alfred Richet; Mother, Eugenie Renouard Richet. NATIONALITY: French. RELIGION: Christian. EDUCATION: Univ. of Paris, France, M.D., 1877; Univ. of Paris, France, D.Sc., 1878. SPOUSE: Amélie Aubry, married 1877. CHILDREN: Georges, son; Jacques, son; Charles, son; Albert, son; Alfred, son; Louise, daughter; Adele, daughter. CAREER: Collège de France, Paris, Professor, 1876-87; Univ. of Paris, France, Professor, 1887-1927. OTHER AWARDS: French Biological Society Institute Award, 1879; Cross of the Legion of Honor, 1926.

Selected Publications: *Physiology and Histology of the Cerebral Convolutions.* New York: W. Wood and Co., 1879. *La Chaleur Animale.* Paris: F. Alcan, 1889. *Dictionnaire de Physiologie.* 10 volumes. Paris: F. Alcan, 1895-1928 (with P. Langlois and L. Lapicque). *Traité de Métapsychique.* Paris: F. Alcan, 1923.

For More Information See: *Biographical Dictionary of Scientists.* New York: Wiley, 1969, 443. *Dictionary of Scientific Biography.* New York: Scribner's, 1975 (Volume 11), 425-32.

Commentary: Charles Richet received the Nobel Prize "in recognition of his work on anaphylaxis," the study of hypersensitivity induced by foreign "bodies" injected into the body. His work led to much of our knowledge of allergic reactions. Richet also studied and wrote extensively on clairvoyance, telepathy, and other psychological phenomena; was an ardent student of aeronautics; author of several literary works; and an active pacifist. (R.K.)

1914

Bárány, Robert 222
PRIZE: Medicine and Physiology, 1914. BORN: April 22, 1876; Vienna, Austria. DIED: April 8, 1936; Uppsala, Sweden. PARENTS: Father, Ignaz Bárány; Mother, Marie Hock Bárány. NATIONALITY: Austrian; later Swedish resident. RELIGION: Jewish. EDUCATION: Univ. of Vienna, Austria, M.D., 1900. SPOUSE: Ida Berger, married 1909. CHILDREN: 2 sons; 1 daughter. CAREER: Univ. of Vienna, Austria, Professor and Researcher, 1903-11; Austrian Army, 1914-17; Univ. of Uppsala, Sweden, Professor and Administrator, 1917-36. OTHER AWARDS: Politzer Prize, 1912; Belgian Academy of Sciences Prize, 1913; ERB Medal, German Neurological Society, 1913; Guyot Prize, 1914; Swedish Medical Society Medal, 1925.

Selected Publications: *Untersuchungen über den Vestibular-Apparat des Ohres.* Berlin: O. Coblentz, 1906. *Physiologie und Pathologie des Bogengang-Apparatus beim Menschen.* Leipzig, Germany: F. Deuticke, 1907. *Funktionelle Prüfung des Vestibular-Apparatus.* Jena, Germany: G. Fischer, 1911 (with K. Wittmaack). *Die Radikaloperation des Ohres ohne Gehoergangsplastik.* Leipzig, Germany: F. Deuticke, 1923.

For More Information See: *Dictionary of Scientific Biography.* New York: Scribner's, 1971 (Volume 1), 446-47. Wodak, Ernst. *Der Báránysche Zeigeversuch.* Berlin: Urban and Schwarzenberg, 1927.

Commentary: Robert Bárány was granted the Nobel Prize "for his work on the physiology and pathology of the vestibular apparatus." This founder of the medicine of the ear also studied the brain in depth. (B.I.M.)

1919

Bordet, Jules Jean Baptiste Vincent 223
PRIZE: Medicine and Physiology, 1919. BORN: June 13, 1870; Soignies, Belgium. DIED: April 6, 1961; Brussels, Belgium. PARENTS: Father, Charles Bordet; Mother, Célestine Vandenabeele Bordet. NATIONALITY: Belgian. RELIGION: Christian. EDUCATION: Univ. of Brussels, Belgium, M.D., 1892. SPOUSE: Marthe Levoz, married 1899. CHILDREN: Simone, daughter; Marguerite, daughter; Paul, son. CAREER: Middlekerke Hospital, Belgium, Physician, 1892-94; Institut Pasteur, Paris, France, Researcher, 1894-1901; Institut Pasteur de Brabant, Univ. of Brussels, Belgium, Professor and Administrator, 1901-40. OTHER AWARDS: Prix de la Vaille, Paris, 1911; Hansen Prize, 1913; Pasteur Medal, Swedish Medical Society, 1913.

Selected Publications: *Studies in Immunity.* New York: Wiley, 1909 (with others). *Traité de l'Immunité dans les Maladies Infectieuses.* Paris: Masson et cie, 1920. *Infection et immunité.* Paris: Flammarion, 1947.

For More Information See: *Biographical Memoirs of the Fellows of the Royal Society.* London: Royal Society, 1962 (Volume 8), 18-25. *Dictionary of Scientific Biography.* New York: Scribner's, 1971 (Volume 2), 300-01.

Commentary: Jules Bordet received the Nobel Prize "for his discoveries in regard to immunity." His work ranged from the elaboration of the constituents of immune serum to the uses of that research in diagnosing various disease states, and from the discovery of the whooping cough bacillus to studies of blood coagulation and bacteriophages. (L.W.)

1920

Krogh, Schack August Steenberg   224
PRIZE: Medicine and Physiology, 1920. BORN: November 15, 1874; Grenaa, Jutland, Denmark. DIED: September 13, 1949; Copenhagen, Denmark. PARENTS: Father, Viggo Krogh; Mother, Marie Drechmann Krogh. NATIONALITY: Danish. RELIGION: Most probably Christian/Protestant. EDUCATION: Univ. of Copenhagen, Denmark, M.Sc., 1899; Univ. of Copenhagen, Denmark, Ph.D., 1903. SPOUSE: Birte Marie Jörgensen, married 1905. CHILDREN: Erik, son; Bodie, daughter; Ellen, daughter; Agnes, daughter. CAREER: Univ. of Copenhagen, Denmark, Professor, 1899-1949. OTHER AWARDS: Seegan Prize, Vienna Academy of Sciences, 1906; Baly Medal, Royal College of Physicians, London, 1945.

Selected Publications: *Meddelelser fra Akademiet for de Tekniske Videnskaber* 1 (1949): 39-50 (complete works).

For More Information See: *Dictionary of Scientific Biography.* New York: Scribner's, 1973 (Volume 7), 501-04. Rehberg, Brandt. "August Krogh, November 15, 1874-September 13, 1949." *Yale Journal of Biology and Medicine* 24 (1951): 83-102.

Commentary: August Krogh's Nobel Prize was presented "for his discovery of the regulation of the motor mechanism of capillaries." His studies of respiration led him to the discovery that the capillaries of the muscles were open during muscular work and partially closed during rest. He later wrote about the importance of capillary control to the economy of the body, and the role of muscles and hormones in capillary control. (B.I.M.)

1922

Hill, Archibald Vivian   225
PRIZE: Medicine and Physiology, 1922. BORN: September 26, 1886; Bristol, Gloucestershire, England. DIED: June 3, 1977; Cambridge, England. PARENTS: Father, Jonathan Hill; Mother, Ada Priscilla Rumney Hill. NATIONALITY: British. RELIGION: Anglican. EDUCATION: Cambridge Univ., England, M.A., 1906; Cambridge Univ., England, Sc.D., 1907. SPOUSE: Margaret Neville Keynes, married June 18, 1913. CHILDREN: Mary Eglantyne, daughter; David Keynes, son; Janet Rumney, daughter; Maurice Neville, son. CAREER: British Army, 1914-19; Univ. of Manchester, England, Profes-

sor, 1920-23; Univ. of London, England, Professor, 1923-51. OTHER AWARDS: Order of the British Empire, 1918; Royal Medal, 1926; Officer of the British Empire, 1927; Medal of Freedom with Silver Palm, U.S., 1947; Companion of Honour, Britain, 1948; Copley Medal, 1948; Chevalier of Legion of Honor, 1950.

Selected Publications: *Muscular Activity.* Baltimore, MD: Williams and Wilkins, 1926. *Living Machinery.* New York: Harcourt Brace, 1927. *Muscular Movement in Man.* New York: McGraw-Hill, 1927. *Trails and Trials in Physiology.* Baltimore, MD: Williams and Wilkins, 1965.

For More Information See: *Biographical Memoirs of the Fellows of the Royal Society.* London: Royal Society, 1978 (Volume 24), 71-149. *Perspectives in Biology and Medicine* 14 (1977): 27-42.

Commentary: Archibald Hill was cited by the Academy "for his discovery relating to the production of heat in the muscles." His other activities included service as a member of Parliament and as a member of the Scientific Advisory Committee in England during the Second World War. (B.I.M.)

Meyerhof, Otto Fritz   226
PRIZE: Medicine and Physiology, 1922. BORN: April 12, 1884; Hanover, Germany. DIED: October 6, 1951; Philadelphia, PA. PARENTS: Father, Felix Meyerhof; Mother, Bettina May Meyerhof. NATIONALITY: German; later American citizen. RELIGION: Jewish. EDUCATION: Univ. of Heidelberg, Germany, M.D., 1909. SPOUSE: Hedwig Schallenberg, married June 4, 1914. CHILDREN: George Geoffrey, son; Walter Ernst, son; Bettina Ida, daughter. CAREER: Univ. of Heidelberg, Germany, Researcher, 1909-11; Univ. of Kiel, Germany, Professor, 1912-24; Kaiser Wilhelm Institute of Biologie, Berlin-Dahlem, Germany, Researcher, 1924-29; Kaiser Wilhelm Institute of Physiology, Heidelberg, Germany, Director, 1929-38; Research Centre Nationale, Paris, France, Director, 1938-40; Univ. of Pennsylvania, Professor, 1940-51.

Selected Publications: *Chemical Dynamics of Life Phenomena.* London: J. B. Lippincott, 1924. *Die Chemischen Vorgänge in Muskel.* Berlin: J. Springer, 1930. *Chimie de la Contraction Musculaire.* Bordeaux: Delmas, 1932.

For More Information See: *Biographical Memoirs. National Academy of Sciences.* New York: Columbia U. Press, 1960 (Volume 34), 152-82. *Dictionary of Scientific Biography.* New York: Scribner's, 1974 (Volume 9), 359.

Commentary: Otto Meyerhof received his Nobel "for his discovery of the fixed relationship between the consumption of oxygen and the metabolism of lactic acid in the muscle." His later studies led to recognition of the similarity of chemical pathways in many biological systems and of the key role in muscle contraction played by adenosine triphosphate. (B.I.M.)

1923

Banting, Frederick Grant, Sir   227
PRIZE: Medicine and Physiology, 1923. BORN: November 4, 1891; Alliston, Ontario, Canada. DIED: February 21, 1941; Newfoundland, Canada. PARENTS: Father, William Thompson Banting; Mother, Margaret Grant Banting. NATIONALITY: Canadian. RELIGION: Methodist. EDUCATION: Victoria College, Canada, M.B., 1916;

Univ. of Toronto, Canada, M.D., 1922. SPOUSE: Marion Robertson, married 1924, divorced 1932; Henrietta Ball, married 1939. CHILDREN: William Robertson, son. CAREER: Western Ontario Univ., London, Canada, Researcher, 1920-21; Univ. of Toronto, Canada, Professor, 1921-41. OTHER AWARDS: Starr Gold Medal, U. of Toronto, Canada, 1922; George Armstrong Peters Prize, U. of Toronto, Canada, 1922; John Scott Medal, American Philosophical Society, 1923; Charles Mickle Fellowship, U. of Toronto, Canada, 1923; Reeve Prize, U. of Toronto, Canada, 1923; Rosenberger Gold Medal, Chicago, IL, 1924; Cameron Prize, Edinburgh, Scotland, 1927; Flavelle Medal, Royal Society of Canada, 1931; Knighthood, 1934; Apothecaries' Medal, London, Canada, 1934.

Selected Publications: "Internal Secretion of Pancreas." *Journal of Laboratory and Clinical Medicine* 7 (February 1922): 251-326 (with C.H. Best). "Pancreatic Extracts in Diabetes." *Journal of the Canadian Medical Association* 12 (March 1922): 141-46 (with others). "Effect of Pancreatic Extract (Insulin) on Normal Rabbits." *American Journal of Physiology* 62 (September 1922): 162-76. "Insulin in Treatment of Diabetes Mellitus." *Journal of Metabolic Research* 2 (November-December 1922): 547-604 (with W.R. Campbell and A.A. Fletcher).

For More Information See: *Dictionary of National Biography.* London: Oxford U. Press, 1959, 54-55. *Dictionary of Scientific Biography.* New York: Scribner's, 1970 (Volume 1), 440-43. Harris, Seale. *Banting's Miracle: The Story of the Discoverer of Insulin.* Philadelphia, PA: Lippincott, 1946. Stevenson, Lloyd. *Sir Frederick Banting.* Toronto: Ryerson Press, 1946.

Commentary: The award to Sir Frederick Banting was "for the discovery of insulin." In collaboration with C.H. Best, J. MacLeod, and J.B. Collip, Banting ligated the pancreatic ducts of dogs and subsequently removed the pancreas. The now-diabetic dogs were given an intravenous solution prepared from the degenerated pancreas, resulting in a reduced blood sugar. Purification of the active substance yielded insulin, which has saved thousands of lives since its introduction in 1922. Banting's later work included research in cancer, coronary thrombosis, silicosis, and altitude sickness. (J.J.S.)

MacLeod, John James Rickard 228

PRIZE: Medicine and Physiology, 1923. BORN: September 6, 1876; Cluny, Scotland. DIED: March 16, 1935; Aberdeen, Scotland. PARENTS: Father, Reverend Robert MacLeod; Mother, no record found. NATIONALITY: Scottish. RELIGION: Presbyterian. EDUCATION: Marischal College, Scotland, M.B., 1898; Marischal College, Scotland, Ch.B., 1898; Cambridge Univ., England, D.P.H., 1902. SPOUSE: Mary Watson McWalter, married 1903. CHILDREN: None. CAREER: Western Reserve Univ., Cleveland, OH, Professor, 1903-18; Univ. of Toronto, Canada, Professor and Administrator, 1918-28; Univ. of Aberdeen, Scotland, Professor, 1928-35. OTHER AWARDS: Cameron Prize, U. of Edinburgh, Scotland, 1923.

Selected Publications: *Practical Physiology.* London: E. Arnold, 1902 (with others). *Recent Advances in Physiology.* New York: Longmans, Green, 1906 (with Leonard Hill). *Diabetes: Its Pathological Physiology.* New York: Longmans, Green, 1913. *Fundamentals of Human Physiology.* St. Louis, MO: C.V. Mosby, 1916 (with R.G. Pearce). *Physiology and Biochemistry in*

Modern Medicine. St. Louis, MO: C.V. Mosby, 1918 (with R.G. Pearce). *Carbohydrate Metabolism and Insulin.* New York: Longmans, Green, 1926.

For More Information See: Best, C.H. "The Late John James Rickard Macleod, M.B., Ch.B., LL.D., F.R.C.P." *Canadian Medical Association Journal* 32 (1935): 556. *Dictionary of Scientific Biography.* New York: Scribner's, 1973 (Volume 8), 614-15.

Commentary: John MacLeod shared the Nobel Prize with Frederick Banting "for the discovery of insulin." Originally concerned with studies of respiration, his interests turned to experimental glycosuria and carbohydrate metabolism. Together with Banting, a new surgeon in his academic department, and C.H. Best, a student in his classes, he carried out the insulin work in the early 20s. His long career continued in further investigations of carbohydrate metabolism and respiration. (C.S.)

1924

Einthoven, Willem 229

PRIZE: Medicine and Physiology, 1924. BORN: May 22, 1860; Semarang, Dutch East Indies. DIED: September 29, 1927; Leiden, Netherlands. PARENTS: Father, Jacob Einthoven; Mother, Louise M.M.C. de Vogel Einthoven. NATIONALITY: Dutch. RELIGION: Jewish. EDUCATION: Univ. of Utrecht, Netherlands, Ph.D., 1855. SPOUSE: Frédérique Jeanne Louise de Vogel, married 1886. CHILDREN: Augusta, daughter; Louise, daughter; Willem, son; Johanna, daughter. CAREER: Univ. of Leiden, Netherlands, Professor, 1885-1927.

Selected Publications: *Stereoscopie door Kleurverschil.* Utrecht, Netherlands: Utrechtsche Drukkerij, 1885. *Over de Beteekenis der Electrophysiologie als een Ouderdeel Van de Leer der Levensverrichtingen.* Leiden, Netherlands: Brill, 1906. *Das Saitengalvenometer und die Messung der Aktionsströme des Herzens.* Stockholm: Norstedt, 1926.

For More Information See: *Dictionary of Scientific Biography.* New York: Scribner's, 1971 (Volume 4), 333-35. Hogenwerf, S. *Leven en Werken van Willem Einthoven.* N.p.: Hoorn, 1925.

Commentary: Willem Einthoven received the Nobel "for his discovery of the mechanism of the electrocardiogram." His knowledge of both physics and medicine led to the development of the string galvanometer and other medically oriented equipment, and extension of his work to the measurement of action currents of the cervical sympathetic nerve and of the heart. (R.K.)

1926

Fibiger, Johannes Andreas Grib 230

PRIZE: Medicine and Physiology, 1926. BORN: April 23, 1867; Silkeborg, Denmark. DIED: January 30, 1928; Copenhagen, Denmark. PARENTS: Father, C.E.A. Fibiger; Mother, Elfride Muller Fibiger. NATIONALITY: Danish. RELIGION: Lutheran. EDUCATION: Univ. of Copenhagen, Denmark, baccalaureate, 1883; Univ. of Copenhagen, Denmark, M.D., 1890; Univ. of Copenhagen, Denmark, Ph.D., 1895. SPOUSE: Mathilde Fibiger, married 1894. CHILDREN: None. CAREER: Univ. of Copenhagen, Denmark, Researcher, 1891-94; Blegdams Hospital for Contagious Diseases, Copenhagen, Denmark, Physician, 1894-97; Univ. of Copenhagen, Denmark, Professor, 1897-1928. OTHER AWARDS: Nordhoff-Jung Cancer Prize, 1927.

Selected Publications: *Bakteriologiske Studier over Diphtheri.* Copenhagen: det Schulothecke Forlag, 1895. *Investigations on the Spiroptera Cancer.* Copenhagen: Andr. Fred. Host and Son, Bianco Lunos Bogtrykkeri, 1918-19. *Experimental Production of Tar Cancer in White Mice.* Copenhagen: Andr. Fred. Host and Son, Bianco Lunos Bogtrykkeri, 1921 (with Fridtjof Bang). *Investigations Upon Immunisation against Metastasis Formation in Experimental Cancer.* Copenhagen: Andr. Fred. Host and Son, Bianco Lunos Bogtrykkeri, 1927 (with Paul Moller).

For More Information See: *Biographical Dictionary of Scientists.* New York: Wiley, 1969, 179-80. Secher, K. *Johannes Fibiger.* Copenhagen: Nordisk Vorlag, 1947.

Commentary: The Academy cited Johannes Fibiger "for his discovery of the *Spiroptera* carcinoma." Fibiger published extensively in this area and was the first to study artificially produced cancer. (B.I.M.)

1927

Wagner von Jaurregg, Julius   231
PRIZE: Medicine and Physiology, 1927. BORN: March 7, 1857; Wels, Austria. DIED: September 27, 1940; Vienna, Austria. PARENTS: Father, Adolf Johann Wagner von Jauregg; Mother, Ludovika Ranzoni von Jauregg. NATIONALITY: Austrian. RELIGION: Christian. EDUCATION: Univ. of Vienna, Austria, Ph.D., 1880. SPOUSE: Anna Koch, married 1899. CHILDREN: Julia, daughter; Theodor, son. CAREER: Univ. of Vienna, Austria, Professor, 1881-1928. OTHER AWARDS: Cameron Prize, 1935; Gold Medal, American Committee for Research on Syphilis, 1937.

Selected Publications: "Über die Einwirkung Fieberhafter Erkrankungen auf Psychosen." *Jahrbuch für Psychiatrie und Neurologie* 7 (1887): 94-131. "Zur Reform des Irrenwesens." *Viennaer Klinische Wochenschrift* 14 (1901): 293-96. *Myxöden und Kretinismus.* Leipzig, Germany: F. Deuticke, 1915. "Über die Einwirkung der Malaria auf die Progressive Paralyse." *Psychiatrischneurologische Wochenschrift* 20 (1918-19): 132-34. *Fieber und Infektionstherapie.* Vienna: Verlag für Medizin, Weidmann, 1936.

For More Information See: *Dictionary of Scientific Biography.* New York: Scribner's, 1976 (Volume 14), 114-16. *Grosse Nervenärzte.* Stuttgart, Germany: G. Thieme, 1956, 254-66.

Commentary: Julius Wagner von Jauregg was granted the Nobel Prize "for his discovery of the therapeutic value of malaria inoculation in the treatment of dementiaparalytica." His long career included other notable work in the areas of the vagus nerve, the thyroid gland, cretinism, and insane patient treatment. (R.K.)

1928

Nicolle, Charles Jules Henri   232
PRIZE: Medicine and Physiology, 1928. BORN: September 21, 1866; Rouen, France. DIED: February 28, 1936; Tunis, Tunisia. PARENTS: Father, Dr. Eugène Nicolle; Mother, no record found. NATIONALITY: French; later

Tunisian resident. RELIGION: Christian. EDUCATION: Rouen School of Medicine, France, M.D., 1893. SPOUSE: Alice Avice, married 1893. CHILDREN: Marcelle, son; Pierre, son. CAREER: Rouen School of Medicine, France, Professor, 1895-1903; Pasteur Institute, Tunis, Tunisia, Director, 1903-36. OTHER AWARDS: Prix Montyon, 1909, 1912, 1914; Prix Osiris, 1927; Gold Medal, Tunis, 1928.

Selected Publications: "Recherches Experimentales sur le Typhus Exanthématique." *Annales de l'Institut Pasteur* 24 (1910): 243-75; 25 (1911): 97-144; 26 (1912): 250-80, 332-35. *Naissance, Vie et Mort des Maladies Infectieuses.* Paris: F. Alcan, 1930. *Biologie de l'Invention.* Paris: F. Alcan, 1932. *Destindes Maladies Infectieuses.* Paris: Presses Universitaires de France, 1939.

For More Information See: *Dictionary of Scientific Biography.* New York: Scribner's, 1978 (Supplement), 453-55. Lot, G. *Charles Nicolle et la Biologie Conquerante.* Paris: Seghers, 1961.

Commentary: The Academy cited Charles Nicolle for his work on typhus, which proved the infectious nature of the blood of typhus fever patients and the transmission of typhus fever by the body louse. Nicolle also demonstrated that serum from patients with measles, typhus fever, or undulant fever could protect uninfected persons from the disease. (R.K.)

1929

Eijkman, Christiaan   233
PRIZE: Medicine and Physiology, 1929. BORN: August 11, 1858; Nijkerk, Netherlands. DIED: November 5, 1930; Utrecht, Netherlands. PARENTS: Father, Christiaan Eijkman; Mother, Johanna Alida Pool Eijkman. NATIONALITY: Dutch. RELIGION: Christian. EDUCATION: Univ. of Amsterdam, Netherlands, M.D., 1883. SPOUSE: Aaltje Wigeri van Edema, married 1883, died 1886; Berthe Julie Louise van der Kemp, married 1888. CHILDREN: Pieter Hendrik, son. CAREER: Dutch Army, 1886-87; Medical School, Java, Indonesia, Director, 1888-96; Univ. of Utrecht, Netherlands, Professor, 1898-1928. OTHER AWARDS: John Scott Medal, Philadelphia, 1923.

Selected Publications: *Specifieke Antistoffen.* Haarlem, Netherlands: de Erven F. Bohn, 1901. *Onzichtbare Smetstoffen.* Haarlem, Netherlands: de Erven F. Bohn, 1904. *Een en Ander over Voeding.* Haarlem, Netherlands: de Erven F. Bohn, 1906. *Hygiënische Strijdvragen.* Rotterdam: W. L. and J. Brusse, 1907.

For More Information See: *Dictionary of Scientific Biography.* New York: Scribner's, 1971 (Volume 4), 310-12. Jansen, Barend Coenraad. *Het Levenswerk van Christiaan Eijkman, 1858-1930.* Haarlem, Netherlands: de Erven F. Bohn, 1959.

Commentary: Christiaan Eijkman won the Nobel "for his discovery of the antineuritic vitamin," by study of the effect of polishings from polished rice on a beri-beri-like disease in fowl. He also studied the physiology of tropical residents and conducted fermentation tests and testing for the colon bacillus in water. (R.K.)

Hopkins, Frederick Gowland, Sir   234
PRIZE: Medicine and Physiology, 1929. BORN: June 30, 1861; Eastbourne, Sussex, England. DIED: May 16, 1947; Cambridge, England. PARENTS: Father, Frederick

Hopkins; Mother, Elizabeth Gowland Hopkins. NA-TIONALITY: British. RELIGION: Anglican. EDUCATION: Univ. of London, England, B.Sc., 1890; Univ. of London, England, M.B., 1894. SPOUSE: Jessie Anne Stevens, married 1898. CHILDREN: Barbara Holmes, daughter; Jacquetta Hawkes, daughter; 1 son. CAREER: Guy's Hospital, London, England, Researcher, 1894-97; Cambridge Univ., England, Professor, 1898-1943. OTHER AWARDS: Baly Medal, Royal College of Physicians, 1915; Royal Medal, Royal Society, 1918; Cameron Prize, U. of Edinburgh, Scotland, 1922; Knighthood, 1925; Copley Medal, 1926; Albert Medal, 1934; Order of Merit, 1935; Harben Medal, 1937.

Selected Publications: *Hopkins and Biochemistry, 1861-1947.* Cambridge: W. Heffer, 1949.

For More Information See: Baldwin, Ernest. *Gowland Hopkins.* London: VandenBerghs, 1961. *Dictionary of Scientific Biography.* New York: Scribner's, 1972 (Volume 6), 498-502.

Commentary: Frederick Hopkins received the Nobel "for his discovery of the growth-stimulating vitamins." Hopkins's work on nutrition was pioneering in that field, but he also contributed to the study of muscle metabolism, glutathione, and uric acid. (R.K.)

1930

Landsteiner, Karl 235

PRIZE: Medicine and Physiology, 1930. BORN: June 14, 1868; Vienna, Austria. DIED: June 26, 1943; New York, NY. PARENTS: Father, Leopold Landsteiner; Mother, Fanny Hess Landsteiner. NATIONALITY: Austrian; later American citizen. RELIGION: Catholic; from Jewish background. EDUCATION: Univ. of Vienna, Austria, M.D., 1891. SPOUSE: Helen Wlatso, married 1916. CHILDREN: Ernst Karl, son. CAREER: Univ. of Vienna, Austria, Professor, 1891-98; Pathological-Anatomical Institute, Vienna, Austria, Researcher, 1898-1907; Wilhelmina Hospital, Vienna, Austria, Physician, 1908-19; R. K. Zickenhuis Hospital, The Hague, Netherlands, Physician, 1919-22; Rockefeller Institute, NY, Researcher, 1922-43. OTHER AWARDS: Chevalier Legion of Honor, France; Hans Aronson Foundation Prize, Berlin, 1926; Paul Ehrlich Gold Medal, 1930; Dutch Red Cross Medal, 1933; Cameron Prize, U. of Edinburgh, Scotland, 1938.

Selected Publications: *Die Spezifizität der Serologischen Reaktionen.* Berlin: Julius Springer, 1933.

For More Information See: *Dictionary of Scientific Biography.* New York: Scribner's, 1973 (Volume 7), 622-25. *Obituary Notices of Fellows of the Royal Society of London.* London: Royal Society, 1947 (Volume 5), 295-324. Speiser, Paul. *Karl Landsteiner.* Vienna: Hallenek Brothers, 1961.

Commentary: Karl Landsteiner was awarded the Nobel Prize "for his discovery of the human blood groups," but his work ranged across chemistry, bacteriology, immunology, and pathology, with important work in each. His efforts in the study of poliomyelitis and syphilis were especially notable. (R.K.)

1931

Warburg, Otto Heinrich 236

PRIZE: Medicine and Physiology, 1931. BORN: October 8, 1883; Freiburg, Germany. DIED: August 1, 1970; Berlin, Germany. PARENTS: Father, Emil Gabriel Warburg; Mother, Elizabeth Gaertner Warburg. NATIONALITY: German. RELIGION: Jewish. EDUCATION: Univ. of Berlin, Germany, Dr. der Chemie, 1906; Univ. of Heidelberg, Germany, Dr. der Medizin, 1911. SPOUSE: None. CHILDREN: None. CAREER: Kaiser-Wilhelm Institute, Germany, Professor, 1913-70. OTHER AWARDS: Paul Ehrlich Prize, 1962; Nordhoff-Jung Prize; Schneider Prize; Gold Medal, U. of Wurzburg; German Order of Merit; Freedom of the City of Berlin.

Selected Publications: *Uber den Stoffwechsel der Tumoren.* Berlin: Springer, 1926 (*The Metabolism of Tumours.* Tr. by Frank Dickens. London: Constable, 1930). *Uber die Katalytischen Wirkungen der Lebendigen Substanz.* Berlin: Springer, 1928. *Schwermetalle als Wirkungsgruppen von Fermenten.* Berlin: W. Saenger, 1948. *Wasserstoffübertragende Fermente.* Berlin: W. Saenger, 1948. *The Prime Cause and Prevention of Cancer.* Wurzburg, Germany: K. Triltsch, 1969.

For More Information See: *Biographical Memoirs of the Fellows of the Royal Society.* London: Royal Society, 1972 (Volume 18), 629-99. *Dictionary of Scientific Biography.* New York: Scribner's, 1976 (Volume 14), 172-77. Krebs, Hans A. *Otto Warburg: Biochemist and Eccentric.* New York: Oxford U. Press, 1981.

Commentary: In a career spanning 65 years and over 500 papers, Otto Warburg distinguished himself as probably the greatest biochemist of this century. His Nobel Prize was awarded for the discovery of "the nature and mode of action of the respiratory enzyme" (cytochrome oxidase's action in cellular respiration). Other major research areas included photosynthesis and the metabolism, prevention, and treatment of cancer. Possibly as important as his research was the fact that Warburg worked with and helped develop three future Nobel Prize winners: Otto Meyerhof, Hans Krelos, and Hugo Theorell, sustaining a legacy which would even further enhance our understanding of the essence of life. (J.J.S.)

1932

Adrian, Edgar Douglas, Baron 237

PRIZE: Medicine and Physiology, 1932. BORN: November 30, 1889; London, England. DIED: August 4, 1977; London, England. PARENTS: Father, Alfred Douglas Adrian; Mother, Flora Lavinia Barton Adrian. NATIONALITY: British. RELIGION: Protestant; from Huguenot background. EDUCATION: Cambridge Univ., England, M.A., 1911; Cambridge Univ., England, M.D., 1915. SPOUSE: Hester Agnes Pinsent, married June 15, 1923. CHILDREN: Anne, daughter; Jennet, daughter; Richard Hume, son. CAREER: British Army, 1916-19; Cambridge Univ., England, Professor and Administrator, 1920-75. OTHER AWARDS: Baly Medal, 1929; Royal Medal, Royal Society, 1934; Order of Merit, England, 1942; Copley Medal, Royal Society, 1946; Hughlings Jackson Medal, Royal Society of Medicine, 1947; Gold Medal, Royal Society of Medicine, 1950; Albert Gold Medal, Royal Society of Arts, 1953; Harben Medal, 1955; Made Baron, 1955; Chevalier Legion of Honour,

France, 1956; Sherrington Memorial Medal, 1957; Medal for Distinguished Merit, British Medical Association, 1958; Jephcott Medal, Royal Society of Medicine, 1963.

Selected Publications: *The Basis of Sensation.* New York: W.W. Norton, 1928. *Mechanism of Nervous Action.* Philadelphia, PA: U. of Pennsylvania Press, 1932. *Physical Background of Perception.* Oxford: Clarendon Press, 1947.

For More Information See: *Biographical Memoirs of Fellows of the Royal Society.* London: Royal Society, 1979 (Volume 25), 1-73. *Current Biography Yearbook.* New York: H.W. Wilson, 1955, 1-3.

Commentary: Edgar Adrian's shared Nobel was for his "discoveries regarding the function of the neurons" in sending nerve messages. His work led to the development of the techniques of electroencephalography. (R.K.)

Sherrington, Charles Scott, Sir   238

PRIZE: Medicine and Physiology, 1932. BORN: November 27, 1857; London, England. DIED: March 4, 1952; Eastbourne, Sussex, England. PARENTS: Father, James Norton Sherrington; Mother, Anne Brookes Sherrington. NATIONALITY: British. RELIGION: Anglican. EDUCATION: Cambridge Univ., England, M.B., 1885. SPOUSE: Ethel Mary Wright, married 1892. CHILDREN: Carr E.R., son. CAREER: Koch Laboratory, Berlin, Germany, Researcher, 1886-87; St. Thomas Hospital, London, England, Physician, 1887-90; Univ. of London, England, Professor and Administrator, 1891-94; Univ. of Liverpool, England, Professor, 1895-1913; Oxford Univ., England, Professor, 1913-35; Univ. of Edinburgh, Scotland, Professor, 1936-38. OTHER AWARDS: Royal Medal, Royal Society, 1905; Knighthood, 1922; Order of Merit, England, 1924; Baly Gold Medal; Retzius Gold Medal, Royal Swedish Academy; Copley Medal, 1927.

Selected Publications: *The Integrative Action of the Nervous System.* New Haven, CT: Yale U. Press, 1906. *Man on His Nature.* London: Cambridge U. Press, 1940. *Selected Writings of Sir Charles Sherrington.* Oxford: Oxford U. Press, 1979.

For More Information See: *Dictionary of Scientific Biography.* New York: Scribner's, 1975 (Volume 12), 395-402. Eccles, John C., and Gibson, William C. *Sherrington. His Life and Thought.* New York: Springer International, 1979. *Obituary Notices of Fellows of the Royal Society.* Cambridge: Royal Society, 1952 (Volume 21), 241-70.

Commentary: Charles Sherrington shared the Nobel Prize for "discoveries regarding the function of the neurons" in the activity of the brain and spinal cord. Although his life's work was in this field, his writings show a broader scope, including poetry and the history of medicine. (R.K.)

1933

Morgan, Thomas Hunt   239

PRIZE: Medicine and Physiology, 1933. BORN: September 25, 1866; Lexington, KY. DIED: December 4, 1945; Pasadena, CA. PARENTS: Father, Charlton Hunt Morgan; Mother, Ellen Key Howard Morgan. NATIONALITY: American. RELIGION: Episcopalian. EDUCATION: State College of Kentucky, B.S., 1886; State College of Kentucky, M.S., 1888; Johns Hopkins Univ., MD, M.D.,

Ph.D., 1890. SPOUSE: Lilian V. Sampson, married June 4, 1904. CHILDREN: Lilian Vaughn, daughter; Isabel Merrick, daughter; Edith Sampson, daughter; Howard Key, son. CAREER: Bryn Mawr College, PA, Professor, 1891-1903; Columbia Univ., NY, Professor, 1904-28; California Institute of Technology, Professor, 1928-45. OTHER AWARDS: Darwin Medal, 1924; Copley Medal, 1939.

Selected Publications: *Regeneration.* New York: Macmillan, 1901. *Heredity and Sex.* New York: Columbia U. Press, 1913. *The Scientific Basis of Evolution.* London: Faber and Faber, 1932. *The Theory of the Gene.* New Haven, CT: Yale U. Press, 1932.

For More Information See: Allan, Garland E. *Thomas Hunt Morgan: The Man and His Science.* Princeton, NJ: Princeton U. Press, 1978. *Biographical Memoirs. National Academy of Sciences.* New York: Columbia U. Press, 1959 (Volume 33), 383-436. *Dictionary of Scientific Biography.* New York: Scribner's, 1974 (Volume 9), 515-26.

Commentary: Thomas Morgan received the Nobel "for his discoveries concerning the function of the chromosome in the transmission of heredity." His life's work on the fruit fly, *Drosophila melanogaster,* led to a broad understanding of genetic principles. (R.K.)

1934

Minot, George Richards   240

PRIZE: Medicine and Physiology, 1934. BORN: December 2, 1885; Boston, MA. DIED: February 25, 1950; Brookline, MA. PARENTS: Father, James Jackson Minot; Mother, Elizabeth Whitney Minot. NATIONALITY: American. RELIGION: Unitarian. EDUCATION: Harvard Univ., MA, B.A., 1908; Harvard Univ., MA, M.D., 1912. SPOUSE: Marian Linzee Weld, married June 29, 1915. CHILDREN: Marian Linzee, daughter; Elizabeth Whitney, daughter; Charles Sedgwick, son. CAREER: Massachusetts General Hospital, Boston, Physician, 1912-13; Johns Hopkins Univ., Baltimore, MD, Researcher, 1913-15; Massachusetts General Hospital, Boston, Physician, 1915-23; Peter Bent Brigham Hospital, MA, Physician, 1923-28; Collis P. Huntington Memorial Hospital, MA, Physician and Administrator, 1923-28; Harvard Univ., MA, Professor and Administrator, 1928-50. OTHER AWARDS: Kober Gold Medal, Association of American Physicians, 1928; Cameron Prize, U. of Edinburgh, Scotland, 1930; Gold Medal, National Institute of Social Sciences, 1930; Gold Medal and Award, Popular Science Monthly, 1930; Moxon Medal, Royal College of Physicians, 1933; John Scott Medal, Philadelphia, 1935; Scroll Award, Association of Grocery Manufacturers of America, 1936.

Selected Publications: "Development of Liver Therapy in Pernicious Anemia." *Lancet* 1 (1935): 361-64. *Pathological Physiology and Clinical Description of the Anemias.* New York: Oxford U. Press, 1936.

For More Information See: *Biographical Memoirs: National Academy of Sciences.* New York: Columbia U. Press, 1974 (Volume 45), 336-83. *Dictionary of Scientific Biography.* New York: Scribner's (Volume 9), 1974, 416-17. Rackemann, F.M. *The Inquisitive Physician: The Life and Times of George Richards Minot.* Cambridge, MA: Harvard U. Press, 1956.

Commentary: George Minot shared the Nobel Prize for "discoveries concerning liver therapy against anemias." Minot's work in anemia and pernicious anemia was only part of his work in blood disorders and was in addition to research in such varied areas as cancer, arthritis, and dietary deficiencies. (R.K.)

Murphy, William Parry 241

PRIZE: Medicine and Physiology, 1934. BORN: February 6, 1892; Stoughton, WI. PARENTS: Father, Thomas Francis Murphy; Mother, Rose Anna Parry Murphy. NATIONALITY: American. RELIGION: Congregationalist. EDUCATION: Univ. of Oregon, A.B., 1914; Harvard Univ., MA, M.D., 1920. SPOUSE: Harriet Adams, married September 10, 1919. CHILDREN: Priscilla Adams, daughter; William Parry, son. CAREER: U.S. Army, 1917-18; Rhode Island Hospital, Physician, 1920-22; Peter Bent Brigham Hospital, MA, Physician and Researcher, 1922-. OTHER AWARDS: Cameron Prize, U. of Edinburgh, Scotland, 1930; Commander Order of White Rose First Rank, Finland, 1934; Bronze Medal for Science Exhibit, American Medical Association, 1934; Gold Medal, Humane Society of Massachusetts, 1935; National Order of Merit Carlos J. Finlay, Cuba, 1952; Distinguished Achievement Award, Boston, MA, 1965; International Bicentennial Symposium Award, 1972; Gold Badge, Massachusetts Medical Society, 1973; Paul Harris Fellow Award, 1980.

Selected Publications: *Anemia in Practice: Pernicious Anemia.* Philadelphia, PA: W.B. Saunders, 1939.

For More Information See: *Asimov's Biographical Encyclopedia of Science and Technology.* Garden City, NY: Doubleday, 1964, 507. *National Cyclopedia of American Biography.* New York: James T. White, 1946 (Volume G), 358-59.

Commentary: William Murphy's shared Nobel was for "discoveries concerning liver therapy against anemias." His work with Minot on pernicious anemia is noted as his most important contribution. (R.K.)

Whipple, George Hoyt 242

PRIZE: Medicine and Physiology, 1934. BORN: August 28, 1878; Ashland, NJ. DIED: February 1, 1976; Rochester, NY. PARENTS: Father, Ashley Cooper Whipple; Mother, Frances Anna Hoyt Whipple. NATIONALITY: American. RELIGION: Baptist/Episcopalian background. EDUCATION: Yale Univ., CT, A.B., 1900; Johns Hopkins Univ., MD, M.D., 1905. SPOUSE: Katherine Ball Waring, married June 24, 1914. CHILDREN: Barbara, daughter; George Hoyt, son. CAREER: Holbrook School, NY, Teacher, 1901; Johns Hopkins Univ., MD, Professor, 1902-14; Univ. of California, San Francisco, Professor and Administrator, 1914-21; Univ. of Rochester, NY, Professor and Administrator, 1921-55. OTHER AWARDS: Warren Triennial Prize, 1910; Popular Science Monthly Award, 1929; William Wood Gerhard Gold Medal, 1934; Charles Mickle Fellowship, U. of Toronto, Canada, 1938; Kober Medal, Georgetown U., 1939; Rochester Civic Medal, NY, 1943; Certificate of Honor, European Society for Hematology, 1959; Gold-Headed Cane Award, American Association of Pathologists and Bacteriologists, 1961; Kovalenko Medal, National Academy of Sciences, 1962; Distinguished Service Award, American Medical Association, 1973; President's Medal, U. of Rochester, NY, 1975.

Selected Publications: "Icterus. A Rapid Change of Hemoglobin to Bile Pigments in the Circulation Outside the Liver." *Journal of Experimental Medicine* 17 (1913): 612-35 (with C.W. Hooper). "Blood Regeneration Following Simple Anemia. IV. Influence of Meat, Liver, and Various Extractives, Alone or Combined with Standard Diets." *American Journal of Physiology* 53 (1920): 236-62 (with C.W. Hooper and F.S. Robscheit). "Pigment Metabolism and Regeneration of Hemoglobin in the Body." *Archives of Internal Medicine* 29 (1922): 711-31. "Blood Regeneration in Severe Anemia. 14. A Liver Fraction Potent in Pernicious Anemia Fed Alone and Combined with Whole Liver, Liver Ash and Fresh Bile." *Journal of Experimental Medicine* 49 (1929): 215-27 (with F.S. Robscheit-Robbins). *The Dynamic Equilibrium of Body Proteins. Hemoglobin, Plasma Proteins, Organ and Tissue Proteins.* Springfield, IL: Thomas, 1956.

For More Information See: Corner, George W. *George Hoyt Whipple and His Friends.* Philadelphia, PA: Lippincott, 1963. *Perspectives in Biology and Medicine* 2 (Spring 1959): 253-89.

Commentary: George Whipple shared his Nobel Prize for "discoveries concerning liver therapy against anemia." In a long and fruitful career, his work on anemia in dogs was landmark, but he also did notable work on bile and bile pigments, black water fever, intestinal obstructions, plasma protein regeneration, and iron metabolism. (R.K.)

1935

Spemann, Hans 243

PRIZE: Medicine and Physiology, 1935. BORN: June 27, 1869; Stuttgart, Würtenberg, Germany. DIED: September 12, 1941; Freiburg-im-Breisgau, Baden, Germany. PARENTS: Father, Johann Willhelm Spemann; Mother, Lisinka Hoffmann Spemann. NATIONALITY: German. RELIGION: Protestant. EDUCATION: Univ. of Würzburg, Germany, doctorate, 1895. SPOUSE: Clara Binder, married 1895. CHILDREN: Fritz, son; Rudo, son. CAREER: Univ. of Würzburg, Germany, Researcher, 1894-1908; Univ. of Rostock, Germany, Professor, 1908-13; Kaiser Wilhelm Institute of Biology, Berlin-Dahlem, Germany, Director, 1914-18; Univ. of Freiburg-im-Breisgau, Germany, Professor, 1919-35.

Selected Publications: *Experimentelle Beiträge zu einer Theorie der Entwicklung.* Berlin: J. Springer, 1936 (*Embryonic Development and Induction.* New Haven, CT: Yale U. Press, 1938).

For More Information See: *Dictionary of Scientific Biography.* Scribner's, 1975 (Volume 12), 567-69. Mangold, Otto. *Hans Spemann, ein Meister der Entwicklungsphysiologie, sein Leben und sein Werk.* Stuttgart, Germany: Wissenschaftlich Verlagsgesellschaft, 1953. Spemann, Hans. *Forschung und Leben, Erinnerungen.* Stuttgart, Germany: J. Engelhorns Nacht, 1943.

Commentary: Hans Spemann was awarded the Nobel Prize "for his discovery of the organizer effect in embryonic development." By developing techniques that permitted implanting embryo sections into another embryo, Spemann was able to show that certain parts of the embryo, which contained specific chemicals, could induce further development, while others could not. (R.K.)

1936

Dale, Henry Hallett, Sir   244
PRIZE: Medicine and Physiology, 1936. BORN: June 9, 1875; London, England. DIED: July 23, 1968; Cambridge, England. PARENTS: Father, Charles James Dale; Mother, Frances Ann Hallett Dale. NATIONALITY: British. RELIGION: Methodist. EDUCATION: Cambridge Univ., England, B. Chir., 1903; Cambridge Univ., England, M.D., 1909. SPOUSE: Ellen Harriet Hallett, married November 5, 1904. CHILDREN: Robert Henry, son; Alison Sarah, daughter; Elinor Mary, daughter. CAREER: Wellcome Physiological Research Laboratories, England, Director, 1904-14; National Institute for Medical Research, Hampstead, England, Researcher and Administrator, 1914-42; Royal Institution of Great Britain, Director, 1942-46. OTHER AWARDS: Gedge Prize, Cambridge U., England, 1900; Walsingham Medal, Cambridge U., England, 1900; Raymond Horton Smith Prize, 1909; Baly Medal, Royal College of Physicians, 1921; Cameron Prize, U. of Edinburgh, Scotland, 1926; Medal of the Society of Apothecaries, 1932; Harrison Memorial Medal, Pharmaceutical Society of Great Britain, 1932; Knighthood, 1932; Addingham Medal, William Hoffmann Wood Trust, Leeds, England, 1935; Royal Medal, Royal Society, 1936; Copley Medal, Royal Society, 1937; Fothergillian Medal, Medical Society of London, 1938; Harben Gold Medal, Royal Institute of Public Health and Hygiene, 1943; Danbury Memorial Medal, Pharmaceutical Society of Great Britain, 1943; Dr. Bimala Churn Law Gold Medal, Indian Association for the Cultivation of Science, 1943; Order of Merit, 1944; USA Medal of Freedom with Silver Palm, 1947; Grand Croix de l'Ordre de la Couronne of Belgium, 1949; Pour le merite, West Germany, 1955; Gold Medal of Honour, Canadian Pharmaceutical Manufacturer's Association, 1955; Gold Albert Medal, Royal Society of the Arts, 1956; Schmiedeberg-Plakette, German Pharmacological Society, 1962.

Selected Publications: *Adventures in Physiology.* London: Pergammon Press, 1953. *An Autumn Gleaning.* London: Pergammon Press, 1954.

For More Information See: *Biographical Memoirs of the Fellows of the Royal Society.* London: Royal Society, 1970 (Volume 16), 77-174. *Dictionary of Scientific Biography.* New York: Scribner's, 1978 (Supplement I), 104-07.

Commentary: Henry Dale shared the Nobel Prize for "discoveries relating to the chemical transmission of nerve impulses." His two major research interests were derived from studies of the action of adrenaline and acetylcholine (chemical transmission of nerve impulses) and studies of the action of histamine (response of the organism and its tissues to various external assaults). (R.K.)

Loewi, Otto   245
PRIZE: Medicine and Physiology, 1936. BORN: June 3, 1873; Frankfurt on the Main, Germany. DIED: December 25, 1961; New York, NY. PARENTS: Father, Jacob Loewi; Mother, Anna Willstädter Loewi. NATIONALITY: German; later American citizen. RELIGION: Jewish. EDUCATION: Univ. of Strasbourg, France, M.D., 1896. SPOUSE: Gulda Goldschmiedt, married April 5, 1908. CHILDREN: Harold, son; Victor, son; Geoffrey W., son; Anna, daughter. CAREER: City Hospital, Frankfurt, Germany, Researcher, 1897-98; Univ. of Marburg,

Germany, Professor, 1898-1904; Univ. of Vienna, Austria, Professor, 1905-09; Univ. of Graz, Austria, Professor, 1909-38; Univ. of Brussels, Belgium, Professor, 1938-39; New York Univ., Professor, 1940-61. OTHER AWARDS: Austrian Distinguished Order for Art and Science, 1936; Cameron Prize, U. of Edinburgh, Scotland, 1944.

Selected Publications: "The Humoral Transmission of Nervous Impulse." *Harvey Lectures* 28 (1934): 218-33. "The Ferrier Lecture on Problems Connected with the Principle of Humoral Transmission of Nervous Impulses." *Proceedings of the Royal Society* 118B (1935): 299-316. "Die Chemische Übertragung der Nervwirkung." *Schweizerische Medizinische Wochenschrift* 67 (1937): 850-55. "The Edward Gamaliel Janeway Lectures: Aspects of the Transmission of Nervous Impulse." *Journal of the Mount Sinai Hospital* 12 (1945): 803-16, 851-65.

For More Information See: *Biographical Memoirs of Fellows of the Royal Society.* London: Royal Society, 1962 (Volume 8), 67-89. *Dictionary of Scientific Biography.* New York: Scribner's, 1973 (Volume 8), 451-56. Lembeck, Fred, and Giere, Wolfgang. *Otto Loewi: Ein Lebensbild in Dokumenten.* New York: Springer, 1968.

Commentary: Otto Loewi's shared Nobel Prize was for "discoveries relating to chemical transmission of nerve impulses." He also produced significant papers on metabolism, the heart, the kidney, the action of insulin, and cocaine's effect on adrenalin. (R.K.)

1937

Szent-Györgyi, Albert von Nagyrapolt   246
PRIZE: Medicine and Physiology, 1937. BORN: September 16, 1893; Budapest, Hungary. PARENTS: Father, Nicholas Szent-Györgyi; Mother, Josephine Lenhossek Szent-Györgyi. NATIONALITY: Hungarian; later American citizen. RELIGION: Belongs to no organized church. EDUCATION: Univ. of Budapest, Hungary, M.D., 1917; Cambridge Univ., England, Ph.D., 1927. SPOUSE: Cornelia Demeny, married 1917, 2nd wife Marta Borbiro, married 1941, 3rd wife Marcia Houston, married 1975. CHILDREN: Cornelia, daughter. CAREER: Austro-Hungarian Army, 1914-18; Researcher at various universities (Prague, Czechoslovakia; Berlin, Germany; Hamburg, Germany; Leiden, Netherlands; Liége, Belgium; Groningen, Germany; Budapest, Hungary; Minnesota; Cambridge, England), 1919-30; Univ. of Szeged, Hungary, Professor and Administrator, 1931-45; Univ. of Budapest, Hungary, Professor, 1945-47; Marine Biology Laboratories, Woods Hole, MA, Director, 1947-75; National Foundation for Cancer Research, Woods Hole, MA, Director, 1975-. OTHER AWARDS: Cameron Prize, U. of Edinburgh, Scotland, 1946; Lasker Award, American Heart Association, 1954.

Selected Publications: *On Oxidation, Fermentation, Vitamins, Health and Disease.* Baltimore, MD: Williams and Wilkins, 1939. *Chemistry of Muscular Contraction.* New York: Academic Press, 1947. *Bioelectronics.* New York: Academic Press, 1968. *The Living State and Cancer.* New York: M. Dekker, 1978.

For More Information See: *Current Biography Yearbook.* New York: H.W. Wilson, 1955, 596-99. *Encyclopedia of World Biography.* New York: McGraw-Hill,

1973 (Volume 10), 314-16. "Lost in the Twentieth Century." *Annual Review of Biochemistry* 32 (1963): 1-14.

Commentary: Albert Szent-Györgyi was granted the Nobel Prize "for his discoveries in connection with the biological combustion processes, with especial reference to Vitamin C and the catalysis of fumaric acid." A prolific researcher and writer, Szent-Györgyi made significant contributions as well in discovering vitamin P, in the biochemistry of muscular contraction, in isolation of ATP, and in the study of cancer. (M.L.)

1938

Heymans, Corneille Jean Francois   247
PRIZE: Medicine and Physiology, 1938. BORN: March 28, 1892; Ghent, Belgium. DIED: July 18, 1968; Knokke, Belgium. PARENTS: Father, Jean-Francois Heymans; Mother, Marie-Henriette Henning Heymans. NATIONALITY: Belgian. RELIGION: Catholic. EDUCATION: Univ. of Ghent, Belgium, M.D., 1920. SPOUSE: Bertha May, married January 18, 1921. CHILDREN: Pierre, son; Marie-Henriette, daughter; Jean, daughter; Berthe, daughter. CAREER: Univ. of Ghent, Belgium, Professor, 1923-68. OTHER AWARDS: Alvarenga Prize, Académie Royale de Médecine, Belgium; Gluge Prize, Académie Royal des Sciences, Belgium; Prix Quinquennal de Médecine du Gouvernement, Belgium; Pius XI Prize, Pontifica Academia Scientiarum, Rome; Purkinje Prize, Academy of Medicine, Czechoslovakia; Bourceret Prize, Académie de Médecine de Paris, France; Monthyon Prize, Institut de France; Schmiedeberg Plakette, Deutsche Pharmakologische Gesellschaft, Germany; Cyon Prize; Academy of Sciences, Bologna, Italy; Burgi Prize, U. of Bern, Switzerland.

Selected Publications: *The Cartoid Sinus and Other Reflexogenic Vasosensitive Zones.* Paris: Press of French Universities, 1929. *Introduction to the Regulation of Blood Pressure and Heart Rate.* Springfield, IL: Thomas, 1950. *Reflexogenic Areas of the Cardiovascular System.* London: Churchill, 1958 (with E. Neil).

For More Information See: *A Biographical History of Medicine.* New York: Grune and Stratton, 1970, 984-86. *Corneel Heymanns: A Collective Biography.* Ghent, Belgium: Archives Internationales de Pharmacodynamie et de Therapie, 1972.

Commentary: Corneille Heymans won the Nobel Prize "for his discovery of the role played by the sinus and aortic mechanisms in the regulation of respiration." This was accomplished by development of new techniques for physiologic investigation, such as cross-circulation (where the carotid artery and jugular vein of one animal were used to perfuse blood in another animal unconnected except for the nerves involved). (M.L. and C.E.)

1939

Domagk, Gerhard   248
PRIZE: Medicine and Physiology, 1939 (refused). BORN: October 30, 1895; Lagow, Brandenburg, Germany. DIED: April 24, 1964; Beirberg, Wurttenburg, Baden, Germany. PARENTS: Father, Paul Domagk; Mother, Martha Reimer Domagk. NATIONALITY: German. RELIGION: Christian. EDUCATION: Univ. of Kiel, Germany, M.D., 1921. SPOUSE: Gertrude Strübe, married 1925.

CHILDREN: Hildegarde, daughter; 3 sons. CAREER: German Army, 1914-18; Univ. of Greifswald, Germany, Professor, 1921-25; Univ. of Müenster, Germany, Professor, 1925-64; I.G. Farberindustrie, Elberfeld, Germany, Director of Research, 1928-64. OTHER AWARDS: Emil Fischer Memorial Plaque, 1937; Gold Medal of the Paris Exposition, 1938; Paul Ehrlich Gold Medal, 1939; Cameron Prize, U. of Edinburgh, Scotland, 1939; Von Klebelsberg Award, U. of Szeged, Hungary.

Selected Publications: "Ein Beitrag zur Chemotherapie der Bakteriellen Infektionen." *Deutsche Medizinische Wochenschrift* 61 (1935): 250-53. *Chemotherapie Bakterieller Infektionen.* Leipzig, Germany: Hirzel, 1940 (with F. Hegler). *Pathologische Anatomie und Chemotherapie der Infektionskrankenheiten.* Stuttgart, Germany: Thieme, 1947. *Chemotherapie der Tuberkulose mit Thiosemikarbazonen.* Stuttgart, Germany: Thieme, 1950.

For More Information See: *Biographical Memoirs of the Fellows of the Royal Society.* London: Royal Society, 1964 (Volume 10), 39-50. *Dictionary of Scientific Biography.* New York: Scribner's, 1971 (Volume 4), 153-56.

Commentary: Gerhard Domagk received the Nobel Prize "for his discovery of the antibacterial effects of prontosil," one of the sulfonamide compounds. It was used against many disease states successfully, and led to the preparation of many related sulfonamides. Domagk continued to work to find medically effective drugs, first for tuberculosis, later for cancer. (C.E.)

1943

Dam, Carl Peter Henrik   249
PRIZE: Medicine and Physiology, 1943. BORN: February 21, 1895; Copenhagen, Denmark. DIED: April 18, 1976; Copenhagen, Denmark. PARENTS: Father, Emil Dam; Mother, Emilie Peterson Dam. NATIONALITY: Danish. RELIGION: Christian. EDUCATION: Polytechnic Institute, Denmark, M.S., 1920; Univ. of Copenhagen, Denmark, D.Sc., 1934. SPOUSE: Inger Olsen, married July 15, 1924. CHILDREN: None. CAREER: Royal School of Agriculture and Veterinary Medicine, Copenhagen, Denmark, Professor, 1920-23; Univ. of Copenhagen, Denmark, Professor, 1923-41; Univ. of Rochester, NY, Researcher, 1942-45; Rockefeller Institute for Medical Research, NY, Researcher, 1945-48; Polytechnic Institute, Copenhagen, Denmark, Professor, 1948-65. OTHER AWARDS: Christian Bohr Award in Physiology, 1939; Norman Medal, German Fat Research Society, 1960.

Selected Publications: *Some Studies on Vitamin E.* Copenhagen: E. Munksgaard, 1941. "Vitamin K, Its Chemistry and Physiology." *Advances in Enzymology* 2 (1942): 285. "Medical Aspects of Vitamin K." *Lancet* 63 (1943): 353.

For More Information See: *Current Biography Yearbook.* New York: H.W. Wilson, 1949, 134-36. *Modern Scientists and Engineers.* New York: McGraw-Hill, 1980 (Volume 1), 258-59.

Commentary: Henrik Dam was cited by the Academy "for his discovery of vitamin K," the blood coagulation factor. Dam's work also included research in cholesterol metabolism, vitamin E, lipids, growth factors, and gallstone formation. (C.E.)

Doisy, Edward Adelbert   **250**
PRIZE: Medicine and Physiology, 1943. BORN: November 13, 1893; Hume, IL. PARENTS: Father, Edward Perez Doisy; Mother, Ada Alley Doisy. NATIONALITY: American. RELIGION: Congregationalist. EDUCATION: Univ. of Illinois, A.B., 1914; Univ. of Illinois, M.S., 1916; Harvard Univ., MA, Ph.D., 1920. SPOUSE: Alice Ackert, married July 20, 1918, died August 1964; Margaret McCormick, married April 19, 1965. CHILDREN: Edward Adelbert, son; Robert A., son; Philip P., son; Richard J., son. CAREER: Harvard Univ., MA, Researcher, 1915-17; U.S. Army, 1917-19; Washington Univ., MO, Professor, 1919-23; St. Louis Univ., MO, Professor, 1923-65. OTHER AWARDS: Gold Medal, St. Louis Medical Society, 1935; Philip A. Conne Medal, Chemist's Club of New York, 1935; St. Louis Civic Award, 1939; Willard Gibbs Award, American Chemical Society, 1941; American Pharmaceutical Manufacturing Association Award, 1942; Squibb Award, 1944; Fleur de Lis, St. Louis U., MO, 1951; Commercial Solvent Award, 1952; Illini Achievement Award, U. of Illinois, 1958; Barren Foundation Medal, 1972.

Selected Publications: "The Constitution and Synthesis of Vitamin K1." *Journal of Biological Chemistry* 131 (1939): 357-69 (with others). "The Isolation of Vitamin K1." *Journal of Biological Chemistry* 130 (1939): 219-34 (with others). "The Isolation of Vitamin K2." *Journal of Biological Chemistry* 131 (1939): 327-44 (with others). *Female Sex Hormones.* Philadelphia, PA: U. of Pennsylvania Press, 1941 (with others).

For More Information See: *Current Biography Yearbook.* New York: H. W. Wilson, 1949, 161-62. *Modern Scientists and Engineers.* New York: McGraw-Hill, 1980 (Volume 1), 298-99.

Commentary: Edward Doisy was granted the Nobel Prize "for his discovery of the chemical nature of vitamin K." In addition to synthesis isolation, and characterization of the K vitamins, Doisy also worked with metabolism, endocrinology, insulin, blood buffers, ovarian hormones, and estrogens. (K.F.)

1944

Erlanger, Joseph   **251**
PRIZE: Medicine and Physiology, 1944. BORN: January 5, 1874; San Francisco, CA. DIED: December 15, 1965; St. Louis, MO. PARENTS: Father, Herman Erlanger; Mother, Sarah Galinger Erlanger. NATIONALITY: American. RELIGION: Jewish. EDUCATION: Univ. of California, B.S., 1895; Johns Hopkins Univ., MD, M.D., 1899. SPOUSE: Aimee Hirstel, married June 21, 1906. CHILDREN: Margaret, daughter; Ruth Josephine, daughter; Herman, son. CAREER: Johns Hopkins Univ., MD, Professor, 1899-1906; Univ. of Wisconsin, Professor, 1906-10; Washington Univ., MO, Professor, 1910-65.

Selected Publications: "A Study of the Metabolism in Dogs with Shortened Small Intestines." *American Journal of Physiology* 6 (1901): 1-30 (with A.W. Hewlett). "On the Physiology of Heart-Block in Mammals, with Especial Reference to the Causation of Stokes-Adams Disease." *Journal of Experimental Medicine* 7 (1905): 676-724. "Studies in Blood Pressure Estimation by Indirect Methods. I. The Mechanism of the Oscillatory Methods." *American Journal of Physiology* 39 (1916): 401-46. "The Compound Nature of the

Action Current of Nerve as Disclosed by the Cathode Ray Oscillograph." *American Journal of Physiology* 70 (1924): 624-66 (with H.S. Gasser).

For More Information See: *Biographical Memoirs. National Academy of Sciences.* New York: Columbia U. Press, 1970 (Volume 41), 111-39. *Dictionary of Scientific Biography.* New York: Scribner's, 1971 (Volume 4), 397-99. "A Physiologist Reminisces." *Annual Review of Physiology* 26 (1964): 1-14.

Commentary: Joseph Erlanger shared his Nobel for "discoveries regarding the highly differentiated functions of single nerve fibers." His career included work on circulation and cardiac physiology, blood pressure and blood volume, neurophysiology, and treatment of wound shock. (B.R.W.)

Gasser, Herbert Spencer   **252**
PRIZE: Medicine and Physiology, 1944. BORN: July 5, 1888; Platteville, WI. DIED: May 11, 1963; New York, NY. PARENTS: Father, Herman Spencer; Mother, Elizabeth Griswold Spencer. NATIONALITY: American. RELIGION: Jewish. EDUCATION: Univ. of Wisconsin, A.B., 1910; Univ. of Wisconsin, A.M., 1911; Johns Hopkins Univ., MD, M.D., 1915. SPOUSE: None. CHILDREN: None. CAREER: Univ. of Wisconsin, Professor, 1911-16; Washington Univ., MO, Professor, 1916-31; Cornell Univ., NY, Professor, 1931-35; Rockefeller Institute for Medical Research, NY, Professor and Administrator, 1935-63. OTHER AWARDS: Kober Medal, American Association of Physicians, 1954.

Selected Publications: "A Study of the Mechanism by Which Muscular Exercise Produces Acceleration of the Heart." *American Journal of Physiology* 34 (1914): 48-71 (with W.J. Meek). "An Experimental Study of Surgical Shock." *Journal of the American Medical Association* 69 (1917): 2089-92 (with J. Erlanger and B.L. Elliott). "The Compound Nature of the Action Current of Nerve as Disclosed by the Cathode Ray Oscillograph." *American Journal of Physiology* 70 (1924): 624-66 (with J. Erlanger). "The Classification of Nerve Fibers." *Ohio Journal of Science* 41 (1941): 145-59.

For More Information See: *Dictionary of Scientific Biography.* New York: Scribner's, 1972 (Volume 5), 290-91. *Herbert Spencer Gasser, 1888-1963: An Autobiographical Memoir.* New York: Academic Press, 1964.

Commentary: Herbert Gasser shared his Nobel Prize for "discoveries regarding the highly differentiated functions of single nerve fibers." Gasser's major work was accomplished with Joseph Erlanger, in wound shock, blood volume, and in neurophysiology, but his later work on nerve fibers helped to clarify many problems in that field. (B.R.W.)

1945

Chain, Ernst Boris, Sir   **253**
PRIZE: Medicine and Physiology, 1945. BORN: June 19, 1906; Berlin, Germany. DIED: August 12, 1979; Mulranny, County Mayo, Ireland. PARENTS: Father, Michael Chain; Mother, Margarete Eisner Chain. NATIONALITY: German; later Italian resident and British citizen. RELIGION: Jewish. EDUCATION: Friedrich-Wilhelms Univ., Germany, Ph.D., 1930. SPOUSE: Anne Beloff, married 1948. CHILDREN: Benjamin, son; Daniel, son; Judith, daughter. CAREER: Charite Hospital, Berlin,

Germany, Researcher, 1930-33; Cambridge Univ., England, Researcher, 1933-35; Oxford Univ., England, Professor, 1935-48; Instituto Superiore di Sanita, Rome, Italy, Professor and Administrator, 1948-61; Univ. of London, England, Professor, 1961-79. OTHER AWARDS: Silver Berzelius Medal, Swedish Medical Society, 1946; Pasteur Medal, Institut Pasteur and Societe de Chimie Biologique, 1946; Harmsworth Memorial Fund, 1946; Paul Ehrlich Centenary Prize, 1954; Gold Medal for Therapeutics, Worshipful Society of Apothecaries, England, 1957; Knighthood, 1969; Marotta Medal, Societa Chimica Italiana, 1972; Carl Neuberg Medal, 1972; Hamburg Memorial Medal, Germany, 1972; Heymans Memorial Medal, 1974.

Selected Publications: "Penicillin as a Chemotherapeutic Agent." *Lancet* 239 (1940): 226-28 (with others). "Further Observations on Penicillin." *Lancet* 241 (1941): 177-89 (with others). *Antibiotics: A Survey of Penicillin, Streptomycin and other Antimicrobial Substances from Fungi, Actinomycetes, Bacteria and Plants*. London: Oxford U. Press, 1949 (with others).

For More Information See: *Biographical Encyclopedia of Scientists*. New York: Facts on File, 1981, 140. *Biographical Memoirs of Fellows of the Royal Society*. London: Royal Society, 1983 (Volume 29), 42-91.

Commentary: Ernst Chain shared the Nobel "for the discovery of penicillin and its curative effect in various infectious diseases." Chain participated in the research that demonstrated the structure of penicillin and used it in successful clinical trials. Other notable work included that on penicillinase, tumor metabolism, and insulin action. (B.I.M.)

Fleming, Alexander, Sir   254

PRIZE: Medicine and Physiology, 1945. BORN: August 6, 1881; Lochfield Farm, Ayrshire, Scotland. DIED: March 11, 1955; London, England. PARENTS: Father, Hugh Fleming; Mother, Grace Morton Fleming. NATIONALITY: Scottish. RELIGION: Presbyterian. EDUCATION: Univ. of London, England, M.D., 1906. SPOUSE: Sarah Marion McElroy, married December 1915, died 1949; Amalia Cotsouris Voureka, married April 1953. CHILDREN: Robert, son. CAREER: Shipping Company, London, Clerk, 1897-1901; St. Mary's Hospital, London, England, Physician and Researcher, 1906-55. OTHER AWARDS: Gold Medal, U. of London, England, 1908; Cheadle Medal, 1908; John Scott Medal, Philadelphia, PA, 1944; Knighthood, 1944; Cameron Prize, U. of Edinburgh, Scotland, 1945; Louis Pasteur Medal, 1947; Medal for Merit, United States, 1947.

Selected Publications: "On the Use of Salvarsan in the Treatment of Syphilis." *Lancet* 1 (1911): 1631-34. "On a Remarkable Bacteriolytic Substance Found in Secretions and Tissues." *Proceedings of the Royal Society* 93B (1922): 306-17. "On the Antibacterial Action of Cultures of a *Penicillium*, with Special Reference to Their Use in the Isolation of *B. Influenzae*." *British Journal of Experimental Pathology* 10 (1929): 226-36. "Penicillin: Its Discovery, Development, and Uses in the Field of Medicine and Surgery." *Journal of the Royal Institute of Public Health and Hygiene* 8 (1945): 36-49, 63-71, 93-105. *Chemotherapy: Yesterday, Today, and Tomorrow*. Cambridge: Cambridge U. Press, 1946.

For More Information See: *Dictionary of Scientific Biography*. New York: Scribner's, 1972 (Volume 5), 28-31. Ludovici, Laurence J. *Fleming, Discoverer of Penicillin*. London: A. Dakers, 1952. Macfarlane, Gwyn. *Alexander Fleming: The Man and the Myth*. Cambridge, MA: Harvard U. Press, 1984. Maurois, Andre. *The Life of Sir Alexander Fleming, Discoverer of Penicillin*. New York: Dutton, 1959.

Commentary: Alexander Fleming received the Nobel Prize "for the discovery of penicillin," which had occurred in 1928. Fleming shared the prize with Florey and Chain, who, after having discovered Fleming's published work on the *Penicillium* mold, had purified penicillin, produced it in quantity, and used it successfully in the treatment of disease. Fleming's work continued with important contributions in the areas of blood chemistry, antiseptics, lysozyme, and antibiotics. (H.L.F.)

Florey, Howard Walter, Sir   255

PRIZE: Medicine and Physiology, 1945. BORN: September 24, 1898; Adelaide, Australia. DIED: February 21, 1968; Oxford, England. PARENTS: Father, Joseph Florey; Mother, Bertha Mary Wadham Florey. NATIONALITY: Australian; later British resident. RELIGION: Most probably Christian/Protestant. EDUCATION: Adelaide Univ., Australia, B.S., 1921; Adelaide Univ., Australia, M.B., 1921; Oxford Univ., England, B.Sc., 1924; Oxford Univ., England, M.A., 1924; Cambridge Univ., England, Ph.D., 1927. SPOUSE: Mary Ethel Reed, married 1926. CHILDREN: Charles, son; Poquita, daughter. CAREER: Cambridge Univ., England, Professor, 1926-31; Univ. of Sheffield, England, Professor, 1931-35; Oxford Univ., England, Professor and Administrator, 1935-65; Australian National Univ., Canberra, Chancellor, 1965-68. OTHER AWARDS: Knighthood, 1944; Lister Medal, Royal College of Surgeons, 1945; Cameron Prize, U. of Edinburgh, Scotland, 1945; Berzelius Silver Medal, Swedish Medical Society, 1945; Commander of the Legion of Honor, 1946; Harmsworth Memorial Award, 1946; Albert Gold Medal, Royal Society of the Arts, 1946; Medal in Therapeutics, Society of Apothecaries, London, England, 1946; Gold Medal, Royal Society of Medicine, 1947; Medal for Merit, United States, 1948; Addingham Gold Medal, 1949; Copley Medal, Royal Society, 1951; Royal Medal, 1951; Gold Medal, British Medical Association, 1964; Lomonossov Medal, USSR Academy of Sciences, 1964.

Selected Publications: "The Secretion of Mucus by the Colon." *British Journal of Experimental Pathology* 11 (1930): 348-61. "Some Properties of Mucus, with Special Reference to Its Antibacterial Functions." *British Journal of Experimental Pathology* 11 (1930): 192-208 (with N.E. Goldsworthy). "Penicillin as a Chemotherapeutic Agent." *Lancet* 239 (1940): 226-28 (with others). "Further Observations on Penicillin." *Lancet* 241 (1941): 177-88 (with others). *Antibiotics: A Survey of Penicillin, Streptomycin, and Other Antimicrobial Substances from Fungi, Actinomycetes, Bacteria and Plants*. London: Oxford U. Press, 1949.

For More Information See: *Biographical Memoirs of the Fellows of the Royal Society*. London: Royal Society, 17 (1971): 255-302. *Dictionary of Scientific Biography*. New York: Scribner's, 1972 (Volume 5), 41-44.

Commentary: Howard Florey shared the Nobel Prize "for the discovery of penicillin and its curative effects in various infectious diseases." His joint research elaborated the structure of penicillin and used it in successful clinical trials. Florey did notable work also in mucous secretions, the cell's role in inflammation, the action of lysozyme, and the development of atherosclerosis. (R.K.)

1946

Muller, Hermann Joseph   256
PRIZE: Medicine and Physiology, 1946. BORN: December 21, 1890; New York, NY. DIED: April 5, 1967; Indianapolis, IN. PARENTS: Father, Hermann Joseph Muller; Mother, Frances Louise Lyons Muller. NATIONALITY: American. RELIGION: Unitarian; from Jewish/Catholic background. EDUCATION: Columbia Univ., NY, B.A., 1910; Columbia Univ., NY, M.A., 1911; Columbia Univ., NY, Ph.D., 1916. SPOUSE: Jessie Marie Jacobs, married June 11, 1923, divorced 1934; Dorothea Johanna Kantorowicz, married May 20, 1939. CHILDREN: David Eugene, son; Helen Juliette, daughter. CAREER: Cornell Univ., NY, Professor, 1911-12; Columbia Univ., NY, Professor, 1912-15; Rice Institute, TX, Professor, 1915-18; Columbia Univ., NY, Professor, 1918-20; Univ. of Texas, Professor, 1920-36; Soviet Academy of Sciences Institute of Genetics, USSR, Researcher, 1933-37; Univ. of Edinburgh, Scotland, Professor, 1937-40; Amherst College, MA, Professor, 1940-45; Indiana Univ., Professor, 1945-67. OTHER AWARDS: Cleveland Research Prize, American Association for the Advancement of Science, 1927; Kimber Award in Genetics, US National Academy of Sciences, 1955; Virchow Medal, Virchow Society of New York, 1956; Darwin Medal, Linnean Society of London, 1958; Darwin Medal, Deutsche Akademie Naturforscher Leopoldina, 1959; Alexander Hamilton Award, Columbia U., NY, 1960; Humanist of the Year, Humanist Association, 1963; City of Hope Medical Centre Research Citation, 1964.
Selected Publications: "Artificial Transmutation of the Gene." *Science* 66 (1927): 84-87. *Out of the Night: A Biologist's View of the Future.* London: V. Gollancz, 1936. *Genetics, Medicine and Man.* Ithaca, NY: Cornell U. Press, 1947 (with C.C. Little and L.H. Snyder). *Studies in Genetics: The Selected Papers of H.J. Muller.* Bloomington, IN: Indiana U. Press, 1962.
For More Information See: *Biographical Memoirs of the Fellows of the Royal Society.* London: Royal Society, 1968 (Volume 14), 349-89. *Dictionary of Scientific Biography.* New York: Scribner's, 1974 (Volume 9), 564-65.
Commentary: Hermann Muller was given the Nobel "for the discovery of the production of mutations by means of x-ray irradiation." His work and writings led to much research on artificial mutation of organisms and to much discussion of the effects of atomic fission. Muller's writings also include papers on genetics, blood transfusion, and the psychological studies of identical twins raised in different environments. (R.K.)

1947

Cori, Carl Ferdinand   257
PRIZE: Medicine and Physiology, 1947. BORN: December 5, 1896; Prague, Czechoslovakia. DIED: October 20, 1984; Cambridge, MA. PARENTS: Father, Carl Isidor Cori; Mother, Maria Lippich Cori. NATIONALITY: Czechoslovakian; later American citizen. RELIGION: Christian. EDUCATION: German Univ. of Prague,

Czechoslovakia, M.D., 1920. SPOUSE: Gerty Theresa Radnitz, married August 5, 1920, died October 26, 1957; Anne Fitzgerald Jones, married March 23, 1960. CHILDREN: Carl Thomas, son. CAREER: Univ. of Graz, Austria, Researcher, 1920-21; State Institute for the Study of Malignant Disease, Buffalo, NY, Researcher, 1922-31; Washington Univ., St. Louis, MO, Professor, 1931-66; Harvard Univ., MA, Professor, 1966-84. OTHER AWARDS: Midwest Award, American Chemical Society, 1946; Lasker Award, 1946; Squibb Award, 1947; Sugar Research Foundation Award, 1947, 1950; Willard Gibbs Medal, American Chemical Society, 1948.
Selected Publications: "Mammalian Carbohydrate Metabolism." *Physiological Reviews* 11 (April 1931). "The Formation of Hexosephosphate Esters in Frog Muscle." *Journal of Biological Chemistry* 116 (1936): 119-28 (with G.T. Cori). "Crystalline Muscle Phosphorylase. III. Kinetics." *Journal of Biological Chemistry* 151 (1943): 39-55 (with A.A. Green and G.T. Cori). "The Enzymatic Conversion of Phosphorylase a to b." *Journal of Biological Chemistry* 158 (1945): 321-32 (with G.T. Cori). "Glucose 6-Phosphatase of the Liver in Glycogen Storage Disease." *Journal of Biological Chemistry* 199 (1952): 661-67 (with G.T. Cori).
For More Information See: *Current Biography Yearbook* New York: H.W. Wilson, 1947, 135-37. Houssay, B.A. "Carl F. and Gerty T. Cori." *Biochimica et Biophysica Acta* 20 (1956): 11-16.
Commentary: Carl Cori, with his wife and colaureate, Gerty, were honored with the Nobel Prize "for their discovery of the course of the catalytic conversion of glycogen." The Coris elucidated the process by which animal starch (glycogen) is converted into utilizable sugar and isolated the enzyme, phosphorylase, which is integral to the process. The laureates also made significant contributions in the studies of sugar utilization and the effects of insulin and epinephrine, tumor glycolysis, carbohydrate metabolism, and the action of pituitary extracts. (B.A. and R.K.)

Cori, Gerty Theresa Radnitz   258
PRIZE: Medicine and Physiology, 1947. BORN: August 15, 1896; Prague, Czechoslovakia. DIED: October 26, 1957; St. Louis, MO. PARENTS: Father, Otto Radnitz; Mother, Martha Neustadt Radnitz. NATIONALITY: Czechoslovakian; later American citizen. RELIGION: Jewish. EDUCATION: German Univ. of Prague, Czechoslovakia, M.D., 1920. SPOUSE: Carl Ferdinand Cori, married August 5, 1920. CHILDREN: Carl Thomas, son. CAREER: Children's Hospital, Vienna, Austria, Researcher, 1920-22; State Institute for the Study of Malignant Diseases, Buffalo, NY, Researcher, 1922-31; Washington Univ., St. Louis, MO, Professor, 1931-57. OTHER AWARDS: Midwest Award, American Chemical Society, 1946; Squibb Award, 1947; Garvan Medal, 1948; Sugar Research Prize, National Academy of Sciences, 1950; Borden Award, Association of Medical Colleges.
Selected Publications: "The Formation of Hexosephosphate Esters in Frog Muscle." *Journal of Biological Chemistry* 116 (1936): 119-28 (with C.F. Cori). "Crystalline Muscle Phosphorylase. II. Prosthetic Group." *Journal of Biological Chemistry* 151 (1943): 31-38. (with A.A. Green). "Crystalline Muscle Phosphorylase. III. Kinetics." *Journal of Biological Chemistry* 151 (1943): 39-55 (with A.A. Green and

C.F. Cori). "The Enzymatic Conversion of Phosphorylase a to b." *Journal of Biological Chemistry* 158 (1945): 321-32 (with C.F. Cori). "Action of Amylo-1,6-Glycosidase and Phosphorylase on Glycogen and Amylopectin." *Journal of Biological Chemistry* 188 (1951): 17-29 (with J. Larner). "Glucose 6-Phosphatase of the Liver in Glycogen Storage Disease." *Journal of Biological Chemistry* 199 (1952): 661-67 (with C.F. Cori). "Glycogen Structure and Enzyme Deficiencies in Glycogen Storage Disease." *Harvey Lectures* 48 (1952-53): 145-71.

For More Information See: Cori, C.F. "The Call of Science." *Annual Review of Biochemistry* 38 (1969): 1-20. *Current Biography Yearbook.* New York: H.W. Wilson, 1947, 135-37. *Dictionary of Scientific Biography.* New York: Scribner's, 1971 (Volume 3), 415-16. Houssay, B.A. "Carl F. and Gerty T. Cori." *Biochimica et Biophysica Acta* 20 (1956): 11-16.

Commentary: Gerty Cori, with her husband and colaureate, Carl, were honored with the Nobel Prize "for their discovery of the course of the catalytic conversion of glycogen." The Coris elucidated the process by which animal starch (glycogen) is converted into usable sugar and isolated the enzyme, phosporylase, which is integral to the process. The Coris also made significant contributions in the study of sugar utilization and the effects of insulin and epinephrine, tumor glycolysis, carbohydrate metabolism, and the action of pituitary extracts. (B.A. and R.K.)

Houssay, Bernardo Alberto   259
PRIZE: Medicine and Physiology, 1947. BORN: April 10, 1887; Buenos Aires, Argentina. DIED: September 27, 1971; Buenos Aires, Argentina. PARENTS: Father, Alberto Houssay; Mother, Clara Laffont Houssay. NATIONALITY: Argentinian. RELIGION: Christian. EDUCATION: Univ. of Buenos Aires, Argentina, Pharmacy Degree, 1904; Univ. of Buenos Aires, Argentina, Doctorate in Medicine, 1910. SPOUSE: Maria Angelica Catan, married December 22, 1920. CHILDREN: Alberto Bernardo, son; Hector Emilio Jose, son; Raul Horacio, son. CAREER: Univ. of Buenos Aires, Argentina, Professor, 1907-69. OTHER AWARDS: National Award of Sciences, Buenos Aires, Argentina, 1923; Charles Mickle Fellowship, Toronto, Canada, 1945; Banting Medal, American Diabetes Association, 1946; Research Award, American Pharmaceutical Manufacturers' Association, 1947; Baly Medal, Royal College of Physicians, England, 1947; James Cook Medal; Sydney Medal, 1948; Dale Medal, Society for Endocrinology, England, 1960; Weizmann Prize, 1967.

Selected Publications: "Carbohydrate Metabolism." *New England Journal of Medicine* 214 (1936): 971. "The Hypophysis and Metabolism." *New England Journal of Medicine* 214 (1936): 961. "Diabetes as a Disturbance of Endocrine Regulation." *American Journal of Medical Science* 193 (1937): 581. "Advancement of Knowledge of the Role of the Hypophysis in Carbohydrate Metabolism During the Last Twenty-Five Years." *Endocrinology* 30 (1942): 884.

For More Information See: *Biographical Memoirs of the Fellows of the Royal Society.* London: Royal Society, 1974 (Volume 20), 247-70. *Current Biography Yearbook.* New York: H.W. Wilson, 1948, 295-97.

Commentary: Argentinian scientist and activist Bernardo Houssay was recognized by the Academy "for his discovery of the part played by the hormone of the anterior pituitary lobe in the metabolism of sugars." Although Houssay's major interest was in the endocrine glands and the pituitary, his research produced significant results on the physiology of circulation and respiration, the process of immunity, the nervous system, digestion, and snake and spider venoms. He was also recognized as an activist leader in the promotion of democracy, education, and scientific research in Argentina. (B.S.S.)

1948

Müller, Paul Hermann   260
PRIZE: Medicine and Physiology, 1948. BORN: January 12, 1899; Olten, Switzerland. DIED: October 12, 1965; Basel, Switzerland. PARENTS: Father, Gottlieb Müller; Mother, Fanny Leypoldt Müller. NATIONALITY: Swiss. RELIGION: Evangelical. EDUCATION: Univ. of Basel, Switzerland, doctorate, 1925. SPOUSE: Friedel Rugsegger, married October 6, 1927. CHILDREN: Henry, son; Niklaus, son; Margaret, daughter. CAREER: Lonza Power Plant, Switzerland, Researcher, 1916-17; J.R. Geigy Company, Basel, Switzerland, Researcher, 1925-65.

Selected Publications: "Uber Konstitution und Toxische Wirkung von Naturlichen und Neuen Synthetischen. Insektentotenden Stoffen." *Helvetica Chimica Acta* 27 (1944): 899-928 (with P. Lauger and H. Martin). "Uber Zusammenhange Zwischen Konstitution und Insektizider Werkung. I." *Helvetica Chimica Acta* 29 (1946): 1560-80.

For More Information See: *Current Biography Yearbook.* New York: H.W. Wilson, 1945, 340-42. *Dictionary of Scientific Biography.* New York: Scribner's, 1974 (Volume 9), 576-77.

Commentary: Paul Müller's Nobel was granted "for his discovery of the high efficiency of DDT as a contact poison against several arthropods." Müller's original research on plant pigments and natural tanning agents led him to the research on disinfectants and pesticides that resulted in his discovery of the effectiveness of DDT as an insecticide. It was later used in tropical areas and in the fight against malaria and typhus. Müller's original articles included a warning about the stability of DDT, which later proved to be warranted when large accumulations of DDT were found in biological organisms. (M.D.C.)

1949

Egas Moniz, Antonio Caetano Abreu Freire   261
PRIZE: Medicine and Physiology, 1949. BORN: November 29, 1874; Avanca, Portugal. DIED: December 13, 1955; Lisbon, Portugal. PARENTS: Father, Fernando De Pina Rezende Abreu; Mother, Maria de Rosario de Almeida e Sousa. NATIONALITY: Portuguese. RELIGION: Catholic. EDUCATION: Univ. of Coimbra, Portugal, M.D., 1899. SPOUSE: Elvira de Macedo Dias, married 1902. CHILDREN: None. CAREER: Univ. of Coimbra, Portugal, Professor, 1902-11; Univ. of Lisbon, Portugal, Professor, 1911-55. OTHER AWARDS: Grand Cross of Isabel la Catolica, Spain; Instrucao Publica, Portugal; Santiago de Espada; Commander, Legion of Honour.

Selected Publications: *Diagnostic des Tumeurs Cérébrales et Epreuve de L'Encephalographie Arterielle.* Paris: Masson, 1931. *A Vida Sexual (Fisiologia e*

Patologia). Lisbon: Abrantes, 1931. *L'Angiographie Cérébrale, Ses Applications et Résultats en Anatomie, Physiologie et Clinique.* Paris: Masson, 1934. *Cérébrale Arteriographie und Phlebographie.* Berlin: J. Springer, 1940.

For More Information See: *Dictionary of Scientific Biography.* New York: Scribner's, 1971 (Volume 4), 286-87. "Egas Moniz, 1874-1955." *Journal of the International College of Surgeons* 36 (1961): 261-71.

Commentary: Egas Moniz was cited by the Academy "for his discovery of the therapeutic value of leucotomy in certain psychoses." His earlier work was concerned with cerebral angiography, a method of studying blood circulation in the brain. In addition, he was an active and important member of the political scene in Portugal throughout his lifetime. (A.C.)

Hess, Walter Rudolph   262
PRIZE: Medicine and Physiology, 1949. BORN: March 17, 1881; Frauenfeld, Switzerland. DIED: August 12, 1973; Locarno, Switzerland. PARENTS: Father, Clemen Hess; Mother, Gertrud Fischer Saxon Hess. NATIONALITY: Swiss. RELIGION: Christian. EDUCATION: Univ. of Zurich, Switzerland, M.D., 1906. SPOUSE: Louise Sandmeyer, married 1909. CHILDREN: Gertrud, daughter; Rudolph, son. CAREER: Zurich, Switzerland, Physician, 1905-12; Bonn, Germany, Physician, 1913-17; Univ. of Zurich, Switzerland, Professor and Administrator, 1917-51. OTHER AWARDS: Marcel Benorst Prize, Switzerland, 1933; Ludwig Medal, German Society for Circulation Research, 1938.

Selected Publications: *Die Funktionelle Organisation des Vegetativen Nervensystems.* Basel, Switzerland: B. Schwabe, 1948. *The Functional Organization of the Diencephalon.* New York: Grune and Stratton, 1957. *The Biology of Mind.* Chicago: U. of Chicago Press, 1964. *Biological Order and Brain Organization: Selected Works of W.R. Hess.* New York: Springer-Verlag, 1981.

For More Information See: *Modern Scientists and Engineers.* New York: McGraw-Hill, 1980 (Volume 2), 52. "W.R. Hess: The Control of the Autonomic Nervous System by the Hypothalamus." *The Lancet* 1 (March 17, 1951): 627-29.

Commentary: Walter Hess received the Nobel "for his discovery of the functional organization of the interbrain as a coordinator of the activities of the internal organs," using strictly localized stimuli as the investigating tool. He also worked in the areas of blood pressure and viscosity and in respiratory function. (R.K.)

1950

Hench, Philip Showalter   263
PRIZE: Medicine and Physiology, 1950. BORN: February 28, 1896; Pittsburgh, PA. DIED: March 31, 1965; Ocho Rios, Jamaica. PARENTS: Father, Jacob Bixler Hench; Mother, Clara John Showalter Hench. NATIONALITY: American. RELIGION: Presbyterian. EDUCATION: Lafayette College, PA, A.B., 1916; Univ. of Pittsburgh, PA, M.D., 1920; Univ. of Minnesota, M.Sc., 1931. SPOUSE: Mary Genevieve Kahler, married July 14, 1927. CHILDREN: Mary Showalter, daughter; Susan Kahler, daughter; Philip Kahler, son; John Bixler, son. CAREER: St. Francis Hospital, Pittsburgh, PA, Physician, 1920-21; Univ. of Minnesota, Professor, 1921-57.

OTHER AWARDS: Heberden Medal, London, 1942; Lasker Award, American Public Health Association, 1949; Page One Award, Newspaper Guild of New York, 1950; Passano Foundation Award, 1950; Scientific Award, American Pharmaceutical Manufacturers Association, 1950; Special Citation, American Rheumatism Association, 1951; Pennsylvania Ambassador Award, 1951; Northwestern U. Centennial Award, 1951; Award of Merit, Masonic Foundation, 1951; Criss Award, 1951; Honor Award, Mississippi Valley Medical Society, 1952; Order of Carlos Finlay, Cuba.

Selected Publications: *Chronic Arthritis: Chronic Infectious Arthritis, Chronic Senescent Arthritis, Gout.* Baltimore, MD: The Williams and Wilkins Company, 1940. "Effects of Cortisone Acetate and Pituitary ACTH on Rheumatoid Arthritis, Rheumatic Fever, and Certain Other Conditions." *Archives of Internal Medicine* 85 (1950): 545-666 (with E. Kendall). *Cortisone, Hydrocortisone, and Corticotropin (ACTH) in the Treatment of Rheumatoid Arthritis.* Basel, Switzerland: Geigy, 1954.

For More Information See: *Current Biography Yearbook.* New York: H.W. Wilson, 1950, 230-32. *Modern Scientists and Engineers.* New York: McGraw-Hill, 1980 (Volume 2), 42-43.

Commentary: Philip Hench shared the Nobel Prize for "discoveries relating to the hormones of the adrenal cortex, their structure, and biological effects." His use of cortisone in the treatment of arthritis, a disease in which he was an acknowledged expert, led to his receiving the award. Hench was also a scholar of the history of yellow fever. (B.W.)

Kendall, Edward Calvin   264
PRIZE: Medicine and Physiology, 1950. BORN: March 8, 1886; Norwalk, CT. DIED: May 4, 1972; Rahway, NJ. PARENTS: Father, George Stanley Kendall; Mother, Eva Frances Abbott Kendall. NATIONALITY: American. RELIGION: Congregationalist. EDUCATION: Columbia Univ., NY, B.S., 1908; Columbia Univ., NY, M.S., 1909; Columbia Univ., NY, Ph.D., 1910. SPOUSE: Rebecca Kennedy, married December 30, 1915. CHILDREN: Hugh, son; Roy, son; Norman, son; Elizabeth, daughter. CAREER: Parke, Davis, and Co., Detroit, MI, Researcher, 1910-11; St. Luke's Hospital, NY, Researcher, 1911-14; Univ. of Minnesota, Professor and Administrator, 1914-51. OTHER AWARDS: John Scott Prize and Premium, Philadelphia, 1921; Chandler Medal, Columbia U., NY, 1925; Squibb Award for Outstanding Research in Endocrinology, 1945; Lasker Award, American Public Health Association, 1949; Page One Award, Newspaper Guild of NY, 1950; John Phillips Memorial Award, American College of Physicians, 1950; Research Corporation Award, Research Corporation of NY, 1950; Remsen Memorial Award, MD section of American Chemical Society, 1950; Research Award, American Pharmaceutical Manufacturers Association, 1950; Edgar F. Smith Award, American Chemical Society, 1950; Passano Award, 1950; Medal of Honor, Canadian Pharmaceutical Manufacturers Association, 1950; Dr. C.C. Criss Award, 1951; Award of Merit, Masonic Foundation for Medical Research and Humane Welfare, 1951; Cameron Award, U. of Edinburgh, Scotland, 1951; Heberden Society Award, London, 1951; Kober Award, Association of American Physicians, 1952; Alexander Hamilton Medal, Alumni of Columbia College, 1961; Scientific Achievement Award, American Medical Association, 1965.

Selected Publications: "The Isolation in Crystalline Form of the Compound Containing Iodin Which Occurs in the Thyroid: Its Chemical Nature and Physiological Activity." *Transactions of the Association of American Physicians* 30 (1914): 420-49. *Oxidative Catalysis.* New York: Columbia U. Press, 1925. "The Identification of a Substance Which Possesses the Qualitative Action of Cortin." *Journal of Biological Chemistry* 116 (1936): 267-76. "Effects of Cortisone Acetate and Pituitary ACTH on Rheumatoid Arthritis, Rheumatic Fever, and Certain Other Conditions." *Archives of Internal Medicine* 85 (1950): 545-666 (with P. Hench).

For More Information See: *Biographical Memoirs. National Academy of Sciences.* Washington, DC: National Academy of Sciences, 1975 (Volume 48), 249-92. *Dictionary of Scientific Biography.* New York: Scribner's, 1978 (Supplement I), 258-59.

Commentary: Edward Kendall shared the Nobel Prize for "discoveries relating to the hormones of the adrenal cortex, their structure, and biological effects." In addition to his research on cortisone and its therapeutic effects, Kendall also did notable work on thyroxine and thyroid extracts, oxidation in animals, and the action of amylases. (B.W.)

Reichstein, Tadeus   265

PRIZE: Medicine and Physiology, 1950. BORN: July 20, 1897; Wloclawek, Poland. PARENTS: Father, Isidor Reichstein; Mother, Gustava Brockman Reichstein. NATIONALITY: Polish; later Swiss citizen. RELIGION: Jewish. EDUCATION: Eidenössische Technische Hochschule, Switzerland, B.S., 1920; Eidenössische Technische Hochschule, Switzerland, Ph.D., 1922. SPOUSE: Louise Henriette Quarls V. Ufford, married July 21, 1927. CHILDREN: Ruth, daughter. CAREER: Eidenössische Technische Hochschule, Switzerland, Professor, 1922-38; Univ. of Basel, Switzerland, Professor and Administrator, 1938-. OTHER AWARDS: Cameron Award, U. of Edinburgh, Scotland, 1951; Copley Medal, Royal Society, 1968.

Selected Publications: *Uber das Offenkettige Tropin und Einige Seiner Homologen.* Weida i. Thür, Germany: Thomas & Hubert, 1924. "Die Hormone der Nebennierenrinde." In *Handbuch der Biologischen Arbeitsmethoden,* by Emil Abderhalden. Berlin, 1938 (Volume 5), 1367-1439. "The Hormones of the Adrenal Cortex." In *Vitamins and Hormones.* New York: Academic Press, 1943, 346-414 (with C.W. Shoppee).

For More Information See: *Current Biography Yearbook.* New York: H.W. Wilson, 1951, 512-14. "Tadeus Reichstein." *Journal of Chemical Education* 26 (1949): 529-30.

Commentary: Tadeus Reichstein shared the Nobel Prize for "discoveries relating to the hormones of the adrenal cortex, their structure, and biological effects." Prior to his work on the hormones of the adrenal cortex, Reichstein researched the composition of roasted coffee and coffee, along with synthesized Vitamin C, and studied plant glycosides. The isolation of cortisone and the discovery of its therapeutic value were the end results of the Nobel Prize-winning work. (R.K.)

1951

Theiler, Max   266

PRIZE: Medicine and Physiology, 1951. BORN: January 30, 1899; Pretoria, South Africa. DIED: August 11, 1972; New Haven, CT. PARENTS: Father, Sir Arnold Theiler; Mother, Emma Jegge Theiler. NATIONALITY: South African; later American resident. RELIGION: Most probably Christian/Protestant. EDUCATION: Univ. of London, England, M.D., 1922. SPOUSE: Lillian Graham, married February 18, 1928. CHILDREN: Elizabeth, daughter. CAREER: Harvard Univ., MA, Professor, 1922-30; Rockefeller Foundation, NY, Researcher and Administrator, 1930-64; Yale Univ., New Haven, CT, Professor, 1964-67; Rockefeller Foundation, NY, Researcher, 1967-72. OTHER AWARDS: Chalmers Medal, Royal Society of Tropical Medicine and Hygiene, England, 1939; Flattery Medal, Harvard U., MA, 1945; Lasker Award, American Public Health Association, 1949.

Selected Publications: "Studies on the Action of Yellow Fever Virus in Mice." *Annals of Tropical Medicine and Parasitology* 24 (1930): 249-72. "The Effect of Prolonged Cultivation in Vitro upon the Pathogenicity of Yellow Fever Virus." *Journal of Experimental Medicine* 65 (1937): 767-86. *Yellow Fever.* Chapter 2. New York: McGraw-Hill, 1951. *The Anthropod-Borne Viruses of Vertebrates: An Account of the Rockefeller Foundation Virus Program.* New Haven, CT: Yale U. Press, 1973.

For More Information See: *Biographical Encyclopedia of Scientists.* New York: Facts on File, 1981, 778-79. *Current Biography Yearbook.* New York: H.W. Wilson, 1952, 586-87.

Commentary: Max Theiler won the Nobel "for his discoveries concerning yellow fever and how to combat it." His contributions to yellow fever research included the theory of transmission, the introduction of a new experimental animal (mice), and the development of a vaccine. During his long career, he also worked on amoebic dysentery, rat bite fever, dengue fever, and Japanese encephalitis. (M.D.C.)

1952

Waksman, Selman Abraham   267

PRIZE: Medicine and Physiology, 1952. BORN: July 2, 1888; Priluka, Ukraine, Russia. DIED: August 16, 1973; Hyannis, MA. PARENTS: Father, Jacob Waksman; Mother, Fradia London Waksman. NATIONALITY: Russian; later American citizen. RELIGION: Jewish. EDUCATION: Rutgers Univ., NJ, B.Sc., 1915; Rutgers Univ., NJ, M.Sc., 1916; Univ. of California, Ph.D., 1918. SPOUSE: Debora B. Mitnik, married August 5, 1916. CHILDREN: Byron H., son. CAREER: Rutgers Univ., NJ, Professor, 1918-73. OTHER AWARDS: Nitrate of Soda Research Award, 1930; Passano Foundation Award, 1947; Award of the Carlsberg Laboratories, Denmark, 1948; New Jersey Agricultural Society Medal, 1948; Lasker Award, American Public Health Association, 1948; Emil Christian Hanson Medal, 1948; Leeuwenhoek Medal, Netherlands Academy of Sciences, 1950; Henrietta Szold Award, 1950; Commander, French Legion of Honour, 1950; British Shalom Humanitarian Award, 1952; Order of Merit of the Rising Sun, Japan, 1952; Great Cross of Public Health, Spain, 1954; St. Vincent Award for Medical Sciences, Academy of Sciences of Torino, Italy, 1954; Instituto Curlo Forlanini Medal, 1959; American Trudeau Medal, 1961; Commendatore Order of Southern Cross of Brazil, 1963.

Selected Publications: *Enzymes: Properties, Distribution, Methods and Applications.* Baltimore, MD: Williams and Wilkins, 1926 (with W.C. Davison). *Humus: Origin, Chemical Composition, and Importance in Nature.* Baltimore, MD: Williams and Wilkins, 1936. *Neomycin: Its Nature, Formation, Isolation and Practical Application.* New Brunswick, NJ: Rutgers U. Press, 1953. *The Actinomycetes.* 3 volumes. Baltimore, MD: Williams and Wilkins, 1959-62. *Scientific Contributions of Selman A. Waksman; Selected Articles Published in Honor of His 80th Birthday.* New Brunswick, NJ: Rutgers U. Press, 1968.

For More Information See: *National Cyclopedia of American Biography.* New York: James T. White, 1960 (Volume I), 312-13. Waksman, Selman. *My Life with the Microbes.* New York: Simon and Schuster, 1954.

Commentary: The Academy cited Selman Waksman "for his discovery of streptomycin, the first antibiotic effective against tuberculosis." His other research was concerned with the microbiology in soil and sea; investigation of organic matter decomposition in various soils; the study of bacteria, fungi, and actinomycetes; and the transformation of nitrogen and carbon compounds. (R.K.)

1953

Krebs, Hans Adolf, Sir   268

PRIZE: Medicine and Physiology, 1953. BORN: August 25, 1900; Hildenschein, Germany. DIED: November 22, 1981; Oxford, England. PARENTS: Father, Georg Krebs; Mother, Alma Davidson Krebs. NATIONALITY: German; later British citizen. RELIGION: Jewish. EDUCATION: Univ. of Hamburg, Germany, M.D., 1925; Cambridge Univ., England, M.S., 1934. SPOUSE: Margaret Cicely Fieldhouse, married 1938. CHILDREN: Paul, son; John, son; Helen, daughter. CAREER: Kaiser Wilhelm Institute, Berlin, Germany, Researcher, 1926-30; Municipal Hospital, Altona, Germany, Physician, 1930-32; Univ. of Freiberg, Germany, Professor, 1932-33; Cambridge Univ., England, Professor, 1933-35; Univ. of Sheffield, England, Professor, 1935-54; Oxford Univ., England, Professor, 1954-67. OTHER AWARDS: Lasker Award, 1953; Royal Medal, Royal Society, 1954; Gold Medal, Netherlands Society for Physics, Medical Science and Surgery, 1958; Knighthood, 1958; Copley Medal, 1961.

Selected Publications: "Metabolism of Acetoacetic Acid in Animal Tissues." *Nature* 154 (August 12, 1944): 209-10 (with L. V. Eggleston). "Urea Synthesis in Mammalian Liver." *Nature* (June 14, 1947): 808-09 (with others). "Tricarboxylic Acid Cycle." *Harvey Lectures* 44 (1950): 165-99. "A Survey of the Energy Transformations in Living Matter." *Ergcbn. Physiol. Biol. Chem. Exp. Pharmak* 49 (1957): 212 (with H. Kornberg). *The Metabolic Roles of Citrate.* London: Academic Press, 1968. *Essays in Cell Metabolism.* New York: Wiley, 1970. *Biographical Memoirs. Royal Society of London.* London: Royal Society, 1984 (Volume 30), 349.

For More Information See: *Current Biography Yearbook.* New York: H. W. Wilson, 1954, 384-85. *Reminiscences and Reflections.* New York: Oxford U. Press, 1982.

Commentary: Hans Krebs's Nobel Prize was granted "for his discovery of the citric acid cycle," now known as the Krebs cycle, which noted the oxidation of pyruvic acid to carbon dioxide and water. Other metabolic paths, especially energy-related (which were major interests), included the ornithine cycle of urea synthesis in liver and the glyoxalate cycle of fat metabolism. (J.E.H.)

Lipmann, Fritz Albert   269

PRIZE: Medicine and Physiology, 1953. BORN: June 12, 1899; Konigsburg, Germany. PARENTS: Father, Leopold Lipmann; Mother, Gertrude Lachmanski Lipmann. NATIONALITY: German; later American citizen. RELIGION: Jewish. EDUCATION: Univ. of Berlin, Germany, M.D., 1924; Univ. of Berlin, Germany, Ph.D., 1927. SPOUSE: Elfreda M. Hall, married June 23, 1931. CHILDREN: Stephen Hall, son. CAREER: Kaiser Wilhelm Institute, Berlin and Heidelberg, Germany, Researcher, 1927-30; Fischer's Laboratory, Berlin, Germany, Researcher, 1930-31; Rockefeller Institute for Medical Research, NY, Researcher, 1931-32; Carlsburg Foundation, Copenhagen, Denmark, Researcher, 1932-39; Cornell Univ., Ithaca, NY, Researcher, 1939-41; Massachusetts General Hospital, Boston, Researcher and Administrator, 1941-57; Harvard Univ., MA, Professor, 1949-57; Rockefeller Univ., NY, Professor, 1957-. OTHER AWARDS: Carl Neuberg Medal, 1948; Mead Johnson and Company Award, 1948; National Medal of Science, 1966.

Selected Publications: "Fermentation of Phosphogluconic Acid." *Nature* (October 3, 1936): 588-89. "Colored Intermediate on Reduction of Vitamin B1." *Nature* (November 13, 1937): 849. "Coupling Between Pyruvic Acid Dehydrogenation and Adenylic Acid Phosphorylation." *Nature* (February 18, 1939): 281. "Biosynthetic Mechanisms." *Harvey Lectures* 44 (1950): 99-123.

For More Information See: *Current Biography Yearbook.* New York: H. W. Wilson, 1954, 413-14. *Wanderings of a Biochemist.* New York: Wiley, 1971.

Commentary: Fritz Lipmann received the Nobel Prize "for his discovery of Coenzyme A and its importance for intermediary metabolism." Lipmann's major work was in the classification of energy-producing phosphates, but his research endeavors also included work with the thyroid gland, fibroblasts and the Pasteur effect, glycolysis in embryo cell metabolism, and the mechanism of peptide and protein synthesis. (R.K.)

1954

Enders, John Franklin   270

PRIZE: Medicine and Physiology, 1954. BORN: February 10, 1897; West Hartford, CT. DIED: September 8, 1985; Waterford, CT. PARENTS: Father, John Ostrom Enders; Mother, Harriet Goulden Whitmore Enders. NATIONALITY: American. RELIGION: Most probably Christian/Protestant. EDUCATION: Yale Univ., CT, A.B., 1920; Harvard Univ., MA, M.A., 1922; Harvard Univ., MA, Ph.D., 1930. SPOUSE: Sarah Frances Bennett, married September 17, 1927, died 1943; Carolyn Keane, married May 12, 1951. CHILDREN: John Ostrom II, son; Sarah Steffian, daughter. CAREER: U.S. Army, 1917-20; Harvard Univ., MA, Professor, 1929-77. OTHER AWARDS: Commander, Order National de la

Republic de Haute Volta; Passano Foundation Award, 1953; Lasker Award, 1954; Kimball Award, 1954; Kyer Award, U.S. Public Health Service, 1955; Chapin Award, 1955; Bruce Award, American College of Physicians, 1956; Cameron Prize, U. of Edinburgh, Scotland, 1960; Howard Taylor Ricketts Memorial Award, U. of Chicago, 1962; New England Israel Freedom Award, 1962; Robert Koch Medal, Germany, 1962; Science Achievement Award, American Medical Association, 1963; Presidential Medal of Freedom, 1963.

Selected Publications: *Immunity: Principles and Application in Medicine and Public Health.* New York: Macmillan, 1939 (with Hans Zinsser and Leroy D. Fothergill). "Cultivation of the Lansing Strain of Poliomyelitis Virus in Cultures of Various Human Embryonic Tissues." *Science* 109 (January 28, 1949): 85-87. "Mumps." In *Viraland Ricketsial Infections of Man.* Philadelphia, PA: Lippincott, 1959, 780-89.

For More Information See: *Biographical Encyclopedia of Scientists.* New York: Facts on File, 1981, 239. *Current Biography Yearbook.* New York: H. W. Wilson, 1955, 182-84.

Commentary: John Enders shared the Nobel Prize for "discovery of the ability of the poliomyelitis virus to grow in cultures of different tissues." He pioneered work in virus study and vaccine development that eventually led to safe vaccines for polio, measles, German measles, and mumps. Enders also worked in the areas of cancer and genetics. (R.K.)

Robbins, Frederick Chapman 271

PRIZE: Medicine and Physiology, 1954. BORN: August 25, 1916; Auburn, AL. PARENTS: Father, Dr. William Jacob Robbins; Mother, Christine F. Chapman. NATIONALITY: American. RELIGION: Presbyterian background. EDUCATION: Univ. of Missouri, B.A., 1936; Univ. of Missouri, B.S., 1938; Harvard Univ., MA, M.D., 1940. SPOUSE: Alice Havemeyer Northrup, married June 19, 1948. CHILDREN: Alice, daughter; Louise, daughter. CAREER: Children's Hospital, Boston, MA, Physician, 1946-52; Harvard Univ., MA, Professor, 1950-52; Case Western Reserve Univ., OH, Professor and Administrator, 1952-. OTHER AWARDS: Bronze Star, 1945; Mead Johnson Prize, 1953; Medical Mutual Honor Award, 1969; Ohio Governor's Award, 1971.

Selected Publications: "Cultivation of the Lansing Strain of Poliomyelitis Virus in Cultures of Various Human Embryonic Tissues." *Science* 109 (January 28, 1949): 85-87 (with T.H. Weller and J.F. Enders). *Proceedings of the Society for Experimental Biology and Medicine* 72 (1949): 153-55 (with T.H. Weller and J.F. Enders). "Studies of the Cultivation of Poliomyelitis Viruses in Tissue Culture. I. The Propagation of Poliomyelitis Viruses in Suspended Cell Cultures of Various Human Tissues." *Journal of Immunology* 69 (1952): 645-71 (with others).

For More Information See: *Biographical Encyclopedia of Scientists.* New York: Facts on File, 1981, 682. *Current Biography Yearbook.* New York: H.W. Wilson, 1955, 182-84.

Commentary: Frederick Robbins received the Nobel jointly for "discovery of the ability of the poliomyelitis virus to grow in cultures of different tissues." His research efforts also included work on the parasitic microorganisms causing Q fever. (R.K.)

Weller, Thomas Huckle 272

PRIZE: Medicine and Physiology, 1954. BORN: June 15, 1915; Ann Arbor, MI. PARENTS: Father, Carl Vernon Weller; Mother, Elsie Huckle Weller. NATIONALITY: American. RELIGION: Most probably Christian. EDUCATION: Univ. of Michigan, B.S., 1936; Univ. of Michigan, M.S., 1937; Harvard Univ., MA, M.D., 1940. SPOUSE: Kathleen R. Fahey, married August 18, 1945. CHILDREN: Peter Fahey, son; Robert Andrew, son; Nancy Kathleen, daughter; Janet Louise, daughter. CAREER: Harvard Univ., MA, Professor and Administrator, 1940-81. OTHER AWARDS: Mead Johnson Award, American Academy of Pediatrics, 1953; Kimble Methodology Award, 1954; George Ledlie Prize, 1963; Weinstein Cerebral Palsy Award, 1973; Bristol Award, Infectious Diseases Society of America, 1980.

Selected Publications: "Cultivation of the Lansing Strain of Poliomyelitis Virus in Cultures of Various Human Embryonic Tissues." *Science* 109 (January 28, 1949): 85-87 (with F.C. Robbins and J.F. Enders). *Proceedings of the Society for Experimental Biology and Medicine* 72 (1949): 153-55 (with F.C. Robbins and J.F. Enders). "Studies of the Cultivation of Poliomyelitis Viruses in Tissue Culture. I. The Propagation of Poliomyelitis Viruses in Suspended Cell Cultures of Various Human Tissues." *Journal of Immunology* 69 (1952): 645-71 (with others).

For More Information See: *Biographical Encyclopedia of Scientists.* New York: Facts on File, 1981, 834. *Current Biography Yearbook.* New York: H.W. Wilson, 1955, 182-84.

Commentary: Thomas Weller's Nobel was shared for "discovery of the ability of the poliomyelitis virus to grow in cultures of different tissues." Prior to this research, Weller had grown both rubella and chickenpox viruses in tissue cultures. His work led to the development of a successful polio vaccine. (R.K.)

1955

Theorell, Axel Hugo Teodor 273

PRIZE: Medicine and Physiology, 1955. BORN: July 6, 1903; Linköping, Sweden. DIED: August 15, 1982; Stockholm, Sweden. PARENTS: Father, Thure Theorell; Mother, Armida Bell Theorell. NATIONALITY: Swedish. RELIGION: Lutheran. EDUCATION: Univ. of Stockholm, Sweden, Bachelor of Medicine, 1924; Univ. of Stockholm, Sweden, M.D., 1930. SPOUSE: Elin Margit Alenius, married 1931. CHILDREN: Klas, son; Henning, son; Tores, son. CAREER: Univ. of Uppsala, Sweden, Professor, 1930-36; Nobel Medical Institute, Stockholm, Sweden, Professor and Administrator, 1937-70. OTHER AWARDS: First Class Commander, Royal Order of North Star; Legion d'Honneur, France; Officer, Order Southern Cross, Brazil.

Selected Publications: "The Heme-Protein Linkage in Hemoglobin and in Horseradish Peroxidase." Arkiv Kemi Mineral. Geol. 16A (1943): 1-18. "Catalases and Peroxidases." In *The Enzymes.* New York: Academic Press, 1951, 397-427. "Function and Structure of Liver Alcohol Dehydrogenase." *Harvey Lectures* 61 (1967): 17-41. "Introduction to Mechanisms of Enzyme Actions." In *Metabolic Regulation and Enzyme Action.* London: Academie Press, 1970, 179-80. "My Life with Proteins and Prosthetic Groups." In *Proteolysis and Physiological Regulation.* New York: Academic, 1975, 1-27.

For More Information See: *Biographical Memoirs of the Fellows of the Royal Society.* London: Royal Society, 1983 (Volume 29), 585-621. *Current Biography Yearbook.* New York: H. W. Wilson, 1956, 622-24.

Commentary: Axel Theorell won the Nobel Prize "for his discoveries concerning the nature and mode of action of oxidation enzymes." In pioneer research, he found that the yellow enzyme isolated from yeast consists of two parts, the first an enzyme of vitamin B2 plus a phosphate group, the second a protein apoenzyme. He further elaborated on the mechanism by which the coenzyme oxidizes glucose. Theorell also studied Cytochrome C, isolated crystalline myoglobin, and researched alcohol dehydrogenase, which resulted in the development of blood tests for alcohol levels. (R.K.)

1956

Cournand, Andre F.   274

PRIZE: Medicine and Physiology, 1956. BORN: September 24, 1895; Paris, France. PARENTS: Father, Jules Cournand; Mother, Marguerite Weber Cournand. NATIONALITY: French; later American citizen. RELIGION: Agnostic; from a Christian background. EDUCATION: Univ. of Paris-Sorbonne, France, B.A., 1913; Univ. of Paris-Sorbonne, France, P.C.B., 1914; Univ. of Paris, France, M.D., 1930. SPOUSE: Sibylle Blumer, married 1924, died 1959; Ruth Fabian, married 1963, died 1973; Beatrice Bishop Berle, married 1975. CHILDREN: Muriel, daughter; Marie-Eve, daughter; Marie Claire, daughter; Pierre, son (adopted). CAREER: French Army, 1915-19; Columbia Univ., NY, Professor and Researcher, 1930-64. OTHER AWARDS: Croix de Guerre, France; Silver Medal, U. of Paris, France, 1930; Andrea Retzius Silver Medal, Swedish Society of Internal Medicine, 1946; Lasker Award, 1949; John Phillips Memorial Award, American College of Physicians, 1952; Gold Medal, Royal Academy of Medicine, Belgium, 1956; Jiminiz Diaz Prize, 1970.

Selected Publications: "Catheterization of the Right Auricle in Man." *Proceedings of the Society for Experimental Biology and Medicine* 46 (1941): 462-66. *Cardiac Catheterization in Congenital Heart Disease: A Clinical and Physiological Study in Infants and Children.* New York: Commonwealth Fund, 1949 (with J.S. Baldwin and A. Himmelstein). *Pulmonary Circulation: Historical Background and Present Day Status of Knowledge in Man.* Leiden, Netherlands: Universitaire Pers, 1959.

For More Information See: *Current Biography Yearbook.* New York: H.W. Wilson, 1957, 117-19. *From Roots to Late Budding: The Intellectual Adventures of a Medical Student.* New York: Gardner Press, 1985.

Commentary: Andre Cournand shared the Nobel for "discoveries concerning heart catheterization and pathological changes in the circulatory systems." Cournand's work with Dickinson Richards was the product of a lifelong interest in the heart and lung systems of the body. His later interests extended to the history of science and scientific ethics and psychology. (R.K.)

Forssmann, Werner Theodor Otto   275

PRIZE: Medicine and Physiology, 1956. BORN: August 29, 1904; Berlin, Germany. DIED: June 1, 1979; Schopfheim, Germany. PARENTS: Father, Julius Forssmann;

Mother, Emmy Hindenberg Forssmann. NATIONALITY: German. RELIGION: Evangelical. EDUCATION: Univ. of Berlin, Germany, M.D., 1929. SPOUSE: Elsbeth Engel, married 1933. CHILDREN: Klaus, son; Knut, son; Jorg, son; Wolf, son; Bernd, son; Renate, daughter. CAREER: Augusta Viktoria Hospital, Eberswalde, Germany, Physician, 1929-30; Ferdinand Sauerbruch Clinic, Berlin, Germany, Physician and Researcher, 1931-32; City Hospital, Dresden, Germany, Physician and Researcher, 1933-38; German Army, Physician, 1939-45; Bad Kreuznach, Germany, Physician, 1946-58; Dusseldorf Evangelical Hospital, Germany, Physician, 1958-79. OTHER AWARDS: Leibnitz Medal, German Academy of Sciences, 1954; Grosses Bundesverdienst Kreuz, 1958, 1964; Gold Medal, Societa Medico Chirurgica di Ferrara, 1968; Ordentliches Mitglied der Rheinisch-Westfallschoen Akademy der Wissenschaften des Landes Nordrhein Westfalen, 1968; Commander, Ordre des Palmes Academiques, 1971.

Selected Publications: "Die Sondierung des Rechten Herzens." *Klinische Wochenschrift* 8 (1929): 2085-87. "Technik und Praktische Bedentung der Herzkatheterung fur die Funktionelle Diagnostik und die Therapie von Herz-und Lungenerkrankungen." *Med. Klin., Berl* 48 (October 30, 1953): 1614-20 (with W. Bolt and H. Rink).

For More Information See: *Current Biography Yearbook.* New York: H.W. Wilson, 1957, 190-92. *Selbstversuch: Erinnerungen Eines Chirurgen.* Düsseldorf, Germany: Droste, 1972 (*Experiments on Myself: Memoirs of a Surgeon in Germany.* Tr. by Hilary Davies. New York: St. Martin's Press, 1974).

Commentary: Werner Forssmann received the Nobel in recognition of "discoveries concerning heart catheterization and pathological changes in the circulatory system." He researched and introduced the process which was later developed further by Richards and Cournand. He specialized both in work and in research as a heart and pulmonary surgeon and urologist. (R.K.)

Richards, Dickinson Woodruff   276

PRIZE: Medicine and Physiology, 1956. BORN: October 30, 1895; Orange, NJ. DIED: February 23, 1973; Lakeville, CT. PARENTS: Father, Dickinson Woodruff Richards; Mother, Sally Lambert Richards. NATIONALITY: American. RELIGION: Presbyterian. EDUCATION: Yale Univ., CT, A.B., 1917; Columbia Univ., NY, M.A., 1922; Columbia Univ., NY, M.D., 1923. SPOUSE: Constance B. Riley, married September 19, 1931. CHILDREN: Ida E., daughter; Ann H., daughter; Constance L., daughter; Gertrude W., daughter. CAREER: Presbyterian Hospital, NY, Physician, 1923-27; National Institute for Medical Research, London, England, Researcher, 1927-28; Columbia Univ., NY, Professor, 1928-73. OTHER AWARDS: Chevalier Legion of Honor, France.

Selected Publications: "The Circulation in Traumatic Shock in Man." *Harvey Lectures* 39 (1943-44): 217. "Cardiac Output by the Catheterization Technique in Various Clinical Conditions." *Federation Proceedings* 4 (1945): 215. "Contributions of Right Heart Catheterization to the Physiology of Congestive Heart Failure." *American Journal of Medicine* 3 (1947): 434.

For More Information See: *Current Biography Yearbook.* New York: H.W. Wilson, 1957, 457-59. *The National Cyclopedia of American Biography.* New York: James T. White, 1960 (Volume I), 336-37.

Commentary: Dickinson Richards shared the Nobel for "discoveries concerning heart catheterization and pathological changes in the circulatory systems." Richards's work with Andre Cournand made feasible the application of the method earlier devised by Werner Forssmann. Throughout a long career, he continued to investigate the problems of pulmonary and cardiac physiology and the diagnosis of clinical disorders in these systems. (R.K.)

1957

Bovet, Daniele   277

PRIZE: Medicine and Physiology, 1957. BORN: March 23, 1907; Neuchatel, Switzerland. PARENTS: Father, Pierre Bovet; Mother, Amy Babut Bovet. NATIONALITY: Swiss; later Italian citizen. RELIGION: Most probably Christian/Protestant. EDUCATION: Univ. of Geneva, Switzerland, D.Sc., 1929. SPOUSE: Filomena Nitti, married March 19, 1938. CHILDREN: 3 sons. CAREER: Institut Pasteur, Paris, France, Researcher, 1929-47; Instituto Superiore di Sanita, Rome, Italy, Researcher, 1947-64; Univ. of Sassari, Italy, Professor, 1964-71; Rome Univ., Italy, Professor, 1971-77. OTHER AWARDS: Chevalier de la Legion d'Honneur, 1946.

Selected Publications: *Structure Chimique et Activité Pharmacodynamique du Systeme Nerveux Vegetatif.* Basel, Switzerland: Karger, 1948 (with F. Bovet-Nitti). *Curare and Curare-like Agents.* Amsterdam: Elsevier Publishing Co., 1959 (with F. Bovet-Nitti and G.B. Marini-Bettolo). *Controlling Drugs.* San Francisco, CA: Jossey-Bass, 1974 (with others).

For More Information See: *Biographical Encyclopedia of Scientists.* New York: Facts on File, 1981, 98-99. *Current Biography Yearbook.* New York: H.W. Wilson, 1958, 55-56.

Commentary: Daniele Bovet was granted the Nobel "for his discoveries relating to synthetic compounds that inhibit the action of certain body substances, and especially their action on the vascular system and the skeletal muscles." Among his contributions are pioneer work on the sulfanilimids, antihistamines, curare-like anesthetics, brain-influencing drugs, and oxytocic substances. (A.N.)

1958

Beadle, George Wells   278

PRIZE: Medicine and Physiology, 1958. BORN: October 22, 1903; Wahoo, NE. PARENTS: Father, Chauncey Elmer Beadle; Mother, Hattie Albro Beadle. NATIONALITY: American. RELIGION: Most probably Christian/Protestant. EDUCATION: Univ. of Nebraska, B.S., 1926; Univ. of Nebraska, M.S., 1927; Cornell Univ., NY, Ph.D., 1931. SPOUSE: Marion Cecile Hill, married August 22, 1928, divorced 1953; Muriel McClure Barnett, married August 12, 1953. CHILDREN: David, son. CAREER: Cornell Univ., Ithaca, NY, Researcher, 1926-31; California Institute of Technology, Professor, 1931-35; Institut de Biologie, Paris, France, Researcher, 1935; Harvard Univ., MA, Professor, 1936-37; Stanford Univ., CA, Professor, 1937-46; California Institute of Technology, Professor, 1946-61; Univ. of Chicago, IL, Professor and Administrator, 1961-70. OTHER AWARDS: Lasker Award, American Public Health Association, 1950; Dyer Award, 1951; Emil C. Hansen Prize, Den-

mark, 1953; Albert Einstein Commemorative Award in Science, 1958; National Award of American Cancer Society, 1959; Kimber Genetics Award, National Academy of Science, 1960; Priestley Memorial Award, 1967; Donald Forsha Jones Medal, 1972.

Selected Publications: *An Introduction to Genetics.* Philadelphia, PA: W.B. Saunders, 1939 (with A.H. Sturtevant). *The Language of the Gene.* London: U. of London Press, 1960. *Genetics and Modern Biology.* Philadelphia, PA: American Philosophical Society, 1963. *The Language of Life.* New York: Doubleday, 1966 (with M.M. Beadle).

For More Information See: *Current Biography Yearbook.* New York: H.W. Wilson, 1956, 37-39. *National Cyclopedia of American Biography.* New York: James T. White, 1964 (Current Volume J), 372-73.

Commentary: George Beadle shared the Nobel Prize for "fundamental contributions in the field of biochemical and microbial genetics." His genetic studies progressed from maize to Drosophila to Neurospora crassa, the red bread mold. In the studies of *Neurospora*, Beadle found mutations by irradiation that could be reversed by Vitamin B6 additions and concluded that specific genes controlled chemical synthesis in cells. The research for which the Nobel was awarded laid the foundations of biochemical genetics. (P.M.)

Lederberg, Joshua   279

PRIZE: Medicine and Physiology, 1958. BORN: May 23, 1925; Montclair, NJ. PARENTS: Father, Zwi H. Lederberg; Mother, Esther Goldenbaum Lederberg. NATIONALITY: American. RELIGION: Jewish. EDUCATION: Columbia Univ., NY, B.A., 1944; Yale Univ., CT, Ph.D., 1947. SPOUSE: Esther Miriam Lederberg, married 1946, divorced 1968; Marguerite Stein Kirsch, married 1968. CHILDREN: David, son; Ann, daughter. CAREER: Univ. of Wisconsin, Professor, 1947-58; Stanford Univ., CA, Professor and Administrator, 1958-78; Rockefeller Univ., NY, President, 1978-. OTHER AWARDS: Eli Lilly Award, 1953; Pasteur Award, Society of Illinois Bacteriologists, 1956; Procter Prize, 1982.

Selected Publications: *Papers in Microbial Genetics.* Madison, WI: U. of Wisconsin Press, 1952. "Viruses, Genes and Cells." *Bacteriological Reviews* 21 (1957): 133-39. "Bacterial Reproduction." *Harvey Lectures* 53 (1959): 69-82. *Tables and Algorithms for Calculating Functional Groups of Organic Molecules in High Mass Spectrometry.* Palo Alto, CA: Stanford U. Press, 1964.

For More Information See: *Biographical Encyclopedia of Scientists.* New York: Facts on File, 1981, 479-80. *Current Biography Yearbook.* New York: H.W. Wilson, 1959, 251-52.

Commentary: Joshua Lederberg's Nobel was granted "for his discoveries concerning genetic recombination and the organization of the genetic material of bacteria." His studies showed that, in some cases, bacteria were sexual, based on the work with *Escherichio coli.* Lederberg also studied bacterial transduction—genetic information transfer across barriers by *Salmonella*—that led to the later work in genetic engineering. (J.C.)

Tatum, Edward Lawrie   280

PRIZE: Medicine and Physiology, 1958. BORN: December 14, 1909; Boulder, CO. DIED: November 5, 1975; New York, NY. PARENTS: Father, Arthur Lawrie Tatum; Mother, Mabel Webb Tatum. NATIONALITY:

American. RELIGION: Most probably Christian/Protestant. EDUCATION: Univ. of Wisconsin, A.B., 1931; Univ. of Wisconsin, M.A., 1932; Univ. of Wisconsin, Ph.D., 1934. SPOUSE: June Alton, married July 28, 1934, divorced 1956; Viola Kantor, married December 16, 1956, died April 21, 1974; Elsie Berglund, married 1974. CHILDREN: Margaret Carol, daughter; Barbara Ann, daughter. CAREER: Univ. of Wisconsin, Researcher, 1935; Univ. of Utrecht, Netherlands, Researcher, 1936-37; Stanford Univ., CA, Professor, 1937-45; Yale Univ., New Haven, CT, Professor, 1948-56; Stanford Univ., CA, Professor, 1956-57; Rockefeller Institute, NY, Professor, 1957-75. OTHER AWARDS: Remsen Award, American Chemical Society, 1953.

Selected Publications: "Genetic Control of Biochemical Reactions in Neurospora." *Proceedings of the National Academy of Sciences* 27 (1941): 499-506 (with G. Beadle). "Genetic Control of Biochemical Reactions in Neurospora: An Aminobenzoicless Mutant." *Proceedings of the National Academy of Sciences* 28 (1942): 234-64 (with G. Beadle). "Gene Recombination in the Bacterium Escherichia Coli." *Journal of Bacteriology* 53 (1947): 673-84 (with J. Lederberg). "Sex in Bacteria: Genetic Studies, 1945-1952." *Science* 118 (1953): 169-74 (with J. Lederberg).

For More Information See: *Current Biography Yearbook.* New York: H.W. Wilson, 1959, 437-39. *National Cyclopedia of American Biography.* New York: James T. White, 1964 (Current Volume J): 475.

Commentary: Edward Tatum shared the Nobel Prize "for discovering that genes act by regulating specific chemical processes." His career included work on the nutrition and metabolism of Drosophila, on inherited defects in eye pigment development in Drosophila, on mutation and hereditary characteristic transmission in relation to genes in *Neurospora crassa*, on biochemical mutations and nutrition of *Escherichia coli*, and on genetic recombination. (P.M.)

1959

Kornberg, Arthur   281

PRIZE: Medicine and Physiology, 1959. BORN: March 3, 1918; Brooklyn, NY. PARENTS: Father, Joseph Kornberg; Mother, Lena Katz Kornberg. NATIONALITY: American. RELIGION: Jewish. EDUCATION: City College of New York, B.S., 1937; Univ. of Rochester, NY, M.D., 1941. SPOUSE: Sylvy R. Levy, married November 21, 1943. CHILDREN: Roger, son; Thomas Bill, son; Kenneth Andrew, son. CAREER: National Institutes of Health, MD, Researcher, 1942-52; Washington Univ., MO, Professor, 1953-59; Stanford Univ., CA, Professor, 1959-. OTHER AWARDS: Paul-Lewis Laboratory Award, American Chemical Society, 1951; Silver Medal, Federal Security Agency, 1952; Lucy Wortham James Award, James Ewing Society, 1968; Max Berg Award, 1968; Science Achievement Award, American Medical Association, 1968; Borden Award, American Association of Medical Colleges, 1968; Albert Gallatin Medal, New York U., 1970; National Medal of Science, United States, 1980.

Selected Publications: *Harvey Lectures* 53 (1957-58): 83. *Enzymatic Synthesis of DNA.* New York: Wiley, 1961. "Enzymatic Synthesis of DNA. XXIII. Synthesis of Circular Replicative Form of Phage Phi X174DNA." *Proceedings of the National Academy of Sciences* 58 (1967): 1723-30 (with M. Goulian). "Enzy-

matic Synthesis of DNA. XXIV. Synthesis of Infectious Phage Phi X174DNA." *Proceedings of the National Academy of Sciences* 58 (1967): 2321-28 (with M. Goulian and R. Sinsheimer). *DNA Replication.* New York: W.H. Freeman, 1980.

For More Information See: *Biographical Encyclopedia of Scientists.* New York: Facts on File, 1981, 448-49. *Current Biography Yearbook.* New York: H.W. Wilson, 1968, 210-12.

Commentary: Arthur Kornberg won the Nobel Prize for his contributions "to the discovery of the mechanisms in the biological synthesis of ribonucleic acid and deoxyribonucleic acid." At the beginning of his career, Kornberg studied the mechanisms of formation of important coenzymes (flavin adenine dinucleotide and nicotinamide adenine dinucleotide). This led to the discovery of the enzyme DNA polymerase, which catalyzes formation of short DNA molecules. Kornberg's later research centered around reactions in the Krebs cycle and on phospholipid synthesis. (R.K.)

Ochoa, Severo   282

PRIZE: Medicine and Physiology, 1959. BORN: September 24, 1905; Luarca, Spain. PARENTS: Father, Severo Ochoa; Mother, Carmen de Albornez Ochoa. NATIONALITY: Spanish; later American citizen. RELIGION: Christian. EDUCATION: Malaga College, Spain, B.A., 1921; Univ. of Madrid, Spain, M.D., 1929. SPOUSE: Carmen Garcia Cobian, married July 8, 1931. CHILDREN: None. CAREER: Kaiser-Wilhelm Institute, Berlin, Germany, Researcher, 1929-37; Marine Biological Laboratory, England, Researcher, 1937; Univ. of Oxford, England, Researcher, 1938-40; Washington Univ., MO, Researcher, 1941-42; New York Univ., Professor, 1942-75; Roche Institute of Molecular Biology, NJ, Researcher, 1975-. OTHER AWARDS: Neuberg Medal Award, Society of European Chemists, 1951; Charles Meyer Price Award, Societé de Chimie Biologique, 1955; Borden Award, Association of American Medical Colleges, 1958; New York U. Medal, 1960; Order of the Rising Sun, 2nd Class Gold Medal, Japan, 1967; Quevedo Gold Medal, Spain, 1969; Albert Gallatin Medal, 1970; National Medal of Science, 1979.

Selected Publications: "Enzymatic Synthesis and Breakdown of Polynucleotides; Polynucleotide Phosphorylase." *Journal of the American Chemical Society* 77 (1955): 3165-66 (with M. Grunberg-Manago). "Enzymatic Synthesis of Nucleic Acidlike Polynucleotides." *Science* 122 (1955): 907-10 (with M. Grunberg-Manago and P.J. Ortiz). "Small Polyribonucleotides with 5^1 Phosphomonoester End-Groups." *Science* 123 (1956): 415-17 (with L.A. Heppel and P.J. Ortiz). *La Clare Genetica, Base Quimica de la Herencia.* Barcelona, Spain: Real Academia de Ciencias y Artes de Barcelona, 1964. *Macromolecules: Biosynthesis and Function.* New York: Academic Press, 1970. *Viruses, Oncogenes, and Cancer.* New York: Karger, 1985.

For More Information See: *Current Biography Yearbook.* New York: H.W. Wilson, 1962, 327-29. *Science* (October 23, 1959): 1099-1100.

Commentary: Severo Ochoa shared the Nobel Prize for his contributions "to the discovery of the mechanisms in the biological synthesis of ribonucleic acid and deoxyribonucleic acid." His research on high-energy phosphates and their role in the body's energy processes resulted in the discovery and application of the enzyme polynucleotide phosphorylase, which catalyzes the synthesis of RNA. Ochoa also studied enzyme catalysis of reactions in the Krebs cycle. (J.C.)

1960

Burnet, Frank MacFarlane, Sir 283

PRIZE: Medicine and Physiology, 1960. BORN: September 3, 1899; Traralgon, Victoria, Australia. DIED: August 31, 1985; Melbourne, Australia. PARENTS: Father, Frank Burnet; Mother, Hadassah MacKay Burnet. NATIONALITY: Australian. RELIGION: Presbyterian. EDUCATION: Melbourne Univ., Australia, M.A., 1922; Melbourne Univ., Australia, M.D., 1923; Univ. of London, England, Ph.D., 1928. SPOUSE: Edith Linda Marston Druce, married July 10, 1928, died 1973; Hazel Jenkin Foletta, married 1976. CHILDREN: Ian, son; Elizabeth, daughter; Deborah, daughter. CAREER: Melbourne Hospital, Australia, Physician, 1923-24; Lister Institute, London, England, Researcher, 1926-27; Walter and Eliza Hall Institute for Medical Research, Melbourne, Australia, Physician and Administrator, 1928-65. OTHER AWARDS: Royal Medal, Royal Society, 1947; Knighthood, 1951; Lasker Award, 1952; Von Behring Prize, Marburg U., Germany, 1952; Galen Medal, Society of Apothecaries, 1958; Copley Medal, Royal Society, 1959.

Selected Publications: *Biological Aspects of Infectious Disease.* New York: Macmillan, 1940. *Virus as Organism.* Cambridge, MA: Harvard U. Press, 1945. *Principles of Animal Virology.* New York: Academic Press, 1955. *Clonal Selection: Theory of Acquired Immunity.* Nashville, TN: Vanderbilt U. Press, 1959. *Immunology, Aging and Cancer.* San Francisco, CA: W.H. Freeman, 1976.

For More Information See: *Changing Patterns.* New York: American Elsevier, 1969. "Fifty Years On." *British Medical Journal* 2 (1964): 1091.

Commentary: MacFarlane Burnet shared the Nobel "for the discovery of acquired immunological tolerance," for which he provided the hypothesis that was the impetus for the experimentation by Sir Peter Medawar. His work on the agglutinins of typhoid fever, his research on influenza virus and other virus biology, and his studies of haemagglutination should also be mentioned. (B.I.M.)

Medawar, Peter Brian, Sir 284

PRIZE: Medicine and Physiology, 1960. BORN: February 28, 1915; Rio de Janeiro, Brazil. PARENTS: Father, Nicholas Medawar; Mother, Edith Muriel Dowling Medawar. NATIONALITY: British. RELIGION: Most probably Christian/Protestant. EDUCATION: Oxford Univ., England, M.A., 1939; Oxford Univ., England, D.Sci., 1945. SPOUSE: Jean Shinglewood Taylor, married February 27, 1937. CHILDREN: Caroline, daughter; Louise, daughter; Charles, son; Alexander, son. CAREER: Oxford Univ., England, Researcher, 1938-47; Birmingham Univ., England, Professor and Administrator, 1947-51; Univ. of London, England, Professor and Administrator, 1951-62; National Institute for Medical Research, Mill Hill, England, Director, 1962-71; Clinical Research Centre, England, Researcher, 1971-. OTHER AWARDS: Edward Chapman Research Prize, 1938; Royal Medal, Royal Society, 1959; Copley Medal, Royal Society, 1969; Hamilton Fairley Medal, Royal College of Physicians, 1971.

Selected Publications: *The Future of Man.* New York: Basic Books, 1960. "Transplantation of Tissues and Organs." *British Medical Bulletin* 27 (1965). *The Life Science: Current Ideas of Biology.* New York: Harper and Row, 1977 (with J.S. Medawar). *Advice to a Young Scientist: Scientific Papers on Growth, Aging, Wound Healing and Transplantation.* New York: Harper Colophon Books, 1981.

For More Information See: *Biographical Encyclopedia of Scientists.* New York: Facts on File, 1981, 541-42. *Current Biography Yearbook.* New York: H.W. Wilson, 1961, 303-05.

Commentary: Peter Medawar shared the Nobel "for the discovery of acquired immunological tolerance," for which he provided the experimental evidence to support MacFarlane Burnet's hypothesis. He also carried out research in the areas of growth, aging, and cellular transformations and contributed notable writings on the philosophy of science. (R.K.)

1961

Von Békésy, Georg 285

PRIZE: Medicine and Physiology, 1961. BORN: June 3, 1899; Budapest, Hungary. DIED: June 13, 1972; Honolulu, HI. PARENTS: Father, Alexander Von Békésy; Mother, Paula Mazaly Von Békésy. NATIONALITY: Hungarian; later American citizen. RELIGION: Christian. EDUCATION: Univ. of Budapest, Hungary, Ph.D., 1923. SPOUSE: None. CHILDREN: None. CAREER: Hungarian Telephone System, Communications Engineer, 1923-46; Karolinska Institute, Stockholm, Sweden, Researcher, 1946-47; Harvard Univ., MA, Professor, 1947-66; Univ. of Hawaii, Professor, 1966-72. OTHER AWARDS: Denker Prize, 1931; Leibniz Medal, Akademie der Wissenschaften, Berlin, Germany, 1937; Academy Award, Academy of Science, Budapest, Hungary, 1946; Shambaugh Prize, 1950; Howard Crosby Warren Medal, Society of Experimental Psychologists, 1955; Gold Medal, American Otological Society, 1957; Achievement Award, Deafness Research Foundation, 1961; Gold Medal, Acoustical Society of America, 1961.

Selected Publications: *Experiments in Hearing.* New York: McGraw-Hill, 1960 (collection of his papers). *Sensory Inhibition.* Princeton, NJ: Princeton U. Press, 1967.

For More Information See: *Biographical Encyclopedia of Scientists.* New York: Facts on File, 1981, 60. *Current Biography Yearbook.* New York: H.W. Wilson, 1962, 36-38.

Commentary: Georg Von Békésy won the Nobel for his "discoveries concerning the physical mechanisms of stimulation within the cochlea," which permitted the explanation of how persons distinguished between sounds. His entire career was devoted to the ear, including the development of instrumentation as well as experimentation. Von Békésy's work was instrumental in advances in measuring deafness, in surgery of the ear, and in working toward restoring hearing. (R.K.)

1962

Crick, Francis Harry Compton 286

PRIZE: Medicine and Physiology, 1962. BORN: June 8, 1916; Northhampton, England. PARENTS: Father, Harry

Crick; Mother, Annie Elizabeth Wilkins Crick. NATION-ALITY: British. RELIGION: Atheist; from Christian background. EDUCATION: Univ. of London, England, B.Sc., 1937; Cambridge Univ., England, Ph.D., 1954. SPOUSE: Ruth Doreen Dodd, married 1940, divorced 1947; Odile Speed, married 1949. CHILDREN: Michael, son; Gabrielle, daughter; Jacqueline, daughter. CAREER: British Admiralty, Researcher, 1939-47; Strangeways Research Laboratory, Cambridge, England, Researcher, 1947-49; Cambridge Univ., England, Professor, 1949-77; Salk Institute for Biological Studies, San Diego, CA, Professor, 1977-. OTHER AWARDS: Warren Triennial Prize, 1959; Albert Lasker Award, 1960; Prix Charles Leopold Mayer, French Academy of Sciences, 1961; Research Corporation Award, 1961; Gairdner Foundation Medal, 1962; Royal Medal, Royal Society, 1972; Copley Medal, Royal Society, 1976; Michelson-Morley Award, Cleveland, OH, 1981.

Selected Publications: "Structure for Deoxyribose Nucleic Acid." *Nature* 171 (April 25, 1953): 737. "Genetical Implications of the Structure of Deoxyribonucleic Acid." *Nature* 171 (May 30, 1953): 964-67. *The Genetic Code. III.* San Francisco, CA: W. H. Freeman, 1966. *Of Molecules and Men.* Seattle, WA: U. of Washington Press, 1966. *Life Itself: Its Origin and Nature.* New York: Simon and Schuster, 1981.

For More Information See: *Asimov's Biographical Encyclopedia of Science and Technology.* Garden City, NY: Doubleday, 1982, 859-61. *Biographical Encyclopedia of Scientists.* New York: Facts on File, 1981, 168-69. *Current Biography Yearbook.* New York: H.W. Wilson, 1983, 68-71.

Commentary: Francis Crick won the Nobel Prize for his work leading to "discoveries concerning the structure of nucleic acids and its significance for information transfer in living material." Originally a physicist who worked on problems of radar and magnetic mines, he entered molecular biology with his colaureate, James Watson, in work which defined the molecular structure of DNA, and explained how it replicated. Crick continued to work on the understanding of the genetic code, proposed the existence of transfer RNAs, and formulated the "central dogma" of molecular genetics. His later research focused on the brain. (R.K.)

Watson, James Dewey   287

PRIZE: Medicine and Physiology, 1962. BORN: April 3, 1928; Chicago, IL. PARENTS: Father, James Dewey Watson; Mother, Jean Mitchell Watson. NATIONALITY: American. RELIGION: Most probably Christian. EDUCATION: Univ. of Chicago, IL, B.S., 1947; Univ. of Chicago, IL, Ph. B., 1947; Indiana Univ., Ph.D., 1950. SPOUSE: Elizabeth Lewis, married 1968. CHILDREN: Duncan James, son; Rufus Robert, son. CAREER: Univ. of Copenhagen, Denmark, Researcher, 1950-51; Cambridge Univ., England, Researcher, 1951-53; California Institute of Technology, Researcher, 1953-55; Harvard Univ., MA, Professor, 1955-76; Cold Spring Harbor Laboratory, NY, Director, 1968-. OTHER AWARDS: John Collins Warren Prize, Massachusetts General Hospital, 1959; Eli Lilly Award, American Chemical Society, 1959; Albert Lasker Prize, American Public Health Association, 1960; Research Corporation Prize, 1962; Carty Medal, National Academy of Sciences, 1971.

Selected Publications: "Structure for Deoxyribase Nucleic Acid." *Nature* 171 (April 25, 1953): 737. "Genetical Implications of the Structure of Deox-

ribonucleic Acid." *Nature* 171 (May 30, 1953): 964-67. *Molecular Biology of the Gene.* Menlo Park, CA: W.A. Benjamin, 1965. *The DNA Story.* San Francisco, CA: W.H. Freeman, 1981 (with J. Tooze). *The Molecular Biology of the Cell.* New York: Garland, 1983 (with others).

For More Information See: *Current Biography Yearbook.* New York: H.W. Wilson, 1963, 458-60. *The Double Helix.* New York: Atheneum, 1968.

Commentary: James Watson shared the Nobel Prize for his contributions to "discoveries concerning the structure of nucleic acids and its significance for information transfer in living material." His landmark collaboration with his colaureate, Francis Crick, resulted in the presentation of a model for the structure of DNA and in the discussion of its genetic implications. In addition, Watson performed notable studies on the molecular structure of viruses and on protein biosynthesis. (R.K.)

Wilkins, Maurice Hugh Frederick   288

PRIZE: Medicine and Physiology, 1962. BORN: December 15, 1916; Pongaroa, New Zealand. PARENTS: Father, Edgar Henry Wilkins; Mother, Eveline Constance Jane Whittaker Wilkins. NATIONALITY: British. RELIGION: Agnostic; from Protestant/Agnostic Buddhist background. EDUCATION: Cambridge Univ., England, B.A., 1938; Cambridge Univ., England, Ph.D., 1940. SPOUSE: Patricia Ann Chidgey, married March 29, 1959. CHILDREN: Sarah Fenella, daughter; Emily Lucy Una, daughter; George Hugh, son; William Henry, son. CAREER: Univ. of California, Berkeley, Researcher, 1944; St. Andrews Univ., Scotland, Professor, 1945; Univ. of London, England, Professor and Administrator, 1946-81. OTHER AWARDS: Albert Lasker Award, American Public Health Association, 1960.

Selected Publications: "Crystallinity in Sperm Heads: Molecular Structure of Nucleoprotein in Vivo." *Biochim. Biophys. Act* 10 (1953): 192-93 (with J.T. Randall). "The Molecular Configuration of Deoxyribonucleic Acid. I. X-ray Diffraction Study of a Crystalline Form of the Lithium Salts." *Journal of Molecular Biology* 2 (1960): 19 (with others). "The Molecular Structure of Deoxyribonucleic Acid (DNA)." *J. Chim. Phys* 58 (1961): 891-98. "Determination of the Helical Configuration of Ribonucleic Acid Molecules by X-ray Diffraction Study of Crystalline Amino-acid Transfer Ribonucleic Acid." *Nature* 194 (1962): 1014 (with others).

For More Information See: *Asimov's Biographical Encyclopedia of Science and Technology.* Garden City, NY: Doubleday, 1982, 1415. *Current Biography Yearbook.* New York: H.W. Wilson, 1963, 465-66.

Commentary: Maurice Wilkins's Nobel Prize was for his research contributing to the "discoveries concerning the structure of nucleic acids and its significance for information transfer in living material." Wilkins began his career as a physicist, working successively on the luminescence of solids, the theory of phosphorescence, radar, and the separation of uranium isotopes. His biophysical research started with the genetic effects of ultrasonic waves, moved to ultraviolet microspectrophotometric study of nucleic acids and viruses, and finally to the laureate work on x-ray diffraction of DNA and later RNA. (R.K.)

1963

Eccles, John Carew, Sir 289

PRIZE: Medicine and Physiology, 1963. BORN: January 27, 1903; Melbourne, Australia. PARENTS: Father, William James Eccles; Mother, Mary Carew Eccles. NATIONALITY: Australian; later British and American resident. RELIGION: Catholic. EDUCATION: Melbourne Univ., Australia, B.S., 1925; Melbourne Univ., Australia, M.B., 1925; Oxford Univ., England, M.A., 1929; Oxford Univ., England, Ph.D., 1929. SPOUSE: Irene Miller, married July 3, 1928, divorced 1968; Helena Táboríková, married April 27, 1968. CHILDREN: Rosamond, daughter; Alice, daughter; Mary, daughter; Judith, daughter; Frances, daughter; Peter, son; William, son; John son; Richard, son. CAREER: Oxford Univ., England, Professor, 1934-37; Kanematsu Memorial Institute of Pathology, Sydney, Australia, Director, 1937-44; Univ. of Otago, Dunedin, New Zealand, Professor, 1944-51; Australian National Univ., Canberra, Australia, Professor, 1951-66; Institute for Biomedical Research, IL, Researcher, 1966-68; State Univ. of NY, Professor and Administrator, 1968-75. OTHER AWARDS: Gotch Memorial Prize, 1927; Rolleston Memorial Prize, 1932; Knighthood, 1958; Baly Medal, 1961; Cothenius Medal, Deutsche Akademie der Naturforscher Leopoldina, 1963.

Selected Publications: *Reflex Activity of the Spinal Cord.* London: Oxford U. Press, 1938. *The Neurophysiological Basis of Mind.* Oxford: Clarendon Press, 1965. *The Cerebellum as a Neuronal Machine.* Berlin: Springer-Verlag, 1967. *The Physiology of Nerve Cells.* Baltimore, MD: Johns Hopkins Press, 1968. *The Inhibitory Pathways of the Central Nervous System.* Liverpool: Liverpool U. Press, 1969.

For More Information See: *Current Biography Yearbook.* New York: H.W. Wilson, 1972, 119-22. Robinson, John. *100 Most Important People in the World Today.* New York: Putnam, 1970, 237-40.

Commentary: John Eccles was cited by the Academy for establishing the relationship between inhibition of nerve cells and repolarization of a cell's membrane, much of which work grew out of the findings of his corecipients, Andrew Huxley and Alan Hodgkin. Eccles's other significant contributions were in the areas of brain research, nerve impulses, and neuromuscular transmissions. (R.K.)

Hodgkin, Alan Lloyd, Sir 290

PRIZE: Medicine and Physiology, 1963. BORN: February 5, 1914; Banbury, Oxfordshire, England. PARENTS: Father, G.L. Hodgkin; Mother, M.F. Wilson Hodgkin. NATIONALITY: British. RELIGION: Most probably Christian/Protestant. EDUCATION: Cambridge Univ., England, no degrees found. SPOUSE: Marion de Kay Rous, married 1944. CHILDREN: 1 son, 3 daughters. CAREER: Air Ministry and Ministry of Aircraft Production, England, Scientific Officer, 1939-45; Cambridge Univ., England, Professor and Administrator, 1945-52; Royal Society, England, Foulerton Research Professor, 1952-69; Cambridge Univ., England, Professor and Administrator, 1970-81. OTHER AWARDS: Baly Medal, 1955; Royal Medal, Royal Society, 1958; Copley Medal, 1965; Knighthood, 1972; Order of Merit, 1973.

Selected Publications: "Ionic Currents Underlying the Activity in the Giant Axon of the Squid." *Arch. Sci. Physiol* 3 (1949): 129-50 (with A. Huxley and B. Katz). "Properties of Nerve Axons. I. Movement of Sodium and Potassium Ions during Nervous Activity." *Cold Spring Harbor Symposia on Quantitative Biology* 17 (1952): 43-52 (with A. Huxley). "Movement of Radioactive Potassium and Membrane Current in a Giant Axon." *Journal of Physiology (London)* 121 (1953): 403-14 (with A. Huxley). *The Conduction of the Nervous Impulse.* Liverpool: Liverpool U. Press, 1971. *The Pursuit of Nature: Informal Essays on the History of Physiology.* Cambridge: Cambridge U. Press, 1977.

For More Information See: *Biographical Encyclopedia of Scientists.* New York: Facts on File, 1981, 386. *Science* 142 (October 25, 1963): 468-70.

Commentary: Alan Hodgkin's Nobel Prize was shared for studies of the ionic mechanisms involved in excitation and inhibition in peripheral and central portions of the nerve cell membrane. The discoveries stemmed from "elegant experiments" that measured the potential across the membrane with activity and without, and explained those measurements as related to sodium concentrations. The sodium hypothesis was later proven by many researchers. Hodgkin also did notable work on muscles and vision. (B.I.M.)

Huxley, Andrew Fielding, Sir 291

PRIZE: Medicine and Physiology, 1963. BORN: November 22, 1917; London, England. PARENTS: Father, Leonard Huxley; Mother, Rosalind Bruce Huxley. NATIONALITY: British. RELIGION: Agnostic; from Christian background. EDUCATION: Cambridge Univ., England, B.A., 1938; Cambridge Univ., England, M.A., 1941. SPOUSE: Jocelyn Richenda Gammell Pease, married July 5, 1947. CHILDREN: Eleanor Bruce, daughter; Henrietta Catherine, daughter; Clare Marjory Pease, daughter; Camilla Rosalind, daughter; Janet Rachel, daughter; Stewart Leonard, son. CAREER: Plymouth Marine Biology Laboratory, MA, Researcher, 1939-40; Cambridge Univ., England, Professor and Administrator, 1941-60; Univ. of London, England, Professor, 1960-83; Cambridge Univ., England, Professor and Administrator, 1983-. OTHER AWARDS: Copley Medal, Royal Society, 1973; Knighthood, 1974.

Selected Publications: "Ionic Currents Underlying the Activity in the Giant Axon of the Squid." *Arch. Sci. Physiol* 3 (1949): 129-50 (with A. Hodgkin and B. Katz). "Properties of Nerve Axons. I. Movement of Sodium and Potassium Ions during Nervous Activity." *Cold Spring Harbor Symposia on Quantitative Biology* 17 (1952): 43-52 (with A. Hodgkin). "Movement of Radioactive Potassium and Membrane Current in a Giant Axon." *Journal of Physiology (London)* 121 (1953): 403-14 (with A. Hodgkin). *Reflections on Muscle.* Princeton, NJ: Princeton U. Press, 1980.

For More Information See: *Biographical Encyclopedia of Scientists.* New York: Facts on File, 1981, 404. *Science* 142 (October 25, 1963): 468-70.

Commentary: Andrew Huxley shared the Nobel Prize for studies of the ionic mechanisms involved in excitation and inhibition in peripheral and central portions of the nerve cell membrane. His earlier formulation of the hypothesis that, during activity, the nerve membrane potential was controlled by sodium levels, was proven to be true by his own studies; studies of others also proved this. Huxley's research extended into muscular contraction and the development of the interference microscope and the ultramicrotome. (R.K.)

1964

Bloch, Konrad E.   292

PRIZE: Medicine and Physiology, 1964. BORN: January 21, 1912; Neisse, Germany. PARENTS: Father, Frederich D. Bloch; Mother, Hedwig Steiner Bloch. NATIONALITY: German; later American citizen. RELIGION: Jewish. EDUCATION: Technische Hochschule, Germany, Chem. Eng., 1934; Columbia Univ., NY, Ph.D., 1938. SPOUSE: Lore Teutsch, married February 15, 1941. CHILDREN: Peter, son; Susan, daughter. CAREER: Columbia Univ., NY, Professor, 1939-46; Univ. of Chicago, IL, Professor, 1946-54; Harvard Univ., MA, Professor, 1954-78. OTHER AWARDS: Medal, Société de Chimie Biologique, 1958; Fritzsche Award, American Chemical Society, 1964; Distinguished Service Award, U. of Chicago School of Medicine, IL, 1964; Centennial Science Award, U. of Notre Dame, IN, 1965; Cardano Medal, Lombardy Academy of Sciences, 1965; William Lloyd Evans Award, Ohio State U., 1968.

Selected Publications: "Biological Conversion of Cholesterol to Cholic Acid." *Journal of Biological Chemistry* 149 (1943): 511-17 (with B. Berg and D. Rittenberg). "The Utilization of AcOH for Fatty Acid Synthesis." *Journal of Biological Chemistry* 154 (1944): 311-12 (with D. Rittenberg). "Biosynthesis of Squaline." *Journal of Biological Chemistry* 200 (1953): 129-34 (with R.G. Langdon). *Lipide Metabolism.* New York: Wiley, 1960.

For More Information See: *Biographical Encyclopedia of Scientists.* New York: Facts on File, 1981, 83. *Science* 146 (October 23, 1964): 504-06.

Commentary: Konrad Bloch shared the Nobel Prize for his "contributions to understanding the mechanism and regulation of cholesterol and fatty acid metabolism." Bloch's early research showed that acetic acid was a major precursor of cholesterol in rats, and he continued to work on explaining the steps in the biosynthesis of sterols, first following the metabolism of acetic acid to squalene, then proposing the cyclization of squalene to lanosterol, and then working on the intermediates of lanosterol conversion to cholesterol. Bloch also made notable contributions in the study of the biosynthesis of glutathione and of the metabolism of the fatty acids. (R.K.)

Lynen, Feodor Felix Konrad   293

PRIZE: Medicine and Physiology, 1964. BORN: April 6, 1911; Munich, Germany. DIED: August 6, 1979; Munich, Germany. PARENTS: Father, Wilhelm L. Lynen; Mother, Frieda Prym Lynen. NATIONALITY: German. RELIGION: Lutheran. EDUCATION: Univ. of Munich, Germany, Dr. Phil., 1937. SPOUSE: Eva Wieland Lynen, married May 17, 1937. CHILDREN: Peter, son; Heinrich, son; Annemarie, daughter; Susanne, daughter; Eva-Marie, daughter. CAREER: Univ. of Munich, Germany, Professor, 1942-79. OTHER AWARDS: Neuberg Medal, American Society of European Chemists and Pharmacists, 1954; Justus von Liebig Medal, Gesellschaft Deutscher Chemiker, 1955; Carus Medal, Deutsche Akademie der Naturforscher Leopoldina, 1961;

Otto Warburg Medal, Gesellschaft für Physiologische Chemie, 1963; Norman Medaille, Deutsche Gesellschaft für Fettnissenschaft, 1967.

Selected Publications: "Acetyl Coenzyme A and the Fatty Acid Cycle." *Harvey Lecture Series* 48 (1953): 210-44. "Der Fettsaurecyclus." *Angewandte Chemie* 67 (1955): 463-70. "Phosphatkreislauf und Pasteur-Effekt." *Proceedings of the International Symposium on Enzyme Chemistry, Tokyo and Kyoto* (1957): 25-34. "Biosynthesis of Fatty Acids." *Proceedings of the Symposium on Drugs Affecting Lipid Metabolism* (1961): 3-15. "Cholesterol und Arteriosklerose." *Naturwiss. Rundschau* 25 (1972): 382-87.

For More Information See: *Current Biography Yearbook.* New York: H.W. Wilson, 1967, 263-65. *Die Aktivierte Essigsaure und Ihre Folgen: Autobiograph.* New York: de Gruyter, 1976.

Commentary: The Nobel Prize was awarded to Feodor Lynen for his "contributions to understanding the mechanism and regulation of cholesterol and fatty acid metabolism." His research on cholesterol, in particular, helped clarify its role as a possible cause of diseases of the heart and the circulatory system. Lynen studied the enzymatic steps of the fatty acid cycle, the role of biotin in fatty substance metabolism, fermentation, the citric acid cycle, phosphorization/oxidation, and the regulation of metabolic rates. (R.K.)

1965

Jacob, Francois   294

PRIZE: Medicine and Physiology, 1965. BORN: June 17, 1920; Nancy, France. PARENTS: Father, Simon Jacob; Mother, Therese Franck Jacob. NATIONALITY: French. RELIGION: Jewish. EDUCATION: Lycée Carnot, France, baccalaureate, 1938; Univ. of Paris, France, M.D., 1951; Univ. of Paris, France, B.S., 1951; Univ. of Paris, France, D.Sc., 1954. SPOUSE: Lysiane Bloch, married 1947. CHILDREN: Pierre, son; Laurent, son; Henri, son; Odile, daughter. CAREER: French Army, 1940-45; Institut Pasteur, Paris, France, Researcher and Administrator, 1950-. OTHER AWARDS: Bronze Medal, French National Scientific Research Center, 1955; Essee Prize, Anti-Cancer League, 1958; Prix Charles Leopold Mayer, Academy des Sciences, 1962; Croix de la Liberation; Grand Croix; Legion d'Honneur.

Selected Publications: "Genetic Regulatory Mechanisms in the Synthesis of Proteins." *Journal of Molecular Biology* 3 (1961): 356 (with Jacques Monod). "On the Regulation of Gene Activity: Beta-Galactosidase Formation in E. Coli." *Cold Spring Harbor Symposia on Quantitative Biology* 26 (1961): 207 (with Jacques Monod). *Sexuality and Genetics of Bacteria.* New York: Academic Press, 1961 (with E. Wollman). "Telenomic Mechanism's Cellular Metabolism, Growth and Differentiation." *Cold Spring Harbor Symposia on Quantitative Biology* 26 (1961): 394-95 (with Jacques Monod).

For More Information See: *Current Biography Yearbook.* New York: H.W. Wilson, 1966, 191-93. *Science* 150 (October 22, 1965): 462-63.

Commentary: Francois Jacob shared the Nobel Prize with Jacques Monod and Andre Lwoff for his contributions "to our knowledge of the fundamental processes in living matter which form the bases for such phenomena as adaptation, reproduction and evolution." Jacob's major contributions came in his explanation of the genetic basis of lysogenic bacteria through inherited sexual differences, in his elucidation of the action of regulator genes which control the behavior of structural and operator genes in enzyme synthesis, and in his work on messenger RNA. (B.S.S.)

Lwoff, Andre Michael 295

PRIZE: Medicine and Physiology, 1965. BORN: May 8, 1902; Allier, France. PARENTS: Father, Salomon Lwoff; Mother, Marie Siminovitch Lwoff. NATIONALITY: French. RELIGION: Jewish. EDUCATION: Univ. of Paris, France, Licencie es Sciences, 1921; Univ. of Paris, France, M.D., 1927; Univ. of Paris, France, D.Sc., 1932. SPOUSE: Marguerite Bourdaleix, married December 5, 1925. CHILDREN: None. CAREER: Institut Pasteur, Paris, France, Researcher and Administrator, 1921-68; Cancer Research Institute, Villejuif, France, Researcher and Administrator, 1968-72. OTHER AWARDS: Medaille de la Resistance, France; Commander Legion d'Honneur, France; Lallemont Award, Academie des Sciences; Noury Award, Academie des Sciences; Longchampt Award, Academie des Sciences; Chaussier Award, Academie des Sciences; Petit d'Ormoy, France; Charles Leopold Mayer Foundation Prize; Leeuwenhoek Medal, Royal Netherlands Academy of Sciences and Arts, 1960; Keilin Medal, British Biochemical Society, 1964; Einstein Award, 1967.

Selected Publications: *L'Evolution Physiologique.* Paris: Hermann, 1944. *The Kinetosomes in Development, Reproduction, and Evolution.* New York: Wiley, 1950. *Problems of Morphogenesis in Ciliates.* New York: Wiley, 1950. *Biochemistry and Physiology of Protozoa.* New York: Academic Press, 1951-64. *Biological Order.* Cambridge, MA: Massachusetts Institute of Technology Press, 1962.

For More Information See: *Asimov's Biographical Encyclopedia of Science and Technology.* Garden City, NY: Doubleday, 1982, 787. *Biographical Encyclopedia of Scientists.* New York: Facts on File, 1981, 514-15. *Science* 150 (October 22, 1965): 462-63.

Commentary: Andre Lwoff was honored, together with his colaureates Francois Jacob and Jacques Monod, for his contributions "to our knowledge of the fundamental processes in living matter which form the bases for such phenomena as adaptation, reproduction, and evolution." Lwoff was active first in elucidating the morphology and biology of the ciliate protozoa, with particular attention paid to how cell structures are genetically continued. He was also a major contributor in the areas of the biology of viruses, the genetics of bacteria, and the mechanisms by which viruses are replicated in the course of a viral infection. (B.S.S.)

Monod, Jacques Lucien 296

PRIZE: Medicine and Physiology, 1965. BORN: February 9, 1910; Paris, France. DIED: May 31, 1976; Cannes, France. PARENTS: Father, Lucien Monod; Mother, Charlotte Todd MacGregor Monod. NATIONALITY: French. RELIGION: Protestant. EDUCATION: Univ. of Paris, France, B.S., 1931; Univ. of Paris, France, D.Sc., 1941. SPOUSE: Odette Bruhl, married 1938. CHILDREN: Olivier, son; Philippe, son. CAREER: Univ. of Paris, France, Professor, 1931-41; Pasteur Institute, Paris, France, Researcher and Administrator, 1945-76. OTHER AWARDS: Montyon Physiology Prize, Paris Academie des Sciences, 1955; Louis Rapkine Medal, London, England, 1958; Chevalier de l'Ordre des Pal-

mes Academiques, 1961; Charles Leopold Mayer Prize, Academie des Sciences, 1962; Officer de la Legion d'Honneur, 1963.

Selected Publications: "Genetic Regulatory Mechanisms in the Synthesis of Proteins." *Journal of Molecular Biology* 3 (1961): 356 (with Francois Jacob). "On the Regulation of Gene Activity: Beta Galactosidase Formation in E. Coli." *Cold Spring Harbor Symposia on Quantitative Biology* 26 (1961): 207 (with Francois Jacob). "Teleonomic Mechanism's Cellular Metabolism, Growth and Differentiation." *Cold Spring Harbor Symposia on Quantitative Biology* 26 (1961): 394-95 (with Francois Jacob). *Chance and Necessity.* New York: Random House, 1971.

For More Information See: *Current Biography Yearbook.* New York: H.W. Wilson, 1971, 277-79. *Science* 150 (October 22, 1965): 462-63.

Commentary: Jacques Monod shared the Nobel Prize with Francois Jacob and Andre Lwoff for his contributions "to our knowledge of the fundamental processes in living matter which form the bases for such phenomena as adaptation, reproduction, and evolution." The subject research elucidated the mechanism by which genes manufacture the proteins necessary for individual development. Monod studied protein metabolism, specifically the synthesis of the bacterial enzyme Beta-galactosidase and its role as a catalyst. He was also a part of the work that identified messenger RNA and its role in protein production and introduced the concept of the operon (working gene cluster). Monod is recognized as well as a philosopher of science. (B.S.S.)

1966

Huggins, Charles Brenton 297

PRIZE: Medicine and Physiology, 1966. BORN: September 22, 1901; Halifax, Canada. PARENTS: Father, Charles Edward Huggins; Mother, Bessie Spencer Huggins. NATIONALITY: Canadian; later American citizen. RELIGION: Baptist. EDUCATION: Acadia Univ., Canada, B.A., 1920; Harvard Univ., MA, M.D., 1924. SPOUSE: Margaret Wellman, married July 29, 1927. CHILDREN: Charles Edward, son; Emily Wellman Fine, daughter. CAREER: Univ. of Michigan Medical School, Surgery Intern and Instructor, 1924-26; Univ. of Chicago Medical School, IL, Professor and Administrator, 1927-. OTHER AWARDS: Gold Medal, American Medical Association, 1936, 1940; Award for Research, American Urological Association, 1948; Francis Amory Award, 1948; Gold Medal, Société Internationale d'Urologie, 1948; American Cancer Society Award, 1953; Bertner Award, M.D. Anderson Hospital, TX, 1953; American Pharmaceutical Manufacturers Award, 1953; Gold Medal, American Association of Genito-Urinary Surgeons, 1955; Borden Award, Association of American Medical Colleges, 1955; Comfort Cruikshank Award, Middlesex Hospital, London, 1957; Cameron Prize, Edinburgh U., 1958; Valentine Prize, New York Academy of Medicine, 1962; Hunter Award, American Therapeutic Society, 1962; Lasker Award for Medical Research, 1963; Gold Medal for Research, Rudolph Virchow Society, 1964; Laurea and Award, American Urological Society, 1969; Gold Medal in Therapeutics, Worshipful Society of Apothecaries of London, 1966; Gairdner Award, Toronto, 1966; Chicago Medical Society Award, 1967; Centennial

Medal, Acadia U., Nova Scotia, 1967; Hamilton Award, Illinois Medical Society, 1967; Bigelow Medal, Boston Surgical Society, 1967; Sheen Award, American Medical Association, 1970; Distinguished Service Award, American Society of Abdominal Surgeons, 1972.

Selected Publications: "The Business of Discovery in the Medical Sciences." *Journal of the American Medical Association* 194 (December 13, 1965): 1211-15. "Endocrine-Induced Regression of Cancers." *Science* 156 (1967): 1050-54. *Experimental Leukemia and Mammary Cancer: Induction, Prevention and Cure.* Chicago: U. of Chicago Press, 1979.

For More Information See: *Current Biography Yearbook.* New York: H.W. Wilson, 1965, 205-08. Talalay, Paul. "The Scientific Contributions of Charles Brenton Huggins." *Journal of the American Medical Association* 192 (June 28, 1965): 1137-40.

Commentary: The Nobel Prize went to Charles Huggins "for his discoveries concerning hormonal treatment of prostate cancer," recognizing 25 years of painstaking investigation of the relationship between hormones and cancer. Huggins first found that androgens (male hormones) can stimulate prostatic cancer, whereas castration or estrogens (female hormones) frequently have the opposite effect. The effectiveness of antiandrogenic treatment was soon confirmed and adopted. Huggins has worked since on producing variants of natural hormones that have little or no feminizing effect. (S.D.S.)

Rous, Francis Peyton   298

PRIZE: Medicine and Physiology, 1966. BORN: October 5, 1879; Baltimore, MD. DIED: February 16, 1970; New York, NY. PARENTS: Father, Charles Rous; Mother, Frances Anderson Wood Rous. NATIONALITY: American. RELIGION: Most probably Christian/Protestant. EDUCATION: Johns Hopkins Univ., MD, B.A., 1900; Johns Hopkins Univ., MD, M.A., 1901; Johns Hopkins Univ., MD, M.D., 1905. SPOUSE: Marie Eckford de Kay, married June 15, 1915. CHILDREN: Marion de Kay, daughter; Ellen de Kay, daughter; Phoebe de Kay, daughter. CAREER: Univ. of Michigan, Professor, 1906-08; Rockefeller Institute, NY, Professor, 1909-45. OTHER AWARDS: John Scott Medal, Philadelphia, PA, 1927; Kobler Medal, Association of American Physicians, 1953; Bertner Foundation Award, U. of Texas, 1954; Jessie Stevenson Kovalenko Award, National Academy of Sciences, 1954; Distinguished Service Award, American Cancer Society, 1957; Lasker Foundation Award, 1958; Karl Landsteiner Award, American Association of Blood Banks, 1958; New York Academy of Medicine Medal, 1959; Judd Award, Memorial Center for Cancer, NY, 1959; United Nations Prize, 1962; Gold-Headed Cane, American Association of Pathologists and Bacteriologists, 1964; National Medal of Science, United States, 1965; Paul Ehrlich-Ludwig Darmstaedter Prize, West Germany, 1966; Gold Medal, British Royal Society of Medicine, 1966.

Selected Publications: "A Sarcoma of the Fowl Transmissible by an Agent Separable from the Tumor Cells." *Journal of Experimental Medicine* 13 (1911): 397-411. "Transmission of a Malignant New Growth by Means of a Cell-Free Filtrate." *Journal of the American Medical Association* 56 (1911): 198. *The Modern Dance of Death.* London: Cambridge U. Press, 1929. "The Virus Tumors and the Tumor Problem."

American Journal of Cancer 28 (1936): 233-71. "Surmise and Fact on the Nature of Cancer." *Nature* 183 (1959): 1357-61.

For More Information See: *Biographical Memoirs of Fellows of the Royal Society.* London: Royal Society, 1971 (Volume 17), 643-62. *Biographical Memoirs of the National Academy of Sciences.* Washington, DC: National Academy of Sciences, 1976 (Volume 48), 275-306. *Current Biography Yearbook.* New York: H.W. Wilson, 1967, 354-57.

Commentary: Peyton Rous's work on tumor-inducing viruses in chickens earned him the Nobel Prize, 55 years after the original report. Rous did notable work also in the fields of blood preservation, the liver and its connection with the biliary system, the gall bladder, and culture techniques for viruses and cells. (R.K.)

1967

Granit, Ragnar Arthur   299

PRIZE: Medicine and Physiology, 1967. BORN: October 30, 1900; Helsinki, Finland. PARENTS: Father, Arthur W. Granit; Mother, Albertina Helena Malmberg Granit. NATIONALITY: Finnish; later Swedish citizen. RELIGION: Lutheran. EDUCATION: Helsingfors Univ., Finland, Mag. phil., 1923; Helsingfors Univ., Finland, M.D., 1927. SPOUSE: Marguerite E. Bruun, married 1929. CHILDREN: Michael, son. CAREER: Pennsylvania Univ., Philadelphia, Fellow, 1929-31; Helsinki Univ., Finland, Professor, 1932-40; Royal Caroline Institute, Stockholm, Sweden, Professor, 1940-67. OTHER AWARDS: Lunsgaard Gold Medal, 1938; Jubilee Medal, Swedish Society of Physicians, 1947; Björkén Prize, Uppsala U., 1948; Retzin Gold Medal, 1957; Donders Medal, 1957; 3rd International St. Vincent Prize, 1961; Jahre Prize, Oslo U., Norway, 1961; Sherrington Memorial Gold Medal, 1967; Purinje Gold Medal, 1969.

Selected Publications: *On the Correlation of Some Sensory and Physiological Phenomena of Vision.* London: George Putman, 1938. *Sensory Mechanisms of the Retina.* New York: Hafner, 1963. *Receptors and Sensory Perception.* Westport, CT: Greenwood Press, 1975. *The Purposive Brain.* Cambridge, MA: Massachusetts Institute of Technology Press, 1980.

For More Information See: *Biographical Encyclopedia of Scientists.* New York: Facts on File, 1981, 330. *Hur det Kom Sig* (A Memoir). N.p., 1983.

Commentary: Ragnar Granit shared the Nobel Prize for his research which illuminated the electrical properties of vision by studying wavelength discrimination by the eye. His pioneer discovery that light waves both excite and inhibit the electric impulse discharge stimulated much research. Granit's other contributions are in the areas of electrical control of nerves in muscle tissues and nerve impulse transmission of pain and touch. (B.I.M.)

Hartline, Halden Keffer   300

PRIZE: Medicine and Physiology, 1967. BORN: December 22, 1903; Bloomsburg, PA. PARENTS: Father, Daniel Schollenberger Hartline; Mother, Harriet Franklin Keffer Hartline. NATIONALITY: American. RELIGION: Most probably Christian/Protestant. EDUCATION: Lafayette College, PA, B.S., 1923; Johns Hopkins Univ., MD, M.D., 1927. SPOUSE: Mary Elizabeth Kraus, married April 11, 1936. CHILDREN: Daniel Keffer, son; Peter Halden, son; Frederick Flanders, son. CAREER: Johns Hopkins Univ., Baltimore, MD, Researcher, 1927-29; Univ. of Pennsylvania, Professor, 1929-49; Johns Hopkins Univ., Baltimore, MD, Professor, 1949-53; Rockefeller Univ., NY, Professor, 1953-74. OTHER AWARDS: William H. Howell Award, 1927; Howard Crosby Warren Medal, 1948; A.A. Michelson Award, Case Institute, 1964; Lighthouse Award, New York City, 1969.

Selected Publications: *Studies on Excitation and Inhibition in the Retina: A Collection of Papers from the Laboratories of H. Keffer Hartline.* New York: Rockefeller U. Press, 1974.

For More Information See: *Biographical Encyclopedia of Scientists.* New York: Facts on File, 1981, 355. *Science* 158 (October 27, 1967): 471-73.

Commentary: Halden Hartline's research on the mechanisms by which we see won him the Nobel Prize. Early in his career, he found that in the process of vision, changes occur in the electrical potential of the retina. By studying individual nerve fibers in the eye of the crab, Hartline demonstrated that the intensity of light affected the speed of the electric impulses generated, and that faint light's effect was cumulated over time. In further research with vertebrates and crabs, he demonstrated complex interactions of the nerve cells and fibers of the eye that helped to explain the intricacies of vision. (B.I.M.)

Wald, George 301

PRIZE: Medicine and Physiology, 1967. BORN: November 18, 1906; New York, NY. PARENTS: Father, Isaac Wald; Mother, Ernestine Rosenmann Wald. NATIONALITY: American. RELIGION: Jewish. EDUCATION: New York Univ., B.S., 1927; Columbia Univ., NY, M.A., 1928; Columbia Univ., NY, Ph.D., 1932. SPOUSE: Frances Kingsley, married May 15, 1931, divorced 1957; Ruth Hubbard, married 1958. CHILDREN: Elijah, son; Michael, son; David, son; Deborah, daughter. CAREER: National Research Council Fellow, 1932-34; Harvard Univ., MA, Professor, 1934-77. OTHER AWARDS: Eli Lilly Prize, American Chemical Society, 1939; Lasker Award, American Public Health Association, 1953; Proctor Medal, Association for Research in Ophthalmology, 1955; Rumford Medal, American Academy of Arts and Sciences, 1959; Ives Medal, Optical Society of America, 1966; Paul Karrer Medal, U. of Zurich, Switzerland, 1967; T. Duckett Jones Award, Helen Hay Whitney Foundation, 1967; Bradford Washburn Medal, Boston Museum Society, 1968; Max Berg Award, 1969; Priestly Medal, Dickinson College, 1970.

Selected Publications: *General Education in a Free Society.* Cambridge, MA: Harvard U. Press, 1945. *Twenty-Six Afternoons of Biology.* Reading, MA: Addison-Wesley, 1966. *Visual Pigments and Photoreceptors: Review and Outlook.* New York: Academic Press, 1974.

For More Information See: *Current Biography Yearbook.* New York: H.W. Wilson, 1968, 412-14. "George Wald: The Man, the Speech." *New York Times Magazine* (August 17, 1969): 28-29+.

Commentary: George Wald's share of the Nobel Prize was for his research on the chemical processes that allow pigments in the retina of the eye to convert light into vision. Wald's original research showed that the eye rod pigment was made up of the protein opsin and retinene, a Vitamin A compound. Light striking

the pigment separated the two components and produced an energy burst that moved along the retina's nerve network. In later work, Wald showed that the eye cones contained three pigments corresponding to the three primary colors, which could be used to explain many phenomena, including color blindness. (B.I.M.)

1968

Holley, Robert William 302

PRIZE: Medicine and Physiology, 1968. BORN: January 28, 1922; Urbana, IL. PARENTS: Father, Charles Elmer Holley; Mother, Viola Esther Wolfe Holley. NATIONALITY: American. RELIGION: Unitarian. EDUCATION: Univ. of Illinois, A.B., 1942; Cornell Univ., NY, Ph.D., 1947. SPOUSE: Anne Lenore Dworkin, married March 3, 1945. CHILDREN: Frederick, son. CAREER: Washington State College, Researcher, 1947-48; Cornell Univ., Ithaca, NY, Professor, 1948-66; Salk Institute of Biological Studies, La Jolla, CA, Researcher, 1968-. OTHER AWARDS: Distinguished Service Award, U.S. Department of Agriculture, 1965; Lasker Award, 1965; U.S. Steel Foundation Award, National Academy of Sciences, 1967.

Selected Publications: "A New Method for Sequence Determination of Large Olegonucleotides." *Biochem. Biophys. Res. Commun.* 17 (1964): 389-94 (with others). "Structure of a Ribonucleic Acid." *Science* 147 (1965): 1462-65 (with others). "Structure of an Alanine Transfer Ribonucleic Acid." *Journal of the American Medical Association* 194 (1965): 868-71. "Experimental Approaches to the Determination of the Nucleotide Sequences of Large Oligonucleotides and Small Nucleic Acids." *Progr. Nucl. Acid Res. Mol. Biol.* (1968): 37-47.

For More Information See: *Current Biography Yearbook.* New York: H.W. Wilson, 1967, 172-74. *Science* 162 (October 25, 1968): 433-36.

Commentary: Robert Holley shared the Nobel Prize for his development of techniques for determining the structure of nucleic acids and for his determination of the complete nucleotide sequence of the alanine transfer ribonucleic acids. His continued research refined techniques, prepared other candidates for study, and elaborated further structures. (K.F.)

Khorana, Har Gobind 303

PRIZE: Medicine and Physiology, 1968. BORN: January 9, 1922; Raipur, India. PARENTS: Father, Shri Ganput Rai Khorana; Mother, Shrimat Krishna Devi Khorana. NATIONALITY: Indian; later American citizen. RELIGION: Hindu. EDUCATION: Punjab Univ., India, B.Sc., 1943; Punjab Univ., India, M.Sc., 1945; Liverpool Univ., England, Ph.D., 1948. SPOUSE: Esther Elizabeth Sibler, married 1952. CHILDREN: Julia, daughter; Emily Anne, daughter; Dave Roy, son. CAREER: Federal Institute of Technology, Zurich, Switzerland, Researcher, 1948-49; Cambridge Univ., England, Researcher, 1950-52; Univ. of British Columbia, Canada, Administrator, 1952-60; Univ. of Wisconsin, Professor and Administrator, 1960-70; Massachusetts Institute of Technology, Professor, 1970-. OTHER AWARDS: Merck Award, Chemical Institute of Canada, 1958; Gold Medal, Professional Institute of Public Service of Canada, 1960; Dannie-Heinneman Preiz, Gottingen, Germany, 1967;

Remsen Award, Johns Hopkins U., 1968; American Chemical Society Award, 1968; Louisa Gross Horowitz Prize, 1968; Lasker Award, 1968.

Selected Publications: *Some Recent Developments in the Chemistry of Phosphate Esters of Biological Interest.* New York: Wiley, 1961. "Studies on Polynucleotides. LXVII. Initiation of Protein Synthesis in Vitro as Studied by Using Ribopolynucleotides with Repeating Nucleotide Sequences as Messengers." *Journal of Molecular Biology* 25 (1967): 275-98 (with others). "Synthesis of Transfer RNA Genes." *Advan. Biosci* (1971): 89-102.

For More Information See: *Current Biography Yearbook.* New York: H.W. Wilson, 1970, 222-24. *Science* 162 (October 25, 1968): 433-36.

Commentary: Har Khorana received the Nobel Award for his work in the genetics area. He succeeded first in synthesizing polynucleotides and extended Nirenberg's nitrocellulose binding technique by testing each of the 64 possible ribonucleotides. This work was followed by other proofs of parts of the genetic code. Prior to his work in genetics, Khorana had done valuable research on alkaloids and on the synthesis of Coenzyme A. After receiving the Nobel, Khorana succeeded in an even more striking accomplishment—the synthesis of an artificial gene. (K.F.)

Nirenberg, Marshall Warren 304

PRIZE: Medicine and Physiology, 1968. BORN: April 10, 1927; New York, NY. PARENTS: Father, Harry Edward Nirenberg; Mother, Minerva Bykowsky Nirenberg. NATIONALITY: American. RELIGION: Jewish. EDUCATION: Univ. of Florida, B.S., 1948; Univ. of Florida, M.S., 1952; Univ. of Florida, Ph.D., 1957. SPOUSE: Perola Zaltzman, married July 14, 1961. CHILDREN: None. CAREER: National Institutes of Health, Bethesda, MD, Researcher and Administrator, 1957-. OTHER AWARDS: Molecular Biology Award, National Academy of Sciences, 1962; Biological Sciences Award, Washington Academy of Sciences, 1962; Paul Lewis Award, American Chemical Society, 1963; Modern Medicine Award, 1963; Medal, Department of Health, Education and Welfare, 1964; Harrison Howe Award, American Chemical Society, 1964; National Medal of Sciences, 1965; Hildebrand Award, American Chemical Society, 1966; Research Corporation Award, 1966; Gairdner Foundation Award of Merit, Canada, 1967; Prix Charles Leopold Meyer, French Academy of Sciences, 1967; Franklin Medal, Franklin Institute, 1968; Lasker Award, 1968; Priestly Award, 1968; Louisa Gross Horowitz Prize, 1968.

Selected Publications: "The Genetic Code." *Scientific American* 208 (March 1963): 80-94. "RNA Code and Protein Synthesis." *Cold Spring Symposium on Quantitative Biology* (1966): 11-24 (with others). "Genetic Memory." *Journal of the American Medical Association* 206 (1968): 1973-77.

For More Information See: *Current Biography Yearbook.* New York: H.W. Wilson, 1965, 305-07. Robinson, Donald. *100 Most Important People in the World Today.* New York: Putnam, 1970, 204-06.

Commentary: Marshall Nirenberg won the Nobel Prize for his development of the procedure for deciphering the genetic code in living cells. He was then able to reveal the exact order of amino acids in protein synthesis as directed by the information stored in DNA (deoxyribonucleic acid). (K.F.)

1969

Delbrück, Max 305

PRIZE: Medicine and Physiology, 1969. BORN: September 4, 1906; Berlin, Germany. DIED: March 9, 1981; Pasadena, CA. PARENTS: Father, Hans Delbrück; Mother, Lina Thiersch Delbrück. NATIONALITY: German; later American citizen. RELIGION: Protestant. EDUCATION: Univ. of Gottingen, Germany, Ph.D., 1930. SPOUSE: Mary Adaline Bruce, married August 2, 1941. CHILDREN: Jonathan, son; Nicola, daughter; Tobias, son; Ludina, daughter. CAREER: Kaiser Wilhelm Institute, Berlin, Germany, Researcher, 1932-37; California Institute of Technology, Researcher, 1937-39; Vanderbilt Univ., TN, Professor, 1940-47; California Institute of Technology, Professor, 1947-76. OTHER AWARDS: Kimber Medal, National Academy of Sciences; Louisa Gross Horowitz Prize, 1969.

Selected Publications: "Mutation of Bacteria from Virus-Sensitive to Virus-Resistant." *Genetics* 28 (1943): 491-511 (with S. Luria). "Induced Mutations in Bacterial Viruses." *Cold Spring Harbor Symposia on Quantitative Biology* 11 (1946): 33-37. *Uber Vererbungschemie.* Cologne: Westdeutscher Verlag, 1963.

For More Information See: *Asimov's Biographical Encyclopedia of Science and Technology.* Garden City, NY: Doubleday, 1982, 817-18. *Biographical Encyclopedia of Scientists.* New York: Facts on File, 1981, 196. *Biographical Memoirs of Fellows of the Royal Society.* London: Royal Society, 1982 (Volume 28), 59-60.

Commentary: Max Delbrück was awarded the Nobel Prize for his share in the "discoveries concerning the replication mechanism and the genetic structure of viruses." Originally a physicist, Delbrück became interested in bacteriophages. He pioneered the use of the plaque technique to study bacteriophage replication and discovered that bacteriophages produced multiple offspring while destroying their hosts. He also showed that genetic material from two different viruses could combine into a third form. His career later turned to the study of sensory physiology. (K.F.)

Hershey, Alfred Day 306

PRIZE: Medicine and Physiology, 1969. BORN: December 4, 1908; Owosso, MI. PARENTS: Father, Robert D. Hershey; Mother, Alma Wilbur Hershey. NATIONALITY: American. RELIGION: Most probably Christian/Protestant. EDUCATION: Michigan State U., B.S., 1930; Michigan State U., Ph.D., 1934. SPOUSE: Harriet Davidson, married November 15, 1946. CHILDREN: Peter Manning, son. CAREER: Washington Univ., MO, Professor, 1934-50; Carnegie Institute at Cold Spring Harbor, NY, Researcher and Administrator, 1950-74. OTHER AWARDS: Lasker Award, American Public Health Association, 1958; Kimber Genetics Award, National Academy of Sciences, 1965.

Selected Publications: "Reproduction of Bacteriophage." *International Review of Cytology* 1 (1952): 119-34. "Nucleic Acid Economy in Bacteria Infected with Bacteriophage T2. II. Phage Precursor Nucleic Acid. *Journal of General Physiology* 37 (1953): 1-23. "Upper Limit to the Protein Content of the Germinal Substance of Bacteriophage T2." *Virology* 1 (1955): 108-27.

For More Information See: *Biographical Encyclopedia of Scientists.* New York: Facts on File, 1981, 370. *Current Biography Yearbook.* New York: H.W. Wilson, 1970, 175-77.

Commentary: Alfred Hershey shared the Nobel Prize for his work in "discoveries concerning the replication mechanism and the genetic structure of viruses." He was instrumental in demonstrating that spontaneous mutations occurred in both bacteriophages and the cells with which they interacted; that the genetic material of different viruses could combine; and that the nucleic acid, not its associated protein, carried genetic information. His early research was on the chemistry of Brucella bacteria and in the area of immunology. Hershey also worked on the development of vaccines for various childhood diseases. (K.F.)

Luria, Salvador Edward 307

PRIZE: Medicine and Physiology, 1969. BORN: August 13, 1912; Turin, Italy. PARENTS: Father, Davide Luria; Mother, Ester Sacerdote Luria. NATIONALITY: Italian; later American citizen. RELIGION: Jewish. EDUCATION: Univ. of Turin, Italy, M.D., 1935. SPOUSE: Zella Hurwitz, married April 18, 1945. CHILDREN: Daniel, son. CAREER: Italian Army, 1935-38; Institute of Radium, Paris, France, Researcher, 1938-40; Columbia Univ., NY, Researcher, 1940-42; Indiana Univ., Professor, 1943-50; Univ. of Illinois, Professor, 1950-59; Massachusetts Institute of Technology, Professor and Administrator, 1959-. OTHER AWARDS: Lepetit Prize, 1935; Lenghi Prize, Academia Nazionale Lincei, 1965; Louisa Gross Horowitz Prize, Columbia U., 1969.

Selected Publications: "Mutation of Bacteria from Virus-Sensitive to Virus-Resistant." *Genetics* 28 (1943): 491-511 (with M. Delbrück). *The Multiplication of Viruses.* Vienna: Springer, 1958. *The Recognition of DNA in Bacteria.* San Francisco, CA: W. H. Freeman, 1969. *A View of Life.* Menlo Park, CA: Benjamin Cummings, 1981 (with S. Gould and S. Singer).

For More Information See: *Current Biography Yearbook.* New York: H. W. Wilson, 1970, 258-60. *A Slot Machine, A Broken Test Tube* (autobiography). New York: Harper and Row, 1984.

Commentary: Salvador Luria shared the Nobel Prize for his part in "discoveries concerning the replication mechanism and the genetic structure of viruses." Luria, working with Delbrück, developed techniques for purifying viruses and discovered that generations of viruses mutate, and that during bacteriophage growth, spontaneous mutations occurred in both the bacteriophages and in the host bacterial cells. He also worked on the phenomena of lysogeny and transduction, as well as being a social conscience of the scientific community, championing a variety of causes. (A.N.)

1970

Axelrod, Julius 308

PRIZE: Medicine and Physiology, 1970. BORN: May 30, 1912; New York, NY. PARENTS: Father, Isadore Axelrod; Mother, Molly Liechtling Axelrod. NATIONALITY: American. RELIGION: Jewish. EDUCATION: City College of New York, B.S., 1933; New York Univ., M.A., 1941; George Washington Univ., Washington, DC,

Ph.D., 1955. SPOUSE: Sally Taub, married August 30, 1938. CHILDREN: Paul Mark, son; Alfred Nathan, son. CAREER: New York Univ., Researcher, 1933-49; National Institutes of Health, MD, Researcher and Administrator, 1950-. OTHER AWARDS: Meritorious Research Award, Association for Research on Nervous and Mental Diseases, 1965; Gairdner Award, 1967; Alumni Distinguished Achievement Award, George Washington U., 1968; Claude Bernard Professorship and Award, U. of Montreal, 1969; Distinguished Service Award, 1970; Distinguished Service Award, Modern Medicine Magazine, 1970; Albert Einstein Award, Yeshiva U., 1971; Rudolph Virchow Medal, 1971; Myrtle Wreath Award, Hadassah, 1972; Torald Sollmann Award, American Society of Pharmacology and Experimental Therapeutics, 1973.

Selected Publications: "Reduction in the Accumulation of Norepinephrine 3H in Experimental Hypertension." *Life Science* 5 (1966): 2283-91 (with others). "Control of Catechol Amine Metabolism." *Progress in Endocrinology, International Congress of Endocrinology, 3rd* (1968): 286-93. *The Pineal.* New York: Academic Press, 1968 (with R. Wurthman and D. Kelly). "Biochemical Pharmacology of Catechol Amines and Its Clinical Implications." *Transactions of the American Neurological Association* 96 (1972): 179-86.

For More Information See: *Biographical Encyclopedia of Scientists.* New York: Facts on File, 34-35. *People* 11 (February 5, 1979): 24.

Commentary: Julius Axelrod shared the Nobel Prize for his role in developing the available knowledge about humoral transmitters in sympathetic nerves. Axelrod used tagged epinephrine and norepinephrine to show that the injected drugs equilibrated with the pool of transmitters in the nerve channels. He studied the action of many drugs and proved that their action was due to the changes they caused in the storage of neurotransmitters. Axelrod also studied the role of two enzymes which degrade the catecholamines, of which norepinephrine is one. With Bernard Brodie, he was responsible for the widely used drug Tylenol. (K.F.)

Katz, Bernard, Sir 309

PRIZE: Medicine and Physiology, 1970. BORN: March 26, 1911; Leipzig, Germany. PARENTS: Father, Max N. Katz; Mother, Eugenie Rabinowitz Katz. NATIONALITY: German; later British citizen. RELIGION: Jewish. EDUCATION: Univ. of Leipzig, Germany, M.D., 1934; Univ. of London, England, Ph.D., 1938. SPOUSE: Marguerite Penly, married October 27, 1945. CHILDREN: David, son; Jonathan, son. CAREER: Sydney Hospital, Australia, Physician, 1939-42; British Army, 1942-45; Univ. of London, England, Professor and Administrator, 1946-78. OTHER AWARDS: Garten Prize, U. of Leipzig, 1934; Feldberg Foundation Award, 1965; Baly Medal, Royal College of Physicians, 1967; Copley Medal, Royal Society, 1967; Knighthood, 1969.

Selected Publications: *Electric Excitation of Nerve: A Review.* London: Oxford U. Press, 1939. *How Cells Communicate.* San Francisco, CA: W. H. Freeman, 1961. *Nerve, Muscle, and Synapse.* New York: McGraw-Hill, 1966. *The Release of Neural Transmitter Substance.* Springfield, IL: Thomas, 1969.

For More Information See: *Biographical Encyclopedia of Scientists.* New York: Facts on File, 1981, 427. *Science* 170 (October 23, 1970): 422-24.

Commentary: Bernard Katz shared the Nobel Prize for his contribution to the knowledge of the mechanisms involved in the release of transmitter substances from nerve terminals. Katz discovered that there was a potential present at a neuromuscular junction even after stimulation and proposed the quantum hypothesis (that nerve endings secrete acetylcholine in quanta, and that stimulation enormously increases the quanta released). He also researched the effects of sodium, potassium, and calcium on activity in the junction. (K.F.)

von Euler, Ulf Svante   310

PRIZE: Medicine and Physiology, 1970. BORN: February 7, 1905; Stockholm, Sweden. DIED: March 10, 1983; Stockholm, Sweden. PARENTS: Father, Hans von Euler; Mother, Astrid Cleve von Euler. NATIONALITY: Swedish. RELIGION: Protestant. EDUCATION: Karolinska Institute, Sweden, M.D., 1930. SPOUSE: Jane Sodenstierna, married April 12, 1930, divorced (no date found); Dagmar Cronstedt, married August 20, 1958. CHILDREN: Leo, son; Christopher, son; Ursula, daughter; Marie, daughter. CAREER: Karolinska Institute, Sweden, Professor and Administrator, 1930-71. OTHER AWARDS: Commander, Order of the North Star, Sweden; Cruzeiro do Sul, Brazil, 1952; Palmes Academiques, France; Gairdner Award, 1961; Jahre Prize, 1965; Stouffer Prize, 1967; Grand Cross Al Merito Civil, Spain, 1979.

Selected Publications: "Hypertension after Bilateral Nephrectomy in the Rat." *Nature* 160 (1947): 905 (with E. Braun-Menendez). *Noradrenaline: Chemistry, Physiology, Pharmacology, and Clinical Aspects.* Springfield, IL: Thomas, 1956. *Prostaglandins.* New York: Academic Press, 1968. *Release and Uptake Functions in Adrenergic Nerve Granules.* Liverpool: Liverpool U. Press, 1982.

For More Information See: *Biographical Encyclopedia of Scientists.* New York: Facts on File, 1981, 815. *Biographical Memoirs of Fellows of the Royal Society.* London: Royal Society, 1985 (Volume 31), 143-70.

Commentary: Ulf von Euler was awarded the Nobel Prize for his contribution to knowledge concerning humoral transmitters in sympathetic nerves. Von Euler was responsible for isolation and identification of norepinephrine as the transmitter in the sympathetic nervous system and elaboration of its role in stress conditions. He also found that stimulation of the nerve to the adrenal gland produced increased adrenal epinephrine and isolated and characterized the norepinephrine storage units in nerves. Von Euler, early in his career, discovered prostaglandin, which would later become a much-studied entity. (K.F.)

1971

Sutherland, Earl Wilbur, Jr.   311

PRIZE: Medicine and Physiology, 1971. BORN: November 19, 1915; Burlingame, KS. DIED: March 9, 1974; Miami, FL. PARENTS: Father, Earl Wilbur Sutherland; Mother, Edith Hartshorn Sutherland. NATIONALITY: American. RELIGION: Protestant. EDUCATION: Washburn College, KS, B.S., 1937; Washington Univ., MO, M.D., 1942. SPOUSE: Mildred Rice, married 1937, divorced 1962; Claudia Sebeste Smith, married 1963. CHILDREN: 2 sons; 2 daughters. CAREER: Washington Univ., MO, Professor, 1940-42; United States Army,

1942-45; Washington Univ., MO, Professor, 1945-53; Case Western Reserve Univ., OH, Professor, 1953-63; Vanderbilt Univ., TN, Professor, 1963-73; Univ. of Miami, FL, Professor, 1973-74. OTHER AWARDS: Lasker Award, 1970; Achievement Award, American Heart Association, 1971; National Medal of Science, United States, 1973.

Selected Publications: "Hormonal Regulatory Mechanisms." *Proceedings of the Third International Congress of Biochemistry.* New York: Academic Press, 1955, 318-27. "The Properties of an Adenine Ribonucleotide Produced with Cellular Particles, ATP, Mg++, and Epinephrine or Glucagon." *Journal of the American Chemical Society* 79 (1957): 3068 (with T.W. Rall). "Formation of a Cyclic Adenine Ribonucleotide by Tissue Particles." *Journal of Biological Chemistry* 232 (1958): 1065-76 (with T.W. Rall). "The Biological Role of Adenosine 3^1, 5^1-Phosphate." *Harvey Lecture Series.* New York: Academic Press, 1962 (Volume 57), 17-33. "The Role of Cyclic 3^1, 5Å-AMP in Responses to Catecholamines and Other Hormones." *Pharmacological Reviews* 18 (1966): 145-61 (with G.A. Robison). *Cyclic AMP.* New York: Academic Press, 1971 (with G.A. Robison and R.W. Butcher).

For More Information See: *Biographical Memoirs of the National Academy of Sciences.* Washington, DC: National Academy of Sciences, 1978 (Volume 49), 319-50. *Time* 98 (October 25, 1971): 63.

Commentary: Earl Sutherland received the Nobel Prize for "his long study of hormones, the chemical substances that regulate virtually every body function." During his career, he investigated the regulation of carbohydrate metabolism by the hormone adrenaline interaction with phosphorylase, the role of the cyclic AMP intermediate in hormonal activities, and the involvement of cyclic AMP in transmission of genetic information and in abnormal cell growth. (B.I.M.)

1972

Edelman, Gerald Maurice   312

PRIZE: Medicine and Physiology, 1972. BORN: July 1, 1929; New York, NY. PARENTS: Father, Edward Edelman; Mother, Anna Freedman Edelman. NATIONALITY: American. RELIGION: Jewish. EDUCATION: Ursinus College, PA, B.S., 1950; Univ. of Pennsylvania, M.D., 1954; Rockefeller Univ., NY, Ph.D., 1960. SPOUSE: Maxine Morrison, married June 11, 1950. CHILDREN: Eric, son; David, son; Judith, daughter. CAREER: Rockefeller Univ., NY, Professor and Administrator, 1957-. OTHER AWARDS: Spencer Morris Award, U. of Pennsylvania, 1954; Eli Lilly Award, Harvey Society, 1965; Annual Alumni Award, Ursinus College, 1969; Albert Einstein Commemorative Award, Yeshiva U., 1974; Buchman Memorial Award, California Institute of Technology, 1975; Rabbi Shai Schaknai Memorial Prize, Hebrew U., 1977.

Selected Publications: "The Structure and Function of Antibodies." *Scientific American* 223 (August 1970): 34-42. *Cellular Selection and Regulation in the Immune Response.* New York: Raven Press, 1974. *Molecular Machinery of the Membrane.* Cambridge, MA: Massachusetts Institute of Technology Press, 1975. *Dynamic Aspects of Neocortical Function.* New York: Wiley, 1985 (with E. Gall and W. Cowan). *Molecular Basis of Neural Development*. New York: Wiley, 1985 (with E. Gall and W. Cowan).

For More Information See: *Biographical Encyclopedia of Scientists*. New York: Facts on File, 1981, 226. *Science* 178 (October 27, 1972): 384-86.

Commentary: Gerald Edelman shared the Nobel Prize for his research on the chemical structure of antibodies. His dissertation used Rodney Porter's methods to cleave and study the structure of human immunoglobulins. Later research led to the cleavage of the large molecules into component polypeptide chains, using urea. Edelman reported two different polypeptides and different antigen-binding properties, which stimulated much of the later work in this field. He also succeeded in determining the structure of human myeloma protein. (B.I.M.)

Porter, Rodney Robert 313

PRIZE: Medicine and Physiology, 1972. BORN: October 8, 1917; Liverpool, England. DIED: September 6, 1985; Winchester, England. PARENTS: Father, Joseph L. Porter; Mother, Isobel M. Porter. NATIONALITY: British. RELIGION: Most probably Christian/Protestant. EDUCATION: Cambridge Univ., England; Liverpool Univ., England. SPOUSE: Julia Frances New, married 1948. CHILDREN: Nigel, son; Tim, son; Susan, daughter; Ruth, daughter; Helen, daughter. CAREER: National Institute for Medical Research, London, England, Researcher, 1949-60; London Univ., England, Professor, 1960-67; Oxford Univ., England, Professor, 1967-85. OTHER AWARDS: Award of Merit, Gairdner Foundation, 1966; Ciba Medal, Biochemistry Society, 1967; Karl Landsteiner Memorial Award, American Association of Blood Banks, 1968; Royal Medal, Royal Society, 1973.

Selected Publications: *Defence and Recognition*. Baltimore, MD: University Park Press, 1973. *Chemical Aspects of Immunology*. Burlington, NC: Carolina Biological Supply Company, 1976. *Contemporary Topics in Molecular Immunology*. Volume 6, New York: Plenum Press, 1976 (with G. Ada). *Biochemistry and Genetics of Complement: A Discussion*. London: Royal Society, 1984.

For More Information See: *Biographical Encyclopedia of Scientists*. New York: Facts on File, 1981, 648-49. *New York Times Biographical Service* (1972): 1779. *Science* 178 (October 27, 1972): 384-86.

Commentary: Rodney Porter won the Nobel Prize for his research on the chemical structure of antibodies. He developed the method of selective cleavage with enzymes and succeeded in separating antibodies into two different parts with the enzyme papain. The activities of the two parts fit the known bivalency of immunoglobulin G. Later, Porter separated rabbit immunoglobulin polypeptides and developed the four-chain model for immunoglobulin G structure. (R.K.)

1973

Lorenz, Konrad Zacharias 314

PRIZE: Medicine and Physiology, 1973. BORN: November 7, 1903; Vienna, Austria. PARENTS: Father, Adolf Lorenz; Mother, Emma Lecher Lorenz. NATIONALITY: Austrian. RELIGION: Most probably Christian/Protestant. EDUCATION: Univ. of Vienna, Austria, M.D., 1928; Univ. of Vienna, Austria, Ph.D., 1933. SPOUSE: Margarethe "Gretl" Gebhardt, married June 24, 1927. CHILDREN: Agnes, daughter; Dagmar, daughter; Thomas, son. CAREER: Univ. of Vienna, Austria, Professor, 1928-40; Univ. of Königsberg, Germany, Professor, 1940-42; German Army, 1942-44; Soviet Armenia, Prisoner of War, 1944-48; Institute of Comparative Ethology, Altenberg, Austria, Administrator, 1949-51; Max Planck Foundation, Germany, Administrator, 1951-73. OTHER AWARDS: Gold Medal, Zoological Society of New York, 1955; City Prize, Vienna, 1959; Gold Bölsche Medal, 1962; Austrian Distinction for Science and Art, 1964; Prix Mondial, Cino de Duca, 1969; Kalinga Prize, UNESCO, 1970; Order Pour le Merité; Grosses Verdienstkreuz, 1974; Bayerischer Verdienstorden, 1974.

Selected Publications: *On Aggression*. New York: Harcourt, Brace and World, 1966. *Evolution and Modification of Behavior*. Chicago: U. of Chicago Press, 1967. *Studies in Animal and Human Behavior*. Cambridge, MA: Harvard U. Press, 1970-71.

For More Information See: *Current Biography Yearbook*. New York: H.W. Wilson, 1977, 274-77. Evans, Richard. *Konrad Lorenz: The Man and His Ideas*. New York: Harcourt, Brace, Jovanovich, 1975.

Commentary: Konrad Lorenz shared the Nobel Prize for his work in ethology (the comparative study of the behavior of animals in their natural environment). He worked mostly with birds, particularly geese, and was especially well known for his study of aggressive behavior, of imprinting (the programed action of following the first moving object seen after hatching), and of the effects of isolation and overcrowding on young primates. (B.I.M.)

Tinbergen, Nikolaas 315

PRIZE: Medicine and Physiology, 1973. BORN: April 15, 1907; The Hague, Netherlands. PARENTS: Father, Dirk Cornelus Tinbergen; Mother, Jeannette Van Eek Tinbergen. NATIONALITY: Dutch. RELIGION: Agnostic; from Protestant background. EDUCATION: Univ. of Leiden, Netherlands, Ph.D., 1932. SPOUSE: Elisabeth "Lies" Amelie Rutten, married April 14, 1932. CHILDREN: Jacob, son; Catharina, daughter; Dirk, son; Jannetje, daughter; Gerardina, daughter. CAREER: Univ. of Leiden, Netherlands, Professor, 1933-49; German Prisoner of War, 1945-47; Oxford Univ., England, Professor, 1949-73. OTHER AWARDS: Bölsche Medal, 1969; Italia Prize for TV Documentaries, 1969; Godman-Salvin Medal, British Ornithology Union, 1969; Jan Swammerdam Medal, 1973.

Selected Publications: *The Animal in Its World: Explorations of an Ethologist, 1932-72*(collected papers). Cambridge, MA: Harvard U. Press, 1972-73. *Early Childhood Autism: An Ethological Approach*. Berlin: P. Parry, 1972 (with E.A. Tinbergen).

For More Information See: *Current Biography Yearbook*. New York: H.W. Wilson, 1975, 414-16. *Psychology Today* (March 1974): 68-71.

Commentary: Nikolaas Tinbergen received the Nobel for his studies of animal behavior, in acknowledgement of the importance of ethological research to the understanding of human behavior. Best known for his studies of the habits of gulls, Tinbergen also researched the homing instincts of digger wasps, the mating rituals of sticklebacks, and the color adaptations of butterflies. His later studies of autism in children were also noteworthy. (B.I.M.)

von Frisch, Karl   316

PRIZE: Medicine and Physiology, 1973. BORN: November 20, 1886; Vienna, Austria. DIED: June 12, 1982; Munich, Germany. PARENTS: Father, Anton Ritter von Frisch; Mother, Marie Exner von Frisch. NATIONALITY: Austrian. RELIGION: Catholic. EDUCATION: Univ. of Munich, Germany, Ph.D., 1910. SPOUSE: Margaret Mohr, married July 20, 1917. CHILDREN: Johanna, daughter; Maria, daughter; Helene, daughter; Otto, son. CAREER: Univ. of Munich, Germany, Professor, 1910-14; Döbling Hospital, Vienna, Austria, Physician, 1914-19; Univ. of Munich, Germany, Professor, 1912-21; Univ. of Rostock, Germany, Professor, 1921-23; Univ. of Breslau, Poland, Professor, 1923-25; Univ. of Munich, Germany, Administrator, 1925-46; Univ. of Graz, Austria, Professor and Administrator, 1946-50; Univ. of Munich, Germany, Professor, 1950-58. OTHER AWARDS: Orden Pour le Merite fur Wissenschaften und Kunste, 1952; Magellan Prize, American Philosophical Society, 1956; Kalinga Prize, UNESCO, 1959; Balzan Prize, 1963.

Selected Publications: *The Dancing Bees: An Account of the Life and Senses of the Honeybee.* New York: Harcourt, Brace, 1955. *Man and the Living World.* New York: Harcourt, 1963. *Bees: Their Vision, Chemical Senses and Language.* Ithaca, NY: Cornell U. Press, 1972. *Animal Architecture.* New York: Van Nostrand Reinhold, 1983.

For More Information See: *A Biologist Remembers.* New York: Pergamon, 1967. *Current Biography Yearbook.* New York: H.W. Wilson, 1974, 130-33. "Karl von Frisch." *Biographical Memoirs of the Fellows of the Royal Society.* London: Royal Society, 1983 (Volume 29), 197-200.

Commentary: Karl von Frisch was awarded the Nobel Prize for his work in ethology (the study of animal behavior). He used conditioned reflex studies to show that bees distinguished among colors and could communicate their findings. Previously, von Frisch had shown that fish could distinguish among colors, light intensities, and sound levels. (B.I.M.)

1974

Claude, Albert   317

PRIZE: Medicine and Physiology, 1974. BORN: August 24, 1898; Luxembourg, Belgium. DIED: May 22, 1983; Brussels, Belgium. PARENTS: Father, Florentin Claude; Mother, no record found. NATIONALITY: Belgian; later American citizen. RELIGION: Most probably Christian. EDUCATION: Univ. of Liège, Belgium, M.D., 1928. SPOUSE: Joy Gilder, married June 20, 1935. CHILDREN: Philippa, daughter. CAREER: Rockefeller Univ., NY, Professor, 1929-72; Univ. of Belgium, Professor, 1950-70; Institute Jules Bordet, Brussels, Belgium, 1948-71. OTHER AWARDS: British War Medal, 1918; Interallied Medal, 1918; Grand Cordon de l'Ordre de Leopold II, Belgium; Prize Fonds National de la Recherche Scientifique, 1965; Medal, Belgian Academie of Medicine; Louisa G. Horowitz Prize, Columbia U., 1970; Paul Ehrlich Award, 1971; Ludwig Darmstaedter Prize, 1971.

Selected Publications: "Fractionation of Chicken Tumor Extracts by Highspeed Centrifugation." *American Journal of Cancer* 30 (1937): 742-45. "Distribution of Nucleic Acids in the Cell and the Morphological Constitution of Cytoplasm." *Biological Symposia* 10

(1943): 111-29. "Fractionation of Mammalian Liver Cells by Differential Centrifugation. I and II." *Journal of Experimental Medicine* 84 (1946): 51-89. "The Nature of the Golgi Apparatus. I and II." *Journal of Morphology* 85 (1949): 35-111 (with G. Palade).

For More Information See: *Biographical Encyclopedia of Scientists.* New York: Facts on File, 1981, 151. *Science* 186 (November 8, 1974): 516-20.

Commentary: Albert Claude won the Nobel Prize for his contributions to the research on the structure and function of the internal components of cells. Claude discovered early that cell components could be separated in a centrifuge and developed the procedures and studied the fractions for several different cells and tissues. He also used electron microscopy to study cell structure. (R.K.)

de Duvé, Christian René Marie Joseph   318

PRIZE: Medicine and Physiology, 1974. BORN: October 2, 1917; Thames Ditton, England. PARENTS: Father, Alphonse de Duvé; Mother, Madeleine Pungs de Duvé. NATIONALITY: Belgian; later American resident. RELIGION: Most probably Christian. EDUCATION: Univ. of Louvain, Belgium, M.D., 1941; Univ. of Louvain, Belgium, M.Sc., 1946. SPOUSE: Janine Herman, married September 30, 1943. CHILDREN: Thierry, son; Alain, son; Anne, daughter; Françoise, daughter. CAREER: Univ. of Louvain, Belgium, Professor, 1947-; Rockefeller Univ., NY, Professor, 1962-. OTHER AWARDS: Prix des Alumni, 1949; Prix Pfizer, 1957; Prix Franqui, 1960; Prix Quinquennal, Belge des Sciences Médicales, Belgium, 1967; International Award of Merit, Gairdner Foundation, Canada, 1967; Dr. H.P. Heineken Prijs, Netherlands, 1973; Grand Cross, Order of Leopold II, 1975.

Selected Publications: "Cytochrome Oxidase and Acid Phosphatase of Isolated Mitochondria." *Congr. Intern. Biochim..,* Resumes Communs., 2e Congr., Paris (1952): 278 (with F. Appelmans and R. Wattiaux). "Lysosomes, a New Group of Cytoplasmic Particles." *Subcellular Particles, Symposium, Woods Hole, MA* (1958): 128-58. "Lysosomes and Chemotherapy." *Biological Approaches to Cancer Chemotherapy* (1960): 101-12. *A Guided Tour of the Living Cell.* New York: Scientific American Books, 1984.

For More Information See: *Biographical Encyclopedia of Scientists.* New York: Facts on File, 1981, 193-94. *Science* 186 (November 8, 1974): 516-20.

Commentary: Christian de Duvé shared the Nobel Prize for his contributions to research on the structure and function of the internal components of cells. Using electron microscopy and biochemical analyses, de Duvé identified and discussed in detail two cytoplasmic enzyme-containing units—the lysosome and peroxisome. His later research also involved work on the relationships of lysosomes and storage diseases in man, on lysosomes in cell pathology, and on drug-lysosome interactions. (B.I.M.)

Palade, George Emil   319

PRIZE: Medicine and Physiology, 1974. BORN: November 19, 1912; Jassi, Rumania. PARENTS: Father, Emil Palade; Mother, Constana Cantemir Palade. NATIONALITY: Rumanian; later American citizen. RELIGION: Most probably Christian. EDUCATION: Univ. of Bucharest, Rumania, M.D., 1940. SPOUSE: Irina Malaxa, married June 12, 1941, died 1969; Marilyn Farquhar, married

1970. CHILDREN: Philip Theodore, son; Georgia Teodora, daughter. CAREER: Univ. of Bucharest, Rumania, Professor, 1935-45; Rockefeller Univ., NY, Professor, 1946-72; Yale Univ., CT, Professor, 1972-. OTHER AWARDS: Passano Award, American Medical Association, 1964; Lasker Award, 1966; Gairdner Special Award, 1967; Horowitz Prize, 1970; Warren Prize, Massachusetts General Hospital.

Selected Publications: "The Nature of the Golgi Apparatus. I and II." *Journal of Morphology* 85 (1949): 35-111 (with A. Claude). "Liver Microsomes. An Integrated Morphological and Biochemical Study." *J. Biophys. Biochem. Cytol.* 2 (1956): 171-200 (with P. Siekovitz). "Pancreatic Microsomes. An Integrated Morphological and Biochemical Study." *J. Biophys. Biochem. Cytol* 2 (1956): 671-90 (with P. Siekovitz). "Functional Changes in the Structure of Cell Components." *Subcellular Particles, Symposium, Woods Hole, MA* (1958): 64-80.

For More Information See: *Biographical Encyclopedia of Scientists.* New York: Facts on File, 1981, 612. *Science* 186 (November 8, 1974): 516-20.

Commentary: George Palade shared the Nobel Prize for his contributions to research on the structure and function of the internal components of cells. Palade used and refined the available techniques of electron microscopy and sedimentation to isolate purified cell functions and study their biochemical nature. His introduction of osmium tetroxide as a fixative made electron microscopy a viable technique for the studies. Palade also studied the synthesis of enzymes on ribosomes and the pathways of resulting protein and provided the first detail studies of mitochondrial fine structure. (B.I.M.)

1975

Baltimore, David   320
PRIZE: Medicine and Physiology, 1975. BORN: March 7, 1938; New York, NY. PARENTS: Father, Richard I. Baltimore; Mother, Gertrude Lipschitz Baltimore. NATIONALITY: American. RELIGION: Jewish. EDUCATION: Swarthmore College, PA, B.A., 1960; Rockefeller Univ., NY, Ph.D., 1964. SPOUSE: Alice S. Huang, married October 5, 1968. CHILDREN: Lauren Rachel, daughter. CAREER: Albert Einstein College of Medicine, NY, Researcher, 1964-65; Salk Institute, CA, Researcher, 1965-68; Massachusetts Institute of Technology, Professor and Administrator, 1968-. OTHER AWARDS: Gustav Stern Award, 1970; Warren Triennial Prize, Massachusetts General Hospital, 1971; Eli Lilly Award, 1971; U.S. Steel Foundation Award, 1974; Gairdner Foundation Annual Award, 1974.

Selected Publications: "Viral RNA-Dependent DNA Polymerase." *Nature (London)* 226 (1970): 1211-13. "RNA-Directed DNA Synthesis and RNA Tumor Viruses." *Advances in Virus Research* 17 (1972): 51-94. *Animal Virology.* New York: Academic Press, 1976 (with others). *Activation and Regulation of Immunoglobin Synthesis in Malignant B Cells.* Copenhagen: Munksgaard, 1979 (with others).

For More Information See: *Current Biography Yearbook.* New York: H.W. Wilson, 1983, 25-28. *Science* 190 (November 14, 1975): 650, 712-13.

Commentary: David Baltimore received the Nobel Prize for his contributions to the "discoveries concerning the interaction between tumor viruses and the

genetic material of the cell." He and Howard Temin independently arrived at an explanation of DNA synthesis in RNA tumor viruses through the proposal of a reverse transcriptase enzyme which allowed DNA synthesis to proceed by copying the RNA element. The theory, although controversial, was later accepted. Baltimore began his career working on RNA virus replication and moved on to poliovirus and leukemia virus research later. His partial synthesis of a mammalian hemoglobin gene led to his activity in support of limitations of genetic engineering research. He also worked successfully in synthetic vaccine research. (B.I.M.)

Dulbecco, Renato   321
PRIZE: Medicine and Physiology, 1975. BORN: February 22, 1914; Catanzaro, Italy. PARENTS: Father, Leonardo Dulbecco; Mother, Maria Virdia Dulbecco. NATIONALITY: Italian; later American citizen. RELIGION: Most probably Christian. EDUCATION: Univ. of Torino, Italy, M.D., 1936. SPOUSE: Guiseppina Salvo, married June 1, 1940, divorced 1963; Maureen Muir, married July 17, 1963. CHILDREN: Peter Leonard, son; Maria Vittoria, daughter; Fiona Linsey, daughter. CAREER: Univ. of Torino, Italy, Researcher, 1936-47; Indiana Univ., Researcher, 1947-49; California Institute of Technology, Professor, 1949-63; Salk Institute, CA, Researcher, 1963-71; Imperial Cancer Research Fund, London, England, Administrator, 1971-77; Salk Institute, CA, Professor, 1977-81. OTHER AWARDS: John Scott Award, City of Philadelphia, PA, 1958; Kimball Award, Conference of Public Health Laboratory Directors, 1959; Albert and Mary Lasker Basic Medical Research Award, 1964; Howard Taylor Ricketts Award, 1965; Paul Ehrlich-Ludwig Darmstaedter Prize, 1967; Horowitz Prize, Columbia U., 1973; Selman Waksman Award, National Academy of Sciences, 1974; Man of the Year, London, 1975; Targo d'oro, Villa San Giovanni, 1978; Italian-American of the Year, San Diego, CA, 1978; Decorated Grand Officiale, Italian Republic, 1981; Mandel Gold Medal, Czechoslovak Academy of Sciences, 1982.

Selected Publications: *The Induction of Cancer by Viruses.* San Francisco, CA: W.H. Freeman, 1967. *The Biology of Small DNA-Tumor Viruses.* New York: MSS Information Corp., 1974. *Induction of Host Systems, Integration and Excision.* Cambridge, MA: Cambridge U. Press, 1975. *Virology.* Hagerstown, MD: Harper and Row, 1980 (with Howard Ginsberg).

For More Information See: *Biographical Encyclopedia of Scientists.* New York: Facts on File, 1981, 219. *Science* 190 (November 14, 1975): 650, 712-13.

Commentary: Renato Dulbecco's Nobel was awarded for his contributions to the "discoveries concerning the interaction between tumor viruses and the genetic material of the cell." He developed many of the techniques used by researchers to study the molecular biology of animal viruses, including those used by his colaureates, who had both worked under him. Dulbecco also did pioneer work on gene transformation by DNA tumor viruses. (B.I.M.)

Temin, Howard Martin   322
PRIZE: Medicine and Physiology, 1975. BORN: December 10, 1934; Philadelphia, PA. PARENTS: Father, Henry Temin; Mother, Annette Lehman Temin. NATIONALITY: American. RELIGION: Jewish. EDUCATION: Swarthmore College, PA, B.A., 1955; California Institute of

Technology, Ph.D., 1959. SPOUSE: Rayla Greenberg, married May 27, 1962. CHILDREN: Sara Beth, daughter; Miriam Judith, daughter. CAREER: California Institute of Technology, Researcher, 1959-60; Univ. of Wisconsin, Professor, 1960-. OTHER AWARDS: Warren Triennial Prize, Massachusetts General Hospital, 1971; Special Commendation, Medical Society of Wisconsin, 1971; PAP Award, Papanicolaou Institute, 1972; Bertner Award, M.D. Anderson Hospital and Tumor Institute, 1972; U.S. Steel Foundation Award, 1972; Waksman Award, Theobald Smith Society, 1972; Griffuel Prize, Association of Developmental Recherche Cancer, Villejuif, France, 1972; Award in Enzyme Chemistry, American Chemical Society, 1973; Award for Distinguished Achievement, Modern Medicine, 1973; Gairdner Foundation International Award, 1974; Albert Lasker Award, 1974; Lucy Wortham James Award, Society of Surgical Oncologists, 1976; Alumni Distinguished Service Award, California Institute of Technology, 1976; Gruber Award, American Academy of Dermatology, 1981.

Selected Publications: "Participation of Deoxyribonucleic Acid (DNA) in Rous Sarcoma Virus Production." *Virology* 22 (1964): 486-94. "Carcinogenesis by Avian Sarcoma Viruses. III. The Differential Effect of Serum and Polyanions on Multiplication of Uninfected and Converted Cells." *Journal of the National Cancer Institute* 37 (1966): 167-75. *RNA-Directed DNA Synthesis.* San Francisco, CA: W.H. Freeman, 1972. "RNA-Directed DNA Synthesis and RNA Tumor Viruses." *Advances in Virus Research* 17 (1972): 51-94 (with D. Baltimore).

For More Information See: *Biographical Encyclopedia of Scientists.* New York: Facts on File, 1981, 776-77. *Science* 190 (November 14, 1975): 650, 712-13.

Commentary: Howard Temin shared the Nobel Prize for his contributions to the "discoveries concerning the interaction between tumor viruses and the genetic material of the cell." He and David Baltimore independently proposed an explanation of the DNA synthesis in RNA tumor viruses. The theory of the reverse transcriptase enzyme said that the DNA synthesis proceeded by copying the RNA element. The theory, contrary to the "central dogma" of molecular biology at that time, was later accepted. Temin worked with Rous sarcoma virus, beginning with graduate work that developed a reproducible assay in vitro for the tumor virus. (B.I.M.)

1976

Blumberg, Baruch Samuel   323
PRIZE: Medicine and Physiology, 1976. BORN: July 28, 1925; New York, NY. PARENTS: Father, Meyer Blumberg; Mother, Ida Simonoff Blumberg. NATIONALITY: American. RELIGION: Jewish. EDUCATION: Union College, NY, B.S., 1946; Columbia Univ., NY, M.D., 1951; Oxford Univ., England, Ph.D., 1957. SPOUSE: Jean Liebesman, married April 4, 1954. CHILDREN: George Micah Connor, son; Noah Francis Baruch, son; Jane Emily, daughter; Anne Francesca, daughter. CAREER: National Institutes of Health, MD, Administrator, 1957-64; Institute for Cancer Research, PA, Administrator, 1964-. OTHER AWARDS: Albion O. Berstein Award, Medical Society of the State of New York, 1969; Grand Scientific Award, Phi Lambda Kappa, 1972; Annual Award, Eastern Pennsylvania Branch of

the American Society for Microbiology, 1972; Eppinger Prize, U. of Freiburg, Germany, 1973; Passano Award, 1974; Distinguished Achievement Award, Modern Medicine, 1975; Gairdner Foundation International Award, 1975; Karl Landsteiner Memorial Award, American Association of Blood Banks, 1975; Scopus Award, American Friends of Hebrew University, 1977; Strittmatter Award, Philadelphia County Medical Society, 1980.

Selected Publications: *Conference on Genetic Polymorphisms and Geographic Variations in Disease. Proceedings.* New York: Grune & Stratton, 1962. *Australia Antigen and Hepatitis.* Cleveland, OH: Chemical Rubber Co., 1972 (with others). *Primary Hepatocellular Carcinoma and Hepatitis B Virus.* Chicago: Yearbook Medical Publishers, 1982. *Hepatitis B: The Virus, the Disease, and the Vaccine.* New York: Plenum Press, 1984 (with K. Eisenstein and I. Milman).

For More Information See: *Current Biography Yearbook.* New York: H. W. Wilson, 1977, 72-74. *Science* 194 (November 26, 1976): 928-29.

Commentary: The Academy cited Barry Blumberg for his work in "discoveries concerning mechanisms involved in the origin and spread of infectious diseases." Blumberg identified Australia antigen as the indicator in the blood of the presence of hepatitis-B, which became the basis for the test for screening out hepatitis-B carriers among blood donors and for vaccine work. His career-long research dealt with how and why people of different backgrounds react differently to disease. (B.I.M.)

Gajdusek, Daniel Carleton   324
PRIZE: Medicine and Physiology, 1976. BORN: September 9, 1923; Yonkers, NY. PARENTS: Father, Karl A. Gajdusek; Mother, Ottilia Dobroczki Gajdusek. NATIONALITY: American. RELIGION: Most probably Christian. EDUCATION: Univ. of Rochester, NY, B.S., 1943; Harvard Univ., MA, M.D., 1946. SPOUSE: None. CHILDREN: 21 adopted children from New Guinea, Ivan Mbagintao; Josede Figirliyong; Jesus Raglmar; Jesus Mororui; Mathias Maradol; Jesus Tamel; Jesus Salalu; John Paul Runman; Yavine Borima; Arthur Yolwa; Joe Yongorimah Kintoki; Thomas Youmog; Toni Wanevi; Toname Ikabala; Magame Prima; Senavayo Anua; Igitava Yariga; Luwi Ivavara; Irvam'bin'ai Undae'mai; Steven Malruio; Susanna Undopmaina. CAREER: Columbia Presbyterian Medical Center, NY, Physician, 1946-47; Pediatrics Children's Hospital, OH, Physician, 1947-48; Harvard Univ., MA, Researcher, 1949-52; Walter Reed Army Institute of Research, Washington, DC, Researcher, 1952-53; Institute Pasteur, Iran, Researcher, 1954-55; Walter and Eliza Hall Institute of Medical Research, Australia, Researcher, 1955-57; National Institutes of Health, MD, Administrator, 1958-. OTHER AWARDS: E. Meade Johnson Award, American Academy of Pediatrics, 1963; Superior Service Award, National Institutes of Health, 1970; Distinguished Service Award, Department of Health, Education and Welfare, 1975; Professor Lucian Dautrebande Prize, Belgium, 1976; Cotzias Prize, American Academy of Neurology, 1979.

Selected Publications: *Journals. Study of Child Growth and Development of Disease Patterns in Primitive Cultures.* Bethesda, MD: National Institute of Neurological Diseases and Blindness, 1963. *Slow Latent and Temperate Virus Infections.* Bethesda, MD: National Institute of Health, 1965 (with C. Gibbs, Jr., and M. Alpers). *Genetic Studies in Relation to Kuru.* Chicago: U. of Chicago Press, 1972-75 (with others). *Kuru.* New York: Raven Press, 1981 (with J. Farquhar).

For More Information See: *Current Biography Yearbook.* New York: H. W. Wilson, 1981, 156-59. *Science* 194 (November 26, 1976): 928-29.

Commentary: Carleton Gajdusek was recognized for his "discoveries concerning mechanisms involved in the origin and spread of infectious diseases," especially for his intensive study of kuru, a brain disease in New Guinea, that showed that slow virus infections were possible in humans, and discovered a new group of viruses, apparently pieces of genetically active nucleic acid bound to fragments of plasma membrane. His work included research in many other medical problems in primitive isolated populations as well as contributions to anthropology and comparative child behavior. (B.I.M.)

1977

Guillemin, Roger   325

PRIZE: Medicine and Physiology, 1977. BORN: January 11, 1924; Dijon, France. PARENTS: Father, Raymond Guillemin; Mother, Blanche Rigollot Guillemin. NATIONALITY: French; later American citizen. RELIGION: Agnostic; from Catholic background. EDUCATION: Univ. of Dijon, France, B.A., 1941; Univ. of Dijon, France, B.Sc., 1942; Faculty of Medicine, France, M.D., 1949; Univ. of Montreal, Canada, Ph.D., 1953. SPOUSE: Lucienne Jeanne Billard, married March 22, 1951. CHILDREN: Chantal, daughter; Francois, son; Claire, daughter; Helene, daughter; Elizabeth, daughter; Cecile, daughter. CAREER: Baylor Univ., Texas, Professor, 1953-70; Salk Institute, CA, Professor, 1970-. OTHER AWARDS: Bonneau and La Caze Awards, Académie des Sciences, 1957, 1960; Legion of Honor, France, 1974; Gairdner International Award, 1974; Lasker Foundation Award, 1975; Dickson Foundation Award, 1975; Dickson Prize, 1976; Passano Award, 1976; Schmitt Medal, 1977; National Medal of Science, USA, 1977; Barren Gold Medal, USA, 1979; Dale Medal, Society for Endocrinology, England, 1980.

Selected Publications: "Humoral Hypothalamic Control of the Anterior Pituitary. A Study which Combined Tissue Cultures." *Endocrinology* 57 (1955): 599 (with Barry Rosenberg). "Hypothalamic Control of the Anterior Pituitary, Study with Tissue Culture Techniques." *Federation Proceedings* 14 (1955): 211. "The Adenohypophysis and Its Hypothalamic Control." *Annual Review of Physiology* 29 (1967): 313. *The Hormones of the Hypothalamus.* San Francisco, CA: W.H. Freeman Co., 1972 (with R. Burgus). "Control of Adenohypophysial Functions by Peptides of the Central Nervous System." *The Harvey Lectures* 71 (1975-76). "Purification, Isolation, and Primary Structure of the Hypothalamic Luteinizing Hormone-releasing Factor of Ovine Origin—a Historical Account." *American Journal of Obstetrics and Gynecology* 129 (1977): 214. *The Brain as an Endocrine Organ.* Cambridge, MA: Massachusetts Institute of Technology Press, 1978. *Hypothalamic Control of Pituitary Functions: The Growth Hormone Releasing Factor.* Liverpool: Liverpool U. Press, 1985.

For More Information See: *The Nobel Duel.* New York: Doubleday, 1981. *Pioneers in Neuroendocrinology II.* New York: Plenum Press, 1978, 351. *Science* 198 (November 11, 1977): 594-95.

Commentary: Roger Guillemin was recognized, with his colaureates, for his work that "opened new vistas within biological and medical research far outside the border of their own spheres of interest." Guillemin's research, both with and independent of Andrew Schally, led to an understanding of the production of peptide hormones in the brain. The two identified and synthesized three brain hormones (thyrotropin-releasing factor, luteinizing-hormone releasing factor, and growth hormone inhibiting factor) that are used by the hypothalamus to direct the release of pituitary hormones. Research on understanding the brain's part in body chemistry and the understanding of the brain's role have been enormously increased as a result of their efforts. (R.K.)

Schally, Andrew Victor   326

PRIZE: Medicine and Physiology, 1977. BORN: November 30, 1926; Wilno, Poland. PARENTS: Father, Casimir Peter Schally; Mother, Maria Lacka Schally. NATIONALITY: Polish; later Canadian and American citizen. RELIGION: No record found. EDUCATION: McGill Univ., Canada, B.Sc., 1955; McGill Univ., Canada, Ph.D., 1957. SPOUSE: Margaret Rachel White, married May 14, 1956, divorced (no date found); Ana Maria de Medeiros Comaru, married August 1976. CHILDREN: Karen, daughter; Gordon, son. CAREER: Baylor Univ., Texas, Professor, 1957-62; VA Hospital, New Orleans, LA, Administrator, 1962-. OTHER AWARDS: Director's Award, VA Hospital, New Orleans, LA, 1968; Van Meter Prize, American Thyroid Association, 1969; Ayerst-Squibb Award, Endocrine Society, 1970; William S. Middleton Award, VA Hospital, New Orleans, LA, 1970; Charles Mickle Award, U. of Toronto, 1974; Gairdner International Award, 1974; Edward T. Tyler Award, 1975; Borden Award, Association of Medical Colleges and Borden Company Foundation, 1975; Lasker Award, 1975; Laude Award, 1975; Award, Spanish Pharmaceutical Society, 1977; Medal of Scientific Merit, Federal U. of Ceara, Brazil, 1977; First Diploma of Merit of St. Luke, Foundation of Social Pioneers, Rio de Janeiro, 1977.

Selected Publications: "The Release of Corticotropin by Anterior Pituitary Tissue in Vitro." *Canadian Journal of Biochemistry and Physiology* 33 (1955): 408 (with M. Saffran). "Stimulation of the Release of Corticotropin from the Adenohypophysis by a Neurohypophysial Factor." *Canadian Journal of Biochemistry and Physiology* 57 (1955): 439 (with M. Saffran). "Isolation of Thyrotropin Releasing Factor (TRF) from Porcine Hypothalamus." *Biochemical and Biophysical Research Communications* 25 (1966): 165 (with others). "Purification of Thyrotropic Hormone Releasing Factor from Bovine Hypothalamus." *Endocrinolgy* 78 (1966): 726 (with others). "The Amino Acid Sequence of a Peptide with Growth Hormone Releasing Activity Isolated from Porcine Hypothalamus." *Journal of Biological Chemistry* 246 (1971): 6647 (with others). *The Hypothalamus and Pituitary in Health and Disease.* Springfield, IL: Thomas, 1972 (with W. Locke).

For More Information See: *The Nobel Duel.* New York: Doubleday, 1981. *Pioneers in Neuroendocrinology II.* New York: Plenum Press, 1978, 351. *Science* 198 (November 11, 1977): 594-95.

Commentary: The Academy cited Andrew Schally and his colaureates for work that "opened new vistas within biological and medical research far outside the border of their own spheres of interest," specifically that research which contributed to the understanding of the production of peptide hormones in the brain. Schally identified and synthesized, along with his colaureate, Roger Guillemin, three brain hormones (thyrotropin-releasing factor, luteinizing-hormone-releasing factor, and growth hormone release inhibiting factor) that the hypothalamus uses to direct the release of pituitary hormones. The resultant understanding of the brain's role in body chemistry and the research therein has been enormously increased as a result of their efforts. (R.K.)

Yalow, Rosalyn Sussman   327

PRIZE: Medicine and Physiology, 1977. BORN: July 19, 1921; New York, NY. PARENTS: Father, Simon Sussman; Mother, Clara Zipper Sussman. NATIONALITY: American. RELIGION: Jewish. EDUCATION: Hunter College, NY, A.B., 1941; Univ. of Illinois, M.S., 1942; Univ. of Illinois, Ph.D., 1945. SPOUSE: A. Aaron Yalow, married June 6, 1943. CHILDREN: Benjamin, son; Elanna, daughter. CAREER: Hunter College, NY, Professor, 1946-50; VA Hospital, NY, Researcher and Administrator, 1950-80; Montefiore Medical Center, NY, Administrator, 1980-. OTHER AWARDS: William S. Middleton Medical Research Award, Veterans Administration, 1960; Eli Lilly Award, American Diabetes Association, 1961; Federal Woman's Award, 1961; Van Slyke Award, American Association of Clinical Chemists, 1968; Award, American College of Physicians, 1971; Dickson Prize, University of Pittsburgh, PA, 1971; Howard Taylor Ricketts Award, University of Chicago, IL, 1971; Gairdner Foundation International Award, 1971; Commemorative Medallion, American Diabetes Association, 1972; Koch Award, Endocrine Society, 1972; Bernstein Award, Medical Society of the State of New York, 1974; Boehringer-Manheim Corporation Award, American Association of Clinical Chemists, 1975; Science Achievement Award, American Medical Association, 1975; Exceptional Service Award, Veterans Administration, 1975; A. Cressy Morrison Award, New York Academy of Sciences, 1975; Distinguished Achievement Award, Modern Medicine, 1976; Lasker Award, 1976; La Madonnina International Prize, Milan, 1977; Golden Plate Award, American Academy Achievement, 1977; G. von Hevesy Medal, 1978; Rosalyn S. Yalow Research and Development Award, American Diabetes Association, 1978; Banting Medal, 1978; Torch of Learning Award, American Friends of Hebrew University, 1978; Virchow Gold Medal, Virchow-Pirquet Medical Society, 1978; Gratum Genus Humanum Gold Medal, World Federation of Nuclear Medicine or Biology, 1978; Jacobi Medallion, Mount Sinai School of Medicine, 1978; Jubilee Medal, College of New Rochelle, 1978; Exceptional Service Award, Veterans Administration, 1978; Sarasota Medical Award, 1979; Gold Medal, Phi Lambda Kappa, 1980; Achievement in Life Award, Encyclopedia Britannica, 1980; Theobald Smith Award, 1982; John and Samuel Bard Award, Bard College, 1982; Distinguished Research Award, Dallas Association of Retarded Citizens, 1982.

Selected Publications: *Peptide Hormones.* New York: American Elsevier, 1973 (with S.A. Berson). *Methods in Radioimmunoassay of Peptide Hormones.* New York: American Elsevier, 1976. *Basic Research and Clinical Medicine.* New York: McGraw-Hill, 1981 (with others). *Radioimmunoassay.* New York: Van Nostrand-Reinhold, 1984.

For More Information See: *Current Biography Yearbook.* New York: H.W. Wilson, 1978, 458-60. "Madame Curie from the Bronx." *New York Times Magazine* (April 9, 1978): 29-31+.

Commentary: Rosalyn Yalow shared the Nobel for her contributions to the discovery and development of radioimmunoassay, a technique which employs radioactive isotopes to detect and measure the levels of insulin and hormones in the blood and body tissues. Yalow's work indicated that diabetes in adults led to an increase of the insulin level, but the sugar-metabolizing action of the insulin was blocked. Radioimmunoassays have been used to test donors' blood for hepatitis virus; to test antibiotic action; and to diagnose thyroid disease, hypertension, hormone-secreting cancers, drug abuse, reproductive failures, and other growth disorders. (R.K.)

1978

Arber, Werner   328

PRIZE: Medicine and Physiology, 1978. BORN: June 3, 1929; Granichen, Switzerland. PARENTS: Father, Julius Arber; Mother, Maria Arber. NATIONALITY: Swiss. RELIGION: Protestant. EDUCATION: Univ. of Geneva, Switzerland, Ph.D., 1958. SPOUSE: Antonia, married June 3, 1966. CHILDREN: Silvia, daughter; Caroline, daughter. CAREER: Univ. of Southern California, Researcher, 1958-59; Univ. of Geneva, Switzerland, Professor, 1960-70; Univ. of Basel, Switzerland, Professor, 1970-.

Selected Publications: "Biological Specificities of Deoxyribonucleic Acid." *Pathol. Microbiol.* 25 (1962): 668-81. "Host-Controlled Restriction and Modification of Bacteriophage." *Symp. Soc. Gen. Microbiol.* 18 (1968): 295-314. "DNA Modification and Restriction." *Prog. Nucleic Acid Res. Mol. Biol.* 14 (1974): 1-37. *Genetic Manipulation: Impact on Men and Society.* New York: Cambridge U. Press, 1984.

For More Information See: *Asimov's Biographical Encyclopedia of Science and Technology.* Garden City, NY: Doubleday, 888-89. *Science* 202 (December 8, 1978): 1069-71.

Commentary: Werner Arber shared the Nobel Prize for his contributions to "the discovery of restriction enzymes and their application to problems of molecular genetics." Arber began to research the molecular basis of the host-controlled variation among bacterial viruses and found that modification involved DNA changes and restriction DNA degradation. His model, later experimentally confirmed, stated that DNA contained specific sites recognizable and cleavable by restriction endonucleases with specificities characteristic of the bacterial strain. The bacterium can methylate within the DNA molecule, protecting it from cleavage, but producing modification. Arber's colaureates (and others) extended his work. (R.K.)

Nathans, Daniel 329

PRIZE: Medicine and Physiology, 1978. BORN: October 30, 1928; Wilmington, DE. PARENTS: Father, Samuel Nathans; Mother, Sarah Levitan Nathans. NATIONALITY: American. RELIGION: Jewish. EDUCATION: Univ. of Delaware, B.S., 1950; Washington Univ., MO, M.D., 1954. SPOUSE: Joanne E. Gomberg, married March 4, 1956. CHILDREN: Eli, son; Jeremy, son; Benjamin, son. CAREER: Columbia Presbyterian Medical Center, NY, Physician, 1954-59; Rockefeller Univ., NY, Professor, 1959-62; Johns Hopkins Univ., MD, Professor and Administrator, 1962-.

Selected Publications: "Purification of a Supernatant Factor That Stimulates Amino Acid Transfer from Soluble Ribonucleic Acid to Protein." *Annals of the New York Academy of Sciences* 88 (1960): 718-21. "Cell-free Protein Synthesis Directed by Coliphage MS2 RNA: Synthesis of Intact Viral Coat Protein and Other Products." *Journal of Molecular Biology* 13 (1965): 521-31. "Natural RNA Coding of Bacterial Protein Synthesis." *Methods of Enzymology* 12 (1968): 787-91. "Restriction Endonucleases in the Analysis and Restructuring of DNA Molecules." *Annual Review of Biochemistry* 44 (1975): 273-93 (with H. O. Smith).

For More Information See: *Biographical Encyclopedia of Scientists.* New York: Facts on File, 1981, 584-85. *Science* 202 (December 8, 1978): 1069-71.

Commentary: Daniel Nathans shared the Nobel Prize for his contribution to the "development of restriction endonucleases, enzymes that can be used to study genetic organization and to manipulate DNA for genetic engineering." Nathans used restriction enzymes to break up the monkey cancer virus SV40 and was able to map the SV40 genes. His techniques were used by others to map various DNA molecules. Nathans also described other possible applications, including the recombinant DNA technique that was the subject of much controversy about potential dangers and benefits in the world's scientific community. (A.D.)

Smith, Hamilton Othanel 330

PRIZE: Medicine and Physiology, 1978. BORN: August 23, 1931; New York, NY. PARENTS: Father, Tommie Harkey Smith; Mother, Bunnie Othanel Smith. NATIONALITY: American. RELIGION: From Baptist background. EDUCATION: Univ. of California, A.B., 1952; Johns Hopkins Univ., MD, M.D., 1956. SPOUSE: Elizabeth Anne Bolton, married May 25, 1957. CHILDREN: Joel, son; Barry, son; Dirk, son; Kirsten, daughter; Bryan, son. CAREER: Barnes Hospital, MO, Physician, 1956-57; U.S. Navy, 1957-59; Henry Ford Hospital, MI, Physician, 1959-62; Univ. of Michigan, Researcher, 1962-67; Johns Hopkins Univ., MD, Professor, 1967-. OTHER AWARDS: Guggenheim Fellow, 1975-76.

Selected Publications: "A Restriction Enzyme from Hemophilus Influenzae: I. Purification and General Properties." *Journal of Molecular Biology* 51 (1970): 379 (with K.W. Wilcox). "A Restriction Enzyme from Hemophilus Influenzae: II. Base Sequence of the Recognition Site." *Journal of Molecular Biology* 51 (1970): 393. "Restriction Endonucleases in the Analysis and Restructuring of DNA Molecules." *Annual Review of Biochemistry* 44 (1975): 273-93 (with D. Nathans).

For More Information See: *Biographical Encyclopedia of Scientists.* New York: Facts on File, 1981, 737-38. *Science* 202 (December 8, 1978): 1069-71.

Commentary: The Academy cited Hamilton Smith for his research on "the discovery of restriction enzymes and their application to problems of molecular genetics." Smith purified and characterized the first specific restriction endonuclease, from Hemophilus influenzae. He also interested his colaureate, Daniel Nathans, in applying the restriction enzyme in "chopping" experiments and supplied the requisite endonuclease to him. (R.K.)

1979

Cormack, Allan MacLeod 331

PRIZE: Medicine and Physiology, 1979. BORN: February 23, 1924; Johannesburg, South Africa. PARENTS: Father, George Cormack; Mother, Amelia MacLeod Cormack. NATIONALITY: South African; later American citizen. RELIGION: Most probably Christian. EDUCATION: Univ. of Cape Town, South Africa, B.Sc., 1944; Univ. of Cape Town, South Africa, M. Sc., 1945. SPOUSE: Barbara Jeanne Seavey, married January 6, 1950. CHILDREN: Margaret Jean, daughter; Jean Barbara, daughter; Robert Allan Seavey, Jr., son. CAREER: Univ. of Cape Town, Rondebosch, South Africa, Professor, 1946-56; Harvard Univ., MA, Researcher, 1956-57; Tufts Univ., MA, Professor, 1957-. OTHER AWARDS: Ballou Medal, Tufts U., 1978; Honorable Mention, Swedish Radiological Society, 1979; Medal of Merit, U. of Cape Town, South Africa, 1980.

Selected Publications: "Representation of a Function by Its Line Integrals, with Some Radiological Applications." *Journal of Applied Physics* 34 (September 1963): 2722-27. "Representation of a Function by Its Line Integrals, with Some Radiological Applications II. *Journal of Applied Physics* 35 (October 1964): 2908-13. "Small-Angle Scattering of 143-mev Polarized Protons." *Nuclear Physics* 56 (1964): 46-64 (with J.N. Palmieri and D.J. Steinberg). "Measurement of Cross Sections with Neutrons as Targets." *Physical Review* 138 (1965): 823-30 (with M.W. Shapiro and A. M. Koehler).

For More Information See: *Physics Today* 32 (December 1979): 19-20. *Science* 206 (November 30, 1979): 1060-62.

Commentary: The Nobel Prize was awarded to Allan Cormack for his contributions to "the invention of the x-ray diagnostic technique, computerized axial tomography." Cormack developed the equations necessary for image reconstruction, the process in which x-ray projections of a sample taken at a variety of different angles are combined, using the computer, to reconstruct the image being viewed. Computer-assisted tomography (CAT) has become a most valuable addition to medical diagnostic techniques. (R.K.)

Hounsfield, Godfrey Newbold, Sir 332

PRIZE: Medicine and Physiology, 1979. BORN: August 28, 1919; Newark, England. PARENTS: Father, Thomas Hounsfield; Mother, no record found. NATIONALITY: British. RELIGION: Most probably Christian. EDUCATION: City and Guilds College, England, Radio Communications Qualification, 1938; Faraday House Electrical Engineering College, England, Degree in Electrical and Mechanical Engineering, 1951. SPOUSE: None. CHILDREN: None. CAREER: Thorn EMI Limited, Middlesex, England, Researcher and Administrator, 1951-. OTHER AWARDS: MacRobert Award, 1972; Barclay Prize, British Institute of Radiology, 1974; Wilhelm Exner Medal, Austrian Industrial Association, 1974; Ziedses des Plantes Medal, Physikalisch-Medizinische Gesellschaft, Würzburg, Germany, 1974; Prince Philip Medal Award, City and Guilds of London Institute, 1975; ANS Radiation Award, Georgia Institute of Technology, 1975; Lasker Award, 1975; Duddell Bronze Medal, Institute of Physics, 1976; Golden Plate Award, American Academy of Achievement, 1976; Churchill Gold Medal, 1976; Gairdner Foundation Award, 1976; Reginald Mitchell Gold Medal, Stoke-on-Trent Association of Engineers, 1976; Ambrogino d'Oro Award, City of Milan, 1980; Deutsche Roentgen Plakette, Deutsche Roentgen Museum, 1980.

Selected Publications: "Magnetic Films for Information Storage." *British Patent 1083673* (September 20, 1967) (with P.H. Brown). "Computerized Transverse Axial Scanning (Tomography)." *British Journal of Radiology* 46 (1973): 1016.

For More Information See: *Current Biography Yearbook.* New York: H.W. Wilson, 1980, 153-55. *Physics Today* 32 (December 1979): 19-20. *Science* 206 (November 30, 1979): 1060-62.

Commentary: Godfrey Hounsfield shared the Nobel Prize for his contributions "to the development of the x-ray scanning system, computerized axial tomography." Hounsfield designed the apparatus that would permit image reconstruction, the process in which x-ray projections of a sample taken at a variety of different angles are combined, using the computer, to reconstruct the image being viewed. The process has revolutionized medical diagnostic techniques employing x-ray methods. Hounsfield was also responsible for significant developments in radar systems, computer design, and large-capacity memory storage in computers, and continues his research in noninvasive medical diagnostic techniques. (R.K.)

1980

Benacerraf, Baruj   333
PRIZE: Medicine and Physiology, 1980. BORN: October 29, 1920; Caracas, Venezuela. PARENTS: Father, Abraham Benacerraf; Mother, Henrietta Lasry Benacerraf. NATIONALITY: Venezuelan; later American citizen. RELIGION: No organized religion; from Jewish background. EDUCATION: Lycée Janson, France, baccalaureate, 1940; Columbia Univ., NY, B.S., 1942; Medical College of Virginia, M.D., 1945. SPOUSE: Annette Dreyfus, married March 24, 1943. CHILDREN: Beryl, daughter. CAREER: Queens General Hospital, NY, Physician, 1945-46; United States Army, 1946-48; Columbia Univ., NY, Researcher, 1948-50; Centre National de Recherche Scientique, France, Administrator, 1950-56; New York Univ., Professor, 1956-68; National Institutes of Health, MD, Administrator, 1968-70; Harvard Univ., MA, Professor and Administrator, 1970-. OTHER AWARDS: Rabbi Shai Schacknai Prize, Hebrew U. of Jerusalem, 1974; T. Duckett Jones Memorial Award, Helen Jay Whitney Foundation, 1976; Waterford Award, 1980.

Selected Publications: "Studies on Hypersensitivity. III. The Relation between Delayed Reactivity to the Picryl Group of Conjugates and Contact Sensitivity." *Immunology* 2 (1959): 219-29 (with P.G.H. Gell). "Studies on Hypersensitivity. IV. The Relation between Contact and Delayed Sensitivity: A Study on the Specificity of Cellular Immune Reactions." *Journal of Experimental Medicine* 113 (1961): 571-85 (with P.G.H. Gell). "Antigenicity of Altered Autologous Proteins, a Mechanism of Autoimmune Reactions." *Annals of the New York Academy of Sciences* 124 (1965): 126-32. *Textbook of Immunology.* Baltimore, MD: Williams and Wilkins, 1979. *Immunogenetics and Immune Regulation.* New York: Masson Publications, 1982.

For More Information See: *New York Times Biographical Service* (October 1980): 1358-59. *Science* 210 (November 7, 1980): 621-23.

Commentary: Baruj Benacerraf shared the Nobel Prize for his contributions to the explanation of the "genetically determined structures of the cell surface that regulate immunological reactions." Benacerraf found that the genes located in the major histocompatibility complex (MHC), which plays a major role in transplant rejection, control the immune cell interactions that are responsible for a human immune response. Benacerraf continues to research the complex system needed for controlling immune responses. (R.K.)

Dausset, Jean Baptiste Gabriel Joachim   334
PRIZE: Medicine and Physiology, 1980. BORN: October 19, 1916; Toulouse, France. PARENTS: Father, Henri Pierre Jules Dausset; Mother, Elizabeth Brullard Dausset. NATIONALITY: French. RELIGION: Agnostic; most probably from Christian background. EDUCATION: Univ. of Paris, France, M.D., 1943. SPOUSE: Rosita Mayoral Lopez, married March 17, 1962. CHILDREN: Enric, son; Irene, daughter. CAREER: National Blood Transfusion Center, France, Administrator, 1946-63; Univ. of Paris, France, Professor, 1958-77; Collége de France, Professor, 1977-. OTHER AWARDS: Grand Prix Scientifique, Ville de Paris, 1970; Stratton Lecture Award, International Hematology Society, 1970; Karl Landsteiner Award, American Association of Blood Banks, 1971; Gairdner Foundation Prize, 1977; Koch Foundation Prize, 1978; Wolf Foundation Prize, 1978.

Selected Publications: *Immuno-Hematologie Biologique et Clinique.* Paris: Flammarion, 1956. *Tissue Typing.* New York: S. Karger, 1966. *Advances in Transplantation.* New York: Williams and Wilkins, 1968. *Human Transplantation.* Orlando, FL: Grune and Stratton, 1968. *Tissue Typing Today.* Orlando, FL: Grune and Stratton, 1971. *Histocompatibility Testing.* New York: Williams and Wilkins, 1973. *Histocompatibility.* San Diego, CA: Academic Press, 1976 (with G. Snell and S. Nathanson). *Immunology.* New York: Academic Press, 1980 (with M. Fougereau). *A Modern Illustration of Experimental Medicine in Action.* New York: Elsevier/North-Holland, 1980 (with Felix Rapaport).

For More Information See: *Current Biography Yearbook.* New York: H.W. Wilson, 1981, 108-11. *Science* 210 (November 7, 1980): 621-23.

Commentary: Jean Dausset received the Nobel Prize for work that led to the explanation of "the genetically determined structures of the cell surface that regulate immunological reactions." Dausset first established the existence in humans of the major histocompatibility complex (MHC), which plays a major role in transplant rejection, and led the way to more success in organ transplants, as well as to research on individual susceptibility to infections, diseases, and tumors. His research stemmed from his previous work with blood-replacement transfusion methods. He was also responsible for developing later systems for classification of antigens. (R.K.)

Snell, George Davis 335

PRIZE: Medicine and Physiology, 1980. BORN: December 13, 1903; Bradford, MA. PARENTS: Father, Cullen Bryant Snell; Mother, Katherine Davis Snell. NATIONALITY: American. RELIGION: Congregationalist. EDUCATION: Dartmouth College, NH, B.S., 1926; Harvard Univ., MA, M.S., 1928; Harvard Univ., MA, Sc.D., 1930. SPOUSE: Rhoda Carson, married July 28, 1937. CHILDREN: Thomas Carleton, son; Roy Carson, son; Peter Garland, son. CAREER: Dartmouth College, NH, Professor, 1929-30; Brown Univ., RI, Professor, 1930-31; Univ. of Texas, Researcher, 1931-33; Washington Univ., MO, Professor, 1933-35; Jackson Laboratory, Bar Harbor, ME, Researcher, 1935-69. OTHER AWARDS: Bertner Foundation Award, 1962; Griffin Award, Animal Care Panel, 1962; Gregor Mendel Award, Czechoslovak Academy of Sciences, 1967; Gairdner Foundation Award, 1976; Wolf Prize, 1978; Award, National Institute for Arthritis and Infectious Disease, National Cancer Institute, 1978.

Selected Publications: *The Biology of the Laboratory Mouse.* Philadelphia, PA: The Blakiston Co., 1941. *Cell Surface Antigens: Studies in Mammals Other Than Man.* New York: MSS Information Corporation, 1973 (with others). *Genetic and Biological Aspects of Histocompatibility Antigens.* Copenhagen: Munksgaard, 1973 (with others). *Histocompatibility.* New York: Academic Press, 1976 (with J. Dausset and S. Nathanson).

For More Information See: *New York Times Biographical Service* (October 1980): 1467. *Science* 210 (November 7, 1980): 621-23.

Commentary: The Nobel Prize was awarded to George Snell for his work on the "genetically determined structures of the cell surface that regulate immunological reactions." Snell's research started with the x-ray induction of mutations in mice and progressed to the breeding of congenic mice, mice that are genetically identical except for a single genetic region. Snell found 10 loci that controlled graft resistance, but one (named Histocompatibility II or H-2) was paramount in determining graft acceptance. It later came to be known as the major histocompatibility complex (MHC), worked on by his colaureates as well. (R.K.)

1981

Hubel, David Hunter 336

PRIZE: Medicine and Physiology, 1981. BORN: February 27, 1926; Windsor, Ontario, Canada. PARENTS: Father, Jesse Hervey Hubel; Mother, Elsie M. Hunter Hubel. NATIONALITY: Canadian; later American citizen. RELIGION: Most probably Christian/Protestant. EDUCATION: McGill Univ., Canada, B.Sc., 1947; McGill Univ., Canada, M.D., 1951. SPOUSE: Shirley Ruth Izzard, married June 20, 1953. CHILDREN: Carl Andrew, son; Eric David, son; Paul Matthew, son. CAREER: Montreal Neurological Institute, Canada, Physician, 1952-54; Johns Hopkins Univ., MD, Physician, 1954-59; Harvard Univ., MA, Professor, 1959-. OTHER AWARDS: Trustees Research to Prevent Blindness Award, 1971; Lewis S. Rosenstiel Award, Brandeis U., MA, 1972;

Friedenwald Award, Association for Research in Vision and Ophthalmology, 1975; Karl Spencer Lashley Prize, American Philosophical Society, 1977; Louisa Gross Horowitz Prize, Columbia U., NY, 1978; Dickson Prize, U. of Pittsburgh, PA, 1979; Ledie Prize, Harvard U., MA, 1980.

Selected Publications: "Receptive Fields of Single Neurones in the Cat's Striate Cortex." *Journal of Physiology* 148 (1959): 574-91 (with T.N. Wiesel). "Receptive Fields, Binocular Interaction and Functional Architecture in the Cat's Visual Cortex." *Journal of Physiology* 160 (1962): 106-54 (with T.N. Wiesel). "Receptive Fields and Functional Architecture in Two Nonstriate Visual Areas (18 and 19) of the Cat." *Journal of Neurophysiology* 28 (1965): 229-89 (with T.N. Wiesel). "Receptive Fields and Functional Architecture of Monkey Striate Cortex." *Journal of Physiology* 195 (1968): 215-43 (with T. N. Wiesel). "The Visual Cortex of Normal and Deprived Monkeys." *American Scientist* 67 (1979): 532-43.

For More Information See: *New York Times Biographical Service* (October 1981): 1362. *Science* 214 (October 30, 1981): 518-20.

Commentary: David Hubel was honored by the Academy for his work on "information processing in the visual system." He discovered, with his fellow laureate Torsten Wiesel, that each neuron in the visual system responds best to a particular stimulus and that a complicated arrangement of cells operates to make vision work. In related research, the team made discoveries relating to binocular vision and the importance of early visual stimulation for proper development. (P.P.H.)

Sperry, Roger Wolcott 337

PRIZE: Medicine and Physiology, 1981. BORN: August 20, 1913; Hartford, CT. PARENTS: Father, Francis Bushnell Sperry; Mother, Florence Kramer Sperry. NATIONALITY: American. RELIGION: Christian. EDUCATION: Oberlin College, OH, B.A., 1935; Oberlin College, OH, M.A., 1937; Univ. of Chicago, IL, Ph.D., 1941. SPOUSE: Norma G. Deupree, married December 28, 1949. CHILDREN: Glen Tad, son; Janeth Hope, daughter. CAREER: Harvard Univ., MA, Researcher, 1941-46; Univ. of Chicago, IL, Professor, 1946-53; California Institute of Technology, Professor, 1954-. OTHER AWARDS: Oberlin College Alumni Citation, 1954; Howard Crosby Warren Medal, Society for Experimental Psychology, 1969; Distinguished Scientist/Contribution Award, American Psychological Association, 1971; California Scientist of the Year, 1972; William Thomas Wakeman Research Award, National Paraplegic Foundation, 1972; Passano Foundation Award, 1972; Claude Bernard Science Journalism Award, 1975; Karl Lashley Award, American Philosophical Society, 1976; Albert Lasker Award, 1979; Ralph Gerard Prize, 1979; Wolf Foundation Prize, 1979.

Selected Publications: "Neurology and the Mind-Brain Problem." *American Scientist* 40 (1952): 291. "On the Neural Basis of the Conditioned Response." *British Journal of Animal Behavior* 3 (1955): 41. "Cerebral Organization and Behavior." *Science* 133 (1961): 1749. "Chemoaffinity in the Orderly Growth of Nerve Fiber Patterns of Connection." *Proceedings of the National Academy of Sciences U.S.A.* 50 (1963): 703. "Mental Unity Following Surgical Disconnection of the Cerebral Hemispheres." *Harvey Lectures* 62 (1968): 293-322. *Science and Moral Priority.* New York: Columbia U. Press, 1983.

For More Information See: *Current Biography Yearbook.* New York: H.W. Wilson, 1986, 53-56. *Science* 214 (October 30, 1981): 517-18.

Commentary: Roger Sperry was cited by the Academy for his split-brain research that separated and identified the functions of the left and right hemispheres of the brain. However, the Nobel Prize also recognized Sperry's relentless pursuit over 40 years for a better understanding of the conscious processes and functions of the human brain through studies in at least three major areas: developmental neurobiology, experimental psychobiology, and human split-brain studies. His later research concentrated on the emotional and social components of the two-sided brain. (D.T.)

Wiesel, Torsten N.   338

PRIZE: Medicine and Physiology, 1981. BORN: June 3, 1924; Uppsala, Sweden. PARENTS: Father, Fritz Samuel Wiesel; Mother, Anna-Lisa Elisabet Bentzer Wiesel. NATIONALITY: Swedish; later American citizen. RELIGION: From Protestant background. EDUCATION: Karolinska Institute, Sweden, M.D., 1954. SPOUSE: Ann Grace Yee, married (no date found). CHILDREN: Sara Elisabet, daughter. CAREER: Karalinska Institute, Sweden, Professor, 1954-55; Johns Hopkins Univ., MD, Professor, 1955-59; Harvard Univ., MA, Professor, 1959-83; Rockefeller Univ., NY, Professor, 1983-. OTHER AWARDS: Jules Stein Award, Trustees for Prevention of Blindness, 1971; Lewis S. Rosenstiel Prize, Brandeis U., MA, 1972; Friedenwald Award, Trustees of Association for Research in Vision and Ophthalmology, 1975; Lashley Prize, American Philosophical Society, 1977; Louisa Gross Horowitz Prize, Columbia U., NY, 1978; Dickson Prize, U. of Pittsburgh, PA, 1979.

Selected Publications: "Receptive Fields of Single Neurones in the Cat's Striate Cortex." *Journal of Physiology* 148 (1959): 574-91 (with D. H. Hubel). "Receptive Fields, Binocular Interaction and Functional Architecture in the Cat's Visual Cortex." *Journal of Physiology* 160 (1962): 106-54 (with D.H. Hubel). "Receptive Fields and Functional Architecture in Two Nonstriate Visual Areas (18 and 19) of the Cat." *Journal of Neurophysiology* 28 (1965): 229-89 (with D.H. Hubel). "Receptive Fields and Functional Architecture of Monkey Striate Cortex." *Journal of Physiology* 195 (1968): 215-43 (with D. H. Hubel). "Anatomical Demonstration of Orientation Columns in Macaque Monkey." *Journal of Comparative Neurology* 177 (1978): 361-80 (with D.H. Hubel and M.P. Stryker).

For More Information See: *New York Times Biographical Service* (October 1981): 1451. *Science* 214 (October 30, 1981): 518-20.

Commentary: Torsten Wiesel shared the Nobel Prize for his work on "information processing in the visual system." With his fellow laureate, D.H. Hubel, he demonstrated that individual neurons respond to specific stimuli and that the cells are organized in columns. Studies of the "ocular dominance columns" showed that the visual response is better to stimulation presented to the dominant eye. Wiesel and Hubel also related ocular dominance to early visual stimulation. (P.P.H.)

1982

Bergström, Sune   339

PRIZE: Medicine and Physiology, 1982. BORN: January 10, 1916; Stockholm, Sweden. PARENTS: Father, Sverker Bergström; Mother, Wera Wistrand Bergström. NATIONALITY: Swedish. RELIGION: Most probably Christian. EDUCATION: Karolinska Institute, Sweden, D.Med.Sci., 1944; Karolinska Institute, Sweden, M.D., 1944. SPOUSE: Maj Gernandt, married July 30, 1943. CHILDREN: 1 son. CAREER: Columbia Univ., NY, Researcher, 1940-41; Squibb Institute, NJ, Researcher, 1941-42; Nobel Institute, Stockholm, Sweden, Researcher, 1942-46; Basel Univ., Switzerland, Researcher, 1946-47; Univ. of Lund, Sweden, Professor, 1947-58; Karolinska Institute, Sweden, Professor and Administrator, 1958-. OTHER AWARDS: Louisa Gross Horowitz Prize, Columbia U., NY, 1975; Lasker Award, 1977.

Selected Publications: *Prostaglandins: Proceedings of the Second Nobel Symposium, Stockholm, June 1966.* New York: Interscience Publishers, 1967 (with Bengt Samuelsson). *Third Conference on Prostaglandins in Fertility Control, January 17-20, 1972.* Stockholm: Karolinska Institutet, 1972 (with K. Green and B. Samuelsson). *Report from the Meeting of the Prostaglandin Task Force Steering Committee, Chapel Hill, June 8-10, 1972, Stockholm, October 2-3, 1972, Geneva, February 26-28, 1973.* Stockholm: Karolinska Institutet, 1973. *Prostacyclin.* New York: Raven Press, 1979 (with John R. Vane).

For More Information See: *New Scientist* 96 (November 14, 1982): 82-83. *Science* 218 (November 19, 1982): 765-68.

Commentary: Sune Bergström won the Nobel Prize for his work on the "discoveries concerning prostaglandins and related biologically active substances." Bergström's work began when he found that exceedingly small amounts of the prostaglandins investigated by Ulf von Euler retained very high activity on muscles and in lowering blood pressure. He succeeded later in the isolation and characterization of the structures of the prostaglandins and in the determination that their biosynthetic origin was arachidonic acid. The availability of prostaglandins for research greatly stimulated this field. (R.K.)

Samuelsson, Bengt Ingemar   340

PRIZE: Medicine and Physiology, 1982. BORN: May 21, 1934; Halmstedt, Sweden. PARENTS: Father, Anders Samuelsson; Mother, Stina Samuelsson. NATIONALITY: Swedish. RELIGION: No record found. EDUCATION: Karolinska Institute, Sweden, D. Med. Sci., 1960; Karolinska Institute, Sweden, M.D., 1961. SPOUSE: Inga Karin Bergstein, married August 19, 1958. CHILDREN: Bo, son; Elisabeth, daughter; Astrid, daughter. CAREER: Karolinska Institute, Sweden, Professor and Administrator, 1961-. OTHER AWARDS: A. Jahres Award, Oslo U., 1970; Louisa Gross Horowitz Prize, Columbia U., 1975; Lasker Award, 1977.

Selected Publications: *Prostaglandins: Proceedings of the Second Nobel Symposium, Stockholm, June 1966.* New York: Interscience Publishers, 1967 (with S. Bergstrom). *Third Conference on Prostaglandins in Fertility Control, January 17-20, 1972.* Stockholm: Karolinska Institutet, 1972 (with K. Green and S. Bergstrom).

For More Information See: *New Scientist* 96 (November 14, 1982): 82-83. *Science* 218 (November 19, 1982): 765-68.

Commentary: Bengt Samuelsson was awarded the Nobel Prize for his efforts in the "discoveries concerning prostaglandins and related biologically active substances." Samuelsson, working along with his co-laureate Sune Bergström, was given credit for structural work, for the detailed description of the role of arachidonic acid, and for clarifying the biosynthetic process that produced the prostaglandins. Samuelsson also discovered thromboxanes, which help blood to clot, and leukotrienes, involved in asthma. (R.K.)

Vane, John Robert   341

PRIZE: Medicine and Physiology, 1982. BORN: March 29, 1927; Tardebigg, Worcestershire, England. PARENTS: Father, Maurice Vane; Mother, Frances Florence Fisher Vane. NATIONALITY: British. RELIGION: Most probably Christian. EDUCATION: Univ. of Birmingham, England, B.Sc., 1946; Oxford Univ., England, B.Sc., 1949; Oxford Univ., England, D.Phil., 1953. SPOUSE: Elizabeth Daphne Page, married April 4, 1948. CHILDREN: Nicola, daughter; Miranda, daughter. CAREER: Yale Univ., CT, Professor, 1953-55; Univ. of London, England, Professor, 1955-73; Wellcome Laboratories, England, Researcher and Administrator, 1973-. OTHER AWARDS: Lasker Award, 1977; Baly Medal, Royal College of Physicians, 1977; Peter Debye Prize, U. of Maastricht, Netherlands, 1980; Feldberg Foundation Prize, 1980; Ciba Geigy Drew Award, Drew U., NJ, 1980; Dale Medal, Society of Endocrinology, 1981; Galen Medal, Apothecaries' Society, 1983; Biological Council Medal, 1983; Louis Pasteur Foundation Prize, CA, 1984.

Selected Publications: *Prostaglandin Synthetase Inhibitors—Their Effects on Physiological Functions and Pathological States.* New York: Raven Press, 1974 (with H. Robinson). *Metabolic Functions of the Lung.* New York: Dekker, 1977 (with Y.S. Bakhle). *Inflammation.* New York: Springer Verlag, 1978 (with S.H. Ferreira). *Anti-Inflammatory Drugs.* New York: Springer Verlag, 1979. *Prostacyclin.* New York: Raven Press, 1979 (with S. Bergstrom). *Interactions Between Platelets and Vessel Walls.* Great Neck, NY: Scholium International, 1981 (with G.V.R. Bonn). *Prostacyclin in Health and Disease.* Edinburgh: Royal College of Physicians, 1982.

For More Information See: *New Scientist* 96 (November 14, 1982): 82-83. *Science* 218 (November 19, 1982): 765-68.

Commentary: John Vane shared the Nobel for his contributions to the "discoveries concerning prostaglandins and related biologically active substances." Vane used the dynamic bioassay method he had developed working with the angiotensins to differentiate the various prostaglandins. He investigated prostaglandin release during anaphylaxis in perfused guinea pig lung and then demonstrated that the release of a contracting substance could be halted with anti-inflammatory drugs. Vane's explanation that aspirin and related drugs acted by inhibiting arachidonic acid conversion to prostaglandins stimulated extensive research on the role of prostaglandins in all sorts of biological systems. (R.K.)

1983

McClintock, Barbara   342

PRIZE: Medicine and Physiology, 1983. BORN: June 16, 1902; Hartford, CT. PARENTS: Father, Thomas Henry McClintock; Mother, Sara Handy McClintock. NATIONALITY: American. RELIGION: Congregationalist. EDUCATION: Cornell Univ., NY, B.S., 1923; Cornell Univ., NY, M.A., 1925; Cornell Univ., NY, Ph.D., 1927. SPOUSE: None. CHILDREN: None. CAREER: Cornell Univ., NY, Researcher, 1924-31; California Institute of Technology, Researcher, 1931-33; Univ. of Freiburg, Germany, Researcher, 1933-34; Cornell Univ., NY, Researcher, 1934-36; Univ. of Missouri, Professor, 1936-41; Carnegie Institution of Washington at Cold Spring Harbor Laboratory, NY, Researcher, 1941-85. OTHER AWARDS: Kimber Award, National Academy of Sciences, 1967; National Medal of Science, 1970; Rosenstiel Award, 1978; Lasker Award, 1978; Wolf Foundation Prize, Israel, 1981; Horowitz Prize, Columbia U., 1982.

Selected Publications: "A Correlation of Cytological and Genetical Crossing Over in Zea Mays." *Proceedings of the National Academy of Sciences* 17 (August 1931): 492-97 (with H. Creighton). "The Relation of a Particular Chromosomal Element to the Development of the Nucleoli in Zea Mays." *A. Zellforsch. U. Mikr. Anat* 21 (1934): 294-328. "Mutable Loci in Maize." *Carnegie Institution of Washington Yearbook* 48 (1949): 142-43.

For More Information See: *Current Biography Yearbook.* New York: H.W. Wilson, 1984, 262-65. Keller, E. *A Feeling for the Organism: The Life and Work of Barbara McClintock.* San Francisco, CA: Freeman, 1983.

Commentary: Barbara McClintock received the Nobel Prize for "discovery of mobile genetic elements of profound importance for our understanding of the organization and function of genes. She carried out this research alone and at a time when her contemporaries were not yet able to realize the generality and significance of her findings." Her early experiments proved that chromosomes exchange genetic information and physical material in crossing over during cell division. Her later work on corn showed that portions of DNA that control other genes can move between chromosome sites. (R.K.)

1984

Jerne, Niels Kaj   343

PRIZE: Medicine and Physiology, 1984. BORN: December 23, 1911; London, England. PARENTS: Father, Hans Jessen Jerne; Mother, Else Marie Lindberg Jerne. NATIONALITY: British; later Danish and Swiss resident. RELIGION: Most probably Christian. EDUCATION: Univ. of Copenhagen, Denmark, doctorate in medicine, 1951. SPOUSE: Ursula Alexandra Kohl, married 1964. CHILDREN: 2 sons. CAREER: Danish State Serum Institute, Researcher, 1943-56; California Institute of Technology, Researcher, 1954-55; World Health Organization, Geneva, Switzerland, Chief Medical Officer, 1956-62; Univ. of Pittsburgh, PA, Administrator, 1962-66; Paul Ehrlich Institute, Frankfurt, Germany, Director, 1966-69; Basel Institute for Immunology,

Switzerland, Director, 1969-. OTHER AWARDS: Marcel Benorst Prize, Berne, Switzerland, 1979; Paul Ehrlich Prize, Frankfurt, Germany, 1982.

Selected Publications: "Immunological Speculation." *Annual Review of Microbiology* 14 (1960): 341-58. "Antibody Formation and Immunological Memory." *Macromolecular Behavior* (1966): 151-57. "Regulation of Antibody Synthesis." *Transplant.* Organum Geweben, Int. Symp., Bad Hamburg v.d. H., Ger. (1966): 81-89. "The Immune System." *Scientific American* 229 (July 1973): 52-60.

For More Information See: *New Scientist* 104 (October 18, 1984): 3-5. *Science* 226 (November 30, 1984): 1025-28.

Commentary: Niels Jerne, cited as the "leading theoretician in immunology during the last 30 years," was recognized for three theories that propelled the science of immunology forward. The first (1955) opposed the view that the body created antibodies as needed and instead proposed that the body contained all the antibodies needed to fight infection. The second explained how a type of immune-system cell, the T lymphocyte, develops in the thymus gland and learns its function. The network theory (1973) postulated that the immune system was a self-regulating functional network of interacting antibodies and lymphocytes. (R.K.)

Koehler, Georges J.F. 344

PRIZE: Medicine and Physiology, 1984. BORN: April 17, 1946; Munich, Germany. PARENTS: No record found. NATIONALITY: German. RELIGION: Most probably Christian. EDUCATION: Univ. of Freiburg, Germany, doctorate, 1974. SPOUSE: No record found. CHILDREN: No record found. CAREER: Cambridge Univ., England, Researcher, 1974-76; Basel Institute for Immunology, Switzerland, Researcher, 1977-84; Max Planck Institute for Immune Biology, Germany, Director, 1985-.

Selected Publications: "Continuous Culture of Fused Cells Secreting Antibody of Predefined Specificity." *Nature (London)* 256 (1975): 495-97 (with C. Milstein). "Immunoglobulin Production by Lymphocyte Hybridomas." *European Journal of Immunology* 8 (1978): 82-88 (with H. Hengartner and M.J. Shulman). "Immunoglobulin Chain Loss in Hybridoma Lines." *Proceedings of the National Academy of Sciences USA* 77 (1980): 2197-99. "The Technique of Hybridoma Production." *Immunological Methods* 2 (1981): 285-98.

For More Information See: *New York Times Biographical Service* (October 16, 1984): 1339. *Science* 226 (November 30, 1984): 1025-28.

Commentary: The Nobel Prize went to Georges J.F. Koehler and his colaureate, César Milstein, for their "pioneering contributions to the theory and techniques of immunology." Koehler helped to develop the techniques for producing monoclonal antibodies, antibodies which have a specific affinity for certain sites in the body that might permit them, for example, to attack diseased cells but leave healthy cells intact. The techniques have been said to lay the basis for medical advances such as cancer treatment and the detection of acquired immune deficiency syndrome (AIDS). (R.K.)

Milstein, César 345

PRIZE: Medicine and Physiology, 1984. BORN: October 8, 1927; Bahia Blanca, Argentina. PARENTS: Father, Lázaro Milstein; Mother, Máxima Milstein. NATIONAL-ITY: Argentinian; later British citizen. RELIGION: Agnostic; from Jewish background. EDUCATION: Univ. of Buenos Aires, Argentina, Licenciado en Ciencias Quimicas, 1952; Univ. of Buenos Aires, Argentina, Doctor en Quimica, 1957; Cambridge Univ., England, Ph.D., 1960. SPOUSE: Celia Prilleltensky, married 1953. CHILDREN: No record found. CAREER: National Institute of Biology, Buenos Aires, Argentina, Researcher, 1961-63; Cambridge Univ., England, Researcher and Administrator, 1963-. OTHER AWARDS: Silver Jubilee Medal, 1977; Ciba Medal, Biochemistry Society, 1978; Rosenstiel Medal, 1979; Avery-Landsteiner Preis, 1979; Rosenberg Prize, 1979; Mattia Award, 1979; Louisa Gross Horowitz Prize, Columbia U., NY, 1980; Koch Preis, 1980; Wolf Prize, 1980; Wellcome Foundation Medal, 1980; Jimenez Diaz Medal, 1981; William Bate Hardy Prize, Cambridge Philosophical Society, England, 1981; Sloan Prize, General Motors Cancer Research Foundation, 1981; Gairdner Award, 1981; Royal Medal, Royal Society, 1982.

Selected Publications: "Expansion and Contraction in the Evolution of Immunoglobulin Gene Pools." *Progr. Immunol.*, Int. Congr. Immunol., 1st (1971): 33-45 (with J. Svasti). "Clonal Variants of Myeloma Cells." *Prog. Immunol., Proc. Intern Congr. Immunol., 2nd* 1 (1974): 173-82 (with others). "Continuous Cultures of Fused Cells Secreting Antibody of Predefined Specificity." *Nature (London)* 256 (1975): 495-97 (with G. Koehler). "Immunoglobulin Genes in a Mouse Myeloma and in Mutant Clones." *Miami Winter Symposium* 9 (1975): 131-52 (with others).

For More Information See: *New York Times Biographical Service* (October 16, 1984): 1361. *Science* 226 (November 30, 1984): 1025-28.

Commentary: César Milstein shared the Nobel Prize for "pioneering contributions to the theory and techniques of immunology," which were said to lay the basis for advances in medical areas such as cancer treatment and the detection of acquired immune deficiency syndrome (AIDS). In work with his colaureate, Georges J. F. Koehler, Milstein developed the techniques for producing monoclonal antibodies, antibodies with a specific affinity for certain sites in the body that might find diseased cells but leave healthy cells intact. (R.K.)

1985

Brown, Michael Stuart 346

PRIZE: Medicine and Physiology, 1985. BORN: April 13, 1941; New York, NY. PARENTS: Father, Harvey Brown; Mother, Evelyn Katz Brown. NATIONALITY: American. RELIGION: Jewish. EDUCATION: Univ. of Pennsylvania, B.A., 1962; Univ. of Pennsylvania, M.D., 1966. SPOUSE: Alice Lapin, married June 21, 1964. CHILDREN: Elizabeth Jane, daughter; Sara Ellen, daughter. CAREER: Massachusetts General Hospital, Boston, Physician, 1966-68; National Institutes of Health, MD, Researcher, 1968-71; Univ. of Texas Health Science Center, Dallas, Professor, 1971-. OTHER AWARDS: Pfizer Award, American Chemical Society, 1976; Passano Award, 1978; Lounsbery Award, National Academy of Sciences, USA, 1979; Lita Annenberg Hazen Award, 1982; Horowitz Prize, Columbia U., NY, 1984.

Selected Publications: "Binding and Degradation of Low Density Lipoproteins by Cultured Human Fibroblasts: Comparison of Cells from a Normal Subject and from a Patient with Homozygous Familial Hypercholesterolemia." *Journal of Biological Chemistry* 249 (1974): 5153-62 (with J.L. Goldstein). "Development of a Cell Culture System for Study of the Basic Defect in Familial Hypercholesterolemia." In *Atherosclerosis III: Proceedings of the Third International Symposium.* Berlin: Springer-Verlag, 1974, 422-25 (with J.L. Goldstein). "Expression of the Familial Hypercholesterolemia Gene in Heterozygotes: Model for a Dominant Disorder in Man." *Transactions of the Association of American Physicians* 87 (1974): 120-31 (with J.L. Goldstein). "Familial Hypercholesterolemia: A Genetic Regulatory Defect in Cholesterol Metabolism." *American Journal of Medicine* 58 (1975): 147-50 (with J.L. Goldstein).

For More Information See: *New York Times* (October 15, 1985): C 1,3. *Science* 231 (January 10, 1986): 126-29.

Commentary: Michael Brown and Joseph Goldstein shared the Nobel Prize for their discoveries which "revolutionized our knowledge about the regulation of cholesterol metabolism and the treatment of diseases caused by abnormally elevated cholesterol levels in the blood." Brown's early work included study of the role of enzymes in the chemistry of the digestive system and of cholesterol production. The Nobel work centered on the causes of familial hypercholesterolemia and the discovery that human body cells have surface receptors which process bloodstream particles that carry cholesterol. (B.S.S.)

Goldstein, Joseph Leonard   347

PRIZE: Medicine and Physiology, 1985. BORN: April 18, 1940; Sumter, SC. PARENTS: Father, Isadore E. Goldstein; Mother, Fannie A. Goldstein. NATIONALITY: American. RELIGION: Jewish. EDUCATION: Washington and Lee Univ., VA, B.S., 1962; Southwestern Medical School, Univ. of Texas, M.D., 1966. SPOUSE: None. CHILDREN: None. CAREER: Massachusetts General Hospital, Boston, Physician, 1966-68; National Institutes of Health, MD, Researcher, 1968-70; Univ. of Washington, Seattle, Researcher, 1970-72; Univ. of Texas Health Science Center, Dallas, Professor, 1972-. OTHER AWARDS: Heinrich-Wieland Prize, 1974; Pfizer Award, American Chemical Society, 1976; Passano Award, 1978; Lounsbery Award, National Academy of Sciences, USA, 1979; Gairdner Foundation Award, 1981; Award, New York Academy of Sciences, 1981; Lita Annenberg Hazen Award, 1982; Horowitz Award, Columbia U., NY, 1984.

Selected Publications: "Familial Hypercholesterolemia: Identification of a Defect in the Regulation of 3-hydroxy-3-methylglutaryl Coenzyme A Reductase Activity Associated with Overproduction of Cholesterol." *Proceedings National Academy of Sciences USA* 70 (1973): 2804-08 (with M.S. Brown). "Expression of the Familial Hypercholesterolemia Gene in Heterozygotes: Mechanism for a Dominant Disorder in Man." *Science* 185 (1974): 61-63 (with M.S. Brown). "Homozygous Familial Hypercholesterolemia: Specificity of the Biochemical Defect in Cultured Cells and Feasibility of Prenatal Detection." *American Journal of Human Genetics* 26 (1974): 199-206 (with M.J.E. Harrod and M.S. Brown). "Familial Hypercholesterolemia: Biochemical, Genetic, and Pathophysiological Considerations." *Advances in Internal Medicine* 20 (1975): 273-96 (with M.S. Brown).

For More Information See: *New York Times* (October 15, 1985): C 1,3. *Science* 231 (January 10, 1986): 126-29.

Commentary: Joseph Goldstein shared the Nobel Prize with Michael Brown for his discoveries which "revolutionized our knowledge about the regulation of cholesterol metabolism and the treatment of diseases caused by abnormally elevated cholesterol levels in the blood." His early work included study of the genetic code and the genetic aspects of heart disease. The Nobel work centered on the causes of familial hypercholesterolemia and the discovery that human body cells have surface receptors that process bloodstream particles that carry cholesterol. (B.S.S.)

Peace

1901

Dunant, Jean Henri   348
PRIZE: Peace, 1901. BORN: May 8, 1828; Geneva, Switzerland. DIED: October 30, 1910; Heiden, Switzerland. PARENTS: Father, Jean Jacques Dunant; Mother, Anne Antoinette Colladeon Dunant. NATIONALITY: Swiss. RELIGION: Anti-church; from Calvinist background. EDUCATION: No college degrees. SPOUSE: None. CHILDREN: None. CAREER: Colonies Suisses de Setif, President, 1853-58; Societé Anonyme des Moulins de Mons-Djemila, President, 1858-60; Societé de l'Omnium Algerien Destine a Favoriser le Developpement de l'Industrie, du Commerce et de l'Agriculture en Algerie, President, 1860-66; Compagnie Algerienne, President, 1866-67. OTHER AWARDS: Order of Saint Maurice and Saint Lazarus, Italy, 1860; Chevalier of the Legion of Honor, France, 1865; Binet-Fendt Prize, Switzerland, 1897; Order of the Crown, Prussia, 1897; Order of Christ, Portugal, 1897; Stuttgart Medal, Germany, 1908.

Selected Publications: *L'Empire de Charlemagne Rétabli ou le Saint-Empire Romain Reconstitué par Napoleon III.* Geneva: Fick, 1859. *Memorandum au Sujet de la Société Financiere et Industrielle des Moulins de Mons-Djémila en Algérie.* Paris: n.p., 1859. *Un Souvenir de Solferino.* Geneva: Fick, 1862 (*A Memory of Solferino.* Tr. by the Red Cross. London: Cassell, 1947). *Project de Société Internationale pour la Renovation de l'Orient.* Paris: n.p., 1866. *Bibliothéque Internationale Universelle.* Paris: n.p., 1867. *Les Prisonniers de Guerre.* Geneva: Improv. H. Jarrys, 1915 (with reproduction of original 1867 edition).

For More Information See: Gumpert, Martin. *Dunant: The Story of the Red Cross.* New York: Blue Ribbon Books, 1942. Hart, Ellen. *Man Born to Live. Life and Work of Henry Dunant.* London: Victor Gollancz, 1953. *Memoires.* Ed. by Bernard Gagnebin. Geneva: n.p., 1970.

Commentary: Henri Dunant shared the first Peace Prize for his work in organizing the Geneva Conventions of 1863 and 1864 and the International Red Cross, which those conventions produced. His memoir of the Battle of Solferino in 1859 stirred Europe as the experience had stirred him. Dunant found himself transformed by the horrors of war as he personally ministered to hundreds of the wounded in the Chiesa Maggiore, a church overlooking the Lombard Plain, which was the site of the battle. His anguished plea for neutralization of the wounded and medical care for friend and foe alike formed the nexus for the Conventions and for Geneva's International Committee of Five, which Gustave Moynier headed and Dunant served as secretary. Though based on his Red Cross efforts, Dunant's prize could have resulted from his longtime devotion to international efforts at human amelioration, including the establishment of a YMCA, the fight to establish a Jewish homeland in Palestine, and championing of the ideas of international arbitration, disarmament, a world court, a universal library, abolition of slavery, and humane treatment for prisoners of war. (R.G.)

Passy, Frederic   349
PRIZE: Peace, 1901. BORN: May 20, 1822; Paris, France. DIED: June 12, 1912; Neuilly-sur-seine, France. PARENTS: No record found. NATIONALITY: French. RELIGION: Protestant; from Catholic background. EDUCATION: Univ. of Paris, France, law degree, 1846. SPOUSE: Married, no record found. CHILDREN: Paul Edouard, son; others, no record found. CAREER: French governmental positions, 1847-49, 1881-89; Writer and Lecturer on Economics.

Selected Publications: *Melanges Economiques.* Paris: Guillaumin, 1857. *Histoire du Travail.* Paris: H. Bellaire, 1873. "The Advance of the Peace Movement throughout the World." *American Monthly Review of Reviews* 17 (February 1898): 183-88. *Pour la Paix: Notes et Documents.* Paris: Charpentier, 1909.

For More Information See: *Biographical Dictionary of Modern Peace Leaders.* Westport, CT: Greenwood, 1985, 730-32. Passy, Paul. *Un Apotre de la Paix: La Viede Fredric Passy.* Paris: n.p., 1927.

Commentary: Frederic Passy won the Nobel Prize for his efforts over 50 years in the peace movement, for which he became known as the apostle of peace. He was instrumental in forming national and international leagues to further the cause of peace. In his legislative efforts in France, he was an advocate of labor, disarmament arbitration, and free trade, and an opponent of colonialism. Passy was also an acknowledged scholar of economics. (R.G.)

1902

Ducommun, Elie   350
PRIZE: Peace, 1902. BORN: February 19, 1833; Geneva, Switzerland. DIED: December 7, 1906; Berne, Switzerland. PARENTS: Father, Jules Ducommun; Mother, no record found. NATIONALITY: Swiss. RELIGION: Most probably Christian. EDUCATION: No college degrees. SPOUSE: No record found. CHILDREN: No record found. CAREER: Geneva Public Schools, Switzerland, Teacher, 1855-57; Journalist and Writer, 1857-1906; political posts, 1855-75; Jura-Bern-Lucern Railroad, Switzerland, Secretary-General, 1875-1903.

Selected Publications: *Precis Historique du Mouvement en Faveur de la Paix.* Berne, Switzerland: 1899. "The Permanent International Bureau of Peace." *The Independent* 55 (March 19, 1903): 660-61. *Derniers Sourires: Poesies Precedees d'une Notice Biographique.* Berne, Switzerland: 1908.

For More Information See: *Biographical Dictionary of Modern Peace Leaders.* Westport, CT: Greenwood Press, 1985, 228-29. *Dictionnaire Historique et Biographique de la Suisse.* Neuchatel, Switzerland: Administration du Dictionnaire Historique et Biographique de la Suisse, 1921-33. *The Independent* 55 (March 5, 1903): 554-57.

Commentary: Elie Ducommun received the Nobel Prize for his work as "the untiring and skillful director of the Berne Peace Bureau and therefore head of the united work of all the peace societies of the world." Although a respected journalist, businessperson, and poet, much of his energy and time was devoted to the cause of peace. He attended many of the meetings which were called on the topic and edited several journals devoted to peace. Ducommun also was an important political figure in Switzerland. (B.S.S.)

Gobat, Charles Albert   351

PRIZE: Peace, 1902. BORN: May 21, 1843; Tramelan, Switzerland. DIED: March 16, 1914; Bern, Switzerland. PARENTS: No record found. NATIONALITY: Swiss. RELIGION: Protestant. EDUCATION: Heidelberg Univ., Germany, Doctor of Law, 1867. SPOUSE: None. CHILDREN: None. CAREER: Berne, Switzerland, Attorney, 1867-82; Berne Univ., Switzerland, Professor, 1882-1912.

Selected Publications: *La Republique de Berne et la France Pendant les Guerres de Religion d'apres des Documents Inedits.* Paris: Gedalge, 1891. *Histore de la Suisse Racontee au Peuple.* Neuchatel, Switzerland: F. Zahn, 1899. *Le Cauchemar de l'Europe.* Paris: Le Soudier, 1911.

For More Information See: *London Times* (March 17, 1914): 10c. *New York Times* (March 17, 1914): 11+.

Commentary: Lawyer and statesman Charles Gobat shared the Nobel for "his general efforts for Peace, and his work as President of the fourth conference of the Interparliamentarian Union at Berne in 1892." After winning the Nobel, Gobat's role in the struggle for peace became even greater. In 1904, he came to America to lead the Inter-Parliamentary Conference in St. Louis, MO. A firm believer in arbitration, he called on the United States to intervene in the Russo-Japanese War. As president of the Bern International Peace Bureau from 1906 and administrative head of the Interparliamentary Union from 1892, he was simultaneously director of the two largest peace organizations in the world. Gobat died "with his boots on" while addressing a meeting of the International Peace Bureau. (K.N.M.)

1903

Cremer, William Randal, Sir   352

PRIZE: Peace, 1903. BORN: March 18, 1828; Fareham, Wiltshire, England. DIED: July 22, 1908; London, England. PARENTS: Father, George Cremer; Mother, Harriet Tutte. NATIONALITY: British. RELIGION: Methodist. EDUCATION: No college degrees. SPOUSE: Charlotte Wilson, married 1860, died 1876; Lucy Coombes, married 1877. CHILDREN: None. CAREER: England, Carpenter and Trade Union Organizer/Worker, 1843-85; British Parliament Member, 1885-1908. OTHER AWARDS: Cross of the Legion of Honor, England, 1890; Commander of the Norwegian Order of Saint Olav, 1904; Knighthood, England, 1907.

Selected Publications: *The Arbitrator*, Journal of the International Arbitration League, Editor and Contributor, 1889-1908.

For More Information See: *Dictionary of National Biography: Twentieth Century Supplement, 1901-1911.* London: Oxford U. Press, 1912, 441-42. Evans, Howard. *Sir Randal Cremer: His Life and Works.* London: T. Fisher Unwin, 1909.

Commentary: William Cremer earned the Nobel Prize for his intensive work in the peace movement and his belief in international arbitration in achieving world peace. His initial efforts, in 1887, led to the drafting of a treaty of international arbitration and to the formation of the Interparliamentary Union for International Courts of Arbitrations after the treaty was not accepted by Britain and the United States in 1889. He had established the precursor of the Interparliamentary Union—the Workmen's Peace Association—in 1870. Later called the International Arbitration League, this organization (and Cremer) formulated the plan for a high court of nations, which eventually materialized in the Hague Tribunal. (D.P.)

1905

von Suttner, Bertha Felicie Sophie Kinsky   353

PRIZE: Peace, 1905. BORN: June 9, 1843; Prague, Austria. DIED: June 21, 1914; Vienna, Austria. PARENTS: Father, Count Franz Joseph Kinsky; Mother, Sophie Wilhelmine Körner Kinsky. NATIONALITY: Austrian. RELIGION: Areligious; from Catholic background. EDUCATION: No college degrees. SPOUSE: Arthur Gundaccar von Suttner, married 1876. CHILDREN: None. CAREER: *Die Waffen nieder*, Editor, 1892-99.

Selected Publications: *Die Waffen nieder.* Dresden, Germany: E. Pierson, 1889 (*Lay Down Your Arms: The Autobiography of Martha von Tilling.* Tr. by T. Holmes. New York: Garland Publishing, 1972). *Memoiren von Bertha von Suttner.* Stuttgart, Germany: Deutsche Verlags-Anstalt, 1909 (*Memoirs of Bertha von Suttner: Records of an Eventful Life.* New York: Garland Publishing, 1972). *Der Kampf um die Vermeidung des Weltkrieges: Randglossen aus zwei Jahrzehnten zu den Ereignissen vor der Katastrophe (1892-1900 und 1907-1914).* Zurich: Orell Fussli, 1917.

For More Information See: Kempf, Beatrix. *Woman for Peace: The Life of Bertha von Suttner.* Park Ridge, NJ: Noyes Press, 1973. Lengyel, Emil. *And All Her Paths Were Peace: The Life of Bertha von Suttner.* Nashville, TN: T. Nelson, 1975. Opfell, Olga S. *The Lady Laureates.* Metuchen, NJ: Scarecrow Press, 1978, 1-17.

Commentary: The Nobel Peace Prize was awarded to Bertha von Suttner "for her sincere peace activities." Her emergence on the international scene began with publication of *Lay Down Your Arms*, which exposed the cruel realities of war, rather than its glory, heroism, and patriotism. Throughout her life, she popularized the quest for peace through her writings—novels, correspondence, newspaper articles (she was one of the first female political journalists); through the pacifist journal she edited; through her activities in peace societies and at international conferences; and through lecturing in Europe and the United States. (M.A.V.C.)

1906

Roosevelt, Theodore   354

PRIZE: Peace, 1906. BORN: October 27, 1858; New York, NY. DIED: January 6, 1919; Oyster Bay, NY. PARENTS: Father, Theodore Roosevelt; Mother, Martha Bulloch Roosevelt. NATIONALITY: American. RELIGION: Presbyterian. EDUCATION: Harvard Univ., MA, A.B., 1880. SPOUSE: Alice Hathaway Lee, married October 27, 1880, died February 14, 1884; Edith Kermit Carow, married December 2, 1886. CHILDREN: Alice Lee, daughter; Theodore, son; Kermit, son; Ethel Carow, daughter; Archibald Bulloch, son; Quentin, son. CAREER: New York Assembly, Member, 1882-84; U.S. Civil Service Commission, 1889-95; New York City, Police Commissioner, 1895; Department of the Navy, Assistant Secretary, 1897-98; U.S. Army, 1898; State of New York, Governor, 1899-1901; U.S. President, 1901-09.

Selected Publications: *The Naval War of 1812.* New York: G.P. Putnam and Sons, 1882. *Hunting Trips of a Ranchman.* Upper Saddle River, NJ: Literature House Gregg Press, 1885. *The Winning of the West 1769-1807.* 4 volumes. New York: G.P. Putnam and Sons, 1889-96. *Oliver Cromwell* New York: Scribner's Sons, 1901. *History as Literature, and Other Essays.* New York: Scribner's Sons, 1913.

For More Information See: Bishop, Joseph Bucklin. *Theodore Roosevelt and His Time Shown in His Own Letters.* 2 volumes. New York: Scribner's Sons, 1920. *Dictionary of American Biography.* 1935 ed. New York: Scribner's (Volume 16), 135-44. Morris, Edmund. *The Rise of Theodore Roosevelt.* New York: Coward, McCann and Geoghegan, 1979. Roosevelt, Theodore. *Theodore Roosevelt: An Autobiography.* New York: Scribner's Sons, 1913.

Commentary: Theodore Roosevelt's mediation of the Russo-Japanese War at a peace conference in Portsmouth, New Hampshire, and his intervention in the dispute between Britain, Germany, and France concerning the roles to be played in Morocco won him the Nobel Peace Prize. He was the first American and the first head of state to win the prize. But his contributions to America and the world neither began nor ended with those events. He is noted as a progressive president who attempted to control trusts, to conserve natural resources, to protect labor, and to provide a "square deal" for all. His foreign policies led most importantly to the securing of the Panama Canal Zone and building of the Canal, and to the expansion of the Monroe Doctrine by statement of the Roosevelt Corollary. (S.W.)

1907

Moneta, Ernesto Teodora   355

PRIZE: Peace, 1907. BORN: September 20, 1833; Milan, Italy. DIED: February 10, 1918; Milan, Italy. PARENTS: No record found. NATIONALITY: Italian. RELIGION:

Catholic. EDUCATION: No college degrees. SPOUSE: Married (no date found). CHILDREN: 2 sons. CAREER: Italy, Traveler, Soldier, Political Activist, 1848-66; *Il Secolo*, Editor, 1866-98; *La Vita Internazionale*, Publisher, 1898-1918.

Selected Publications: *Patria i Umanita.* Milan: Sonzogno, 1899. *Le Guerre, le Insurrezioni e la Pace nel Secolo Decimonono.* 4 volumes. Milan: Societe Tip. Editrice Popolare, 1903-10. *La Nostra Pace.* Milan: Bellini, 1909.

For More Information See: Combi, Maria. *Ernesto Teodoro Moneta: Premio Nobel per la Pace.* Milan: Mursia, 1968. Pinardi, Giuseppe. *La Carriere d'un Pacifiste: E.T. Moneta.* Le Havre, France: L'Universel, 1904.

Commentary: Ernesto Moneta, a "militant pacifist," won the Nobel Prize for his work in founding the Lombard Peace Union in 1887, his peace conferences in Italy, and his role in presiding over the International Peace Congress in Milan in 1906. A rugged Italian soldier in campaigns between 1848 and 1866, Moneta advocated fighting for freedom in Italy while working continuously for peace. He was also well known for remarkable journalistic skill in a variety of publishing ventures. (S.M.)

Renault, Louis   356

PRIZE: Peace, 1907. BORN: May 21, 1843; Autun, Saône-et-Loire, France. DIED: February 8, 1918; Barbizon, France. PARENTS: No record found. NATIONALITY: French. RELIGION: Most probably Christian/Protestant. EDUCATION: Univ. of Dijon, France, bachelor's degree, 1861; Univ. of Paris, France, doctorate in law, 1868. SPOUSE: Juliette Thiaffait, married February 22, 1873. CHILDREN: 4 daughters (2 survived, Germaine and Marie); 1 son. CAREER: Univ. of Dijon, France, Professor, 1868-73; Univ. of Paris, France, Professor, 1873-1918.

Selected Publications: *Précis de Droit Commercial.* 2 volumes. Paris: F. Pinchon, 1884-85. *Manuel de Droit Commercial.* Paris: F. Pinchon, 1887. *Traité de Droit Commercial.* 8 volumes. Paris: F. Pinchon, 1889-99.

For More Information See: *Encyclopedia of the Social Sciences.* New York: Macmillan, 1937 (Volume 13), 287-88. Fauchille, Paul. *Louis Renault.* Paris: A. Pedone, 1918. Scott, James. "In Memoriam: Louis Renault." In *American Journal of International Law* 12 (July 1918), 606-10.

Commentary: Louis Renault, French jurist, scholar, diplomat, and judge, won the Nobel Prize for his efforts as "principal worker" at the Hague Peace Conferences in 1899 and 1907. Although the conferences did not succeed in limiting armaments, they did establish the Hague Permanent Court of Arbitration, which provided an avenue for peaceful resolution of disputes between countries. Renault is also considered to be the founder of international law as a legal science in France. (M.J.H.)

1908

Arnoldson, Klas Pontus   357

PRIZE: Peace, 1908. BORN: October 27, 1844; Goteborg, Sweden. DIED: February 20, 1916; Stockholm, Sweden. PARENTS: Father, Olaf Andersson Arnoldson; Mother, Inga Hagbom von Seth Arnoldson. NATIONALITY:

Swedish. RELIGION: Christian/Protestant; with Unitarian views. EDUCATION: No college degrees. SPOUSE: Eva Bernhardina Wahlgren, married May 15, 1869, dissolved April 7, 1903; Edit Viktoria Blomskold, married May 4, 1903. CHILDREN: No record found. CAREER: Railroad Worker, 1860-81; Swedish Parliament, 1882-87; Political Activist, Writer, and Peace Worker, 1888-1916.

Selected Publications: *Ar Varldsfred Majlig.* Stockholm: Froleen, 1890 (*Pax Mundi.* London: Swan Sonnenschein, 1890). *Religionen i Forskningens Ljus* (*Religion in the Light of Research*). Sundsvall, Sweden: Forlagsforeningen Fria Ordet, 1891. *Seklernas Hopp* (*Hope of the Centuries*). Stockholm: Wilhelmsson, 1901. *Maria Magdalena.* Stockholm: Bohlin, 1903.

For More Information See: Svenson, Axel. *En Lifsgerning for Freden: Nagra Erinrande Ord Pa K. P. Arnoldson Sixtioarsdag den 27 Oktober 1904.* Stockholm: n.p., 1904. *Svenst Biografiskt Lexikon.* Stockholm: Albert Bonniers Forlag, 1920 (Volume 2), 248-53.

Commentary: Klas Arnoldson was granted the Nobel Prize for 35 years of working for peace. His outstanding contributions in this regard, in addition to his influential writings, were the founding of the Swedish Society of Arbitration and Peace, the accomplishment of a peaceful separation of Norway and Sweden, and the willingness of Sweden to consider permanent neutrality. Arnoldson was also a powerful member of the Swedish Parliament for many years. (B.S.S.)

Bajer, Fredrik   358

PRIZE: Peace, 1908. BORN: April 21, 1837; Vester Egede, Denmark. DIED: January 22, 1922; Copenhagen, Denmark. PARENTS: Father, Alfred Bayer; Mother, Cecilie Luise Crone Bayer. NATIONALITY: Danish. RELIGION: Protestant. EDUCATION: No college degrees. SPOUSE: Pauline Matilde Schluter, married October 8, 1867. CHILDREN: No record found. CAREER: Danish Army, 1856-65; Writer and Teacher, 1865-72; Politician and Writer, 1872-95.

Selected Publications: *Nordiske Neutralitetsforbund.* Copenhagen: Studentersamfund Forlag, 1885. *Tactics for the Friends of Peace.* Tr. by P. H. Peckover. Wisbech, England: Poyser, 1891. *Idéen til Nordens, Saerlig Danmarks, Vedvarende Neutralitet.* Copenhagen: 1900. *A Serious Drama of Modern History: How Danish Slesvig Was Lost.* Tr. by P. H. Peckover. London: Peace Society, 1907. *Nordens, Saerlig Danmarks, Neutralitet under Krimkrigen.* Copenhagen: Schultz, 1914.

For More Information See: *Dansk Biografisk Leksikon.* Copenhagen: J.H. Schultz Forlag, 1933 (Volume II), 34-39. Schou, August. *Histoire de l'Internationalisme III: Du Congres de Vienne Jusqu'a la Premiere Guerre Mondiale.* Oslo: Aschehoug, 1963.

Commentary: Fredrik Bajer's political and writing activities in support of peace won him the Nobel Prize. An accomplished military figure in his early years, Bajer became an outstanding spokesperson for arbitration and peace later. He was also an outstanding figure in Danish education, a leading spokesperson for women's equality, and a fervent promoter of Scandinavian unity. (B.S.S.)

1909

Beernaert, Auguste Marie Francois   359

PRIZE: Peace, 1909. BORN: July 26, 1829; Ostend, Belgium. DIED: October 6, 1912; Lucerne, Switzerland. PARENTS: Father, Bernard Beernaert; Mother, Euphrosine-Josepha Rayon Beernaert. NATIONALITY: Belgian. RELIGION: Catholic. EDUCATION: Univ. of Louvain, Belgium, Doctor of Law, 1851. SPOUSE: Mathilde-Wilhelmine-Marie Borel, married August 6, 1870. CHILDREN: None. CAREER: Brussels, Belgium, Attorney, 1853-73; Belgian and international politics, 1873-1907.

Selected Publications: *De l'État de l'Enseignement du Droit en France et en Allemagne: Rapport Adressé à M. le Ministre de l'Intérieur.* Brussels: Lesigne, 1854. *Discours Prononcé à l'Occasion de l'Inauguration des Quais d'Anvers, le 26 Juillet 1885.* Paris: Chaix, 1885.

For More Information See: Carton de Wiart, Henri. *Beernaert et Son Temps.* Brussels: La Renaissance du Livre, 1945. Carton de Wiart, Henri. "Notice sur Auguste Beernaert," *Annuaire de l'Académic Royale de Belgique* 105 (1939): 293-364. *Notices: Biographiques & Bibliographiques.* Brussels: Hayez, Imprimeur de L'Academie Royale de Belgique, 1909, 315-25.

Commentary: Auguste Beernaert was awarded the Nobel Prize for his untiring efforts for peace in the last third of his long, active life. He was a prominent member of all the peace conferences from 1889 until his death in 1912, his work with the Mexican question in 1902 and enemy property inviolability in 1907 being especially noteworthy. Early in his career he was also instrumental in introducing general suffrage and efficient elections in Belgium and in the establishment of the Belgian Congo. (L.S.)

d'Estournelles, Paul Henri Benjamin Balleut de Constant, Baron   360

PRIZE: Peace, 1909. BORN: November 22, 1852; La Fleche, Sarthe, France. DIED: May 15, 1924; Bordeaux, France. PARENTS: Father, Léonce Balluet d'Estournelles; Mother, Louise de Constant d'Estournelles. NATIONALITY: French. RELIGION: Most probably Christian. EDUCATION: Lycée Louis le Grand, France, licence in law, 1875. SPOUSE: Daisy Sedwick-Berend, married (no date found). CHILDREN: 2 sons; 3 daughters. CAREER: French diplomatic corps and political establishment, 1876-1924. OTHER AWARDS: Officer of the Legion of Honor, France.

Selected Publications: *La Rapprôchement Francoallemand.* Paris: Delagrave, 1909. *America and Her Problems.* New York: Macmillan, 1915. *Les Reparations: Les Ruines de Fargniers et la Dotation Carnegie.* La Flèche, Sarthe, France: La Conciliation Internationale, 1922.

For More Information See: *Biographical Dictionary of Modern Peace Leaders.* Westport, CT: Greenwood Press, 1985, 265-66. Wild, Adolph. *Baron d'Estournelles de Constant (1852-1924). Hamburg: Stiftung Europa-Kolleg, 1973.*

Commentary: Paul d'Estournelles received the Nobel Prize for his services to the cause of international peace and goodwill. His talents in arbitration among nations were notable and were used in avoiding confrontation between France and Britain in the 1893 Siam/French Siam border dispute and in numerous arbitrations and/or treaties involving France, Britain, and Germany. d'Estournelles founded the Conciliation Internationale and worked with Andrew Carnegie toward peace. (C.B.B.)

1911

Asser, Tobias Michael Carel   361
PRIZE: Peace, 1911. BORN: April 29, 1838; Amsterdam, Netherlands. DIED: July 29, 1913; The Hague, Netherlands. PARENTS: Father, Carel Daniel Asser; Mother, (no first name) Godefroi Asser. NATIONALITY: Dutch. RELIGION: Jewish. EDUCATION: Atheneum, Netherlands, Doctor of Laws, 1860. SPOUSE: (No first name found) Asser, married (no date found). CHILDREN: No record found. CAREER: Univ. of Amsterdam, Netherlands, Professor, 1862-93. OTHER AWARDS: Recipient of decorations from the governments of Holland, Austria, Italy, and Belgium.

Selected Publications: *Schets van Het Nederlandsch Handelsrecht.* Haarlem, Netherlands: Erven F. Bohn, 1873. *Schets van Het International Privaatrecht.* Haarlem, Netherlands: Erven F. Bohn, 1880.

For More Information See: *The Jewish Encyclopedia.* New York: Funk and Wagnalls, 1925 (Volume 2), 229. "Tobias Asser." In *Jaarboeken der Koninklyke Akademie.* Amsterdam: G.G. Vander Post, 1914.

Commentary: Tobias Asser was recognized by the Committee as a "practical legal statesman" and "pioneer in the field of international legal relations." An authority on international law, he believed that peace depended on a uniformity in international private law which nations could emulate in their national legislation. To this end, he persuaded the Dutch government to convene and presided over four conferences at The Hague on international private law (1893, 1894, 1900, 1904). He was one of the founders of the Institute of International Law and the Review of International Law and Comparative Legislation. (D.S.)

Fried, Alfred Hermann   362
PRIZE: Peace, 1911. BORN: November 11, 1864; Vienna, Austria. DIED: May 6, 1921; Vienna, Austria. PARENTS: No record found. NATIONALITY: Austrian. RELIGION: Jewish. EDUCATION: No college degrees. SPOUSE: No record found. CHILDREN: No record found. CAREER: Austria, Bookdealer and Publisher.

Selected Publications: *Handbuch der Friedensbewegung.* Vienna; Leipzig, Germany: Oesterveichische Friendensgesellschaft, 1905. *Die Grundlogen des Revolutionaeren Pacifismus.* Tubingen, Germany: Mohr Reichenbachsche Buchhandlung, 1908. *Der Kaiser und der Weltfrieden.* Berlin: Maritima, Verlagsges, 1910. *Der Weltprotest gegen den Versailler Frieden.* Leipzig, Germany: P. Reinhold, 1920.

For More Information See: *Encyclopedia Judaica.* Jerusalem: Macmillan, 1971 (Volume 7), 171. Goldscheid, R. *Alfred Fried.* Leipzig, Germany: P. Reinhold, 1922.

Commentary: Alfred Fried was recognized by the Committee as perhaps "the most industrious literary pacifist in the past twenty years." Trained as a bookseller, Fried believed that the existing international anarchy would decrease and disappear if international legal and political organizations could be established. To this end, he founded the German and Austrian

Peace Societies and edited and published several pacifist periodicals in both Germany and Austria. He worked closely with pacifist Bertha von Suttner (Nobel Peace Prize winner in 1905). Accused of high treason in Austria for his pacifist work, he emigrated to Switzerland to work with prisoners of war. (D.S.)

1912

Root, Elihu   363
PRIZE: Peace, 1912. BORN: February 15, 1845; Clinton, NY. DIED: February 7, 1937; New York, NY. PARENTS: Father, Oren Root; Mother, Nancy Whitney Buttrick Root. NATIONALITY: American. RELIGION: Protestant. EDUCATION: Hamilton College, NY, A.B., 1864; New York Univ., law degree, 1867. SPOUSE: Clara Frances Wales, married January 1878. CHILDREN: Edith, daughter; Elihu, Jr., son; Edward Wales, son. CAREER: New York, Attorney, 1867-99; United States political offices, 1899-1915. OTHER AWARDS: Roosevelt Medal, 1924; Woodrow Wilson Foundation Medal, 1926; Civic Forum Medal, 1927; Eleanor van Rensselaer Fairfax Medal, 1930.

Selected Publications: *The Citizen's Part in Government.* New Haven, CT: Yale U. Press, 1907. *Experiments in Government and the Essentials of the Constitution.* Princeton, NJ: Princeton U. Press, 1913. *Addresses on Government and Citizenship.* Cambridge, MA: Harvard U. Press, 1916. *Addresses on International Subjects.* Cambridge, MA: Harvard U. Press, 1916. *Military and Colonial Policy of the U.S.* Cambridge, MA: Harvard U. Press, 1916. *Latin America and the U.S.* Cambridge, MA: Harvard U. Press, 1917. *Miscellaneous Addresses.* Cambridge, MA: Harvard U. Press, 1917. *Men and Policies.* Cambridge, MA: Harvard U. Press, 1925.

For More Information See: Jessup, Philip C. *Elihu Root.* New York: Dodd, Mead and Co., 1938. Leopold, Richard W. *Elihu Root and the Conservative Tradition.* Boston: Little, Brown and Co., 1954. *The National Cyclopedia of American Biography.* New York: J. T. White and Co., 1937 (Volume 26), 1-5.

Commentary: Elihu Root won the Nobel Prize for a number of efforts that were applauded by the Academy, including his championing of the Taft proposal for an unconditional arbitration treaty with Britain, his support of no special privileges for American shipping in the Panama Canal, and his presidency of the Carnegie Peace Foundation. In addition to his peace efforts, Root served his country well in many years of public service, with notable successes in organizing US involvement in Cuba and the Philippines after the Spanish-American War, in promoting understanding between South American countries and between the countries of South and North America, and in dealing with Japan in the dispute over the status of Japanese immigrants. (B.S.)

1913

La Fontaine, Henri Marie   364
PRIZE: Peace, 1913. BORN: April 22, 1854; Brussels, Belgium. DIED: May 14, 1943; Brussels, Belgium. PARENTS: No record found. NATIONALITY: Belgian. RELIGION: Christian. EDUCATION: Univ. of Brussels, Belgium, law doctorate, 1877. SPOUSE: Mathilde Lhoest,

married 1903. CHILDREN: No record found. CAREER: Attorney, 1877-93; Univ. of Brussels, Belgium, Professor, and Belgian Senator, 1894-1940.

Selected Publications: *Des Droits et Obligations des Entrepreneurs de Travaux Publics Nationaux, Provinciaux, et Communaux.* Brussels: Ferdinand Larcier, 1885. *La Femme et le Barreau.* Brussels: Ferdinand Larcier, 1901. *Histoire Sommaire et Chronologique des Arbitrages Internationaux (1794-1900).* Brussels: Bureau de la Revue de Droit International et de Législation Comparée, 1902. *Bibliographie de la Paix et de l'Arbitrage International.* Brussels: Institut International de Bibliographie, 1904. *The Great Solution: Magnissima Charta.* Boston: World Peace Foundation, 1916.

For More Information See: *Biographical Dictionary of Modern Peace Leaders.* Westport, CT: Greenwood Press, 1985, 538-39. *Biographie Nationale.* Brussels: Bruylant, 1973-74 (Volume 38): cols. 213-21.

Commentary: For his efforts at establishing and furthering the principles of international cooperation and understanding among the peoples of the world, Henri La Fontaine was awarded the Nobel Prize. His early support of the idea of a world bibliography and a universal index to information, in order to bring about understanding among the nations, led to his lifelong devotion to the principle of bringing freedom to the whole world. The goal, he felt, would be achieved by "the great solution," a "magnissima charta" which would create a "United States of the World." (F.L.T.)

1919

Wilson, Thomas Woodrow 365
PRIZE: Peace, 1919. BORN: December 28, 1856; Staunton, VA. DIED: February 3, 1924; Washington, DC. PARENTS: Father, Joseph Ruggles Wilson; Mother, Jessie Janet Woodrow Wilson. NATIONALITY: American. RELIGION: Presbyterian. EDUCATION: Princeton Univ., NJ, B.A., 1879; Univ. of Virginia, LLB., 1881; Johns Hopkins Univ., MD, Ph.D., 1886. SPOUSE: Ellen Louise Axson, married June 24, 1885, died August 6, 1914; Edith Bolling Galt, married December 18, 1915. CHILDREN: Margaret Woodrow, daughter; Jessie Woodrow, daughter; Eleanor Randolph, daughter. CAREER: Atlanta, GA, Attorney, 1882-83; Bryn Mawr College, PA, Professor, 1885-88; Wesleyan Univ., Middletown, CT, Professor, 1888-90; Princeton Univ., NJ, Professor and President, 1890-1910; New Jersey, Governor, 1911-13; U.S. President, 1913-21.

Selected Publications: *Congressional Government.* New York: Meridian Books, 1902. *A History of the American People.* 5 volumes. New York: Harper and Brothers, 1902. *Constitutional Government in the United States.* New York: Columbia U. Press, 1908. *The New Freedom.* New York: Doubleday, Page, and Company, 1913. *A Day of Dedication: The Essential Writings and Speeches of Woodrow Wilson.* Edited with an introduction by Alan Fried. New York: Macmillan, 1965.

For More Information See: Baker, Ray Stannard. *Woodrow Wilson: Life and Letters.* 8 volumes. Garden City, NY: Doubleday, Doran and Co., 1927-39. Blum, John Morton. *Woodrow Wilson and the Politics of Morality.* Boston: Little, Brown, 1956. Buehrig, Edward Henry. *Wilson's Foreign Policy in Perspective.* Bloomington, IN: Indiana U. Press, 1957. *Encyclopedia of American Biography.* New York: Harper and

Row, 1974, 1214-17. *Encyclopedia of World Biography.* New York: McGraw-Hill, 1973, 403-06. Link, Arthur Stanley. *Woodrow Wilson.* 5 volumes. Princeton, NJ: Princeton U. Press, 1947-65. White, William Allen. *Woodrow Wilson.* Boston: Houghton-Mifflin, 1924.

Commentary: The Nobel Peace Prize was awarded to Woodrow Wilson "for his sincere attempts at peace negotiations"; this statement has been generally thought to refer to his "Fourteen Points" speech to Congress that was aimed at securing a lasting peace at the end of the First World War and was instrumental in the establishment of the League of Nations. President Wilson's efforts to ensure peace in the world followed a long academic career as a writer and teacher of political science, as president of Princeton University, as governor of New Jersey, and as President of the United States, enacting major bills dealing with areas such as tariffs, banking, and anti-trust. (D.B.)

1920

Bourgeois, Léon-Victor Auguste 366
PRIZE: Peace, 1920. BORN: May 29, 1851; Paris, France. DIED: September 29, 1925; Epernay, France. PARENTS: No record found. NATIONALITY: French. RELIGION: Catholic. EDUCATION: Univ. of Paris, France, Docteur en Droit, 1875. SPOUSE: No record found. CHILDREN: No record found. CAREER: French Public Offices, 1876-1923.

Selected Publications: *Solidarité.* Paris: A. Colin, 1896. *L'Education de la Démocratie Française.* Paris: E. Cornély, 1897. *Le Declaration des Droits de l'Homme.* Paris: E. Cornély, 1902. *Pour la Société des Nations.* Paris: Bibliothèque Charpentier, 1910. *La Pacte de 1919 et la Société des Nations.* Paris: Bibliothèque Charpentier/E. Fasquelle, 1919. *L'Oeuvre de la Société des Nations, 1920-1923.* Paris: Payot, 1923.

For More Information See: Hamburger, M. *Léon Bougeois, 1851-1925.* Paris: Librairie des Sciences Politiques et Sociales, 1932. Minnich, Lawrence A. "Social Problems and Political Alignments in France, 1893-1898: Leon Bourgeois and Solidarity." (Ph.D. dissertation, Cornell U., 1949).

Commentary: Léon Bourgeois was awarded the Nobel Prize in recognition of his status as the spiritual father of the League of Nations, in that he drafted the original document which described such an organization. In addition to his yeoman efforts for the League, Bourgeois devoted his life to the service of France, occupying a series of major offices and spearheading major reforms in education, finances, and the conduct of government. (B.L.)

1921

Branting, Karl Hjalmar 367
PRIZE: Peace, 1921. BORN: November 23, 1860; Stockholm, Sweden. DIED: February 24, 1925; Stockholm, Sweden. PARENTS: Father, Lars Gabriel Branting; Mother, Emerentia Maria Charlotta Georgii Branting. NATIONALITY: Swedish. RELIGION: Most probably Christian/Protestant. EDUCATION: Univ. of Uppsala, Sweden, baccalaureate, 1882. SPOUSE: Anna Matilda Charlotta Jaderin, married April 4, 1884. CHILDREN: No record found. CAREER: Stockholm Observatory,

Sweden, Astronomer, 1882-84; *Tiden*, Editor, 1884-86; *Socialdemokraten*, Editor, 1886-1917; Political Activist and Prime Minister, 1889-1925.

Selected Publications: *Socialdemokratiens Arhundrade.* 2 volumes. Stockholm: Aktiebolaget Ljus, 1904-06. *Varfor det var Ratt Antaga Pensionforsakringslagen.* Stockholm: Tidens Forlag, 1913. *Den Politiska Krisen: Dess Innebord, Uppkomst och Forsta Forlopp.* Stockholm: Tidens Forlag, 1914. *Tal och Skrifter i Urval.* Stockholm: Tidens Forlag, 1927-30.

For More Information See: Branting, Anna. *Min Langa Resa: Boken om Hjalmar Och Mig.* Stockholm: Meden, 1945. Hoglund, Zeth. *Hjalmar Branting.* Stockholm: Folket i Bilds Forlag, 1949. *Svenskt Biografiskt Lexikon.* Stockholm: Albert Bonniers Forlag, 1926 (Volume 6), 14-37.

Commentary: Hjalmar Branting won the Nobel Prize for his lifelong commitment to constitutional pacifism and the activities in which he involved himself as a result. He was a fervent supporter of Swedish neutrality and saw the role of Sweden as arbitrator and conciliator in international disputes. An involved worker for and at the League of Nations, Branting participated in many disarmament debates, was involved actively in the settlement of the Greek-Italian conflict of 1923 and the British-Turkish dispute in 1924, and helped in the drafting of the Geneva Protocol for international security. Branting was also the father of socialism in Sweden and served in the Parliament from 1886 until his death, including three terms as Prime Minister. (B.S.S.)

Lange, Christian Lous 368

PRIZE: Peace, 1921. BORN: September 17, 1869; Stavanger, Norway. DIED: December 11, 1938; Oslo, Norway. PARENTS: Father, Halvard Lange; Mother, Thora Lous. NATIONALITY: Norwegian. RELIGION: Most probably Christian/Protestant. EDUCATION: Univ. of Oslo, Norway, M.A., 1893; Univ. of Oslo, Norway, Ph.D., 1919. SPOUSE: Bertha Manthey, married December 27, 1894. CHILDREN: 3 sons; 2 daughters. CAREER: Norway and International, Writer, Journalist, and Political Activist, 1893-1938.

Selected Publications: *Den Europaeiske Borgerkrig.* Oslo: Aschehoug, 1915. *The Conditions of a Lasting Peace.* Oslo: Interparliamentary Union, 1917. *Histoire de l'Internationalisme.* 3 volumes. Oslo: Aschehoug, 1919, 1954, 1963.

For More Information See: Falnes, Oscar J. "Christian L. Lange and His Work for Peace." *American-Scandinavian Review* 57 (1969): 266-74. *Norsk Biografisk Leksikon.* Oslo: Aschehoug, 1938 (Volume 8), 172-74.

Commentary: A leader in the practice of internationalism, both in words and action, Christian Lange received the Nobel Prize for a lifetime focused on peace and international affairs. Lange was a founder and officer of the Interparliamentary Union and of the Norwegian Nobel Institute. His work for the Union was especially noteworthy. He also participated actively in two international peace conferences and was a delegate to the League of Nations from its founding until his death. In addition, he was a leader of liberal thought, fighting for free speech, free trade, universal suffrage, and the rights of labor. (B.S.S.)

1922

Nansen, Fridtjof 369

PRIZE: Peace, 1922. BORN: October 10, 1861; Store fróen, Vestre Aker, Norway. DIED: May 13, 1930; Polhogda, Norway. PARENTS: Father, Baldur Nansen; Mother, Adelaide Wedel Jarlsberg Nansen. NATIONALITY: Norwegian. RELIGION: Agnostic; from Lutheran background. EDUCATION: Univ. of Kristiania, Norway, Dr. Philos., 1888. SPOUSE: Eva Sars, married 1889, died 1907; Sigrunn Munthe Sandberg, married 1919. CHILDREN: Liv, daughter; Irmelin, daughter; Odd, son; Kåre, son; Asmund, son. CAREER: Bergen Museum, Norway, Curator, 1882-87; Greenland Expedition Leader, 1888-89; Kristiania Zootomic Collection, Norway, Curator, 1889-93; Polar Expedition Leader, 1893-96; Univ. of Kristiania, Norway, Professor, 1897-1919. OTHER AWARDS: Jaachim Friele's Gold Medal; Vega Medal, Sweden, 1889.

Selected Publications: *Eskimo Life.* London: Longmans, 1893. *Farthest North.* New York: Harper, 1897. *In Northern Mists.* New York: Stokes, 1911.

For More Information See: *Encyclopedia of World Biography.* New York: McGraw-Hill, 1973 (Volume 8), 59-60. Sorensen, Jon. *Fridtjof Nansen.* New York: W. W. Norton, 1932.

Commentary: Fridtjof Nansen received the Nobel Prize "for his activities in behalf of peace and science." A Renaissance man with accomplishments in zoology, anatomy, geology, oceanography, anthropology, and art, he gained early fame as a polar explorer and, during the first few years after Norway's independence in 1905, as a statesman. It was, however, as a delegate to the League of Nations that he began his crusade against suffering and for peace. For instance, he personally organized the repatriation of over 425,000 prisoners of war after World War I, assisted the Armenians, and helped save millions of Russians from starvation. And with a "Nansen passport," political refugees and displaced persons gained an internationally recognized document of identification enabling them to apply for admission to a new home country. Nansen's service to humanity affected countless lives all over the world. (S.O.)

1925

Chamberlain, Joseph Austen, Sir 370

PRIZE: Peace, 1925. BORN: October 16, 1863; Birmingham, England. DIED: March 16, 1937; London, England. PARENTS: Father, Joseph Chamberlain; Mother, Harriet Kenrick Chamberlain. NATIONALITY: British. RELIGION: Anglican. EDUCATION: Cambridge Univ., England, baccalaureate, 1885. SPOUSE: Ivy Muriel Dundas; married 1906. CHILDREN: Diane, daughter; Joseph, son; Lawrence Endicott, son. CAREER: Britain, Member of Parliament and other posts, 1892-1937. OTHER AWARDS: Knighthood, 1925.

Selected Publications: *Peace in Our Time.* London: Allan, 1928. *The Permanent Bases of Foreign Policy.* New York: Council of Foreign Relations, 1931 (with others). *Down the Years.* London: Cassell, 1935. *Politics from the Inside, an Epistolary Chronicle, 1906-1914.* London: Cassell, 1936. *Seen in Passing.* London: Cassell, 1937.

For More Information See: *The Dictionary of National Biography, 1931-1940.* London: Oxford U. Press, 1949, 163-68. Petrie, Sir Charles. *Life and Letters of the Rt. Hon. Sir Austen Chamberlain.* 2 volumes. London: Cassell, 1939-40.

Commentary: Austen Chamberlain received the Nobel Prize for his work on the Locarno Pacts of 1925, an activity highly acclaimed also in England. The Locarno Treaty, of which he was the principal architect, set to rest many of the hatreds of World War I by guaranteeing the frontiers of Western Europe, establishing the idea of collective security, and preparing the way for Germany's entrance into the League of Nations. In his 45 years of office, Chamberlain also was responsible for many advances in fiscal policy and for establishing future patterns for dealings with China and Egypt. (F.L.T.)

Dawes, Charles Gates   371

PRIZE: Peace, 1925. BORN: August 27, 1865; Marietta, OH. DIED: April 23, 1951; Evanston, IL. PARENTS: Father, Rufus R. Dawes; Mother, Mary Beman Gates Dawes. NATIONALITY: American. RELIGION: Most probably Christian/Protestant. EDUCATION: Marietta College, OH, B.A., 1884; Cincinnati Law School, OH, L.L.B., 1886; Marietta College, OH, M.A., 1887. SPOUSE: Carol D. Blymyer, married 1889. CHILDREN: Rufus Fearing, son; Dana McCutcheon, son; Carolyn, daughter; Virginia, daughter. CAREER: Lincoln, NE, Attorney, 1887-94; Utility business development, 1894-97; United States, Comptroller of Currency, 1897-1901; Central Trust Co., Chicago, IL, President and Chair, 1902-25; United States Government, positions to Vice President, 1925-35. OTHER AWARDS: Distinguished Service Medal, United States; Companion of the Bath, England; Commander of S.S. Maurice and Lazarus, Italy; Order of Leopold, Belgium, 1919; Commander Legion d'Honneur, France, 1919.

Selected Publications: *The Banking System of the United States and Its Relation to the Money and Business of the Country.* Chicago: Rand-McNally, 1894. *Notes as Vice President.* Boston: Little, Brown and Company, 1935. *A Journal of Reparations.* London: Macmillan, 1939.

For More Information See: *Dictionary of American Biography. Supplement 5.* New York: Scribner's, 1977, 159-60. Timmons, Bascom. *Portrait of an American: Charles G. Dawes.* New York: Henry Holt, 1953.

Commentary: Charles Dawes was the Nobel recipient for his work in drafting the Dawes Plan. The apotheosis of American capitalism, Dawes acquired wealth and public influence as an innovative financier and Republican Party stalwart. From McKinley's administration to Hoover's, he held varied federal executive and diplomatic positions, capping his career as Coolidge's vice president from 1929-31. A picturesque figure, possessed of an unusual "dramatic sense" and a penchant for "direct action," Dawes chaired the Reparations Committee of Experts, convened in 1924 to resolve the crisis which threatened peace in Europe, and he popularized its report. An imaginative agreement among the former combatants to settle German reparations payments, the Dawes Plan broke the impasse among the European powers, extending back to 1914, and seemed to lay the foundations for their economic recovery. (S.W.)

1926

Briand, Aristide   372

PRIZE: Peace, 1926. BORN: March 28, 1862; Nantes, France. DIED: March 7, 1932; Paris, France. PARENTS: Father, Pierre-Guillaume Briand; Mother, Magdeleine Boucheau Briand. NATIONALITY: French. RELIGION: Christian. EDUCATION: Univ. of Paris, France, law degree, 1881. SPOUSE: None. CHILDREN: None. CAREER: Attorney, Journalist, political office through Premier (12 times), 1881-1932.

Selected Publications: Journalist efforts appeared in *Le Peuple, La Lanterne, La Petite Republique,* and *L'Humanité,* 1901-32.

For More Information See: Aubert, Alfred. *Briand.* Paris: Chiron, 1928. Baumont, Maurice. *Aristide Briand: Diplomat and Idealist.* Gottingen, Germany: Munsterschmidt, 1966. Suarez, Georges. *Briand, sa Vie, son Oeuvre.* 6 volumes. Paris: Plon, 1938-52. Thomson, Valentine. *Briand: Man of Peace.* New York: Covici-Friede, 1930.

Commentary: The great French politician, Aristide Briand, a member of 21 cabinets and 12 times Premier of France, shared the Nobel Prize for his work on the Locarno Pacts of 1925, which included treaties, guarantees, and nonaggression agreements that involved Germany, France, Poland, Belgium, and Czechoslovakia. A lifelong enemy of war, Briand nonetheless led France through a critical period in World War I but returned to peace efforts after the war. Locarno represented a peak in his performance in this regard and was followed by an even greater victory, the signing by 15 nations of the Kellogg-Briand Pact in 1928, which established arbitration as a viable concept and renounced war. Briand also proposed, in 1930, the concept of a European Union. In addition to his other efforts, Briand was noted as a supporter of labor unions and as the man who guided the Government Commission that wrote the law separating church and state, won its passage in the Chamber, and enforced it as the Cabinet Minister of Public Instruction and Worship. (B.S.S.)

Streseman, Gustav   373

PRIZE: Peace, 1926. BORN: May 10, 1878; Berlin, Germany. DIED: October 3, 1929; Berlin, Germany. PARENTS: Father, Ernest Streseman; Mother, no record found. NATIONALITY: German. RELIGION: Lutheran. EDUCATION: Univ. of Berlin, Germany, Ph.D., 1900. SPOUSE: Käthe Kleefeld, married 1906. CHILDREN: Gert Wolfgang, son; Haus Joachim, son. CAREER: German and international political offices, 1900-29. OTHER AWARDS: Deutscher Ring, Foreign Institute.

Selected Publications: *Essays and Speeches.* Freeport, NY: Books for Libraries Press, 1930.

For More Information See: Olden, Rudolf. *Streseman.* New York: E.P. Dutton, 1930. Von Rheinbaben, Rochus. *Streseman: The Man and the Statesman.* New York: D. Appleton, 1929.

Commentary: Gustav Streseman was awarded the Nobel Prize for his successful efforts on behalf of peace. Streseman's involvement in German politics after World War I was characterized by his attempt to reestablish order and peace. He succeeded in curbing the rampant inflation, and was involved in the negotiations leading to the Dawes Plan, the Locarno Pact, and the admission of Germany to the League of Nations. Streseman strove to alleviate the harsh conditions imposed upon Germany after World War I, while improving relations internationally, especially with France. He was the most prominent and influential statesman of the Weimar Republic and respected abroad as a man of goodwill. (S.O.)

1927

Buisson, Ferdinand Edouard   374
PRIZE: Peace, 1927. BORN: December 20, 1841; Paris, France. DIED: February 16, 1932; Thieuloy-Saint-Antoine, France. PARENTS: Father, Pierre Buisson; Mother, (no first name found) Ribaucourt Buisson. NATIONALITY: French. RELIGION: Protestant. EDUCATION: Univ. of Paris, France, Ph.D., 1892. SPOUSE: No name found, married 1866. CHILDREN: 2 sons, 1 daughter. CAREER: Academie du Neuchatel, Switzerland, Professor, 1866-70; French government positions, 1870-96; Sorbonne Univ., Paris, France, 1896-1901; French government and international positions, 1902-26.

Selected Publications: *Dictionnaire de Pedagogie et d'Instruction Primarie.* Paris: Hachette, 1878-87.

For More Information See: *Dictionnaire de Biographie Francaise.* Paris: Librairie Letouzey, 1956 (Volume 7), 645-46. Talbott, John E. *The Politics of Educational Reform in France, 1918-1940.* Princeton, NJ: Princeton U. Press, 1969, 57-59, 75-77, 106-07.

Commentary: Ferdinand Buisson has been called "the world's most persistent pacifist," and in the Nobel presentation statement, his prominence as a progressive educator and statesman was also acknowledged in that "...great organized work for peace must be preceded by the education of the people...." Buisson dedicated his life to peace by working consistently toward reconciliation between former adversary nations France and Germany in particular and through his efforts to reverse the Dreyfus decision; his advocacy of universal suffrage; and by helping to found human rights and peace organizations, La Ligue Internationale de la Paix et de la Liberte (1867) and La Ligue des Droits des Hommes (1898). (C.B.B.)

Quidde, Ludwig   375
PRIZE: Peace, 1927. BORN: March 23, 1858; Bremen, Germany. DIED: March 4, 1941; Geneva, Switzerland. PARENTS: No record found. NATIONALITY: German. RELIGION: Most probably Christian/Protestant. EDUCATION: No college degrees. SPOUSE: Margarethe Jacobson, married 1882. CHILDREN: None. CAREER: Independently wealthy, but served in various political, editorial, and societal roles.

Selected Publications: *Caligula: Eine Studie Über Römischen Caesarenwahnsinn.* Leipzig, Germany: Wilhelm Friedrich, 1894. "Shall There Be a Germany Irredenta?" *Living Age* 302 (September 6, 1919): 583-85. *Die Schuldfrage.* Berlin: Schwetschke, 1922. "The Future of Germany." *Living Age* 321 (April 5, 1924): 635-38.

For More Information See: Taube, Utz-Friedebert. *Ludwig Quidde: Ein Beitrag Zur Geschichte des Demokratischen Gedankens in Deutschland.* Kallmünz über Regensburg: Lassleben, 1963. Wehberg, Hans.

Ludwig Quidde: Ein Deutscher Demokrat und Vorkämpfer der Völkersverständigung. Offenbach am Main: Ballwerk, 1948.

Commentary: Ludwig Quidde received the Nobel Prize in recognition of his "long and arduous service in the course of peace." His publication of *Caligula* in 1894, seen as an attack on the Kaiser, led to his jailing and subsequent lifelong involvement in pacifist movements. During his career, he founded the Munich Peace Society, opposed German policies in 1914 and fled to Switzerland, wrote against secret military training in Germany in the 20s (and was again jailed), and was forced into exile a second time on Hitler's assumption of power in 1933. (S.K.A.)

1929

Kellogg, Frank Billings   376
PRIZE: Peace, 1929. BORN: December 22, 1856; Potsdam, NY. DIED: December 21, 1937; St. Paul, MN. PARENTS: Father, Asa F. Kellogg; Mother, Abigail Billings Kellogg. NATIONALITY: American. RELIGION: Christian. EDUCATION: No high school or college degrees; read law and admitted to bar, 1877. SPOUSE: Clara M. Cook, married 1896. CHILDREN: None. CAREER: Minnesota, Attorney, 1877-1916; Senator from Minnesota, 1917-23; Ambassador to Great Britain, 1924-25; Secretary of State, 1925-29; Minnesota, Attorney, 1929-37; Permanent Court of International Justice, Judge, 1930-35. OTHER AWARDS: Grand Cross French Legion of Honor, 1929; Order of Olive Branch of Argentina, 1930.

For More Information See: Bryn-Jones, David. *Frank B. Kellogg: A Biography.* New York: G.P. Putnam's Sons, 1937. Ellis, L. Ethan. *Frank B. Kellogg and American Foreign Relations, 1925-1929.* New Brunswick, NJ: Rutgers U. Press, 1961. Ferrell, Robert H. *Peace in Their Time: The Origins of the Kellogg-Briand Pact.* New Haven, CT: Yale U. Press, 1952. *The McGraw-Hill Encyclopedia of World Biography.* New York: McGraw-Hill Book Company, 1973 (Volume 6), 157-58.

Commentary: Frank Kellogg won the Nobel Prize for his efforts in concluding the Pact of Paris (Kellogg-Briand Treaty) in 1928. The treaty, which Kellogg moved from a proposed bilateral agreement with France to one that involved all the major nations of the world, outlawed war as an instrument of national policy. During Kellogg's tenure as secretary of state, he also improved U.S. relations with Mexico, contributed to settlement of a territorial dispute between Chile and Peru, and sought the end of a revolution in Nicaragua. He signed 80 treaties including conciliation treaties with all of the Latin American countries except Argentina and with 15 other nations. He also concluded 19 arbitration treaties. (W.K.)

1930

Söderblom, Nathan (Söderblom, Lars Olof Jonathan)   377
PRIZE: Peace, 1930. BORN: January 15, 1866; Trönö, Sweden. DIED: July 12, 1931; Uppsala, Sweden. PARENTS: Father, Jonas Söderblom; Mother, Sophia Blume Söderblom. NATIONALITY: Swedish. RELIGION: Lutheran. EDUCATION: Uppsala Univ., Sweden, B.A.,

1886; Univ. of Paris-Sorbonne, France, Doctor of Theology, 1901. SPOUSE: Anna Forsell, married 1897. CHILDREN: 7 sons; 3 daughters. CAREER: Swedish Church, positions to Archbishop, 1894-1901; Univ. of Uppsala, Sweden, Professor, 1901-12; Univ. of Leipzig, Germany, Professor, 1912-14.

Selected Publications: *Die Religionen der Erde (The Religions of the World)*. Halle, Germany: Gebauer-Schwetschke, 1905. *Einführung in die Religionsgeschichte (Introduction to the History of Religion)*. Leipzig, Germany: Quelle and Meyer, 1920. *Christian Fellowship*. New York: Fleming H. Revell, 1923.

For More Information See: *Encyclopedia of World Biography*. New York: McGraw Hill, 1973 (Volume 10), 120-21. Sundkler, Bengt. *Nathan Söderblom: His Life and Work*. Lynd, Sweden: Gleerup, 1968.

Commentary: Swedish theologian Nathan Söderblom was awarded the 1930 Nobel Prize for "his promotion of international understanding." An outspoken pacifist and leader in the ecumenical movement, he authored numerous theological works. Söderblom's dissertation, *La Vie Future d'Apres le Mazdaisme*, established him as a religious scholar. Perhaps his outstanding success was the realization of the Universal Christian Conference on Life and Work in 1925. (L.S.)

1931

Addams, Laura Jane   378

PRIZE: Peace, 1931. BORN: September 6, 1860; Cedarville, IL. DIED: May 21, 1935; Chicago, IL. PARENTS: Father, John Huy Addams; Mother, Sarah Weber Addams. NATIONALITY: American. RELIGION: Presbyterian. EDUCATION: Rockford Female Seminary, IL, A.B., 1882. SPOUSE: None. CHILDREN: None. CAREER: Hull House, Chicago, IL, Founder and Director, 1889-1935. OTHER AWARDS: Thomas Prize, Bryn Mawr College, 1931; Pictorial Reviews Annual Achievement Award, 1931; American Education Award, National Education Association, 1935.

Selected Publications: *Democracy and Social Ethics*. New York: Macmillan, 1902. *Newer Ideals of Peace*. New York: Macmillan, 1907. *The Spirit of Youth and the City Streets*. New York: Macmillan, 1909. *The Excellent Becomes the Permanent*. New York: Macmillan, 1932.

For More Information See: Addams, Jane. *The Second Twenty Years at Hull House*. New York: Macmillan, 1930. Addams, Jane. *Twenty Years at Hull House*. New York: Macmillan, 1910. Farrell, John C. *Beloved Lady: A History of Jane Addams' Ideas on Reform and Peace*. Baltimore, MD: Johns Hopkins Press, 1967. Levine, Daniel. *Jane Addams and the Liberal Tradition*. Stevens Point, WI: Worzalla Publishing Co., 1971.

Commentary: Both 1931 recipients of the Peace Prize, Jane Addams and Nicholas Murray Butler were cited by the committee for a lifetime spent "in trying to raise the ideal of peace in their people and in the whole world." The committee further noted for Jane Addams that "we also pay homage to the work which women can do for the cause of peace and fraternity among nations" and that "for twenty-five years she has been the faithful spokesman of the idea of peace." Her most notable contributions were the establishment of the internationally famous settlement house, Chicago's Hull House, and her work with the National American Woman Suffrage Association and the Women's International League for Peace and Freedom. (M.K.)

Butler, Nicholas Murray   379

PRIZE: Peace, 1931. BORN: April 2, 1862; Elizabeth, NJ. DIED: December 7, 1947; New York, NY. PARENTS: Father, Henry Leny Butler; Mother, Mary J. Murry Butler. NATIONALITY: American. RELIGION: Episcopalian. EDUCATION: Columbia Univ., NY, A.B., 1882; Columbia Univ., NY, A.M., 1883; Columbia Univ., NY, Ph.D., 1884. SPOUSE: Susanna Edwards Schyler, married 1887, died 1903; Kate La Montagne, married 1907. CHILDREN: 1 daughter. CAREER: Columbia Univ., NY, Professor and Administrator, 1885-1945. OTHER AWARDS: Goethe Gold Medal, 1932; Grand Cross of the Legion of Honor, 1937; Alexander Hamilton Award, 1947.

Selected Publications: *The International Mind: An Argument for the Judicial Settlement of International Disputes*. New York: Scribner's, 1912. *Building the American Nation: An Essay of Interpretation*. New York: Scribner's, 1923. *The Path to Peace: Essays and Addresses on Peace and Its Making*. New York: Scribner's, 1930. *The Family of Nations: Its Need and Its Problems. Essays and Addresses*. New York: Scribner's, 1938. *Why War? Essays and Addresses on War and Peace*. New York: Scribner's, 1940. *Liberty-Equality-Fraternity: Essays and Addresses on the Problems of Today and Tomorrow*. New York: Scribner's, 1942. *The World Today: Essays and Addresses*. New York: Scribner's, 1946.

For More Information See: *Across the Busy Years: Recollections and Reflections*. 2 volumes. New York: Scribner's, 1939-40. *Current Biography Yearbook*. New York: H. W. Wilson, 1940, 130-32. Marrin, Albert. *Nicholas Murray Butler*. Boston: Twayne, 1976.

Commentary: Nicholas Murray Butler—educator, innovative university administrator, and political activist in the Republican party—won the Nobel in that "during his twenty-five years of work for peace Dr. Butler has shown almost matchless strength and indefatigable energy." Through his long association with the Carnegie Endowment for International Peace he achieved world-wide influence for his ideas. Friend to the world's statesmen, in 1930 he personally gained the support of Pope Pius XI for the Kellogg-Briand pact outlawing war as an instrument of national policy. (F.L.T.)

1933

Angell, Norman, Sir (Lane, Ralph Norman Angell)   380

PRIZE: Peace, 1933. BORN: December 26, 1874; Holbeach, Lincolnshire, England. DIED: October 7, 1967; Croydon, Surrey, England. PARENTS: Father, Thomas Lane; Mother, Mary Angell Lane. NATIONALITY: British. RELIGION: Anglican. EDUCATION: No college degrees. SPOUSE: None. CHILDREN: None. CAREER: Writer and Journalist. OTHER AWARDS: Knighthood, 1931.

Selected Publications: *Patriotism Under Three Flags*. London: Unwin, 1903. *The Great Illusion*. London: Heinemann, 1910. *The Fruits of Victory*. London: Collins, 1921. *The Unseen Assassins*. London: Hamish

Hamilton, 1932. *Peace with the Dictators?* London: Hamish Hamilton, 1938. *The Steep Places.* London: Hamish Hamilton, 1947.

For More Information See: *After All: The Autobiography of Norman Angell.* New York: Farrar, Straus and Young, 1952. Marrin, Albert. *Sir Norman Angell.* Boston: Twayne, 1979.

Commentary: Journalist, author, and activist Norman Angell was awarded the Nobel Prize for his writings on peace. In 1909, he published a pamphlet which was expanded to become his most famous work, *The Great Illusion.* The book preached what was to be his continuing theme, the futility of wars of conquest as a means to achieve economic benefits and human happiness. Denounced by many during World War I as an unpatriotic pacifist, he worked steadfastly during and after the war for international cooperation through collective security. In 1932, he published *The Unseen Assassins,* a masterful and timely analysis of the issues of war and peace. Opposed to war, Angell did, however, believe that the fascist dictators should be resisted in defense of freedom. He worked against the policy of appeasement and supported the war effort during World War II. After the war, he promoted a union of the Western democracies and the international control of atomic energy. (F.L.T.)

1934

Henderson, Arthur   381

PRIZE: Peace, 1934. BORN: September 13, 1863; Glasgow, Scotland. DIED: October 20, 1935; London, England. PARENTS: Father, David Henderson; Mother, no record found. NATIONALITY: British. RELIGION: Methodist. EDUCATION: No college degrees. SPOUSE: Eleanor Percy Watson, married 1888. CHILDREN: David, son; William Watson, son; Arthur, Jr., son; Eleanor, daughter. CAREER: Foundry Worker and Union Officer, England, 1875-1903; Darlington, England, Mayor, 1903; British Parliament, Member, 1903-35. OTHER AWARDS: Wateler Peace Prize, Carnegie Foundation, 1933.

Selected Publications: *British Finance and Prussian Militarism.* New York: Hodder and Stoughton, 1917. *The Aims of Labor.* London: Headley, 1919. *Report of the Labour Commission to Ireland.* London: The Labour Party, 1921. *Consolidating World Peace.* Oxford: Clarendon Press, 1931.

For More Information See: *The Dictionary of National Biography, 1931-1940.* London: Oxford U. Press, 1949, 417-20. Hamilton, Mary. *Arthur Henderson.* London: W. Heinemann, 1938.

Commentary: Arthur Henderson was awarded the Nobel prize in recognition of the role he played as president of the League of Nation's World Disarmament Conference. During his years as president, his tireless efforts, bolstered by his firm conviction in a world commonwealth, were responsible for holding together this conference long after it had become apparent that it was doomed to failure by the rapid growth of nationalism that preceded World War II. Although Henderson's dedication to the cause of world peace was to have little influence, his other achievements were to have far-reaching effects. The greater part of his life was dedicated to the establishment, and suc-

cess, of a strong British working class party; today he is remembered as a founding father of the Labour Party. (E.G.)

1935

Ossietzky, Carl von   382

PRIZE: Peace, 1935. BORN: October 3, 1889; Hamburg, Germany. DIED: May 4, 1938; Berlin, Germany. PARENTS: Carl Ignatius von Ossietzky; Mother, Rosalie Marie Pratska von Ossietzky. NATIONALITY: German. RELIGION: Christian. EDUCATION: No college degrees. SPOUSE: Maud Woods, married May 22, 1914. CHILDREN: Rosalinde, daughter. CAREER: Germany, Journalist, 1918-38.

Selected Publications: *Schriften* (*Writings*). 2 volumes. Berlin: Aufbau, 1966.

For More Information See: Frei, Bruno. *Carl v. Ossietzky: Ritter ohne Furcht und Tadel.* Berlin: Aufbau, 1966. Grossman, Kurt R. *Ossietzky: Ein Deutscher Patriot.* Munich: Kindler, 1963. Ossietzky, Maud von. *Maud v. Ossietzky Erzahlt: Ein Lebensbild.* Berlin: Buchverlag der Morgen, 1966.

Commentary: The Academy cited Carl von Ossietzky for "his valuable contribution to the cause of peace" but noted his value as "a symbol of the struggle for peace rather than its champion." An accomplished journalist dedicated to liberalism, Ossietzky became a confirmed fighter for peace after his sad experiences as a soldier in World War I. He was a leader of the German Peace Society for many years, but his major contributions took the form of brilliant essays in a number of journals. It was as a symbol, however, that he became an international force. Beginning in 1926, he fearlessly exposed German military activities, which led to his imprisonment several times. His attacks on Hitlerism and Nazi policies, beginning in 1933, led to his banishment to concentration camp life until his death. Ossietzky's receipt of the Prize, which he was prevented from accepting, resulted in Hitler's decree that no German in the future could accept any Nobel Prize. (B.S.S.)

1936

Saavedra Lamas, Carlos   383

PRIZE: Peace, 1936. BORN: November 1, 1878; Buenos Aires, Argentina. DIED: May 5, 1959; Buenos Aires, Argentina. PARENTS: Father, Mariano Saavedra Zavaleta; Mother, Luisa Lamas. NATIONALITY: Argentinian. RELIGION: Christian. EDUCATION: National Univ., Argentina, Doctorate of Laws, 1903. SPOUSE: Rosa Saenz Pena, married 1903. CHILDREN: Carlos Roque, son. CAREER: Univ. of La Plata and Univ. of Buenos Aires, Argentina, Professor and Administrator (to President), 1903-46; concurrently served in a number of political posts. OTHER AWARDS: International Medal, Pan-American Society, NY, 1933; Star of the German Red Cross, 1936; Grand Cross of the Legion of Honor, France.

Selected Publications: *Traites Internationaux de Type Social: Les Conventions sur L'Emigration et le Travail Perspective Qu'elles Offrent aux Pays Sud-Americains et Specialement a la Republique Argentine.* Paris: Pedone, 1924. *Centro de Legislacion Social y del Trabajo.* Buenos Aires: Imprenta de la Universidad,

1927. *La Crise de la Codification et de la Doctrine Argentine de Droit International.* Paris: Pedone, 1931. *Codigo Nacional del Trabajo.* 3 volumes. Buenos Aires: Roldan, 1933.

For More Information See: *Encyclopedia of World Biography.* New York: McGraw-Hill, 1973 (Volume 9), 346-47. Oro Maini, Atilio dell. *Carlos Saavedra Lamas.* Buenos Aires: Anales de la Academia Nacional de Derecho y Ciencias Sociales, 1960.

Commentary: In a dual career as a distinguished professor of law and political leader, Carlos Saavedra Lamas earned the Nobel Prize through his espousal of an Antiwar Pact born in Latin America and submitted to the League of Nations, as well as for his work in the League of Nations. Saavedra Lamas had served Argentina in a number of important posts from 1906-32, sponsoring legislation that clarified policies on water rights, agriculture, immigration, and finances. His international prominence began in 1932 when, as foreign minister, he succeeded in ending the Chaco War between Paraguay and Bolivia; he also developed the foundation for and presented the South American Antiwar Pact first to the American nations and later to the League of Nations. He was President of the League in 1936. (R.A.)

1937

Cecil, Edgar Algernon Robert Gascoyne, Sir   384

PRIZE: Peace, 1937. BORN: September 14, 1864; London, England. DIED: November 24, 1958; Turnbridge Wells, England. PARENTS: Father, Robert Arthur Talbot Cecil; Mother, Georgiana Alderson Cecil. NATIONALITY: British. RELIGION: Episcopalian. EDUCATION: Oxford Univ., England, baccalaureate, 1881; Oxford Univ., England;, law degree, 1884. SPOUSE: Eleanor Lambton, married 1889. CHILDREN: None. CAREER: Private Secretary, 1886-88; Attorney, 1888-1906; British Parliament and other political positions, 1906-27. OTHER AWARDS: Knighthood, 1923.

Selected Publications: *Our National Church.* London: F. Warne & Co., 1913 (with H. J. Clayton). *The Moral Basis of the League of Nations.* London: Lindsey Press, 1923. *The Co-operation of Nations.* London: U. of London Press, 1928. *The Way of Peace.* London: P. Allan & Co., 1928. *All the Way.* London: Hodder & Stoughton, 1949.

For More Information See: *A Great Experiment: An Autobiography.* New York: Oxford U. Press, 1941. Jackson, Jere Langdon. "Apostle of the League: Lord Robert Cecil and the Fight for the League of Nations, 1916-1924." (Ph.D. dissertation, U. of North Carolina at Chapel Hill, 1974).

Commentary: Edgar Cecil was awarded the Nobel Prize for his work as one of the architects of the League of Nations and as its faithful defender. The League occupied much of his life, while at the same time he served his country in a variety of important government posts. Cecil had the distinction of being an important figure in the founding of the League, in its history throughout its existence, and in the final meetings in Geneva in 1946, when he said "The League is dead; long live the United Nations." (B.L.)

1945

Hull, Cordell   385

PRIZE: Peace, 1945. BORN: October 2, 1871; Overton County, TN. DIED: July 23, 1955; Bethesda, MD. PARENTS: Father, William Hull; Mother, Elizabeth Riley Hull. NATIONALITY: American. RELIGION: Protestant. EDUCATION: Cumberland Univ., TN, law degree, 1891. SPOUSE: Rose Frances Witz Whitney, married 1917. CHILDREN: None. CAREER: Tennessee, House of Representatives, Member, 1893-97; Tennessee, Infantry Captain, 1898-99; Attorney, 1899-1903; Tennessee, Judge, 1903-07; United States, House of Representatives, Member, 1907-31; United States, Senator, 1931-33; United States, Secretary of State, 1933-44. OTHER AWARDS: Woodrow Wilson Medal, 1937; Theodore Roosevelt Distinguished Service Medal, 1945.

Selected Publications: *Economic Barriers to Peace.* New York: Woodrow Wilson Foundation, 1937.

For More Information See: Hinton, Harold B. *Cordell Hull: A Biography.* Garden City, NY: Doubleday, Doran and Company, 1942. *The Memoirs of Cordell Hull.* 2 volumes. New York: The Macmillan Company, 1948. Pratt, Julius. *Cordell Hull, 1933-44.* 2 volumes. New York: Cooper Square Publishers, 1964.

Commentary: The award to Cordell Hull was "for his long and indefatigable work for understanding between nations." Hull was cited for his prominent role in laying the groundwork for the United Nations as an organization dedicated to the maintenance of peace following World War II. The Nobel Committee also recognized Hull's lifelong efforts at lowering trade barriers as a means to improve international relations and remove one of the causes of war; and his promotion of peace among the nations of the American continents through the implementation of Franklin D. Roosevelt's "good neighbor policy." (G.S.)

1946

Balch, Emily Greene   386

PRIZE: Peace, 1946. BORN: January 8, 1867; Boston, MA. DIED: January 7, 1961; Cambridge, MA. PARENTS: Father, Francis Vergnies Balch; Mother, Ellen Noyes Balch. NATIONALITY: American. RELIGION: Unitarian. EDUCATION: Bryn Mawr College, PA, A.B., 1889. SPOUSE: None. CHILDREN: None. CAREER: Children's Aid Society, Boston, MA, Social Worker, 1891; Denison House Settlement, Boston, MA, Headworker, 1892-93; Wellesley College, MA, Professor, 1896-1918; *The Nation*, NY, Editor, 1918-19.

Selected Publications: *Public Assistance of the Poor in France.* Baltimore, MD: American Economic Association, 1893. *Our Slavic Fellow Citizens.* New York: Charities Publication Committee, 1910. *Approaches to the Great Settlement.* New York: B.W. Huebsch, 1918. *The Miracle of Living.* New York: Island Press, 1941.

For More Information See: *Current Biography Yearbook.* New York: H.W. Wilson, 1948, 32-34. Randall, Mercedes M. *Improper Bostonian: Emily Greene Balch.* New York: Twayne Publishers, 1964.

Commentary: The Nobel Award to Emily Greene Balch recognized her important contributions as a leader of the international women's movement for peace. Her activism began in 1915 when she served as a delegate to the International Congress of Women, and later as an official spokesperson to the then-neutral Scandinavian countries, Russia, and the United States. She continued her work as a founder, officer, and lifelong worker of the Women's International League for Peace and Freedom. In 1919, after 22 years of her teaching, Wellesley College declined to reappoint her because of her pacifist views. (J.M.S.)

Mott, John R.   **387**
PRIZE: Peace, 1946. BORN: May 25, 1865; Livingston Manor, NY. DIED: January 31, 1955; Orlando, FL. PARENTS: Father, John Stitt Mott; Mother, Elmira Dodge Mott. NATIONALITY: American. RELIGION: Methodist. EDUCATION: Cornell Univ., NY, Ph.B., 1888. SPOUSE: Leila Ada White, married November 26, 1891; died September 28, 1952; Agnes Peter, married July 28, 1953. CHILDREN: John Livingstone, son; Irene, daughter; Frederick Dodge, son; Eleanor, daughter. CAREER: Young Men's Christian Association, Administrator, 1888-1931. OTHER AWARDS: Distinguished Service Medal, United States, 1919; Order of the Crown, Siam, 1919; Chevalier, French Legion of Honor, 1919; Chevalier, Order of the Crown of Italy, 1920; Imperial Order of the Sacred Treasure, Japan, 1920 and 1929; Star of the Hungarian Red Cross, 1923; Order of Polona Restituta, Poland, 1924; Order of the Holy Sepulchre, Jerusalem, 1924; Order of the Savior, Greece, 1924; Order of the White Lion, Czechoslovakia, 1930; Order of the Jade, China, 1938; Order of the White Rose, Finland, 1946; Prince Carl Medal, Sweden, 1946; Commander's Cross, Order of Merit of the Federated Republic of Germany, 1954.

Selected Publications: *Liberating the Lay Forces of Christianity.* New York: Macmillan, 1932. *Five Decades and a Forward View.* New York: Harper and Brothers, 1939. *Addresses and Papers.* 6 volumes. New York: Association Press, 1946-1947.

For More Information See: *Current Biography Yearbook.* New York: H.W. Wilson, 1947, 453-56. *Dictionary of American Biography. Supplement 5 (1951-1955).* New York: Scribner's, 1977, 506-08. Hopkins, Charles Howard. *John R. Mott, 1865-1955: A Biography.* Grand Rapids, MI: Eerdmans, 1979.

Commentary: John Mott was neither a politician nor an active participant in peace organizations but was awarded the Nobel Prize for his steadfast commitment to spreading the word of Christ, as well as his inspiration to youth, his leading role in five world church and missionary movements, his demonstrated respect for individual differences, and humanitarian efforts in time of war. A recognized leader of the Christian ecumenical movement and an organizer at his best when dealing with diverse elements, Mott was also instrumental in founding the World Council of Churches. (M.L.L.)

1949

Orr, John Boyd (Orr, Boyd, Lord)   **388**
PRIZE: Peace, 1949. BORN: September 23, 1880; Kilmaurs, Ayrshire, Scotland. DIED: June 25, 1971; Brechin, Angus, Scotland. PARENTS: Father, Robert Clark Orr; Mother, Annie Boyd Orr. NATIONALITY: Scottish. RELIGION: Presbyterian. EDUCATION: Glasgow Univ., Scotland, M.A., 1902; Glasgow Univ., Scotland, B.Sc., 1910; Glasgow Univ., Scotland, M.B., Ch.B., 1912; Glasgow Univ., Scotland, M.D., 1914; Glasgow

Univ., Scotland, D.Sc., 1920. SPOUSE: Elizabeth Pearson Callum, married 1915. CHILDREN: Elizabeth Joan, daughter; Helen Ann, daughter; Donald Noel, son. CAREER: British Military Service, 1914-19; Rowett Institute, England, Director and Publisher, 1914-45; Glasgow Univ., Scotland, Rector and Chancellor, 1945-71; Food and Agriculture Organization, United Nations, Director, 1946-48. OTHER AWARDS: Knighthood, 1935; Raised to peerage, 1948; Legion d'Honneur, 1949; Harben Medal, Royal Institute of Public Health, 1949; Gold Medal, International Federation of Agricultural Producers, 1949; Gold Medal, National Farmers Union of America, 1951; Borden Gold Medal, U.S.A., 1958.

Selected Publications: *Food, Health and Income.* London: Macmillan, 1936. *Food and the People.* London: Pilot Press, 1943. *The White Man's Dilemma.* London: Allen and Unwin, 1953. *Feast and Famine.* London: Rathbone Books, 1957. *As I Recall: The 1880's to the 1960's.* London: MacGibbon and Kee, 1966.

For More Information See: *Current Biography Yearbook.* New York: H.W. Wilson Co., 1946, 440-43. Cuthbertson, D.P. "Lord Boyd Orr (1880-1971): A Biographical Sketch." *Journal of Nutrition.* 105 (May 1975): 519-24. Kay, H.D. "John Boyd Orr, Baron Boyd Orr of Brechin Mearns." In *Biographical Memoirs of Fellows of the Royal Society* (Volume 18), 43-81. London: The Royal Society of London, 1972.

Commentary: John Boyd Orr was recognized by the Academy for his efforts to eliminate world hunger and to promote global unity and peace. A nutritionist, Orr learned early that it was easier to persuade farmers to feed animals well than it was to convince people of the importance of human nutrition. As the first director-general of the Food and Agriculture Organization, he tried, unsuccessfully, to establish a world food plan. Much of his later life was spent working toward a "United States of the World" that would allow such a plan to exist. "There can be no peace in the world so long as a large proportion of the population lack the necessities of life...," John Boyd Orr stated in his Nobel lecture. (M.L.L.)

1950

Bunche, Ralph Johnson   **389**
PRIZE: Peace, 1950. BORN: August 7, 1904; Detroit, MI. DIED: December 9, 1971; New York, NY. PARENTS: Father, Fred Bunche; Mother, Olive Agnes Johnson Bunche. NATIONALITY: American. RELIGION: Protestant. EDUCATION: Univ. of California, Los Angeles, A.B., 1927; Harvard Univ., MA, A.M., 1928; Harvard Univ., MA, Ph.D., 1934. SPOUSE: Ruth Ethel Harris, married June 23, 1930. CHILDREN: Joan Harris, daughter; Jane Johnson, daughter; Ralph Johnson, Jr., son. CAREER: Howard Univ., Washington, DC, Professor, 1929-41; United States government positions, 1942-47; United Nations positions, 1947-71. OTHER AWARDS: Spingarm Medal, National Association for the Advancement of Colored People, 1949; Medal of Freedom, 1963.

Selected Publications: *A World View of Race.* Washington, DC: Associates in Negro Folk Education, 1936. "What America Means to Me." *American Magazine*

149 (February 1950): 19, 122-26. *The Political Status of the Negro in the Age of FDR.* Chicago: U. of Chicago Press, 1973.

For More Information See: *Current Biography Yearbook.* New York: H. W. Wilson, 1948, 77-79. Kugelmass, J. A. *Ralph J. Bunche: Fighter for Peace.* New York: Julian Messner, 1952. Mann, Peggy. *Ralph Bunche: UN Peacemaker.* New York: Coward, McCann and Geoghegan, 1975.

Commentary: Ralph Bunche earned the Nobel Prize for mediating the war among Israel, Egypt, Jordan, Lebanon, and Syria, a war which had followed the United Nation's plan in 1947 for partitioning Palestine. As personal representative of the UN Secretary General, Bunche accompanied Count Folke Bernadotte, UN mediator, to the Middle East. Following Bernadotte's assassination, Bunche became acting mediator and directed the difficult and complex negotiations between Israeli and Arab delegations which culminated in the signing of armistice agreements between these countries in 1949. Bunche was earlier an outstanding academic, a civil rights activist, and a leading United States government service employee. His career ended with 25 years of service to the United Nations. (D.N.S.)

1951

Jouhaux, Leon   390

PRIZE: Peace, 1951. BORN: July 1, 1879; Paris, France. DIED: April 28, 1954; Paris, France. PARENTS: No record found. NATIONALITY: French. RELIGION: Christian. EDUCATION: No college degrees. SPOUSE: (No first name found) Jouhaux, married (no date found). CHILDREN: None. CAREER: Match Company, Paris, France, Unskilled Laborer, 1895-1900; Paris, France, Unskilled Laborer, 1900-02; France, Union Activist and Leader, 1902-54. OTHER AWARDS: Medal of the French Resistance, 1946.

Selected Publications: *The International Federation of Trade Unions and Economic Reconstruction.* Amsterdam: IFTU, 1922. *Le Desarmement.* Paris: Alcan, 1927. *Le Mouvement Syndical en France.* Berlin: Federation Syndicale Internationale, 1931.

For More Information See: *Current Biography Yearbook.* New York: H.W. Wilson, 1948, 329-31. *Living Age* 352 (July 1937): 419-25. Millet, Raymond. *Jouhaux et la C.G.T.* Paris: Denoel et Steele, 1937.

Commentary: Leon Jouhaux was recognized for his "work and struggle to elevate the working class, and first of all to improve their conditions." He received the Prize "because from his earliest years he has time after time thrown himself into the fight for peace and against war...." Jouhaux, forced into work at a match factory at age 13, became a leader of the French trade-union movement and an officer in the national organization, The Confederation Generale du Travail (C.G.T.) from 1909-51. He used his power to lead the C.G.T. into peace programs which included support of arms limitation, international arbitration, respect for all nationalities, and open treaties. (T.B.)

1952

Schweitzer, Albert   391

PRIZE: Peace, 1952. BORN: January 14, 1875; Kayersburg, Alsace. DIED: September 4, 1965; Lambaréné, Gabon, French Equatorial Africa. PARENTS: Father, Louis Schweitzer; Mother, Adele Schillinger Schweitzer. NATIONALITY: French; later French Equatorial African resident. RELIGION: Lutheran. EDUCATION: Univ. of Strasbourg, France, Ph.D., 1899; Univ. of Strasbourg, France, Licentiate, 1900; Univ. of Strasbourg, France, Doctorate in Medicine, 1913. SPOUSE: Helene Bresslau, married June 18, 1912. CHILDREN: Rhena Fanny Suzanne Schweitzer Eckert Miller, daughter. CAREER: Chapel of St. Nicholas, Strasbourg, France, Preacher, 1899-1900; Univ. of Strasbourg, France, Principal of Theological College, 1901-12; Schweitzer Hospital, Gabon, France, Founder and Director, 1913-65. OTHER AWARDS: Goethe Memorial Prize, Frankfurt, 1928; Wellcome Medal, Royal African Society, 1952; Grand Gold Medal, Paris, 1955; Pour le Merite, Germany, 1955; Order of Merit, England, 1955.

Selected Publications: *J.S. Bach, le musicien-poete.* Paris: Costallat, 1905 (Tr. by Ernest Newman. Neptune, NJ: Paganiniana, 1980). *Deutsche und Franzosische Orgelbaukunstund Orgelkunst.* Leipzig, Germany: Breitkopf und Hartel, 1906 (*Organ Playing and Organ Building in France and Germany.* Tr. by William D. Turner, Braintree, MA: Organ Literature). *Von Reimarus zu Wrede.* Tübingen, Germany: J.C.B. Mohr, 1906 (*The Quest of the Historical Jesus: A Critical Study of Its Progress from Reimarus to Wrede.* Tr. by W. Montgomery. New York: Macmillan, 1968). *Zwischen Wasser und Urwald.* Upsala, Sweden: Lindblad Publishing House, 1921 (*On the Edge of the Primeval Forest.* Tr. by C.T. Campion. New York: AMS Press, 1976). *Kultur und Ethik.* Munich: C.H. Beck, 1923 (*Civilization and Ethics.* Tr. by C.T. Campion. London: A. & C. Black, 1923). *Aus Meiner Kindheit und Jugendzeit.* Bern, Switzerland: Paul Haupt, 1924 (*Memoirs of Childhood and Youth.* Tr. by C.T. Campion. New York: Macmillan, 1949). *Die Mystik des Apostels Paulus.* Tübingen, Switzerland: J.C.B. Mohr (Siebeck), 1930 (*The Mysticism of Paul the Apostle.* Tr. by W. Montgomery. New York: Crossroad, 1968). *Aus Meinem Leben und Denken.* Leipzig, Germany: Felix Meiner, 1931 (*Out of My Life and Thought.* Tr. by C.T. Campion, New York: Holt, 1933).

For More Information See: Anderson, Erica. *Albert Schweitzer's Gift of Friendship.* New York: Harper, 1964. Brabazon, James. *Albert Schweitzer: A Biography.* New York: Putnam, 1975. Cousins, Norman. *Dr. Schweitzer of Lambaréné.* New York: Harper, 1960. *Current Biography Yearbook.* New York: H.W. Wilson, 1965, 375-78. *Encyclopedia of World Biography.* New York: McGraw-Hill, 1973 (Volume 9), 477-80. Schweitzer, Albert. *Memoirs of Childhood and Youth.* Tr. by C.T. Campion. New York: Macmillan, 1949. Schweitzer, Albert. *Out of My Life and Thought.* Tr. by C.T. Campion. New York: Holt, 1933. Seaver, George. *Albert Schweitzer, the Man and his Mind.* New York: Harper, 1955.

Commentary: Albert Schweitzer, musician, theologian, philosopher, doctor, earned the respect and admiration of the world as a humanitarian, receiving the Nobel Prize for his efforts in behalf of "the Brotherhood of Nations." The author of scholarly books on

Bach and theology, a renowned organ builder and organist, he became known to the world as the founder and director of the Schweitzer Hospital in Lambaréné, Gabon, French Equatorial Africa. His "Reverence for Life" philosophy left a profound mark on the world. (M.K.)

1953

Marshall, George Catlett   392
PRIZE: Peace, 1953. BORN: December 31, 1880; Union-town, PA. DIED: October 16, 1959; Bethesda, MD. PARENTS: Father, George Catlett Marshall; Mother, Laura Bradford Marshall. NATIONALITY: American. RELIGION: Episcopalian. EDUCATION: Virginia Military Institute, graduate, 1901. SPOUSE: Elizabeth Carter Coles, married 1902, died 1927; Katharine Tupper Brown, married 1930. CHILDREN: None. CAREER: U.S. Army and Government Posts, 1902-51. OTHER AWARDS: Gold Medal, Distinguished Service Medal, and Victory Medal, USA; Croix de Guerre Montenegro; Grand Croix Legion of Honor, France; Officer, Order of the Crown, Italy; Knight Grand Cross, Order of the Bath, England; Order of Suvarov, USSR; Theodore Roosevelt Distinguished Service Medal, 1945; Humanitarian Award, Varieties Clubs, 1947; Freedom House Award, 1947; Gold Medal, National Planning Association, 1949; National Civic Service Award, 1949; New York Board of Trade Award, 1949; Distinguished Public Service Award, Conference of Mayors, 1949; Citizenship Award, Disabled American Veterans, New York Chapter, 1950; Distinguished Service Medal, American Legion, 1951; Four Freedoms Foundation Award, 1952.

Selected Publications: *Memories of My Service in the World War, 1917-18.* Boston: Houghton-Mifflin, 1976. Bland, Larry I. (ed.), *The Papers of George Catlett Marshall.* Baltimore, MD: Johns Hopkins U. Press, 1981-.

For More Information See: Ferrell, Robert H. *George C. Marshall.* New York: Cooper Square Publishers, 1966. Mosley, Leonard. *Marshall, Hero for Our Times.* New York: Hearst Books, 1982. Pogue, Forrest C. *George C. Marshall.* Multivolume set. New York: Viking Press, 1963-.

Commentary: To later generations, General George Catlett Marshall's selection for the Nobel Peace Prize seems anomalous. The seemingly contradictory selection of a military man, the first ever chosen to receive the Peace Prize, is more apparent than real. While serving as Secretary of State, Marshall promoted peace in the aftermath of the most devastating war in history and received the Nobel honor most probably for the Marshall Plan, which provided American loans and technical assistance to any European states pursuing recovery. Throughout his career, Marshall covered himself in glory, especially as Chief of Staff of the U.S. Army (1939-45), Secretary of State (1947-49), and Secretary of Defense (1950-51). (R.S.L.)

1957

Pearson, Lester Bowles   393
PRIZE: Peace, 1957. BORN: April 23, 1897; Newton Brook, Canada. DIED: December 27, 1972; Ottawa, Canada. PARENTS: Father, Edwin Arthur Pearson;

Mother, Annie Sarah Bowles Pearson. NATIONALITY: Canadian. RELIGION: Methodist. EDUCATION: Univ. of Toronto, Canada, B.A., 1919; Oxford Univ., England, B.A., 1923; Oxford Univ., England, M.A., 1925. SPOUSE: Maryon Elspeth Moody, married 1925. CHILDREN: Geoffrey Arthur, son; Patricia Lillian Hannah, daughter. CAREER: Univ. of Toronto, Canada, Professor, 1926-28; Canadian Government, positions through Prime Minister, 1928-68. OTHER AWARDS: Order of Merit, England, 1962; Medallion of Valor, Israel.

Selected Publications: *Democracy in World Politics.* Princeton, NJ: Princeton U. Press, 1955. *Diplomacy in the Nuclear Age.* Cambridge, MA: Harvard U. Press, 1959. *Peace in the Family of Man.* New York: Oxford U. Press, 1969. *Words and Occasions.* Toronto: U. of Toronto Press, 1970.

For More Information See: Bothwell, Robert. *Pearson, His Life and World.* New York: McGraw-Hill, 1978. *Current Biography Yearbook.* New York: H.W. Wilson, 1963, 319-21. *Mike: The Memoirs of the Right Honourable Lester B. Pearson.* Toronto: U. of Toronto Press, 1972-75.

Commentary: Lester Pearson was the Nobel recipient for lifelong work in pursuit of peace, culminating in his efforts to resolve the Suez Canal Crisis of 1956. An immensely likeable person, quick in mind, and buoyant in spirit, "Mike" Pearson spent 40 years at the center of Canadian foreign policy development, the first 20 as an increasingly respected professional diplomat, the latter 20 as a successful Liberal Party leader. For nearly 10 years, as Minister for External Affairs (1948-57), he presided over a veritable golden age of Canadian leadership in the postwar quest for world peace, and he culminated his distinguished political career as prime minister (1963-68). Following the combined British, French, and Israeli attack upon Egypt in 1956, Pearson took the lead in United Nations efforts to resolve the Suez Canal Crisis. His long diplomatic experience, familiarity with principal actors, and highly respected "personal qualities" enabled him to fashion a solution acceptable to all parties, ending the armed conflict and restoring peace to the region. (S.W.)

1958

Pire, Dominique, Reverend (François, Georges Charles Clement Ghislain Eugéne)   394
PRIZE: Peace, 1958. BORN: February 10, 1910; Dinant, Belgium. DIED: January 30, 1969; Louvain, Belgium. PARENTS: Father, Georges Pire; Mother, Berthe Ravet Pire. NATIONALITY: Belgian. RELIGION: Catholic. EDUCATION: Colegio Angelico, Italy, Doctor of Sacred Theology, 1936. SPOUSE: None. CHILDREN: None. CAREER: Dominican Priest, 1934-69; Studium de la Sarte-Huy, Professor, 1937-47; Crusader for the successful settlement of displaced persons, 1947-69. OTHER AWARDS: Croix de Guerre with palms, Belgium; Croix d'Honneur du Merite Civique Français; Medaille de la Résistance with crossed swords; Legion d'Honneur, France; Cross of Merit Order of Merit, Germany; Medaille de la Reconnaissance Nationale; Sonning Prize, Denmark, 1964.

Selected Publications: *The Story of Father Dominique Pire, Winner of the Nobel Peace Prize, as Told to Hugues Vehenne.* Tr. by John L. Skeffington. New York: Dutton, 1961. *Building Peace.* Tr. by Graeme

M. Ogg. London: Transworld Publishers, 1967. *Vivre ou Mourir Ensemble.* Brussels: Presses Academiques Europeennes, 1969.

For More Information See: *Current Biography Yearbook.* New York: H.W. Wilson, 1959, 362-64. Houart, Victor. *The Open Heart: The Inspiring Story of Father Pire and the Europe of the Heart.* Tr. by Mervyn Savill. London: Souvenir Press, 1959. Kent, George. "Father Pire: Nobel Prize Winner." *Catholic World* 189 (April 1959): 26-31.

Commentary: Father Dominique Pire was awarded the Nobel Prize for his work with European refugees. He organized a sponsorship program which put refugee families living in camps in touch with private families elsewhere and founded four homes for elderly refugees and seven European villages for the resettlement of refugees. The international society L'Aide aux Personnes Deplacées (Aid to Displaced Persons) was also established by Father Pire to assist stateless refugees with material and moral support. (J.C.H.)

1959

Noel-Baker, Philip John   395

PRIZE: Peace, 1959. BORN: November 1, 1889; London, England. DIED: October 8, 1982; London, England. PARENTS: Father, Joseph Allen Baker; Mother, Elizabeth B. Moscrip Baker. NATIONALITY: British. RELIGION: Quaker. EDUCATION: Cambridge Univ., England, baccalaureate, 1912; Cambridge Univ., England, M.A., 1914. SPOUSE: Irene Noel, married 1915. CHILDREN: Francis Edward, son. CAREER: Ruskin College, England, Vice-Principal, 1914; Cambridge Univ., England, Fellow and War Service, 1915-19; British Government Offices, 1919-24; Univ. of London, England, Professor, 1924-29; British Parliament and Government, various positions, 1929-70. OTHER AWARDS: Mons Star, 1915; Croce di Guerra, 1918; Howland Prize, Yale U., CT, 1934; Silver Medal, 1947; Albert Schweitzer Book Prize, 1960.

Selected Publications: *The Geneva Protocol for the Pacific Settlement of International Disputes.* London: King, 1925. *Disarmament.* London: Hogarth, 1926. *The League of Nations at Work.* London: Nisbet, 1926. *Disarmament and the Coolidge Conference.* London: Leonard and Virginia Woolf, 1927. *The Private Manufacture of Armaments.* London: Gollancz, 1936. *The Arms Race: A Programme for World Disarmament.* London: Stevens, 1958. *The Way to World Disarmament—Now!* London: Union of Democratic Control, 1963.

For More Information See: *Annual Obituary.* New York: St. Martin's Press, 1982. Russell, Bertrand. "Philip Noel-Baker: A Tribute." *International Relations* 2 (1960): 1-2.

Commentary: Philip Noel-Baker was awarded the Nobel for his contributions as a tireless worker for world peace through disarmament. For 53 years, he worked for peace in his speeches, writings, and participation in every international disarmament conference. His service to Britain was equally impressive, both as an Olympic medal winner and Captain of Britain's team and in a long career in Parliament and a succession of government offices. (A.J. and B.S.S.)

1960

Luthuli, Albert John   396

PRIZE: Peace, 1960. BORN: 1898 (?); Rhodesia. DIED: July 21, 1967; Groutville, South Africa. PARENTS: Father, John Luthuli; Mother, Mtonya Luthuli. NATIONALITY: South African. RELIGION: Congregationalist. EDUCATION: No college degrees. SPOUSE: Nokukhanya Bhengu, married 1927. CHILDREN: 2 sons; 5 daughters. CAREER: Adam's Mission Station College, South Africa, Teacher, 1921-36; Abasemakholweni Tribe, South Africa, Chief, 1936-53; African National Congress, President-General, 1953-67. OTHER AWARDS: United Nations Human Rights Prize, 1968.

Selected Publications: "What I Would Do If I Were Prime Minister." *Ebony* 17 (February 1962): 21-29. *Africa's Freedom.* London: Allen and Unwin, 1964.

For More Information See: Benson, Mary. *Chief Albert Luthuli of South Africa.* London: Oxford U. Press, 1963. *Current Biography Yearbook.* New York: H.W. Wilson, 1962, 271-73. *Let My People Go.* New York: McGraw-Hill, 1962. *New York Times* (October 24, 1961): 22.

Commentary: Albert Luthuli was cited by the Academy for his leadership in peaceful resistance to apartheid in South Africa, noting that "in his fight against racial discrimination he had always worked for nonviolent methods." A longtime teacher, tribal chieftain, President of the African National Congress, and a leader of Christianity in South Africa, Luthuli was a forceful figure of international stature in affairs within South Africa, despite being harassed and under internal exile for a good part of his career. (B.S.S.)

1961

Hammarskjold, Dag Hjalmar Agne Carl   397

PRIZE: Peace, 1961 (posthumous). BORN: July 29, 1905; Jonkoping, Sweden. DIED: September 17, 1961; Northern Rhodesia. PARENTS: Father, Hjalmar Hammarskjold; Mother, Agnes Almquest Hammarskjold. NATIONALITY: Swedish. RELIGION: Lutheran. EDUCATION: Uppsala Univ., Sweden, B.A., 1925; Uppsala Univ., Sweden, LLB, 1930; Univ. of Stockholm, Sweden, Ph.D., 1934. SPOUSE: None. CHILDREN: None. CAREER: Commission on Unemployment, Sweden, Secretary, 1930-34; Bank of Sweden, Secretary, 1935-36; Ministry of Finance, Sweden, 1936-45; Ministry of Foreign Affairs, Sweden, 1946; Organization of European Economic Cooperation, Executive Committee Vice-Chair, 1948-49; General Assembly, U.N., 1949-61.

Selected Publications: *The Servant of Peace.* New York: Harper and Row, 1962. *Markings.* New York: Knopf, 1964.

For More Information See: *Current Biography Yearbook.* New York: H.W. Wilson Co., 1953, 241-43. *Encyclopedia of World Biography.* New York: McGraw-Hill, 1973 (Volume 5), 65-66. Stolpe, Sven. *Dag Hammarskjold.* New York: Scribner's Sons, 1966.

Commentary: Although the award to Dag Hammarskjold did not mention any specific achievement, it was widely speculated at the time that the award was presented posthumously for his work toward peace in the Congo. The recipient drew upon 18 years of distinguished service in the Swedish government and for the Organization for European Economic Cooperation to develop the office of the Secretary General of the United Nations as a nonpolitical arena which could serve as a channel of communication and an impartial consultant in international conflicts. Hammarskjold proved the effectiveness of this philosophy in 1955 when he secured the release of 15 American aviators shot down and held by the Chinese; in his role as mediator during the 1956 Middle East crisis; and during the 1960-61 problems in the new Republic of the Congo. (E.G.)

1962

Pauling, Linus Carl *see* **entry 56**

1964

King, Martin Luther, Jr.   **398**
PRIZE: Peace, 1964. BORN: January 15, 1929; Atlanta, GA. DIED: April 4, 1968; Memphis, TN. PARENTS: Father, Martin Luther King, Sr.; Mother, Alberta Williams King. NATIONALITY: American. RELIGION: Baptist. EDUCATION: Morehouse College, GA, A.B., 1948; Crozer Theological Seminary, PA, B.D., 1951; Boston Univ., MA, Ph.D., 1955. SPOUSE: Coretta Scott, married June 18, 1953. CHILDREN: Youlanda Denise, daughter; Martin Luther, III, son; Dexter Scott, son; Bernice Albertine, daughter. CAREER: Ebenezer Baptist Church, Atlanta, GA, Pastor, 1947-54; Dexter Avenue Baptist Church, Montgomery, AL, Pastor, 1954-60; Ebenezer Baptist Church, Atlanta, GA, Pastor, 1960-68. OTHER AWARDS: Pearl Plafker Award, Crozer Theological Seminary, PA, 1951; Spingarn Medal, National Association for the Advancement of Colored People, 1957; Man of the Year, *Time*, 1963.
    Selected Publications: *Stride Toward Freedom.* New York: Harper and Row, 1958. *Strength to Love.* New York: Harper and Row, 1963. *Why We Can't Wait.* New York: Harper and Row, 1964. *Where Do We Go from Here: Chaos or Community.* New York: Harper and Row, 1967. *The Trumpet of Conscience.* New York: Harper and Row, 1968.
    For More Information See: Ansbro, John. *Martin Luther King, Jr.: The Making of a Mind.* Maryknoll, NY: Orbis Books, 1982. *Current Biography Yearbook.* New York: H.W. Wilson, 1965, 220-23. King, Coretta Scott. *My Life with Martin Luther King, Jr.* New York: Holt, Rinehart and Winston, 1969.
    Commentary: Nobel recipient Martin Luther King, Jr., received his award for his efforts to bring about integration within the United States without violence. Beginning with the successful boycott of the Montgomery, AL, transit company that ended segregated seating on buses in the community, King led Black Americans into a new era of achievement of civil rights based on a nonviolent philosophy and a return of love for hate. He was also later a leader in the movement to end the Vietnam War. (B.S.)

1968

Cassin, Rene-Samuel   **399**
PRIZE: Peace, 1968. BORN: October 5, 1887; Bayonne, France. DIED: February 20, 1976; Paris, France. PARENTS: Father, Henri Cassin; Mother, Gabrielle Dreyfus

Cassin. NATIONALITY: French. RELIGION: Jewish. EDUCATION: Univ. of Aix-en-Provence, France, degree in humanities, 1908; Univ. of Aix-en-Provence, France, degree in law, 1908; Univ. of Aix-en-Provence, France, doctorate, 1914. SPOUSE: Simone Yzombard, married 1917. CHILDREN: None. CAREER: Paris, France, Attorney, 1909-14; French Army, 1914-16; Univ. of Aix-en-Provence, France, Professor, 1916-20; Univ. of Lille, France, Professor, 1920-29; Univ. of Paris, France, Professor, 1929-60. OTHER AWARDS: Human Rights Prize, United Nations, 1968; Goethe Prize, 1973; Grand Croix Legion d'Honneur; Croix de Guerre.
    Selected Publications: *La Conception des Droits de L'Etat dans les Successions d'apres le Code Civil Suisse.* Paris: Sirey, 1914. *L'Inegalite entre l'Homme et la Femme dans la Legislation Civile.* Marseille: Barlatier, 1919. *Pour la Defense de la Paix.* Paris: n.p., 1936. "How the Charter on Human Rights was Born." *UNESCO Courier* 21 (January 1968): 4-6.
    For More Information See: *Encyclopedia Judaica.* New York: Macmillan, 1971 (Volume 5), 231. *New York Times* (October 10, 1968): 1, 14.
    Commentary: Rene Cassin was awarded the Nobel Prize "primarily for his contribution to the protection of human worth and the rights of man, as set forth in the Universal Declaration of Human Rights." Renowned as a jurist, humanitarian, and internationalist, Cassin brought to all of his activities a profound respect for human rights. His legal scholarship included notable work on contracts, inheritance, domicile, and the inequality between men and women. He was a major force in French politics during World Wars I and II and especially in his work with Charles DeGaulle. Cassin occupied important positions in France, Europe, and the United Nations throughout his long career. He founded the French Federation of Disabled War Veterans and guided it as well as the High Council for Wards of the Nation for many years. But he will be remembered primarily as a charter member of the United Nations Commission on Human Rights, its chair or vice-chair for much of its existence, and the one most responsible for drafting the Declaration of Human Rights. (T.B. and B.S.S.)

1970

Borlaug, Norman Ernest   **400**
PRIZE: Peace, 1970. BORN: March 25, 1914; Cresco, IA. PARENTS: Father, Henry O. Borlaug; Mother, Clara Vaala Borlaug. NATIONALITY: American. RELIGION: Lutheran. EDUCATION: Univ. of Minnesota, B.S., 1937; Univ. of Minnesota, M.S., 1940; Univ. of Minnesota, Ph.D., 1941. SPOUSE: Margaret G. Gibson, married September 24, 1937. CHILDREN: Norma Jean Rhoda, daughter; William Gibson, son. CAREER: DuPont, DE, Microbiologist, 1942-44; Rockefeller Foundation, NY, Research Scientist and Administrator working primarily in Mexico, 1944-. OTHER AWARDS: Agricultural Editors Association Award, 1967; International Agronomy Award, 1968; Distinguished Service Medal, Pakistan, 1968.
    For More Information See: *Champions of Peace.* Birmingham, England: Paddington Press, 1976, 290-92. *Current Biography Yearbook.* New York: H.W. Wilson, 1971, 50-52. Gray, Tony.

Commentary: Norman Borlaug was cited by the Nobel Committee for his leadership in the "Green Revolution" in developing countries in that "he has helped to provide bread for a hungry world. We have made this choice in the hope that providing bread will also give the world peace." Borlaug's contribution was finding a high-yield, dwarf, disease-resistant wheat strain, capable of cultivation in a wide range of climatic conditions, to provide relief from famine in developing countries. (M.J.H.)

1971

Brandt, Willy (Frahm, Herbert Ernst Karl)   401

PRIZE: Peace, 1971. BORN: December 18, 1913; Lübeck, Germany. PARENTS: Father, Unknown; Mother, Martha Frahm; Stepfather, Emil Kuhlman. NATIONALITY: German. RELIGION: Anti-religious; from Christian background. EDUCATION: No college degrees. SPOUSE: Carlotta Thorkildsen, married 1940, divorced 1948; Rut Hansen Bergaust, married 1948, divorced 1980; Brigitte Seebacher, married 1983. CHILDREN: Ninja, daughter; Peter, son; Lars, son; Matthias, son. CAREER: *Lübecker Volksbote*, Reporter, 1927-33; Lübeck, Germany, Shipbroker, 1933-34; Student and miscellaneous activities, 1934-39; Norwegian Army, 1940; Stockholm, Reporter, 1940-48; Berlin, Germany, Political Offices to Mayor and in Social Democratic Party, 1948-66; Germany, Political Offices to Chancellor, 1966-. OTHER AWARDS: Grosskreuz des Verdienstorden der Bundesrepublik Deutschland, 1959; Grand Cross, Order of St. Olaf, Norway, 1960; Freedom Prize, Freedom House Organization, 1961; Man of the Year, *Time*, 1970; Order of Pius IX, Vatican, 1970; Reinhold-Niebuhr Prize, 1972; Aspen Institute for Humanistic Studies Prize, 1973; Gold Medal, B'nai Brith, 1981; Third World Prize, 1985.

Selected Publications: *My Road to Berlin.* Garden City, NY: Doubleday, 1960. *The Ordeal of Coexistence.* Cambridge, MA: Harvard U. Press, 1963. *A Peace Policy for Europe.* New York: Holt, Rinehart and Winston, 1969. *In Exile: Essays, Reflections and Letters, 1933-47.* Philadelphia, PA: U. of Pennsylvania Press, 1971. *People and Politics: The Years 1960-1975.* Boston: Little, Brown, 1978.

For More Information See: Binder, David. *The Other German: Willy Brandt's Life & Times.* Washington, DC: New Republic Books, 1975. *Current Biography Yearbook.* New York: H.W. Wilson, 1958, 57-58. Harpprecht, Klaus. *Willy Brandt: Portrait and Self-Portrait.* Los Angeles: Nash Publishing Co., 1971. Prittie, Terence. *Willy Brandt: Portrait of a Statesman.* New York: Schocken Books, 1974.

Commentary: The Nobel Committee unanimously selected Willy Brandt, citing his "efforts to obtain for the people of West Berlin the fundamental human rights of personal security and full freedom of movement" and his "outstanding efforts in order to create conditions for peace in Europe." In a long and respected career, he fought Naziism, wrote in Norway and Germany, and led postwar Germany back to some measure of economic and political health, working toward normal relations between East and West. (S.K.A.)

1973

Kissinger, Henry Alfred   402

PRIZE: Peace, 1973. BORN: May 27, 1923; Fuerth, Germany. PARENTS: Father, Louis Kissinger; Mother, Paula Stern Kissinger. NATIONALITY: German; later American citizen. RELIGION: Jewish. EDUCATION: Harvard Univ., MA, A.B., 1950; Harvard Univ., MA, M.A., 1952; Harvard Univ., MA, Ph.D., 1954. SPOUSE: Ann Fleischer, married February 6, 1949, divorced 1964; Nancy Maginnes, married March 30, 1974. CHILDREN: Elizabeth, daughter; David, son. CAREER: U.S. Army, 1943-46; Harvard Univ., MA, Professor, 1954-69; U.S. Government, Special Assistant to the President and Secretary of State, 1969-77; Kissinger Associates, Chair, 1978-. OTHER AWARDS: Woodrow Wilson Book Prize, 1958; Guggenheim Fellowship, 1965-66; Gold Medal, National Institute of Social Sciences, 1972; *Time* Man of the Year, 1972; American Institute for Public Service Award, 1973; Jefferson Award, 1973; Theodore Roosevelt Award, 1973; American Legion Distinguished Service Medal, 1974; Wateler Peace Prize, 1974; Presidential Medal of Freedom, 1977.

Selected Publications: *Nuclear Weapons and Foreign Policy.* New York: Harper, 1957. *A World Restored: Metternich, Castlereagh and the Problem of Peace.* Boston: Houghton-Mifflin, 1957. *The Necessity for Choice: Prospects of American Foreign Policy.* New York: Harper, 1961. *The Troubled Partnership: A Re-Appraisal of the Atlantic Alliance.* New York: McGraw-Hill, 1965. *American Foreign Policy.* 3d ed. New York: Norton, 1977. *White House Years.* Boston: Little, Brown, 1979.

For More Information See: *Current Biography Yearbook.* New York: H.W. Wilson Co., 1972, 254-57. Dickson, Peter W. *Kissinger and the Meaning of History.* Cambridge: Cambridge U. Press, 1978. *Encyclopedia of American Biography.* New York: Harper and Row, 1974, 623-25. Graubard, Stephen R. *Kissinger: Portrait of a Mind.* New York: Norton, 1973. Hersh, Seymour M. *The Price of Power: Kissinger in the White House.* New York: Summit Books, 1983. Morris, Roger. *Uncertain Greatness: Henry Kissinger and American Foreign Policy.*

Commentary: Henry Kissinger received the Nobel Prize for his work in "negotiating an end to the war in Vietnam," together with Le Duc Tho of North Vietnam. The awards generated a storm of protests and led to the resignation of two committee members. Kissinger is known for his scholarly and practical work in international relations and for his development, as a government consultant and secretary of state, of American defense and foreign policy. He is also remembered for his long efforts toward a negotiated peace between Israel and the Arab countries. (D.B.)

Le Duc Tho (Phan Dinh Khai)   403

PRIZE: Peace, 1973 (refused). BORN: October 14, 1911; Dich Le, Vietnam. PARENTS: No record found. NATIONALITY: Vietnamese. RELIGION: No record found. EDUCATION: No college degrees. SPOUSE: Married twice. CHILDREN: No record found. CAREER: Vietnam, Communist Party Positions, 1930-.

Selected Publications: No record found.

For More Information See: *Current Biography Yearbook.* New York: H.W. Wilson, 1975, 235-38. *New York Times Biographical Edition* (October 1973): 1683.

Commentary: Le Duc Tho shared the Nobel Prize with Henry Kissinger for his work in negotiating the Vietnam armistice. He refused the award on the grounds that there was no peace in Vietnam. Others bitterly resented the award made to a man dedicated to communism and to wars of liberation. Though his public presence in the long and arduous sessions of negotiation with Kissinger won him international recognition, Le Duc Tho had been known since 1930 as one of the founders of the Indochinese Communist Party and as a powerful figure in the Vietnamese political arena. (R.J.)

1974

MacBride, Sean   404
PRIZE: Peace, 1974. BORN: January 26, 1904; Paris, France. PARENTS: Father, John MacBride; Mother, Maud Gonne MacBride. NATIONALITY: Irish. RELIGION: Catholic. EDUCATION: National Univ., Ireland, law study, 1937. SPOUSE: Catalina Bulfin, married 1926. CHILDREN: Tiernan, son; Anna, daughter. CAREER: Irish Republican Army, 1918-24; Ireland, Journalist, 1924-37; Ireland, Attorney, 1937-47; Ireland and United Nations, Attorney and Politician, 1947-83. OTHER AWARDS: International Gaelic Hall of Fame, 1974; Man of the Year, Irish United Societies, 1975; Lenin International Prize, 1977; Medal of Justice, U.S., 1978; International Institute of Human Rights Medal, 1978; UNESCO Silver Medal, 1980.

Selected Publications: *Civil Liberty.* N.p., 1948. *Our People—Our Money.* 3 lectures. Dublin: Browne and Nolan, 1949. *Ireland; Economy; Report on Italian Economic Situation.* N.p., 1955. *Report on Current Economic Situation in Western Europe.* N.p., 1956.

For More Information See: *New York Times Biographical Edition.* (October 1974): 1459. *Time* 104 (October 21, 1974): 18.

Commentary: Sean MacBride was awarded the Nobel Prize for his lifelong commitment to rights actions, including his work on human rights, on peace and disarmament, and on the liberation of Namibia from South African rule. MacBride's youthful militancy in the Irish Republican Army, his years as a successful attorney, and his political prowess were invaluable assets in a number of important international posts, including committee responsibilities and officerships in the Council of Ministers of the Council of Europe, the Council of OEEC, the Pan European Union, the International Commission of Jurists, the Council of Minorities Rights Group, the International Peace Bureau, Amnesty International, the U.N. Commission for Namibia, and the UNESCO Study Group on Communication Problems. (T.N.B.)

Sato, Eisaku   405
PRIZE: Peace, 1974. BORN: March 27, 1901; Tabuse, Yamaguchi, Japan. DIED: June 2, 1975; Tokyo, Japan. PARENTS: Father, Hidesuke Sato; Mother, Moyo Sato. NATIONALITY: Japanese. RELIGION: Shinto. EDUCATION: Tokyo Imperial Univ., Japan, law degree, 1924.

SPOUSE: Hiroku Sato, married February 25, 1926. CHILDREN: Ryotaro, son; Shinji, son. CAREER: Japanese Government, posts to Prime Minister, 1924-72.

For More Information See: *Current Biography Yearbook.* New York: H.W. Wilson Co., 1965, 361-64, and 1975-76, 473. Gray, Tony. *Champions of Peace.* New York: Paddington Press, 1976, 302-05. *New York Times.* June 3, 1975, 1:36.

Commentary: Eisaku Sato was awarded the Nobel Peace Prize for his determined antimilitarism and a "reconciliation policy that contributed to a stabilization of conditions in the Pacific area." His winning of the Nobel Prize capped a 48-year career of service to Japan, including eight years as prime minister. (W.E.W.)

1975

Sakharov, Andrei Dmitriyevich   406
PRIZE: Peace, 1975. BORN: May 21, 1921; Moscow, USSR. PARENTS: No record found. NATIONALITY: Russian. RELIGION: Christian; most probably Eastern Orthodox. EDUCATION: Moscow State Univ., USSR, B.A., 1942; Lebedev Institute of Physics, USSR, Ph.D., 1947. SPOUSE: First wife, no record found; Yelena G. Bonner, married 1971. CHILDREN: 1 son; 1 daughter. CAREER: Lebedev Institute of Physics, USSR, Professor, 1945-80; Internal Exile, 1980-. OTHER AWARDS: Eleanor Roosevelt Peace Award, 1974; Cino del Duca Prize, 1974; Reinhold Niebohr Prize, U. of Chicago, IL, 1974; Order of Lenin, USSR; Fritt Ord Prize, 1980.

Selected Publications: *Progress, Coexistence, and Intellectual Freedom.* New York: Norton, 1968. *Sakharov Speaks.* New York: Knopf, 1974. *My Country and the World.* New York: Knopf, 1975. *Alarm and Hope.* New York: Vintage Books, 1978.

For More Information See: Babyonyshev, Alexander. *On Sakharov.* New York: Knopf, 1982. *Current Biography Yearbook.* New York: H. W. Wilson, 1971, 361-63.

Commentary: Andrei Sakharov was cited by the Committee in that "Sakharov's fearless personal commitment in upholding the fundamental principles for peace between men is a powerful inspiration for all true work for peace." Sakharov was a brilliant physicist, noted as the father of the Soviet hydrogen bomb, before embarking in the 1960s on his lifelong pursuit of, first, educational and scientific thought reform in the Soviet Union, and, later, intellectual freedom and a democratic socialism that would bring the United States and the Soviet Union together in cooperative efforts. (S.K.)

1976

Corrigan, Mairead   407
PRIZE: Peace, 1976. BORN: January 27, 1944; Belfast, Northern Ireland. PARENTS: Father, Andrew Corrigan; Mother, Margaret Corrigan. NATIONALITY: Irish. RELIGION: Catholic. EDUCATION: No college degrees. SPOUSE: Jack Maguire, married September 8, 1981. CHILDREN: None. CAREER: Textile factory, Belfast, Ireland, Bookkeeper, 1960-65; Guiness Son and Company, Belfast, Ireland, Secretary, 1965-76; Peace People, Founder and Administrator, 1976-. OTHER

AWARDS: Carl von Ossietzky Medal, Berlin, 1976; People's Peace Prize, Norway, 1976; Hall of Fame, United States, 1977.

For More Information See: *Current Biography Yearbook.* New York: H.W. Wilson, 1978, 88-91. Deutsch, Richard. *Mairead Corrigan, Betty Williams.* Translated by Jack Bernard. Woodbury, NY: Barron's, 1977. Hershey, Robert D. "Nobels Go to 2 Ulster Women and to Amnesty International." *New York Times* (October 11, 1977): 1+.

Commentary: The award citation praised both Mairead Corrigan and Betty Williams because they had "acted from a profound conviction that the individual can make a meaningful contribution to peace through constructive reconciliation" and had "paved the way for the strong resistance against violence and misuse of power, which was present in broad circles of the people." Corrigan's impetus for starting the Irish group Peace People came from the killing of three of her nieces and nephews by a car driven by a terrorist who had been shot. After her sister committed suicide, she married her brother-in-law, Jack Maguire. She remains an active worker for peace. (K.J.H.)

Williams, Elizabeth 408

PRIZE: Peace, 1976. BORN: May 22, 1943; Andersonstown, Belfast, Northern Ireland. PARENTS: No record found. NATIONALITY: Irish. RELIGION: Catholic (mother)/Protestant (father) background. EDUCATION: No college degrees. SPOUSE: Ralph Williams, married June 14, 1961, dissolved (no date found); James T. Perkins, married 1982. CHILDREN: Paul, son; Deborah, daughter. CAREER: Ireland, Clerk and Waitress, 1961-76; Community of Peace People, Ireland, Leader, 1976-. OTHER AWARDS: Carl von Ossietsky Medal for Courage, 1976; Norwegian People's Peace Prize, 1976.

Selected Publications: Occasional Writer for *Peace by Peace*, 1976-86.

For More Information See: *Current Biography Yearbook.* New York: H.W. Wilson, 1979, 434-37. Deutsch, Richard. *Mairead Corrigan, Betty Williams.* Translated by Jack Bernard. Woodbury, NY: Barron's, 1977.

Commentary: Betty Williams shared the Nobel Prize with Mairead Corrigan in recognition of the fact that "their initiative paved the way for the strong resistance against violence and misuse of power which was present in broad circles of the people." Shocked into action by her witnessing of the accidental death (caused by police action) of Mairead Corrigan's sister, Anne Maguire, and her three children, Betty Williams and Mairead Corrigan launched the organization, Peace People, with the goal of ending the fighting and killing in Ireland. The organization, under Williams's leadership, has remained a force in Ireland and in the world. (T.B.)

1978

Begin, Menachim Wolfovitch 409

PRIZE: Peace, 1978. BORN: August 16, 1913; Brest-Litovsk, Poland. PARENTS: Father, Zeev-Dov Begin; Mother, Hassia Kossovsky Begin. NATIONALITY: Polish; later Israeli citizen. RELIGION: Jewish. EDUCATION: Warsaw Univ., Poland, Masters of Jurisprudence, 1935. SPOUSE: Aliza Arnold, married 1939. CHILDREN: Benjamin, son; Hassia, daughter; Leah, daughter. CA-

REER: Betar Zionist Youth Movement, Staff and Administrator, 1929-40; Israeli Affairs and Politics, 1942-83.

Selected Publications: *The Revolt: Story of the Irgun.* Tr. by Shmuel Katz. New York: Schuman, 1951. *White Nights: The Story of a Prisoner in Russia.* Tr. by Katy Kaplan. London: MacDonald, 1957.

For More Information See: *Current Biography Yearbook.* New York: H. W. Wilson Co., 1978, 41-45. Gervasi, Frank Henry. *The Life and Times of Menahem Begin: Rebel to Statesman.* New York: Putnam, 1979. Herschler, Gertrude, and Eckman, Lester S. *Menahem Begin: From Freedom Fighter to Statesman.* New York: Shengold Publishers, 1979. Silver, Eric, *Begin: A Biography.* London: Weidenfeld and Nicolson, 1984.

Commentary: Menachim Begin shared the Nobel Prize for his "contribution to the two frame agreements on peace in the Middle East, and on peace between Egypt and Israel, which were signed at Camp David on September 17, 1978." Begin's entire public career was dedicated to the achievement and perpetuation of a Jewish state, first as a rebel, then as a Knesset hawk, and finally as prime minister and peace negotiator. (I.S.Z.)

El-Sadat, Muhammed Anwar 410

PRIZE: Peace, 1978. BORN: December 25, 1918; Mit Abul-Kum, Minufiyah Province, Egypt. DIED: October 6, 1981; Cairo, Egypt. PARENTS: Father, Muhammed El-Sadat; Mother, no record found. NATIONALITY: Egyptian. RELIGION: Islamic. EDUCATION: Royal Military Academy, Egypt, baccalaureate, 1938. SPOUSE: Married 1938; Jihan Safwat Raouf, married 1949. CHILDREN: 3 daughters by first wife; with second wife, Gamal, son; Lubna, daughter; Noha, daughter; Jihan, daughter. CAREER: Egyptian Army and Politics, 1938-81. OTHER AWARDS: Sinai Medal, 1974; Man of the Year, *Time*, 1977; Methodist Peace Prize, 1978.

Selected Publications: *Revolt on the Nile.* Tr. by Thomas Graham. London: A. Wingate, 1957. *In Search of Identity: An Autobiography.* New York: Harper and Row, 1978. *Speeches and Interviews by President Anwar el-Sadat.* Cairo: Arab Republic of Egypt, Ministry of Information, 1971-79. *The Public Diary of President Sadat.* Ed. by Raphael Israeli. Leiden, Netherlands: Brill, 1979.

For More Information See: *Current Biography Yearbook.* New York: H.W. Wilson Co., 1971, 358-61. Hirst, David, and Beeson, Irene. *Sadat.* London: Faber and Faber, 1981. Narayan, B.K. *Anwar el-Sadat: Man with a Mission.* New Delhi: Vikas Publishers, 1977.

Commentary: Anwar Sadat shared the Nobel Prize for his "contribution to the two frame agreements on peace in the Middle East, and on peace between Egypt and Israel, which were signed at Camp David on September 17, 1978." In the wake of the October War of 1973, Sadat increasingly sought conciliation with the Israelis, culminating in his historic trip to Jerusalem in November 1977. Substantive agreements were reached at the Camp David talks and a peace treaty was signed in March 1979. This was the highlight of a career-long involvement in Egyptian military and political life, which included a role in the overthrow of the Farouk monarchy. (I.S.Z.)

1979

Teresa, Mother (Bojaxhiu, Agnes Gonxha)   411
PRIZE: Peace, 1979. BORN: August 27, 1910; Skopje, Yugoslavia. PARENTS: Father, Nikola Bojaxhiu; Mother, Dranofile Bernai Bojaxhiu. NATIONALITY: Yugoslavian; later Indian citizen. RELIGION: Catholic. EDUCATION: No formal college degrees; educated for teaching in the novitiate in Darjeeling, India. SPOUSE: None. CHILDREN: None. CAREER: Sisters of Loretto, Teacher and Principal, 1928-48; Missionary, 1948-. OTHER AWARDS: Padma Shri Lotus Order, 1962; Magsaysay Prize, 1963; Good Samaritan Prize, 1970; Joseph Kennedy Jr. Foundation Award, 1971; Pope John XXIII Peace Prize, 1971; Jawaharlal Nehru Award of India, 1972; Templeton Prize for Progress in Religion, 1973; Saint Louise de Marillac Award, 1973; Albert Schweitzer Award, 1975; Balzan Award, Italy, 1979; Bharat Ratna Award, 1980.
For More Information See: *Current Biography Yearbook.* New York: H.W. Wilson, 1973, 403-06. Egan, Eileen. *Such a Vision of the Street.* New York: Doubleday, 1985. Muggeridge, Malcolm. *Something Beautiful for God.* New York: Walker, 1984. Rae, Daphne. *Love Until It Hurts: The Work of Mother Teresa and Her Missionaries of Charity.* New York: Harper and Row, 1981. Spink, Kathryn. *The Miracle of Love: Mother Teresa of Calcutta, Her Missionaries of Charity and Her Co-Workers.* New York: Harper and Row, 1982.
Commentary: In announcing Mother Teresa of Calcutta as the winner of the 1979 Nobel Peace Prize, the Committee said, "This year, the world has turned its attention to the plight of children and refugees, and these are precisely the categories for whom Mother Teresa has for many years worked so selflessly." As a Sister of Loretto, she taught and was principal of St. Mary's High School in Calcutta for 20 years before being inspired to leave the cloister to work among the destitute, the dying, and the orphaned children in the slums of Calcutta. Since founding her order, the Society of the Missionaries of Charity, in 1950, Mother Teresa's work among the poorest of the poor has spread to 50 Indian cities and more than 25 countries. The order operates schools, hospitals, youth centers, and orphanages, and 53,000 lepers are among the patients treated at medical centers in Africa and Asia. (P.E.J.)

1980

Perez Esquivel, Adolfo   412
PRIZE: Peace, 1980. BORN: November 26, 1931; Buenos Aires, Argentina. PARENTS: No record found. NATIONALITY: Argentinian. RELIGION: Catholic. EDUCATION: National School of Fine Arts, Argentina, graduate, 1956. SPOUSE: Amanda Perez, married 1956. CHILDREN: Leopoldo, son; 2 other sons. CAREER: Manuel Belgrano Escuela Nacional de Bellas Artes, Buenos Aires, Argentina, Professor, 1956-73; Service for Justice and Peace in Latin America, Founder and Secretary General, 1973-. OTHER AWARDS: Premio La Nacion de Escultura; Memorial Juan XXIII, Instituto de Polelogia Victor Seix, Barcelona, Spain, 1977.
Selected Publications: *Paz y Justicia,* Founder and Editor, 1973-.

For More Information See: *Current Biography Yearbook.* New York: H.W. Wilson, 1981, 321-24. *New York Times Biographical Service* (October 14, 1980): 1455-56. *1980 Vela de Armas.* Mexico City: Las Ediciones del Tiempo, 1980, 315-16, 473.
Commentary: Adolfo Perez Esquivel was honored as "a spokesman of a revival of respect of human rights...having shone a light through the darkness" of Argentina's military rule. Perez Esquivel left a distinguished career as a sculptor to become a human rights activist and Catholic church lay leader coordinating human rights efforts in Argentina and in all of Latin America. He was mistreated and jailed by the Argentinian military government for 14 months early in his career without charge or trial but has persisted in his efforts through the Service for Justice and Peace, which he founded, and through a women's group, Las Locas de Mayo. (R.A.)

1982

Garcia Robles, Alfonso   413
PRIZE: Peace, 1982. BORN: March 20, 1911; Zamora, Michoacan, Mexico. PARENTS: Father, Quirino Garcia; Mother, Teresa Robles. NATIONALITY: Mexican. RELIGION: Catholic. EDUCATION: Univ. of Mexico, law degree, 1938(?); Univ. of Paris, France, law degree, 1938(?); Academy of International Law, Netherlands, law degree, 1938(?). SPOUSE: Juana Maria de Szyslo, married 1950. CHILDREN: Alfonso, son; Fernando, son. CAREER: Mexican Government, various posts in Embassies, United Nations, and in Mexico, 1939-.
Selected Publications: *La Anchura del Mar Territorial.* Mexico: Collegio de Mexico, 1966. *Se Anos de la Politica Exterior de Mexico (Six Years of Mexican Foreign Policy).* Tlateloco, Mexico: Secretaria de Relaciones Exteriores, 1976. *La Conferencia de Revision del Tratado Sobre la No Proliferation de las Armas Nucleares (The Review Conference on the Non-Proliferation Treaty).* Mexico City: Editorial de El Colegio Nacional, 1977. *338 Dias de Tlateloco (338 Days of Tlateloco).* Mexico: Fondo de Cultura Economica, 1977.
For More Information See: *Christian Century* (November 3, 1982): 1097. *New York Times Biographical Service* (October 14, 1982): 1305.
Commentary: The Nobel Prize awarded to Alfonso Garcia Robles was "not only a reward for almost twenty years of work on disarmament, but also vindication of the virtues of patient and methodical negotiation." Garcia Robles's major contribution was the Treaty of Tlateloco, written to ban nuclear weapons from Latin America in the 60s, and signed by 22 nations. Although dedicated to disarmament, he has also been a national and international spokesperson for Mexico in a number of important government and United Nations posts that date back to 1939. His documents on Mexico's position on the Law of the Sea in the late 50s are notable as well. (R.A.)

Myrdal, Alva Reimer   414
PRIZE: Peace, 1982. BORN: January 31, 1902; Uppsala, Sweden. DIED: February 1, 1986; Stockholm, Sweden. PARENTS: Father, Albert Reimer; Mother, Lova Larsson Reimer. NATIONALITY: Swedish. RELIGION: Lutheran. EDUCATION: Univ. of Stockholm, Sweden, B.A., 1924;

Univ. of Uppsala, Sweden, M.A., 1934. SPOUSE: Gunnar Myrdal, married October 8, 1924. CHILDREN: Jan, son; Sissela Bok, daughter; Kaj Ffolster, daughter. CAREER: Stockholm, Sweden, Teacher, 1924-32; Central Prison, Stockholm, Sweden, Psychologist, 1932-34; Training College for Preschool Teachers, Stockholm, Sweden, Director, 1935-48; United Nations, New York, Administrator, 1949-55; Swedish Government, Ambassador and Minister, 1955-73; Center for the Study of Democratic Institutions, Santa Barbara, CA, Researcher, 1973-74; Massachusetts Institute of Technology, Professor, 1974-75; Wellesley College, MA, Professor, 1976-77; Institute for Research on Poverty, Madison, WI, Researcher, 1977-78. OTHER AWARDS: West German Peace Prize, 1970; Wateler Prize, Hague Academy of International Peace, 1973; Prize, Royal Swedish Institute of Technology, 1975; Monismanien Prize, 1976; Gold Medal, Royal Swedish Academy of Science, 1977; Albert Einstein Peace Prize, 1980; People's Peace Prize, Norway, 1981.

Selected Publications: *Crisis in the Population Question.* Stockholm: A. Bonnier, 1934 (with Gunnar Myrdal). *Women in the Community.* Copenhagen: TARP, 1943. *Women's Two Roles: Home and Work.* Copenhagen: Routledge and Kegan Paul, 1956. *Our Responsibility for the Poor Peoples: Development Problems at Close View.* Copenhagen: Raben and Sjoegren, 1961. *The Game of Disarmament.* New York: Pantheon, 1977.

For More Information See: *Contemporary Authors.* Detroit, MI: Gale, 1978 (Volume 69-72), 448-50. *New York Times Biographical Service* (October 1982): 1367-68.

Commentary: Alva Myrdal received the Nobel Prize for her obsessive work in the latter part of her life in pursuit of disarmament. Her early career included many years as a teacher and as a director of teachers' colleges in Sweden, while at the same time working with her husband, Gunnar, also a Nobel Prize winner, in their sociological work on the population problem and in general areas of social philosophy. A later interest was the role of women. Appointed to important United Nations and Swedish posts, Myrdal became a force in national and international policy. (J.G.)

1983

Walesa, Lech 415

PRIZE: Peace, 1983. BORN: September 29, 1943; Popow, Poland. PARENTS: Father, Boleslaw Walesa; Mother, Feliksa Walesa. NATIONALITY: Polish. RELIGION: Catholic. EDUCATION: No college degrees. SPOUSE: Miroslawa Walesa, married 1969. CHILDREN: 4 sons; 3 daughters. CAREER: Lenin Shipyard, Gdansk, Poland, Electrician, 1963-76; Polish Labor Leader, 1976-. OTHER AWARDS: Man of the Year, *Time,* 1981; Love International Award, 1981; Freedom Medal, U.S.A., 1981; Medal of Merit, 1981; Social Justice Award, 1983.

For More Information See: *Current Biography Yearbook.* New York: H.W. Wilson, 1981, 436-39. *New York Times Biographical Service* (October 1983): 1271-72.

Commentary: Lech Walesa was granted the Nobel Prize for his efforts through negotiation and nonviolent protest to gain the right for Polish workers to organize freely. Walesa was involved in labor unrest almost from his first working day and eventually

(1976) lost his electrician's position because of his activities. He was one of the founders of the free trade union on the Baltic Coast in 1979, the forerunner of the large union Solidarity which Walesa has guided since its beginnings. Harassed constantly and jailed by Polish leaders, Walesa remains a symbol to Polish labor and the Polish people, with his activities "characterized by a determination to solve his country's problems through negotiation and cooperation without resorting to violence." (J.H.S.)

1984

Tutu, Desmond Mpilo 416

PRIZE: Peace, 1984. BORN: October 7, 1931; Klerksdorp, Witwatersrand, Transvaal, South Africa. PARENTS: Father, Zachariah Tutu; Mother, Aletta Tutu. NATIONALITY: South African. RELIGION: Anglican. EDUCATION: Bantu Normal College, South Africa, Teacher's Diploma, 1953; Univ. of South Africa, B.A., 1954; St. Peter's Theological College, South Africa, L.Th., 1960; King's College (Univ. of London), England, B.D., 1966; King's College (Univ. of London), England, M.Th., 1966. SPOUSE: Leah Nomalizo Shenxane, married July 2, 1955. CHILDREN: Trevor, son; Naomi, daughter; Mpho, daughter; Thandi, daughter. CAREER: South Africa, Schoolmaster, 1954-57; Anglican Church, South Africa, Parish Priest and various administrative positions, 1960-. OTHER AWARDS: Athena Prize, Onassis Foundation, Greece, 1980; Family of Man Gold Medallion, 1983.

Selected Publications: *Crying in the Wilderness: The Struggle for Justice in South Africa.* London: A.R. Mowbray and Co., 1982. *Hope and Suffering: Sermons and Speeches.* Johannesburg: Skotaville Publishers, 1983.

For More Information See: *Current Biography Yearbook.* New York: H.W. Wilson, January 1985, 40-44. "Gifts Seen and Heard." *Commonweal* III (November 30, 1984): 645-46. Hammer, Joshua. "Urging Nonviolent Change in His Tortured Land: South Africa's Desmond Tutu Wins the Nobel Prize." *People* 22 (December 17, 1984): 185-87.

Commentary: The Nobel Prize Committee indicated that Bishop Desmond Tutu's recognition "should be regarded not only as a gesture of support to him and to the South African Council of Churches of which he is leader, but also to all individuals and groups in South Africa who, with their concern for human dignity, fraternity and democracy, incite the admiration of the world." Tutu has been outspoken for much of his life against apartheid, South Africa's system of strict race separation. In 1984 and 1985, he became personally involved in intervening to defuse violence and in advocating the withdrawal of foreign investments from South Africa. (P.P.F.)

Physics

1901

Roentgen, Wilhelm Conrad   417

PRIZE: Physics, 1901. BORN: March 27, 1845; Lennep, Germany. DIED: February 10, 1923; Munich, Germany. PARENTS: Father, Friedrich Conrad Roentgen; Mother, Charlotte Constanze Frowein Roentgen. NATIONALITY: German. RELIGION: Lutheran. EDUCATION: Polytechnic, Switzerland, engineering diploma, 1868; Polytechnic, Switzerland, Ph.D., 1869. SPOUSE: Anna Bertha Ludwig, married January 19, 1872. CHILDREN: None; but adopted wife's niece, Josephina Bertha. CAREER: Univ. of Zurich, Switzerland, Researcher, 1869; Univ. of Wurzburg, Germany, Researcher, 1870-72; Univ. of Strasbourg, Germany, Professor, 1872-75; Agricultural Academy, Hohenheim, Germany, Professor, 1875-76; Univ. of Strasbourg, Germany, Professor, 1876-79; Univ. of Giessen, Germany, Professor, 1879-88; Univ. of Wurzburg, Germany, Professor, 1888-1900; Univ. of Munich, Germany, Professor, 1900-23. OTHER AWARDS: Rumford Medal, Royal Society, 1896; Royal Order of Merit, Bavaria, 1896; Baumgaertner Prize, Vienna Academy, 1896; Elliot-Cresson Medal, Franklin Institute, Philadelphia, PA, 1897; Prize Lacaze, Paris, 1897; Mattencei Medal, Rome, 1897; Otto-Wahlbuch-Stiftung Prize, Hamburg, 1898; Order of Merit of St. Michael, I class, 1900; Silver Medal of Prince Regent Luitpold, 1900; Barnard Medal, Columbia U., NY, 1900; Komitur of the Order of the Italian Crown, 1900; Order Pour le Merite for Science and Art, France, 1911; Helmholtz Medal, Germany, 1919.

Selected Publications: "On a New Kind of Rays, a Preliminary Communication." *Sitzungsberichte Phys.-Med. Ges. Wurzburg* (1895): CXXXVII. "On a New Kind of Rays, Continued." *Sitzungsberichte Phys.-Med. Ges. Wurzburg* (1896): XI. "Further Observations on the Properties of X-rays." *Math. u. Naturw. Mitt. a.d. Sitzungsberichte Preuss. Akad. Wiss., Physik.-Math. Kl.*(1897): 392.

For More Information See: *Dictionary of Scientific Biography.* New York: Scribner's, 1975 (Volume 11), 529-31. Glasser, Otto. *Dr. W.C. Roentgen.* Springfield, IL: Thomas, 1945. Nitske, W. Robert. *The Life of Wilhelm Conrad Roentgen, Discoverer of the X-ray.* Tucson, AZ: U. of Arizona Press, 1971.

Commentary: Wilhelm Roentgen, first recipient of the Nobel Prize in Physics, was cited "in recognition of the extraordinary merit gained by the discovery of the special rays bearing his name." Although the award was made for a single surprise discovery, Roentgen had spent 28 years quietly contributing carefully done work that laid part of the foundation for much of the theory of thermodynamics, mechanics, and electricity. His discovery of X-rays remains his stunning contribution in that it opened the doors to modern physics and, in great measure, to modern surgery and medical treatment. (T.S.)

1902

Lorentz, Hendrik Antoon   418

PRIZE: Physics, 1902. BORN: July 18, 1853; Arnhem, Netherlands. DIED: February 4, 1928; Haarlem, Netherlands. PARENTS: Father, Gerrit Frederik Lorentz; Mother, Geertruida van Ginkel Lorentz. NATIONALITY: Dutch. RELIGION: Protestant. EDUCATION: Univ. of Leiden, Netherlands, B.Sc., 1871; Univ. of Leiden, Netherlands, Ph.D., 1875. SPOUSE: Aletta Kaiser, married 1881. CHILDREN: Geertruida Luberta, daughter; Johanna Wilhelmina, daughter; Rudolf, son. CAREER: Univ. of Leiden, Netherlands, Professor, 1878-1912; Teyler Laboratory, Haarlem, Netherlands, Director, 1912-23. OTHER AWARDS: Rumford Medal, Royal Society, 1908; Copley Medal, Royal Society, 1918.

Selected Publications: *Lectures on Theoretical Physica.* 8 volumes. London: Macmillan and Co., 1927-31. *H.A. Lorentz, Collected Papers.* 9 volumes. The Hague: M. Nijhoff, 1934-39.

For More Information See: de Haas-Lorentz, G.L. *H.A. Lorentz. Impressions of His Life and Work.* Tr. by Joh. C. Fagginger Auer. Amsterdam: North-Holland Publishing Co., 1957. *Dictionary of Scientific Biography.* New York: Scribner's, 1973 (Volume 8), 487-500.

Commentary: Hendrik Lorentz shared the Nobel Prize with Pieter Zeeman "in recognition of the extraordinary service they rendered by their researches into the influence of magnetism upon radiation phenomena." Beginning with his doctoral work on reflection and refraction of light, Lorentz changed the face of optics and electricity in a long and fruitful career. His first major contribution was a formula relating light velocity to the density and composition of the medium through which it passed. His general theory of the electrical and optical properties of moving bodies followed. Next came the concept of the electron, which paved the way for molecular and quantum theories. Lorentz's work in electromagnetism and motion led to the Einstein theory of relativity. He also pioneered in the science of hydraulics. (A.S.)

Zeeman, Pieter   419

PRIZE: Physics, 1902. BORN: May 25, 1865; Zonnemaire Zeeland, Netherlands. DIED: October 9, 1943; Amsterdam, Netherlands. PARENTS: Father, Catharinus Farandinus Zeeman; Mother, Wilhelmina Worst Zeeman.

NATIONALITY: Dutch. RELIGION: Lutheran. EDUCATION: Univ. of Leiden, Netherlands, Ph.D., 1893. SPOUSE: Johanna Elisabeth Lebret, married 1895. CHILDREN: 3 daughters; 1 son. CAREER: Univ. of Leiden, Netherlands, Professor, 1893-97; Univ. of Amsterdam, Netherlands, Professor, 1897-1935. OTHER AWARDS: Gold Medal, Netherlands Scientific Society of Haarlem, 1892; Rumford Medal, Royal Society, 1922.

Selected Publications: *Researches in Magneto-Optics.* London: Macmillan, 1913. *Verhandelingen van Dr. P. Zeeman over Magneto-Optische Verschijnselen.* Leiden, Netherlands: E. Ijdo, 1921.

For More Information See: *Dictionary of Scientific Biography.* New York: Scribner's, 1973 (Volume 10), 524-26. *Obituary Notices of Fellows of the Royal Society of London* 4 (1944): 591-95.

Commentary: Pieter Zeeman and Hendrik Lorentz received the Nobel Prize "in recognition of the extraordinary service they rendered by their researches into the influence of magnetism upon radiation phenomena." Zeeman devoted his early career to studying the interrelationships between magnetism and light. The Zeeman effect refers to the widening and splitting of spectral lines by a magnetic field and added to the evidence for an electromagnetic theory of light. Zeeman also studied the absorption and motion of electricity in fluids, magnetic fields on the sun's surface, the Doppler effect, the effect of nuclear magnetic moments on spectral lines, and mass spectrography of Ar-38 and Ni-64. (A.S.)

1903

Becquerel, Antoine Henri   420

PRIZE: Physics, 1903. BORN: December 15, 1852; Paris, France. DIED: August 25, 1908; Le Croisic, France. PARENTS: Father, Alexander Edmond Becquerel; Mother, no record found. NATIONALITY: French. RELIGION: Most probably Christian. EDUCATION: Ecole des Pontes-et-Chaussees, France, ingenieur, 1877; Ecole des Pontes-et-Chaussees, France, docteur-es-sciences, 1888. SPOUSE: Lucie-Zoe-Marie Jamin, married 1874, died 1878; (No first name found) Lorieux, married 1890. CHILDREN: Jean, son. CAREER: Museum of Natural History, Paris, France, Professor, 1878-95; Polytechnic, Paris, France, Professor, 1895-1908. OTHER AWARDS: Legion of Honour, France, 1900; Rumford Medal, 1908; Barnard Medal, 1908; Helmholtz Medal, 1908.

Selected Publications: "Emission de Radiations Nouvelles par l'Uranium Metallique." *Comptes Rendus de l'Academie des Sciences, Paris* 122 (1896): 1086-88. "Sur Diverses Proprietes des Rayons Uraniques." *Comptes Rendus de l'Academie des Sciences, Paris* 123 (1896): 855-58. "Sur le Rayonnement des Corps Radio-Actifs." *Comptes Rendus de l'Academie des Sciences, Paris* 129 (1899): 1205-07. "Sur la Radioactivite de l'Uranium." *Comptes Rendus de l'Academie des Sciences, Paris* 133 (1901): 977-80. "Recherches sur Une Propriete Nouvelle de la Matiere. Activite Radiante Spontanee ou Radioactivite de la Matiere." *Memories de l'Academie des Sciences, Paris* 46 (1903).

For More Information See: *Dictionary of Scientific Biography.* New York: Scribner's, 1970 (Volume 1), 558-61. Ranc, Albert. *Henri Becquerel et la Decouverte de la Radioactivite.* Paris: Éditiones de la Liberté, 1946.

Commentary: Henri Becquerel was cited by the Academy "in recognition of the extraordinary services he has rendered by his discovery of spontaneous radioactivity." In addition to that monumental discovery, Becquerel performed pioneer research in the areas of light polarization, light absorption, phosphorescence, and terrestrial magnetism. (B.S.S.)

Curie, Marie (Sklodowska, Maria) *see* entry 11

Curie, Pierre   421

PRIZE: Physics, 1903. BORN: May 15, 1859; Paris, France. DIED: April 19, 1906; Paris, France. PARENTS: Father, Eugene Curie; Mother, Sophie-Claire Depoully Curie. NATIONALITY: French. RELIGION: Anticlerical; from Protestant background. EDUCATION: Univ. of Paris-Sorbonne, France, licence es sciences, 1875; Univ. of Paris-Sorbonne, France, licence in physical sciences, 1877; Univ. of Paris-Sorbonne, France, doctor of science, 1895. SPOUSE: Marie Sklodowska, married July 25, 1895. CHILDREN: Irene, daughter; Eve, daughter. CAREER: Univ. of Sorbonne, France, Researcher, 1878-82; Univ. of Sorbonne, France, Professor, 1882-1906. OTHER AWARDS: La Caze Prize, Academie des Sciences, 1901; Davy Medal, Royal Society, 1903; Matteuci Gold Medal, Italian Society of Sciences, 1904.

Selected Publications: *Oeuvres de Pierre Curie.* Paris: Gauthier-Villars, 1908.

For More Information See: Curie, M. *Pierre Curie.* Tr. by Charlotte and Vernon Kellogg. New York: Macmillan, 1923. *Dictionary of Scientific Biography.* New York: Scribner's, 1971 (Volume 3), 503-08.

Commentary: Pierre Curie shared the Nobel Prize with Marie Curie and A. Becquerel "in recognition of the special services rendered by them in the work they jointly carried out in investigating the phenomena of radiation discovered by Professor Becquerel." Curie was also responsible for pioneer magnetic studies. The Curie point, the temperature at which a substance changes its magnetic properties, is named after him. He also studied the piezo-electric properties of crystals and developed sensitive instrumentation to permit such study. (V.C.)

1904

Strutt, John William (Lord Rayleigh)   422

PRIZE: Physics, 1904. BORN: November 12, 1842; Lanford Grove, Essex, England. DIED: June 30, 1919; Witham, Essex, England. PARENTS: Father, John James Strutt; Mother, Elizabeth Vicars Strutt. NATIONALITY: British. RELIGION: Spiritualist; from Anglican background. EDUCATION: Cambridge Univ., England, B.A., 1865. SPOUSE: Evelyn Balfour, married 1871. CHILDREN: Robert John, son; Arthur Charles, son; Julian, son. CAREER: Cambridge Univ., England, Laboratory Director, 1879-84; Royal Institute, England, Professor, 1887-1905; Cambridge Univ., England, Chancellor, 1908-19. OTHER AWARDS: Royal Medal, 1882; Bressa Prize, Italy, 1891; Hodgkins Prize, Smithsonian, 1895; Matteuci Medal, Italy, 1895; Barnard Medal, Columbia U., NY, 1895; Faraday Medal, Chemical Society, 1895; Copley Medal, 1899; Albert Medal, Royal Society of the Arts, 1905; Rumford Medal, 1914; Cresson Medal, Franklin Institute, 1914.

Selected Publications: *The Theory of Sound.* 2 volumes. London: Macmillan, 1877-78. *Scientific Papers.* 6 volumes. Cambridge: Cambridge U. Press, 1899-1920.

For More Information See: *Dictionary of Scientific Biography.* New York: Scribner's, 1976 (Volume 13), 100-07. Strutt, Robert John. *Life of John William Strutt.* Madison, WI: U. of Wisconsin Press, 1965.

Commentary: Lord Rayleigh received the Nobel Prize "for his investigations into the density of the most important gases, and for his discovery of argon in connection with these investigations." His success was attributable to both his development of new experimental techniques and his ability to explain the experimental results obtained. In his career, he touched many facets of physics-electricity, optics, capillarity, the gas laws, and sound. Probably his most-remembered contribution is the explanation of why the sky is blue. (L.M.)

1905

Lenard, Philipp Edward Anton   423
PRIZE: Physics, 1905. BORN: June 7, 1862; Pressburg, Hungary. DIED: May 20, 1947; Messelhausen, Germany. PARENTS: Father, Philipp Lenard; Mother, Antonia Baumann Lenard. NATIONALITY: Hungarian; later German citizen. RELIGION: Protestant. EDUCATION: Univ. of Heidelberg, Germany, Ph.D., 1886. SPOUSE: Katherine Schlehner, married 1897. CHILDREN: Werner, son; others, no record found. CAREER: Univ. of Heidelberg, Germany, Researcher, 1887-90; Univ. of Bonn, Germany, Researcher, 1891-94; Univ. of Breslau, Germany, Professor, 1894-95; Technische Hochschule, Aachen, Germany, Professor, 1895-96; Univ. of Heidelberg, Germany, Professor, 1896-98; Univ. of Kiel, Germany, Professor, 1898-1907; Univ. of Heidelberg, Germany, Professor, 1907-31. OTHER AWARDS: Rumford Medal, Royal Society, 1904; Franklin Medal, Franklin Institute, 1905.

Selected Publications: *Uber Kathodenstrahlen.* Leipzig, Germany: J. A. Barth, 1906. *Uber Aether und Materie.* Heidelberg, Germany: C. Winter, 1911. *Uber Relativitatsprinzip, Aether, Gravitation.* Leipzig, Germany: S. Hirzel, 1920.

For More Information See: *A Biographical Dictionary of Scientists.* New York: Wiley, 1982, 321-22. *Dictionary of Scientific Biography.* New York: Scribner's, 1973 (Volume 8), 180-83.

Commentary: The Committee cited Philipp Lenard "for his work in connection with cathode rays," in which he studied their magnetic deflection and electrostatic properties. Lenard also made significant contributions to the theory of the structure of atoms, to falling drop theory, to the phenomena of magnetism and luminescence, and to the understanding of spectral lines. His ability to contribute, however, was sadly marred by his lifelong pathological anti-Semitism, which did not allow him to accept the work of the Jewish giants in physics and later made him a willing supporter of Hitler and "Aryan Physics." (M.N.C.)

1906

Thomson, Joseph John, Sir   424
PRIZE: Physics, 1906. BORN: December 18, 1856; Manchester, England. DIED: August 30, 1940; Cambridge, England. PARENTS: Father, Joseph James Thomson; Mother, Emma Swindells Thomson. NATIONALITY: British. RELIGION: Anglican. EDUCATION: Owens College, England, engineering degree, 1876; Cambridge Univ., England, B.A., 1880. SPOUSE: Rose Elisabeth Paget, married 1890. CHILDREN: George Paget, son; Joan, daughter. CAREER: Cambridge Univ., England, Professor, 1883-1918. OTHER AWARDS: Royal Medal, Royal Society, 1894; Hughes Medal, 1902; Hodgkins Medal, Smithsonian Institution, 1902; Knighthood, 1908; Order of Merit, 1912; Copley Medal, Royal Society, 1914; Franklin Medal, 1923; Scott Medal, 1923; Mescart Medal, Paris, 1927; Guthrie Medal and Prize, 1928; Dalton Medal, 1931; Faraday Medal, Institution of Civil Engineers, 1938.

Selected Publications: *A Treatise on the Motion of Vortex Rings.* London: Macmillan, 1883. *Elements of the Mathematical Theory of Electricity and Magnetism.* Cambridge: Cambridge U. Press, 1895. *The Conduction of Electricity Through Gases.* Cambridge: Cambridge U. Press, 1903. *Electricity and Matter.* Westminster, England: Constable, 1904. *The Corpuscular Theory of Matter.* New York: Scribner's, 1907. *Atomic Theory.* Oxford: Clarendon Press, 1914.

For More Information See: *Biographical Memoirs of the Fellows of the Royal Society.* London: Royal Society, 1939-41 (Volume 3), 587-609. *Dictionary of Scientific Biography.* New York: Scribner's, 1976 (Volume 13), 362-72. *Obituary Notices of Fellows of the Royal Society.* London: Royal Society, 1941 (Volume 3), 587. Rayleigh, Robert J.S. *The Life of J.J. Thomson.* Cambridge: Cambridge U. Press, 1943.

Commentary: The Nobel award to J.J. Thomson was "in recognition of his merits for the theoretic and experimental study of the conduction of electricity through gases." During his long career at Cambridge, Thomson established a center for experimental work on the discharge of electricity through gases and on chemical analysis with the aid of positive electric rays. He also carried out significant investigations on the structure of atoms and developed a model of atomic structure which was important to theoretical physics until it was replaced by the Rutherford model in 1913. (S.G.)

1907

Michelson, Albert Abraham   425
PRIZE: Physics, 1907. BORN: December 19, 1853; Strelno, Germany. DIED: May 9, 1931; Pasadena, CA. PARENTS: Father, Samuel Michelson; Mother, Rosalie Przlubska Michelson. NATIONALITY: German; later American citizen. RELIGION: Jewish. EDUCATION: United States Naval Academy, MD, baccalaureate, 1873. SPOUSE: Margaret McLean Hemingway, married April 10, 1877, divorced, 1897; Edna Stanton, married December 23, 1899. CHILDREN: Albert Hemingway, son; Truman, son; Elsa, daughter; Madeline, daughter; Dorothy, daughter; Beatrice, daughter. CAREER: United States Naval Academy, MD, Professor, 1875-79; Germany and France, Student, 1879-82; Case School of

Applied Science, Cleveland, OH, Professor, 1883-89; Clark Univ., MA, Professor, 1889-92; Univ. of Chicago, IL, Professor, 1892-1929. OTHER AWARDS: Rumford Medal, Royal Society, 1889; Grand Prix, Paris Exposition, 1900; Matteuci Medal, Rome, Italy, 1904; Copley Medal, Royal Society, 1907; Elliott Cresson Medal, 1912; Draper Medal, National Academy of Sciences, 1916.

Selected Publications: *Velocity of Light.* Chicago: U. of Chicago Press, 1902 *Light Waves and Their Uses.* Chicago: U. of Chicago Press, 1903. *Studies in Optics.* Chicago: U. of Chicago Press, 1927.

For More Information See: *Biographical Memoirs. National Academy of Sciences.* Washington, DC: National Academy of Sciences, 1938 (Volume 19), 120-47. *Dictionary of Scientific Biography.* New York: Scribner's, 1974 (Volume 9), 371-74. Livingston, Dorothy M. *The Master of Light: A Biography of Albert A. Michelson.* New York: Scribner's, 1973.

Commentary: Albert Michelson was the recipient of the Nobel Prize "for his optical precision instruments and the spectroscopic and metrological investigations carried out with their aid." Although remembered for his painstaking measurements of the velocity of light, Michelson was responsible for the development of the echelon spectrograph and astrophysical spectroscopy, measured the rigidity of the Earth, and was a leader in producing high-quality optical gratings. (C.G. and L.S.)

1908

Lippman, Gabriel Jonas   426
PRIZE: Physics, 1908. BORN: August 16, 1845; Hollerich, Luxembourg. DIED: July 13, 1921; at sea. PARENTS: No record found. NATIONALITY: French. RELIGION: Jewish. EDUCATION: Univ. of Paris-Sorbonne, France, doctorate, 1875. SPOUSE: (No first name found) Cherbuliez, married 1888. CHILDREN: None. CAREER: Sorbonne Univ., Paris, France, Professor, 1878-1921.

Selected Publications: "Extension du Principe de Carnot à la Theorie des Phenomenes Electriques." *Comptes Rendus de l'Academie des Sciences* 82 (1876): 1425. "Photographies Colorées du Spectre, sur Albumine et sur Gelatine Bichromatees." *Comptes Rendus de l'Academie des Sciences* 115 (1892): 575. "Sur un Coelostat." *Comptes Rendus de l'Academie des Sciences* 120 (1895): 1015.

For More Information See: *Annales de Physique* 16 (1921): 156. *Dictionary of Scientific Biography.* New York: Scribner's, 1981 (Volume 7), 387-88.

Commentary: Gabriel Lippman was awarded the Nobel Prize "for his method, based on the interference phenomenon, for reproducing colours photographically." Lippman possessed a far-ranging research mind which contributed to the fundamental principles of optics, photochemistry, electricity, and thermodynamics. In addition to his photographic work, his development of a sensitive capillary electrometer and his research with pendulum clocks and astronomical devices are usually mentioned. (V.A.H.)

1909

Braun, Karl Ferdinand   427
PRIZE: Physics, 1909. BORN: June 6, 1850; Fulda, Germany. DIED: April 20, 1918; Brooklyn, NY. PARENTS:

Father, Konrad Braun; Mother, Franziska Gohring Braun. NATIONALITY: German. RELIGION: Christian. EDUCATION: Univ. of Berlin, Germany, Ph.D., 1872. SPOUSE: Amelie Bühler, married 1885. CHILDREN: Conrad, son; 1 other son; 2 daughters. CAREER: Univ. of Wurzburg, Germany, Researcher, 1872-74; St. Thomas Gymnasium, Leipzig, Germany, Professor, 1874-76; Univ. of Marburg, Germany, Professor, 1876-80; Univ. of Strasbourg, France, Professor, 1880-83; Technical High School, Karlsruhe, Germany, Professor, 1883-85; Univ. of Tübingen, Germany, Professor, 1885-95; Univ. of Strasbourg, France, Professor, 1895-1915.

Selected Publications: *Ueber den Einfluss von Steifigkeit, Befestigung und Amplitude auf die Schwingungen von Saiten.* Berlin: Druck von G. Schade, 1872. *Über Elektrische Kraftübertragung Inbesondere über Drehstrom.* Tübingen, Germany: H. Laupp'sche Buchhandlung, 1892. *Drahtlose Telegraphie durch Wasser und Luft.* Leipzig, Germany: Veit and Co., 1901. *Anleitung fur das Photographieren von Tieren.* Berlin: Deutsche Landwirtschafts-Gesellschaft, 1927.

For More Information See: *Asimov's Biographical Encyclopedia of Science and Technology.* Garden City, NY: Doubleday, 1982, 523-24. *Dictionary of Scientific Biography.* New York: Scribner's, 1970 (Volume 2), 427-28.

Commentary: Karl Braun was cited by the Academy, along with his colaureate, Guglielmo Marconi, for "contributions to the development of wireless telegraphy." Braun refined cathode-ray tubes, invented the oscillograph, and introduced crystal rectifiers, but he is remembered principally for his modification of the Marconi transmitting system to permit greater range. He also made significant contributions in his study of the oscillations of strings and elastic rods, of thermodynamics, and of electricity (specifically, the theory of Ohm's Law and the calculation of the electromotive force of reversible galvanic elements from thermal sources). (C.S.)

Marconi, Guglielmo   428
PRIZE: Physics, 1909. BORN: April 25, 1874; Bologna, Italy. DIED: July 20, 1937; Rome, Italy. PARENTS: Father, Guiseppi Marconi; Mother, Annie Jameson Marconi. NATIONALITY: Italian. RELIGION: Catholic. EDUCATION: No college degrees. SPOUSE: Beatrice O'Brien, married March 16, 1905, divorced 1924; Maria Cristina Bezzi-Scali, married 1927. CHILDREN: 1 son; Degna, daughter, 3 other daughters. CAREER: Inventor and Entrepreneur, Italy. OTHER AWARDS: Order of Saint Anne, Russia; Commander of the Order of Saint Maurice and Saint Lazarus, 1902; Grand Cross of the Order of the Crown of Italy, 1902; Freedom of the City of Rome, 1903; Grand Cross Order of Alphonso XII; Grand Cordon Order of the Rising Sun; Albert Medal, Royal Society of Arts.

Selected Publications: "Wireless Telegraphy." *Proceedings of the Institution of Electrical Engineers* 28 (1899): 273. "Wireless Telegraphy." *Proceedings of the Royal Institution of Great Britain* 16 (1899-1901): 247-56. "Syntonic Wireless Telegraphy." *Royal Society of Arts Journal* 49 (1901): 505. "The Progress of Electric Space Telegraphy." *Proceedings of the Royal Institution of Great Britain* 17 (1902-04): 195-210. "Recent Advances in Wireless Telegraphy." *Proceedings of the Royal Institution of Great Britain* 18 (1905-07): 31-45.

For More Information See: Boinod, B.L. Jacot de, and Collier, D.M.B. *Marconi: Master of Space.* London: Hutchinson, 1935. *Dictionary of Scientific Biography.* New York: Scribner's, 1974 (Volume 9), 98-99. Dunlap, Orrin E., Jr. *Marconi: The Man and His Wireless.* New York: Macmillan Publishing Co., 1937. Marconi, Degna. *My Father, Marconi.* New York: McGraw-Hill Book Co., Inc., 1962.

Commentary: The Nobel Prize given to Guglielmo Marconi recognized his "contributions to the development of wireless telegraphy." A privately educated inventor, Marconi became the inventor of the first practical system of wireless telegraphy, working in a laboratory on his father's estate. He spent his lifetime refining the invention, acquiring key patents and forming his own company. Marconi's demonstrations and inventions made possible the electronic communications systems of the modern world. (C.G. and L.S.)

1910

Van der Waals, Johannes Diderik   429

PRIZE: Physics, 1910. BORN: November 23, 1837; Leiden, Netherlands. DIED: March 9, 1923; Amsterdam, Netherlands. PARENTS: Father, Jacobus van der Waals; Mother, Elisabeth van den Burg van der Waals. NATIONALITY: Dutch. RELIGION: Christian. EDUCATION: Leiden Univ., Netherlands, doctorate, 1873. SPOUSE: Anna Magdelana Smit, married 1864. CHILDREN: Anne Madeleine, daughter; Jacqueline Elisabeth, daughter; Johanna Diderica, daughter; Johannes Diderik, son. CAREER: Univ. of Amsterdam, Netherlands, Professor, 1877-1907.

Selected Publications: *Over de Continuiteit van den Gasen-Vloeistoftoestand.* Leiden, Netherlands: A.W. Sijthoff, 1873. *La Continuität des Gasförmigen und Flüssigen Zustandes.* Leipzig, Germany: J.A. Barth, 1881. *Lehrbuch der Thermodynamik in Ihrer Anwendung auf das Gleichgewicht von Systemen mit Gasförmig-flüssigen Phasen.* Leipzig, Germany: Maas and van Suchtelen, 1908. *De Relativiteitstheorie.* Haarlem, Netherlands: F. Bohn, 1923. *Lehrbuch der Thermostatik, das Heisst, des Thermischen Gleich Gewichtes Materieller Systeme.* Leipzig, Germany: J.A. Barth, 1927.

For More Information See: *Dictionary of Scientific Biography.* New York: Scribner's, 1976 (Volume 14), 109-11. Oesper, R.E. "Johannes Diderik van der Waals." *Journal of Chemical Education* 31 (1954): 599.

Commentary: The Academy recognized Johannes Diderik van der Waals "for his work on the equation of state for gases and liquids," which relates pressure, absolute temperature, and volume through the use of three constants. Van der Waals was also well known for his theory of binary solutions and thermodynamic theory of capillarity. (C.S.)

1911

Wien, Wilhelm Carl Werner Otto Fritz Franz   430

PRIZE: Physics, 1911. BORN: January 13, 1864; Gaffken, Germany. DIED: August 30, 1928; Munich, Germany. PARENTS: Father, Carl Wien; Mother, Caroline Gertz Wien. NATIONALITY: German. RELIGION: Christian. EDUCATION: Univ. of Berlin, Germany, Ph.D., 1886. SPOUSE: Luise Mehler, married 1898. CHILDREN: Waltraut, son; Karl, son; Gerda, daughter; Hildegard, daughter. CAREER: Germany, Landowner, 1886-90; State Physico-Technical Institute, Germany, Researcher, 1890-96; Technische Hochschule, Auchen, Germany, Professor, 1896-99; Univ. of Giessen, Germany, Professor, 1899-1900; Univ. of Würzburg, Germany, Professor, 1900-20; Univ. of Munich, Germany, Professor, 1920-28.

Selected Publications: *Lehrbuch der Hydrodynamik.* Leipzig, Germany: S. Hirzel, 1900. *Kanalstrahlen.* Leipzig, Germany: Akademische Verlagsgesellschaft, 1917. *Aus Dem Leben und Wirken eines Physikers.* Leipzig, Germany: J.A. Barth, 1930.

For More Information See: *Deutsches Biographisches Jahrbuch.* Berlin: Deutsches Verlags, 1931 (Volume 10), 302-10. *Dictionary of Scientific Biography.* New York: Scribner's, 1976 (Volume 14), 337-42. Steenbeck, Max. *Wilhelm Wien und Sein Einfluss auf die Physik Seiner Zeit.* Berlin: Akademie-Verlag, 1964.

Commentary: Wilhelm Wien was awarded the Nobel Prize "for his discoveries regarding the laws governing the radiation of heat." In 1893 he developed the law of displacement which states that the wavelength of radiation emitted from bodies varies with temperature; for instance, moderately hot bodies radiate in the infrared, while extremely hot bodies radiate in the ultraviolet ends of the spectrum. He did further research on black bodies, which absorb all radiation. Although his work in this area proved valid only for short waves, Wien's theories enables Max Planck to devise the quantum theory. Wien's further researches took him into the areas of cathode rays, canal rays, light diffraction, color of refracted light, metal permeability to light and heat, measurement of high temperatures, and thermodynamics. (M.H.)

1912

Dalén, Nils Gustaf   431

PRIZE: Physics, 1912. BORN: November 30, 1869; Skaraborg, Sweden. DIED: December 9, 1937; Stockholm, Sweden. PARENTS: No record found. NATIONALITY: Swedish. RELIGION: Christian. EDUCATION: Chalmers Tekniska Högskola, Sweden, Civil Engineering Degree, 1896. SPOUSE: Elma Axelia Persson, married July 13, 1901. CHILDREN: Gunnar, son; Anders, son; 2 daughters. CAREER: Laval Steam Turbine Co., Sweden, Researcher, 1897-1900; Swedish Carbide and Acetylene Co., Sweden, Administrator and Researcher, 1901-03; Gas Accumulator Co., Engineer and Researcher, 1906-12. OTHER AWARDS: Morehead Medal, International Acetylene Association, 1933.

Selected Publications: *Chemische Technologie des Papiers.* Leipzig, Germany: J.A. Barth, 1911.

For More Information See: *Biographical Encyclopedia of Scientists.* New York: Facts on File, 1981, 179. *Svenskt Biografiskt Lexikon.* Stockholm: Albert Bonners Forlag, 1931 (Volume 3), 36-50.

Commentary: The award to Gustaf Dalén was "for his invention of automatic regulators for use in conjunction with gas accumulators for illuminating lighthouses and buoys." His inventions to improve coastal lighting were actually threefold: (1) he discovered a method for storing acetylene gas in small containers without fear of explosion; (2) he constructed an apparatus which allowed one liter of gas to provide thousands of rapid flashes; and (3) he developed a "sunset" or "solar" valve which allowed unstaffed lights to be lit as soon as the sun set and extinguished as soon as the sun rose. This last development made operation of lighthouses and beacons entirely automatic for months at a time. Blinded in an industrial accident in 1912, Dalén was unable to attend the presentation of his award. His research did not stop, though: he was awarded the contract for lighting the Panama Canal, worked with hot air turbines and air compressors, and invented an efficient cooking stove. (M.H.)

1913

Kamerlingh Onnes, Heike 432
PRIZE: Physics, 1913. BORN: September 21, 1853; Gröningen, Netherlands. DIED: February 21, 1926; Leiden, Netherlands. PARENTS: Father, Harm Kamerlingh Onnes; Mother, Anne Gerdina Coers Kamerlingh Onnes. NATIONALITY: Dutch. RELIGION: Christian. EDUCATION: Univ. of Gröningen, Netherlands, Candidaats Degree, 1873; Univ. of Heidelberg, Germany, Ph.D., 1879. SPOUSE: Maria Adriana Wilhelmina Elisabeth Bijleveld, married 1887. CHILDREN: Albert, son. CAREER: Univ. of Leiden, Netherlands, Professor, 1882-1923. OTHER AWARDS: Rumford Medal, Royal Society, 1912.

Selected Publications: "Algemeene Theorie der Vloeistoffen" (*General Theory of Fluids*). *Verhandelingen der Kon. Akademie van Wetenschappen (Amsterdam)*21 (1881): 9 p. "On the Cryogenic Laboratory at Leiden and on the Production of Very Low Temperatures." *Communications from the Laboratory of Physics at the University of Leiden* 14 (1894). "The Liquefaction of Helium." *Communications from the Physical Laboratory at the University of Leiden* 108 (August 1908) (Translated from *Bijvoegsel aan het Verslag van de Gewone Vergadering der Wis-en Naturkundige Afdeeling der Kon. Akademie van Wetenschappen te Amsterdan* (June 1908): 163-79). "Further Experiments with Liquid Helium. D. On the Change of the Electrical Resistance of Pure Metals at Very Low Temperatures, etc. V. The Disappearance of the Resistance of Mercury." *Communications from the Physical Laboratory of the University of Leiden* 122b (May 1911) (Translated from *Verslagen van de Afdeeling Natuurkunde der Kon. Akademie van Wetenschappen te Amsterdam* (May 1911): 81-83). "Further Experiments with Liquid Helium. G. On the Electrical Resistance of Pure Metals, etc. VI. On the Sudden Change in the Rate at Which the Resistance of Mercury Disappears." *Communications from the Physical Laboratory of the University of Leiden* 124c (December 1911) (Translated from *Verslagen van de Afdeeling Natuurkunde der Kon. Akademie van Wetenschappen te Amsterdam* (December 30, 1911): 799-802). "Further Experiments with Liquid Helium. P. On the Lowest Temperature Yet Obtained." *Transactions of the Faraday Society* 18, Part 2 (December 1922). Reprinted in *Communications from the Physical Laboratory of the University of Leiden* 159 (1922): 3-32.

For More Information See: *Dictionary of Scientific Biography*. New York: Scribner's, 1973 (Volume 7), 220-22. "Heike Kamerlingh Onnes—1853-1926." *Proceedings of the Royal Society* A113 (January 1927): i-vi.

Commentary: Considered the "father of cryogenics," Heike Kamerlingh Onnes received the Nobel Prize for "researches on the properties of matter at low temperatures...." Working in his world-renowned laboratory at Leiden and ever-mindful of his motto, "through measuring to knowing," he astonished the scientific community in 1908 by liquifying helium, a feat which opened up the whole field of cryogenics. Continued experimentation in this area brought him to the discovery of the phenomenon of "supraconductivity" (later called superconductivity) in 1911, as well as that of Helium II. Less well known are his efforts during World War I to aid starving children in every country suffering from food shortages. (C.H.W.)

1914

Laue, Max Theodor Felix von 433
PRIZE: Physics, 1914. BORN: October 9, 1879; Pfaffendorf, Germany. DIED: April 24, 1960; Berlin, Germany. PARENTS: Father, Julius von Laue; Mother, Minna L. Zerrenner von Laue. NATIONALITY: German. RELIGION: Protestant. EDUCATION: Univ. of Berlin, Germany, Dr. Phil., 1903. SPOUSE: Magdalene Deger, married October 6, 1910. CHILDREN: Theodor Hermann, son; Hildegard Minna, daughter. CAREER: Univ. of Berlin, Germany, Professor, 1906-09; Univ. of Munich, Germany, Professor, 1909-12; Univ. of Zurich, Switzerland, Professor, 1912-14; Univ. of Frankfurt am Main, Germany, Professor, 1914-18; Univ. of Berlin, Germany, Professor and Administrator, 1919-43; Univ. of Göttingen, Germany, Professor and Administrator, 1946-51; Fritz Haber Institute of Physical Chemistry, Berlin, Germany, Director, 1951-58. OTHER AWARDS: Max Planck Medal, German Physical Society, 1932; Bimala-Churn-Law Gold Medal, Indian Association for the Cultivation of Science, India, 1950; Knight, Order Pour le Mérite, 1952; Grand Cross with Star for Federal Service, 1953; Officer of the Legion of Honour, France, 1957.

Selected Publications: "Interferenzerscheinungen bei Röntgenstrahlen." *Bayerische Akademie der Wissenschaften zu Munchen. Sitzungsberichte Mathematisch-Physikalischen Klasse* (June 1912): 303-22 (with W. Friedrich and P. Knipping). "Eine Quantitative Prüfung der Theorier fü die Interferenzerscheinungen bei Röntgenstrahlen." *Bayerische Akademie der Wissenschaften zu Munchen. Sitzungsberichte Mathematisch-Physikalischen Klasse* (July 1912): 363-73. *Bayerische Akademie der Wissenschaften zu Munchen. Sitzungsberichte Mathematisch-Physikalischen Klasse* (1913): 971-88. *Über die Auffindung der Röntgenstrahlinterferenzen.* Karlsruhe, Germany: C. F. Müllersche Hofbuchhandlung, 1920. *Die Relativitätstheorie* (*The Theory of Relativity*). 2 volumes. Braunschweig, Germany: F. Vieweg & Sohn, 1921. *Röntgenstrahlinterferenzen* (*X-ray Interference*). Leipzig, Germany: Akademische Verlagsgesellschaft, 1941. *Geschichte der Physik*. Bonn: Universitats Verlag, 1946 (*History of Physics*. Tr. by Ralph Oesper. New York: Academic Press, 1950). *Theorie der Supraleitung*. Berlin: Springer, 1947 (*Theory of Superconductivity*. Tr. by Lothar Meyer and William Band. New York: Academic Press, 1952).

For More Information See: *Biographical Memoirs of Fellows of the Royal Society*. London: Royal Society, 1960 (Volume 6), 135-56. *Dictionary of Scientific Biog-*

raphy. New York: Scribner's, 1973 (Volume 8), 50-53. "My Development as a Physicist: An Autobiography." In *Fifty Years of X-ray Diffraction,* by Peter Paul Ewald, 278-307. Utrecht, Netherlands: N.V.A. Obsthoek's Uitgeversmaatschappÿ, 1962.

Commentary: Max von Laue provided the mathematical formulations in 1912 that demonstrated that a narrow beam of X-rays is diffracted by the orderly array of atoms in a crystal lattice. He won the Nobel award for this "discovery of the diffraction of X-rays in crystals," which was described by Einstein as one of the most beautiful discoveries in physics. It enabled the development of two new branches of science: x-ray crystallography and x-ray spectroscopy. Laue's other important accomplishments both before and after his prize-winning work were his thinking and writings on the theory of relativity and superconductivity. (C.H.W.)

1915

Bragg, William Henry, Sir   434
PRIZE: Physics, 1915. BORN: July 2, 1862; Westword, Cumberland, England. DIED: March 12, 1942; London, England. PARENTS: Father, Robert John Bragg; Mother, Mary Wood Bragg. NATIONALITY: British. RELIGION: Anglican. EDUCATION: Cambridge Univ., England, M.A., 1884. SPOUSE: Gwendoline Todd, married 1889. CHILDREN: William Lawrence, son; Robert Charles, son; Gwendolyn Mary, daughter. CAREER: Univ. of Adelaide, Australia, Professor, 1885-1909; Leeds Univ., England, Professor, 1909-15; Univ. of London, England, Professor, 1915-25; Royal Institution, England, Professor and Administrator, 1923-42. OTHER AWARDS: Barnard Gold Medal, Columbia U., NY, 1915; Rumford Medal, Royal Society, 1915; Gold Medal, Societa Italiana de Scienze, 1917; Knighthood, 1920; Copley Medal, Royal Society, 1930; Franklin Medal, Franklin Institute, Philadelphia, PA, 1930; Faraday Medal, Institution of Electrical Engineers, 1936; John J. Carty Medal, National Academy of Sciences, 1938; Institute of Metals Medal, 1939.

Selected Publications: *Studies in Radioactivity.* London: Macmillan, 1912. "X-rays and Crystal Structure." *Science* (December 14, 1914): 795-802. *An Introduction to Crystal Analysis.* London: Bell and Sons, Ltd., 1928. *The Crystalline State.* 4 volumes. London: G. Gell, 1933-53 (with W.L. Bragg). *Atomic Structure of Minerals.* London: Oxford U. Press, 1937 (with W.L. Bragg).

For More Information See: Caroe, Gwendolyn M. *William Henry Bragg, 1862-1942.* Cambridge: Cambridge U. Press, 1978. *Dictionary of Scientific Biography.* New York: Scribner's, 1970 (Volume 2), 397-400. *Obituary Notices of the Fellows of the Royal Society.* London: Royal Society, 1943 (Volume 4): 277-300.

Commentary: William Henry Bragg and his son, William Lawrence Bragg, were jointly awarded the Nobel Prize "for the value of their contribution to the study of crystal structures by means of x-rays." W.H. Bragg began his career studying the properties of alpha, beta, and gamma rays, contributing greatly to the understanding of radioactivity. He built the first x-ray spectrometer and established the field of x-ray spectroscopy. W.L. Bragg found that the phenomenon of x-ray diffraction in crystals could be treated mathematically, and together with his father determined crystal

structures, using the x-ray spectrometer. The Braggs reduced the problem of crystal structure analysis to a standard procedure, and their discoveries and techniques became fundamental to the field of molecular biology as well. (M.N.K.)

Bragg, William Lawrence, Sir   435
PRIZE: Physics, 1915. BORN: March 31, 1890; Adelaide, Australia. DIED: July 1, 1971; Ipswich, England. PARENTS: Father, William Henry Bragg; Mother, Gwendoline Todd Bragg. NATIONALITY: British. RELIGION: Anglican. EDUCATION: Univ. of Adelaide, Australia, M.A., 1908; Cambridge Univ., England, M.A., 1912. SPOUSE: Alice Grace Jenny Hopkinson, married 1921. CHILDREN: Stephen, son; David, son; Margaret, daughter; Patience, daughter. CAREER: Cambridge Univ., England, Professor, 1914-15; British Army, 1915-19; Manchester Univ., England, Professor, 1919-37; National Physical Laboratory, England, Director, 1937-38; Cambridge Univ., England, Professor, 1938-53; Royal Institution, England, Professor and Administrator, 1954-65. OTHER AWARDS: Barnard Gold Medal, Columbia U., NY, 1915; Gold Medal, Societa Italiana di Scienze, 1917; Military Cross, 1918; Hughes Medal, Royal Society, 1931; Knighthood, 1941; Royal Medal, Royal Society, 1946; Roebling Medal, Mineral Society of America, 1948; Commander, Order of Leopold of Belgium, 1961.

Selected Publications: *X-rays and Crystal Structure.* London: G. Bell and Sons, 1915 (with W.H. Bragg). *The Crystalline State.* 4 volumes. London: G. Bell, 1933-53 (with W.H. Bragg). *Atomic Structure of Minerals.* London: Oxford U. Press, 1937 (with W.H. Bragg). *The Development of X-Ray Analysis.* London: G. Bell, 1975.

For More Information See: *Dictionary of Scientific Biography.* New York: Scribner's, 1978 (Volume 15), 61-64. "Reminiscences of Fifty Years of Research." *Proceedings of the Royal Institution of Great Britain* 41 (1966): 92-100.

Commentary: William Lawrence Bragg and his father, William Henry Bragg, were jointly awarded the Nobel Prize "for the value of their contribution to the study of crystal structures by means of x-rays." W.L. Bragg found that the phenomenon of x-ray diffraction in crystals, discovered by Von Laue, could be treated mathematically. His simplification of the mathematical method made possible an experimental attack on the problem of crystal structures using the x-ray spectrometer, first constructed by W.H. Bragg. The Braggs reduced the problem of crystal structure analysis to a standard procedure, and their discoveries and techniques became fundamental to the field of molecular biology as well. (M.N.K.)

1917

Barkla, Charles Glover   436
PRIZE: Physics, 1917. BORN: June 27, 1877; Widness, Lancashire, England. DIED: October 23, 1944; Edinburgh, Scotland. PARENTS: Father, John Martin Barkla; Mother, Sarah Glover Barkla. NATIONALITY: British. RELIGION: Methodist. EDUCATION: Univ. of Liverpool, England, B.Sc., 1898; Univ. of Liverpool, England, M.Sc., 1899; Univ. of Liverpool, England, D.Sc., 1904. SPOUSE: Mary Esther Cowell, married 1907. CHILDREN: Michael, son; 1 other son; 1 daughter. CAREER: Univ.

of Liverpool, England, Researcher, 1905-09; Univ. of London, England, Professor, 1909-13; Univ. of Edinburgh, Scotland, Professor, 1913-44. OTHER AWARDS: Hughes Medal, 1917.

Selected Publications: "Secondary Roentgen Radiation." *Philosophical Magazine,* 6th series, 11 (June 1906): 812-28. "The Spectra of the Fluorescent Roentgen Radiations." *Philosophical Magazine* 22 (September 1911): 396-412. *Radiation and Matter.* Greenock, England: Telegraph Printing Works, 1920.

For More Information See: *Dictionary of Scientific Biography.* New York: Scribner's, 1970 (Volume 1), 456-59. Stephenson, Reginald. "The Scientific Career of Charles Glover Barkla." *American Journal of Physics* 35 (February 1967): 141-52.

Commentary: The Nobel Prize was awarded to Charles Glover Barkla "for his discovery of the characteristic Roentgen radiation of the elements." Barkla showed that when a sample of a chemical element is placed in the path of X-rays, secondary X-rays are emitted. Although some of this emitted radiation is in fact a scattering of primary X-rays, Barkla was able to distinguish a secondary emission which produced a spectrum characteristic of each chemical element involved and could be used to deduce much about the structures of atoms. Barkla's career, except in a very small way, was totally devoted to the study of Roentgen radiation. (J.L.K.)

1918

Planck, Max Karl Ernst Ludwig 437

PRIZE: Physics, 1918. BORN: April 23, 1858; Kiel, Germany. DIED: October 3, 1947; Göttingen, Germany. PARENTS: Father, Julius Wilhelm Planck; Mother, Emma Patzig Planck. NATIONALITY: German. RELIGION: Protestant. EDUCATION: Univ. of Munich, Germany, Ph.D., 1879. SPOUSE: Marie Merck, married 1885, died 1909; Marga von Hosslin, married 1911. CHILDREN: Karl, son; Hermann, son; another son; Margarete, daughter; Emma, daughter. CAREER: Univ. of Munich, Germany, Professor, 1880-85; Univ. of Kiel, Germany, Professor, 1885-89; Univ. of Berlin, Germany, Professor, 1889-1926. OTHER AWARDS: Copley Medal, Royal Society, 1929.

Selected Publications: *Vorlesungen uber Thermodynamik.* Leipzig, Germany: Veit, 1897. "Zur Theorie des Gesetzes der Energieverteilung im Normalspektrum." *Verhandlungen der Deutschen Physikalischen Gesellschaft* 2 (1900): 237-45. "Uber die Elementarquanta der Materie und der Elektrizitat." *Annalen der Physik* 4 (1901): 564-66. *Vorlesungen uber die Theorie der Warmestrahlung.* Leipzig, Germany: Barth, 1906.

For More Information See: *Dictionary of Scientific Biography.* New York: Scribner's, 1975 (Volume 11), 7-17. Hermann, A. *Max Planck in Selbstzeugnissen und Bilddokumenten.* Hamburg: Rowohlt, 1973.

Commentary: Max Planck was awarded the Nobel Prize "for his work on the establishment and development of the theory of elementary quanta." Planck's earliest research was in the thermodynamics of irreversible processes. He later turned to the study of electromagnetic radiation, which represented his major contribution to science. Planck put forth the thesis that a body emits radiation in the form of discrete quanta of energy equal to the frequency times a constant, h, later named Planck's Constant, and thus introduced quantum theory. He also contributed to the development of the theory of relativity, soon after Einstein introduced it. (J.L.K.)

1919

Stark, Johannes 438

PRIZE: Physics, 1919. BORN: April 15, 1874; Schickenhof, Bavaria, Germany. DIED: June 21, 1957; Traunstein, Bavaria, Germany. PARENTS: No record found. NATIONALITY: German. RELIGION: Most probably Christian/Protestant. EDUCATION: Univ. of Munich, Germany, Ph.D., 1897. SPOUSE: Louise Uepler, married (no date found). CHILDREN: 5 children. CAREER: Univ. of Munich, Germany, Professor, 1897-1900; Univ. of Gottingen, Germany, Professor, 1900-06; Technische Hochschule, Hanover, Germany, Professor, 1906-09; Technische Hochschule, Aachen, Germany, Professor, 1909-17; Univ. of Greifswald, Germany, Professor, 1917-20; Univ. of Wurzburg, Germany, Professor, 1920-22. OTHER AWARDS: Baumgartner Prize, Vienna Academy of Sciences, 1910; Vahlbruch Prize, Gottingen Academy of Sciences, 1914; Matteuci Medal, Rome.

Selected Publications: *Die Elektrizität in Gasen.* Leipzig, Germany: J.A. Barth, 1902. "Der Doppler-Effekt bei den Kanalstrahlen und die Spektra der Positiven Atomionen." *Physikalische Zeitschrift* 6 (1905): 892-97. "Elementarquantum der Energie, Modell der Negativen und Positiven Elektrizität." *Physikalische Zeitschrift* 8 (1907): 881-84. *Prinzipien der Atomdynamik.* 3 volumes. Leipzig, Germany: S. Hirzel, 1910-15.

For More Information See: *Asimov's Biographical Encyclopedia of Science and Technology.* Garden City, NY: Doubleday, 1982, 649-50. *Dictionary of Scientific Biography.* New York: Scribner's, 1975 (Volume 12), 613-66.

Commentary: Johannes Stark's award was "for his discovery of the Doppler effect in canal rays and the splitting of spectral lines in electrical fields." The latter phenomenon became known as the Stark effect and was an early confirmation of the quantum theory of atoms. Stark was an important experimental physicist with a talent for conceptualization. His main area of interest was electrical conduction in gases, and he did valuable speculative work regarding the nature of chemical forces and the problems of atomic and molecular structure. In 1904, Stark founded the *Jahrbuch der Radioaktivität und Elektronik* to publish research papers in the area of particle physics. Stark is also known for his modification of the photo-equivalence law proposed by Albert Einstein in 1906. Now known as the Stark-Einstein law, it states that each molecule involved in a photochemical reaction absorbs only one quantum of the radiation that causes the reaction. (B.L.)

1920

Guillaume, Charles Edouard 439

PRIZE: Physics, 1920. BORN: February 15, 1861; Fleurier, Switzerland. DIED: June 13, 1938; Paris, France. PARENTS: Father, Edouard Guillaume; Mother, no record found. NATIONALITY: Swiss; later French citizen. RELIGION: Christian. EDUCATION: Zurich Polytechnic, Switzerland, Ph.D., 1883. SPOUSE: A.M. Taufflieb, married 1888. CHILDREN: 3 children. CAREER: International Bureau of Weights and Measures, France, Administrator and Researcher, 1883-1936. OTHER AWARDS: Grand Officer, Legion of Honour.

Selected Publications: *Traité Pratique de Thermométrie de Précision.* Paris: Gauthier-Villars, 1889. "Recherches sur les Aciers au Nickel. Propriétés Metrologiques." *Comptes Rendus Hebdomadaires des Séances de l'Académie des Sciences* 124 (1897): 752. "Recherches sur les Aciers au Nickel. Propriétés Magnétiques et Déformations Permanentes." *Comptes Rendus Hebdomadaires des Séances de l'Académie des Sciences* 124 (1897): 1515. "Recherches sur les Aciers au Nickel. Dilatations aux Températures Élevées: Résistance Electrique." *Comptes Rendus Hebdomadires des Séances de l'Académie des Sciences* 125 (1897): 235. "Recherches sur les Aciers au Nickel. Variations de Volumes des Alliages Irréversibles." *Comptes Rendus Hebdomadaires des Séances de l'Académie des Sciences* 126 (1898): 738. *Les États de la Matiére.* Paris: Societé Astronomique de France, 1908.

For More Information See: *Asimov's Biographical Encyclopedia of Science and Technology.* Garden City, NY: Doubleday, 1982, 586-87. *Dictionary of Scientific Biography.* New York: Scribner's, 1972 (Volume 5), 582-83.

Commentary: Charles Edouard Guillaume was awarded the Nobel Prize "in recognition of the service he has rendered to precision measurements in physics by his discovery of anomalies in nickel steel alloys." During his years with the Bureau International des Poids et Mesures, his work was concerned with increasing the precision of standard measures. He was known for discovering Invar, an iron and nickel alloy which has a very small coefficient of expansion in relation to temperature change. Invar is used in clockmaking and, among other precise instruments, surveyors' tapes. Guillaume was also known for redetermining the volume of the liter; for his work on the mercury thermometer; and for discovery of another alloy, elinvar, which does not change its elasticity within a wide temperature change. (B.N.L.)

1921

Einstein, Albert   440
PRIZE: Physics, 1921. BORN: March 14, 1879; Ulm, Germany. DIED: April 18, 1955; Princeton, NJ. PARENTS: Father, Hermann Einstein; Mother, Pauline Koch Einstein. NATIONALITY: German; later Swiss and American citizen. RELIGION: Jewish. EDUCATION: Univ. of Zurich, Switzerland, Ph.D., 1905. SPOUSE: Mileva Maric, married 1901, divorced 1916; Elsa Einstein, married 1917. CHILDREN: Hans Albert, son; Edward, son. CAREER: Swiss Patent Office, Berne, Switzerland, Patent Examiner, 1902-08; Univ. of Zurich, Switzerland, Professor, 1909-11; German Univ., Prague, Austria, Professor, 1911-12; Technische Hochschule, Switzerland, Professor, 1912-14; Kaiser Wilhelm Institute, Germany, Director, 1914-33; Princeton Univ., NJ, Professor, 1933-55. OTHER AWARDS: Barnard Medal, Columbia U., 1920; Copley Medal, Royal Society,

1925; Gold Medal, Royal Astronomical Society, 1926; Max Planck Medal, 1929; Franklin Medal, Franklin Institute, Philadelphia, PA, 1935.

Selected Publications: *Relativity, The Special and the General Theory: A Popular Exposition.* Tr. by Robert W. Lawson. London: Methuen, 1920. *The Meaning of Relativity: Four Lectures Delivered at Princeton University, May 1921.* Tr. by Edwin Plimpton Adams. London: Methuen, 1921. *Investigations on the Theory of the Brownian Movement.* Tr. by A.D. Cowper. London: Methuen, 1926. *The Evolution of Physics: The Growth of Ideas from Early Concepts to Relativity and Quanta.* Written with Leopold Infeld. New York: Simon and Schuster, 1938.

For More Information See: Clark, Ronald W. *Einstein: The Life and Times.* New York: World Publishing, 1971. *Current Biography Yearbook.* New York: H.W. Wilson, 1953, 178-81. *Dictionary of Scientific Biography.* New York: Scribner's, 1971 (Volume 4), 312-33. Frank, Philipp. *Einstein, His Life and Times.* Tr. by G. Rosen. New York: A.A. Knopf, 1947. Hoffmann, Banesh, and Dukas, Helen. *Albert Einstein—Creator and Rebel.* New York: Viking, 1972. Reiser, Anton. *Albert Einstein, a Biographical Portrait.* New York: Boni, 1930.

Commentary: Although the theory of relativity is synonymous with Albert Einstein, the Nobel Prize was awarded for his work on the photoelectric effect as described in his 1905 paper "The Quantum Law of the Emission and Absorption of Light" (*Annalen der Physik*). Einstein's Law of the Photoelectric Effect became the basis of quantitative photochemistry. Einstein was nominated for the award every year from 1910-22 except for 1911 and 1915, and the Nobel Prize in 1921 notes his contributions to theoretical physics in the area of quantum theory. Albert Einstein's work changed contemporary thinking and formed the basis for the modern science of physics. (J.S.)

1922

Aston, Francis William   441
PRIZE: Physics, 1922. BORN: September 1, 1877; Harborne, Birmingham, England. DIED: November 20, 1945; Cambridge, England. PARENTS: Father, William Aston; Mother, Fanny Charlotte Hallis Aston. NATIONALITY: British. RELIGION: Anglican. EDUCATION: Cambridge Univ., England, B.A., 1912. SPOUSE: None. CHILDREN: None. CAREER: British Brewery, Chemist, 1901-03; Univ. of Birmingham, England, Researcher, 1903-09; Cambridge Univ., England, Researcher, 1909-14; Royal Aircraft Establishment, England, Researcher, 1914-18; Cambridge Univ., England, Researcher, 1919-45. OTHER AWARDS: Mackenzie Davidson Medal, Roentgen Society, 1920; Hughes Medal, Royal Society, 1922; John Scott Medal, Franklin Institute, PA, 1923; Paterno Medal, 1923; Royal Medal, Royal Society, 1938; Duddell Medal, Physical Society, 1941.

Selected Publications: "Constitution of Atmospheric Neon." *Philosophical Magazine* 39 (1920): 449-55. "The Mass Spectra of Chemical Elements." *Philosophical Magazine* 40 (1920): 628-34. *Isotopes.* London: E. Arnold and Co., 1922. *Structural Units of the Material Universe.* London: Oxford U. Press, 1925. *Mass-Spec-*

tra and Isotopes. London: Arnold, 1933. "Masses of Some Light Atoms Measured by Means of a New Mass Spectrometer." *Nature* 137 (1936): 357-58.

For More Information See: *Dictionary of Scientific Biography.* New York: Scribner's, 1970 (Volume 1), 320-22. *Obituary Notices of Fellows of the Royal Society.* Cambridge: Royal Society, 1945-48 (Volume 5), 635-51.

Commentary: Francis Aston's Nobel Prize was granted "for his discovery, by means of his mass spectrograph, of isotopes in a large number of non-radioactive elements, and for his enunciation of the whole-number rule." Beginning in the field of optical properties of organic compounds and in brewery chemistry, Aston moved on to study phenomena in gas discharge tubes and discovered the Aston Dark Space. His studies of positive rays led him to the identification of two isotopes of neon and eventually to the invention of the mass spectrograph. With this instrument, Aston identified 212 naturally occurring isotopes and stated the Whole Number Rule, which says that all isotopes have very nearly whole number masses relative to the defined mass of the oxygen isotope. (B.S.S.)

Bohr, Niels Henrik David   442

PRIZE: Physics, 1922. BORN: October 7, 1885; Copenhagen, Denmark. DIED: November 18, 1962; Copenhagen, Denmark. PARENTS: Father, Christian Bohr; Mother, Ellen Adler Bohr. NATIONALITY: Danish. RELIGION: Jewish. EDUCATION: Univ. of Copenhagen, Denmark, baccalaureate, 1907; Univ. of Copenhagen, Denmark, M.S., 1909; Univ. of Copenhagen, Denmark, Ph.D., 1911. SPOUSE: Margrethe Norlund, married 1912. CHILDREN: Christian, son; Hans, son; Erik, son; Aage, son; Ernest, son; 1 other son. CAREER: Cambridge Univ., England, Professor, 1911-12; Univ. of Manchester, England, Professor, 1912-13; Univ. of Copenhagen, Denmark, Professor, 1913-14; Victoria Univ., England, Professor, 1914-16; Univ. of Copenhagen, Denmark, Professor and Administrator, 1916-62. OTHER AWARDS: Gold Medal, Royal Danish Academy of Sciences, 1907; Hughes Medal, Royal Society, 1921; H. C. Oerstad Medal, Society for the Propagation of Natural Science, 1924; Norwegian Gold Medal, U. of Oslo, 1924; Barnard Medal, Columbia U., NY, 1925; Matteuci Medal, Societa Italiana della Scienze, Rome, Italy, 1925; Franklin Medal, Franklin Institute, Philadelphia, PA, 1926; Faraday Medal, Chemical Society of London, England, 1930; Planck Medal, Deutsche Physikalische Gesellschaft, 1930; Copley Medal, Royal Society, 1938.

Selected Publications: *The Theory of Spectra and Atomic Constitution: Three Essays.* Cambridge: Cambridge U. Press, 1922. *Atomic Theory and the Description of Nature.* New York: Macmillan, 1934. *Atomic Physics and Human Knowledge.* New York: Wiley, 1958. *Essays, 1958-1962, on Atomic Physics and Human Knowledge.* New York: Interscience, 1963. *On the Constitution of Atoms and Molecules, Papers of 1913 Reprinted from the Philosophical Magazine.* New York: Benjamin, 1963.

For More Information See: *Dictionary of Scientific Biography.* New York: Scribner's, 1970 (Volume 2), 239-54. Moore, Ruth E. *Niels Bohr: The Man, His Science, and the World They Changed.* New York: Knopf, 1966. *Niels Bohr, His Life and Work as Seen by His Friends and Colleagues.* Edited by S. Rozental. New York: Wiley, 1967.

Commentary: "The investigation of the structure of atoms, and of the radiation emanating from them" were recognized as leading to Niels Bohr's Nobel Prize. Bohr's theories on the existence of stationary states of an atomic system and the transition of the system from one stationary state to another laid the foundation for much of the understanding of the physical and chemical properties of the elements. Bohr provided exemplary leadership throughout his career in the development of the field of quantum physics. (J.N.S.)

1923

Millikan, Robert Andrews   443

PRIZE: Physics, 1923. BORN: March 22, 1868; Morrison, IL. DIED: December 19, 1953; Pasadena, CA. PARENTS: Father, Silas Franklin Millikan; Mother, Mary Jane Andrews Millikan. NATIONALITY: American. RELIGION: Congregationalist. EDUCATION: Oberlin College, OH, A.B., 1891; Oberlin College, OH, A.M., 1893; Columbia Univ., NY, Ph.D., 1895. SPOUSE: Greta Irvin Blanchard, married April 10, 1902. CHILDREN: Clark Blanchard, son; Glenn Allen, son; Max Franklin, son. CAREER: Univ. of Chicago, IL, Professor, 1896-1921; California Institute of Technology, Professor and Administrator, 1921-46. OTHER AWARDS: Comstock Prize, National Academy of Sciences, 1913; Edison Medal, American Institute of Electrical Engineers, 1922; Hughes Medal, Royal Society, 1923; Faraday Medal, Chemical Society of London, 1924; Matteuci Medal, Societa Italiana della Scienze, 1925; Gold Medal, American Society of Mechanical Engineers, 1926; Messel Medal, Society of Chemical Industry, 1928; Gold Medal, Holland Society, 1928; Gold Medal, Radiological Society of North America, 1930; Gold Medal, Roosevelt Memorial Association, 1932; Newman Medal, 1934; Legion of Honor, France, 1936; Gold Medal, Franklin Institute, PA, 1937; Gold Medal, Ulster-Irish Association of NY, 1938; Joy Kissen Mookerjee Gold Medal, Indian Association for the Cultivation of Science, 1939; Oersted Medal, American Association of Physics Teachers, 1940; Order of the Jade, China, 1940; Order Al Merito, Chile, 1944.

Selected Publications: "Quantum Theory and Its Relation to Photoelectric Phenomena." *Physik. Z.* 17 (1916): 217-21. *Electron: Its Isolation and Measurement and the Determination of Some of Its Properties.* Chicago: U. of Chicago Press, 1917. "Radiation and the Electron." *Nature* 101 (1918): 234-37, 254-57. "High-Frequency Rays of Cosmic Origin." *Science* 62 (1925): 445-48. *Electrons, Protons, Photons, Neutrons and Cosmic Rays.* Chicago: U. of Chicago Press, 1935.

For More Information See: *The Autobiography of Robert A. Millikan.* New York: Prentice-Hall, 1950. *Dictionary of Scientific Biography.* New York: Scribner's, 1974 (Volume 9), 395-400.

Commentary: The Academy honored Robert Millikan "for his work on the elementary charge of electricity and on the photoelectric effect." In addition to his determination of the charge of the electron, his verification of Einstein's photoelectric equation, and his determination of Planck's constant, Millikan contributed major work on Brownian movement, the ultraviolet spectrum, the law of motion of a falling particle, and cosmic radiation. (I.H.G.)

1924

Siegbahn, Karl Manne Georg   444
PRIZE: Physics, 1924. BORN: December 3, 1886; Örebro, Sweden. DIED: September 26, 1978; Stockholm, Sweden. PARENTS: Father, Georg Siegbahn; Mother, Emma Zetterberg Siegbahn. NATIONALITY: Swedish. RELIGION: Most probably Christian/Protestant. EDUCATION: Univ. of Lund, Sweden, master's degree, no date found; Univ. of Lund, Sweden, Dr.Sc., 1911. SPOUSE: Karin Hoegbom, married 1914. CHILDREN: Kai, son; Bo, son. CAREER: Univ. of Lund, Sweden, Professor, 1911-23; Univ. of Uppsala, Sweden, Professor, 1923-37; Swedish Royal Academy of Sciences, Professor and Administrator, 1937-64. OTHER AWARDS: Hughes Medal, Royal Society, 1934; Rumford Medal, Royal Society, 1940; Duddel Medal, Physical Society of London, 1948.

Selected Publications: *The Spectroscopy of X-rays*(collected papers). London: Oxford U. Press, 1925.

For More Information See: *Asimov's Biographical Encyclopedia of Science and Technology.* Garden City, NY: Doubleday, 1982, 707-08. *Biographical Encyclopedia of Scientists.* New York: Facts on File, 1981, 733-34.

Commentary: Karl Siegbahn received his Nobel Prize "for his discoveries and research in the field of x-ray spectroscopy." After briefly studying electricity and magnetism, Siegbahn developed techniques for accurate measurement of x-ray wavelengths and showed that x-ray spectra were valuable for identification, as well as lending credence to the Bohr ideas of structure. In later research, Siegbahn turned to problems of nuclear physics. (C.S.)

1925

Franck, James   445
PRIZE: Physics, 1925. BORN: August 26, 1882; Hamburg, Germany. DIED: May 21, 1964; Göttingen, Germany. PARENTS: Father, Jacob Franck; Mother, Rebecca Drucker Franck. NATIONALITY: German; later American citizen. RELIGION: Jewish. EDUCATION: Univ. of Berlin, Germany, Ph.D., 1906. SPOUSE: Ingrid Josephson, married December 23, 1906, died 1942; Hertha Sponer, married June 29, 1946. CHILDREN: Dagmar, daughter; Elisabeth, daughter. CAREER: Univ. of Berlin, Germany, Professor, 1906-18; Kaiser Wilhelm Institute, Germany, Professor, 1918-20; Univ. of Göttingen, Germany, Professor, 1920-33; Univ. of Copenhagen, Denmark, Professor, 1934; Johns Hopkins Univ., MD, Professor, 1935-38; Univ. of Chicago, IL, Professor, 1938-47. OTHER AWARDS: Max Planck Medal, German Physical Society, 1953; Rumford Medal, American Academy of Arts and Sciences, 1955.

Selected Publications: *Anregung von Quantensprüngen durch Stösse.* Berlin: J. Springer, 1926 (with P. Jordan). *Photosynthesis in Plants.* Ames, IA: Iowa State College Press, 1949 (with W. E. Loomis).

For More Information See: *Biographical Memoirs of the Fellows of the Royal Society.* London: Royal Society, 1965 (Volume 11), 53-74. *Current Biography Yearbook.* New York: H. W. Wilson, 1957, 192-94. *Dictionary of Scientific Biography.* New York: Scribner's, 1972 (Volume 5), 117-18.

Commentary: The award to James Franck was for his contributions to the "discovery of the laws governing the impact of an electron upon an atom." He also was one of the formulators of the Franck-Condon Principle, which permitted the prediction of most-favored vibrational transitions in a bond system. His later work dealt with a model for photosynthesis. Franck was also prominent on the political/moral scene in his objections to the Hitler regime in Germany in the early 30s and in the Franck report of 1945, which was prepared by a group of atomic scientists and which called for an open demonstration of the atomic bomb in an uninhabited locale, rather than its surprise use in Japan. (F.K.)

Hertz, Gustav Ludwig   446
PRIZE: Physics, 1925. BORN: July 22, 1887; Hamburg, Germany. DIED: October 30, 1975; Berlin, Germany. PARENTS: Father, Gustav Hertz; Mother, Augusta Arning Hertz. NATIONALITY: German. RELIGION: From Jewish background. EDUCATION: Univ. of Berlin, Germany, Ph.D., 1911. SPOUSE: Ellen Dihlmann, married 1919, died 1941; Charlotte Jollasse, married 1943. CHILDREN: Hellmuth, son; Johannes, son. CAREER: Univ. of Berlin, Germany, Researcher, 1913-14; German Army, 1914-17; Univ. of Berlin, Germany, Researcher, 1917-20; Philips Incandescent Lamp Factory, Netherlands, Researcher, 1920-25; Univ. of Halle, Germany, Professor and Administrator, 1925-28; Charlottenburg Technological Univ., Berlin, Germany, Professor and Administrator, 1928-35; Siemans Company, Germany, Researcher and Administrator, 1935-45; Research Laboratory, USSR, Researcher and Administrator, 1945-54; Karl Marx Univ., Leipzig, Germany, Professor and Administrator, 1955-61. OTHER AWARDS: Max Planck Medal, German Physical Society.

Selected Publications: "Impacts Between Gas Molecules and Slowly Moving Electrons." *Ber. Physike. Geog* (1913): 373-91 (with J. Franck). "A Connection Between Impact Ionization and Electron Affinity." *Verh. Deut. Physik. Geo* 15: 929-34 (with J. Franck). "Collisions Between Electrons and Molecules of Mercury Vapor and the Ionizing Voltage for the Same." *Verh. Deut. Physik. Geo* 16: 457-67. *Lehrbuch der Kernphysik.* 3 volumes. Leipzig, East Germany: B.G. Teubner, 1958-62.

For More Information See: *Biographical Dictionary of Scientists.* New York: Wiley, 1982, 595-96. *Physics Today* 29 (January 1976): 83-85.

Commentary: Gustav Hertz shared the Nobel Prize for his contributions to the "discovery of the laws governing the collision of an electron with an atom." Hertz, in his earliest research, worked on the infrared absorption of CO_2 and the ionization potentials of several gases. His study of the relationships between electron energy losses in collisions and spectral lines provided needed data for Bohr to develop his theory of atomic structure and for Planck to develop his ideas on quantum theory. (F.K.)

1926

Perrin, Jean Baptiste   447
PRIZE: Physics, 1926. BORN: September 30, 1870; Lille, France. DIED: April 17, 1942; New York, NY. PARENTS: No record found. NATIONALITY: French. RELIGION: Christian. EDUCATION: École Normale Supér-

ieure, France, Ph.D., 1897. SPOUSE: Henriette Duportal, married 1897. CHILDREN: Aline, daughter; Francis, son. CAREER: École Normale Superieure, France, Researcher, 1894-97; Univ. of Paris, France, Professor, 1897-1940. OTHER AWARDS: Joule Prize, Royal Society, 1896; La Caze Prize, French Academy of Sciences, 1914.

Selected Publications: "Rayons Cathodiques et Rayons de Roentgen." *Annales de Chimie et de Physique* 11 (1897): 496-554. *Traite de Chimie Physique. Les Principes.* Paris: Gauthier-Villars, 1903. "Mouvement Brownien et Realite Moleculaire." *Annales de Chimie et de Physique* 18 (1909): 1-114. *Les Atomes.* Paris: Alcan, 1913. *Oeuvres Scientifiques de Jean Perrin.* Paris: Centre National de la Recherche Scientifique, 1950.

For More Information See: *Dictionary of Scientific Biography.* New York: Scribner's, 1973 (Volume 10), 524-26. Nye, Mary Jo. *Molecular Reality.* London: MacDonald, 1972.

Commentary: Jean Perrin was cited by the Academy "for his work on the discontinuous structure of matter, and especially for his discovery of sedimentation equilibrium." Perrin began his career studying the nature of cathode rays and proved they were negative particles. His further studies were of x-ray effects on gas conductivity, fluorescence, radium disintegration, and sound. But his major work was in the exploration of the world of colloids, during which he further developed the theory of Brownian movement and was able to calculate the value of the Avogadro number (the number of molecules per grammolecule of a gas). Perrin was also responsible for the creation of much of the scientific establishment in France. (A.S.)

1927

Compton, Arthur Holly   448

PRIZE: Physics, 1927. BORN: September 10, 1892; Wooster, OH. DIED: March 15, 1962; Berkeley, CA. PARENTS: Father, Elias Compton; Mother, Otelia Catherine Augspurger Compton. NATIONALITY: American. RELIGION: Presbyterian. EDUCATION: College of Wooster, OH, B.S., 1913; Princeton Univ., NJ, M.A., 1914; Princeton Univ., NJ, Ph.D., 1916. SPOUSE: Betty Charity McCloskey, married June 28, 1916. CHILDREN: Arthur Alan, son; John Joseph, son. CAREER: Univ. of Minnesota, Professor, 1916-17; Westinghouse Lamp Co., PA, Researcher, 1917-19; Cambridge Univ., England, Researcher, 1919-20; Washington Univ., St. Louis, MO, Professor, 1920-23; Univ. of Chicago, IL, Professor, 1923-45; Washington Univ., St. Louis, MO, Chancellor, 1945-54. OTHER AWARDS: Rumford Medal, American Academy of Arts and Sciences, 1927; Gold Medal, Radiological Society of North America, 1928; Matteuci Medal, Italian Academy of Sciences, 1933; Franklin Medal, Franklin Institute, PA, 1940; Hughes Medal, Royal Society, 1940; Washington Award, Western Society of Engineers, 1945; Franklin Medal, American Philosophical Society, 1945; Congressional Medal of Merit, 1946.

Selected Publications: "A Quantum Theory of the Scattering of X-Rays by Light Elements." *Physical Review* 21 (1923): 483-502. "Polarization of Secondary X-Rays." *Journal of the Optical Society of America* 8 (1924): 487-91 (with C.F. Hagenow). "X-Ray Spectra from a Ruled Reflection Grating." *Proceedings of the*

National Academy of Sciences, USA 11 (1925): 598-601 (with R.L. Doan). *X-Rays and Electrons.* Princeton, NJ: D. Van Nostrand Company, 1926. *X-Rays in Theory and Experiment.* Princeton, NJ: D. Van Nostrand Company, 1935 (with S.K. Allison).

For More Information See: *The Cosmos of Arthur Holly Compton.* New York: Knopf, 1967. *Dictionary of Scientific Biography.* New York: Scribner's, 1971 (Volume 3), 366-72. *National Cyclopaedia of American Biography.* New York: James T. White, 1946 (Volume G), 363-64.

Commentary: Arthur Compton won his Nobel Prize "for his discovery of the effect named after him." The Compton effect referred to the increase of wavelength of X-rays caused by scattering of the incident radiation by electrons. It was important in the developing theories of quantum versus wave nature. Compton also developed the coincidence method for studying x-ray scattering and studied x-ray reflection and polarization, x-ray spectra and wavelength measurement, and geographic variations of cosmic-ray intensity. (I.H.G.)

Wilson, Charles Thomson Rees   449

PRIZE: Physics, 1927. BORN: February 14, 1869; Glencorse, Midlothian, Scotland. DIED: November 15, 1959; Carlops, Peeblesshire, Scotland. PARENTS: Father, John Wilson; Mother, Annie Clerk Harper Wilson. NATIONALITY: Scottish. RELIGION: Protestant. EDUCATION: Owens College, England, B.Sc., 1887; Cambridge Univ., England, B.A., 1892. SPOUSE: Jessie Fraser Dick, married 1908. CHILDREN: 2 sons; 2 daughters. CAREER: Cavendish Laboratory, England, Researcher, 1892-96; Bradford Grammar School, Yorkshire, England, Teacher, 1894; Cambridge Univ., England, Professor, 1896-1934. OTHER AWARDS: Hughes Medal, Royal Society, 1911; Hopkins Prize, Cambridge Philosophical Society, England, 1920; Gunning Prize, Royal Society of Edinburgh, Scotland, 1921; Royal Medal, Royal Society, 1922; Howard Potts Medal, Franklin Institute, 1925; Copley Medal, Royal Society, 1935.

Selected Publications: "A Method of Making Visible the Paths of Ionizing Particles Through a Gas." *Proceedings of the Royal Society of London* Series A. 85 (1911): 285-88. "An Expansion Apparatus for Making Visible the Track of Ionizing Particles in Gases and Some Results Obtained by Its Use." *Proceedings of the Royal Society of London* Series A. 87 (1913): 277-92. "The Acceleration of Beta-Particles in Strong Electrical Fields Such as Those of Thunderclouds." *Proceedings of the Cambridge Philosophical Society* 22 (1925): 534-38.

For More Information See: *Biographical Memoirs of the Fellows of the Royal Society.* London: Royal Society, 1960 (Volume 6), 269-95. *Dictionary of Scientific Biography.* New York: Scribner's, 1981 (Volume 14), 420-23.

Commentary: The award to Charles Wilson was "for his method of making the paths of electrically charged particles visible by condensation of vapour." He invented the cloud chamber, later referred to as the Wilson Cloud Chamber, which Ernest Rutherford called "the most original apparatus in the whole history of physics." It became vital to the study of radioactivity and the development of nuclear physics. Wilson's work was on condensation phenomena, the conductivity of air, and atmospheric electricity. (F.K.)

1928

Richardson, Owen Willans, Sir 450

PRIZE: Physics, 1928. BORN: April 26, 1879; Dewsbury, Yorkshire, England. DIED: February 15, 1959; Alton, Hampshire, England. PARENTS: Father, Joshua Henry Richardson; Mother, Charlotte Maria Willans Richardson. NATIONALITY: British. RELIGION: Anglican. EDUCATION: Cambridge Univ., England, B.A., 1900; Univ. of London, England, D.Sc., 1904. SPOUSE: Lilian Maud Wilson, married 1906, died 1945; Henrietta Maria G. Rupp, married 1948. CHILDREN: Harold, son; John, son; 1 daughter. CAREER: Cavendish Laboratory, England, Researcher, 1900-06; Princeton Univ., NJ, Professor, 1906-14; Univ. of London, England, Professor, 1914-44. OTHER AWARDS: Hughes Medal, Royal Society, 1920; Royal Medal, Royal Society, 1930; Knighthood, 1939.

Selected Publications: *The Electron Theory of Matter.* Cambridge: Cambridge U. Press, 1914. *The Emission of Electricity from Hot Bodies.* London: Longmans, Green and Co., 1916. *Molecular Hydrogen and Its Spectrum.* New Haven, CT: Yale U. Press, 1934.

For More Information See: *Biographical Memoirs of the Fellows of the Royal Society.* London: Royal Society, 1959 (Volume 5), 207-15. *Dictionary of Scientific Biography.* New York: Scribner's, 1981 (Volume 11), 419-23.

Commentary: The award to Owen Richardson was "for his work on the thermionic phenomenon and especially for the discovery of the law named after him." "Richardson's Law" or the "Richardson Effect," also known as the "thermionic effect," quantified the theory of electron emission from hot bodies and enabled the development of devices like radio tubes and television tubes. Richardson coined the term "thermion." He also made important contributions through his analysis of the molecular hydrogen spectrum. (F.K.)

1929

Broglie, Louis-Victor Pierre Raymond de 451

PRIZE: Physics, 1929. BORN: August 15, 1892; Dieppe, France. PARENTS: Father, Victor de Broglie; Mother, Pauline d'Armaillé de Broglie. NATIONALITY: French. RELIGION: Catholic. EDUCATION: Univ. of Paris, France, licence in history, 1910; Univ. of Paris, France, licence in science, 1913; Univ. of Paris, France, D.Sc., 1924. SPOUSE: None. CHILDREN: None. CAREER: Univ. of Paris, France, Professor, 1926-62. OTHER AWARDS: Henri Poincaré Medal, Académie des Sciences, 1929; Max Planck Medal, German Physical Society, 1938; Kalinga Prize, UNESCO.

Selected Publications: "Recherches sur la Théorie des Quanta." *Annales de Physique* 3 (January-February 1925): 22-128. *La Mécanique Ondulatoire.* Paris: Gauthier-Villars, 1928 (*Selected Papers on Wave Mechanics.* Tr. by W.M. Deans. London: Blackie & Son Limited, 1928 (with L. Brillouin)). *An Introduction to the Study of Wave Mechanics.* Tr. by H.T. Flint. London: Methuen & Co., Ltd., 1930. *Matter and Light: The New Physics.* Tr. by W.H. Johnston. New York: W.W. Norton, 1939. *Non-linear Wave Mechanics: A Causal Interpretation.* Tr. by Arthur J. Knodel and Jack C. Miller. New York: Elsevier, 1960. *The Current*

Interpretation of Wave Mechanics, a Critical Study. Tr. by Express Translation Service. New York: Elsevier, 1964.

For More Information See: *Current Biography Yearbook.* New York: H. W. Wilson, 1955, 67-69. *Modern Scientists and Engineers.* New York: McGraw-Hill, 1980 (Volume 1), 143-44.

Commentary: Louis de Broglie was awarded the Nobel Prize for his discovery of the wave nature of the electron. He showed that both matter and radiation displayed the properties of both particles and waves, which fit the Einstein theory that matter is merely a form of energy and the two can be converted into each other. Schrödinger and Bohr then used the idea of the wave nature of matter in the development of quantum mechanics. In later work, de Broglie attempted to determine a causal, rather than probabilistic, theory of wave mechanics. As a member of the French Commission on Atomic Energy, he actively promoted the peaceful use of atomic power and was an influence on public opinion toward it in France. (L.A.)

1930

Raman, Chandrasekhara Venkata, Sir 452

PRIZE: Physics, 1930. BORN: November 7, 1888; Trichinopoly, India. DIED: November 21, 1970; Bangalore, India. PARENTS: Father, Chandrasekhara Aiyar Raman; Mother, Parvati Ammal Raman. NATIONALITY: Indian. RELIGION: Hindu. EDUCATION: Presidency College, India, B.A., 1902; Presidency College, India, M.A., 1907. SPOUSE: Lokasundari Raman, married June 6, 1907. CHILDREN: Chandrasekhara, son; Radhakrishnan, son. CAREER: Indian Finance Department, Researcher, 1907-17; Calcutta Univ., India, Professor, 1917-33; Indian Institute of Science, Bangalore, Professor, 1933-48; Raman Institute of Research, Bangalore, India, Director, 1948-70. OTHER AWARDS: Knighthood, 1929; Mateucci Medal, Italy, 1929; Hughes Medal, Royal Society, 1930; Franklin Medal, Franklin Institute, PA, 1941.

Selected Publications: "Dynamical Theory of the Motion of Bowed Strings." *Bulletin Indian Association for the Cultivation of Science* 11 (1914). "On the Molecular Scattering of Light in Water and the Color of the Sea." *Proceedings of the Royal Society* 64 (1922). "A New Radiation." *Indian Journal of Physics* 2 (1928): 387. "Crystals and Photons." *Proceedings of the Indian Academy of Science* 13A (1941): 1. *The Physiology of Vision.* Bangalore, India: Indian Academy of Sciences, 1968.

For More Information See: *Current Biography Yearbook.* New York: H.W. Wilson, 1948, 510-12. *Dictionary of Scientific Biography.* New York: Scribner's, 1975 (Volume 11), 264-67.

Commentary: Chandrasekhara Venkata Raman was cited by the Academy "for his work on the scattering of light and for the discovery of the effect named after him." Raman discovered that, given the proper circumstances, the light scattered by mercury and other elements and compounds is scattered with a different frequency. He explained the observations, using quantum theory. The Raman effect became a powerful tool for studies of molecular structure and chemical analysis. Raman also contributed major work on the theory of musical instruments, the optics of colloids, electrical and magnetic anisotropy, the physiology of human vision, light diffraction by acoustic waves, x-ray effects on infrared vibrations in light-irradiated crystals, and crystal structure and dynamics. (B.S.S.)

1932

Heisenberg, Werner Karl 453

PRIZE: Physics, 1932. BORN: December 5, 1901; Würzburg, Germany. DIED: February 1, 1976; Munich, Germany. PARENTS: Father, August Heisenberg; Mother, Annie Wecklein Heisenberg. NATIONALITY: German. RELIGION: Protestant. EDUCATION: Univ. of Munich, Germany, Ph.D., 1923; Univ. of Gottingen, Germany, Dr. Phil. Habil., 1924. SPOUSE: Elisabeth Schumacher, married April 29, 1937. CHILDREN: Wolfgang, son; Jochem, son; Martin, son; Anna Maria, daughter; Barbara, daughter; Christine, daughter; Verena, daughter. CAREER: Univ. of Copenhagen, Denmark, Professor, 1924-26; Univ. of Leipzig, Germany, Professor, 1927-41; Univ. of Berlin, Germany, Professor, 1942-45; Univ. of Göttingen, Germany, Professor, 1946-58; Univ. of Munich, Germany, Professor, 1958-70. OTHER AWARDS: Barnard Medal, Columbia U., NY, 1930; Max Planck Medal, German Physical Society, 1933; Grotius Medal, Hugo Grotius Stiftung, 1956; Sigmund Freud Prize, Deutsche Akademie für Sprache und Dichtung, 1970; Niels Bohr Gold Medal, Dansk Ingeniorforening, 1970.

Selected Publications: "Über Quantentheoretische Umdeutung Kinematischer und Mechanischer Beziehungen." *Zeitschrift für Physik* 33 (1925): 879-983. "Mehrkörperproblem und Resonanz in der Quantenmechanik." *Zeitschrift für Physik* 38 (1926): 411-26; 41 (1927): 239-67. "Über den Anschaulichen Inhalt der Quantentheoretischen Kinematik und Mechanik." *Zeitschrift für Physik* 43 (1927): 172-98. *The Physical Principles of the Quantum Theory.* Tr. by Carl Eckart and Frank C. Hoyt. Chicago: U. of Chicago Press, 1930. *Philosophic Problems of Nuclear Science.* Tr. by F.C. Hayes. New York: Pantheon, 1952. *Physics and Philosophy: The Revolution in Modern Science.* New York: Harper, 1958.

For More Information See: *Biographical Memoirs of Fellows of the Royal Society.* London: Royal Society, 1977 (Volume 22), 213-51. Heisenberg, Elisabeth. *Inner Exile: Recollections of a Life with Werner Heisenberg.* Tr. by Steve Capalari. Boston: Birkhäuser, 1984. Hermann, Armin. *Werner Heisenberg, 1901-1976.* Tr. by Timothy Nevill. Bonn-Bad Godesberg, Germany: Inter Nationes, 1976. Weber, Robert L. *Pioneers of Science: Nobel Prize Winners in Physics.* Bristol, England: The Institute of Physics, 1980, 95-96.

Commentary: Werner Heisenberg received the Nobel Prize "for the creation of quantum mechanics, the application of which has, among other things, led to the discovery of the allotropic forms of hydrogen." He is probably better known for his formulation in 1927 of the uncertainty principle that bears his name, which states that it is impossible *simultaneously* to determine both the position and the momentum of a particle. Heisenberg also investigated problems in ferromagnetism and quantum electrodynamics and was among the first to suggest that the atomic nucleus consisted of protons and neutrons. In later life, he worked on a unified field theory of elementary particles. (L.A.)

1933

Dirac, Paul Adrien Maurice 454

PRIZE: Physics, 1933. BORN: August 8, 1902; Bristol, England. DIED: October 20, 1984; Tallahassee, FL. PARENTS: Father, Charles Adrien Ladislas Dirac; Mother, Florence Hannah Holten Dirac. NATIONALITY: British; later American resident. RELIGION: Catholic. EDUCATION: Bristol Univ., England, B.Sc., 1921; Cambridge Univ., England, Ph.D., 1926. SPOUSE: Margit Wigner, married 1937. CHILDREN: Mary Elizabeth, daughter; Florence Monica, daughter. CAREER: Cambridge Univ., England, Professor, 1927-68; Florida State Univ., Professor, 1971-84. OTHER AWARDS: Royal Medal, Royal Society, 1939; Copley Medal, Royal Society, 1952; Max Planck Medal, German Institute, 1952.

Selected Publications: *The Principles of Quantum Mechanics.* London: Clarendon Press, 1930. *The Development of Quantum Theory.* New York: Gordon and Breach Science Publishers, 1971. *Spinors in Hibert Space.* New York: Plenum Press, 1974. *General Theory of Relativity.* New York: Wiley, 1975.

For More Information See: *Asimov's Biographical Encyclopedia of Science and Technology.* Garden City, NY: Doubleday, 1964, 484-85. *Modern Scientists and Engineers.* New York: McGraw-Hill, 1980 (Volume 1), 292-93.

Commentary: Paul Dirac shared the Nobel Prize "for the discovery of new productive forms of atomic theory." His mathematical treatment of electronic properties predicted the existence of positrons, previously unobserved, at an early stage of his career. Dirac continued to develop the new field of quantum mechanics, his great contribution being the Dirac wave equations which included special relativity in the Schrödinger equation. (V.A.H.)

Schrodinger, Erwin 455

PRIZE: Physics, 1933. BORN: August 12, 1887; Vienna, Austria. DIED: January 4, 1961; Alpbach, Austria. PARENTS: Father, Rudolf Schrodinger; Mother, M. Bauer Schrodinger. NATIONALITY: Austrian. RELIGION: Catholic. EDUCATION: Univ. of Vienna, Austria, Ph.D., 1910. SPOUSE: Annemarie Bertel, married April 6, 1920. CHILDREN: None. CAREER: Univ. of Vienna, Austria, Researcher, 1910-14; Austrian Army, 1914-20; Univ. of Stuttgart, Germany, Professor, 1920; Univ. of Jena, Germany, Professor, 1920-21; Univ. of Breslau, Germany, Professor, 1921; Univ. of Zurich, Switzerland, Professor, 1921-27; Univ. of Berlin, Germany, Professor, 1927-33; Oxford Univ., England, Researcher, 1933-36; Univ. of Graz, Austria, Professor, 1936-39; Fondation Francqui, Belgium, Professor, 1939-40; Royal Irish Academy, Professor, 1940; Dublin Institute for Advanced Studies, Ireland, Professor, 1940-56; Univ. of Vienna, Austria, Professor, 1956-58. OTHER AWARDS: Matteuci Medal; Planck Medal.

Selected Publications: "Quantisierung als Eigenwertproblem. Erste Mitteilung." *Ann. Phys.* 79 (1926): 361. "Quantisierung Zweite Mitteilung." *Ann. Phys.* 79 (1926): 489. "Quantisierung Dritte Mitteilung." *Ann. Phys.* 80 (1926): 437. "Quantisierung Vierte Mitteilung." *Ann. Phys.* 81 (1926): 109. *What is Life?* Cambridge: Cambridge U. Press, 1945. *Space-Time Structure.* Cambridge: Cambridge U. Press, 1950. *Statistical Thermodynamics.* Cambridge: Cambridge U. Press, 1952.

For More Information See: *Dictionary of Scientific Biography.* New York: Scribner's, 1975 (Volume 12), 217-22. *Encyclopedia of World Biography.* New York: McGraw-Hill, 1973 (Volume 9), 461-63.

Commentary: Erwin Schrodinger was granted the Nobel Prize "for the discovery of new productive forms of atomic theory." Early in his career, Schrodinger worked on specific heats of solids, thermodynamics, atomic spectra, and physiological studies of color, culminating this period with the development of his wave equations. Later he worked on the problem of a unified field theory (of gravitation and electromagnetism) and on other foundational studies in atomic physics. (A.S.)

1935

Chadwick, James, Sir   **456**

PRIZE: Physics, 1935. BORN: October 20, 1891; Bollington, England. DIED: July 24, 1974; Cambridge, England. PARENTS: Father, John Joseph Chadwick; Mother, Anne Mary Knowles Chadwick. NATIONALITY: British. RELIGION: Christian. EDUCATION: Univ. of Manchester, England, baccalaureate, 1911; Univ. of Manchester, England, M.Sc., 1912. SPOUSE: Aileen Stewart-Brown, married 1925. CHILDREN: 2 daughters. CAREER: Cambridge Univ., England, Researcher, 1919-35; Univ. of Liverpool, England, Professor, 1935-48; Manhattan Project, British Mission, England, Administrator, 1943-48; Cambridge Univ., England, Professor, 1948-59. OTHER AWARDS: Hughes Medal, Royal Society, 1932; MacKenzie Davidson Medal, 1932; Knighthood, 1945; United States Medal for Merit, 1946; Transenter Medal, 1946; Melchett Medal, 1946; Faraday Medal, Institution of Electrical Engineers, 1950; Copley Medal, Royal Society, 1950; Franklin Medal, Franklin Institute, PA, 1951; Guthrie Medal, 1967.

Selected Publications: *Radioactivity and Radioactive Substances.* London: Sir Isaac Pitman and Sons, 1921. "The Existence of a Neutron." *Proceedings of the Royal Society of London* A136 (1929): 692-708. *Radiations from Radioactive Substances.* Cambridge: Cambridge U. Press, 1930 (with E. Rutherford and C.D. Ellis). "The Neutron." (Bakerian Lecture) *Proceedings of the Royal Society of London* A142 (1933): 1-25. "The Neutron and its Properties." *British Journal of Radiology* 6 (1933): 24-32. "Evidence for a New Type of Disintegration Produced by Neutrons." *Proceedings of the Cambridge Philosophical Society* 30 (1934): 357-64 (with N. Feather and W.T. Davies).

For More Information See: *Biographical Memoirs of Fellows of the Royal Society.* London: Royal Society, 1976 (Volume 22), 11-70. "Chadwick's Neutron." *Contemporary Physics* 6 (1974): 565-712.

Commentary: James Chadwick's Nobel was granted "for his discovery of the neutron." In a repetition of the Joliot-Curie experiments on alpha-ray bombardment, Chadwick showed that the rays produced traveled at 1/10 the speed of light (too slow to be gamma rays) and that they occasionally struck nitrogen atoms with great force (something a gamma ray could not do). He went on to demonstrate that these rays were neutral and could not be deflected by a magnet; that they were particles and could be absorbed; and that they had a mass of one, like a proton. In discovering the neutron, Chadwick solved the problem of extra

mass in the nucleus and laid the groundwork for the release of energy from the atom. He continued to research in the general area of particle bombardment and nuclear structure. (S.H.S.)

1936

Anderson, Carl David   **457**

PRIZE: Physics, 1936. BORN: September 3, 1905; New York, NY. PARENTS: Father, Carl David Anderson; Mother, Emma Adolfina Ajaxson Anderson. NATIONALITY: American. RELIGION: Most probably Christian/Protestant. EDUCATION: California Institute of Technology, B.S., 1927; California Institute of Technology, Ph.D., 1930. SPOUSE: Lorraine Elvira Bergman, married 1946. CHILDREN: Marshall David Lee, son; David Andrew Keith, son. CAREER: California Institute of Technology, Professor and Administrator, 1930-77. OTHER AWARDS: Gold Medal, American Institute of the City of New York, 1935; Elliott Cresson Medal, Franklin Institute, PA, 1937; Presidential Certificate of Merit, 1945; John Ericsson Gold Medal, American Society of Swedish Engineers, 1960.

Selected Publications: "Energies and Cosmic-Ray Particles." *Physical Review* (August 15, 1932): 405-21. "Positive Electron." *Physical Review* 43 (March 15, 1933): 491-94. "Cosmic-Ray Positive and Negative Electrons." *Physical Review* 44 (September 1, 1933): 406-16. "Mechanism of Cosmic-Ray Counter Action." *Physical Review* 45 (March 15, 1934): 352-63 (with others). "The Positron." *Nature* 133 (March 1934): 313-16.

For More Information See: *Asimov's Biographical Encyclopedia of Science and Technology.* Garden City, NY: Doubleday, 1982, 805-06. *Current Biography Yearbook.* New York: H.W. Wilson, 1951, 15-17.

Commentary: Carl Anderson was recognized by the Academy "for his discovery of the positron." Using a Wilson cloud chamber set in a magnetic field powerful enough to deflect high-energy particles, Anderson photographed charged particles set in motion by cosmic rays. In August 1932, Anderson photographed a charged particle moving upward, and because cosmic rays only move downward, he concluded that this must be a positively charged particle released inside the cloud chamber. The particle appeared to have the mass of an electron, and its ionizing power was too weak to be a proton or alpha particle. Carl Anderson had discovered the positive electron which would become a significant contribution to the understanding of atomic structure. Anderson was also known for his research on cosmic rays and for proving the existence of the meson in 1938. (S.H.S.)

Hess, Victor Franz   **458**

PRIZE: Physics, 1936. BORN: June 24, 1883; Schloss Waldstein, Austria. DIED: December 17, 1964; Mount Vernon, NY. PARENTS: Father, Vincenz Hess; Mother, Serafine Grossbauer Hess. NATIONALITY: Austrian; later American citizen. RELIGION: Catholic. EDUCATION: Univ. of Graz, Austria, Ph.D., 1906. SPOUSE: Berta Waermer Breisky, married 1920, died 1955; Elizabeth Hoencke, married 1955. CHILDREN: None. CAREER: Univ. of Graz, Austria, Researcher, 1906-08; Vienna Veterinary College, Austria, Professor, 1908-10; Univ. of Vienna, Austria, Professor, 1910-20; Univ. of Graz, Austria, Professor, 1920-21; U.S. Radium Corp., NY,

Researcher, 1921-23; Univ. of Graz, Austria, Professor, 1923-31; Univ. of Innsbruck, Austria, Professor, 1931-37; Univ. of Graz, Austria, Professor, 1937-38; Fordham Univ., NY, Professor, 1938-58. OTHER AWARDS: Lieben Prize, Austrian Academy of Sciences, 1919; Abbe Prize, Carl Zeiss Foundation, 1932.

Selected Publications: *Die Elektrische Leitfahigkeit der Atmosphare und Ihre Ursachen.* Brunswick, Germany: F. Viewig and Sohn, 1926. *Die Weltraumstrahlung und Ihre Biologischen Wirkungen.* Zurich: Drell Füssli, 1940. "The Discovery of Cosmic Radiation." *Thought* (1940): 1-12. "Work in the USA." *Oesterreichische Hochschulzeitung* (January 15, 1955): 4.

For More Information See: *Dictionary of Scientific Biography.* New York: Scribner's, 1972 (Volume 6), 354-56. Wilson, J.G. "Obituary Notice." *Nature* 207 (1965): 352.

Commentary: Victor Hess won the Nobel Prize "for his discovery of cosmic radiation." Hess developed the instrumentation and, in a series of daring ascents in balloons and careful study over a period of many years, showed that there was a source of powerful radiation beyond the galaxy which flooded the earth constantly and produced radiation greater in intensity and power than sources on earth. Hess continued to study cosmic radiation throughout his career. (R.J.)

1937

Davisson, Clinton Joseph   459

PRIZE: Physics, 1937. BORN: October 22, 1881; Bloomington, IL. DIED: February 1, 1958; Charlottesville, VA. PARENTS: Father, Joseph Davisson; Mother, Mary Calvert Davisson. NATIONALITY: American. RELIGION: Christian. EDUCATION: Univ. of Chicago, IL, B.S., 1908; Princeton Univ., NJ, Ph.D., 1911. SPOUSE: Charlotte Sara Richardson, married 1911. CHILDREN: Clinton Owen Calvert, son; James Willans, son; Richard Joseph, son; Elizabeth Mary, daughter. CAREER: Carnegie Institute of Technology, Pittsburgh, PA, Professor, 1911-17; Bell Telephone Laboratories, NJ, Researcher, 1917-46; Univ. of Virginia, Charlottesville, Professor, 1947-49. OTHER AWARDS: Comstock Prize, National Academy of Sciences, U.S., 1928; Elliot Cresson Medal, Franklin Institute, PA, 1931; Hughes Medal, Royal Society, 1935; Alumni Medal, U. of Chicago, IL, 1941.

Selected Publications: "Dispersion of Hydrogen and Helium on Bohr's Theory." *Physical Review, 2nd Series* 8 (1916): 20-27. "Scattering of Electrons by Nickel." *Science, New Series* 54 (1921): 522-24 (with C.H. Kunsman). "Thermionic Work Function of Tungsten." *Physical Review, 2nd Series* 20 (1922): 300-30 (with L.H. Germer). "Reflection and Refraction of Electrons by a Crystal of Nickel." *Proceedings of the National Academy of Sciences, USA* 14 (1928): 619-27 (with L.H. Germer).

For More Information See: *Biographical Memoirs. National Academy of Sciences.* Washington, DC: National Academy of Sciences, 1962 (Volume 36), 51-84. *Dictionary of Scientific Biography.* New York: Scribner's, 1971 (Volume 3), 597-98.

Commentary: Clinton Davisson shared the Nobel Prize with George Paget Thomson "for their experimental discovery of the diffraction of electrons by crystals." Davisson studied electron diffraction by nickel crystals and confirmed the De Broglie theory of the wave nature of particles. At the same time that Davisson was studying electron diffraction, he was also doing landmark research in thermal radiation and thermionics. His later research focused on the theory of electron optics and its application, the theory of electronic devices, and solid state physics. (B.S.S.)

Thomson, George Paget, Sir   460

PRIZE: Physics, 1937. BORN: May 3, 1892; Cambridge, England. DIED: September 10, 1975; Cambridge, England. PARENTS: Father, Joseph John Thomson; Mother, Rose Elisabeth Paget. NATIONALITY: British. RELIGION: Anglican. EDUCATION: Cambridge Univ., England, baccalaureate, 1914. SPOUSE: Kathleen Adam Smith, married September 18, 1924. CHILDREN: John Adam, son; Lilian Clare, daughter; David Paget, son; Rose Buchanan, daughter. CAREER: Cambridge Univ., England, Professor, 1919-22; Univ. of Aberdeen, Scotland, Professor, 1922-30; Imperial College of Science, England, Professor, 1930-52; Cambridge Univ., England, Professor and Administrator, 1952-62. OTHER AWARDS: Hughes Medal, Royal Society, 1939; Knighthood, 1943; Royal Medal, Royal Society, 1949; Faraday Medal, Institution of Electrical Engineers, 1960.

Selected Publications: *The Atom.* London: Oxford U. Press, 1930 (with J.J. Thomson). *Wave Mechanics of Free Electrons.* New York: McGraw-Hill, 1930. *Theory and Practise of Electron Diffraction.* New York: Macmillan, 1939 (with W. Cochrane). *The Foreseeable Future.* London: Cambridge U. Press, 1955. *The Inspiration of Science.* London: Oxford U. Press, 1961.

For More Information See: *Biographical Memoirs of Fellows of the Royal Society.* London: Royal Society, 1977 (Volume 23), 529-56. *Current Biography Yearbook.* New York: H.W. Wilson, 1947, 635-37.

Commentary: George Thomson was awarded the Nobel Prize "for the experimental discovery of the interference phenomenon in crystals irradiated by electrons," which provided ammunition for those who believed in the wave properties of electrons. He developed the techniques of electron diffraction and moved to the study of nuclear physics, becoming involved in fission studies and the atomic bomb development. (T.M.)

1938

Fermi, Enrico   461

PRIZE: Physics, 1938. BORN: September 29, 1901; Rome, Italy. DIED: November 28, 1954; Chicago, IL. PARENTS: Father, Alberto Fermi; Mother, Ida de Gattis Fermi. NATIONALITY: Italian; later American citizen. RELIGION: Agnostic; from Jewish background. EDUCATION: Univ. of Pisa, Italy, Ph.D., 1922. SPOUSE: Laura Capon, married 1928. CHILDREN: Giulio, son; Nella, daughter. CAREER: Univ. of Florence, Italy, Professor, 1924-26; Univ. of Rome, Italy, Professor, 1926-38; Columbia Univ., NY, Professor, 1939-45; Univ. of Chicago, IL, Professor, 1945-54. OTHER AWARDS: Franklin Medal, Franklin Institute, PA, 1947; Barnard Gold Medal, Columbia U., NY, 1950; Fermi Prize, 1954.

Selected Publications: *Collected Papers.* 2 volumes. Chicago: U. of Chicago Press, 1962-65.

For More Information See: *Dictionary of Scientific Biography.* New York: Scribner's, 1971 (Volume 4), 576-83. Fermi, Laura. *Atoms in the Family.* Chicago: U. of Chicago Press, 1954. Segre, Emilio. *Enrico Fermi, Physicist.* Chicago: U. of Chicago Press, 1970.

Commentary: A physicist who was both a theoretician and an experimentalist, Enrico Fermi received the Nobel Prize "for his demonstrations of the existence of new radioactive elements produced by neutron irradiation, and for his related discovery of nuclear reactions brought about by slow neutrons." His accomplishments were foundation points for many branches of physics, including studies of the statistics of particles obeying the exclusion principle, quantum electrodynamics, beta-decay, artificial radioactivity, pionnucleon collisions, and nuclear chain reactions. (A.N. and B.S.S.)

1939

Lawrence, Ernest Orlando   462
PRIZE: Physics, 1939. BORN: August 8, 1901; Canton, SD. DIED: August 27, 1958; Palo Alto, CA. PARENTS: Father, Carl Gustavus Lawrence; Mother, Gunda Jacobson Lawrence. NATIONALITY: American. RELIGION: Lutheran. EDUCATION: Univ. of South Dakota, B.A., 1922; Univ. of Minnesota, M.A., 1923; Yale Univ., CT, Ph.D., 1925. SPOUSE: Mary Kimberly Blumer, married May 1932. CHILDREN: John Eric, son; Margaret Bradley, daughter; Mary Kimberley, daughter; Robert Don, son; Barbara Hundale, daughter; Susan, daughter. CAREER: Yale Univ., CT, Professor, 1925-28; Univ. of California, Berkeley, Professor, 1928-58. OTHER AWARDS: Elliott Cresson Medal, Franklin Institute, PA, 1937; Comstock Prize, National Academy of Sciences, U.S., 1937; Hughes Medal, Royal Society, 1937; Duddell Medal, Royal Physical Society, 1940; Faraday Medal, 1952; American Cancer Society Medal, 1954; Enrico Fermi Award, 1957; Sylvanus Thayer Award, 1958.

Selected Publications: "On the Production of High Speed Protons." *Science* 72 (1930): 376-77 (with N.E. Edlefsen). "Disintegration of Lithium by Swiftly Moving Protons." *Physical Review* 42 (1932): 150-51 (with M.S. Livingston and M.G. White). "An Improved Cyclotron." *Science* 86 (1937): 411 (with Donald Cooksey). "High Energy Physics." *American Scientist* 36 (1948): 41-49. "High-Current Accelerators." *Science* 122 (1955): 1127-32.

For More Information See: *Biographical Memoirs. National Academy of Sciences.* Washington, DC: National Academy of Sciences, 1970 (Volume 41), 251-94. Childs, Herbert. *An American Genius: The Life of Ernest Lawrence.* New York: Dutton, 1968. *Dictionary of Scientific Biography.* New York: Scribner's, 1973 (Volume 8), 93-96.

Commentary: Ernest Lawrence was honored by the Academy "for the invention and development of the cyclotron and for results obtained with it, especially with regard to artificial radioactive elements." The cyclotron permitted nuclear particle acceleration to very high velocities. The particles were used to bombard atoms, leading to many new isotopes and elements, some of which were adapted by Lawrence and his brother to medical and biological applications. Lawrence was a prolific researcher and writer who led the way to many advances. He was an important part

of the Atomic Bomb Project and the attempt to suspend atomic-bomb testing. He also contributed in the areas of ionization potentials of metals, measurement of small time intervals, and the measurement of the electron's e/m ratio. (B.S.S.)

1943

Stern, Otto   463
PRIZE: Physics, 1943. BORN: February 17, 1888; Sorau, Germany. DIED: August 17, 1969; Berkeley, CA. PARENTS: Father, Oskar Stern; Mother, Eugenie Rosenthal Stern. NATIONALITY: German; later American citizen. RELIGION: Jewish. EDUCATION: Univ. of Breslau, Germany, Ph.D., 1912. SPOUSE: None. CHILDREN: None. CAREER: Technische Hochschule, Zurich, Switzerland, Professor, 1913-14; Univ. of Frankfurt, Germany, Professor, 1914-21; Univ. of Rostock, Germany, Professor, 1921-22; Univ. of Hamburg, Germany, Professor, 1923-33; Carnegie Institute of Technology, PA, Professor, 1933-45.

Selected Publications: "Zur Kinetischen Theorie des Dampfdrucks Einatomiger Fester Stoffe und uber die Entropiekonstante Einatomiger Gase." *Physikalische Zeitschrift* 14 (1913): 629-32. "Die Entropie Fester Losungen." *Annalen der Physik, 4th Series* 49 (1916): 823-41. "Ein Weg zur Experimentellen Prufung der Richtungsquantelung im Magnetfeld." *Zeitschrift fur Physik* 7 (1921): 249-53. "Das Magnetische Moment des Silberatoms." *Zeitschrift fur Physik* 9 (1922): 353-55 (with W. Gerlach). "Uber die Richtungsquantelung im Magnetfeld." *Annalen der Physik, 4th Series* 74 (1924): 673 (with W. Gerlach).

For More Information See: *Dictionary of Scientific Biography.* New York: Scribner's, 1976 (Volume 13), 40-43. Estermann, I. *Recent Research in Molecular Beams.* New York: Academic Press, 1959, 1-7.

Commentary: Otto Stern received the Nobel Prize "for his contribution to the development of the molecular ray method and his discovery of the magnetic moment of the proton." Stern's early work was theoretical, in the areas of statistical thermodynamics and quantum theory. As noted in the Academy's citation, Stern's major contribution was in the development of the molecular beam method and its application in studying the characteristics of molecules and atoms. His later research, with Gerlach, was on atom deflection by magnetic field action on the magnetic moment and also on the magnetic moments of subatomic particles. His finding of a proton magnetic moment two to three times larger than expected was a stimulus to much research. Stern also studied the wave nature of atoms and molecules. (B.S.S.)

1944

Rabi, Isidor Isaac   464
PRIZE: Physics, 1944. BORN: July 29, 1898; Rymanov, Austria. PARENTS: Father, David Robert Rabi; Mother, Jennie Teig Rabi. NATIONALITY: Austrian; later American citizen. RELIGION: Jewish. EDUCATION: Columbia Univ., NY, Ph.D., 1927. SPOUSE: Helen Newark, married August 17, 1926. CHILDREN: Nancy Elizabeth, daughter; Margaret Joella, daughter. CAREER: Columbia Univ., NY, Professor, 1929-67. OTHER AWARDS: Sigma Xi Semicentennial Prize, 1936; Elliott Cresson Medal,

Franklin Institute, PA, 1942; United States Medal for Merit, 1948; King's Medal, England, 1948; Commander, Order of the Southern Cross, Brazil, 1952; Henrietta Szold Award, 1956; Barnard Medal, 1960; Priestley Memorial Award, Dickinson College, PA, 1964; Niels Bohr International Gold Medal, 1967; Atoms for Peace Award, 1967; Tribute of Appreciation, United States State Department, 1978; Pupin Gold Medal, Columbia U., 1981; Franklin D. Roosevelt Four Freedoms Medal, 1985; Public Welfare Medal, National Academy of Sciences, 1985.

Selected Publications: "The Principal Magnetic Susceptibilities of Crystals." *Physical Review* 29 (1927): 174-85. "Nuclear Spin in Isotopic Mixtures." *Physical Review* 45 (1934): 334. "A New Method of Measuring Nuclear Magnetic Moment." *Physical Review* 53 (1938): 318 (with others). "Molecular Beam Resonance Method for Measuring Nuclear Magnetic Moments. The Magnetic Moments of 3-LI-6, 3-Li-7, and 9-F-19." *Physical Review* 55 (1939): 526-35 (with others). "The Radiofrequency Spectra of Atoms." *Physical Review* 57 (1940): 765-80 (with P. Kusch and S. Millman). *Science: The Center of Culture.* New York: World Publishing, 1970.

For More Information See: *Current Biography Yearbook.* New York: H.W. Wilson, 1948, 509-10. *Modern Men of Science.* New York: McGraw-Hill, 1966, 385-86. *My Life and Times as a Physicist.* Claremont, CA: Claremont College, 1960.

Commentary: Isidor Isaac Rabi won the Nobel Prize for his atomic- and molecular-beam work and for his discovery of the resonance method—a precise means of determining the magnetic moments of fundamental particles. He assisted in the development of radar and the atomic bomb, and his work in defining the properties of atomic nuclei contributed to the invention of the laser, maser, and atomic clock. Rabi is one of the founders of Brookhaven National Laboratory in Upton, New York, and, while a member of UNESCO, he originated the movement that led to the foundation of the international laboratory for high-energy physics in Geneva called CERN. (L.N.W.)

1945

Pauli, Wolfgang Ernst 465

PRIZE: Physics, 1945. BORN: April 25, 1900; Vienna, Austria. DIED: December 15, 1958; Zurich, Switzerland. PARENTS: Father, Wolfgang Joseph Pauli; Mother, Bertha Schutz Pauli. NATIONALITY: Austrian; later Swiss citizen. RELIGION: Catholic. EDUCATION: Univ. of Munich, Germany, Ph.D., 1921. SPOUSE: Franciska Bertram, married April 4, 1934. CHILDREN: None. CAREER: Univ. of Gottingen, Germany, Researcher, 1921-22; Univ. of Copenhagen, Denmark, Researcher, 1922-23; Univ. of Hamburg, Germany, Professor, 1923-28; Eidgenossische Technishe Hochschule, Zurich, Switzerland, Professor, 1928-58. OTHER AWARDS: Lorentz Medaille, 1930; Franklin Medal, 1952; Max Planck Medal, 1958.

Selected Publications: "Relativitatstheorie." *Encyklopadie der Mathematischen Wissenschaften.* Leipzig, Germany: 1921 (Volume 2), 539-775 (*Theory of Relativity.* Tr. by G. Field. New York: Pergamon Press, 1958). "Uber den Zusammenhang des Abschlusses der Elektronengruppen im Atom mit der Komplexstruktur der Spektren." *Zeitschrift fur Physik* 31

(1925): 765. *Naturerklarung und Psyche.* Zurich: Rascher, 1952 (with C.G. Jung). *Collected Scientific Papers.* Ed. by R. Kronig and V.F. Weisskopf. New York: Interscience Publishers, 1964.

For More Information See: *Current Biography Yearbook.* New York: H.W. Wilson, 1946, 468-70. *Dictionary of Scientific Biography.* New York: Scribner's, 1974 (Volume 10), 422-25. *Theoretical Physics in the Twentieth Century: A Memorial Volume to Wolfgang Pauli.* Ed. by Markus Fierz and V.F. Weisskopf. New York: Interscience Publishers, 1960.

Commentary: Wolfgang Pauli was given the Nobel Prize "for his decisive contribution through his discovery in 1925 of a new law of nature, the exclusion principle, or Pauli Principle." This principle states that no two electrons in the same atom can exist in the same state. It is important in understanding the periodic system of the elements and in all theories of atomic and nuclear structure. Pauli's contributions to modern theoretical physics spanned a lifetime. He studied under Arnold Sommerfeld in Munich and, while only 20 years of age, wrote a 200-page article on the theory of relativity which remains highly regarded today. He did much research in quantum field theory and postulated the neutrino—a subatomic particle—in 1931 to explain energy anomalies in emission of beta particles from atoms. Through his scientific publications, he exerted a decisive influence in the evolution of quantum theory. (L.N.W.)

1946

Bridgman, Percy Williams 466

PRIZE: Physics, 1946. BORN: April 21, 1882; Cambridge, MA. DIED: August 20, 1961; Randolph, NH. PARENTS: Father, Raymond Landon Bridgman; Mother, Ann Maria Williams Bridgman. NATIONALITY: American. RELIGION: Most probably Christian. EDUCATION: Harvard Univ., MA, B.A., 1904; Harvard Univ., MA, M.A., 1905; Harvard Univ., MA, Ph.D., 1908. SPOUSE: Olive Ware, married July 16, 1912. CHILDREN: Jane, daughter; Robert Ware, son. CAREER: Harvard Univ., MA, Professor, 1908-54. OTHER AWARDS: Rumford Medal, American Academy of Arts and Sciences, 1929; Cresson Medal, Franklin Institute, Philadelphia, PA, 1932; Comstock Prize, National Academy of Sciences, 1933; Bakhius-Roozeboom Medal, Royal Academy of Sciences, Amsterdam, Netherlands, 1933; Bingham Medal, Society of Rheology; Research Corporation of America Award, 1937.

Selected Publications: *The Logic of Modern Physics.* New York: Macmillan, 1927. *The Physics of High Pressure.* New York: Macmillan, 1931. *The Nature of Thermodynamics.* Cambridge, MA: Harvard U. Press, 1941. *The Thermodynamics of Electrical Phenomena in Metals and a Condensed Collection of Thermodynamic Formulas.* New York: Dover Publications, 1961. *Collected Experimental Papers.* Cambridge, MA: Harvard U. Press, 1964.

For More Information See: *Biographical Memoirs of Fellows of the Royal Society.* London: Royal Society, 1962 (Volume 8), 26-40. *Dictionary of Scientific Biography.* New York: Scribner's, 1971 (Volume 2), 457-61. *Reflections of a Physicist.* New York: Philosophical Library, 1950.

Commentary: Percy Bridgman was awarded the Nobel Prize "for the invention of apparatus for obtaining very high pressures and for discoveries which he made by means of this apparatus in the field of high pressure physics." His development of a chamber capable of withstanding higher pressures than ever before realized opened the way for new experiments of immense scientific value and resulted, with his other work, in major advances in thermodynamics, the properties of matter, crystallography, and electric conduction in metals. He also was responsible for the production of synthetic diamonds by General Electric. In addition to Bridgman's long and distinguished career at Harvard working in high pressure physics, he was also involved in the philosophical aspects of physics, as seen in his works *The Logic of Physics* and *The Nature of Physical Theory*. (S.G.)

1947

Appleton, Edward Victor, Sir   467

PRIZE: Physics, 1947. BORN: September 6, 1892; Bradford, England. DIED: April 21, 1965; Edinburgh, Scotland. PARENTS: Father, Peter Appleton; Mother, Mary Appleton. NATIONALITY: British. RELIGION: Protestant. EDUCATION: Cambridge Univ., England, B.A., 1913. SPOUSE: Jessie Longson, married 1915, died 1964; Helen F. Allison, married 1965. CHILDREN: Marjery, daughter; Rosalind, daughter. CAREER: Cambridge Univ., England, Researcher, 1917-24; London Univ., England, Professor, 1924-36; Cambridge Univ., England, Professor, 1936-49; Univ. of Edinburgh, Scotland, Administrator, 1949-65. OTHER AWARDS: Knighthood, 1941; Medal of Merit, U.S., 1947; French Legion of Honor, 1947; Albert Medal, Royal Society of Arts, 1950; Gunning Victoria Jubilee Prize, Royal Society, Edinburgh, Scotland, 1960; Medal of Honor, Institute of Radio Engineers of America, 1962.

Selected Publications: "Equivalent Heights of the Atmospheric Ionized Regions in England and America." *Nature* 123 (1929): 445. *The Thermionic Value*. London: Methuen, 1931. *Thermionic Vacuum Tubes*. New York: E.P. Dutton, 1933. "Some Problems of Atmospheric Physics. Atmospheric Ozone." *Journal of the Royal Society of Arts* 85 (1937): 299-307. "New Material for Old." *J. Inst. Civil Engrs. (London)* 8 (1939-40): 448-68.

For More Information See: *Biographical Memoirs of Fellows of the Royal Society*. Cambridge: Royal Society, 1966 (Volume 12), 1-21. *Dictionary of Scientific Biography*. New York: Scribner's, 1970 (Volume 1), 195-96.

Commentary: Edward Appleton was awarded the Nobel Prize "for his investigations of the physics of the upper atmosphere, especially for the discovery of the so-called Appleton layer." Appleton first proved the existence of the ionosphere, 60 miles above ground, and his radiolocation experiments led to the development of radar. He later discovered the Appleton layer, 150 miles above ground, and showed that it reflected short waves around the earth. His research introduced the prospects of round-the-world broadcasting. Appleton also helped develop cathode ray oscillography and showed that sunspots emit short radio waves. (B.S.S.)

1948

Blackett, Patrick Maynard Stuart   468

PRIZE: Physics, 1948. BORN: November 18, 1897; London, England. DIED: July 13, 1974; London, England. PARENTS: Father, Arthur Stuart Blackett; Mother, Caroline Frances Maynard Blackett. NATIONALITY: British. RELIGION: Anglican. EDUCATION: Cambridge Univ., England, B.A., 1921; Cambridge Univ., England, M.A., 1923. SPOUSE: Constanza Bayon, married 1924. CHILDREN: Giovanna, daughter; Nicholas, son. CAREER: British Navy, 1914-19; Cambridge Univ., England, Professor, 1923-33; Univ. of London, England, Professor, 1933-37; Univ. of Manchester, England, Professor, 1937-53; Imperial College of Science and Technology, London, England, Professor, 1953-65. OTHER AWARDS: Royal Medal, Royal Society of London, 1940; American Medal for Merit, 1946; Dalton Medal, 1949; Copley Medal, Royal Society, 1956; Order of Merit, 1967.

Selected Publications: "Some Photographs of the Tracks of Penetrating Radiation." *Proceedings of the Royal Society of London* A139 (1934): 699 (with G.P.S. Occhialini). "Some Experiments on the Production of Positive Electrons." *Proceedings of the Royal Society of London* A144 (1934): 235 (with J. Chadwick and G.P.S. Occhialini). *Cosmic Rays. The Halley Lecture*. Oxford: Clarendon Press, 1936. *Military and Political Consequences of Atomic Energy*. London: Turnstile Press, 1948. "The Elementary Particles of Nature." *British Journal of Radiology* 31 (1958): 1.

For More Information See: *Biographical Memoirs of Fellows of the Royal Society*. London: Royal Society, 1975 (Volume 21), 1-115. Lovell, Bernard. *PMS Blackett: A Biographical Memoir*. London: Royal Society, 1976.

Commentary: The award to Patrick Maynard Stuart Blackett was for "his development of the Wilson cloud chamber and his discoveries therewith in the field of nuclear physics and cosmic radiation." Blackett's other scientific contributions include the theories of pair production and annihilation radiation, a confirmation of the existence of the positron, the discovery of strange particles, and a new theory explaining the earth's magnetism. He was also active in public affairs and an intense opponent of nuclear weapons. (V.C.)

1949

Yukawa, Hideki   469

PRIZE: Physics, 1949. BORN: January 23, 1907; Tokyo, Japan. DIED: September 8, 1981; Kyoto, Japan. PARENTS: Father, Takuji Ogawa; Mother, Koyuki Ogawa; Adopted by Gen'yo Yukawa and his wife, Michi, in 1932. NATIONALITY: Japanese. RELIGION: Buddhist (of the Jodo sect). EDUCATION: Kyoto Imperial Univ., Japan, M.S., 1929; Osaka Univ., Japan, Doctor of Science, 1938. SPOUSE: Sumiko Yukawa, married April 1932. CHILDREN: Harumi, son; Takaaki, son. CAREER: Kyoto Imperial Univ., Japan, Professor, 1932-70. OTHER AWARDS: Imperial Prize, Japan Academy, 1940; Decoration of Cultural Merit, 1943.

Selected Publications: "On the Interaction of Elementary Particles. I." *Proceedings of the Physical-Mathematical Society of Japan* 17 (1935): 48. *Introduction to Quantum Mechanics*. Tokyo: Kobundo, 1947.

Introduction to the Theory of Elementary Particles. 2 volumes. Tokyo: Iwanami Shoten, 1948. *Yukawa Hideki Jishenshu (Selected Works of Hideki Yukawa).* 5 volumes. Tokyo: Asahi Shimbunsha, 1971. *Creativity and Intuition: A Physicist Looks at East and West.* Tr. by J. Bester. Tokyo: Kodansha International, 1973. *Hideki Yukawa Scientific Works.* Tokyo: Iwanami Shoten, 1979.

For More Information See: *Current Biography Yearbook.* New York: H.W. Wilson, 1950, 636-37. *New York Times* (November 4, 1949): 1. *New York Times* (September 10, 1981): D23. *Tabibito, the Traveler.* (autobiography). Tr. by L. Brown and R. Yoshida. Singapore: World Scientific, 1982.

Commentary: Hideki Yukawa won the Nobel Prize "for his prediction of the existence of mesons on the basis of theoretical work on nuclear forces." His research continued on the meson theory and on the general theory of elementary particles related to the concept of the non-local field. Yukawa's pioneering research on the mesons and their essential properties provided "an enormous stimulus to the theoretical as well as experimental physics." In addition, he was a scientist with a broad vision, well versed in classical literature, and keenly aware of social responsibilities of scientists. As a result, he worked as an activist for peace, a world government, and nuclear disarmament. (J.V.S.)

1950

Powell, Cecil Frank   470

PRIZE: Physics, 1950. BORN: December 5, 1903; Tonbridge, Kent, England. DIED: August 9, 1969; Bellano, Lake Como, Italy. PARENTS: Father, Frank Powell; Mother, Elizabeth Caroline Bisacre Powell. NATIONALITY: British. RELIGION: Protestant. EDUCATION: Cambridge Univ., England, baccalaureate, 1925; Cambridge Univ., England, Ph.D., 1927. SPOUSE: Isobel Therese Artner, married 1932. CHILDREN: 2 daughters. CAREER: Bristol Univ., England, Professor, 1928-69. OTHER AWARDS: Charles Vernon Boys Prize, 1947; Hughes Medal, Royal Society, 1949; Rutherford Medal and Prize, 1960; Royal Medal, Royal Society, 1961; Lomonosov Gold Medal, Soviet Academy of Sciences, 1967; Guthrie Medal and Prize, Institute of Physics and Physical Society, 1969.

Selected Publications: *The Study of Elementary Particles by the Photographic Method.* London: Pergamon Press, 1959. "Cosmic Radiation." *Proceedings of the Institute of Electrical Engineers* 107B (1960): 389-94. "The Role of Pure Science in European Civilization." *Physics Today* 18 (1965): 56-64. "Promise and Problems of Modern Science." *Nature* 216 (1967): 543-46. *Selected Papers of Cecil Frank Powell.* Ed. by E.H.S. Burhop, W.O. Lock, and M.G.K. Menon. Amsterdam: North-Holland, 1972.

For More Information See: *Asimov's Biographical Encyclopedia of Science and Technology.* Garden City, NY: Doubleday, 1982, 797-98. *Dictionary of Scientific Biography.* New York: Scribner's, 1975 (Volume 11), 117-18.

Commentary: C.F. Powell received the Nobel Prize "for his development of the photographic method in the study of nuclear processes and for his discoveries concerning mesons." His work in the use of photographic emulsions to track electrically charged particles began in the 1930s, following his work with Tyndall on ionic mobility in gases. Powell's technique led to the discovery of a new particle, the pi-meson, followed by many successive discoveries of unstable elementary particles. His research school at Bristol played a dominant role in particle physics through 1956. Powell was also committed to the social responsibility of the scientist and to international cooperation, founding the Pugwash Movement for Science and World Affairs, and serving as president of the World Federation of Scientific Workers. (S.G.)

1951

Cockcroft, John Douglas, Sir   471

PRIZE: Physics, 1951. BORN: May 27, 1897; Todmorden, Yorkshire, England. DIED: September 18, 1967; Cambridge, England. PARENTS: Father, J.A. Cockcroft; Mother, A.M. Fielden Cockcroft. NATIONALITY: British. RELIGION: Anglican. EDUCATION: Univ. of Manchester, England, M.Sc.Tech., 1922; Cambridge Univ., England, B.A., 1924. SPOUSE: Eunice Elizabeth Crabtree, married August 26, 1925. CHILDREN: 4 daughters; 1 son. CAREER: Cambridge Univ., England, Professor, 1928-39; British Government Service, 1939-44; British Atomic Energy Projects, 1944-59; Cambridge Univ., England, Professor, 1959-67. OTHER AWARDS: Hughes Medal, 1938; American Freedom Medal, 1947; Knighthood, 1948; Chevalier de la Legion d'Honneur, 1950; Royal Medal, Royal Society, 1954; Faraday Medal, 1955; Kelvin Gold Medal, 1956; Niels Bohr International Gold Medal, 1958; Grand Cross, Order of Alfonso X, Spain, 1958; Atoms for Peace Award, 1961.

Selected Publications: "The Design of Coils for the Production of Strong Magnetic Fields." *Philosophical Transactions of the Royal Society* A227 (1928): 317-43. "Experiments with High Velocity Positive Ions." *Proceedings of the Royal Society* A129 (1930): 477-89 (with E.T.S. Walton). "Experiments with High Velocity Positive Ions. I. Further Developments in the Method of Obtaining High Velocity Positive Ions." *Proceedings of the Royal Society* A136 (1932): 619-30 (with E.T.S. Walton). "Experiments with High Velocity Positive Ions. II. The Disintegration of Elements by High Velocity Protons." *Proceedings of the Royal Society* A137 (1932): 229-42.

For More Information See: *Biographical Memoirs of Fellows of the Royal Society.* London: Royal Society, 1968 (Volume 14), 139-88. *Dictionary of Scientific Biography.* New York: Scribner's, 1971 (Volume 3), 328-31. Hartcup, Guy, and Allibone, T.E. *Cockcroft and the Atom.* Bristol, England: Adam Hilger, 1984.

Commentary: John Cockcroft shared the Nobel Prize for his "pioneer work on the transmutation of atomic nuclei by artificially accelerated atomic particles." Beginning with his interest in producing intense magnetic fields and low temperatures, Cockcroft soon began to collaborate with his colaureate, E.T.S. Walton, in accelerating protons by high voltages, and also studied radioactivity and elements produced by high-energy protons and deuterons. A gifted administrator, Cockcroft was also involved in wartime research and in the British Atomic Energy Projects. (C.G. and L.S.)

Walton, Ernest Thomas Sinton   **472**

PRIZE: Physics, 1951. BORN: October 6, 1930; Dungorvan, Ireland. PARENTS: Father, John Arthur Walton; Mother, Anna Elizabeth Sinton Walton. NATIONALITY: Irish. RELIGION: Methodist. EDUCATION: Trinity College, Ireland, B.A., 1926; Trinity College, Ireland, M.Sc., 1927; Cambridge Univ., England, Ph.D., 1930. SPOUSE: Winifred Isabel Wilson, married 1934. CHILDREN: Alan, son; Marian, daughter; Philip, son; Jean, daughter. CAREER: Lord Rutherford's Research Assistant, 1927-34; Trinity College, Dublin, Ireland, Professor, 1934-. OTHER AWARDS: Hughes Medal, Royal Society, 1938.

Selected Publications: "Production of High Speed Electrons by Indirect Means." *Cambridge Philosophical Society Proceedings* (October 1929): 469-81. "Experiments with High Velocity Positive Ions." *Royal Society Proceedings* A (November 3, 1930): 477-89 (with J. Cockcroft). "Transmutation of Lithium and Boron." *Royal Society Proceedings* A (September 1, 1933): 733-42 (with P.I. Dee). "High Velocity Positive Ions, Part 3: Disintegration of Li, B, and C by Diplons." *Royal Society Proceedings* A (May 1, 1934): 704-20 (with J. Cockcroft). "Part 4: Production of Induced Radioactivity by Protons and Diplons." *Royal Society Proceedings* A (January 1, 1935): 225-40 (with J. Cockcroft and C.W. Gilbert).

For More Information See: *Current Biography Yearbook.* New York: H.W. Wilson, 1952, 618-20. *Modern Men of Science.* New York: McGraw-Hill, 1966, 509-10.

Commentary: The Academy cited Ernest Walton (along with John Cockcroft) "for their pioneer work on the transmutation of atomic nuclei by artificially accelerated atomic particles." While working for Rutherford at Cambridge, Walton built a linear accelerator which became a prototype for subsequent atom-smashers. Using voltages of about 400 kilowatts, with a proton current of a few microamperes, Walton and Cockcroft were able to bombard lithium atoms with sufficient force to transform each lithium nucleus into two helium nuclei—the first successful transmutation of elements by human means. Their experiments demonstrated the enormous energies available in atomic nuclei and provided the first experimental confirmation of Einstein's equations showing the equivalence of mass and energy. (L.R.S.)

1952

Bloch, Felix   **473**

PRIZE: Physics, 1952. BORN: October 23, 1905; Zurich, Switzerland. DIED: September 10, 1983; Zurich, Switzerland. PARENTS: Father, Gustav Bloch; Mother, Agnes Mayer Bloch. NATIONALITY: Swiss; later American citizen. RELIGION: Jewish. EDUCATION: Univ. of Leipzig, Germany, Ph.D., 1928. SPOUSE: Lore Clara Misch, married March 14, 1940. CHILDREN: George, son; Daniel, son; Frank, son; Ruth, daughter. CAREER: Univ. of Zurich, Switzerland, Researcher, 1928-29; Univ. of Utrecht, Netherlands, Researcher, 1929-30; Univ. of Leipzig, Germany, Researcher, 1930-31; Univ. of Copenhagen, Denmark, Researcher, 1931-32; Univ. of Leipzig, Germany, Professor, 1932-33; Stanford Univ., CA, Professor, 1934-71.

Selected Publications: "The Magnetic Moment of the Neutron." *Ann. Inst. Henri Poincare* 8 (1938): 63-78. "Nuclear Induction." *Physical Review* 70 (1946): 460-74. "Chemical Analysis by Nuclear Inductions." *U.S. Patent 2, 561, 481.* July 24, 1951 (with William W. Hansen). "Dynamical Theory of Nuclear Induction. II." *Physical Review* 102 (1956): 104-35.

For More Information See: *Current Biography Yearbook.* New York: H.W. Wilson, 1954, 93-95. *National Cyclopedia of American Biography.* New York: James T. White, 1960 (Volume I), 310-12.

Commentary: The Academy honored Felix Bloch for his "development of high precision methods in the field of nuclear magnetism and the discoveries which were made through the use of these methods." Bloch introduced the techniques of nuclear magnetic resonance, used initially to measure the magnetic moments of the proton and neutron, but utilized later for analysis of organic molecules. Bloch also was a major figure in research on electron behavior in crystals, the properties of ferromagnetic domains, x-ray phenomena, quantum electrodynamics, and superconductivity. (L.I.S.)

Purcell, Edward Mills   **474**

PRIZE: Physics, 1952. BORN: August 30, 1912; Taylorville, IN. PARENTS: Father, Edward A. Purcell; Mother, Mary Elizabeth Mills Purcell. NATIONALITY: American. RELIGION: Most probably Christian/Protestant. EDUCATION: Purdue Univ., IN, B.S.E.E., 1933; Harvard Univ., MA, A.M., 1935; Harvard Univ., MA, Ph.D., 1938. SPOUSE: Beth C. Busser, married January 22, 1937. CHILDREN: Dennis W., son; Frank B., son. CAREER: Harvard Univ., MA, Professor, 1938-40; Massachusetts Institute of Technology, Researcher, 1941-45; Harvard Univ., MA, Professor, 1946-86. OTHER AWARDS: Oersted Medal, American Association of Physics Teachers, 1968; National Medal of Science, 1980.

Selected Publications: "Relaxation Effects in Nuclear Magnetic Resonance Absorption." *Physical Review* 73 (1948): 679-712 (with N. Bloembergen and R.V. Pound). "Structural Investigations by Means of Nuclear Magnetism. I. Rigid Crystal Lattices." *Journal of Chemical Physics* 17 (1949): 972-81 (with others). "A Precise Determination of the Proton Magnetic Moment in Bohr Magnetons." *Physical Review* 76 (1949): 1262-63 (with J.H. Gardner). "Interactions between Nuclear Spins in Molecules." *Physical Review* 85 (1952): 143-44 (with N.F. Ramsey).

For More Information See: *Asimov's Biographical Encyclopedia of Science and Technology.* Garden City, NY: Doubleday, 1982, 845. *Current Biography Yearbook.* New York: H.W. Wilson, 1954, 519-21.

Commentary: Edward Purcell shared the Nobel Prize for "development of new methods of nuclear magnetic precision measurements and discoveries in connection therewith." He independently discovered a method of measuring nuclear magnetism with radio waves, without affecting the structure being examined. Previous methods, particularly those of I.I. Rabi, depended on vaporizing the substance to be examined. Purcell's method also provided for much more accurate values of nuclear magnetic moments. By 1949, Purcell had completed the research for which he won the prize. He continued to make contributions in the fields of nuclear magnetism, radio astronomy, astrophysics, and biophysics. (M.H.)

1953

Zernike, Frits   **475**

PRIZE: Physics, 1953. BORN: July 16, 1888; Amsterdam, Netherlands. DIED: March 10, 1966; Naarden, Netherlands. PARENTS: Father, Carl Frederick August Zernike; Mother, Anne Dieperink Zernike. NATIONALITY: Dutch. RELIGION: Protestant. EDUCATION: Univ. of Amsterdam, Netherlands, Ph.D., 1915. SPOUSE: Dora van Bommel van Vloten, married 1929, died 1944; L. Koperberg-Baanders, married 1954. CHILDREN: 2 children. CAREER: Univ. of Groningen, Netherlands, Professor, 1913-58. OTHER AWARDS: Gold Medal, Dutch Society for Sciences, 1912; Rumford Medal, Royal Society, 1952.

Selected Publications: "Die Beugung von Rontgenstrahlen in Flussigkeiten als Effect der Molekulanordnung." *Z. Phys.* 41 (1927): 184 (with J.A. Prins). "Diffraction Theory of the Knife-Edge Test and Its Improved Form, the Phase-Contrast Method." *Mon. Nat. Roy. Astron. Soc.* 94 (1934): 377. "Das Phasenkontrastverfahren bei der Mikroskopschen Beobachtung." *Z. Techn. Phys.* 16 (1935): 454. "The Propagation of Order in Cooperative Phenomena." *Physica* 7 (1940): 565. "A Precision Method for Measuring Small Phase Differences." *Journal of the Optical Society of America* 40 (1950): 326.

For More Information See: *Biographical Memoirs of Fellows of the Royal Society.* Cambridge: Royal Society, 1967 (Volume 13), 393-402. *Dictionary of Scientific Biography.* New York: Scribner's, 1976 (Volume 14), 616-17.

Commentary: The Academy cited Frits Zernike "for his demonstration of the phase-contrast method, especially for his invention of the phase-contrast microscope." Zernike was able to show that there were indeed phase differences between incident and refracted light, required by the concept of light as a wave motion. He then used this phenomenon to develop a microscope capable of viewing otherwise invisible particles, such as bacteria and cells. Zernike was also a significant contributor to the development of photography, statistics theory, the galvanometer, and optics. (R.J.)

1954

Born, Max   **476**

PRIZE: Physics, 1954. BORN: December 11, 1882; Breslau, Germany. DIED: January 5, 1970; Goettingen, Germany. PARENTS: Father, Gustav Born; Mother, Margaretta Kauffman Born. NATIONALITY: German; later British citizen. RELIGION: Jewish. EDUCATION: Univ. of Gottingen, Germany, Ph.D., 1907. SPOUSE: Hedwig Ehrenberg, married August 2, 1913. CHILDREN: Irene, daughter; Margaret, daughter; Gustav, son. CAREER: Cambridge Univ., England, Researcher, 1907-08; Univ. of Breslau, Germany, Researcher, 1908-09; Univ. of Gottingen, Germany, Professor, 1909-12; Univ. of Chicago, IL, Researcher, 1912-15; Univ. of Berlin, Professor, 1915-19; German Army, 1915-19; Univ. of Frankfurt, Germany, Professor, 1919-21;

Univ. of Gottingen, Germany, Professor, 1921-33; Cambridge Univ., England, Professor, 1933-36; Univ. of Edinburgh, Scotland, Professor, 1936-53. OTHER AWARDS: Stokes Medal, England, 1934; Macdougall-Brisbane and Gunning-Victoria Jubilee Prize, Royal Society of Edinburgh, Scotland, 1945, 1950; Max Planck Medaille, Germany, 1948; Hughes Medal, Royal Society, 1950; Grotius Medal, Munich, Germany, 1956.

Selected Publications: *Zur Begrundung der Matrizenmechanik.* Stuttgart, Germany: E. Battenberg, 1962. *Zur Statistischen Deutung der Quantentheorie.* 2 volumes. Stuttgart, Germany: E. Battenberg, 1962. *Ausgewoehlte Abhandlungen* (collected works). 2 volumes. Goettingen, Germany: Vandenhoek and Ruprecht, 1963.

For More Information See: *Dictionary of Scientific Biography.* New York: Scribner's, 1978 (Volume 15), 39-44. *Mein Leben. Die Errinerungen des Nobelpreistragers.* Munich: Nymphenburger Verlagshandlung, 1975. *Physics in My Generation.* New York: Pergamon Press, 1956.

Commentary: Max Born was cited by the Academy for his statistical interpretation of the quantum theory. His early work on vibrations and lattice energies in crystals was followed by his pioneer efforts in the areas of quantum theory and matrix mechanics. Born was also a leading figure in the early explanations of the wave-particle ambiguities of physics. (M.N.)

Bothe, Walther Wilhelm Georg   **477**

PRIZE: Physics, 1954. BORN: June 8, 1891; Oranienburg, Germany. DIED: February 8, 1957; Heidelberg, Germany. PARENTS: Father, Friedrich Bothe; Mother, Charlotte Hartung Bothe. NATIONALITY: German. RELIGION: Lutheran. EDUCATION: Univ. of Berlin, Germany, Ph.D., 1914. SPOUSE: Barbara Below, married July 6, 1920. CHILDREN: Elena, daughter; Johanna, daughter. CAREER: German Army, 1915-20; Univ. of Berlin, Germany, Professor, 1920-31; Giessen Univ., Germany, Professor, 1931-34; Max Planck Institute, Germany, Researcher and Administrator, 1934-57. OTHER AWARDS: Order pour le Merite, peace class, 1952; Max Planck Prize, 1953; Grossen Verdeinstkreuz Bundesrepublik, 1954.

Selected Publications: "Ein Weg zur Experimentellen Nachprufund der Theorie von Bohr, Kraners und Slater." *Zeitschrift fur Physik* 26 (1924): 44. "Uber des Wesen des Comptoneffekts." *Zeitschrift fur Physik* 32 (1925): 639. *Atlas Typischer Nebelkammerbilder.* Berlin: J. Springer, 1940 (with Wolfgang Gentner). "Das Wesen der Hohenstrahlung." *Zeitschrift fur Physik* 56 (1959): 75.

For More Information See: *Current Biography Yearbook.* New York: H.W. Wilson, 1955, 55-56. *Dictionary of Scientific Biography.* New York: Scribner's, 1973 (Volume 2), 337-39.

Commentary: The Nobel Committee honored Walther Bothe for "the coincidence method and his discoveries with this method" and cited him for his leadership in the "new physics." The coincidence method Bothe used was based on the fact that a single particle passing through two or more counters produces pulses from each counter practically coincident in time. The method was used to study angular distribution of cosmic rays, the Compton Effect, and many other physics problems. Bothe also contributed significantly in his research on the corpuscular theory of light, light quanta and interference, and fission products. (M.N.C.)

1955

Kusch, Polycarp   478

PRIZE: Physics, 1955. BORN: January 26, 1911; Blankenburg, Germany. PARENTS: Father, John Matthias Kusch; Mother, Henrietta Van der Haas Kusch. NATIONALITY: American. RELIGION: Lutheran. EDUCATION: Case Institute of Technology, OH, B.S., 1931; Univ. of Illinois, M.S., 1933; Univ. of Illinois, Ph.D., 1936. SPOUSE: Edith Starr McRoberts, married August 12, 1935, died December 1959; Betty Jane Pezzoni, married 1960. CHILDREN: Kathryn, daughter; Judith, daughter; Sara, daughter; Diana, daughter; Maria, daughter. CAREER: Univ. of Minnesota, Researcher, 1936-37; Columbia Univ., NY, Professor, 1937-41; Westinghouse Electric and Manufacturing Company, Researcher, 1941-42; Columbia Univ., NY, Researcher, 1942-44; Bell Technical Laboratories, NJ, Researcher, 1944-46; Columbia Univ., NY, Professor and Administrator, 1946-71; Univ. of Texas at Dallas, Professor, 1972-. OTHER AWARDS: Illinois Achievement Award, U. of Illinois, 1975.

Selected Publications: "The Radiofrequency Spectra of Atoms." *Physical Review* 57 (1940): 765-80 (with S. Millman and I. I. Rabi). "The Magnetic Moment of the Electron." *Physical Review* 74 (1948): 250-63 (with H. M. Foley). "The Magnetic Moment of the Proton." *Physical Review* 75 (1949): 1481-92 (with H. Taub). "The World of Science and the Scientist's World." *Bulletin of the Atomic Scientists* 24 (October 1968): 38-43. "A Personal View of Science and the Future." In *The Future of Science; 1975 Nobel Conference Organized by Gustavus Adolphus College.* New York: John Wiley & Sons, 1977, 39-55.

For More Information See: *Current Biography Yearbook.* New York: H. W. Wilson, 1956, 348-50. *National Cyclopedia of American Biography.* New York: James T. White, 1960 (Volume I), 35.

Commentary: Polycarp Kusch made careful analyses of the magnetic moment of the electron based on the structure of energy levels in various elements and was, thereby, able to disprove the long-prevailing calculations of Dr. P.M.A. Dirac. These results led to the development of new scientific principles serving as the basis of quantum electrodynamics. The importance of Kusch's "precision determination of the magnetic moment of the electron" merited him the Nobel Prize, which he shared with William Lamb, a colleague who had performed experiments related to Kusch's. In later years Kusch also devoted much effort to promoting science education. (C.H.W.)

Lamb, Willis Eugene, Jr.   479

PRIZE: Physics, 1955. BORN: July 12, 1913; Los Angeles, CA. PARENTS: Father, Willis Eugene Lamb; Mother, Marie Helen Metcalf Lamb. NATIONALITY: American. RELIGION: No religious affiliation. EDUCATION: Univ. of California, B.S., 1934; Univ. of California, Ph.D., 1938. SPOUSE: Ursula Schaefer, married June 5, 1939. CHILDREN: None. CAREER: Columbia Univ., NY, Professor, 1938-51; Stanford Univ., CA, Professor, 1951-56; Oxford Univ., England, Professor, 1956-62; Yale Univ., CT, Professor, 1962-74; Univ. of

Arizona, Professor, 1974-. OTHER AWARDS: Rumford Award, American Academy of Arts, 1953; Research Corporation Award, 1955; Yeshiva Award, 1962.

Selected Publications: "Fine Structure of the Hydrogen Atom by a Microwave Method." *Physical Review* 72 (1947): 241-43 (with Robert C. Retherford). "Formation of Metastable Hydrogen Atoms by Electron Bombardment of H-2." *Physical Review* 75 (1949): 1332 (with Robert C. Retherford). "The Fine Structure of Singly Ionized Helium." *Physical Review* 78 (1950): 539-50 (with Miriam Skinner). "Fine Structure of n-3 Hydrogen by a Radio-Frequency Method." *Physical Review* 103 (1956): 313-14 (with T.M. Sanders). *Laser Physics.* Reading, MA: Addison-Wesley Publishing Co., 1974 (with M. Sargent and M.O. Scully).

For More Information See: *Current Biography Yearbook.* New York: H.W. Wilson, 1956, 357-58. *National Cyclopedia of American Biography.* New York: James T. White, 1963 (Volume J), 238.

Commentary: Willis Lamb received the Nobel Prize for his "discoveries regarding the hyperfine structure of the hydrogen spectrum." His accurate studies showed that the two possible energy states of hydrogen, rather than being equal as predicted by Dirac, differed by a very small amount. The "Lamb shift" required a revision of the theory of interaction of the electron with electromagnetic radiation. Lamb also contributed significantly in theoretical physics, atomic and nuclear structure, microwave spectroscopy, and maser and laser physics. (L.I.S.)

1956

Bardeen, John   480

PRIZE: Physics, 1956; Physics, 1972. BORN: May 23, 1908; Madison, WI. PARENTS: Father, Charles Russell Bardeen; Mother, Althea Homer Bardeen. NATIONALITY: American. RELIGION: "Hardly any"; from Christian background. EDUCATION: Univ. of Wisconsin, B.S., 1928; Univ. of Wisconsin, M.A., 1929; Princeton Univ., NJ, Ph.D., 1936. SPOUSE: Jane Maxwell, married 1938. CHILDREN: James Maxwell, son; William Allen, son; Elizabeth Ann Bardeen Greytak, daughter. CAREER: Gulf Research and Development, Geophysicist, 1930-33; Harvard Univ., MA, Fellow, 1935-38; Univ. of Minnesota, Professor, 1939-41; U.S. Naval Ordinance Laboratory, Physicist, 1941-45; Bell Telephone Laboratories, NJ, Physicist, 1945-51; Univ. of Illinois, Professor, 1951-. OTHER AWARDS: Ballantine Medal, Franklin Institute, 1952; Buckley Prize, American Physical Society, 1954; John Scott Medal, City of Philadelphia, 1955; Fritz London Award, 1962; Vincent Bendix Award, American Society of Engineering Education, 1966; Michelson-Morley Award, Case Western Reserve U., OH, 1968; Medal of Honor, Institute of Electrical and Electronic Engineering, 1971; James Madison Medal, Princeton U., NJ, 1973; Franklin Institute Medal, 1975; Presidential Medal of Freedom, 1977.

Selected Publications: "Interaction between Electrons and Lattice Vibrations." *Canadian Journal of Physics* 34 (1956): 1171-89. "Research Leading to the Point-Contact Transistor." *Science* 126 (1957): 105-13. "Theory of Superconductivity." *Physical Review* 108 (1957): 1175-204. "Critical Fields and Currents in Superconductors." *Reviews of Modern Physics* 34

(1962): 667-75. "Review of the Present Status of the Theory of Superconductivity." *IBM Journal of Research* 6 (1962): 3-11. "Electron-phonon Interactions and Superconductivity." *Science* 181 (1973): 1209-14.

For More Information See: *Modern Men of Science.* 2 volumes. New York: McGraw-Hill, 1966-68 (Volume 1), 19-20. Weinraub, Bernard. "Six Americans Win Nobel Prizes in Physics and Chemistry Fields." *New York Times* (October 21, 1972): 1, 14.

Commentary: John Bardeen was the third Nobel laureate to win the prize twice, the first time (1956) for cooperative research on "semiconductors and...discovery of the transistor effect" and the second time (1972) for a cooperative development of a theory of superconductivity. His initial work has been the basis for the emergence of the solid state electronics industry. His later work permitted a theoretical explanation of the disappearance of electrical resistance in materials at temperatures close to absolute zero. (L.M.W.)

Brattain, Walter Houser   481

PRIZE: Physics, 1956. BORN: February 10, 1902; Hsiamen, China. PARENTS: Father, Ross R. Brattain; Mother, Ottilie Houser Brattain. NATIONALITY: American. RELIGION: Most probably Christian/Protestant. EDUCATION: Whitman College, WA, B.S., 1924; Univ. of Oregon, M.A., 1926; Univ. of Minnesota, Ph.D., 1929. SPOUSE: Keren Gilmore, married July 5, 1935, died April 1957; Emma Jane Kirsch Miller, married May 10, 1958. CHILDREN: William Gilmore, son. CAREER: Bureau of Standards, Washington, DC, Researcher, 1928-29; Bell Telephone Laboratories, NJ, 1929-67; Whitman College, Walla Walla, WA, Professor, 1967-72. OTHER AWARDS: Stuart Ballantine Medal, Franklin Institute, PA, 1952; John Scott Medal, Philadelphia, PA, 1955; National Inventors Hall of Fame, 1974.

Selected Publications: "Nature of the Forward Current in Germanium Point Contacts." *Physical Review* 74 (1948): 231-32 (with J. Bardeen). "The Transistor, a Semi-Conductor Triode." *Physical Review* 74 (1948): 230-31 (with J. Bardeen). "Physical Principles Involved in Transistor Action." *Physical Review* 75 (1949): 1208-25 (with J. Bardeen). "Surface Properties of Semiconductors." *Science* 126 (1957): 151-53. "The Distribution of Potential Across the Low-Index Crystal Planes of Germanium Contacting on Aqueous Solution." *Proceedings of the National Academy of Sciences* 48 (1962): 2005-12 (with P.J. Boddy).

For More Information See: *Current Biography Yearbook.* New York: H.W. Wilson, 1957, 68-70. *National Cyclopedia of American Biography.* New York: James T. White, 1960 (Volume 1), 404-05.

Commentary: Walter Houser Brattain shared the Nobel Prize for his "investigations on semiconductors and the discovery of the transistor effect." While engaged in semiconductor research at Bell Laboratories to find a substitute for vacuum tubes in radios, he and his colaureates invented the transistor and showed that certain semiconductors could rectify and amplify currents and voltages. Brattain's contributions to solid state physics also include his work on the photoeffect at the free surface of a semiconductor. During World War II, Brattain worked on the magnetic detection of submarines. (B.N.L.)

Shockley, William Bradford   482

PRIZE: Physics, 1956. BORN: February 13, 1910; London, England. PARENTS: Father, William Hillman Shockley; Mother, May Bradford Shockley. NATIONALITY: American. RELIGION: Atheist; from Protestant background. EDUCATION: California Institute of Technology, B.S., 1932; Massachusetts Institute of Technology, Ph.D., 1936. SPOUSE: Jean Alberta Bailey, married 1933, divorced 1955; Emily I. Lanning, married 1955. CHILDREN: Alison, daughter; William, son; Richard, son. CAREER: Bell Telephone Laboratories, NJ, Researcher, 1936-42; United States Navy, Research Director, 1942-44; Bell Telephone Laboratories, NJ, Researcher, 1945-55; Shockley Semiconductor Laboratories, Director, 1955-58; Shockley Transistor Corporation, President, 1958-60; Shockley Transistor Unit, Director, 1960-63; Consultant, 1963-65; Stanford Univ., CA, Professor, 1965-75. OTHER AWARDS: Medal of Merit, United States, 1946; Morris Liebmann Prize, Institute of Radio Engineers, 1951; O.E. Buckley Prize, American Physical Society, 1953; Comstock Prize, National Academy of Sciences, 1954; Wilhelm Exner Medal, Oesterreichischer Gewerberein, 1963; Holley Medal, American Society of Mechanical Engineers, 1963; Public Service Achievement Award, National Aeronautics and Space Administration, 1969; Gold Medal, Institute of Electrical and Electronics Engineers, 1972; National Inventors Hall of Fame, 1974; Medal of Honor, Institute of Electrical and Electronics Engineers, 1980.

Selected Publications: "Density of Surface States on Silicon Deduced from Contact Potential Measurements." *Physical Review* 72 (1947): 345 (with W. Brattain). "Modulation of Conductance of Thin Films of Semiconductors by Surface Charges." *Physical Review* 74 (1948): 232-33 (with G.L. Pearson). "Investigation of Hole Injection in Transistor Action." *Physical Review* 75 (1949): 691 (with J.R. Haynes). *Electrons and Holes in Semiconductors.* New York: D. Van Nostrand Co., 1950. "The Mobility and Life of Injected Holes and Electrons in Germanium." *Physical Review* 81 (1951): 835-43 (with J.R. Haynes). "Statistics of the Recombinations of Holes and Electrons." *Physical Review* 87 (1952): 835-42 (with W.T. Read).

For More Information See: *Current Biography Yearbook.* New York: H.W. Wilson, 1953, 569-71. *Modern Men of Science.* New York: McGraw-Hill, 1966, 430.

Commentary: William Shockley won the Nobel Prize for his "researches on semiconductors and discovery of the transistor effect." Shockley advanced the hypothesis which led the way to the invention of the transistor, which freed electronics from the disadvantages of the vacuum tube, and provided a device which could rectify extremely high-frequency signals with great reliability. (D.A.K.)

1957

Lee, Tsung-dao   483

PRIZE: Physics, 1957. BORN: November 24, 1926; Shanghai, China. PARENTS: Father, Tsing-Kong Lee; Mother Ming-Chong Chong Lee. NATIONALITY: Chinese; later American citizen. RELIGION: No religious affiliation. EDUCATION: National Chekiang Univ., China, baccalaureate, 1944; Univ. of Chicago, IL, Ph.D., 1950. SPOUSE: Jeanette Hui-Chung Chin, married 1950. CHILDREN: James, son; Stephen, son. CAREER: Univ. of

California, Berkeley, Researcher, 1950-51; Institute for Advanced Study, Princeton, NJ, Researcher, 1951-53; Columbia Univ., NY, Professor, 1953-. OTHER AWARDS: Albert Einstein Commemorative Award in Science, Yeshiva U., 1957; Science Award, Newspaper Guild of NY, 1957.

Selected Publications: "Interaction of Mesons with Nucleons and Light Particles." *Physical Review* 75 (1949): 905 (with C.N. Yang and M. Rosenbluth). "Mass Degeneracy of the Heavy Mesons." *Physical Review* 102 (1956): 290-91 (with C.N. Yang). "Question of Parity Conservation in Weak Interactions." *Physical Review* 104 (1956): 254-58 (with C.N. Yang). "Parity Nonconservation and a Two-Component Theory of the Neutrino." *Physical Review* 105 (1957): 1671-75 (with C.N. Yang). "Remarks on Possible Noninvariance under Time Reversal and Charge Conjugation." *Physical Review* 106 (1957): 340-45 (with C.N. Yang). *Particle Physics and Introduction to Field Theory.* New York: Harwood Academic Press, 1981.

For More Information See: *Current Biography Yearbook.* New York: H.W. Wilson, 1958, 240-41. *Physics Teacher* 20 (May 1982), 281-88.

Commentary: The award to Tsung-dao Lee and Chen Ning Yang was "for their penetrating investigation of the so-called parity laws which has led to important discoveries regarding the elementary particles." The parity principle had held that there was no difference between right and left or that the mirror image of a nuclear reaction was identical to the reaction. Lee and Yang could not make the K-meson particles fit this accepted theory. They questioned the underlying theory of symmetry and proposed experiments to check their ideas. In addition to his work on parity nonconservation, Lee's work was noteworthy in the areas of statistical mechanics, nuclear and subnuclear physics, field theory, astrophysics, and turbulence. (F.K.)

Yang, Chen Ning   484

PRIZE: Physics, 1957. BORN: September 22, 1922; Hofei, Anwhei, China. PARENTS: Father, Ke Chuan Yang; Mother, Meng Hwa Loh Yang. NATIONALITY: Chinese; later American citizen. RELIGION: No religious affiliation; parents are also unaffiliated. EDUCATION: National Southwest Associated Univ., China, B.Sc., 1942; Tsinghua Univ., China, M.Sc., 1944; Univ. of Chicago, IL, Ph.D., 1948. SPOUSE: Chih Li Tu, married 1950. CHILDREN: Franklin, son; Gilbert, son; Eulee, daughter. CAREER: Univ. of Chicago, IL, Professor, 1948-49; Institute for Advanced Study, Princeton, NJ, Professor, 1949-65; State Univ. of New York, Stony Brook, Professor and Administrator, 1965-. OTHER AWARDS: Albert Einstein Commemorative Award, 1957.

Selected Publications: "Interaction of Mesons with Nucleons and Light Particles." *Physical Review* 75 (1949): 905 (with T.D. Lee and M. Rosenbluth). "Reflection Properties of Spin 1/2 Fields and a Universal Fermi-Type Interaction." *Physical Review* 79 (1950): 495-98 (with J. Tiomno). "Mass Degeneracy of the Heavy Mesons." *Physical Review* 102 (1956): 290-91 (with T.D. Lee). "Question of Parity Conservation in Weak Interactions." *Physical Review* 104 (1956): 254-58 (with T.D. Lee). "Parity Nonconservation and a Two-Component Theory of the Neutrino." *Physical Review* 105 (1957): 1671-75 (with T.D. Lee). "R-

emarks on Possible Noninvariance under Time Reversal and Charge Conjugation." *Physical Review* 106 (1957): 340-45 (with T.D. Lee).

For More Information See: *Asimov's Biographical Encyclopedia of Science and Technology.* Garden City, NY: Doubleday, 1982, 877. *Biographical Encyclopedia of Scientists.* New York: Facts on File, 1981, 866.

Commentary: Chen Ning Yang shared the Nobel Prize with Tsung-dao Lee "for their penetrating investigation of the so-called parity laws which has led to important discoveries regarding the elementary particles." Yang and Lee could not make K-mesons fit the accepted theory of parity conservation, so they experimented to demonstrate parity nonconservation. In addition to the research on parity nonconservation, Yang's major interests were in the areas of statistical mechanics and symmetry principles. (B.S.S.)

1958

Cherenkov, Pavel Alekseyevich   485

PRIZE: Physics, 1958. BORN: July 28, 1904; Voronezh Oblast, Russia. PARENTS: Father, Aleksei Cherenkov; Mother, Mariya Cherenkov. NATIONALITY: Russian. RELIGION: Most probably Christian/Eastern Orthodox. EDUCATION: Voronezh Univ., USSR, graduate, 1928; Physics Institute, USSR Academy of Science, Doctorate of Physico-Mathematical Sciences, 1940. SPOUSE: Marya Putintseva, married 1930. CHILDREN: Aleksei, son; Elena, daughter. CAREER: Lebedev Physical Institute, Moscow, USSR, Researcher and Administrator, 1930-. OTHER AWARDS: Stalin Prize, 1946; Order of Lenin, 1964.

Selected Publications: "Visible Glow of Pure Liquids under the Influence of Gamma-rays." *Compt. Rend. Acad. Sci. U.R.S.S.* 2 (1934): 451-54. "Visible Radiation Produced by Electrons Moving in a Medium with Velocities Exceeding that of Light." *Physical Review* 52 (1937): 378-79. "Visible Radiation of Pure Liquids under the Action of Fast Electrons." *Bull. Acad. Sci. U.R.S.S., Classe sci. Mat. Nat., Ser. Phys* (1937): 455-91. "Absolute Output of Radiation Caused by Electrons Moving within a Medium with Super-Light Velocity." *Compt. Rend. Acad. Sci. U.R.S.S.* 21 (1938): 116-21. "Radiation of Electrons Moving with Super-Light Speed." *Trudy Fiz. Inst. Im. P.N. Lebedeva, Akad. Nauk. S.S.S.R.* 2 (1944): 3-62.

For More Information See: *Asimov's Biographical Encyclopedia of Science and Technology.* Garden City, NY: Doubleday, 1982, 801. *Encyclopedia of World Biography.* New York: McGraw-Hill, 1973 (Volume 2), 548-49.

Commentary: Pavel Cherenkov shared the Nobel for his work on "the discovery and the interpretation of the Cherenkov effect." Cherenkov observed the emission of blue light from water bombarded by gamma-rays. This Cherenkov effect, produced by charged atomic particles moving at velocities greater then the speed of light, and the Cherenkov detector for observing high-speed particles became standards for work on nuclear physics and cosmic rays. Cherenkov also contributed to the development and construction of electron accelerators and study of photo-nuclear and photo-meson reactions. (G.E.M.)

Frank, Ilya Mikaylovich 486

PRIZE: Physics, 1958. BORN: October 23, 1908; Leningrad, Russia. PARENTS: Father, Mikhail Luydvigovic Frank; Mother, Yelizaveta Mikhailovna Gratsianova Frank. NATIONALITY: Russian. RELIGION: No record found. EDUCATION: Moscow State Univ., USSR, baccalaureate, 1930; Moscow State Univ., USSR, Doctor of Physio-mathematical Sciences, 1935. SPOUSE: Ella Abramovna Beilikhis, married 1937. CHILDREN: Alexander, son. CAREER: State Optical Institute, USSR, Professor, 1931-34; Lebedev Institute of Physics, USSR, Professor, 1934-. OTHER AWARDS: Stalin Prize, 1946; Order of Lenin, 1946; Vavilov Gold Medal, 1979; Lenin Prize.

Selected Publications: "The Excitation Function and the Absorption Curve in the Optical Dissociation of Thallium Iodide." *Physik Z. Sowjetunion* 2 (1932): 319-36. "Coherent Visible Radiation of Fast Electrons Passing through Matter." *Compt. Rend. Acad. Sci. U.R.S.S.* 14 (1937): 109-14 (with I. Tamm). "Visible Radiation of Pure Liquids under the Action of Rapid Electrons." *Bull. Acad. Sci. U.R.R.S., Classe Sci. Math, Nat., Ser. Phys* (1938): 29-30. (with I. Tamm and P.A. Cherenkov). "A New Type of Nuclear Reactions (The Splitting of Uranium and Thorium Nuclei under the Influence of Neutrons)." *Priroda* 9 (1939): 20-27.

For More Information See: *Biographical Encyclopedia of Scientists.* New York: Facts on File, 1981, 280-81. *Modern Men of Science.* New York: McGraw-Hill, 1966, 182.

Commentary: The Nobel Prize was shared by Ilya Frank for his contributions to "the discovery and interpretation of the Cherenkov effect." Frank's work on the interpretation of the Cherenkov effect, produced by charged atomic particles moving at velocities greater than the speed of light, made it possible for the Cherenkov effect and Cherenkov detector to become standards for work in nuclear physics and cosmic rays. Frank also carried out significant research on photoluminescence, photochemistry, pair production by gamma-rays, reactions of light nuclei, and nuclear fission by mesons. (G.E.M.)

Tamm, Igor Evgenevich 487

PRIZE: Physics, 1958. BORN: July 8, 1895; Vladivostok, Russia. DIED: April 12, 1971; Moscow, USSR. PARENTS: Father, Evgen Tamm; Mother, Olga Davidova Tamm. NATIONALITY: Russian. RELIGION: Jewish. EDUCATION: Moscow Univ., USSR, Ph.D., 1918. SPOUSE: Natalie Shuskaia, married September 16, 1917. CHILDREN: Irene, daughter; Eugen, son. CAREER: Crimean Univ., USSR, Professor and Administrator, 1918-20; Odessa Polytechnical Institut, USSR, Professor, 1920-22; Sverdlov Communist Univ., USSR, Professor, 1922-24; Moscow Univ., USSR, Professor and Administrator, 1924-71. OTHER AWARDS: Order of Lenin (twice); Order of Red Banner of Labor; Stalin Prize, 1946.

Selected Publications: "Exchange Forces Between Neutrons and Protons, and Fermi's Theory." *Nature* 133 (1934): 981. "Nuclear Magnetic Moments and the Properties of the Neutron." *Nature* 134 (1934): 380. "Izluchenie Elektrona pri Ravnomernom Ovizhenii v Prelomliaiushchei Srede" ("Theory of the Electron in Uniform Motion in a Refracting Medium"). *Trudy Fizicheskago Instituta* 2 (1944): 63. "K Reliativistskoi Teorii Vzaimodeistvia Nuklonov" ("Toward a Relativ-istic Theory of the Mutual Interaction of Nucleons.") *Zhurnal Eksperimentalnogo i Teoricheskogo Fizika* 24 (1954): 3. "Teorii Magnitnykh Termoiadernykh Reaktsy" ("Theory of Magnetic Thermodynamic Reactors"). *Fizika Plazmy i Problemy Upravliaemykh Termoiadernykh Reaktsy* (1958): 3-19, 31-41. *Osnovy Teorii Elektrichestva (Principles of the Theory of Electricity).* Moscow: n.p., 1966.

For More Information See: *Current Biography Yearbook.* New York: H.W. Wilson, 1963, 412-14. *Dictionary of Scientific Biography.* New York: Scribner's, 1973 (Volume 13), 239-42. *Prominent Personalities in the USSR.* Metuchen, NJ: Scarecrow, 1968, 618-19.

Commentary: Igor Tamm shared the Nobel Prize for his contributions to the distinguished work on the Cherenkov radiation effect. Tamm and his colaureates developed a theory of the radiation of the electron based on a classical interpretation that a charged particle moving through a medium at a velocity greater than that of light produces an electromagnetic shock-wave effect. Tamm's other work included a quantum theory for acoustical vibrations and light scattering in solid bodies, a theory of light diffusion by free electrons, transistor electronics, the theory of elementary particles, and the theory of gas discharge in a powerful magnetic field. (T.B.)

1959

Chamberlain, Owen 488

PRIZE: Physics, 1959. BORN: July 10, 1920; San Francisco, CA. PARENTS: Father, W. Edward Chamberlain; Mother, Genevieve Lucinda Owen Chamberlain. NATIONALITY: American. RELIGION: Most probably Christian/Protestant. EDUCATION: Dartmouth Univ., NH, B.S., 1941; Univ. of Chicago, IL, Ph.D., 1949. SPOUSE: Babette Cooper, married 1943, divorced 1978. CHILDREN: Karen, daughter; Lynn, daughter; Pia, daughter; Darol, son. CAREER: Manhattan Project, United States, Researcher, 1942-46; Univ. of California, Berkeley, Professor, 1948-.

Selected Publications: "Observation of Antiprotons." *Physical Review* 100 (1955): 947-50 (with others). "Antiproton Star Observed in Emulsion." *Physical Review* 101 (1956): 909-10 (with others). "Example of an Antiproton Nucleon Annihilation." *Physical Review* 102 (1956): 921-23 (with others).

For More Information See: *Current Biography Yearbook.* New York: H.W. Wilson, 1960, 83-85. *Modern Scientists and Engineers.* New York: McGraw-Hill, 1980 (Volume 1), 191.

Commentary: Owen Chamberlain shared the Nobel Prize for his confirmation of the existence of the antiproton, using the Bevatron particle accelerator. Chamberlain's early work was on the atomic bomb project, alpha particle decay, neutron diffraction, and high-energy nuclear reactions. He also confirmed existence of the antineutron. (V.A.H.)

Segré, Emilio Gino 489

PRIZE: Physics, 1959. BORN: February 1, 1905; Rome, Italy. PARENTS: Father, Giuseppe Segré; Mother, Amelia Treves Segré. NATIONALITY: Italian; later American citizen. RELIGION: Jewish. EDUCATION: Univ. of Rome, Italy, Ph.D., 1928. SPOUSE: Elfriede Spiro, married February 2, 1936, died 1970; Rosa Mines, married

February 12, 1972. CHILDREN: Claudio, son; Amelia, daughter; Fausta, daughter. CAREER: Univ. of Rome, Italy, Professor, 1932-36; Univ. of Palermo, Italy, Researcher, 1936-38; Univ. of California, Berkeley, Researcher, 1938-43; Los Alamos Laboratory of the Manhattan Project, Researcher, NM, 1943-46; Univ. of California, Berkeley, Professor, 1946-72; Univ. of Rome, Italy, Professor, 1974-. OTHER AWARDS: Hofmann Medal, German Chemical Society, 1954; Cannizzaro Medal, Academie Nazionale dei Lincei, 1956; Commander of Merit, Republic of Italy, 1959.

Selected Publications: "Observation of Antiprotons." *Physical Review* 100 (1955): 947-50 (with others). "Antiproton Star Observed in Emulsion." *Physical Review* 101 (1956): 909-10 (with others). "Antiprotons." *Nature* 177 (1956): 11-12 (with others). "Proton-Antiproton Elastic and Charge Exchange Scattering at About 120 Mev." *Physical Review* 110 (1958): 994-95 (with others). *Nuclei and Particles.* New York: W.A. Benjamin, 1964. *Enrico Fermi, Physicist.* Chicago: U. of Chicago Press, 1970.

For More Information See: *Asimov's Biographical Encyclopedia of Science and Technology.* Garden City, NY: Doubleday, 1982, 803-04. *Current Biography Yearbook.* New York: H.W. Wilson, 1960, 369-71.

Commentary: For the 1955 discovery of the antiproton, "a nuclear ghost which has haunted the world's physicists for a generation," Emilio Segré was awarded the 1959 Nobel Prize for Physics, along with Owen Chamberlain. The antiproton, a negatively charged proton that destroys itself as well as the matter it strikes, was only one of Segré's discoveries. Included in his research findings throughout his career were the role of the neutron in the splitting of the atom; the discovery of new elements (technetium, astatine, and plutonium-239); and the development of a chemical method for dividing nuclear isomers. Segré's later interests also include writings on the history and contributions of classical and modern physicists. (J.B.T.)

1960

Glaser, Donald Arthur   490

PRIZE: Physics, 1960. BORN: September 21, 1926; Cleveland, OH. PARENTS: Father, William Joseph Glaser; Mother, Lena Glaser. NATIONALITY: American. RELIGION: Jewish. EDUCATION: Case Institute of Technology, OH, B.S., 1946; California Institute of Technology, Ph.D., 1950. SPOUSE: Ruth Louise Thompson, married November 28, 1960; divorced 1969. CHILDREN: William, son; Louise, daughter. CAREER: Univ. of Michigan, Professor, 1949-59; Univ. of California, Berkeley, Professor, 1959-. OTHER AWARDS: Henry Russel Award, U. of Michigan, 1955; Charles Vernon Bays Prize, Institute of Physics, 1958; American Physics Society Prize, 1959; Gold Medal, Case Institute of Technology, 1967; Alumni Distinguished Service Award, California Institute of Technology, 1967.

Selected Publications: "Some Effects of Ionizing Radiation on the Formation of Bubbles in Liquids." *Physical Review* 87 (August 15, 1952): 665. "Progress Report on the Development of Bubble Chambers." *Nuovo Cimento Supplement* 11 (1953): 361-68. "Characteristics of Bubble Chambers." *Physical Review* 97 (January 15, 1955): 474-79 (with D.C. Rahm). "Bubble Counting for the Determination of the Velocities of

Charged Particles in Bubble Chambers." *Physical Review* 102 (July 15, 1956): 1653-58 (with D.C. Rahm and C. Dodd).

For More Information See: *Biographical Encyclopedia of Scientists.* New York: Facts on File, 1981, 316. *Current Biography Yearbook.* New York: H.W. Wilson, 1961, 176-78.

Commentary: The Academy cited Donald Glaser "for the invention of the bubble chamber." The chamber, built in 1952, allowed the tracing of movement of high-energy atomic particles as they passed through a chamber filled with heated liquid through the track of tiny bubbles (which could be photographed for further study). Bubble chambers have been used to study high-energy particles in the way that cloud chambers have been used to study low-energy particles. Bubble chambers have also played a part in the discovery of new atomic particles (such as the rho and omega minus particles); in visualization of charged particle interaction; and in the study of particle mass, lifetime, and decay modes. Glaser's later interests changed to the application of physics to molecular biology. (S.H.S.)

1961

Hofstadter, Robert   491

PRIZE: Physics, 1961. BORN: February 5, 1915; New York, NY. PARENTS: Father, Louis Hofstadter; Mother, Henrietta Koenigsberg Hofstadter. NATIONALITY: American. RELIGION: Jewish. EDUCATION: City College of New York, B.S., 1935; Princeton Univ., NJ, M.A., 1938; Princeton Univ., NJ, Ph.D., 1938. SPOUSE: Nancy Givan, married May 9, 1942. CHILDREN: Douglas Richard, son; Laura James, daughter; Mary Hinda, daughter. CAREER: Univ. of Pennsylvania, Researcher, 1940-42; National Bureau of Standards, Washington, DC, Researcher, 1942-43; Norden Laboratories Corporation, NY, Researcher, 1943-46; Princeton Univ., NJ, Professor, 1946-50; Stanford Univ., CA, Professor and Administrator, 1950-. OTHER AWARDS: Kenyon Prize in Mathematics and Physics, 1935; California Scientist of the Year, 1958; Townsend Harris Medal, City College of New York, 1962.

Selected Publications: "High-Energy Electron Scattering and the Charge Distributions of Selected Nuclei." *Physical Review* 101 (1956): 1131-42 (with B. Hahn and D.G. Ravenhall). *High Energy Electron Scattering Tables.* Stanford, CA: Stanford U. Press, 1960 (with Robert C. Herman). *Nuclear and Nucleon Structure.* Stanford, CA: Stanford U. Press, 1963. *Nucleon Structure: Proceedings.* Stanford, CA: Stanford U. Press, 1964.

For More Information See: *Asimov's Biographical Encyclopedia of Science and Technology.* Garden City, NY: Doubleday, 1982, 853-54. *Current Biography Yearbook.* New York: H.W. Wilson, 1962, 212-14.

Commentary: Robert Hofstadter was cited by the Academy "for his pioneering studies of electron scattering in atomic nuclei and for his thereby achieved discoveries concerning the structure of the nucleons." Among Hofstadter's major contributions were the development of the sodium iodide-thallium scintillation counter for gamma rays and other detectors for neutrons and X-rays; the study of electron scattering, cosmic rays, and cascade showers from high-speed electron interactions; and determination of nuclear charge distributions, the charge and magnetic moments of protons and neutrons, the size and surface thickness of nuclei, and the nucleon form factors. (J.B.T.)

Moessbauer, Rudolf Ludwig 492

PRIZE: Physics, 1961. BORN: January 31, 1929; Munich, Germany. PARENTS: Father, Ludwig Moessbauer; Mother, Cerna Ernst Moessbauer. NATIONALITY: German. RELIGION: Most probably Christian. EDUCATION: Technische Hochschule, Germany, B.S., 1952; Technische Hochschule, Germany, M.S., 1955; Technische Hochschule, Germany, Ph.D., 1958. SPOUSE: Elizabeth Pritz, married 1957. CHILDREN: Peter, son; Regine, daughter; 1 other daughter. CAREER: Max Planck Institute, Heidelberg, Germany, Researcher, 1955-57; Institute of Technology, Munich, Germany, Researcher, 1958-60; California Institute of Technology, Researcher, 1960-64; Technische Universitat, Munich, Germany, Professor and Administrator, 1964-. OTHER AWARDS: Research Corporation Award, New York, 1960; Roentgen Award, U. of Giesson, Germany, 1961; Elliot Cresson Medal, Franklin Institute, PA, 1961; Bavarian Order of Merit, 1962; Guthrie Medal, Institute of Physics, London, 1974.

Selected Publications: "Nuclear Resonance Absorption of Gamma-Rays in Iridium-191." *Naturwissenschaften* 45 (1958): 538-39. "Nuclear Resonance Fluorescence of Gamma-Radiation in Iridium-191." *Z. Physik* 151 (1958): 124-43. "Nuclear Resonance Absorption of Gamma-Rays in Iridium-191." *Z. Naturforsch.* 14a (1959): 211-16. "Nuclear Resonance Absorption of Gamma-Radiation in Re-87 Not Broadened by Doppler Effect." *Z. Physik* 159 (1960): 33-48 (with Herbert W. Wiedemann). "Hyperfine Structure Splitting of Recoil-Free Gamma-Lines." *Z. Physik* 161 (1961): 388-91 (with F.W. Stanek and H.W. Wiedemann).

For More Information See: *Current Biography Yearbook.* New York: H.W. Wilson, 1962, 306-08. *Physics Today* 15 (December 1962): 56.

Commentary: Rudolf Moessbauer won the Nobel Prize "for his researches concerning the resonance absorption of gamma-radiation and his discovery in this connection of the effect which bears his name." Moessbauer's discovery of recoilless nuclear resonance absorption by atoms bound in a solid led to the verification of some predictions of the Einstein theory of relativity and to the possibility of studying small phenomena related to the separation and displacement of nuclear energy levels. The Moessbauer effect has become an important tool of physics, especially in the application known as Moessbauer spectroscopy. (C.N.B.)

1962

Landau, Lev Davidovich 493

PRIZE: Physics, 1962. BORN: January 22, 1908; Baku, Russia. DIED: April 1, 1968; Moscow, USSR. PARENTS: Father, David Landau; Mother, Lubov Landau. NATIONALITY: Russian. RELIGION: Jewish. EDUCATION: Leningrad Univ., USSR, baccalaureate, 1924; Kharkov Institute of Mechanical Engineering, USSR, Ph.D., 1934. SPOUSE: Konkordia Landau, married 1939. CHILDREN: Igor, son. CAREER: Kharkov Univ., USSR, Researcher and Administrator, 1932-37; Institute of

Physical Problems of the USSR Academy of Sciences, USSR, Researcher, 1937-68. OTHER AWARDS: Fritz London Award, 1960; Lenin Prize, 1962; Stalin Prize.

Selected Publications: *Teoriia Polia (Field Theory).* Moscow: n.p., 1941 (with E. Lifshits). "Teoriia Sverkhtekuchesti Gelia-2" ("Theory of the Superfluidity of Helium II"). *Zhurnal Eksperimentalnoe i Theoreticheskoi Fiziki* 11 (1941): 592. *Kvantovaia Mekhanika (Quantum Mechanics).* Moscow: n.p., 1948 (with E. Lifshits). "O Zakonakh Sokhranenia pri Slabykh Vzaimodeistviakh" ("On the Laws of Conservation in Weak Interactions"). *Zhurnal Eksperimentalnoe i Theoreticheskoi Fiziki* 32 (1957): 2.

For More Information See: *Current Biography Yearbook.* New York: H.W. Wilson, 1963, 231-33. *Dictionary of Scientific Biography.* New York: Scribner's, 1973 (Volume 7), 616-19.

Commentary: Lev Landau's work with Helium III at low temperatures won the Nobel Prize for him. In the 1950s, building on P.L. Kapitsa's work, he developed mathematical physical theories to explain the behavior of superfluid Helium III at temperatures near absolute zero. Helium at this temperature flows more easily than a gas, and since it does not behave like a solid, liquid, or a gas, it has been called the "fourth" state. He predicted the possibility of sound wave propagation at two different speeds. Landau was also known for his work in quantum mechanics and for fundamental research in magnetism, elasticity, and plasma oscillations. (T.B.)

1963

Jensen, Johannes Hans Daniel 494

PRIZE: Physics, 1963. BORN: June 25, 1907; Hamburg, Germany. DIED: February 11, 1973; Heidelburg, Germany. PARENTS: Father, Karl Jensen; Mother, Helene J. Ohm Jensen. NATIONALITY: German. RELIGION: Most probably Christian/Protestant. EDUCATION: Univ. of Hamburg, Germany, Dr. rerum naturalium, 1932. SPOUSE: None. CHILDREN: None. CAREER: Univ. of Hamburg, Germany, Professor, 1937-41; Hanover Institute of Technology, Germany, Professor, 1941-48; Univ. of Heidelberg, Germany, Professor, 1949-69.

Selected Publications: "Systematics of the Binding Energies of Atomic Nuclei." *Naturwissenschaften* 33 (1946): 249-50 (with H. Steinwedel). "Interpretation of Preferred Nucleon Numbers in the Structure of Atom Nuclei." *Naturwissenschaften* 36 (1949): 153-55 (with H. E. Suess and O. Haxel). "Electromagnetic Effects Due to Spin-Orbit Coupling." *Physical Review* 85 (1952): 1040-41 (with M. Goeppert-Mayer). "Nuclear Structure and Nuclear Transformation." *Zeitschrift fur Elektrochemie* 58 (1954): 546-53. *Elementary Theory of Nuclear Shell Structure.* New York: Wiley, 1955 (with M. Goeppert-Mayer).

For More Information See: *Modern Men of Science.* New York: McGraw-Hill, 1966, 257. *Physics Today* 16 (December 1963): 21.

Commentary: The Nobel Committee awarded the Prize to Hans Jensen for his work with Maria Goeppert-Mayer on developing the shell model of the atomic nucleus, citing it as "a most striking advance in the correlation of nuclear properties." According to the Academy, their work "has inspired an ever increasing number of new investigations and has been indispensable for later work, both experimental and theoretical, on atomic nuclei." Jensen also studied the recoil distribution of nuclear radiation, the giant resonance in the nuclear photoeffect, and the gamma-5 invariance of the weak interaction. (M.N.C.)

Mayer, Maria Goeppert 495

PRIZE: Physics, 1963. BORN: June 28, 1906; Kattowitz, Poland. DIED: February 20, 1972; San Diego, CA. PARENTS: Father, Friedrich Goeppert; Mother, Maria Wolff Goeppert. NATIONALITY: German; later American citizen. RELIGION: Christian. EDUCATION: Univ. of Gottingen, Germany, Ph.D., 1930. SPOUSE: Joseph Edward Mayer, married January 19, 1930. CHILDREN: Maria Anne, daughter; Peter Conrad, son. CAREER: Johns Hopkins Univ., Baltimore, MD, Volunteer Researcher, 1930-39; Columbia Univ., NY, Volunteer Lecturer, 1939-45; Sarah Lawrence College, NY, Professor, 1942-45; Univ. of Chicago, Fermi Institute, IL, Professor, 1946-60; Univ. of California, San Diego, Professor, 1960-72.

Selected Publications: *Statistical Mechanics.* New York: Wiley, 1940 (with J.E. Mayer). "Nuclear Configurations in the Spin-Orbit Coupling Model." *Physical Review* Series 2, 78 (April 1, 1950): 16-23. "The Structure of the Nucleus." *Scientific American* 184 (March 1951): 22-26. "Electromagnetic Effects Due to Spin-Orbit Coupling." *Physical Review* 85 (1952): 1040-41 (with J.H.D. Jensen). *Elementary Theory of Nuclear Shell Structure.* New York: Wiley, 1955 (with J.H.D. Jensen).

For More Information See: *Biographical Memoirs. National Academy of Sciences.* Washington, DC: National Academy of Sciences, 1979 (Volume 50), 310-28. Dash, Joan. *A Life of One's Own.* New York: Harper and Row, 1973, 226-369. *Physics Today* 25 (May 1972): 77, 79.

Commentary: Maria Goeppert Mayer was cited, with J. Hans D. Jensen, "for their discoveries concerning nuclear shell structure." Mayer first published evidence that atomic nuclei with 2, 8, 20, 28, 50, 82, or 126 nucleons (protons and/or neutrons) show unusual stability; the integers in this context are known as "magic numbers." Later, independently of Jensen, Mayer demonstrated the theoretical basis for a shell model of atomic nuclei, with each magic number corresponding to a completed nuclear shell. She also worked on the absorption spectra of organic molecules and isotope separation by chemical methods. Mayer and Marie Curie were the only two women who won a Nobel Prize in Physics. (J.W.)

Wigner, Eugene Paul 496

PRIZE: Physics, 1963. BORN: November 17, 1902; Budapest, Hungary. PARENTS: Father, Anthony Wigner; Mother, Elisabeth Einhorn Wigner. NATIONALITY: Hungarian; later American citizen. RELIGION: Lutheran. EDUCATION: Technische Hochschule, Germany, Chemical Engineering Degree, 1924; Technische Hochschule, Germany, Doctorate in Engineering, 1925. SPOUSE: Amelia Z. Frank, married December 23, 1936, died 1937; Mary Annette Wheeler, married June 4, 1941, died November 1977; Eileen C.P. Hamilton, married 1979. CHILDREN: David Wheeler, son; Martha Faith, daughter. CAREER: Technische Hochschule, Berlin, Germany, Professor, 1926; Univ. of Gottingen, Germany, Professor, 1927; Technische Hochschule, Berlin, Ger-

many, Professor, 1930-36; Univ. of Wisconsin, Professor, 1936-38; Princeton Univ., NJ, Professor, 1938-71. OTHER AWARDS: Medal of Merit, 1946; Franklin Medal, Franklin Institute, PA, 1950; Enrico Fermi Award; Atoms for Peace Award; Max Planck Medal, German Physical Society, 1961; George Washington Award; Semmelweiss Medal; National Science Medal, 1969; Pfizer Award, 1971; Albert Einstein Award, 1972; Golden Plate Medal; Wigner Medal, 1978; Founders Medal, International Cultural Foundation, 1982.

Selected Publications: *Gruppentheorie und Ihre Anwendung auf die Quantenmechanik der Atomspektren.* Braunschweig, Germany: Vieweg, 1931 (*Group Theory and Its Application to the Quantum Mechanics of Atomic Spectra.* Tr. by J.J. Griffin. New York: Academic Press, 1959). *Nuclear Structure.* Princeton, NJ: Princeton U. Press, 1958 (with Leonard Eisenbud). *The Physical Theory of Neutron Chemical Reactors.* Chicago: U. of Chicago Press, 1958 (with Alvin Martin Weinberg). *Symmetries and Reflections: Scientific Essays of Eugene P. Wigner.* Bloomington, IN: Indiana U. Press, 1967.

For More Information See: *Current Biography Yearbook.* New York: H.W. Wilson, 1954, 657-59. *McGraw-Hill Encyclopedia of World Biography.* New York: McGraw-Hill Book Co., 1973 (Volume 11), 357-58.

Commentary: Eugene Paul Wigner, who has been called one of the great physicists of the twentieth century, shared the Nobel Prize for "systematically improving and extending the methods of quantum mechanics and applying them widely." He formulated symmetry principles and with group theory, applied them in atomic, nuclear, and elementary particle physics. Wigner worked out the theory of neutron absorption and showed that nuclear forces did not depend on electric charge. His work also included research in theories of chemical reaction rates and the solid state and part of the design of the first large-scale nuclear reactor in 1943. In the late 1930s and early 1940s, along with other physicists, he convinced the U.S. government of the need for an atomic bomb project. His book *Gruppentheorie und Ihre Anwendung auf die Quantenmechanik der Atomspektren* was widely used as an advanced text in quantum mechanics. (L.N.W.)

1964

Basov, Nikolai Gennadievich 497

PRIZE: Physics, 1964. BORN: December 14, 1922; Usman, USSR. PARENTS: Father, Gennady Fedorovich Basov; Mother, Zinaida Andreevna Molchanova Basov. NATIONALITY: Russian. RELIGION: Most probably Eastern Orthodox. EDUCATION: Moscow Institute of Engineering Physics, USSR, Candidaat, 1950; Lebedev Institute of Physics, Soviet Academy of Sciences, USSR, Ph.D., 1956. SPOUSE: Qsenia Tikhonova Nasarova, married July 18, 1950. CHILDREN: Genadii, son; Dmitrii, son. CAREER: P.N. Lebedev Physical Institute, Researcher and Administrator, Moscow, USSR, 1953-. OTHER AWARDS: Lenin Prize, 1959, 1964; Order of Lenin, 1967; Gold Medal, Czechoslovakian Academy of Sciences, 1975; A. Volta Gold Medal, Italian Physical Society, 1977.

Selected Publications: "Application of Molecular Beams to the Radio Spectroscopic Study of the Rotation Spectra of Molecules." *Zh. Eksp. Teor. Fiz.* 27

(1954): 431-38 (with A.M. Prokhorov). "Possible Methods of Obtaining Active Molecules for a Molecular Oscillator." *Soviet Physics-JETP* 1 (1956): 184-85 (with O.N. Krokhin and Y.M. Popov). "Theory of the Molecular Generator and the Molecular Power Amplifier." *Zh. Eksp. Teor. Fiz.* 30 (1956): 560-63 (with A.M. Prokhorov). "Generation, Amplification, and Detection of Infrared and Optical Radiation by Quantum Mechanical Systems." *Soviet Physics-Uspekhi* 3 (March-April 1961): 702-28 (with O.N. Krokhin and Y.M. Popov).

For More Information See: *New York Times* (October 30, 1964): 23. Perlado, J.M. "N.G. Basov and Laser Technology in the USSR." *Arbor* 121 (1985): 87-97.

Commentary: Nikolai Gennadievich Basov, together with his teacher Alexander Prokhorov, was awarded the Nobel Prize for "basic researches in the field of experimental physics, which led to the discovery of the maser and the laser." They deduced that quantum mechanics, which governs the behavior of atoms at different energy levels, permits the amplification of microwaves and light waves. They then developed principles and refinements for the construction of first the maser (microwave amplification by stimulated emission of radiation) and then the laser (optical maser), starting in 1954. Such devices collect energy waves, amplify them hundreds of times, and produce a beam whose waves are almost perfectly parallel with little or no interference or static. The work was done independently of, and simultaneously with, the work of C.H. Townes, with whom Basov and Prokhorov shared the 1964 Nobel Prize in Physics. (M.N.K.)

Prokhorov, Alexander Mikhailovich 498

PRIZE: Physics, 1964. BORN: July 11, 1916; Atherton, Australia. PARENTS: Father, Mikhail Ivanovich Prokhorov; Mother, Mariya Ivanovna Prokhorov. NATIONALITY: Australian; later Russian citizen. RELIGION: Most probably Eastern Orthodox. EDUCATION: Leningrad Univ., USSR, baccalaureate, 1939; Institute of Physics, Academy of Sciences, USSR, doctorate, 1946. SPOUSE: Galina Alekeyevna Shelepina, married 1941. CHILDREN: 1 son. CAREER: Institute of Physics, Academy of Sciences, USSR, Researcher and Administrator, 1939-. OTHER AWARDS: Lenin Prize, 1959.

Selected Publications: "Application of Molecular Beams to the Radio Spectroscopic Study of the Rotation Spectra of Molecules." *Zh. Eksp. Teor. Fiz.* 27 (1954): 431-38 (with N.G. Basov). "Theory of the Molecular Generator and the Molecular Power Amplifier." *Zh. Eksp. Teor. Fiz.* 30 (1956): 560-63 (with N.G. Basov). "Quantum Electronics." *Fiz. Mat. Spisanie, Bulgar. Akad. Nauk.* 8 (1965): 165-71. "Quantum Electronics." *Usp. Fiz. Nauk* 85 (1965): 599-604.

For More Information See: *The Great Soviet Encyclopedia.* New York: Macmillan, 1978 (Volume 21), 257. *New York Times* (October 30, 1964): 23.

Commentary: Alexander Prokhorov won his Nobel for contributing to a new method for generating electromagnetic waves using quantum systems and for devising the first molecular generator using ammonia molecule beams (maser). He later created paramagnetic masers and proposed the use of ruby in quantum electronics and the concepts of open resonators and

gas dynamic lasers. Prokhorov further investigated the resonance and nonresonance interactions of laser radiation with matter. (G.E.M.)

Townes, Charles Hard 499

PRIZE: Physics, 1964. BORN: July 28, 1915; Greenville, SC. PARENTS: Father, Henry Keith Townes; Mother, Ellen Sumter Hard Townes. NATIONALITY: American. RELIGION: Presbyterian. EDUCATION: Furman Univ., SC, B.A., 1935; Furman Univ., SC, B.S., 1935; Duke Univ., NC, M.A., 1936; California Institute of Technology, Ph.D., 1939. SPOUSE: Frances H. Brown, married May 4, 1941. CHILDREN: Linda Lewis, daughter; Ellen Screven, daughter; Carla Keith, daughter; Holly Robinson, daughter. CAREER: Bell Telephone Laboratories, NJ, Researcher, 1939-48; Columbia Univ., NY, Professor, 1948-61; Massachusetts Institute of Technology, Professor and Administrator, 1961-67; Univ. of California, Berkeley, Professor, 1967-.

Selected Publications: "Molecular Microwave Oscillator and New Hyperfine Structure in the Microwave Spectrum of NH_3." *Physical Review* Series 2, 95 (July 1, 1954): 282-84 (with J.P. Gordon and H.J. Zeiger). *Microwave Spectroscopy.* New York: McGraw-Hill, 1955 (with A.L. Schawlow). *Quantum Electronics: A Symposium.* New York: Columbia U. Press, 1960. *Venus: Strategy for Exploration.* Report of a study by the Space Science Board. C.H. Townes, chair. Washington, DC: National Academy of Sciences, 1970.

For More Information See: *Asimov's Biographical Encyclopedia of Science and Technology.* Garden City, NY: Doubleday, 855-57. *Current Biography Yearbook.* New York: H.W. Wilson, 1963, 423-25.

Commentary: Charles H. Townes was awarded the Nobel Prize "for fundamental work in the field of quantum electronics, which has led to the construction of oscillators and amplifiers based on the maser-laser principle." Townes and two coworkers completed the first successful maser in 1954. It was based on excited ammonia molecules which, when struck by photons of the appropriate energy, were stimulated into emitting additional photons of the same energy. The amount of energy in question was equal to the energy level difference between an excited ammonia molecule and a ground-level ammonia molecule. This quantum of energy falls into the microwave portion of the electromagnetic spectrum—hence, the name of the device m(icrowave) a(mplification by) s(timulated) e(mission of) r(adiation). Townes's later research was in radio and infrared astronomy. (J.W.)

1965

Feynman, Richard Phillips 500

PRIZE: Physics, 1965. BORN: May 11, 1918; New York, NY. PARENTS: Father, Melville Arthur Feynman; Mother, Lucille Phillips Feynman. NATIONALITY: American. RELIGION: Jewish. EDUCATION: Massachusetts Institute of Technology, B.S., 1939; Princeton Univ., NJ, Ph.D., 1942. SPOUSE: Arlene H. Greenbaum, married June 29, 1942, died June 1945; Mary Louise Bell, married June 28, 1952; Gweneth Howarth, married 1960. CHILDREN: 2 children. CAREER: Princeton Univ. Atomic Bomb Project, NJ, Researcher, 1941-42; Los Alamos Atomic Bomb Project, NM, Researcher, 1942-45; Cornell Univ., NY, Professor, 1945-50; California Institute of Technology, Professor,

1951-. OTHER AWARDS: Einstein Award, 1954; Oersted Medal, 1972; Niels Bohr International Gold Medal, 1973.

Selected Publications: *Quantum Electrodynamics.* Reading, MA: Benjamin/Cummings, Advanced Book Program, 1961. *Theory of Fundamental Processes.* New York: W. A. Benjamin, 1961. *Feynman Lectures on Physics.* 3 volumes. Reading, MA: Addison-Wesley Pub. Co., 1963-69. *Quantum Mechanics and Path Integrals.* New York: McGraw-Hill, 1965. *The Character of Physical Law.* Cambridge, MA: M.I.T. Press, 1967. *Photon Hadron Interactions.* Reading, MA: W. A. Benjamin, 1972. *Statistical Mechanics.* Reading, MA: W. A. Benjamin, 1972.

For More Information See: *Current Biography Yearbook.* New York: H.W. Wilson, 1955, 205-07. *Science* 150 (October 29, 1965): 588-89.

Commentary: Richard Feynman, with his two co-laureates, shared the Nobel Prize for their development of the theory of quantum electrodynamics. His contributions in scientific work included an important role in the atomic bomb project, the development of a quantum theory of electricity and magnetism, the presentation of the Feynman diagram (for possible particle transformations), and the quantum mechanical explanation of the properties of liquid helium. (B.M.)

Schwinger, Julian Seymour   501

PRIZE: Physics, 1965. BORN: February 12, 1918; New York, NY. PARENTS: Father, Benjamin Schwinger; Mother, Belle Rosenfeld Schwinger. NATIONALITY: American. RELIGION: Jewish. EDUCATION: Columbia Univ., NY, BA, 1936; Columbia Univ., NY, Ph.D., 1939. SPOUSE: Clarice Carrol, married 1947. CHILDREN: None. CAREER: Univ. of California, Berkeley, Researcher, 1939-41; Purdue Univ., IN, Professor, 1941-43; Univ. of Chicago, IL, Researcher, 1943; Massachusetts Institute of Technology, Researcher, 1943-45; Harvard Univ., MA, Professor, 1945-75; Univ. of California, Los Angeles, Professor, 1975-. OTHER AWARDS: C. L. Mayer Nature of Light Award, 1949; University Medal, Columbia U., NY, 1951; Einstein Prize, 1951; National Medal of Science for Physics, 1964.

Selected Publications: "Quantum Electrodynamics." *Physical Review* 74 (November 15, 1948): 39-61. "On Gauge Invariance and Vacuum Polarization." *Physical Review* 82 (1951): 664-79. "A Theory of the Fundamental Interactions." *Annals of Physics* 2 (1957): 407-34. *Quantum Electrodynamics.* New York: Dover, 1958. "Gauge Invariance and Mass II." *Physical Review* 128 (1962): 2425-29. *Particles Sources and Fields.* Reading, MA: Addison-Wesley Pub. Co., 1970.

For More Information See: *Current Biography Yearbook.* New York: H.W. Wilson, 1967, 379-81. *Science* 150 (October 29, 1965): 588-89.

Commentary: Julian Schwinger and his two co-laureates received the Nobel Prize for their development of the theory of quantum electrodynamics. Earlier work by Paul Dirac applied quantum mechanics to an analysis of the electromagnetic field and predicted that particles such as the electron would have an infinite quantity of energy, which contradicted observed fact. Schwinger reworked the mathematics in the theory so that the infinite quantities no longer appeared and made it consistent with observation, capable of

predicting the magnetic and other properties of particles and radiation. He later worked on the properties of synchrotron radiation. (J.L.K.)

Tomonaga, Shinichiro   502

PRIZE: Physics, 1965. BORN: March 31, 1906; Tokyo, Japan. DIED: July 8, 1979; Tokyo, Japan. PARENTS: Father, Sanjuro Tomonaga; Mother, Hide Tomonaga. NATIONALITY: Japanese. RELIGION: Most probably Buddhist. EDUCATION: Kyoto Imperial Univ., Japan, B.A., 1929; Kyoto Imperial Univ., Japan, D.Sc., 1939. SPOUSE: Ryoko Sekiguchi, married 1940. CHILDREN: Atsushi, son; Makoto, son; Shigeko, daughter. CAREER: Tokyo Univ., Japan, Professor, 1939-69. OTHER AWARDS: Japan Academy Prize, 1948; Lomonosov Medal, Russia, 1964.

Selected Publications: *Quantum Mechanics.* Tokyo: Misuzu Publishing Company, 1949. (English publication in two volumes. Amsterdam: North-Holland Publishing Company, 1962-66). *Scientific Papers of Tomonaga.* 2 volumes. Tokyo: Misuzu Shobo Publishing Company, 1971-76.

For More Information See: *Modern Men of Science.* New York: McGraw-Hill, 1966: 483-84. Weber, Robert L. *Pioneers of Science, Nobel Prize Winners in Physics.* London: Institute of Physics, 1980, 205-06.

Commentary: The Nobel Prize was awarded to Shinichiro Tomonaga, jointly with Richard Feynman and Julian Schwinger, for his research on a theoretical basis for quantum electrodynamics which was consistent with both observable behavior of particles and the theory of relativity. Tomonaga also worked in the areas of quantum dynamics, the theory of neutrons, and electromagnetics. (D.P.N.)

1966

Kastler, Alfred   503

PRIZE: Physics, 1966. BORN: May 3, 1902; Alsace, France. DIED: January 7, 1984; Bandol, France. PARENTS: Father, Frederic Kastler; Mother, Anna Frey Kastler. NATIONALITY: French. RELIGION: Most probably Christian. EDUCATION: Univ. of Bordeaux, France, Docteur des Sciences Physiques, 1936. SPOUSE: Elise Cosset, married December 24, 1924. CHILDREN: Daniel, son; Claude-Yves, son; Mireille, daughter. CAREER: Clermont-Ferrant Univ., France, Professor, 1936-38; Univ. of Bordeaux, France, Professor, 1938-41; Ecole Normale Superieure, France, Professor, 1941-72. OTHER AWARDS: Holweck Prize, London Physical Society, 1954; C.E.K. Mees International Medal, Optical Society of America, 1962; Award in Scientific Research, Academy of Sciences; Science Prize, City of Paris, 1963.

Selected Publications: *La Diffusion de la Lumière par les Milieux Troubles.* Paris: Hermann, 1952. *Polarisation, Matière et Rayonnement, Volume Jubilaire en l'Honneur d'Alfred Kastler.* Paris: Presses Universitaires de France, 1969. *Cette Etrange Matière.* Paris: Stock, 1976.

For More Information See: *Current Biography Yearbook.* New York: H.W. Wilson, 1967, 216-18. *New York Times* (November 4, 1966): 1,28. "Notices sur les membres décèdès: Kastler (Alfred)." Association Amicale des Anciens élèves de l'Ecole Normale Supèrieure (*Annuaire*), 1985, 60-65.

Commentary: Alfred Kastler was awarded the Nobel prize for "the discovery and development of optical methods for studying Herzian resonances in atoms." He not only provided a stimulus to further research by other scientists, but his work also resulted in practical applications, namely the developments of the laser, magnetometers, and atomic clocks. The double resonance technique, which uses optical and Herzian resonances (light and radiowaves), and the optical pumping technique to orient atoms and atomic fields made it possible to detect with precision the spectrum of Herzian resonances. Kastler was also well known for his humanitarian, social, and political activities. He took stands against the French occupation of Algeria, against the Soviet treatment of Sakharov and Solzhenitsyn, and against cruel and inhuman treatment of livestock. (J.U.S.)

1967

Bethe, Hans Albrecht   504

PRIZE: Physics, 1967. BORN: July 2, 1906; Strasbourg, Germany. PARENTS: Father, Albrecht Theodore Julius Bethe; Mother, Anna Kuhn Bethe. NATIONALITY: German; later American citizen. RELIGION: Jewish. EDUCATION: Univ. of Munich, Germany, Ph.D., 1928. SPOUSE: Rose Ewald, married September 14, 1939. CHILDREN: Henry George, son; Monica, daughter. CAREER: Univ. of Frankfurt, Germany, Professor, 1928-29; Univ. of Stuttgart, Germany, Professor, 1929-30; Univ. of Munich and Univ. of Tubingen, Germany, Professor, 1930-33; Univ. of Manchester, England, Professor, 1933-34; Univ. of Bristol, England, Professor, 1934-35; Cornell Univ., NY, Professor, 1937-75. OTHER AWARDS: Morrison Prize, New York Academy of Science, 1938; U.S. Medal of Merit, 1946; Draper Medal, National Academy of Sciences, 1948; Max Planck Medal, 1955; Enrico Fermi Prize, 1961; Eddington Medal, Royal Astronomical Society, 1963; National Medal of Science, 1975.

Selected Publications: "Energy Production in Stars." *Physical Review* 55 (1939): 434. *Elementary Nuclear Theory*. New York: John Wiley and Sons, Inc., 1947. *Quantum Mechanics of One- and Two-Electron Atoms*. New York: Plenum Publishing Co., 1958 (with E.E. Salpeter). *Splitting of Atoms in Crystals*. New York: Plenum Publishing Co., 1962. *Intermediate Quantum Mechanics*. San Francisco, CA: Benjamin-Cummings Co., 1968 (with Roman W. Jackiw).

For More Information See: *Modern Men of Science*. New York: McGraw Hill, 1966, 37-39. *National Cyclopedia of American Biography*. New York: James T. White, 1960 (Volume I), 320-21.

Commentary: Hans Bethe won the Nobel Prize for his several contributions to nuclear reaction theory, with special reference to the energy production of stars. He was unique among his contemporaries in making diverse contributions to the field of physics, ranging from fundamental particles to ballistic missiles. Bethe was best known for developing a theoretical description of deuteron fusion and using the carbon cycle as a mechanism to explain the rate of energy production in the sun's interior balanced against surface energy losses. He contributed to the theory of nuclear reactors and developed the first theory of electron-positron pair creation. The early work of Bethe and others led to our present-day understanding of core nuclear reactions in the sun. (G.W.)

1968

Alvarez, Luis Walter   505

PRIZE: Physics, 1968. BORN: June 13, 1911; San Francisco, CA. PARENTS: Father, Walter Clement Alvarez; Mother, Harriet Skidmore Smyth Alvarez. NATIONALITY: American. RELIGION: Congregationalist background. EDUCATION: Univ. of Chicago, IL, B.S., 1932; Univ. of Chicago, IL, M.Sc., 1934; Univ. of Chicago, IL, Ph.D., 1936. SPOUSE: Geraldine Smithwick, married April 15, 1937; Janet L. Landin, married December 28, 1958. CHILDREN: Walter S., son; Donald L., son; Jean S., daughter; Helen L., daughter. CAREER: Univ. of California, Berkeley, Professor, 1936-78. OTHER AWARDS: Collier Trophy, 1946; Medal for Merit, 1948; John Scott Medal, 1953; California Scientist of the Year, 1960; Einstein Medal, 1961; National Medal of Science, 1964; Michelson Award, 1965; National Inventors Hall of Fame, 1978; Wright Prize, 1981.

Selected Publications: "The Lifetime of the t-Meson." *Nuovo Cimento* 2 (1955): 344 (with S. Goldhaber). "Catalysis of Nuclear Reactions by u Mesons." *Physical Review* 105 (1957): 1127 (with others). "K-Interactions in Hydrogen." *Nuovo Cimento* 5 (1957): 1026 (with others). "Elastic Scattering of 1.6-Mev Gamma Ray from H, Li, C, and Al Nuclei." *Physical Review* 112 (1958): 1267 (with F.S. Crawford and M.L. Stevenson). *Strong Interactions*. New York: Academic Press, 1966. "Recent Developments in Particle Physics." *Science* 165 (September 12, 1969): 1071.

For More Information See: *Current Biography Yearbook*. New York: H.W. Wilson, 1947, 9-10. *Science* 162 (November 8, 1968): 645.

Commentary: The award to Luis Alvarez was for his "decisive contributions to elementary particle physics, in particular the discovery of a large number of resonance states made possible through his development of the technique of using hydrogen bubble chambers and data analysis." He also made important contributions in many other areas of physics: he codiscovered the east-west effect in cosmic rays, demonstrated orbital electron capture by nuclei, collaborated on building the first proton linear accelerator based on the use of cavity resonators, and developed the ground-controlled-approach blind landing system, which uses microwave radar. (C.D.)

1969

Gell-Mann, Murray   506

PRIZE: Physics, 1969. BORN: September 15, 1929; New York, NY. PARENTS: Father, Arthur Gell-Mann; Mother, Pauline Reichstein Gell-Mann. NATIONALITY: American. RELIGION: Nonbeliever; from Jewish background. EDUCATION: Yale Univ., CT, B.S., 1948; Massachusetts Institute of Technology, Ph.D., 1951. SPOUSE: J. Margaret Dow, married April 19, 1955. CHILDREN: Elizabeth, daughter; Nicholas, son. CAREER: Princeton Univ., NJ, Professor, 1951-52; Univ. of Chicago, IL, Professor, 1952-55; California Institute of Technology, Pasadena, Professor, 1955-. OTHER AWARDS: Daniel Heinemann Prize, American Physical

Society and American Institute of Physics, 1959; Franklin Medal, Franklin Institute, PA, 1967; Research Corporation Award, 1969.

Selected Publications: "Isotopic Spin and New Unstable Particles." *Physical Review* 92 (1953): 833. *Lectures on Weak Interactions of Strongly Interacting Particles, Delivered at the Summer School in Theoretical Physics, Bangalore, 1961.* Bombay: Tata Institute of Fundamental Research, 1961. *Lecture Notes on Special Topics in Relativistic Quantum Theory.* Cambridge, MA: Massachusetts Institute of Technology Press, 1963. "A Schematic Model of Baryons and Mesons." *Physics Letters* 8 (February 1, 1964): 214. *The Eightfold Way: A Review with a Collection of Reprints.* New York: W.A. Benjamin, 1964 (with Y. Ne'eman).

For More Information See: *Asimov's Biographical Encyclopedia of Science and Technology.* Garden City, NY: Doubleday, 1982, 889. *Current Biography Yearbook.* New York: H.W. Wilson, 1966, 124-66.

Commentary: The award to Murray Gell-Mann was "for his contributions and discoveries concerning the classification of elementary particles and their interactions." Gell-Mann's earlier contribution was the introduction of the strangeness principle, which classified the elementary particles in the atomic nucleus, based on properties related to charge and spin. Later, using symmetry group theory, he devised the Eightfold Way, a scheme for classification, based on eight quantum numbers. His predictions of the existences of particles led to many discoveries, including those in the world of quarks. (C.D.)

1970

Alfven, Hannes Olof Gösta   507

PRIZE: Physics, 1970. BORN: May 30, 1908; Norrkoeping, Sweden. PARENTS: Father, Johannes Alfven; Mother, Anna-Clara Romanus Alfven. NATIONALITY: Swedish. RELIGION: Lutheran. EDUCATION: Univ. of Uppsala, Sweden, Ph.D., 1934. SPOUSE: Kerstin Maria Erikson, married 1935. CHILDREN: 5 children. CAREER: Univ. of Uppsala, Sweden, Professor, 1934-37; Nobel Institute of Physics, Sweden, Researcher, 1937-40; Royal Institute of Technology, Professor, 1945-67; Univ. of California, San Diego, Professor, 1967-. OTHER AWARDS: Gold Medal, Royal Astronomical Society, 1967; Lomonosov Gold Medal, Soviet Academy of Sciences, 1971; Franklin Medal, Franklin Institute, PA, 1971.

Selected Publications: *Cosmical Electrodynamics.* Oxford: Clarendon Press, 1950. *On the Origin of the Solar System.* Oxford: Clarendon Press, 1954. *Cosmical Electrodynamics: Fundamental Principles.* Oxford: Clarendon Press, 1963 (with Carl-Gunne Falthammar). *Worlds-Antiworlds: Antimatter in Cosmology.* San Francisco, CA: W. H. Freeman, 1966. *Structure and Evolutionary History of the Solar System.* Dordrecht, Netherlands: D. Reidel, 1975 (with Gustaf Arrhenius).

For More Information See: *New York Times Biographical Edition* (October 28, 1970): 2707-08. *Physics Today* 23 (December 1970): 61-63.

Commentary: One of the founders of the field of plasma physics, Hannes Alfven shared the Nobel Prize "for fundamental work in magnetohydrodynamics with fruitful applications in different parts of plasma phys-

ics." His work on the motion of electrically conducting fluids in a magnetic field was concerned primarily with geophysics and astrophysics. It led to the development of the concept of "Alfven's waves," transverse hydromagnetic waves transmitted by the plasma. Alfven's work helped provide an understanding of the solar system and was instrumental in the development of controlled thermonuclear reactors and space travel. (J.N.S.)

Neel, Louis Eugene Felix   508

PRIZE: Physics, 1970. BORN: November 22, 1904; Lyon, Rhone, France. PARENTS: Father, Louis Antoine Neel; Mother, Marie Antoinette Hartmayer Neel. NATIONALITY: French. RELIGION: Catholic. EDUCATION: École Normale Supérieure, France, Agrege de l'Université, 1928; Univ. of Strasbourg, France, Docteur es Sciences, 1932. SPOUSE: Helene Hourticq, married 1931. CHILDREN: Marie-Françoise, daughter; Marguerite Guely, daughter; Pierre, son. CAREER: Univ. of Strasbourg, France, Professor, 1937-45; Univ. of Grenoble, France, Professor, 1945-76. OTHER AWARDS: Prix Holweck, 1952; Gold Medal (C.N.R.S.)., 1965; Croix de Guerre, 1940; Grand Croix, Legion d'Honneur.

Selected Publications: *Exposés sur l'Energie.* Paris: Institute de France, 1978. *Ouevres Scientifique de Louis Neel.* Paris: Centre National de la Recherche Scientifique, 1978.

For More Information See: *Modern Scientists and Engineers.* New York: McGraw-Hill, 1980 (Volume 2), 351-52. *New York Times Biographical Edition.* (October 28, 1970): 2707-08.

Commentary: Louis Neel received the Nobel Prize "for his pioneering studies of the magnetic properties of solids." His early studies explained antiferromagnetism, the magnetic effect deriving from electron alignments in opposite directions. He also studied the magnetic memory of certain mineral deposits which explained observed changes in the Earth's magnetic field. Neel's research on the ferrimagnetics has provided new materials for microwave electronics. (V.A.H.)

1971

Gabor, Dennis   509

PRIZE: Physics, 1971. BORN: June 5, 1900; Budapest, Hungary. DIED: February 8, 1979; London, England. PARENTS: Father, Berthold Gabor; Mother, Adrienne Jacobovits Gabor. NATIONALITY: Hungarian; later British citizen. RELIGION: Jewish. EDUCATION: Technische Hochschule, Germany, diploma, 1924; Technische Hochschule, Germany, Dr. Elect. Eng., 1927. SPOUSE: Marjorie Louise Butler, married August 8, 1936. CHILDREN: None. CAREER: Siemens and Halske, Berlin, Germany, Researcher, 1927-33; British Thomson-Houston Co., Rugby, England, Researcher, 1933-48; Imperial College, London, England, Professor, 1949-67. OTHER AWARDS: Thomas Young Medal and Prize, 1967; Cristoforo Columbo Prize, Genoa, Italy, 1967; Rumford Medal, Royal Society, 1968; Michelson Medal, Franklin Institute, PA, 1968; Medal of Honor, Institute of Electrical and Electronics Engineers, 1970; Semmelweis Medal, American Hungarian Medical Association, 1970; Holweck Prize, French Physical Society, 1971; George Washington Award, American Hungarian Studies Foundation, 1973.

Selected Publications: "A New Microscopic Principle." *Nature* (May 15, 1948): 777-78. "Microscopy by Reconstructed Wave-Fronts." *Proceedings of the Royal Society* A197 (1949): 454. "Microscopy by Reconstructed Wave Fronts: II." *Proceedings of the Royal Society* B64 (1951): 244. *Inventing the Future.* New York: Knopf, 1964. *Innovations: Scientific, Technological, and Social.* London: Oxford U. Press, 1970.

For More Information See: *Current Biography Yearbook.* New York: H.W. Wilson, 1972, 168-70. *New York Times* (November 3, 1971): 1, 28.

Commentary: Dennis Gabor was one of the few inventors who received the Nobel Prize, "for his invention and development of holography," a lenseless system of three-dimensional photography. His contributions extended into many other areas—the high-speed cathode ray oscillograph, the shrouded magnetic lens, theories of communication, information theory, the physics of optics, predicting machines, plasmas, gas discharge tubes, and television. Gabor was also a thinker about the discipline of physics itself, writing thoughtfully about its applications and societal issues. (G.W.)

1972

Bardeen, John *see* entry 480

Cooper, Leon Neil   510

PRIZE: Physics, 1972. BORN: February 28, 1930; New York, NY. PARENTS: Father, Irving Cooper; Mother, Anna Zola Cooper. NATIONALITY: American. RELIGION: No record found. EDUCATION: Columbia Univ., NY, A.B., 1951; Columbia Univ., NY, A.M., 1953; Columbia Univ., NY, Ph.D., 1954. SPOUSE: Kay Anne Allard, married 1969. CHILDREN: Kathleen, daughter; Coralie, daughter. CAREER: Princeton Univ., NJ, Researcher, 1954-55; Univ. of Illinois, Researcher, 1955-57; Ohio State Univ., Professor, 1957-58; Brown Univ., RI, Professor, 1958-. OTHER AWARDS: Comstock Prize, National Academy of Science, 1968; Descartes Medal, Academy de Paris, 1977.

Selected Publications: "Microscopic Theory of Superconductivity." *Physical Review* 106 (1957): 162-64 (with J. Bardeen and J.R. Schrieffer). "Theory of Superconductivity." *Physical Review* 108 (1957): 1175-1204 (with J. Bardeen and J.R. Schrieffer). "Specific Heat Measurements and the Energy Gap in Superconductors." *Physical Review Letters* 3 (1959): 17. "Superconductivity in the Neighborhood of Metallic Contacts." *Physical Review Letters* 6 (1961): 689-90. *An Introduction to the Meaning and Structure of Physics.* New York: Harper and Row, 1968.

For More Information See: *Physics Today* 25 (December 1972): 73-75. *Science* 178 (November 3, 1972): 489-91.

Commentary: Leon Cooper shared, with John Bardeen and John Schrieffer, the Nobel Prize for work on the theory of superconductivity. Cooper showed that at low temperatures electrons in a conductor could act in bound pairs (called Cooper pairs). With his colaureates, he demonstrated that the Cooper pair action resulted in no electrical resistance to electron flow through solids. The BCS theory stimulated much work in physics. Cooper also contributed significantly in the

areas of nuclear physics, the superfluid state at low temperatures, and the theory of the central nervous system. (P.S.)

Schrieffer, John Robert   511

PRIZE: Physics, 1972. BORN: May 31, 1931; Oak Park, IL. PARENTS: Father, John Henry Schrieffer; Mother, Louise Anderson Schrieffer. NATIONALITY: American. RELIGION: Most probably Christian. EDUCATION: Massachusetts Institute of Technology, B.S., 1953; Univ. of Illinois, M.S., 1954; Univ. of Illinois, Ph.D., 1957. SPOUSE: Anne Grete Thomson, married 1960. CHILDREN: Paul Karsten, son; Anne Bolette, daughter; Anna Regina, daughter. CAREER: Univ. of Chicago, IL, Professor, 1957-59; Univ. of Illinois, Professor, 1959-62; Univ. of Pennsylvania, Professor, 1962-79; Univ. of California, Santa Barbara, Professor, 1979-. OTHER AWARDS: Buckley Prize, 1968; Comstock Prize, National Academy of Sciences, 1968; John Ericsson Medal, American Society of Swedish Engineers, 1976.

Selected Publications: "Microscopic Theory of Superconductivity." *Physical Review* 106 (1957): 162-64 (with L.N. Cooper and J. Bardeen). "Theory of Superconductivity." *Physical Review* 108 (1957): 1175-1204 (with J. Bardeen and L.N. Cooper). "Recent Advances in the Theory of Superconductivity." *Physica* 26 (1960): S1-S16. *Theory of Superconductivity.* Reading, MA: W.A. Benjamin, 1964.

For More Information See: *Physics Today* 25 (December 1972): 73-75. *Science* 178 (November 3, 1972): 489-91.

Commentary: John Schrieffer received the Nobel Prize with his colaureates, John Bardeen and Leon Cooper, for their development of the BCS theory of superconductivity, which related the superconducting state to the bound pair actions of electrons at low temperature in the conductor. His later work was in the areas of particle physics, metal impurities, spin fluctuations, and chemisorption. (P.S.)

1973

Esaki, Leo   512

PRIZE: Physics, 1973. BORN: March 12, 1925; Osaka, Japan. PARENTS: Father, Soichiro Esaki; Mother, Niyoko Ito Esaki. NATIONALITY: Japanese. RELIGION: Buddhist. EDUCATION: Univ. of Tokyo, Japan, B.S., 1947; Univ. of Tokyo, Japan, Ph.D., 1959. SPOUSE: Masako Araki, married November 21, 1959. CHILDREN: Eugene Leo, son; Nina Yvonne, daughter; Anna Eileen, daughter. CAREER: Kobe Kogyo Corporation, Japan, Researcher, 1947-56; Sony Corporation, Japan, Researcher, 1956-60; International Business Machines, Researcher, 1960-. OTHER AWARDS: Nishina Memorial Award, 1959; Asahi Press Award, 1960; Toyo Rayon Foundation Award, 1961; Morris N. Liebmann Memorial Prize, 1961; Stuart Ballantine Medal, Franklin Institute, PA, 1961; Japan Academy Award, 1965; Order of Culture, Japan, 1974; Science Achievement Award, U.S.-Asia Institute, 1983.

Selected Publications: "Properties of Heavily-Doped Ge and Narrow p-n Junctions." *Solid State Phys. Electronics Telecommun., Proc. Intern. Conf., Brussels* 1 (1958): 514-23. "New Horizons in Semimetal Alloys." *IEEE Spectrum* 3 (1966): 74-80, 85-86. "Tunneling Studies on the Group 5 Semimetals and the 4-6 Semiconductors." *Journal of the Physical Society of Japan,*

Supplement 21 (1966): 589-97. "Tunneling in Solids." *Electron. Struct. Solids, Lect. Chania Conf., 2nd* (1968): 1-40.

For More Information See: *Modern Men of Science.* New York: McGraw-Hill, 1966, 156-57. *New York Times Biographical Edition* (October 24, 1973): 1640.

Commentary: Leo Esaki shared the 1973 prize for his discovery of tunneling in semiconductors. Tunneling is a quantum mechanical effect in which an electron passes through a potential barrier (a solid region), even though classical theory predicted that it could not. His research at the Sony Corporation in the late 1950s led to the creation of the Esaki diode, an important component of solid state physics. Because of its simplicity and sensitivity, it has practical applications in high-speed circuits, such as those in computers, communications networks, and other electronic equipment. Esaki applied a tunneling technique in spectroscopic studies, known as tunneling spectroscopy. (D.P.N.)

Giaever, Ivar   513

PRIZE: Physics, 1973. BORN: April 5, 1929; Bergen, Norway. PARENTS: Father, John A. Giaever; Mother, Gudrun M. Skaarud Giaever. NATIONALITY: Norwegian; later American citizen. RELIGION: No affiliation; from Lutheran background. EDUCATION: Norwegian Institute of Technology, Norway, Bachelor of Engineering, 1952; Rensselaer Polytechnical Institute, NY, Ph.D., 1964. SPOUSE: Inger Skramstad, married 1952. CHILDREN: John, son; Guri, son; Anne Kari, daughter; Trine, daughter. CAREER: Norwegian Army, 1952-53; Norwegian Patent Office, Oslo, Patent Examiner, 1953-54; General Electric Company, Canada, Engineer, 1954-56; General Electric Company, United States, Researcher, 1956-. OTHER AWARDS: Oliver E. Buckley Prize, American Physical Society, 1965; Guggenheim Fellow, 1970; V.K. Zworykin Award, National Academy of Engineering, 1974.

Selected Publications: "Energy Gap in Superconductors Measured by Electron Tunneling." *Physical Review Letters* 5 (1960): 147. "Electron Tunneling between Two Superconductors." *Physical Review Letters* 5 (1960): 464. "Detection of the A. C. Josephson Effect." *Physical Review Letters* 14 (1965): 904. "Magnetic Coupling Between Two Adjacent Superconductors." *Physical Review Letters* 15 (1965): 825.

For More Information See: *Asimov's Biographical Encyclopedia of Science and Technology.* Garden City, NY: Doubleday, 1982, 888. *Biographical Encyclopedia of Scientists.* New York: Facts on File, 1981, 311-12.

Commentary: Ivar Giaever was cited by the Academy for his work on tunneling effects in semiconductors and superconductors. His research studying the behavior of electrons in solids when a superconducting metal is present laid the foundation for Josephson's discovery of the Josephson effect, which has been heavily applied in microelectronics. Giaever's interest has shifted to biology, and he has studied stress reactions and antibody-antigen reactions while working as a researcher in immunology at General Electric and at the Albany Medical Center. (L.D.)

Josephson, Brian David   514

PRIZE: Physics, 1973. BORN: January 4, 1940; Cardiff, Wales. PARENTS: Father, Abraham Josephson; Mother, Mimi Josephson. NATIONALITY: British. RELIGION: Jewish. EDUCATION: Cambridge Univ., England, B.A., 1960; Cambridge Univ., England, M.A., 1964; Cambridge Univ., England, Ph.D., 1964. SPOUSE: Carol Anne Oliver, married 1976. CHILDREN: 1 daughter. CAREER: Cambridge Univ., England, Professor, 1965-. OTHER AWARDS: New Scientist Award, 1969; Research Corporation Award, 1969; Fritz London Medal, 1970; Guthrie Medal, 1972; van der Pol Medal, 1972; Elliott Cresson Medal, 1972; Hughes Medal, 1972; Holweck Medal, 1973; Faraday Medal, 1982; Sir George Thompson Medal, 1984.

Selected Publications: "Potential Differences in the Mixed State of Type II Superconductors." *Physics Letters* 16 (1965): 242-43. "Macroscopic Field Equations for Metals in Equilibrium." *Physical Review* 152 (1966): 211-17. "Inequality for the Specific Heat. I. Derivation." *Proceedings of the Physical Society* 92 (1967): 269-75. "Inequality for the Specific Heat. II. Application to Critical Phenomena." *Proceedings of the Physical Society* 92 (1967): 276-84. "Equation of State Near the Critical Point." *Proceedings of the Physical Society, London (Solid State Physics)* 2 (1969): 1113-15. *Consciousness and the Physical World.* New York: Pergamon Press, 1980.

For More Information See: *Asimov's Biographical Encyclopedia of Science and Technology.* Garden City, NY: Doubleday, 1982, 898. *Biographical Encyclopedia of Scientists.* New York: Facts on File, 1981, 420.

Commentary: Brian Josephson shared the Nobel Prize for work in developing theories that advanced and expanded the world of miniature electronics. Specifically, Josephson was cited by the Academy for his theoretical predictions of the properties of supercurrent through a tunnel barrier, particularly phenomena called "Josephson effects." One of the youngest Nobel laureates, the physicist was only 22 and in graduate school when he made his discoveries while doing research on semiconductivity in 1963. He has contributed significantly to studies of superconductivity, critical phenomena, and the theory of intelligence. (L.D.)

1974

Hewish, Antony   515

PRIZE: Physics, 1974. BORN: May 11, 1924; Fowey, England. PARENTS: Father, Ernest William Hewish; Mother, Frances Grace Lanyon Pinch Hewish. NATIONALITY: British. RELIGION: Most probably Christian/ Protestant. EDUCATION: Cambridge Univ., England, B.A., 1948; Cambridge Univ., England, M.A., 1950; Cambridge Univ., England, Ph.D., 1952. SPOUSE: Marjorie Elizabeth Catherine Richards, married 1950. CHILDREN: 1 son; 1 daughter. CAREER: Cambridge Univ., England, Professor, 1952-. OTHER AWARDS: Hamilton Prize, Cambridge U., England, 1951; Eddington Medal, Royal Astronomical Society, 1968; Charles Vernon Boys Prize, Institute of Physics and Physical Sciences, 1970; Dellinger Gold Medal, International Union of Radio Sciences, 1972; Michelson Medal, Franklin Institute, PA, 1973; Hopkins Prize, Cambridge Philosophical Society, 1973; Holweck Medal and Prize, Institute of Physics and French Physical Society, 1974.

Selected Publications: *Seeing Beyond the Visible.* London: English Universities Press, 1970. "Small Stars Raise Large Problems." *Physics Bulletin* 25 (1974): 459-61.

For More Information See: *Biographical Encyclopedia of Scientists.* New York: Facts on File, 1981, 376-77. *Science* 186 (November 15, 1974): 620-21.

Commentary: Antony Hewish was honored for his pioneering research in radio astrophysics, which led to the discovery of pulsars (compact radio sources emitting regular pulses). Although questioned by some scientists, Hewish's delay in announcing the discovery allowed principal scientific facts to be established and clarified, averting what has been called the "little green men" speculation. Hewish's earlier research was on radio scintillation, and he was involved in the study of all three types of radio scintillation, i.e., that due to radio wave deflection by ionized gases in the interstellar medium, in the interplanetary medium, and in the earth's atmosphere. (D.H.)

Ryle, Martin, Sir   516

PRIZE: Physics, 1974. BORN: September 27, 1918; Brighton, England. DIED: October 14, 1984; Cambridge, England. PARENTS: Father, J.A. Ryle; Mother, Miriam Scully Ryle. NATIONALITY: British. RELIGION: Christian. EDUCATION: Oxford Univ., England, baccalaureate, 1945. SPOUSE: Ella Rowena Palmer, married 1947. CHILDREN: 1 son; 2 daughters. CAREER: Telecommunications Research Establishment, England, Researcher, 1939-45; Cambridge Univ., England, Professor and Administrator, 1945-. OTHER AWARDS: Hughes Medal, Royal Society, 1954; Gold Medal, Royal Astronomical Society, 1964; Henry Draper Medal, National Academy of Sciences, U.S.A., 1965; Knighthood, 1966; Royal Medal, Royal Society, 1973.

Selected Publications: "The New Cambridge Radio Telescope." *Nature* 194 (May 12, 1962): 517-18. "High-Resolution Observations of the Radio Sources in Cygnus and Cassiopeia." *Nature* 205 (March 27, 1965): 1259-62 (with B. Elsmore and Ann C. Neville). "Observations of Radio Galaxies with the One-Mile Telescope at Cambridge." *Nature* 207 (September 4, 1965): 1024-27 (with B. Elsmore and Ann C. Neville). "The 5-km Radio Telescope at Cambridge." *Nature* 239 (October 20, 1972): 435-38.

For More Information See: *Current Biography Yearbook.* New York: H.W. Wilson, 1973, 368-71. *New York Times Biographical Edition* (October 16, 1974): 1491.

Commentary: Martin Ryle shared the Nobel Prize for his creative research in the area of radio astrophysics. Ryle developed the aperture synthesis technique, which combines radiotelescopes with computers to see deeply into space. Using the techniques and instrumentation he developed, Ryle was able to map the skies with a thoroughness previously not possible. His research elucidated the characteristics of radio stars, analyzed the pulsars and eliminated "little green men" conjectures about them, and explained the origin of radio scintillation. His studies have also strengthened the belief in the "big bang" theory of the origination of the universe. (D.H.)

1975

Bohr, Aage Niels   517

PRIZE: Physics, 1975. BORN: June 19, 1922; Copenhagen, Denmark. PARENTS: Father, Niels Bohr; Mother, Margrethe Norlund Bohr. NATIONALITY: Danish. RELIGION: Jewish. EDUCATION: Univ. of Copenhagen, Denmark, Ph.D., 1954. SPOUSE: Marietta Bettina Soffer, married (no date found), died 1978; Bente Meyer Scharff, married 1981. CHILDREN: 2 sons; 1 daughter. CAREER: Department of Scientific and Industrial Research, London, England, Researcher, 1943-45; Univ. of Copenhagen, Denmark, Professor and Administrator, 1946-. OTHER AWARDS: Daniel Heinemann Prize, American Physical Society and American Institute for Physics, 1960; Pope Pius XI Medal, 1963; Atoms for Peace Award, Ford Motor Company Fund, 1969; H.C. Örsted Medal, 1970; Rutherford Medal and Prize, Institute of Physics, London, 1972; John Price Wetherill Medal, Franklin Institute, PA, 1974; Ole Römer Medal, 1976.

Selected Publications: "On the Quantization of Angular Momenta in Heavy Nuclei." *Physical Review* 81 (January 1, 1951): 134-38. "Nuclear Magnetic Moments and Atomic Hyperfine Structure." *Physical Review* 81 (February 1, 1951): 331-35. *Rotational States of Atomic Nuclei.* Copenhagen: Munksgaard, 1954. *Collective and Individual-Particle Aspects of Nuclear Structure.* Copenhagen: Munksgaard, 1957 (with B. Mottelson). *Nuclear Structure.* 2 volumes. New York: W.A. Benjamin, 1969-75 (with B. Mottelson).

For More Information See: *Physics Today* 28 (December 1975): 69-71. *Science* 190 (November 28, 1975): 868-70.

Commentary: Aage Bohr shared the Nobel Prize for his contributions to the "discovery of the connection between collective motion and particle motion in the atomic nucleus and the development of the structure of the atomic nucleus based on this connection." Through their own research as well as through their influence on experimental studies pursued at nuclear laboratories throughout the world, Bohr and his colaureate, Ben Mottelson, were instrumental in developing a qualitative and quantitative understanding of the nonspherical (deformed) shape of atomic nuclei postulated in 1950 by their colaureate James Rainwater. Bohr and Mottelson identified the properties of the spheroidal nucleus and provided a clearer picture of nuclear structural dynamics. (J.C.H.)

Mottelson, Benjamin Roy   518

PRIZE: Physics, 1975. BORN: July 9, 1926; Chicago, IL. PARENTS: Father, Goodman Mottelson; Mother, Georgia Blum Mottelson. NATIONALITY: American; later Danish citizen. RELIGION: Jewish. EDUCATION: Purdue Univ., IN, B.S., 1947; Harvard Univ., MA, M.A., 1948; Harvard Univ., MA, Ph.D., 1950. SPOUSE: Nancy Jane Reno, married May 31, 1948. CHILDREN: 2 sons; 1 daughter. CAREER: Institute for Theoretical Physics, Denmark, Researcher, 1950-51; U.S. Atomic Energy Commission, Researcher, 1951-53; CERN, Theoretical Study Group, Researcher, 1953-56; Nordic Institute for Theoretical Atomic Physics, Denmark, Director, 1957-.

Selected Publications: *Collective and Individual-Particle Aspects of Nuclear Structure.* Copenhagen: Munksgaard, 1957 (with A. Bohr). *Lectures on Selected Top-*

ics in Nuclear Structure. Bombay: Tata Institute of Fundamental Research, 1964. *Nuclear Structure.* 2 volumes. New York: W. A. Benjamin, 1969-75 (with A. Bohr). "Elementary Modes of Excitation in the Nucleus." *Reviews of Modern Physics* 48 (July 1976): 375-83.

For More Information See: Asimov's Biographical Encyclopedia of Science and Technology. Garden City, NY: Doubleday, 1982, 883. *Kraks Blaa Bog 1984.* Copenhagen: Krak, 1985, 754. *Physics Today* 28 (December 1975): 69, 71-72.

Commentary: Ben Mottelson was awarded the Nobel Prize for "the discovery of the connection between collective motion and particle motion in atomic nuclei and the development of the theory of the structure of the atomic nucleus based on this connection." Mottelson and Bohr, paying close attention to new experimental results, found the means to combine two previously discrete models of nuclear structure—the liquid-drop and the nuclear shell models—into one unified theory. (J.W.)

Rainwater, Leo James   519

PRIZE: Physics, 1975. BORN: December 9, 1917; Council, ID. DIED: May 31, 1986; Yonkers, NY. PARENTS: Father, Leo J. Rainwater; Mother, Edna E. Teague Rainwater. NATIONALITY: American. RELIGION: Presbyterian. EDUCATION: California Institute of Technology, B.S., 1939; Columbia Univ., NY, M.A., 1941; Columbia Univ., NY, Ph.D., 1946. SPOUSE: Emma Louise Smith, married March 7, 1942. CHILDREN: James Carlton, son; Robert Stephen, son; William George, son; Elizabeth, daughter. CAREER: Columbia Univ., NY, Professor, 1946-. OTHER AWARDS: Ernest Orlando Lawrence Memorial Award, Atomic Energy Commission, 1963.

Selected Publications: "Nuclear Energy Level Argument for a Spheroidal Nuclear Model." *Physical Review* 79 (August 10, 1950): 432-34. "Mu-Meson Physics." *Annual Review of Nuclear Science* 7 (1957): 1-30. "Increasing Synchrocyclotron Currents and the Space Charge Limit." *AD 636708* (1965): 1-8.

For More Information See: *Biographical Encyclopedia of Scientists.* New York: Facts on File, 1981, 662-63. *Science* 190 (November 28, 1975): 868-70.

Commentary: James Rainwater and his colaureates, Aage Bohr and Ben Mottelson, shared the Nobel Prize "for their discovery of the connection between collective motion and particle motion in the atomic nucleus and the development of the structure of the atomic nucleus based on this connection." Rainwater postulated the nonspherical (deformed) shape of atomic nuclei, for which Bohr and Mottelson developed a qualitative and quantitative understanding. The work of the three laureates resolved the apparent conflict between the prevailing liquid drop and nuclear shell models of nuclear structure, and provided the base for an understanding of the low-lying states of all nuclei. (J.C.H.)

1976

Richter, Burton   520

PRIZE: Physics, 1976. BORN: March 22, 1931; Brooklyn, NY. PARENTS: Father, Abraham Richter; Mother, Fanny Pollack Richter. NATIONALITY: American. RELI-

GION: Jewish. EDUCATION: Massachusetts Institute of Technology, B.S., 1952; Massachusetts Institute of Technology, Ph.D., 1956. SPOUSE: Laurose Becker, married July 1, 1960. CHILDREN: Elizabeth, daughter; Matthew, son. CAREER: Stanford Univ., CA, Professor, 1956-. OTHER AWARDS: Ernesto Orlando Lawrence Medal, 1975.

Selected Publications: "Low Mass Anomaly in Photoproduction of Pion Pairs." *Physical Review Letters* 9 (1962): 217-20. *Instabilities in Stored Particle Beams.* Springfield, VA: CFSTI, 1965 (with M. Sands and A. M. Sessler). "High-energy Photoproduction." *U.S. Atomic Energy Commission CONF-670923* (1967): 309-36. "Two-body Photoproduction." *U.S. Atomic Energy Commission SLAC-PUB-501* (1968): 1-57. "Plenary Report on e(+)e(-) Hadrons." *Proceedings of the International Conference on High Energy Physics* 17th (1974): 20-35.

For More Information See: *Biographical Encyclopedia of Scientists.* New York: Facts of File, 1981, 678-79. *Current Biography Yearbook.* New York: H. W. Wilson, 1977, 359-62.

Commentary: Burton Richter's award was for the discovery of a subatomic particle three times heavier than the proton with a life span 10,000 times longer than could be predicted by prior discoveries. These characteristics led to drastic revisions in the quark theories. Richter calls his particle "psi" because "it's the only unassigned Greek letter in particle physics"; colaureate Samuel Ting refers to the particle as "J." The scientific community has not yet resolved the nomenclature. J/psi has been called "the greatest discovery ever in the field of particle physics." The properties of the particle are consistent with a fourth type of quark and support the concept of charm. (R.P.)

Ting, Samuel Chao Chung   521

PRIZE: Physics, 1976. BORN: January 27, 1936; Ann Arbor, MI. PARENTS: Father, K.H. Ting; Mother, T.S. Wang Ting. NATIONALITY: American. RELIGION: Christian. EDUCATION: Univ. of Michigan, B.S.E., 1959; Univ. of Michigan, M.S., 1960; Univ. of Michigan, Ph.D., 1962. SPOUSE: Kay Louise Kuhne, married 1960. CHILDREN: Jeanne Min, daughter; Amy Min, daughter. CAREER: Columbia Univ., NY, Professor, 1964-69; Massachusetts Institute of Technology, Professor, 1969-. OTHER AWARDS: Ernest Orlando Lawrence Award, 1976; A.E. Eringen Medal, 1977.

Selected Publications: "Timelike Momenta in Quantum Electrodynamics." *Physical Review* 145 (1966): 1018-22 (with Stanley J. Brodsky). "Leptonic Decays of Vector Mesons." *United States Atomic Energy Commission CONF-670923* (1967): 452-83. "Electrodynamics at Small Distances, Leptonic Decays of Vector Mesons, and Photoproduction of Vector Mesons." *Int. Conf. High-Energy Phys., Proc. 14th* (1968): 43-71. "Summary of Photoproduction and Leptonic Decays of Vector Mesons." *United States Atomic Energy Commission DESY-68/29* (1968): 1-18. *The Search for Charm, Beauty and Truth at High Energies.* New York: Plenum Press, 1984 (with G. Bellini).

For More Information See: *Physics Today* 29 (December 1976): 17+. *Science* 194 (November 19, 1976): 825-26+.

Commentary: Samuel Ting's award was for the discovery of a subatomic particle three times heavier than the proton with a life span 10,000 times longer than could be predicted by prior discoveries. Ting called the particle "J" after the physical symbol for angular momentum; his colaureate Burton Richter referred to the particle as "psi." The discovery of the particle forced revisions in the existent theory of quarks to accommodate the previously predicted charmed quark. Since the discovery, a family of such particles has been found. (R.P.)

1977

Anderson, Philip Warren 522
PRIZE: Physics, 1977. BORN: December 13, 1923; Indianapolis, IN. PARENTS: Father, Harry W. Anderson; Mother, Elsie Osborne Anderson. NATIONALITY: American. RELIGION: Most probably Christian. EDUCATION: Harvard Univ., MA, B.S., 1943; Harvard Univ., MA, M.A., 1947; Harvard Univ., MA, Ph.D., 1949. SPOUSE: Joyce Gothwaite, married July 31, 1947. CHILDREN: Susan Osborne, daughter. CAREER: Bell Telephone Laboratories, NJ, Researcher, 1949-. OTHER AWARDS: Oliver E. Buckley Prize, 1964.

Selected Publications: "The Limits of Validity of the Van Vleck-Weisskopf Line Shape Formula." *Physical Review* 76 (1949): 471. "An Approximate Quantum Theory of the Antiferromagnetic Ground State." *Physical Review* 86 (1952): 694-701. "New Method in the Theory of Superconductivity." *Physical Review* 110 (1958): 985-86. "New Approach to the Theory of Superexchange Interactions." *Physical Review* 115 (1959): 2-13. "Generalized B.C.S. States and Aligned Orbital Angular Momentum in the Proposed Low-Temperature Phase of Liquid Helium-3." *Physica* 26 (1960): 5137-42. *Concepts in Solids.* New York: W.A. Benjamin, 1963.

For More Information See: *Biographical Encyclopedia of Scientists.* New York: Facts on File, 1981, 18-19. *Physics Today* 30 (December 1977): 77-78.

Commentary: Philip Anderson shared the Nobel Prize with John Van Vleck and Nevill Mott "for their fundamental theoretical investigation of the electronic structure of magnetic and disordered systems." Anderson was responsible for a number of important contributions: the pressure broadening of spectral lines; the theory of superexchange; further explanations of antiferromagnetics, ferroelectrics, and superconductors; the model of metals with impurity atoms (the Anderson model); the treatment of impurity migration in crystals (the Anderson localization); discussions of superconductivity and superfluidity; Helium-3 superfluid state treatment; and work on low-temperature properties of glass. (C.T.)

Mott, Nevill Francis, Sir 523
PRIZE: Physics, 1977. BORN: September 30, 1905; Leeds, England. PARENTS: Father, Charles Francis Mott; Mother, Lilian Mary Reynolds Mott. NATIONALITY: British. RELIGION: Anglican. EDUCATION: Cambridge Univ., England, BA, 1927; Cambridge Univ., England, MA, 1930. SPOUSE: Ruth Horder, married March 21, 1930. CHILDREN: Elizabeth, daughter; Alice, daughter. CAREER: Cambridge Univ., England, Professor, 1930-33; Univ. of Bristol, England, Professor, 1933-54; Cambridge Univ., England, Professor, 1954-

71. OTHER AWARDS: Hughes Medal, 1941; Royal Medal, 1953; Knighthood, 1962; Copley Medal, 1972; Ordre Nationale Mérite, 1977.

Selected Publications: *The Theory of Atomic Collisions.* Oxford: Clarendon Press, 1933 (with H.S.W. Massey). *The Theory of Properties of Metals and Alloys.* New York: Dover, 1936 (with H. Jones). *Electronic Processes in Ionic Crystals.* Oxford: Clarendon Press, 1948 (with R. W. Gurney).

For More Information See: *A Life in Science.* Philadelphia, PA: Taylor and Francis, 1986. *Physics Today* 30 (December 8, 1977): 77-78. *Science* 198 (November 18, 1977): 713-15.

Commentary: The Nobel Prize was awarded to Nevill Mott, along with his two colaureates, for their "fundamental theoretical investigations of the electronic structure of magnetic and disordered systems." Mott began his career working on the quantum theory of atomic collisions and scattering. His fields of interest were multiple and included significant work on models of the solid state, electronic processes in metal-insulator transitions, the photographic process in relation to surface and defect properties, crystal strength, liquid metals, semiconductors, and glassy semiconductors. (C.T.)

Van Vleck, John Hasbrouck 524
PRIZE: Physics, 1977. BORN: March 13, 1899; Middletown, CT. DIED: October 27, 1980; Cambridge, MA. PARENTS: Father, Edward Burr Van Vleck; Mother, Hester Lawrence Raymond Van Vleck. NATIONALITY: American. RELIGION: Christian. EDUCATION: Univ. of Wisconsin, B.S., 1920; Harvard Univ., MA, M.A., 1921; Harvard Univ., MA, Ph.D., 1922. SPOUSE: Abigail June Pearson, married June 10, 1927. CHILDREN: None. CAREER: Harvard Univ., MA, Professor, 1922-23; Univ. of Minnesota, Professor, 1923-28; Univ. of Wisconsin, Professor, 1928-34; Harvard Univ., MA, Professor, 1934-69. OTHER AWARDS: Chevalier Legion of Honor, France; Albert A. Michelson Award, Case Institute of Technology, 1963; Irving Langmuir Award, General Electric Foundation, 1965; National Medal of Science, 1966; Distinguished Service Award, U. of Wisconsin Alumni Association, 1967; Cresson Medal, Franklin Institute, PA, 1971; Lorentz Medal, Netherlands Academy, 1974.

Selected Publications: "Quantum Theory of the Specific Heat of Hydrogen. I. Relation to the New Mechanics, Band Spectra and Chemical Constants." *Physical Review* 28 (1926): 980-1021. "Dielectric Constants and Magnetic Susceptibilities in the New Quantum Mechanics. Part I. A General Proof of the Langevin-Debye Formula." *Physical Review* 29 (1927): 727-44. "The New Quantum Mechanics." *Chemical Reviews* 5 (1928): 467-507. *The Theory of Electric and Magnetic Susceptibilities.* New York: Oxford U. Press, 1932. "The Theory of Antiferromagnetism." *Journal of Chemical Physics* 9 (1941): 85-90.

For More Information See: *Physics Today* 30 (December 8, 1977): 77-78. *Science* 198 (November 18, 1977): 713-15.

Commentary: John Van Vleck shared the Nobel Prize for "fundamental theoretical investigations of the electronic structure of magnetic and disordered systems." Van Vleck was specifically cited for his research on electron correlation, which was important in the development of the laser. His early work focused on magnetism, both from the standpoint of classical quantum theory and the new wave mechanics. Van Vleck developed the concept of temperature-independent magnetic susceptibility. He also contributed significantly in the areas of molecular structure and bonding, the properties of an atom or ion in a crystal, and radar and radioastronomy. (C.T.)

1978

Kapitsa, Pyotr Leonidovich   525

PRIZE: Physics, 1978. BORN: July 8, 1894; Kronstadt, Russia. DIED: April 8, 1984; Moscow, USSR. PARENTS: Father, Leonid Kapitsa; Mother, Olga Stebnitsckiy Kapitsa. NATIONALITY: Russian. RELIGION: Jewish. EDUCATION: Petrograd Polytechnical Institute, USSR, baccalaureate, 1919; Cambridge Univ., England, Ph.D., 1926. SPOUSE: Nadezhda Tschernosvitova, married 1916, died 1920; Anna Alekseyevna Krylova, married 1926. CHILDREN: Andrei, son; Sergei, son. CAREER: Petrograd Polytechnical Institute, USSR, Professor, 1918-21; Cambridge Univ., England, Researcher and Professor, 1921-35; USSR Academy of Sciences, Institute for Physical Problems, Director, 1935-46, 1955-84; Physiotechnical Institute, Moscow, USSR, Professor, 1947-84. OTHER AWARDS: Stalin Prize, 1941, 1943; Faraday Medal, Council of Electrical Engineers of England, 1942; Five Orders of Lenin, 1943; Order of the Red Banner of Labor; Franklin Medal, 1944.

Selected Publications: *Collected Papers.* Oxford: Oxford U. Press, 1946-47. *Elektronika Bol shikh Moshchnostei.* Moscow: n.p., 1962. *Teoriia, Eksperiment, Praktika (Theory, Experiment, Practice).* Moscow: n.p., 1966.

For More Information See: *Current Biography Yearbook.* New York: H.W. Wilson, 1955, 317-18. *Science* 202 (December 1, 1978): 960-62.

Commentary: The Nobel Prize was awarded to Pyotr Kapitsa for his work in low temperature physics, including studies of electrical properties of matter and the liquefaction of gases. Kapitsa invented a new method for liquefying gases and studied the unusual properties of flow and conduction of Helium II. His invention of a simple turbine device to substitute oxygen for air in blast furnaces revolutionized the Soviet steel industry. He was also known for his research with ball lightning, standing waves, atomic energy, and space research. Kapitsa's career in the Soviet Union remains shrouded in mystery since his detention there in 1934, when he was director of the Cavendish Laboratory in England. (T.B.)

Penzias, Arno Allan   526

PRIZE: Physics, 1978. BORN: April 26, 1923; Munich, Germany. PARENTS: Father, Karl Penzias; Mother, Justine Inge Eisenreich Penzias. NATIONALITY: German; later American citizen. RELIGION: Jewish. EDUCATION: City College of New York, B.S., 1954; Columbia Univ., NY, M.A., 1958; Columbia Univ., NY, Ph.D., 1962. SPOUSE: Anne Pearl Barras, married November 25, 1954. CHILDREN: David Simon, son; Mindy Gail, daughter; Laurie Ruth, daughter. CAREER: Bell Laboratories, NJ, Researcher and Administrator, 1961-. OTHER AWARDS: Henry Draper Medal, 1977; Herschel Medal, 1977.

Selected Publications: "Interstellar Carbon Monoxide, Carbon-13 Monoxide, and Carbon Monoxide-Oxygen-18." *Astrophysics Journal* 165 Part I (1971): L63 (with Keith B. Jefferts and Robert W. Wilson). "Interstellar Carbon Monosulfide." *Astrophysics Journal* 168 Part 2 (1971): L53-L58 (with others). "Interstellar C N Excitation at 2.64 mm." *Physics Review Letters* 28 (1972): 772-75 (with Keith B. Jefferts and Robert W. Wilson). "Millimeter-Wavelength Radio-Astronomy Techniques." *Annu. Rev. Astron. Astrophys* 11 (1973): 51-72 (with C.A. Burrus).

For More Information See: *Current Biography Yearbook.* New York: H.W. Wilson, 1985, 328-31. *New York Times* (October 18, 1978): 5.

Commentary: Arno Penzias and his colleague, Robert W. Wilson, were awarded the Nobel Prize for their detection of microwave background radiation, which supported the theory that the universe was created by a "big bang" that took place some 20 billion years ago, as opposed to the "Steady State" theory which held that the universe continually expanded and collapsed upon itself. The findings indicated that the universe is an "open" system continually expanding from the initial "bang" until it loses momentum and becomes still and lifeless. Penzias and Wilson continued their research collaboration and discovered large amounts of the fossil element deuterium in the Milky Way galaxy. The team's discoveries have stimulated extensive further research. (B.M.)

Wilson, Robert Woodrow   527

PRIZE: Physics, 1978. BORN: January 10, 1936; Houston, TX. PARENTS: Father, Ralph Woodrow Wilson; Mother, Fannie May Willis Wilson. NATIONALITY: American. RELIGION: Most probably Christian. EDUCATION: Rice Univ., Texas, B.A., 1957; California Institute of Technology, Ph.D., 1962. SPOUSE: Elizabeth Rhoads Sawin, married September 4, 1958. CHILDREN: Philip Garrett, son; Suzanne Katherine, daughter; Randal Woodrow, son. CAREER: Owens Laboratories, United States, 1962-63; Bell Laboratories, NJ, 1963-. OTHER AWARDS: Henry Draper Medal, Royal Astronomy Society, 1977; Herschel Medal, National Academy of Sciences, 1977.

Selected Publications: "Isotropy of Cosmic Background Radiation at 4080 Megahertz." *Science* 156 (1967): 1100-01 (with A.A. Penzias). "Measurement of the Flux Density of CAS A at 4080 Ma/s." *Astrophysical Journal* 142 (1965): 1149-56 (with A.A. Penzias). "Interstellar CN Excitation at 2.64 mm." *Physics Review Letters* 28 (1972): 772-75 (with A.A. Penzias and K.B. Jefferts).

For More Information See: "The 1978 Nobel Prize in Physics." *Science* 205 (December 1, 1978): 962-65. "Nobel Prizes: Research with an Impact." *Science News* 114 (October 14, 1978): 276.

Commentary: Robert Wilson's Nobel Prize was for work that "made it possible to obtain information about cosmic processes that took place a very long time ago, at the time of the creation of the universe." Wilson's studies of radio noise in the sky led to the observation of a ubiquitous background radiation which fit the spectrum of a blackbody at a temperature about 3 degrees K. The discovery lent credence to the "big bang" theory of the beginning of the universe, which would predict such a background. (L.M.)

1979

Glashow, Sheldon 528

PRIZE: Physics, 1979. BORN: December 5, 1932; New York, NY. PARENTS: Father, Lewis Glashow; Mother, Bella Rubin Glashow. NATIONALITY: American. RELIGION: Jewish. EDUCATION: Cornell Univ., NY, A.B., 1954; Harvard Univ., MA, M.A., 1955; Harvard Univ., MA, Ph.D., 1958. SPOUSE: Joan Shirley Alexander, married 1972. CHILDREN: Jason David, son; Jordan, son; Brian Lewis, son; Rebecca Lee, daughter. CAREER: Institute of Theoretical Physics, Copenhagen, Denmark, Researcher, 1958-60; California Institute of Technology, Researcher, 1960-61; Stanford Univ., CA, Professor, 1961-62; Univ. of California, Berkeley, Professor, 1962-66; Harvard Univ., MA, Professor, 1966-83; Texas A & M, Professor, 1983-. OTHER AWARDS: J.R. Oppenheimer Memorial Prize, 1977; George Ledlie Prize, 1978; Castiglione di Silica Prize, 1983.

Selected Publications: "Symmetries of Strong Interactions." In *Proceedings of the International School of Physics "Enrico Fermi" Course XXXIII, Varenna, 6th-18th July 1964*, pp.189-225. New York: Academic Press, 1966. "Divergencies of Massive Yang-Mills Theories: Higher Groups." *Physical Review D: Particles and Fields* 4 (September 15, 1971): 1918-19 (with J. Iiopoulos). "Toward a Unified Theory: Threads in a Tapestry." *Science* 210 (1980): 1319-23.

For More Information See: *Physics Today* 32 (December 1979): 17-19. *Science* 206 (December 14, 1979): 1290-92.

Commentary: Sheldon Glashow shared the Nobel Prize with Abdus Salam and Steven Weinberg "for their contribution to the theory of the unified weak and electromagnetic interaction between elementary particles, including, *inter alia,* the prediction of the weak neutral current." Glashow extended the Weinberg-Salam theory (which introduced the unity of the electromagnetic interaction and the weak interaction—two of the four fundamental forces) to several elementary particles (among them the baryons and mesons) by defining a new characteristic which he called charm. The concept of charm has been used since in work on the quark theory and in explanations of properties of the J/psi particle. (M.N.)

Salam, Abdus 529

PRIZE: Physics, 1979. BORN: January 29, 1926; Jhang, Pakistan. PARENTS: Father, Ch. Muhammed Hussain; Mother, Hajira Hussain. NATIONALITY: Pakistani; later British resident. RELIGION: Islamic. EDUCATION: Univ. of Punjab, Pakistan, M.A., 1946; Cambridge Univ., England, B.A., 1948; Cambridge Univ., England, Ph.D., 1952; Cambridge Univ., England, D.Sc., 1957. SPOUSE: No record found. CHILDREN: 4 daughters; 2 sons. CAREER: Institute for Advanced Study, Princeton, NJ, Researcher, 1951; Univ. of Punjab, Lahore, Pakistan, Professor, 1951-54; Cambridge Univ., England, Professor, 1954-56; Imperial College, London, England, Professor, 1957-. OTHER AWARDS: Hopkins Prize, Cambridge U., England, 1957; Adams Prize, 1958; Pride of Performance Award, Pakistan, 1959; Maxwell Medal, Physical Society, London, England, 1961; Hughes Medal, 1964; Atoms for Peace Award, 1968; Guthrie Medal and Prize, 1976; Royal Medal, Royal Society, 1978; Matteuci Medal, Academia Nazionale di Lincei, Rome, Italy, 1978; John Tate Medal, American Institute of Physics, 1978.

Selected Publications: "Gauge Unification of Fundamental Forces." *Proc.-Eur. Conf. Part. Phys. (9th)* 2 (1977): 1187-1207. "Gauge Unification of Fundamental Forces." *Proc. Int. Conf. Winter Sch. Front. Theor. Phys.* (1977): 29-35. "Gauge Unification of the Four Fundamental Forces." *Phys. Contemp. Needs* 2 (1978): 419-56. "The Electroweak Force, Grand Unification and Superunification." *Phys. Scr.* 20 (1979): 227-34.

For More Information See: *Physics Today* 32 (December 1979): 17-19. *Science* 206 (December 14, 1979): 1290-92.

Commentary: Abdus Salam and his two colaureates, Sheldon Glashow and Steven Weinberg, shared the Nobel Prize "for their contributions to the theory of the unified weak and electromagnetic interaction between elementary particles, including *inter alia* the prediction of the weak neutral current." The Weinberg-Salam theory treated the unification of two of the four fundamental forces (the electromagnetic interaction and the weak interaction) for certain particles and was a major step toward an overall unified field theory. The theory also predicted neutral currents (elementary particle interactions with no exchange of electric charge). Salam continues his work on theories describing the behavior and properties of elementary particles. (L.I.S.)

Weinberg, Steven 530

PRIZE: Physics, 1979. BORN: May 3, 1933; New York, NY. PARENTS: Father, Fred Weinberg; Mother, Eva Israel Weinberg. NATIONALITY: American. RELIGION: Jewish. EDUCATION: Cornell Univ., NY, A.B., 1954; Princeton Univ., NJ, Ph.D., 1957. SPOUSE: Louise Goldwasser, married 1954. CHILDREN: 1 daughter. CAREER: Columbia Univ., NY, Professor, 1957-59; Univ. of California, Berkeley, Professor, 1959-69; Massachusetts Institute of Technology, Professor, 1969-73; Harvard Univ., MA, Professor, 1973-83; Univ. of Texas, Austin, Professor, 1983-. OTHER AWARDS: J.R. Oppenheimer Prize, 1973; Dannie Heineman Mathematical Physics Prize, 1977; American Institute of Physics—U.S. Steel Foundation Science Writing Award, 1977; Elliot Cresson Medal, Franklin Institute, PA, 1979.

Selected Publications: *Gravitation and Cosmology: Principles and Applications of the General Theory of Relativity.* New York: Wiley, 1972. "Recent Progress in Gauge Theories of the Weak, Electromagnetic and Strong Interactions." *Reviews of Modern Physics* 46 (1974): 255-77. *The First Three Minutes: A Modern View of the Origin of the Universe.* New York: Basic Books, 1977. "Limits of Massless Particles." *Physics Letters. B* 96 (1980): 59-62. "Charges from Extra Dimensions." *Physics Letters. B* 125 (1983): 265-69. *The Discovery of Subatomic Particles.* New York: Scientific American Library, 1983.

For More Information See: *Physics Today* 32 (December 1979): 17-19. *Science* 206 (December 14, 1979): 1290-92.

Commentary: Steven Weinberg and his two colaureates, Abdus Salam and Sheldon Glashow, shared the Nobel Prize "for their contributions to the theory of the unified weak and electromagnetic interaction between elementary particles, including, *inter alia,* the prediction of the weak neutral current." The

Weinberg-Salam theory dealt with the unification of two of the four fundamental forces (the electromagnetic interaction and the weak interaction) for certain particles and was a significant step toward the overall unified field theory. The theory predicted neutral currents (elementary particle interactions with no exchange of electric charge). Weinberg has also written on the problems of astrophysics and cosmology. (M.N.)

1980

Cronin, James Watson   531

PRIZE: Physics, 1980. BORN: September 25, 1931; Chicago, IL. PARENTS: Father, James Farley Cronin; Mother, Dorothy Watson Cronin. NATIONALITY: American. RELIGION: Most probably Christian. EDUCATION: Southern Methodist Univ., TX, B.S., 1951; Univ. of Chicago, IL, Ph.D., 1955. SPOUSE: Annette Martin, married 1954. CHILDREN: Dan, son; Emily, daughter; Kathryn, daughter. CAREER: Brookhaven National Laboratory, Researcher, 1955-58; Princeton Univ., NJ, Professor, 1958-71; Univ. of Chicago, IL, Professor, 1971-. OTHER AWARDS: Research Corporation Award, 1968; Ernest Orlando Lawrence Award, 1977; John Price Wetherill Medal, Franklin Institute, PA, 1975.

Selected Publications: "Experimental Status of CP Violation." *AEC Accession Number 19428, Report Number ANL-7130* (1965): 17-28. "Coupling Constant Relations for 1 (+/−) and Induced 0 (+/−) Mesons." *Nuovo Cimento* 41A (1966): 380-85 (with Y. Nambu). "Experimental Developments in Weak Interactions." *Proc. Int. Conf. Particles Fields* (1967): 3-20. "Weak Interactions and CP Violation-Experimental." *Int. Conf. High-Energy Phys., Proc., 14th* (1968): 281-303.

For More Information See: *New York Times Biographical Service* (October 1980): 1374. *Science* 210 (November 7, 1980): 619-21.

Commentary: James Cronin and Val Fitch shared the Nobel Prize for their demonstration that the K-mesons resulting from proton collisions did not obey the absolute principle of symmetry. Specifically, they found that the rates of switching of K-mesons from particle to antiparticle and from antiparticle to particle were different, which represented deviation from the theory of absolute symmetry. Cronin continued his work in the area of the nature and characteristics of elementary particles. (J.N.B.)

Fitch, Val Logsdon   532

PRIZE: Physics, 1980. BORN: March 10, 1923; Merriman, NE. PARENTS: Father, Fred B. Fitch; Mother, Frances M. Logsdon Fitch. NATIONALITY: American. RELIGION: Most probably Christian. EDUCATION: McGill Univ., Canada, B.S., 1948; Columbia Univ., NY, Ph.D., 1954. SPOUSE: Elsie Cunningham, married 1949, died 1974; Daisy Harper, married 1976. CHILDREN: 2 sons. CAREER: Columbia Univ., NY, Professor, 1953-54; Princeton Univ., NJ, Professor, 1954-. OTHER AWARDS: Research Corporation Award, 1968; Ernest Orlando Lawrence Award, 1968; John Wetherill Medal, Franklin Institute, PA, 1976.

Selected Publications: "Mass Difference of Neutral K Meson." *Nuovo Cimento* 22 (1961): 1160-70 (with P.A. Piroue and R.B. Perkins). "The K(+) Decay Probability." *Physical Review* 140B (1965): 1088-91 (with C.A. Quarles). "Experiments on Time-Reversal In-

variance." *Nucl. Particle Phys. Annu* 1 (1967): 117-20. "Charge Assymetries." *Comments Nucl. Particle Phys* 2 (1968): 6-9.

For More Information See: *Physics Today* 33 (December 1980): 17-19. *Science* 210 (November 7, 1980): 619-21.

Commentary: Val Fitch shared the Nobel Prize with James Cronin for their discovery that the elementary particles K-mesons, resulting from proton collisions, did not obey the absolute principle of symmetry. Specifically, they found that the rates of switching of K-mesons from particle to antiparticle and from antiparticle to particle were different. This represented a deviation from the theory of absolute symmetry. Fitch continued to work in the area of the nature and characteristics of elementary particles. (J.N.B.)

1981

Bloembergen, Nicolaas   533

PRIZE: Physics, 1981. BORN: March 11, 1920; Dordrecht, Netherlands. PARENTS: Father, Auke Bloembergen; Mother, Sophia M. Quint Bloembergen. NATIONALITY: Dutch; later American citizen. RELIGION: Dutch Mennonite. EDUCATION: Univ. of Utrecht, Netherlands, B.A., 1941; Univ. of Utrecht, Netherlands, M.A., 1943; Leiden Univ., Netherlands, Ph.D., 1948. SPOUSE: Huberta D. Brink, married June 26, 1950. CHILDREN: Antonia, daughter; Juliana, daughter; Brink, son. CAREER: Harvard Univ., MA, Professor, 1949-80. OTHER AWARDS: Guggenheim Fellow, 1957; Buckley Prize, American Physical Society, 1958; Morris Liebman Award, IEEE, 1959; Ballantine Medal, Franklin Institute, PA, 1961; Half Moon Trophy, Netherlands Club, NY, 1972; National Medal of Science, 1975; Lorentz Medal, Royal Dutch Academy, 1978; Frederic Ives Medal, Optical Society of America, 1979; von Humboldt Senior Scientist Award, Munich, Germany, 1980; Medal of Honor, IEEE, 1983; Dirac Medal, U. of New South Wales, Australia, 1983.

Selected Publications: *Nuclear Magnetic Relaxation.* The Hague: M. Nijhoff, 1948. "Nuclear Magnetic Relaxation in Semiconductors." *Physica* 20 (1954): 1130-33. "Proposal for a New-Type Solid-State Maser." *Physical Review* 104 (1956): 324-27. "The Zero-Field Solid-State Maser as a Possible Time Standard." *Quantum Electronics Symposium, High View, New York* (1959): 160-66. *Nonlinear Optics.* Reading, MA: W.A. Benjamin, 1965.

For More Information See: *Biographical Encyclopedia of Scientists.* New York: Facts on File, 1981, 83. *Science* 214 (November 4, 1981): 629-33.

Commentary: Nicolaas Bloembergen shared the Nobel Prize with Arthur Schawlow "for their contribution to the development of laser spectroscopy," the use of laser beams as analytical tools. A number of Bloembergen's major contributions are in the field of nonlinear optics (phenomena that occur when a laser beam is intensive enough to make the target resonate, revealing the spectral properties of entire molecules). He also did pioneering work in the development of the maser. (C.M.)

Schawlow, Arthur Leonard   534

PRIZE: Physics, 1981. BORN: May 5, 1921; Mt. Vernon, NY. PARENTS: Father, Arthur Schawlow; Mother,

Helen Mason Schawlow. NATIONALITY: American. RELIGION: Congregationalist. EDUCATION: Univ. of Toronto, Canada, B.A., 1941; Univ. of Toronto, Canada, M.A., 1942; Univ. of Toronto, Canada, Ph.D., 1949. SPOUSE: Aurelia Keith Townes, married May 19, 1951. CHILDREN: Arthur Keith, son; Helen Aurelia, daughter; Edith Ellen, daughter. CAREER: Columbia Univ., NY, Researcher, 1949-51; Bell Telephone Laboratories, NJ, Researcher, 1951-61; Stanford Univ., CA, Professor, 1961-. OTHER AWARDS: Ballentine Medal, Franklin Institute, PA, 1962; Thomas Young Medal and Prize, Institution of Physics and the Physics Society of London, England, 1963; Liebmann Prize, IEEE, 1964; California Scientist of the Year, 1973; Frederick Ives Medal, Optical Society of America, 1976.

Selected Publications: "Significance of the Results of Microwave Spectroscopy for Nuclear Theory." *Annals of the New York Academy of Sciences* 55 (1952): 955-65. "Infrared and Optical Masers." *Physical Review* 112 (1958): 1940-49 (with Charles H. Townes). "Simultaneous Optical Maser Action in Two Ruby Satellite Lines." *Physical Review Letters* 6 (1961): 605-07 (with G.E. Devlin). *Microwave Spectroscopy.* New York: McGraw-Hill, 1955 (with Charles H. Townes).

For More Information See: *Physics Today* 34 (December 1981): 17-20. *Science* 214 (November 6, 1981): 629-33.

Commentary: Arthur Schawlow shared the Nobel Prize with Nicolaas Bloembergen "for their contribution to the development of laser spectroscopy," the use of laser beams as analytical tools. One of Schawlow's best known applications of laser spectroscopy has been in determining the energy that binds an electron to the proton of a hydrogen atom (the Rydberg constant). Schawlow worked with Charles Townes in maser development and then in extending the maser principle to the optical region. Schawlow's group has researched the applications of the laser in depth since, including the Rydberg constant determination and the observation of the Doppler-free optical spectra of hydrogen. (C.M.)

Siegbahn, Kai Manne Boerje 535

PRIZE: Physics, 1981. BORN: April 20, 1918; Lund, Sweden. PARENTS: Father, Karl Manne Georg Siegbahn; Mother, Karin Hoegbom Siegbahn. NATIONALITY: Swedish. RELIGION: Most probably Christian. EDUCATION: Univ. of Uppsala, Sweden, B.Sc., 1939; Univ. of Uppsala, Sweden, Licentiate of Philosophy, 1942; Univ. of Stockholm, Sweden, Ph.D., 1944. SPOUSE: Anna-Brita Rhedin, married 1944. CHILDREN: Per, son; Hans, son; Nils, son. CAREER: Nobel Institute of Physics, Sweden, Researcher, 1942-51; Univ. of Stockholm, Sweden, Professor, 1951-54; Uppsala Univ., Sweden, Professor, 1954-. OTHER AWARDS: Knight of the Order of the North Star; Bjoerken Prize, 1955, 1977; Celsius Medal, 1962; Sixten Heyman Award, 1971; Harrison Howe Award, 1973; Maurice F. Hasler Award, 1975; Charles Frederick Chandler Medal, 1976; Torbern Bergman Medal, 1979; Pittsburgh Award of Spectroscopy, 1982.

Selected Publications: "ß-Ray Spectroscopy in the Precision Range of 1:10^5." *Nuclear Physics* 1 (1956): 137-59 (with K. Edvarson). *ESCA—Atomic, Molecular and Solid State Structure Studied by Means of Electron Spectroscopy.* Nova Acta Regiae Societatis Scientarium Upsaliensis, Series IV, Volume 20. Uppsala, Sweden: Almquist and Wiksells Boktryckeri Ab, 1967 (with others). *ESCA—Applied to Free Molecules.* Amsterdam; London: North-Netherlands, 1969 (with others). "ESCA Applied to Liquids." *Journal of Electron Spectroscopy and Related Phenomena* 2 (1973): 319-25 (with Hans Siegbahn). "Electron Spectroscopy for Atoms, Molecules, and Condensed Matter." *Review of Modern Physics* 54 (July 1982): 709-28.

For More Information See: Hecht, J., and Brookfield, R. "Physicists Keep Nobel Prizes in the Family." *New Scientist* 92 (October 22, 1981): 224-25. Hollander, Jack M., and Shirley, David. "The 1981 Nobel Prize in Physics." *Science* 214 (November 6, 1981): 629-31. Sullivan, Walter. "Physics: To the Heart of the Matter." *New York Times* (20 October 1981): Sec. 3, p. 2.

Commentary: Kai Siegbahn received his Nobel Prize in recognition of "his contribution to the development of high-resolution spectroscopy" in developing the technique of ESCA—electron spectroscopy for chemical analysis. He subsequently led a team of researchers who refined the technique and extended its application to gases and liquids in addition to solids. His father, Manne, won the 1924 prize for physics for the development of high-resolution X-ray spectroscopy. (N.R.H.)

1982

Wilson, Kenneth Geddes 536

PRIZE: Physics, 1982. BORN: June 8, 1936; Waltham, MA. PARENTS: Father, Edgar Bright Wilson, Jr.; Mother, Emily Fisher Buckingham Wilson. NATIONALITY: American. RELIGION: Most probably Christian. EDUCATION: Harvard Univ., MA, B.A., 1956; California Institute of Technology, Ph.D., 1961. SPOUSE: Alison Brown, married October 1982. CHILDREN: None. CAREER: Harvard Univ., MA, Fellow, 1959-62; Ford Foundation Fellow, 1962-63; Cornell Univ., NY, Professor, 1963-. OTHER AWARDS: Heinemann Prize, 1973; Boltzmann Medal, 1975; Wolf Prize, 1980.

Selected Publications: "Renormalization Group and Critical Phenomena. I. Renormalization Group and the Kadanoff Scaling Picture." *Physics Reviews* B4 (November 1, 1971): 3174-83. "Renormalization Group and Critical Phenomena. II. Phase-Space Cell Analysis of Critical Behavior." *Physics Reviews* B4 (November 1, 1971): 3184-05.

For More Information See: *Current Biography Yearbook.* New York: H.W. Wilson, 1983, 446-48. *Physics Today* 35 (December 1982): 17-19.

Commentary: Kenneth Wilson received his award "for his theory for critical phenomena in connection with phase transitions." His further development of the "renormalization group" method, a mathematical technique which allows working with problems that contain mathematical infinities, was applied in investigating various critical phenomena in physical systems, moving toward a general theory. The method is widely applicable to many fields of research. (S.D.)

1983

Chandrasekhar, Subrahmanyan 537

PRIZE: Physics, 1983. BORN: October 19, 1910; Lahore, India. PARENTS: Father, Subrahmanyan Chandrasekhar;

Mother, Sita Balakrishnan Chandrasekhar. NATIONALITY: Indian; later American citizen. RELIGION: Hindu. EDUCATION: Madras Univ., India, M.A., 1930; Cambridge Univ., England, Ph.D., 1933. SPOUSE: Lalitha Doraiswamy, married September 1936. CHILDREN: None. CAREER: Cambridge Univ., England, Professor, 1933-37; Univ. of Chicago, Professor, 1937-. OTHER AWARDS: Bruce Medal, Astronomical Society of the Pacific, 1952; Gold Medal, Royal Astronomical Society, 1953; Rumford Medal, American Academy of Arts and Sciences, 1957; Royal Medal, Royal Society, 1962; National Science Medal, 1966.

Selected Publications: *An Introduction to the Study of Stellar Structure.* Chicago: U. of Chicago Press, 1939. *Principles of Stellar Dynamics.* Chicago: U. of Chicago Press, 1942. *Hydrodynamic and Hydromagnetic Stability.* London: Clarendon, 1961. *Ellipsoidal Figures of Equilibrium.* New Haven, CT: Yale U. Press, 1969. *The Mathematical Theory of Black Holes.* London: Clarendon, 1983.

For More Information See: *Current Biography Yearbook.* New York: H.W. Wilson, March 1986: 6-9. *New York Times Biographical Service* (October 1973): 1176-77. *Science* 222 (November 25, 1983): 883+.

Commentary: In honoring Subrahmanyan Chandrasekhar, the Academy noted his lifetime of scientific contributions, but cited in particular his study of the structure of white dwarfs as his "possibly best-known achievement." In that early work, Chandrasekhar noted that only smaller stars (with a mass less than 1.44 times that of the sun) would stabilize into white dwarfs. Larger stars would continually compress, due to the large gravitational forces and their effect on speeding up electrons toward the speed of light (relativistic degeneracy). This original work later would be used in the explanation of neutron stars and black holes. Chandrasekhar was also a major contributor in the areas of stellar dynamics, hydromagnetics, and radiative transfer. (B.S.S.)

Fowler, William Alfred   538

PRIZE: Physics, 1983. BORN: August 9, 1911; Pittsburgh, PA. PARENTS: Father, John McLeod Fowler; Mother, Jennie Summers Watson Fowler. NATIONALITY: American. RELIGION: Presbyterian. EDUCATION: Ohio State U., B.Eng., 1933; California Institute of Technology, Ph.D., 1936. SPOUSE: Ardiane Foy Olmstead, married August 24, 1940. CHILDREN: Mary Emily, daughter; Martha Summers Fowler Schoenemann, daughter. CAREER: California Institute of Technology, Professor and Administrator, 1936-. OTHER AWARDS: Naval Ordinance Development Award, United States Navy, 1945; Medal of Merit, 1948; Lamme Medal, Ohio State U., 1952; Medal, U. Liege, 1955; Scientist of the Year Award, CA, 1958; Barnard Medal, Columbia U., NY, 1965; Apollo Achievement Award, National Aeronautics and Space Administration, 1969; Bonner Prize, American Physics Society, 1970; Vettlesen Prize, 1973; National Medal of Science, 1974; Benjamin Franklin Fellow, Royal Society of the Arts; Eddington Medal, Royal Astronomical Society, 1978; Bruce Gold Medal, Astronomical Society of the Pacific, 1979.

Selected Publications: "Synthesis of the Elements in Stars." *Review of Modern Physics* 29 (1957): 547 (with E.M. Burbridge, G.R. Burbridge, and F. Hoyle). *Nucleosynthesis in Massive Stars and Supernovae.* Chi-

cago: U. of Chicago Press, 1964 (with F. Hoyle). *Nuclear Astrophysics.* Philadelphia, PA: American Philosophical Society, 1967.

For More Information See: *New Scientist* 100 (October 27, 1983): 254-55. *Science* 222 (November 25, 1983): 881-83.

Commentary: William Fowler's shared Nobel Prize was "for his theoretical and experimental studies of the nuclear reactions of importance in the formation of the chemical elements in the universe." Fowler's research led to what is now the generally accepted theory for synthesis of the heavier elements in stellar explosions or supernovas. Together, Fowler and his co-recipient, Subrahmanyan Chandrasekhar, have detailed the steps leading to the synthesis of the entire roster of substances from which stars, planets, and people are formed. (S.D.)

1984

Rubbia, Carlo   539

PRIZE: Physics, 1984. BORN: March 31, 1934; Georizia, Italy. PARENTS: Father, Silvio R. Rubbia; Mother, Bice Liceni Rubbia. NATIONALITY: Italian. RELIGION: Catholic. EDUCATION: Univ. of Pisa, Italy, Lauréa di Fisica, 1958. SPOUSE: Marrissa Romé, married 1957. CHILDREN: Laura, daughter, André, son. CAREER: European Organization of Nuclear Research, Geneva, Switzerland, Researcher, 1961-; concurrently associated with Harvard Univ., MA, Professor, 1970-.

Selected Publications: "The Physics of the Proton-Antiproton Collider." *Proc. HEP83, Int. Europhys. Conf. High Energy Phys.* (1983): 860-79. "The HPW Proton-Decay Experiment." *AIP Conf. Proc.* (1984): 77-88 (with others).

For More Information See: *Current Biography Yearbook.* New York: H.W. Wilson (June 1985), 26-29. *New York Times* (October 18, 1984): B13.

Commentary: Carlo Rubbia and Simon van der Meer shared the Nobel Prize for their contributions to the discovery of three subatomic particles that moved physics closer to the ultimate goal of a single theory for all natural forces. The team designed and built a colliding-beam accelerator which permitted observation of the then-hypothetical W(−), W(+), and Z particles. The work of the two laureates confirmed the unification of two of the four basic forces of nature—the electromagnetic force that relates electricity and magnetism and the weak force that controls phenomena like radioactivity. In 1984, Rubbia also announced the discovery of the sixth (top) quark, another long-sought particle. (S.M. and B.S.S.)

Van der Meer, Simon   540

PRIZE: Physics, 1984. BORN: November 24, 1925; The Hague, Netherlands. PARENTS: Father, Pieter van der Meer; Mother, Jetske van der Meer. NATIONALITY: Dutch. RELIGION: Agnostic; from Protestant background. EDUCATION: Technical Univ., Netherlands, physical engineering degree, 1955. SPOUSE: Catharina M. Koopman, married 1966. CHILDREN: Esther, daughter; Mathijs, son. CAREER: Dutch Philips Company, Researcher, 1952-56; European Organization for Nuclear Research, Researcher, 1956-.

Selected Publications: "Stochastic Cooling Theory and Devices." *Lawrence Berkeley Laboratory Report LBL-7574* (1978): 93-97. "Stochastic Cooling in the CERN Antiproton Accumulator." *IEEE Trans. Nucl. Sci.* NS28-3 Part I (1981): 1994-98. "Recent Experience with Antiproton Cooling." *IEEE Trans. Nucl. Sci.* 30-4 Part I (1983): 2587-89 (with others). "Antiproton Production and Collection for the CERN Antiproton Accumulator." *IEEE Trans. Nucl. Sci.* 30-4 Part I (1983): 2778-80 (with others).

For More Information See: *New York Times* (October 18, 1984): B13. *Science* 227 (January 11, 1985): 131-34.

Commentary: Simon Van der Meer shared the Nobel Prize with Carlo Rubbia for their contributions to the discovery of three subatomic particles that provided another link in developing a single theory for all natural forces. Van der Meer was the engineering force in the design and construction of a colliding-beam accelerator which permitted observation of the then-hypothetical W(–), W(+), and Z particles. The work of the two laureates confirmed the unification of two of the four basic forces of nature—the electromagnetic force that relates electricity and magnetism and the weak force that controls phenomena like radioactivity. (B.S.S.)

1985

Von Klitzing, Klaus   541

PRIZE: Physics, 1985. BORN: June 28, 1943; Schroda, Germany. PARENTS: Father, Bogislav von Klitzing; Mother, Anny Ulbrich von Klitzing. NATIONALITY: German. RELIGION: Most probably Christian. EDUCATION: Technical Univ., Germany, baccalaureate, 1969; Wurzburg Univ., Germany, Ph.D., 1972. SPOUSE: Renate Falkenberg, married 1971. CHILDREN: Andreas, son; Christine, daughter. CAREER: Technical Univ., Munich, Germany, Professor, 1978-80; Max Planck Institute, Stuttgart, West Germany, Researcher, 1980-. OTHER AWARDS: Walter-Schotty Prize, 1981; Hewlett Packard Europhysics Prize, 1982.

Selected Publications: "Resonance Structure in the High Field Magnetoresistance of Tellurium." *Solid State Communications* 9 (1971): 1251-54 (with G. Landwehr). "An Observation by Photoconductivity of Strain Splitting of Shallow Bulk Donors Located Near to the Surface in Silicon MOS Devices." *Solid State Communications* 20 (1976): 77-80 (with R. J. Nicholas and R.A. Stradling). "New Method for High-Accuracy Determination of the Fine-Structure Constant Based on Quantized Hall Resistance." *Physical Review Letters* 45 (1980): 494 (with G. Dorda and M. Pepper). "Electron Spin Resonance on GaAs-Al(x)Ga(1-x) As Heterostructures." *Physical Review Letters* 51 (1983): 130-33 (with D. Stein).

For More Information See: *New York Times* (October 17, 1985): 1. *Science* 231 (February 21, 1986): 820-22.

Commentary: Klaus von Klitzing received the Nobel Prize for his discovery of the quantized Hall effect, which occurs in semiconductor devices at low temperatures in strong magnetic fields. The discovery not only caused major revision of the theory of electric conduction in strong magnetic fields but also provided a highly accurate laboratory standard of electrical resistance. Von Klitzing also researched the electrical properties of tellurium in strong magnetic fields, silicon inversion layers in strong magnetic fields and unixial stress, and the properties of two-dimensional electron systems. (L.S.S.)

INDEXES

Name Index

Note: Numbers refer to entry accession numbers located in the upper right-hand corner of each entry.

Education Index

Punjab Univ., India

Khorana, Har Gobind, 303

Purdue Univ., IN

Mottelson, Benjamin Roy, 518
Purcell, Edward Mills, 474

Randolph-Macon College, VA

Buck, Pearl Comfort Sydenstricker, 161

Rensselaer Polytechnical Institute, NY

Giaever, Ivar, 513

Rice Univ., Texas

Wilson, Robert Woodrow, 527

Rockefeller Univ., NY

Baltimore, David, 320
Edelman, Gerald Maurice, 312

Rockford Female Seminary, IL

Addams, Laura Jane, 378

Rostov Univ., USSR

Solzhenitsyn, Alexander, 190

Rouen School of Medicine, France

Nicolle, Charles Jules Henri, 232

Royal Caroline Institute, Sweden

Gullstrand, Allvar, 219

Royal Military Academy, Egypt

El-Sadat, Muhammed Anwar, 410

Royal Military College, England

Churchill, Winston Leonard Spencer, Sir, 172

Royal Woman's Superior Training College, Sweden

Lagerlöf, Selma Ottilian Lovisa, 134

Rutgers Univ., NJ

Friedman, Milton, 113
Waksman, Selman Abraham, 267

San Carlos Univ., Guatemala

Asturias, Miguel Angel, 187

South Dakota State College

Schultz, Theodore William, 118

Southern Methodist Univ., TX

Cronin, James Watson, 531

Southwestern Medical School, Univ. of Texas

Goldstein, Joseph Leonard, 347

St. Bartholomew's Medical School Hospital, England

Ross, Ronald, Sir, 208

St. Mary's College, British West Indies

Lewis, William Arthur, Sir, 117

St. Peter's Theological College, South Africa

Tutu, Desmond Mpilo, 416

State College of Kentucky

Morgan, Thomas Hunt, 239

Swarthmore College, PA

Anfinsen, Christian Boehmer, 80
Baltimore, David, 320
Temin, Howard Martin, 322

Technical Univ., Germany

Von Klitzing, Klaus, 541

Technical Univ., Netherlands

Van der Meer, Simon, 540

Technische Hochschule, Germany

Bloch, Konrad E., 292
Gabor, Dennis, 509
Haber, Fritz, 17
Moessbauer, Rudolf Ludwig, 492
Ruzicka, Leopold Stephen, 39
Wigner, Eugene Paul, 496

Tokyo Imperial Univ., Japan

Kawabata, Yasunari, 188
Sato, Eisaku, 405

Trinity College, Ireland

Beckett, Samuel Barclay, 189
Walton, Ernest Thomas Sinton, 472

Tsinghua Univ., China

Yang, Chen Ning, 484

Union College, NY

Blumberg, Baruch Samuel, 323

United States Naval Academy, MD

Michelson, Albert Abraham, 425

Univ. of Adelaide, Australia

Bragg, William Lawrence, Sir, 435

Univ. of Aix-en-Provence, France

Cassin, Rene-Samuel, 399
Mistral, Frederic, 129

Univ. of Algiers, Algeria

Camus, Albert, 176

Univ. of Amsterdam, Netherlands

Eijkman, Christiaan, 233
Zernike, Frits, 475

Univ. of Basel, Switzerland

Müller, Paul Hermann, 260
Spitteler, Carl Friedrich Georg, 144

Univ. of Berlin, Germany

Bothe, Walther Wilhelm Georg, 477
Braun, Karl Ferdinand, 427
Diels, Otto Paul Herman, 50
Euler-Chelpin, Hans Karl August Simon von, 25
Forssmann, Werner Theodor Otto, 275
Franck, James, 445
Hassel, Odd, 77

Hertz, Gustav Ludwig, 446
Laue, Max Theodor Felix von, 433
Leontief, Wassily W., 108
Lipmann, Fritz Albert, 269
Streseman, Gustav, 373
Von Baeyer, Adolf Johann Friedrich Wilhelm, 5
Warburg, Otto Heinrich, 236
Wien, Wilhelm Carl Werner Otto Fritz Franz, 430
Windaus, Adolf Otto Reinhold, 24

Univ. of Berne, Switzerland

Kocher, Emil Theodor, 217

Univ. of Birmingham, England

Vane, John Robert, 341

Univ. of Bonn, Germany

Fischer, Emil Herman, 2
Heyse, Paul Johann Ludwig von, 135
Pirandello, Luigi, 158

Univ. of Bordeaux, France

Kastler, Alfred, 503
Mauriac, Francois, 171
Saint-John Perse, 179

Univ. of Breslau, Germany

Stern, Otto, 463

Univ. of Brussels, Belgium

Bordet, Jules Jean Baptiste Vincent, 223
La Fontaine, Henri Marie, 364

Univ. of Bucharest, Rumania

Palade, George Emil, 319

Univ. of Budapest, Hungary

Szent-Györgyi, Albert von Nagyrapolt, 246
Von Békésy, Georg, 285

Univ. of Buenos Aires, Argentina

Houssay, Bernardo Alberto, 259
Leloir, Luis Federico, 78
Milstein, César, 345

Univ. of California

Erlanger, Joseph, 251
Giauque, William Francis, 48
Klein, Lawrence Robert, 119
Lamb, Willis Eugene, Jr., 479
Libby, Willard Frank, 63
Seaborg, Glenn Theodore, 52
Smith, Hamilton Othanel, 330
Taube, Henry, 98
Urey, Harold Clayton, 31
Waksman, Selman Abraham, 267

Univ. of California, Los Angeles

Bunche, Ralph Johnson, 389
Merrifield, Robert Bruce, 99
Seaborg, Glenn Theodore, 52

Univ. of Cape Town, South Africa

Cormack, Allan MacLeod, 331
Klug, Aaron, 97

Univ. of Missouri
Robbins, Frederick Chapman, 271

Univ. of Montana
Urey, Harold Clayton, 31

Univ. of Munich, Germany
Bethe, Hans Albrecht, 504
Buchner, Eduard, 7
Debye, Peter Josephus Wilhelmus, 34
Fischer, Ernst Otto, 83
Fischer, Hans, 27
Heisenberg, Werner Karl, 453
Kuhn, Richard, 37
Lynen, Feodor Felix Konrad, 293
Pauli, Wolfgang Ernst, 465
Planck, Max Karl Ernst Ludwig, 437
Stark, Johannes, 438
von Frisch, Karl, 316
Wieland, Heinrich Otto, 23
Willstäter, Richard Martin, 16
Zsigmondy, Richard Adolf, 21

Univ. of Nebraska
Beadle, George Wells, 278

Univ. of Oregon
Brattain, Walter Houser, 481
Murphy, William Parry, 241

Univ. of Oslo, Norway
Frisch, Ragnar Kittil, Anton, 102
Hassel, Odd, 77
Lange, Christian Lous, 368

Univ. of Padua, Italy
Golgi, Camillo, 212

Univ. of Paris, France
Bergson, Henri Louis, 152
Bourgeois, Léon-Victor Auguste, 366
Briand, Aristide, 372
Broglie, Louis-Victor Pierre
  Raymond de, 451
Buisson, Ferdinand Edouard, 374
Cournand, Andre F., 274
Dausset, Jean Baptiste Gabriel
  Joachim, 334
Debreu, Gerard, 122
Garcia Robles, Alfonso, 413
Jacob, Francois, 294
Joliot-Curie, Frédéric, 32
Joliot-Curie, Irène, 33
Lwoff, Andre Michael, 295
Moissan, Ferdinand Frederick Henri,
  6
Monod, Jacques Lucien, 296
Passy, Frederic, 349
Renault, Louis, 356
Richet, Charles Robert, 221

Univ. of Paris-Sorbonne, France
Cournand, Andre F., 274
Curie, Marie, 11
Curie, Pierre, 421
Lippman, Gabriel Jonas, 426
Seferis, Giorgos, 182
Söderblom, Nathan, 377

Univ. of Pennsylvania
Anfinsen, Christian Boehmer, 80
Brown, Michael Stuart, 346
Edelman, Gerald Maurice, 312

Univ. of Pisa, Italy
Carducci, Giosuè Alessandro
  Guiseppe, 131
Fermi, Enrico, 461
Rubbia, Carlo, 539

Univ. of Pittsburgh, PA
Hench, Philip Showalter, 263

Univ. of Punjab, Pakistan
Salam, Abdus, 529

Univ. of Rochester, NY
Du Vigneaud, Vincent, 57
Gajdusek, Daniel Carleton, 324
Kornberg, Arthur, 281

Univ. of Rome, Italy
Modigliani, Franco, 124
Segré, Emilio Gino, 489

Univ. of Saskatchewan, Canada
Taube, Henry, 98

Univ. of Sidney, Australia
Cornforth, John Warcup, Sir, 86

Univ. of South Africa
Tutu, Desmond Mpilo, 416

Univ. of South Dakota
Lawrence, Ernest Orlando, 462

Univ. of St. Petersburg, Russia
Metchnikoff, Elie, 216

Univ. of Stockholm, Sweden
Hammarskjold, Dag Hjalmar Agne
  Carl, 397
Myrdal, Alva Reimer, 414
Myrdal, Karl Gunnar, 110
Ohlin, Bertil Gotthard, 115
Siegbahn, Kai Manne Boerje, 535
Theorell, Axel Hugo Teodor, 273

Univ. of Strasbourg, France
Fischer, Emil Herman, 2
Kossel, Karl Martin Leonhard
  Albrecht, 218
Laveran, Charles Louis Alphonse,
  214
Loewi, Otto, 245
Neel, Louis Eugene Felix, 508
Schweitzer, Albert, 391

Univ. of Tokyo, Japan
Esaki, Leo, 512

Univ. of Torino, Italy
Dulbecco, Renato, 321

Univ. of Toronto, Canada
Banting, Frederick Grant, Sir, 227
Pearson, Lester Bowles, 393
Schawlow, Arthur Leonard, 534

Univ. of Tübingen, Germany
Ramsay, William, Sir, 4

Univ. of Turin, Italy
Luria, Salvador Edward, 307

Univ. of Uppsala, Sweden
Alfven, Hannes Olof Gösta, 507
Arrhenius, Svante August, 3
Branting, Karl Hjalmar, 367
Karlfeldt, Erik Axel, 143
Myrdal, Alva Reimer, 414
Siegbahn, Kai Manne Boerje, 535
Svedberg, Theodor H.E., 22
Tiselius, Arne Wilhelm Kaurin, 47

Univ. of Utrecht, Netherlands
Bloembergen, Nicolaas, 533
Einthoven, Willem, 229
Koopmans, Tjalling Charles, 112
Van't Hoff, Jacobus Henricus, 1

Univ. of Vienna, Austria
Bárány, Robert, 222
Canetti, Elias, 202
Hayek, Friedrich August Von, 109
Landsteiner, Karl, 235
Lorenz, Konrad Zacharias, 314
Schrodinger, Erwin, 455
Wagner von Jaurregg, Julius, 231

Univ. of Virginia
Wilson, Thomas Woodrow, 365

Univ. of Washington
Stigler, George Joseph, 121

Univ. of Wilno, Poland
Milosz, Czeslaw, 201

Univ. of Wisconsin
Bardeen, John, 480
Gasser, Herbert Spencer, 252
Moore, Stanford, 81
Schultz, Theodore William, 118
Tatum, Edward Lawrie, 280
Van Vleck, John Hasbrouck, 524

Univ. of Witwatersrand, South Africa
Klug, Aaron, 97

Univ. of Würzburg, Germany
Nernst, Walther Hermann, 18
Spemann, Hans, 243

Univ. of Zaragoza, Spain
Ramón y Cajal, Santiago, 213

Univ. of Zurich, Switzerland
Einstein, Albert, 440
Hess, Walter Rudolph, 262
Karrer, Paul, 36
Werner, Alfred, 14

Universität zu Kiel, Germany
Mommsen, Christian Matthias
  Theodor, 127

Nationality or Citizenship Index

Note: Those names preceded by asterisk are indexed under more than one nationality or citizenship category.

American

Addams, Laura Jane, 378
Alvarez, Luis Walter, 505
Anderson, Carl David, 457
Anderson, Philip Warren, 522
Anfinsen, Christian Boehmer, 80
Arrow, Kenneth Joseph, 106
Axelrod, Julius, 308
Balch, Emily Greene, 386
Baltimore, David, 320
Bardeen, John, 480
Beadle, George Wells, 278
*Bellow, Saul, 197
*Benacerraf, Baruj, 333
Berg, Paul, 93
*Bethe, Hans Albrecht, 504
*Bloch, Felix, 473
*Bloch, Konrad E., 292
*Bloembergen, Nicolaas, 533
Blumberg, Baruch Samuel, 323
Borlaug, Norman Ernest, 400
Brattain, Walter Houser, 481
Bridgman, Percy Williams, 466
*Brown, Herbert Charles, 91
Brown, Michael Stuart, 346
Buck, Pearl Comfort Sydenstricker, 161
Bunche, Ralph Johnson, 389
Butler, Nicholas Murray, 379
Calvin, Melvin, 64
Chamberlain, Owen, 488
*Chandrasekhar, Subrahmanyan, 537
*Claude, Albert, 317
Compton, Arthur Holly, 448
Cooper, Leon Neil, 510
*Cori, Carl Ferdinand, 257
*Cori, Gerty Theresa Radnitz, 258
*Cormack, Allan MacLeod, 331
*Cournand, Andre F., 274
Cronin, James Watson, 531
Davisson, Clinton Joseph, 459
Dawes, Charles Gates, 371
*Debreu, Gerard, 122
*Debye, Peter Josephus Wilhelmus, 34
*Delbrück, Max, 305
Doisy, Edward Adelbert, 250
Du Vigneaud, Vincent, 57
*Dulbecco, Renato, 321
Edelman, Gerald Maurice, 312
*Einstein, Albert, 440
*Eliot, Thomas Stearns, 167
Enders, John Franklin, 270
Erlanger, Joseph, 251
Faulkner, William Cuthbert, 168

*Fermi, Enrico, 461
Feynman, Richard Phillips, 500
Fitch, Val Logsdon, 532
Flory, Paul John, 85
Fowler, William Alfred, 538
*Franck, James, 445
Friedman, Milton, 113
Gajdusek, Daniel Carleton, 324
Gasser, Herbert Spencer, 252
Gell-Mann, Murray, 506
*Giaever, Ivar, 513
Giauque, William Francis, 48
Gilbert, Walter, 94
Glaser, Donald Arthur, 490
Glashow, Sheldon, 528
Goldstein, Joseph Leonard, 347
*Guillemin, Roger, 325
Hartline, Halden Keffer, 300
Hauptman, Herbert Aaron, 100
Hemingway, Ernest Miller, 173
Hench, Philip Showalter, 263
Hershey, Alfred Day, 306
*Hess, Victor Franz, 458
*Hoffman, Roald, 96
Hofstadter, Robert, 491
Holley, Robert William, 302
*Hubel, David Hunter, 336
*Huggins, Charles Brenton, 297
Hull, Cordell, 385
Karle, Jerome, 101
Kellogg, Frank Billings, 376
Kendall, Edward Calvin, 264
*Khorana, Har Gobind, 303
King, Martin Luther, Jr., 398
*Kissinger, Henry Alfred, 402
Klein, Lawrence Robert, 119
*Koopmans, Tjalling Charles, 112
Kornberg, Arthur, 281
Kusch, Polycarp, 478
*Kuznets, Simon Smith, 105
Lamb, Willis Eugene, Jr., 479
*Landsteiner, Karl, 235
Langmuir, Irving, 30
Lawrence, Ernest Orlando, 462
Lederberg, Joshua, 279
*Lee, Tsung-dao, 483
*Leontief, Wassily W., 108
Lewis, Harry Sinclair, 155
Libby, Willard Frank, 63
*Lipmann, Fritz Albert, 269
Lipscomb, William Nunn, 88
*Loewi, Otto, 245
*Luria, Salvador Edward, 307
*Mann, Paul Thomas, 154
Marshall, George Catlett, 392

*Mayer, Maria Goeppert, 495
McClintock, Barbara, 342
McMillan, Edwin Mattison, 51
Merrifield, Robert Bruce, 99
*Meyerhof, Otto Fritz, 226
*Michelson, Albert Abraham, 425
Millikan, Robert Andrews, 443
*Milosz, Czeslaw, 201
Minot, George Richards, 240
*Modigliani, Franco, 124
Moore, Stanford, 81
Morgan, Thomas Hunt, 239
Mott, John R., 387
*Mottelson, Benjamin Roy, 518
Muller, Hermann Joseph, 256
Mulliken, Robert Sanderson, 71
Murphy, William Parry, 241
Nathans, Daniel, 329
Nirenberg, Marshall Warren, 304
Northrop, John Howard, 43
*Ochoa, Severo, 282
O'Neill, Eugene Gladstone, 159
*Onsager, Lars, 75
*Palade, George Emil, 319
Pauling, Linus Carl, 56
*Penzias, Arno Allan, 526
Purcell, Edward Mills, 474
*Rabi, Isidor Isaac, 464
Rainwater, Leo James, 519
Richards, Dickinson Woodruff, 276
Richards, Theodore William, 15
Richter, Burton, 520
Robbins, Frederick Chapman, 271
Roosevelt, Theodore, 354
Root, Elihu, 363
Rous, Francis Peyton, 298
Samuelson, Paul Anthony, 104
*Schally, Andrew Victor, 326
Schawlow, Arthur Leonard, 534
Schrieffer, John Robert, 511
Schultz, Theodore William, 118
Schwinger, Julian Seymour, 501
Seaborg, Glenn Theodore, 52
*Segré, Emilio Gino, 489
Shockley, William Bradford, 482
Simon, Herbert Alexander, 116
*Singer, Isaac Bashevis, 199
Smith, Hamilton Othanel, 330
Snell, George Davis, 335
Sperry, Roger Wolcott, 337
Stanley, Wendell Meredith, 44
Stein, William Howard, 82
Steinbeck, John Ernst, 181
*Stern, Otto, 463
Stigler, George Joseph, 121

Krogh, Schack August Steenberg, 224
*Mottelson, Benjamin Roy, 518
Pontoppidan, Henrik, 142
*Undset, Sigrid, 153

Dutch

Asser, Tobias Michael Carel, 361
*Bloembergen, Nicolaas, 533
*Debye, Peter Josephus Wilhelmus, 34
Eijkman, Christiaan, 233
Einthoven, Willem, 229
Kamerlingh Onnes, Heike, 432
*Koopmans, Tjalling Charles, 112
Lorentz, Hendrik Antoon, 418
Tinbergen, Jan, 103
Tinbergen, Nikolaas, 315
Van der Meer, Simon, 540
Van der Waals, Johannes Diderik, 429
Van't Hoff, Jacobus Henricus, 1
Zeeman, Pieter, 419
Zernike, Frits, 475

Egyptian

El-Sadat, Muhammed Anwar, 410

Finnish

*Granit, Ragnar Arthur, 299
Sillanpää, Frans Eemil, 162
Virtanen, Artturi Ilmari, 42

French

Becquerel, Antoine Henri, 420
Bergson, Henri Louis, 152
Bourgeois, Léon-Victor Auguste, 366
Briand, Aristide, 372
Broglie, Louis-Victor Pierre Raymond de, 451
Buisson, Ferdinand Edouard, 374
Camus, Albert, 176
Carrel, Alexis, 220
Cassin, Rene-Samuel, 399
*Cournand, Andre F., 274
*Curie, Marie, 11
Curie, Pierre, 421
Dausset, Jean Baptiste Gabriel Joachim, 334
*Debreu, Gerard, 122
d'Estournelles, Paul Henri Benjamin Balleut de Constant, Baron, 360
France, Anatole, 146
Gide, André Paul Guillaume, 166
Grignard, Francois Auguste Victor, 12
*Guillaume, Charles Edouard, 439
*Guillemin, Roger, 325
Jacob, Francois, 294
Joliot-Curie, Frédéric, 32
Joliot-Curie, Irène, 33
Jouhaux, Leon, 390
Kastler, Alfred, 503
Laveran, Charles Louis Alphonse, 214
Lippman, Gabriel Jonas, 426
Lwoff, Andre Michael, 295
Martin du Gard, Roger, 160
Mauriac, Francois, 171
Mistral, Frederic, 129

Moissan, Ferdinand Frederick Henri, 6
Monod, Jacques Lucien, 296
Neel, Louis Eugene Felix, 508
Nicolle, Charles Jules Henri, 232
Passy, Frederic, 349
Perrin, Jean Baptisfe, 447
Prudhomme, René-François-Armend, 125
Renault, Louis, 356
Richet, Charles Robert, 221
Rolland, Romain, 139
Sabatier, Paul, 13
Saint-John Perse, 179
Sartre, Jean-Paul Charles Aymard, 183
Schweitzer, Albert, 391
Simon, Claude Eugene Henri, 206
*Werner, Alfred, 14

German

Alder, Kurt, 49
Bergius, Friedrich Karl Rudolph, 28
*Bethe, Hans Albrecht, 504
*Bloch, Konrad E., 292
Böll, Heinrich, 192
*Born, Max, 476
Bosch, Carl, 29
Bothe, Walther Wilhelm Georg, 477
Brandt, Willy, 401
Braun, Karl Ferdinand, 427
Buchner, Eduard, 7
Butenandt, Adolf Friedrick Johann, 38
*Chain, Ernst Boris, Sir, 253
*Delbrück, Max, 305
Diels, Otto Paul Herman, 50
Domagk, Gerhard, 248
Ehrlich, Paul, 215
Eigen, Manfred, 72
*Einstein, Albert, 440
Eucken, Rudolph Christoph, 133
*Euler-Chelpin, Hans Karl August Simon von, 25
Fischer, Emil Herman, 2
Fischer, Ernst Otto, 83
Fischer, Hans, 27
Forssmann, Werner Theodor Otto, 275
*Franck, James, 445
Haber, Fritz, 17
Hahn, Otto, 41
Hauptmann, Gerhart Johann, 137
Heisenberg, Werner Karl, 453
Hertz, Gustav Ludwig, 446
*Herzberg, Gerhard, 79
*Hesse, Herman, 165
Heyse, Paul Johann Ludwig von, 135
Jensen, Johannes Hans Daniel, 494
*Katz, Bernard, Sir, 309
*Kissinger, Henry Alfred, 402
Koch, Heinrich Hermann Robert, 211
Koehler, Georges J.F., 344
Kossel, Karl Martin Leonhard Albrecht, 218
*Krebs, Hans Adolf, Sir, 268
*Kuhn, Richard, 37
Laue, Max Theodor Felix von, 433

*Lenard, Philipp Edward Anton, 423
*Lipmann, Fritz Albert, 269
*Loewi, Otto, 245
Lynen, Feodor Felix Konrad, 293
*Mann, Paul Thomas, 154
*Mayer, Maria Goeppert, 495
*Meyerhof, Otto Fritz, 226
*Michelson, Albert Abraham, 425
Moessbauer, Rudolf Ludwig, 492
Mommsen, Christian Matthias Theodor, 127
Nernst, Walther Hermann, 18
Ossietzky, Carl von, 382
*Ostwald, Friedrich Wilhelm, 9
*Penzias, Arno Allan, 526
Planck, Max Karl Ernst Ludwig, 437
Quidde, Ludwig, 375
Roentgen, Wilhelm Conrad, 417
*Sachs, Leonie Nelly, 186
Spemann, Hans, 243
Stark, Johannes, 438
Staudinger, Hermann, 55
*Stern, Otto, 463
Streseman, Gustav, 373
Von Baeyer, Adolf Johann Friedrich Wilhelm, 5
von Behring, Emil Adolph, 207
Von Klitzing, Klaus, 541
Wallach, Otto, 10
Warburg, Otto Heinrich, 236
Wieland, Heinrich Otto, 23
Wien, Wilhelm Carl Werner Otto Fritz Franz, 430
Willstäter, Richard Martin, 16
Windaus, Adolf Otto Reinhold, 24
Wittig, Georg Friedrich Karl, 92
Ziegler, Karl, 68

Greek

Elytis, Odysseus, 200
Seferis, Giorgos, 182

Guatemalan

Asturias, Miguel Angel, 187

Hungarian

*Gabor, Dennis, 509
*Hevesy, George Charles von, 40
*Lenard, Philipp Edward Anton, 423
*Szent-Györgyi, Albert von Nagyrapolt, 246
*Von Békésy, Georg, 285
*Wigner, Eugene Paul, 496

Icelandic

Laxness, Halldor Kiljan, 174

Indian

*Chandrasekhar, Subrahmanyan, 537
*Khorana, Har Gobind, 303
Raman, Chandrasekhara Venkata, Sir, 452
Tagore, Rabindranath, Sir, 138
*Teresa, Mother, 411

Irish

Beckett, Samuel Barclay, 189
Corrigan, Mairead, 407
MacBride, Sean, 404
Shaw, George Bernard, 150

Religion Index

Planck, Max Karl Ernst Ludwig, 437
Powell, Cecil Frank, 470
Richards, Theodore William, 15
Root, Elihu, 363
Rutherford, Ernest, Sir, 8
Seaborg, Glenn Theodore, 52
Spemann, Hans, 243
Steinbeck, John Ernst, 181
Sutherland, Earl Wilbur, Jr., 311

von Euler, Ulf Svante, 310
Wilson, Charles Thomson Rees, 449
Woodward, Robert Burns, 70
Zernike, Frits, 475

Quaker

Noel-Baker, Philip John, 395

Shinto

Sato, Eisaku, 405

Unitarian

Balch, Emily Greene, 386
Holley, Robert William, 302
Minot, George Richards, 240
Muller, Hermann Joseph, 256
Simon, Herbert Alexander, 116
Sumner, James Batcheller, 45